The Struggle for the Eu

This book explores the Eurasian borderlands as contested "shatter zones" which have generated some of the world's most significant conflicts. Analyzing the struggles of the Habsburg, Russian, Ottoman, Iranian, and Qing empires, Alfred J. Rieber surveys the period from the rise of the great multicultural, conquest empires in the late medieval/early modern period to their collapse in the early twentieth century. He charts how these empires expanded along moving, military frontiers, competing with one another in war, diplomacy, and cultural practices, while the subjugated peoples of the borderlands strove to maintain their cultures and to defend their autonomy. The gradual and fragmentary adaptation of Western constitutional ideas, military reforms, cultural practices, and economic penetration began to undermine these ruling ideologies and institutions, leading to the collapse of all five empires in revolution and war within little more than a decade between 1911 and 1923.

Alfred J. Rieber is University Research Professor of History at the Central European University, Budapest, Hungary, and Professor Emeritus at the University of Pennsylvania.

The Struggle for the Eurasian Borderlands

From the Rise of Early Modern Empires
to the End of the First World War

Alfred J. Rieber

CAMBRIDGE
UNIVERSITY PRESS

CAMBRIDGE
UNIVERSITY PRESS

University Printing House, Cambridge CB2 8BS, United Kingdom

Published in the United States of America by Cambridge University Press, New York

Cambridge University Press is part of the University of Cambridge.

It furthers the University's mission by disseminating knowledge in the pursuit of education, learning and research at the highest international levels of excellence.

www.cambridge.org
Information on this title: www.cambridge.org/9781107618305

First published 2014

A catalogue record for this publication is available from the British Library

Library of Congress Cataloging-in-Publication Data
Rieber, Alfred J.
The struggle for the Eurasian borderlands : from the rise of early modern empires to the end of the First World War / Alfred J. Rieber.
    pages   cm
Includes bibliographical references and index.
ISBN 978-1-107-04309-1 (hardback : alkaline paper)
1. Borderlands – Eurasia – History.   2. Eurasia – History.   3. Eurasia – Relations.
4. Eurasia – History, Military.   5. Imperialism – History.   6. Imperialism – Social
aspects – Eurasia – History.   7. Cultural pluralism – Eurasia – History.   8. Culture
conflict – Eurasia – History.   9. Indigenous peoples – Eurasia – History.   I. Title.
DS5.R54   2014
950–dc23

2014002739

ISBN 978-1-107-04309-1 Hardback
ISBN 978-1-107-61830-5 Paperback

To Marsha: "... like gold to airy thinness beat ..."

Contents

Maps

Acknowledgments

All books have histories; big books have long histories. Thinking back I uncover shards of memories scattered over a lifetime. A grandfather's tales of visits to the sites of ancient empires; the discovery of Owen Lattimore and undergraduate papers on the Crimean Tatars, Afghanistan, and Mongolia, Manchuria and the Soviet Far East as a regional system; Halil Inalcik's first lecture course in the United States; the Interdisciplinary Seminar on Multicultural Societies at the University of Pennsylvania inspired by Lee Benson; seminars on the Comparative History of Bureaucracies with Martin Wolfe and Robert Hartwell; supervising graduate students at the Central European University from the borderlands, Croatia to the Buryat Mongol Republic. All of it pieced together with generous support as University Research Professor at the Central European University from the Open Society (Soros) Foundation in New York. In addition, I benefited from a fellowship in the History of Comparative Empires at Glamorgan University, Wales; brief teaching stints back at Penn and at the University of Maryland; a term as Senior Research Fellow at St. Antony's College, Oxford; and as IREX Senior Exchange Fellow in Russia. My thanks also to the staff of the library of the Central European University for their invaluable assistance in ordering books and obtaining materials through inter-library loan.

Parts of the book were read at different stages by Fikret Adenir, Virginia Aksan, Charles Ingrao, Andreas Kappeler, Michael Khodarkovsky, Alexei Miller, Christine Philliou, Evelyn Rawski, and Richard Wortman, all of whom deserve my thanks for their critical comments and helpful suggestions. Two anonymous readers for Cambridge University Press stimulated me to make extensive revisions. I am grateful to Emily Gioielli and Lyn Flight for help in preparing the manuscript. Michael Watson of Cambridge University Press was most supportive of the project. I bear sole responsibility for any errors that may remain.

My gratitude to Marsha Siefert, hinted at in the dedication, extends to all aspects of our shared intellectual life: her patient listening to often half-formed ideas, helping them to take shape, rescuing me from computer-induced despair, tolerating the personal idiosyncrasies that arise during long immersion in writing, and for just being there.

I am grateful to colleagues for invitations to explore some of these themes at the universities of Chicago, Carnegie-Mellon, Loyola (Chicago), Michigan, the Harriman Institute at Columbia University, the University of Cambridge, St. Antony's, Oxford, and the University of Zagreb. David Cox transformed my rough sketches into excellent maps.

Note on Romanization

In wrestling with this perennial problem, I offer solutions that will surely not satisfy everyone. The Library of Congress system has been followed in general for Russian, Serbian, Bulgarian, Ottoman Turkish, and Persian. The pinyin system has been adopted (reluctantly) for Chinese. I have retained diacritical marks in Hungarian, Polish, and Romanian. When the same term appears in two languages, such as *qizilbashi* (Persian) and *kizilbaşi* (Turkish), I have tried to use one consistently, in this case Persian, reflecting the primary cultural context in which the subject appears. The spelling ulama has been used throughout, reflecting its Arabic origins. Exceptions abound, mainly due to the frequency with which words have become familiar in English language texts. But this too is rather arbitrary. In transliterating Ukrainian names I have generally used the Russian spellings of place names to acknowledge the imperial structure, and Ukrainian spellings of individuals to acknowledge ethnic identities. The exception is Map 6.1 showing the independent Ukraine after the Treaty of Brest-Litovsk, where I have retained the Ukrainian spellings of place names.

Introduction

This study argues that the great crises of the twentieth century – the two world wars and the Cold War – had common origins in a complex historical process I call the struggle over the Eurasian borderlands. The struggle is conceived as having taken place on two levels: from above, in the course of state-building; from below, in the reaction of the subjugated peoples. The main actors in imperial state-building in Eurasia in the first phase were the Habsburg, Ottoman, Russian, Iranian (Safavid and Qajar), and Qing multicultural empires. In their competition for territory and resources they expanded from their early centers of power along moving, military frontiers, engaging one another in war, diplomacy, and cultural practices for hegemony over the borderlands on their peripheries. From below, the peoples of the borderlands brought under imperial rule strove to maintain their cultures, defend their autonomy, regain or achieve independence either by resisting or accommodating to imperial rule.

The impetus and inspiration for this study came from many years of teaching European, Russian, and comparative history, in the course of which a number of challenging questions kept reoccurring along lines familiar to every student of international relations and global history. How is it possible to explain that, with the exception of the wars of Italian and German unification, all the major wars and some minor ones fought in Europe and Asia from the Congress of Vienna in 1815 to the mid-twentieth century began in the Eurasian borderlands, those territories located on the peripheries of the multinational continental empires, which, after the civil wars and interventions from 1918 to 1920, became successor states? The list of such conflicts is impressive: the Crimean War (1854–1856); the Russo-Turkish War (1877–1878); the Second Afghan War (1879); the Sino-Japanese War (1894–1895); the Russo-Japanese War (1904–1905); two Balkan Wars (1913–1914); the First (1914–1918) and Second (1939–1945) World Wars; the Chinese Civil War (1946–1949); and the Korean War (1950–1953). How further to explain that the continental empires, Habsburg, Ottoman, Romanov, Safavid–Qajar, and Qing, having survived their rivalry over these same territories for centuries, collapsed in revolution and war within little more than a decade between 1911 and 1923? Why was it, finally, that Imperial Russia was involved directly or indirectly in most of these conflicts? By posing and seeking to answer these questions in the context of *la longue durée*, the struggle over the borderlands may help to put in a new perspective the major conflicts of the twentieth century as well. The Eurasian borderlands were the multiple sites of the origins of the Cold War – the prelude to a third world war that happily was never fought – as well as the end of the Cold War with the disintegration of the East European bloc, the secession of the Soviet borderlands, and the break up of the successor states of Czechoslovakia and Yugoslavia. But these are aspects of the struggle that require separate studies. The complexity of the struggle during the imperial phase from the early modern period to the twentieth century demands a broad comparative and transnational approach. This explains the thematic organization of the book and justifies, I hope, its great length.

Chapter 1 explains and illustrates what is meant by a geocultural approach, and then applies it to three spatial concepts, Eurasia, borderlands, and frontiers shaped by complex historical processes over long periods of time. Interpreted as place, process, and symbol, these concepts reflect the changing nature of politics, warfare, and cultural practices within different physical landscapes from the early modern period to the twentieth century. The chapter also outlines the dynamic interaction between strategies of imperial expansion: conquest, colonization, and conversion, and the strategies of response:– accommodation and resistance.

Chapter 2 deals with the evolution of imperial ideologies and cultural practices as political theologies. Dynasts and ruling elites of the multicultural states designed them to endow imperial rule with legitimacy, provide an overarching principle of authority, and unify the divergent populations brought under their control. Chapter 3 examines the institutional foundations of imperial rule, focusing on the army, bureaucracy, and co-optation of elites as the instruments for mobilizing the human and material resources necessary to maintain a competitive position in the imperial rivalries.

Chapter 4 analyzes the prolonged struggle over the borderlands along seven Eurasian frontiers: the Baltic littoral, the Danubian frontier, the Pontic steppe, the Caucasian isthmus, Trans Caspia, and Inner Asia, locating many of the sites that will later become "hot spots" in the coming of the two world wars and the Cold War. In the period up to the last quarter of the eighteenth century, the Habsburg, Ottoman, Russian, Safavid, and Qing empires occupied relatively equal power positions with respect to one another, while some minor competitors, Sweden and Dzungaria, and a major one, the Polish–Lithuanian Commonwealth, were eliminated. During this period resistance to imperial rule by the subjugated populations foreshadowed the full-blown nationalist movements and class conflicts of the following period. At the same time, the Russian Empire began to emerge as the hegemonic power in Eurasia. In this period, for the first time, Russia's expansion was seriously challenged from outside the parameters of Eurasia by Napoleonic France, Great Britain, and Prussia/Germany. Yet it maintained its ascendancy, despite the temporary setback of the Crimean War, until the early years of the twentieth century. Finally, during this period the gradual and fragmentary adaptation of Western constitutional ideas and cultural practices, as well as economic penetration, began to undermine the reigning ideologies and institutions of imperial rule in the Ottoman, Qajar, and Qing empires, creating internal tensions that weakened their resistance to Russian and, to a lesser extent, Habsburg expansion.

Chapter 5 analyzes the mounting internal contradictions of imperial rule in all the multicultural states. Attempts by the ruling elites to adopt measures borrowed from abroad in the fields of education, military training, and administration, culminating in the introduction of constitutional experiments, yielded ambiguous results in dealing with rising dissension among the subjugated peoples of the borderlands. They constituted the main causes of the constitutional crises that broke out almost simultaneously in the Russian, Habsburg, Iranian, Ottoman, and Qing empires, shaking the foundations of imperial power. The concluding chapter illustrates how persistent factors in the struggle over the borderlands survived the rupture of war, revolution, and civil wars from 1914 to 1920.

This book does not seek to evoke nostalgia for empire; still less is it a celebration of nationalism, sentiments all too prevalent in historical writing since the end of the Cold War. If there are a few guiding threads through the web of circumstance and structure that alternate in this narrative, they are the complexity of state-building Eurasia; the persistence of problems that geographical and cultural diversity posed to the rulers and the ruled in their different aspirations; and the variety of responses – reform, repression, revolt – that they devised to resolve these problems. The three threads weave continuity into the narrative, which even apparent ruptures do not entirely break, allowing them to be re-knit as it were by different hands.

At this point, two brief apologies are in order. By making comparisons, demonstrating transfers, and transnational (or preferably transcultural) influences, this study seeks to analyze events and issues from multiple perspectives, which require a mix of thematic and chronological chapters. This involves some repetition, which it is hoped will instruct rather than annoy the reader. For example, colonization is treated in Chapter 1 as a key factor in defining Eurasian frontiers; in Chapter 4, it is reintroduced as an instrument of state policy in the struggle over the borderlands. Similarly, the role of religious institutions appears in different contexts: as a force for conversion, as the underpinning of imperial ideologies, and as an element in the crises of imperial systems.

Instead of appending a bibliography, the notes identify sources and provide commentary on the main historiographical disputes that continue to enliven scholarship on the many issues raised in the study. In a synthesis of this sort, reliance on secondary works is inevitable, and is not after all a bad thing. Over the past generation the discovery and exploration of new archival sources, the introduction of new theoretical approaches, and the relatively modest but noticeable shift away from a Eurocentric bias in historiography have greatly enriched the scholarship on empires without which the present study would not have been possible. Although the notes may appear to be abundant, they do not include all the sources consulted, and I apologize for any significant omissions.

1   Imperial space

The concept of space has become a much disputed topic in the world of scholarship. At one extreme, the "spatial turn" has replaced the physical grounding of geography with symbolic meaning. One result has been a cartography in which space surrenders its independent existence to mental mapping. Terms such as frontiers, borders, boundaries, and place are widely employed to delineate virtually all aspects of culture. Another less radical result has been to repair the long-frayed bonds between geography and history by reintroducing the cultural factor. This is the approach used in this chapter to designate Eurasia, borderlands, and frontiers, the key components of imperial space.

My treatment differs from two widely accepted theoretical approaches: the geopolitical and the civilizational. Both stress a single factor underpinning international politics, whether physical geography or ideology. In practice they come close to endorsing determinism. Both also divide space by static linear borders. By contrast, the present study will interpret Eurasia, its frontiers, and borderlands as spaces shaped by complex historical processes forming a geocultural context in which the great conflicts of the twentieth century will be situated. My preference for the geocultural over the geopolitical and civilizational is also based in part on the fact that the discourses of geopolitics and civilization as applied to Eurasia have been ideologically complicit in the coming of the Cold War.

Three approaches

The term geopolitics has intellectual roots in the work of German geographers in the nineteenth century.[1] Subsequently, an Anglo-American school of publicists and scholars shaped these ideas into a new theory of international relations that focused on the perceived Russian bid for control over the Eurasian land mass that would provide the natural

---

[1] Rudolph Kjellen, *Grundriss zu einem System der Politik* (Leipzig: S. Hirzel, 1920), p. 40.

resources and strategic advantage necessary to achieve global hegemony. In a much revised, but recognizable, form, their views gained widespread acceptance in the early years of the twentieth century and again in the post-Second World War debates over Soviet foreign policy, particularly in the work of influential scholars, highly placed advisors, and politicians like Nicholas Spykman, Isaiah Bowman, George Kennan, and J. William Fulbright. These ideas became the common coin of the containment policy.[2]

At the same time, in the late nineteenth and early twentieth centuries, another group of American publicists was building on the influential frontier thesis of Frederick Jackson Turner in order to promote an American overseas empire. Their advocacy merged geopolitics, Social Darwinism, Manifest Destiny, and the Open Door Policy.[3] This cluster of ideas also displayed a strong anti-Russian bias, and acquired a prominent place in the debates during the Paris Peace Conference of 1919 and in the interwar period.[4] The perceived geopolitical threat of Russian domination of Eurasia became entangled with the ideology of an American mission, laying the foundations for American foreign policy during the early years of the Cold War. It continues to inform the historiography of Russia and Eurasia.

The civilizational approach to Eurasia also has its roots in the works of nineteenth-century theorists. One line, represented by Russian pan-Slav philosophers and publicists such as Nikolai Danilevsky and Fedor Dostoevsky, extolled the uniqueness and messianic destiny of a Russian civilization that spanned both Europe and Asia, producing something different from both. Although pan-Slavism never became an official ideology, its precepts strongly influenced a generation of Russian military

---

[2] Nicholas Spykman, *The Geography of the Peace* (New York: Harcourt Brace, 1944); Michael P. Gerace, "Between MacKinder and Spykman. Geopolitics, Containment and After," *Comparative Strategy* 10(4) (1991): 347–64; Randall Bennett Woods, *Fulbright. A Biography* (Cambridge University Press, 2006), p. 141. The work of Spykman and MacKinder still occupied an important place in the education of American military officers in the latter years of the Cold War. See Department of Geography, *Readings in Military Geography* (West Point: United States Military Academy, 1981). For the geopolitical approach, see, for example, Dominic Lieven, *Empire. The Russian Empire and its Rivals from the Sixteenth Century to the Present* (London: Pimlico, 2003), esp. ch. 6; John LeDonne, *The Russian Empire and the World, 1700–1917. The Geopolitics of Expansionism and Containment* (Oxford University Press, 1997); and Milan Hauner, *What is Asia to Us? Russia's Asian Heartland Yesterday and Today* (London: Routledge, 1992).

[3] Walter LaFeber, *The New Empire. An Interpretation of American Expansion, 1860–1898* (Ithaca, NY: Cornell University Press, 1963), on Turner, pp. 62–72, 95–101. For Turner's influence on Woodrow Wilson, see William A. Williams, "The Frontier Thesis and American Foreign Policy," *Pacific Historical Review* (November 1955): 379–95.

[4] Cf. Gerry Kearns, *Geopolitics and Empire. The Legacy of Halford Mackinder* (Oxford University Press, 2009).

proconsuls and geographers in the course of Russia's expansion to the east. The pan-Slav bugbear was taken even more seriously by statesmen and publicists in the West, reinforcing the geopolitical version of the Russian threat in the decades before the Russian Revolution.

After the fall of tsarism, two avatars of the civilizational idea appeared in Russia, apparently diametrically opposed to one another. A small group of émigré Russian intellectuals, dubbing themselves Eurasianists, interpreted the historical role of Russia as a civilization-blending element of the European and Asian cultures destined to bring spiritual unity of the world. Largely ignored in their time and repressed in the Soviet Union, a new Eurasianism has re-surfaced in the post-Soviet period as a powerful voice in the reconstruction of a new national myth within the Russian Federation.[5]

A second offshoot of the civilizational thesis was Stalin's doctrine of socialism in one country, a radical reinterpretation of Marxism–Leninism. The centerpiece of this theory was his proclamation that the success of the world revolution depended upon the building of socialism in backward Russia rather than vice versa. To the extent that this was an unacknowledged version of Eurasianism, it caused a minor scandal in the interparty struggles in the Soviet Union in the 1920s.[6] Western observers were quick to demonstrate what they regarded as an organic link between pre-revolutionary and post-revolutionary ideas of Russia's unique universal destiny as proof of its innate messianism. This myth of unlimited Russian expansionism also became part of the Cold War lore.[7]

Though the term geocultural has not enjoyed the same vogue as geopolitical, it has its own intellectual pedigree in the pioneering work of the

[5] Nicholas V. Riasanovsky, "The Emergence of Eurasianism," *California Slavic Studies* 4 (1967): 39–72; Ilya Vinkovetsky and Charles Schlacks, Jr. (eds.), *Exodus to the East. Forebodings and Events. An Affirmation of the Eurasians* (Idyllwild, CA: Charles Schlacks, 1996); and Ilya Vinkovetsky, "Classical Eurasianism and its Legacy," *Canadian–American Slavic Studies* 34(2) (Summer 2000): 125–40. The revival began even earlier with the work of Lev Gumilov, *Iz istorii Evrazii* (Moscow: Issskustvo, 1993) and *Drevnaia Rus' i velikaia step'* (Moscow: DI-DIK, 1997). See also Aleksandr Dugin, *Misterii Evrazii* (Moscow: Arktogeia, 1996) and the journal *Vestnik Evrazii.*
[6] S. V. Tsakunov, "NEP: evoliutsiia rezhima i rozhdenie natsional-bolshevisma," in Iu. N. Afanas'ev (ed.), *Sovetskoe obshchestvo. Vozniknoveniie, razvitie, istorichestkii final,* 3 vols. (Moscow: RGGU, 1997), vol. I, pp. 100–12.
[7] See, for example, Thomas Masaryk, *The Spirit of Russia*, 2 vols. (London: Allen & Unwin, 1919); Hans Kohn, *Pan Slavism. Its History and Ideology* (South Bend, IN: Notre Dame University Press, 1953); Carl J. Friederich and Zbigniew Brzezinski, *Totalitarian Dictatorship and Democracy* (Cambridge, MA: Harvard University Press, 1956); James Billington, *The Icon and the Ax* (New York: Knopf, 1966).

precursors and early theorists of the Annales School.[8] The basic assumption underlying the geocultural outlook is that climate and soil, the contours of the land, abundance or lack of navigable rivers, proximity to seas, all present possibilities as well as imposing constraints on human action. But they do not determine historical development, the distribution and concentration of power, or specific policy choices. Geocultural factors may shape what Lucian Febvre has called "privileged places for the birth of viable political entities, regions that favor the growth of states."[9] However, even privileged places are not bound by natural frontiers, but emerge from the interaction of cultures, the evolution of collective communities, and the rationalizing action of rulers and ruling elites. For centuries societies and polities have sought to fix their outer limits in the search to satisfy basic needs for group identity, stability, and security.[10] Yet, by its very nature, the process of locating "the other" on the far side of a real or imaginary demarcation line has constituted a potential threat. Thus, boundary maintenance became an ambiguous process.[11] In light of these insights the Eurasian frontiers and borderlands will be treated in this study as fluid rather than fixed and immutable concepts, subject to change over time, not wholly imagined, yet endowed with ideological meaning by intellectuals and politicians to serve statist aims, whether imperial or national.[12] By treating Eurasia as a contested geocultural space, Russian expansion is placed in a different context, as a product of a centuries-old struggle among rival imperial powers.

From the geocultural perspective, four interrelated but distinct processes shaped Eurasian space. First, over long periods of time, from the sixteenth to the early twentieth centuries, large-scale population movements – migration, deportation, flight, and colonization – scattered a great variety of culture groups drawn from Germanic, Slavic, Turkic, Mongol, and Chinese ethnolinguistic groups, and Christian (Roman Catholic,

---

[8] Paul Vidal de la Blache, *Tableau de la géographie de la France* (Paris: Librairie Hachette, 1903, reprinted 1979 and 1994) and André-Louis Sanguin, *Vidal de la Blache. Une génie de la géographie* (Paris: Belin, 1993), pp. 327–33. For a similar analysis by a sociologist, see Martina Löw, *Raumsoziologie* (Frankfurt am Main: Suhrkamp, 2001).

[9] Lucian Febvre, *La terre et l'évolution humaine* (Paris: A. Michel, [1922] 1949), p. 339. See also the work of Carl O. Sauer summarized in his presidential address to the American Association of Geographers in December 1940, "Foreword to Historical Geography," available at: www.colorado.edu/geography/giw/sauer-co/1941_fhg/1941_fhg.html.

[10] Michel Foucher, *Fronts et frontières. Un tour du monde géopolitique*, new edn (Paris: Fayard, 1991), pp. 77–79.

[11] Cf. Frederik Barth (ed.), *Ethnic Groups and Boundaries. The Social Organization of Culture Differences* (Boston, MA: Little Brown, 1969), who stresses the importance of boundaries in maintaining the stability and continuity of ethnic units.

[12] Cf. Benedict Anderson, *Imagined Communities. Reflections on the Origin and Spread of Nationalism*, rev. edn (New York: Verso, 1991).

Orthodox, and Protestant), Judaic, Muslim, and Buddhist believers over vast distances. The result was, in metaphoric terms, a demographic kaleidoscopic of unparalleled variety and complexity rather than a mosaic. In the course of these movements, certain areas acquired the characteristics of what anthropologists have called shatter zones where numerous ethno-religious groups intermingled with one another in close proximity, creating conditions of potential conflict.[13] Second, beginning in the sixteenth century, a number of major centers of political power (Sweden, the Polish–Lithuanian Commonwealth, Muscovy, the Habsburg, Ottoman, Safavid, and, later in the seventeenth century, the Qing empires), seeking to enhance their security, stability, and resource base, expanded on the margins of their core lands into territories separating them from one another, here to be called complex frontiers, with shifting, contested, and often blurred boundaries, reflecting the changing outcomes of the military, demographic, and cultural competition. Third, the attempt to conquer these disputed territories and incorporate them as borderlands within the body politic of the increasingly multicultural state systems became an external struggle that profoundly affected the process of state-building in Eurasia. Fourth, within the borderlands an internal struggle developed as the subjugated peoples continuously sought ways to defend against linguistic assimilation and religious conversion, and to preserve local autonomy or regain their independence. They adopted a variety of strategies ranging along a broad spectrum from violent revolution to cooperation. The centers of power reacted with an equally varied set of strategies ranging from compromise and toleration to repression. Both the external and internal struggles over the borderlands were frequently entangled as the rival states encouraged subversion among their enemies and the conquered populations sought support from the outside, thus blurring the conventional distinction between foreign and domestic policies within imperial space.

These four processes unfolded unevenly over time, and involved different combinations of multicultural states, marked by a rough chronological division into three periods. From the earliest recorded history to approximately the sixteenth to mid-seventeenth centuries, a cyclical pattern

---

[13] By virtue of their ethnic, religious, and linguistic complexity the shatter zones of the Eurasian borderlands have no counterpart in Western Europe, where frontier zones are almost invariably characterized by the encounter of only two ethnolinguistic groups, as in Alsace, Schleswig, Savoie, Istria, Flanders, or the Scottish Highlands. For a similar view, see Omer Bartov and Eric D. Weitz (eds.), *Shatterzone of Empires. Coexistence and Violence in the German, Habsburg, Russian and Ottoman Borderlands* (Bloomington, IN: Indiana University Press, 2013), which appeared too late for me to take advantage of its rich content.

defined the relations between nomadic and sedentary societies. In the second period, the emerging, relatively centralized multicultural states began to expand into the frontier areas and incorporate conquered peoples into borderlands. In the third period, beginning in the late eighteenth century, the Russian Empire gained ascendancy over its main imperial rivals in the struggle to acquire and to consolidate new borderlands. The fourth and shortest period, lasting a few decades before the First World War, was marked by a series of imperial crises culminating in the collapse of the major multicultural dynastic states, the Russian, Habsburg, Ottoman, Qajar, and Qing empires.

Geocultural diversity in Eurasia

From the earliest period Eurasian space was shaped by the encounter between diverse types of pastoral nomadic societies practicing a great variety of economic strategies, and sedentary societies engaged in an equally broad range of agricultural systems and small manufacturing. Nomadic groups ranged from the tundra and taiga of the northern latitudes, south through the mixed forests and treeless grasslands to the semi-arid steppe, deserts, and eastern highlands, extending in broad, irregularly shaped bands from the Danube delta to the coasts of the Sea of Japan. The appearance of pastoral nomads may have been the result of a long process of interaction between the forest, oases, and fringe of the steppe with cultivated lands.[14] Owen Lattimore described the "flanks of the main body of steppe society" as "an almost infinite series of combinations of steppe-nomadic, hunting, agricultural and town life."[15] Similarly, historians of the Ottoman Empire have pointed out the fallacy of dividing nomads and settled peasants into rigidly separate categories. Their interaction depended much on the physical geography, fertility of the soil, climatic factors, and crop yields.[16]

In the early period, the physical environment of Eurasia was more favorable to a nomadic than to a sedentary way of life. The continental climate, with long winters and dry hot summers, the inadequate supplies

[14] Owen Lattimore, *Inner Asian Frontiers of China*, 2nd edn (New York: Capitol Publications, 1951), esp. pp. 113–14, 158–63, 450–54.

[15] Owen Lattimore, *Studies in Frontier History. Collected Papers* (London: Oxford University Press, 1962), p. 248. See also Joseph Fletcher, "The Mongols: Ecological and Social Perspectives," *Harvard Journal of Asiatic Studies* 46(1) (1986): 11–52; and Peter Perdue, *China Marches West. The Qing Conquest of Central Eurasia* (Cambridge, MA: Belknap Press), pp. 30–32.

[16] Rhoads Murphey, "Some Features of Nomadism in the Ottoman Empire. A Survey Based on Tribal Census and Judicial Appeal Documentation from Archives in Istanbul and Damascus," *Journal of Turkish Studies* 8 (1984): 190–92.

of water, and the brevity of the growing season discouraged until recent times cultivation of the land outside the scattered oases or on the margins. The latitudinal landscape offered few barriers to the free movement of herds, and the rainfall was generally sufficient to maintain the pasturage. Mountain ranges forming a broken arc around the southern rim of the steppe and deserts rise gradually, permitting grazing up to high elevations. Running mainly from the southwest to northwest, they do not break up the grasslands into discrete ecological niches.[17]

All along the Eurasian frontiers warfare and peaceful exchanges alternated in irregular and unpredictable rhythms. For two millennia the equine culture of the steppe nomads gave them a military advantage over the sedentary populations on the margins of the grasslands and steppe. In the words of Peter Perdue, "the horse was both the mainstay of the nomadic economy and the one essential element in warfare which the sedentary civilizations could not breed in sufficient numbers for their own needs." With the invention of the compound reflex bow, the stirrup, and the archer's saddle, the mounted warrior long maintained the supremacy of nomadic life in the steppe.[18] Until the sedentary peoples could produce a superior weapons technology, they could not break this dominance. The breakthrough came only with the gunpowder revolution and the manufacture of effective firearms perfected under the centralized leadership of the multicultural agrarian empires.

The best cavalry in the world, however, could not have guaranteed the nomadic predominance. The herds of sheep and cattle were indispensable to the nomadic warrior as a mobile source of food, supplementing their superiority in military technology.[19] Thus, the nomads enjoyed considerable logistical advantages over their sedentary neighbors in large-scale military operations over great distances until military conquests and colonization by intrepid settlers often, but not always, under the protection of centralized bureaucratic states penetrated the steppe.

The stability of commercial relations on the Eurasian frontiers rested on the mutual needs of the nomadic and sedentary populations. The latter sought to obtain mounts bred on the steppes and furs from nomadic hunters and trappers in the northern taiga. The former desired to

---

[17] Robert Taafe, "The Geographical Setting," in *The Cambridge History of Early Inner Asia* (Cambridge University Press, 1990), pp. 23–27.

[18] Heerlee G. Cree, *Studies in Early Chinese Culture* (Baltimore, MD: Waverley Press, 1937), pp. 195–96; Lattimore, *Inner Asian Frontiers*, pp. 465–66; and especially William Hardy McNeill, *The Pursuit of Power. Technology, Armed Force and Society since A.D. 1000* (University of Chicago Press, 1982), pp. 15–21.

[19] Anatoly Khazanov, *Nomads and the Outside World*, 2nd edn (Cambridge University Press, 1994), pp. 28–40, 44–53, 69–72.

obtain tea and manufactured articles from the sedentary population. In addition to trade there were many forms of exchange, ranging from gifts to tribute, that regularized the intercourse between the two ecologies. Aside from the lively exchange in the frontier zones, longer trade patterns developed over the centuries along the margins of the two ecologies. A double track north and south of the Tarim Basin in present-day Xinjiang led through the oases of Transoxenia (Trans Caspia) into Iran, Anatolia, and the Balkans. A "slender dual thread" in the words of René Grousset, the Silk Route (and, after the rise of Islam, the road of pilgrimage), wound its way across deserts, anchored by oases, across high passes and along the central Iranian and Anatolian plateaus to the Mediterranean.[20] From time immemorial it had provided a link between the Chinese, Iranian, Indian, and Roman civilizations. Along these same paths Buddhism spread from India to China and, in more spectacular fashion, Arab armies bore the green standard of Islam into western China less than a hundred years after Mohammed. Under their protection Nestorian Christians penetrated into Mongolia. Along these new frontiers of faith a fateful split opened up between the Sunnite and Shi'ia branches of Islam, adding a new dimension to the cultural diversity of Eurasia.

Along this route the tempo of the caravan trade fluctuated over time, but it remained remarkably vital in the frontier economies at least into the seventeenth century. When local political intermediaries failed to provide adequate protection, merchants continued to trade across the borders of the competing states through Sufi brotherhoods, especially the Naqshbandi networks.[21] In the debate over its subsequent decline, S. A. M. Adshead has provided an ingenious solution. He argues that the worldwide depression of the seventeenth century severely contracted the basic luxury trade along the central land route, but this decline stimulated the ecologically different north–south trade in necessities between the nomadic and sedentary societies. The east–west trade then recovered briefly and weakly in the eighteenth century. By this time, the main north–south trading route had become firmly established under Russian

---

[20] René Grousset, *The Empire of the Steppes. A History of Trans Caspia* (New Brunswick, NJ: Rutgers University Press, 1970), pp. xxii, 39–41, 48–52, 95–98, quotation on p. 22; Thomas T. Allsen, *Culture and Conquest in Mongol Eurasia* (Cambridge University Press, 2001), pp. 10–13.

[21] Isenbike Togan, "Inner Asian Muslim Merchants at the Closure of the Silk Routes in the Seventeenth Century," in Vadime Elisseff (ed.), *The Silk Roads. Highways of Culture and Commerce* (New York: Berghahn, 2000), pp. 247–63.

protection, a fact of enormous importance in understanding the subsequent advance of the Russians into the steppe.[22]

A more serious threat to the peace of the frontiers erupted in the form of large-scale migrations of pastoral nomads forced by unfavorable climatic factors or the demographic pressure of more powerful neighbors seeking better grasslands. Each successive wave absorbed remnants of previous migrations, increasing cultural diversity. Sweeping from east to west, periodic population movements disrupted the stable pattern of seasonal meridianal migration determined by the availability of grass for the herds. Once the migrating populations had spent their force and the tribal confederations that held them together had broken up, the nomads returned to the north–south pattern of grazing. This cyclical pattern repeated itself until once again, like the movement of trade, the cycle was broken by the conquest states that gradually brought to an end the dominance of the nomadic societies.

Among the earliest recorded mass migration of peoples that sent tremors throughout the sedentary fringes of the grasslands, the Scythians and Huns (Hsiung-nu) were described by both Greco-Roman and Chinese chroniclers, recording their impressions at opposite ends of the Eurasian frontiers. The Chinese did not often differentiate among the nomads to the north, referring to them as *hu* or *ti*, the latter term being especially derogatory, meaning animal-like.[23] Incursions into western Eurasia gave rise to often terrifying images of the nomads that became deeply embedded in the oral culture of the Slavic and Germanic peoples, as exemplified in the epic *Igor Tale* and the *Niebelungenlied*.[24] In the process of shaping

---

[22] Morris Rossabi, "The 'Decline' of the Trans Caspian Caravan Trade," in James Tracy (ed.), *The Rise of the Merchant Empires. Long Distance Trade in the Early Modern World, 1350–1750* (Cambridge University Press, 1990), pp. 351–70. See also S. A. M. Adshead, *Central Asia in World History* (London: St. Martin's Press, 1993), pp. 178–79; Niels Steensgaard, *Carracks, Caravans and Companies. The Structural Crisis in the European–Asia Trade in the Early Seventeenth Century* (Lund: Studentenlitteratur, 1973), p. 170; Janet Abu-Lughod, *Before European Hegemony. The World System A.D. 1250–1350* (New York: Oxford University Press, 1989); and André Gunder Frank, *The Centrality of Trans Caspia* (Amsterdam: V.U. University Press, 1992). For a discussion of the literature, see André Gunder Frank, "Trans Caspia's Continuing Role in the World Economy to 1800," in Michael Gervers and Wayne Schlepp (eds.), *Historical Themes and Current Change in Central and Inner Asia. Toronto Studies in Central and Inner Asia*, No. 3 (Toronto: University of Toronto Press, 1998), pp. 14–38.

[23] Sechin Jagghid and Van Jay Symons, *Peace, War, and Trade Along the Great Wall* (Bloomington, IN: Indiana University Press, 1989), pp. 172–73.

[24] The Huns were differently mythologized by the Germans as "the scourge of God" and by the Hungarians as the model of a polity. H. de Boor, *Das Attilabild in Geschichte, Legende und der heroisches Dichtung* (Darmstadt: Wissenschaftliche Buchgesellschaft, 1963), vol. II, p. 8; and Winder McConnell, *The Lament of the Niebelungen* (Columbia, SC: Camden House, 1994).

14   Imperial space

frontiers, the great ancient civilizations of Rome, Persia, and China gave them symbolic as well as military character by distinguishing the "civilized" from the "barbarian."[25] The self-defined "civilized" empires built walls at different times for different purposes. In the Sasanian Empire walls were constructed to defend against Huns, Khazars, and other migrations coming from the Caucasus. In China during the early period of the Warring States (403–221 BC), argues Nicola di Cosmo, "the walls were part of an overall expansionist strategy by Chinese northern states meant to support and protect their penetration into areas thus far alien to the Chou world." By contrast, Roman walls (limes) served both to keep the civilized in and the barbarians outside their perimeters.[26]

The formation of nomadic states again demonstrates the abilities of nomad societies to alter their relationship with the agricultural societies on the fringes of the steppe. The transformation of a confederation into a nomadic state required a political organization operating at a relatively high level, ruling over an extensive territory, and incorporating both pastoral and agricultural populations under a strong military leader who succeeded, however briefly, in establishing a dynastic succession. The death of the leader or internal rivalries would then lead to a break up of the confederation and a reversion to a fragmented politics. This was the cyclical process first analyzed by Ibn Khaldûn. Unless nomadic states underwent a transformation along sedentary lines like the Qing, Safavid, and Ottoman dynastic empires, they were unlikely to enjoy a long life. The productive process, that is, the management of herds, required a freedom of action that subverted superordinate authority. This was the main reason for "the instability and impermanence of nomadic politics."[27] Moreover, the stronger the residue of nomadic practices in the construction of a sedentary empire, the greater the resistance to centralized control and the weaker the capacity of the state to compete in the struggle over the Eurasian borderlands.

---

[25] The Chinese idea of an inner and outer zone can be traced to remote antiquity. Lien-sheng Yang, "Historical Notes on the Chinese World Order," in John K. Fairbank (ed.), *The Chinese World Order* (Cambridge, MA: Harvard University Press, 1968), p. 21.

[26] Arthur Waldron, *The Great Wall of China* (Cambridge University Press, 1990), pp. 68–69, 84, 110, 120–39; Richard N. Frye, *The Golden Age of Persia* (London: Phoenix Press, 2000), p. 14; C. R. Whittaker, *Frontiers of the Roman Empire. A Social and Economic Study* (Baltimore, MD: Johns Hopkins University Press, 1994); Brian J. Boeck, "Containment vs. Colonization. Muscovite Approaches to Settling the Steppe," in Nicholas B. Breyfogle, Abby Schrader, and Willard Sunderland (eds.), *Peopling the Russian Periphery. Borderland Colonization in Eurasian History* (London: Routledge, 2007), pp. 41–60.

[27] Khazanov, *Nomads*, pp. 44–53, 149–52, 164 ff.

Political unity under the Mongols

The Mongols were the most successful of the nomadic peoples in over-coming the obstacles posed by ecological and cultural diversities to create a vast land empire stretching over the 6,000-mile longitudinal expanse of Eurasia. After the rise of the multicultural bureaucratic empires, only the Russians would duplicate that feat, first under the tsars and then under the Bolsheviks. For this reason, perhaps, the two imperial enterprises have been conflated into an oversimplified concept of Eurasia, exaggerating the organic link between them. The image of the "Mongol yoke" runs like a guiding thread through the writing of Russian history. The earliest image of a wholly destructive Mongol impact on Russia was assiduously pro-moted by the so-called Muscovite book men of the sixteenth century who sought to weaken Tatar influences in the court. It was later embellished by nationalist Russian historians and became common currency in the grand narrative of Russian history.[28] It inspired the first Russian Eurasianists. It was then taken up by the Bolsheviks, enshrined in Stalin's famous speech denouncing Russia's backwardness, and surfaced again during the Sino-Soviet polemics over their disputed frontier.[29] Whatever the Mongol influence on Russian administrative and financial practices, or even con-cepts of rulership, its powerful presence and the myths that it spawned played an indisputable role in the subsequent struggle over the borderlands.[30]

The uniqueness of the Mongol Empire has been attributed by Thomas Barfield to its high degree of centralization; it was not "the culmination of a long evolving steppe tradition, but a deviation from it."[31] Three factors underlay the success of the Mongol conquest: the superior command structure and tactics of the army; the incorporation of weapons technol-ogy borrowed from China that enabled them to conduct siege warfare; and their synthesis of Turkic and Chinese styles of statecraft and ideo-logical legitimization. Their success in governance also reflected their understanding of two distinctive ecologies. "In the north the Mongols revived and extended older tributary relationships between steppe and

[28] Donald Ostrowski, *Muscovy and the Mongols. Cross-Cultural Influences on the Steppe Frontier, 1304–1589* (Cambridge University Press, 1998), "Introduction" and pp. 244–45.
[29] Charles J. Halperin, "The Tatar Yoke and Tatar Oppression," *Russia Mediaevalis* 5 (1984): 25. See also Stephen Kotkin, "Mongol Commonwealth? Exchange and Governance in Post Mongol Space," *Kritika* 8(3) (2007): 487–531.
[30] David Christian, *A History of Russia, Central Asia and Mongolia* (Malden, MA: Blackwell Publishers, 1998), vol. I, esp. pp. 412–18.
[31] Thomas Barfield, *The Perilous Frontier. Nomadic Empires and China, 221 BC to AD 1757* (Cambridge, MA: Harvard University Press, 1989), p. 197.

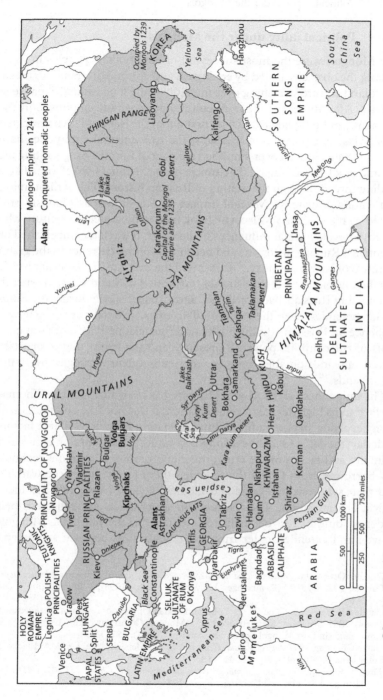

Map 1.1 The Mongol Empire, 1241

forest long characterized by indirect and intermittent methods of control." To the south they imposed new political structures on the agrarian societies they conquered. Perhaps their most important innovation was the "transfer of technicians of governance" between the Islamic and Chinese civilizations.[32] Interpretations of their conquest as having either saddled peoples with a Mongol yoke or presided over a Pax Mongolica reveal the complexity of its impact.[33] But both interpretations admit its initial devastating impact on societies as widely dispersed as North China, Kievan Rus, Iran, the Caucasus, and Hungary, encompassing a wide arc all along the frontiers of the grasslands. In a series of campaigns lasting from 1213 to 1234, the Mongols subjugated the major cities of North China, inflicting heavy losses on both the urban and rural populations, and imposing a heavy burden of labor conscription and taxes. They were not interested in rebuilding at the local level. But they fashioned a multi-cultural administration out of a complex amalgam of Chinese, Jürchen, Khitan, Uighur, and Mongol peoples that "was typical of the hybrid politics that had formed along China's steppe frontier since the collapse of the Han dynasty."[34] Over the following century, the Mongol rulers of the new Yuan dynasty hardly adapted at all to Chinese customs. But when they withdrew from China in 1368 many of their Inner Asian allies remained behind, testifying to the assimilating power of Chinese culture.[35]

Moving west, the Mongols devastated the two major centers of Russian urban and commercial life: the towns scattered along the upper Volga, Oka, and western Dvina, and those in the southwest along the Dnieper and its tributaries. Only Novgorod on the Baltic littoral was spared. Ruined centers like Kursk and Voronezh in the wooded steppe were not

---

[32] See the essays in David Sneath (ed.), *Imperial Statecraft. Political Forms and Techniques of Governance in Inner Asia, Sixth–Twentieth Centuries* (Bellingham, WA: Center for East Asian Studies, Western Washington University, 2006), esp. Thomas T. Allsen, "Technologies of Governance in the Mongolian Empire: A Geographic Overview," pp. 117–39, quotations pp. 135, 138.

[33] A more balanced picture has emerged. See, for example, Larry Moses, *The Political Role of Mongol Buddhism* (Bloomington, IN: Indiana University Press, 1977), pp. 1–82, who stresses Mongol policies of religious toleration, and, more generally, Charles J. Halperin, *Russia and the Golden Horde* (Bloomington, IN: Indiana University Press, 1985), esp. pp. 21–43, stressing skillful diplomacy and administrative practices.

[34] Thomas T. Allsen, "The Rise of the Mongolian Empire and Mongolian Rule in North China," in Herbert Franke and Denis Twitchett (eds.), *The Cambridge History of China, vol. 6: Alien Regimes and Border States, 907–1368* (Cambridge University Press, 1994), pp. 359–64, quotation on p. 362; and David O. Morgan, "Mongols," in H. A. R. Gibb *et al.* (eds.), *The Encyclopedia of Islam*, new edn (Leiden: Brill, 1993), vol. VII, p. 232.

[35] Frederick W. Mote, "Chinese Society under Mongol Rule, 1215–1368," in *Cambridge History of China*, vol. 6, pp. 644–48.

re-founded for three centuries; Kiev was reduced to a virtual ghost town, its vibrant economic life crippled for two centuries.[36] The Mongol domination over the Russian principalities, although indirect, deprived them of their sovereignty, and imposed heavy financial burdens. It shifted the political center of Russian life from the steppe to the forest zone, facilitating the rise of Muscovy with profound consequences for Eurasian history.

The Mongol invasion of Poland was brief. The country was not occupied like Hungary or incorporated into the Mongol (Qipchak) Empire like the Russian principalities. It was not even systematically looted. Although the Mongols defeated the Poles at the battle of Legnica (Liegnitz), the Poles converted defeat into a moral victory. The gallantry of their heavy cavalry inspired the Polish nobility to assume the mantle of defender of European civilization against the barbarism of the East, one of those enduring historical myths that resurfaced from time to time in Polish history. More concretely, the Poles joined with their Lithuanian neighbors to take advantage of the devastation of the Kievan lands in order to occupy territories ruled by west Russian princes and incorporate them into their expanding multicultural state.[37]

The two invasions of Hungary in 1241–1242 and 1285, and Mongol raids thereafter into the mid-fourteenth century, had long-term damaging material and psychological effects.[38] Widespread destruction, virtual depopulation of some regions, and a shift in the international trade routes from the east hampered recovery that was further delayed by a prolonged struggle between royal and noble authority. In order to repopulate large areas of the country, the monarchy invited another nomadic people, the Cumans, to settle in the Great Plain, further delaying the evolution of formal juridical and property rights. It also granted German "guests" extensive privileges in the royal manors of the north, foreshadowing the subsequent domination of urban life by non-Magyars. Even greater

---

[36] While the north recovered more rapidly, the ruined towns of the steppe remained exposed to nomadic raids. Cf. M. N. Tikhomirov, *The Towns of Ancient Rus'* (Moscow: Foreign Languages Publishing House, 1959), who stresses the destructive aspect; and R. A. French, "The Urban Network of Later Medieval Russia," in George Demko and Roland J. Fuchs (eds.), *Geographic Studies on the Soviet Union. Essays in Honor of Chauncey D. Harris* (University of Chicago Press, 1984), who gives a figure of forty new towns in northeast Russia for the end of the thirteenth century. The discrepancy is reconciled by J. L. I. Fennel, *The Crisis of Medieval Russia, 1200–1304* (London: Longman, 1983), pp. 86–89, who argues for serious but patchy destruction.

[37] A. Bruce Boswell, "Territorial Division and the Mongol Invasion, 1202–1300," in W. F. Reddaway (ed.), *The Cambridge History of Poland from the Origins to Sobieski (to 1696)* (Cambridge University Press, 1950), pp. 92–93.

[38] Peter Jackson, *The Mongols and the West* (Harlow: Longmans, 2004), pp. 68–70, 202–5, 212. From this time Hungarians considered themselves a "front-line state" against the barbarians to the east, *ibid.*, p. 200.

numbers of Slav and Vlach immigrants poured in from the north and southeast. Although many were assimilated, many were not.[39]

The south Caucasus endured three Mongol invasions in the early thirteenth century that crushed local resistance, reduced the power of the Georgian kings, and splintered political authority in the region. By engaging in periodic raiding throughout the south Caucasus, the Mongols uprooted local inhabitants, further jumbling the already highly mixed population of the region. As a strategic land bridge and a mountain refuge from nomadic raids, the region had a long history as a frontier between the Roman-Byzantine and Persian Empires, and the early Christian kingdoms and the Islamic conquest. Repeatedly ravaged by invasion and destabilized by migration and flight, the region displayed the classic features of a shatter zone with its heterogeneous population, contested identities, and rapidly shifting frontiers.[40] The Mongols controlled the region indirectly, as in Russia, collecting tribute and playing the local princes against one another. Here, as elsewhere, the Mongols spared those who accepted their authority. The Armenians, as dependent allies, were able to expand their mountain kingdom into the plains of Mesopotamia and Syria after the Mongols had destroyed the Muslim principalities that offered them resistance.[41] Another series of Tatar–Mongol invasions in the fourteenth century led by Timur-i-lang brought an end to a brief revival of Georgian royal power and cut a wide swath of destruction. The decline of urban life was catastrophic. Severely weakened and internally split into warring factions, the Georgian princes were no match for the Ottomans and Iranians advancing in the early fifteenth century on their southwestern and southeastern flanks.[42]

[39] Pal Engel, "The Age of the Angevins, 1301–1382," in Peter Sugar (ed.), *A History of Hungary* (Bloomington, IN: Indiana University Press, 1990), p. 48; Lázsló Kuntler, *Millennium in Central Europe. A History of Hungary* (Budapest: Atlantisz, 1999), pp. 80–81; András Pálóczi Horváth, *Pechenegs, Cumans, Iasians* (Budapest: Corvina, 1989), pp. 54–61.

[40] Hayrapet Margarian, "The Nomads and Ethnopolitical Realities of Transcaucasus in the 11–14th Centuries," in *Iran and the Caucasus* (Leiden: Brill, 2001), vol. V, pp. 75–78; Cyril Toumanoff, "Armeno-Georgian Marchlands," in *Studies in Christian Caucasian History* (Washington, DC: Georgetown University Press, 1963), pp. 437–84.

[41] Peter B. Golden, "The Turkic Peoples and Caucasia," in Ronald Grigor Suny (ed.), *Transcaucasus, Nationalism and Social Change. Essays in the History of Armenia, Azerbaijan and Georgia*, rev. edn (Ann Arbor, MI: University of Michigan Press, 1996), pp. 62–66; Angus David Stewart, *The Armenian Kingdom and the Mamluks. War and Diplomacy during the Reign of Het'um II* (The Hague: Mouton, 2001), pp. 43–46.

[42] W. E. D. Allen, *A History of the Georgian People from the Beginning to the Russian Conquest in the Nineteenth Century* (New York: Barnes & Noble, 1971), pp. 125–27, 137–39; Ronald Grigor Suny, *The Making of the Georgian Nation* (Bloomington, IN: Indiana University Press, 1994), pp. 40–46.

In Trans Caspia, the Mongol conquest of Khwarazm (Qwarezm), a Muslim state based on the great oases cities of Transoxania, leveled such flourishing centers as Balkh, Nishapur, and Herat. After a short siege Bukhara was reduced to such a pitiable state, according to Muslim chroniclers, that not enough people were left to populate a single neighborhood in the city.[43] The second generation of Mongol conquerors, the successors of Chingghis Khan, invaded Iran, inflicting enormous damage on Baghdad and other urban centers. Iran never fully recovered economically from the destruction of its extensive irrigation system.[44]

In the south Caucasus, south Russia, and Hungary the short-term Mongol impact was, with a few local exceptions, to weaken or destroy established institutions and patterns of socioeconomic life. But elsewhere the picture was not uniform, and continues to be much disputed by scholars and myth makers. On the positive side, under a Pax Mongolica the Mongol princes preserved and expanded the ancient trade routes, forming close alliances with international merchants not only to promote exchange, but also to gather intelligence.[45] Under their aegis a Turko-Persian culture flourished in Trans Caspia and parts of Inner Asia, although its homogeneity has been questioned. After their conversion to Islam, the Mongol princes observed a policy of tolerance toward other religions. Mongol arts and crafts contributed to the development of a highly refined Eurasian style.[46] But the political unity imposed by the Mongols on Eurasia only lasted a hundred years. Their attempt to create a unitary empire with a strong central government was undermined by the policy of parceling out territories and armies to the descendants of Chingghis Khan, which contributed to the revival of earlier ethnic and tribal loyalties, and the increased Turkification of many of the successor states. The result was a cultural decline and the restoration of nomadic

[43] Luc Kwanten, *Imperial Nomads. A History of Central Asia, 500–1500* (Philadelphia, PA: University of Pennsylvania Press, 1979), pp. 118–20.

[44] Morgan, "Mongols," p. 231; John A. Boyle (trans.), *The Successors of Ghengis Khan* (New York: Columbia University Press, 1971); and Berthold Spüler, *Die Mongolen in Iran. Politik, Verwaltung und Kultur de Ilchane-Zeit, 1220–1350* (Berlin: Academie Verlag, 1955).

[45] Thomas T. Allsen, "Mongol Princes and their Merchant Partners, 1200–1260," *Asia Major*, 2nd series, 2 (1989): 83–125; and E. Endicott-West, "Merchant Associations in Yuan China. The Ortoy," *Asia Major*, 3rd series, 2 (1989): 127–45.

[46] Robert L. Canfield, "Introduction: The Turko-Persian Tradition," in *Turko-Persia in Historical Perspective* (Cambridge University Press, 2001); Reuven Amitai-Preiss and David Morgan (eds.), *The Mongol Empire and its Legacy* (Leiden: Brill, 2000), esp. the essays by Amitai-Preiss and Ann K. S. Lambton; Thomas T. Allsen, *Mongol Imperialism. The Policies of the Grand Qan Möngke in China, Russia and the Islamic Lands, 1251–1259* (Berkeley, CA: University of California Press, 1987).

ways of life in the steppes and oases of the Inner Asian core of imperial power.[47]

Following the break up of the Mongol Empire, a number of Mongol or Turko-Mongol successor states established themselves on its former territory: the Yuan dynasty in China; the Il-khans in Iran; the khanates of Sibir, Kazan, and Astrakhan; and smaller khanates in the oases of Trans Caspia and the south Caucasus. But none of them sought to restore the unity of Eurasia. They proved to be relatively short-lived. By the late fifteenth and early sixteenth centuries the new major centers of power were beginning to emerge that would dominate the history of Eurasia and the struggle over the borderlands over the following 400 years. Although nomadic tribes founded three of them, the Ottoman, Safavid, and Qing empires, they rapidly adapted, shifting their centers of power to the agricultural lands to the south of the steppe, and adopted the bureaucratic structures and cultural trappings of imperial rule. Like the agrarian states of Muscovy, the Polish–Lithuanian Commonwealth, and the (Austrian) Habsburg Empire, they built their power on the periphery of the Mongol Empire and expanded militarily along their outer frontiers, incorporating new territories as imperial borderlands by applying a variety of strategies ranging from dynastic alliances to conquest, colonization, and conversion. This process profoundly affected the course of state-building. The following section explores imperial frontier strategies as an introduction to the evolution of imperial ideologies and institutions to be taken up in the next two chapters.

The Ottoman Empire

The Ottoman Empire had its origins in one of the great migrations of Turkic tribes and tribal confederations coming out of Trans Caspia. In the tenth and eleventh centuries, Turkic tribes, already dominant in the sedentary areas of Trans Caspia, moved west and south. Within a century, they were pressing against the frontiers of the Byzantine Empire in eastern Anatolia. The Byzantines who bore the brunt of this massive migration did not see them as one nation. They referred to them by many names, and attributed to them different, even obscure, religious practices. The Turks were conscious of being one people.[48] In Anatolia, Armenia,

---

[47] Peter B. Golden, "'I Will Give the People Unto Thee.' The Činggisid Conquests and their Aftermath in the Turkish World," *Journal of the Royal Asiatic Society*, 3rd series, 10(1) (April 2000): 21–41.
[48] N. Oikonomides, "The Turks in the Byzantine Rhetoric of the Twelfth Century," in C. E. Farah (ed.), *Decision Making and Change in the Ottoman Empire* (Kirksville, MO: Thomas Jefferson Press, 1993), pp. 140–60.

Kurdistan, and northern Syria their tribal dynasties established semi-independent principalities, which were unified by the Seljuk dynasty (1040–1118). The Turkic nomadic cavalry formed part of the Seljuk armies that reunited the Islamic lands from the Mediterranean to Trans Caspia. When the Mongols overwhelmed the Seljuk Empire, their ranks were swelled by new groups of Islamicized Turkic tribes who settled along the old Byzantine–Seljuk frontier. Among the smaller Muslim principalities, the Turkic Osmanlı were by no means the most powerful. But under skillful leadership they absorbed other tribal groups, forming the basis of the Ottoman Empire. Beginning in the fourteenth century, the Ottoman Turks crossed from Anatolia into the Balkans, advancing over the following two centuries into the Danubian Basin, Pontic steppe, the Caucasus, and Trans Caspia, where they subsequently encountered the expanding power of the Habsburgs, Russians, and Iranians.

The Ottoman conquest of the Byzantine Empire, and the smaller kingdoms and principalities in the Balkans, culminated in their capture of Constantinople in 1453. To consolidate their imperial rule they employed a combination of colonization, conversion, and the co-optation of elites. The Ottoman conquest of the Balkans took place in two stages, from 1352 to 1402 and from 1415 to 1467 as a gradual process, beginning with a series of raids that forced the local ruler to accept Ottoman suzerainty and pay tribute. When circumstances permitted, the ruling elites were replaced by Ottoman administrators and soldiers.[49] There is still considerable debate among historians over the relative weight to be assigned to colonization and conversion in explaining the imposition of Ottoman control. The idea that the Ottoman state promoted and directed a mass Turkic colonization to inundate the local population has been refuted and replaced by a more complex picture of piecemeal and spontaneous movement of nomads and semi-nomads into the Balkans.[50] The indisputable result was the creation of a vast shatter zone.

During the early period of Ottoman expansion, the sultans preserved, and in some cases expanded, the role of nomadic tribes, creating, in the felicitous expression of Reşat Kasaba, "a moveable empire."[51] The rulers devised special rules for regulating tribal affairs, classified the tribes, and

---

[49] Halil Inalcık, "Ottoman Methods of Conquest," *Studia Islamica* 2 (1954): 103–29.
[50] Antonina Zhelyazkova, "Islamization in the Balkans," in Fikret Adanir and Suraiya Faroqui (eds.), *The Ottomans and the Balkans. A Discussion of Historiography* (Leiden: Brill, 2002), pp. 231–35. Cf. Omar Barkan, "Déportation comme méthode de peuplement et de colonisation dans l'empire Ottoman," *İstanbul Üniversitesi İktisat Fakültesi Memuası* (1946–1950), vol. XI, pp. 524–69; vol. XIII, pp. 56–79; vol. XV, pp. 209–329.
[51] Reşat Kasaba, *A Moveable Empire. Ottoman Nomads, Migrants and Refugees* (Seattle, WA: University of Washington Press, 2009).

appointed tribal officials to administer and collect taxes. They governed relations between the nomads and the sedentary population, and protected the migratory routes. The nomadic tribes performed important functions throughout the empire in providing networks of trade and communications, but were especially valued on the expanding frontiers. They were used to occupy conquered areas where the political structures were weak and local communities disrupted or dispersed. They operated as a powerful military force in the early centuries when cavalry was the dominant branch of armies. In the fourteenth century in the Balkans the spontaneous migration of 10,000 nomads linking up with Vlachs and Albanians prepared the way for subsequent conquest by the regular army. In the fifteenth century, Çepni Turkmens from the Black Sea region were resettled in northern Albania. The government also resorted to forced migration to punish recalcitrants. In 1502, landed families in frontier districts of eastern Anatolia who sympathized with the Iranian Safavids from eastern Anatolia were forcibly resettled in the Morea, and in the 1570s rebellious tribesmen from eastern Anatolia were transported to Cyprus.[52]

During the evolution from a nomadic-tribal organization to a sedentary-imperial state, especially after the conquest of Constantinople, population transfers were also used to strengthen urban economies. Having conquered Constantinople with its depleted Greek population, Mehmed II ordered the mass resettlement of peasants from the newly conquered lands of Serbia and Morea to the neighborhood of his new capital, renamed Istanbul. In 1455, he uprooted all the Jewish communities in the Balkans and resettled them in Istanbul to stimulate its economic life. Throughout his reign he continued to bring in other ethnic groups, Armenians, Greeks, and Muslims, to repopulate the capital.[53]

Conversion to the Sunni branch of Islam seems to have played a larger role in Islamicization of the Balkans than colonization, although firm numbers are hard to come by. The process of conversion too has engendered a vigorous debate between historians who emphasize either voluntary, "social conversion," or forced conversion. There is evidence on both sides. Beginning in the early fifteenth century, the conscription of non-Muslim, mainly peasant, boys to fill the ranks of the elite military formation of the Janissary Corps provided about 200,000 forced converts to Islam, although the institution was also regarded by some Christian families as a means of upward social mobility.

[52] Rudi Paul Lindner, *Nomads and Ottomans in Medieval Anatolia* (Bloomington, IN: Indiana University Press, 1983), p. 109.
[53] Halil Inalcik, "Istanbul," *Encyclopedia of Islam*, 2nd edn, vol. IV, pp. 224–48.

With the exception of the janissaries, conversion began slowly, according to Anton Minkov, passing through three periods: "the innovators" and "early adopters," complete by the 1530s; and the "early majority," accelerating in the 1640s and reaching its peak in the second quarter of the eighteenth century when an estimated 50 percent of the Muslim population of the Balkans were converts. In the eighteenth century, conversion came to a sudden halt. This was due in part to a rise in fundamentalism, which placed greater demands upon the convert, and in part to social and economic changes, which whittled away the practical advantages of conversion. By 1831, the total percentage of Muslims in the Balkans had declined to 37 percent. But the pattern of distribution varied greatly. Muslims were particularly strong in the borderlands facing the Habsburg Empire: reaching figures of over 70 percent in Albania and Kosovo; almost 40 percent in Macedonia; and 50 percent in Bosnia and Hercegovina.[54]

The widespread voluntary conversion of the Bosnian nobility and peasantry to Islam was exceptional in the long frontiers between Christianity and Islam. There is some debate about why this should have been so. A number of factors appear to have played a role; all of them were, however, due to "the privileged position Bosnia had acquired as already in the sixteenth century as the crucial frontier province of Ottoman Europe." In part, the decision to convert reflected the peculiar features of Bosnian socioeconomic life. The Ottoman policy of granting *timars* (land in return for service to the state) to the local Christian elite and their conversion to Islam was followed by the conversion of their peasants and dependent people. Concurrently, peasants converted to escape the heavy labor services of their Christian landlords.[55] In part, conversion was facilitated by the lack of a well-defined frontier of faith in the region. At the outer edges

---

[54] Anton Minkov, *Conversion to Islam in the Balkans* (Leiden: Brill, 2004), pp. 43–61, 195–98. For a critique of the view that there were large-scale conversions in the Sofia region and, by implication, elsewhere in the eastern Balkans, see Géza Dávid, "Limitations of Conversion: Muslims and Christians in the Balkans in the Sixteenth Century," in Eszter Andor and István György Tóth (eds.), *Frontiers of Faith. Religious Exchange and the Constitution of Religious Identities 1400–1750* (Budapest: European Science Foundation, 2001), pp. 149–54. Under the reign of Mehmed IV (1648–1687), who united his personal piety with his military prowess, conversions spread to new borderlands of Crete and Podolia in Poland. It was said that even his hunting expeditions brought converts into the fold. Marc David Baer, *Honored by the Glory of Islam. Conversion and Conquest in Ottoman Europe* (New York: Oxford University Press, 2008), pp. 160–61, 177–78.

[55] Fikret Adanir, "The Formation of a Muslim Nation in Bosnia-Hercegovina. A Historiographic Discussion," in Fikret Adanir and Suraiya Faroqui (eds.), *The Ottomans and the Balkans. A Discussion of Historiography* (Leiden: Brill, 2002), pp. 267–304, quotation on p. 295.

of the ancient division between Greek and Latin Christianity, "no faith had a strong organization to bind its flock to the church either through faith or beliefs or a sense of community," in the words of John V. A. Fine, "changing religion was a general multidirectional phenomenon."[56] Local folk traditions common to both Christianity and Islam coexisted and mingled. The boundary between them was easily crossed.

In the regions of Dalmatia and Slavonia the main lines of religious struggle did not take place between Muslims and Christians, but between the Christian churches. Throughout the sixteenth and seventeenth centuries the Orthodox and Catholic hierarchies competed fiercely for spiritual care over the Christian population and the right to collect taxes from them.[57] By contrast, the Ottomans were even-handed in their treatment of the established Christian churches. Soon after the Ottoman conquest of Bosnia, Mehmed II gave permission for the Franciscan Order to establish monasteries, which became centers of learning in the region. By the seventeenth century, the Bosnian Franciscans, who had been born subjects of the sultan, enjoyed greater freedom of action in their missionary activities than their main Catholic rivals, the Jesuits, who were considered by the Ottomans to be agents of the Habsburg Empire and therefore the enemy. Their linguistic abilities also gave the Franciscans the edge in the Banat, where the majority of the population spoke either a south Slavic tongue or Romanian, which was close to the Italian spoken by the Franciscans coming from Dalmatia. In Hungary, they could fall back on Latin which was still the lingua franca in what was otherwise a Babel of tongues. As late as the nineteenth century, the monks were the first in the province, and apparently in the empire, to compile a modern Turkish dictionary and develop a center of Turkology.[58]

The role of Ottoman frontiers in state-building emerged from the fusion of three cultural streams: Islamic messianism; the Turkic warrior ethos; and the Byzantine imperial tradition. The founders of the Ottoman

---

[56] John V. A. Fine, "The Medieval and Ottoman Roots of Modern Bosnian Society," in Mark Pinson (ed.), *The Muslims of Bosnia and Hercegovina. The Historic Development from the Middle Ages to the Dissolution of Yugoslavia* (Cambridge, MA: Harvard University Press, 1996), pp. 13, 16.

[57] Milo Bogović, *Katolička crkva i pravoslavlje u Dalmaciji za vrijeme mletačke vladavine* (Zagreb: Kršćanska sadašnjost, 1993); Josip Buturac, *Katolička crkva u Slavoniji za turskoga vladanja* (Zagreb: Kršćanska sadašnjost, 1982). I am grateful to Drago Roksandic for bringing these sources to my attention.

[58] István-György Tóth, "Les missionnaires franciscains venus de l'étranger en Hongrie au XVIIe siècle avant la période de reconquête catholique," *XVIIe siècle* 50 (1998): 222, 225–29; Ekrem Čaušević, "A Church of Bosnian Turkology. The Franciscans and the Turkish Language," in Markus Kaller and Kemal H. Karpat (eds.), *Ottoman Bosnia. A History in Peril* (Madison, WI: University of Wisconsin Press, 2004), pp. 241–53.

frontier thesis, Paul Wittek and Mehmed Fuad Köprülü, made a distinction in the early period of Ottoman expansion between the core and the frontier in terms of social structure and cultural characteristics. Köprülü, influenced by the Annales School, took a broader view of the frontier, embracing its distinctive religious, legal, economic, and artistic institutions. Wittek stressed the *gazi* warrior milieu rooted in Islamic religious zeal. By the thirteenth century, warrior cultures had appeared on both sides of the contested Turkic–Byzantine frontier. They were originally composed of Islamic *gazis* and Greek *akritai*, but were increasingly replaced by Turkmen tribesmen recruited from the other side. In this intermediate zone war and trade often alternated in a pattern similar to that on the ancient Roman and Chinese frontiers, and facilitated the penetration and conquest of the Byzantine Empire by the Ottoman Turks.[59]

Research in frontier narratives and subsequent Islamic religious texts have now demonstrated that the *gazi* concept of the early Ottoman state meant different things to different people, reflecting various interests that were vigorously promoted by rulers, frontier warriors, and the ulama. Historians now substitute for the "Ghazi Thesis" an Islamo-Christian syncretism.[60] Although the early Ottoman state can no longer be equated with the idea of jihad or holy war, there is no denying that it represented the spirit of conquest that lay at the foundations of Ottoman state-building.

The Ottoman ruling elite employed the term *Jihad*, derived from the precepts of Islam and imbued with both military and spiritual aspects, to represent the division of the world into two cultural spheres, the *dār ul-Islām*, the abode of Islam, and the *dār ul-harb*, the abode of war. Between them stretched contested space where warriors fought the just war consecrated by Islam. This provided the ruling elites with a justification for expansion in all directions. But this rigid duality could not be strictly maintained.

[59] Paul Wittek, *La formation de l'empire ottoman* (London: Valorium Reprints, 1982). See also Halil Inalcik (a student of Köprülü), "The Impact of the Annales School on Ottoman Studies and New Findings," *Journal of the Fernand Braudel Center* 1(3/4) (1978): 69–96. Reviews of Wittek's critics and defenders are Cemal Kafadar, *Between Two Worlds. The Construction of the Ottoman State* (Berkeley, CA: University of California Press, 1995), pp. 35–59; Colin Heywood, "The Frontier in Ottoman History: Old Ideas and New Myths," in Daniel Power and Naomi Standen (eds.), *Frontiers in Question. Eurasian Borderlands, 700–1700* (New York: St. Martin's Press, 1999), pp. 228–50.

[60] Heath W. Lowry, *The Nature of the Early Ottoman State* (Albany, NY: State University of New York Press, 2003), pp. 142–43; Linda T. Darling, "Contested Territory: Ottoman Holy War in Comparative Context," *Studia Islamica* (2000): 133–63. See also Kafadar, *Between Two Worlds*; Colin Imber, *Studies in Ottoman History and Law* (Istanbul: Isis, 1996).

The Ottoman rulers created frontier marches (*uc*) under the leadership of frontier lords who enjoyed considerable autonomy. In return they were obliged to furnish armed men, both Muslims and Christians, as frontier troops.[61] The image of the Islamic warrior tradition eroded over the following centuries, changing the process and rationalization of state-building.

The conquest of Constantinople in 1453 was the first major turning point that spelled the beginning of the end of the Ottoman concept of the ever-expanding frontier and the beginning of an imperial state system.[62] Soon thereafter the Ottoman sultans began to authorize the demarcation of boundary lines with Christian states, first with the Venetian Republic. From the fifteenth to the seventeenth centuries, the Ottomans signed a series of peace agreements with Hungary, Poland, and the Habsburgs signifying at least temporarily the existence of a power equilibrium. Even more pragmatically, they recognized the autonomy of vassal borderlands adjoining complex frontiers, such as the Crimean khanate and the principalities of Moldavia and Wallachia, to avoid the costs and uncertainties of military expeditions far from their home bases.

The second major turning point in the Ottoman concept of frontiers was the Treaty of Karlowitz in 1699. Bringing to an end a long war with the Habsburgs, it signaled another step away from the concept of the ever-expanding frontier justified by jihad to a more defensive posture relying more on mediation and fixed boundaries recognized by international treaties with Christian states. As Virginia Aksan has written, "the psychological impact of the abandonment of the idea of the 'ever expanding frontier' of Islam should not be underestimated."[63] That this treaty signified "a formal closure of the Ottoman frontier" is, however, somewhat misleading.[64] Once the forward movement of the Ottoman *gazi* warriors had been checked, internal forces worked to weaken the Ottoman frontier defenses and reverse the process, creating new frontiers and accelerating the process of internal instability.

After Karlowitz, the sultans began to restrict the movement of nomads and attempted to settle them on vacant or under-populated land. The

---

[61] Colin Imber, "The Legend of the Osman Gazi," in E. Zachariadou (ed.), *The Ottoman Emirate (1300–1389)* (Rethymnon: University of Crete Press, 1993), pp. 67–75; Heywood, "The Frontier," pp. 233–35.

[62] Kafadar, *Between Two Worlds*, p. 152.

[63] Virginia H. Aksan, "Locating the Ottomans among Early Modern Empires," *Journal of Early Modern History* 2 (1999): 110.

[64] Cf. Rifaat A. Abou-el-Haj, "The Formal Closure of the Ottoman Frontier in Europe: 1699–1703," *Journal of the American Oriental Society* 89(3) (July–September 1969): 467–70.

central authorities were already concerned about the effect of the wandering population in the internal provinces. Between around 1600 to the mid-nineteenth century there was a general movement from the plains into the mountains primarily in order to escape irregular demands for tribute and taxes related to frontier wars. The continuous presence of nomads added to the deteriorating sense of security.[65] The flight of the tax-paying population to less accessible environments created both a fiscal and security problem. The burden of taxes fell on a diminishing population, increasing their discontent and resistance; the mountains provided not only a refuge, but hospitable terrain for armed bands. In periods following the wars of the sixteenth and seventeenth centuries against the Habsburgs, discharged Muslim peasants recruited into paramilitary bands roamed the countryside, forming bandit gangs that terrorized the countryside.

As the frontier receded further in the eighteenth century, nomadic warriors who continued the *gazi* tradition and lived from booty were forced to retreat, thereby losing the source of their livelihood. Disdainful of agricultural pursuits, they turned to brigandage and periodically incited rebellion. They were joined by elements of the local peasantry who were protesting against the growing tax burden. This was the origin of the *hayduk* (bandit) movement. Even before the national liberation movements in the early nineteenth century, armed bands raised the level of violence in this vast shatter zone to new levels.

The Ottoman Empire faced similar problems in defending its Islamic frontiers. In the first decades of the seventeenth century, Turkmen migrations repeatedly created friction between the Ottomans and the Iranians. The long-disputed frontier between the Ottoman and Safavid empires was a shatter zone par excellence, inhabited by Arabs, Kurds, Muslim Georgians (*Adjary*), and Laz; nor was there a clear-cut line dividing the Sunni and Shi'ia populations. The population was mainly nomadic because the climate of the region was inhospitable to sedentary life. Both the Ottoman and Safavid empires sought to recruit local tribes in the endemic warfare between them over a century and a half. Pastoral nomads called Boz-Ulus virtually paralyzed the Ottoman government when the Iranians counterattacked in their long war with the Ottomans.[66] After the peace of Zuhab in 1639 the frontier remained fairly

---

[65] Wolf-Dieter Hüteroth, "Ecology of the Ottoman Lands," in Suraiya N. Faroqui (ed.), *The Cambridge History of Turkey, vol. 3: The Later Ottoman Empire, 1603–1839* (Cambridge University Press, 2006), pp. 32–35.

[66] Halil Inalcik, *The Ottoman State, Economy and Society, 1300–1600* (Cambridge University Press, 1994), pp. 24, 32, 40, 96, 165–66; Inalcik, "Military and Fiscal Transformation in the Ottoman Empire, 1600–1700," *Archivum Ottomanicum* VI (1980): 284–87.

stable, though not clearly delimited between Iraq and Iran until the twentieth century.[67]

After Mehmed II conquered the Greek Empire of Trebizond, the last of the Greek successor states to Byzantium, most of the Christian population converted to Sunni Islam. Only a minority remained in the Orthodox Church. Under Ottoman rule Turkmen tribes occupied the arable valleys, driving the remaining Greeks into the highlands where they remained until the population exchanges following the First World War. Migrations of Turkmen nomads into eastern Anatolia continued into the eighteenth century. The arrival of the Çepni Turkmens in the eighteenth century corresponded with the rise of the great dynasties of the lords of the valley (derebeys). They long enjoyed virtually complete local independence from the Ottoman center of power, continuing an ancient tradition going back to Byzantine times.[68] Once at the cutting-edge of imperial expansion, increasingly Turkmen nomads became one of the most destabilizing social elements not only in the borderlands, but in the imperial center of power.[69]

In the south Caucasus, Ottoman frontier policy achieved greater success along the Black Sea coast than in the highlands of Armenia and Kurdistan. The Circassians and Georgians were drawn into the commercial life of the Black Sea dominated by the Turks, and they supplied highly valued slaves to the armies and harems of the sultan. But once the Turks attempted to drive the Iranians out of the highlands they encountered stiff resistance from the mountain tribes. Subsequently, the Russians, much to their grief, inherited this resistance to their establishment of a secure southern frontier.[70]

The third major turning point in the Ottoman concept of frontiers occurred at the end of the eighteenth century. The reconquest of Belgrade from the Habsburgs in 1739 was the last gasp of Ottoman expansion, followed by a period of deceptive calm along the west Balkan and Danubian frontiers, which was brought to an end by the massive intervention of Russia on the frontiers. This dramatic turning point in the struggle over the borderlands is taken up in Chapter 4.

---

[67] Rudi Matthee, "The Safavid–Ottoman Frontier. Iraq-i Arab as seen by the Safavids," Kemal Karpat with Robert W. Zens (eds.), *Ottoman Borderlands. Issues, Personalities and Political Changes* (Madison, WI: University of Wisconsin Press, 2003), pp. 170–71.

[68] Anthony Bryer, "The Last Laz Risings and the Downfall of the Pontic Derebeys, 1812–1840," in *Peoples and Settlements in Anatolia and the Caucasus, 800–1900* (London: Variorum Reprints, 1988), pp. 191–99.

[69] Lindner, *Nomads and Ottomans*.

[70] Carl Max Kortepeter, *Ottoman Imperialism during the Reformation. Europe and the Caucasus* (New York University Press, 1972); B. A. Gardanova *et al.* (eds.), *Narody Kavkaza*, 2 vols. (Moscow: Akademiia nauk, 1962), vol. II, p. 376.

The Iranian empires

In Iran the early stage of state-building under the Safavid dynasty was, like the Ottoman, launched by a nomadic military enterprise operating from a frontier environment. Like its Qajar successors, the founders of the dynasty were Turkic tribesmen from the rich pasture lands of the Iranian frontier province of Azerbaijan in the south Caucasus. Still in touch with their nomadic heritage, they retained their faith in the radical and chiliastic sects related to the Shi'ite branch of Islam. The Safavid dynasty, like its imperial predecessors, confronted a threatening nomadic presence on its frontiers from three directions: the Caucasian isthmus; the north, facing the Turkmens; and the northeast, facing the Afghans. The defense and expansion of its frontiers depended upon the ability of charismatic Turkic tribal leaders, like Shah Ismail and Shah Abbas, to conquer the outer lands by combining military skills with universalist claims of Shi'ia messianism. Tribal allegiances fluctuated depending on frontier conditions. The Kurds in particular were notorious for switching loyalties. The Shahsevan tribal confederacy turned to cross-border banditry when their traditional way of life was threatened and their pastoral territory was divided after two Russo-Iranian wars in the first quarter of the nineteenth century. By the early twentieth century they had become one of the most highly unstable social groups in Iran.[71] In the early twentieth century, a quarter of the population was still nomadic. As one leading authority put it: "tribal groups have occupied Iran's borders for centuries because the peripheries of state power were where the tribal formations flourished and tribal groups endured."[72]

Aside from the tribal frontiers, there were also several religious frontiers: Shi'ia–Sunni in the west, with the Ottomans and in Trans Caspia with the Uzbeks; and Islamic–Christian in the Caucasus with Georgia. Yet here, too, the confessional lines were not rigid even though the early Safavids attempted to convert the non-Shi'ia population. The existence of the mystical Sufi sects of Sunni Islam added another complexity to Iran's religious frontiers. Though persecuted, they survived among the tribes in the frontier zone. There they became involved in frequent

---

[71] Richard Tapper, *Frontier Nomads of Iran. A Political and Social History of the Shahsevan* (Cambridge University Press, 1997).
[72] Lois Beck, "Tribes and the State in Nineteenth and Twentieth Century Iran," in Philip Khoury and J. Kostiner, *Tribes and State Formation in the Middle East* (Berkeley, CA: University of California Press, 1990), p. 201.

rebellions against the authority of a centralized state.[73] Passing through a belt of shatter zones, Iranian frontiers were among the most ill-defined, porous, and fluctuating among the Islamic states, indeed, of all Eurasia.

Although similarly vague and changing, the concept of *Iranshahr* has nonetheless persisted from the fall of the Sasanian Empire until the present day. It was highly fluid without reference to ethnic or religious boundaries. As in the Ottoman Empire, the idea of the ever-expanding frontier prevailed among the rulers well into the nineteenth century. At its height in the 1660s Iranshahr extended in the east from the oasis of Merv in Transoxenia and Qandahar in Afghanistan to Daghestan, Armenia, and Kurdistan in the west. At times the concept was infused with delusions of grandeur: "The hunger for empire emerged vividly in Qajar narratives." The founder of the dynasty, Aqa Muhammad Khan, admitted to seeking to restore Iran's "natural boundaries" from the mountains of the Caucasus to the Punjab. Qa'im Maqam Farahani, the chief minister of the heir to the throne, Abbās Mīrzā, urged the crown prince to seize the occasion of Tsar Alexander I's death in 1825 "to seize Crimea and Moscow from the Tsar and proceed to conquer Russia and Rum." Even after the Iranians were forced to renounce all claims on Afghan territory in the mid-nineteenth century, many Iranians continued to view Herat as part of their patrimony.[74] The idea died hard among Iranian intellectuals and officials that the acquisition and defense of land was the symbolic measure of imperial rule.[75]

Like the Ottoman Empire, Iran suffered large territorial losses and a contraction of its frontiers in the eighteenth and nineteenth centuries, which will be discussed in Chapter 4. Retreat was accompanied by a greater secularization of the state. In both cases, this meant a withering away of the last vestiges of messianism and the real end to the ever-expanding frontier of Iranshahr.

The Chinese empires

Before the advent of the Qing dynasty (1644–1918), the Chinese had devised, in the words of A. I. Johnston, two alternating "strategic

---

[73] Hamid Algar, "Religious Forces in Eighteenth and Nineteenth Century Iran," in *The Cambridge History of Iran* (Cambridge University Press, 1991), vol. 7, pp. 705–31; Lawrence Lockhart, *The Fall of the Safavid Dynasty and the Afghan Occupation of Persia* (Cambridge University Press, 1958), pp. 11–12, 102.

[74] Nikki R. Keddie, *Qajar Iran and the Rise of Reza Khan, 1796–1925* (Costa Mesa, CA: Mazda, 1999), pp. 32–33.

[75] Firoozeh Kashani-Sabet, *Frontier Fictions. Shaping the Iranian Nation, 1804–1946* (Princeton University Press, 1999), pp. 15–16, 19, 22–23.

cultures" to deal with the outer world in general and the Inner Asian frontiers in particular. The first he labeled "Confucian," which emphasizes defensive warfare and a preference for negotiation in dealing with barbarians. The second he calls *parabellum*, which assumes the inevitability of violent conflict.[76] On the tactical level, the Chinese resorted to a multiple approach: sustaining trade and tribute relations; launching punitive raids or full-scale military campaigns into nomadic territory; playing barbarians against barbarians; and constructing defensive walls. A permanent resolution to the nomadic problem appeared difficult, if not impossible, in the era preceding modern methods of communication and transportation. Faced with superior Chinese strength on the frontier, the nomads could always withdraw deep into the steppe where pursuit was limited by logistical considerations.

Throughout the four centuries from the end of the Tang dynasty until the Mongol conquest, the two strategies and the four tactics worked largely because China was shielded from a massive invasion of the steppe nomads by several semi-nomadic states that occupied the region north of the Yellow River. The organization of a powerful Mongol confederacy under Chingghis Khan dramatically changed the strategic balance. The Mongol Yuan dynasty failed in its ambitious effort to fuse the Chinese and steppe cultures. Following their established practice, the Mongols consolidated their power, adopted the culture and imperial structure of the vanquished, but then forfeited the loyalty of the tribal leaders without winning over the Chinese population. In the words of F. W. Mote: "They failed in the steppe pattern of failure."[77] After they were overthrown by a domestic rebellion, the region north of the Yellow River reverted to its traditional state as a complex frontier where the new, purely Chinese Ming dynasty (1368–1644), the Mongols, and Jürchen (later Manchu) peoples competed for supremacy. Unlike the sites of other state-building projects in Eurasia, ethnic and religious hostility played no role here, in part because the Confucian ethical system had no place for either prejudice.[78]

From the very earliest period of Chinese history, the river civilization to the south of the Yellow River with its intensive agriculture organized in cellular villages was distinct from the arid and semi-arid steppe to the

---

[76] Alastair Iain Johnston, *Cultural Realism. Strategic Culture and Grand Strategy in Ming China* (Princeton University Press, 1995), p. ix. Cf. Peter C. Perdue, "Culture, History and Imperial Chinese Strategy. Legacies of the Qing Conquests," in Hands van de Ven (ed.), *Warfare in Chinese History* (Leiden: Brill, 2000), pp. 252–87.

[77] F. W. Mote, *Imperial China, 900–1800* (Cambridge, MA: Harvard University Press, 1999), p. 397.

[78] Mote, *Imperial China*, p. 559.

north where nomadic cultures predominated. But as Owen Lattimore argued, there was no clear-cut boundary line separating the two cultures. Lattimore's central thesis was that frontiers are formed at the margins of socioeconomic systems defined by their "optimal limit of growth." In stressing the dynamics of frontier exchange in Chinese nomadic relations, he coined the term "frontier feudalism." The key to the system was the shift from a clan to a territorial-based organization of the nomads on the margins. This was the result of a Chinese policy of creating a patron–client relationship with the frontier nomads. Although Lattimore believed that the nomad could always withdraw into the steppe if necessary, his famous aphorism, "the pure nomad is a poor nomad," illustrates the preference for a symbiotic relationship along the frontier.[79] For Lattimore Manchuria occupied a unique niche on China's frontiers: a reservoir region with an inner-facing frontier. Under the Qing dynasty the population beyond the Great Wall was composed of tribal elements "who remained outside of the conquered territory but were identified with the alien dynasty within the Wall." In periods of alternating barbarian and Chinese ascendancy, Manchuria served as a reservoir of officials and troops. Thus, the indigenous population and the colonists from the south looked back to China rather than forward to settling new territories.[80] As the key to governing China, it was a prize that, beginning in the late nineteenth century, the Russians and the Japanese fought to seize from China and bring under their control.

Lattimore's thesis stood virtually alone until the 1970s when Western scholars began to move away from an interpretation that emphasized the Western challenge as the main factor in shaping Chinese frontier policy.[81] The revisionists argued that the interaction of the sedentary population with the nomads along an age-old Inner Asian frontier established the precedents for subsequent dealings with the Western maritime powers on China's coastal frontier. The process was guided by bargaining for mutual benefit. Its main features were the regulation of trade and the establishment of a tribute system. Inner Asian imperial policy also displayed a high degree of religious toleration, especially toward Lamaism, introduced

[79] Owen Lattimore, "Inner Asian Frontiers. Chinese and Russian Margins of Expansion," in *Studies in Frontier History*, pp. 134–45. The quotation is from "The Geographic Factor in Mongol History," *ibid.*, p. 257.

[80] Owen Lattimore, "Chinese Colonization in Manchuria," in *Studies in Frontier History*, pp. 308–11.

[81] Paul A. Cohen, *Discovering History in China. American Historians Writing on the Recent Chinese Past* (New York: Columbia University Press, 1984). Cf. Maurice Rossabi, "The Tea and Horse Trade with Inner Asia during the Ming," *Journal of Asian History* 42 (1970): 136–68, and more generally his *China and Inner Asia. From 1368 to the Present Day* (New York: Pika Press, 1975).

different administrative systems for the outer provinces, and promoted various projects of resettlement, some of which involved an element of coercion.[82] Inspired by the scholarship of Joseph Fletcher, Thomas J. Barfield, and Sechin Jagchid, a richer picture emerged of the interdependence of nomads and agriculturalists along the Inner Asian frontiers.[83] From these studies the nomads emerge as more dependent and, hence, more committed than the imperial power to the maintenance of an exchange culture on the frontiers. They clearly preferred trading to raiding. As long as the nomads accepted Chinese cultural superiority and tributary status peace was assured. But stability in the steppe was a chancy thing. Climactic change, the Chinese decision to close or restrict markets, or the breakdown of order "in the fluid and often chaotic frontier zones" could lead to war.[84]

Long experience had also taught the ruling elites in China the importance of preparing for war. Traditionally, their military policy rested on a combination of active and static defenses. Military campaigns supplemented by forced population movements were a recourse of last resort in maintaining control along the Inner Asian frontiers. Such a strategy was costly and, due to logistical problems, incursions into the steppe could not be sustained for long periods. A more static form of defense was the construction of walls. From the earliest times earthen walls served the dual purpose of protecting frontiers against outside attack and facilitating centralization and unification in the core provinces. The building of the Great Wall of China at the end of the sixteenth century signaled the retreat of the Ming dynasty from a policy of active defense of the frontiers against the steppe nomads. The shift foreshadowed its political decline. In 1644, it was no longer able to contain the invasion of the "barbarian" Manchus.

Conquest was the foundation of state-building by the Manchus. After subjugating the core of Ming China, their expansion into Mongolia and

---

[82] Peter C. Perdue, "Manchu Colonialism," *International History Review* 2 (1998): 255–62; Peter C. Perdue, "Empire and Nation in Comparative Perspective. Frontier Administration in Eighteenth Century China," *Journal of Early Modern History* (2001): 282–304. Perhaps the first to suggest the reciprocal influence of the frontier on Chinese administrative practice was Joseph Fletcher, "Ch'ing Inner Asia *c.* 1800," in John K. Fairbank and Dennis Twitchet (eds.), *The Cambridge History of China, vol. 10: Late Ching, 1800–1911* (Cambridge University Press, 1978), p. 378.

[83] Joseph Fletcher, "China and Trans Caspia, 1368–1884," in John K. Fairbank (ed.), *The Chinese World Order. Traditional China's Foreign Relations* (Cambridge, MA: Harvard University Press, 1968); Joseph Fletcher, "The Mongols. Ecological and Social Perspectives," *Harvard Journal of Asiatic Studies* 6 (1986): 11–50; Barfield, *The Perilous Frontier*; Sechin Jagchid and Van Jay Symons, *Peace, War and Trade along the Great Wall. Nomadic–Chinese Interaction through Two Millennia* (Bloomington, IN: Indiana University Press, 1989).

[84] Jagchid and Symons, *Peace, War and Trade*, pp. 13–15.

west Turkestan was the first time a ruling dynasty in China had brought these borderlands under control since the Tang in the seventh century CE. Conversion played no role at all; but co-optation of the Mongol and Han elites was vital to their success. Colonization proved to be more problematic.

The Manchus were determined to alter radically the older pattern of frontier policies toward the steppe in order to make certain that men of their origin would never again conquer China. They adopted two strategies to break the cycle of invasion from the steppe. For at least a century after they conquered China, they enforced a strict policy of quarantining their homeland in the northeast against the penetration of cultural and economic influences from the old centers of Chinese power to the south. Their aim was to keep intact the warrior traditions that they believed had given them the edge over the sedentary Han people.[85] At the same time, they created the Eight Banner system. This was a mixed frontier force of Manchus, Mongols, and Han peoples to defend against subsequent attacks from the steppe. By co-opting military elites, the Qing facilitated their rule over China, enabling them to split and weaken the Mongol tribes who constituted their major rivals for control over the Inner Asian frontier in the early years of the new dynasty.

The Manchus began their domination of Inner Asia by securing control over the Liao River valley, and then consolidated it by occupying the remaining key frontier points in the northwest and northeast.[86] In Mongolia, which became, in the words of Owen Lattimore, "China's frontier province par excellence," the Qing government sought to divide the Mongols along both class and tribal lines, while allowing considerable latitude to the more independent tribes in the region. Mongol political unity had not existed since the heyday of the great steppe empires of the thirteenth and fourteenth centuries, although there had been periodic attempts to restore it.[87] But in the 1630s and 1640s when the Manchus were forcing the northern frontiers of Ming China, a constellation of west Mongol tribes (Oirat in Russian or Olot in Chinese) succeeded in bringing all the northern part of western Turkestan (Dzhungaria) under their control. At first they denied any intention of restoring the empire of

---

[85] Robert H. G. Lee, *The Manchurian Frontier in Ch'ing History* (Cambridge University Press, 1970), pp. 8–11, 39–40.

[86] Lattimore, *Inner Asian Frontiers*, pp. 115–17, 157, 171.

[87] Owen Lattimore, *Nationalism and Revolution in Mongolia* (New York: Oxford University Press, 1955), pp. 6–7, exploded the myth of Mongol "nationalism" based on an illusory image of unity, noting that "they neither adhered to the Manchus as a united people nor resisted the imposition of Manchu authority in the manner of a nation defending itself against foreigners."

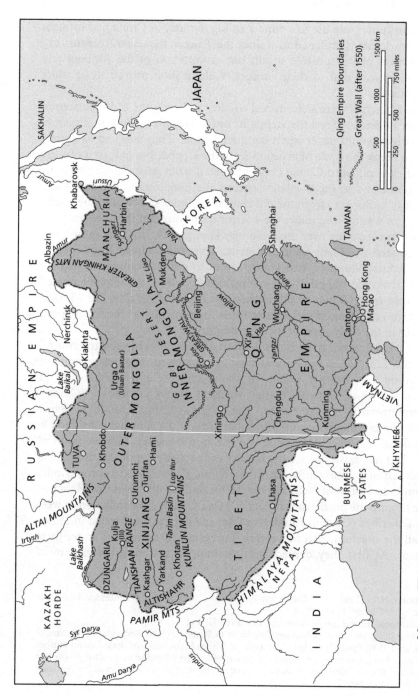

Map 1.2 The Qing Empire at its height, c. 1850

Chingghis Khan. They accepted the decision of the great Mongol congress (*chulgan*) of 1640 to uphold the confederation of tribes, adopt a Mongol code of laws, and avoid internecine warfare in order to present a common front against external enemies. Dzhungaria was not merely a nomadic confederation. It had some of the earmarks of an early modern state. Pastoral and agricultural communities were based on a restored irrigation system. In a few urban centers handicrafts flourished and, thanks to Russian fugitives, guns, cannon, and powder were manufactured. Dzhungaria gradually became a center of attraction for all Mongols. Then in the 1650s and 1660s, a series of succession struggles and tribal rivalries plunged the country into civil war. The emergence of a strong leader, the famous Galdan, precipitated an expansionist policy aimed at unifying the Mongols of Turkestan and north Mongolia (the Khalka tribes). This brought in the Qing.[88]

By this time the Manchus had already subjugated Inner Mongolia. In the 1670s they took advantage of tribal wars in order to take the northern Mongols (Khalkas) under their protection. Confronted by a determined effort by the Oirats to expand their Dzhungarian khanate into a pan-Mongol empire, the Qing sent powerful armies to the northwest where they finally defeated their rivals after 50 years of intermittent fighting. These wars revealed all the complexities of a struggle for western Turkestan between the Manchus and Mongols with the Russians hovering in the wings. The Khalkas shifted back and forth between the Chinese and Oirats, at one point seeking help from the Russians. Characteristic of nomadic tactics, they claimed that their oaths of allegiance, and acceptance of titles and seals from the Qing emperors, did not constitute vassalage but only an alliance, while Qing officials claimed the opposite.[89] The Qing strategy was to split the Mongol tribes before launching a final assault on Dzhungaria. In the 1690s, the Kangxi emperor took personal charge of the bargaining and intimidation. He finally persuaded the Khalka khans to recognize the sovereignty of the Qing dynasty.[90]

Having secured their flank, the Qing launched a military campaign that by mid-century reached their deepest penetration into Inner

[88] O. V. Zotov, *Kitai i vostochnyi Turkestan v XV–XVIII vv. Mezhdugosudarstvennye otnosheniia* (Moscow: Nauka, 1991), pp. 102–3, and I. Ia. Zlatkin, *Istoriia Dzhungarskogo Khanstva* (Moscow: Nauka, 1983), pp. 97–100.

[89] This has given rise to a prolonged historiographical controversy between Soviet (now Russian) and Chinese historians over whether the Mongol–Chinese relations were that of sovereign and vassal or "intergovernmental." For a summary of the debate, see Zotov, *Kitai i vostochnyi Turkestan*, especially the historiographical introduction and pp. 116–21 defending the older Soviet tradition in rather more sophisticated terms.

[90] I. S. Ermachenko, *Politika man'chzhurskoi dinastii Tsin v Iuzhnoi i Severnoi Mongolii v XVII v.* (Moscow: Nauka, 1974), pp. 102–4.

Asia.[91] The Oirats retreated, moving north and west, and bringing Uighurs and Kirghiz under their control. Their expansion represented the last attempts to construct a Mongol empire between Russia and China. It stretched from the lower Irtysh in the north to the borders of Tibet in the south, and from Tashkent, which it occupied in 1723, to western Turkestan. To destroy Dzhungaria, the Qing alternated between the two strategies that had long characterized China's relations with "the barbarians." They traded with the Oirats, but prepared for war by building forts in the steppe and settling military colonists. Throughout the early decades of the eighteenth century, they continued to launch military expeditions into the major oases of Turkestan. In mid-century, the Qing mounted a series of powerful offensives. In 1755–1759, with the help of the Khalka Mongols, the armies of Kangxi destroyed the Dzhungarian khanate and scattered the Oirats throughout Eurasia. The victorious Qing armies then campaigned against the Kazakhs deep into the mountainous Altai region, expanding the frontiers of China to their greatest extent in a thousand years.

The growth of scholarly interest in the western expansion of the Manchus has led to a new conceptualization of the frontier in Inner Asia. The importance of cities in frontier defense was first suggested by G. William Skinner, who argued that cities in the frontier regions of the west were obliged to assume broader military-administrative responsibilities in dealing with their vulnerable and diverse regions.[92] His analysis of complex macro-regional economies with their cores located in river valley lowlands and centered on major cities not only served as the basis for his cyclical interpretation of Chinese history, but provided a structural framework for delimiting internal frontiers. Urban clusters at the core were surrounded by sparsely populated peripheries.[93] The administrative division of China into provinces duplicated some of the core–periphery characteristics of macroeconomic systems. At sites where the peripheries of one macro-region or province met others, the administrative control of the urban cores was weakest and the possibilities for rural protest greater. In the nineteenth century, internal rebellions often began or expanded rapidly at the peripheries where the borders of several

[91] This section is based mainly on Perdue, *China Marches West*, chs. 6 and 7.
[92] G. William Skinner, "Urban Development in Imperial China," and "Cities and the Hierarchy of Local Systems," in *The City in Late Imperial China* (Stanford University Press, 1977), pp. 3–31 and 211–49. See also Piper Rae Gaubatz, *Beyond the Great Wall. Urban Form and Transformation on the Chinese Frontiers* (Stanford University Press, 1996), who expands this thesis.
[93] G. William Skinner, "The Structure of Chinese History," *Journal of Asian Studies* 44(2) (February 1985): 271–92.

provinces met.[94] In the twentieth century after the Long March of the Communists, their most successful organizational activities, the establishment of base areas, were carried out in internal border areas.

Like the other Eurasian empires, the Qing was virtually encircled by frontier shatter zones. The next important stage in the reconceptualization of the Chinese frontier policy came in the 1990s from a group of scholars headed by Pamela Crossley, Evelyn Rawski, and James A. Millward. They insisted that the Qing was an Inner Asian empire rather than a Chinese dynasty. They argued that a Manchu ethnic identity did not diminish, but grew stronger throughout the nineteenth century as the new ruling elite maintained the frontier between their homeland and China. For them Sinicization was based on the mistaken view of the Han people as a homogeneous ethnic group.[95] Their revisionist view of the frontier in Chinese history has attached new and unprecedented importance to the complex interaction between the core provinces of China and the Inner Asian frontiers.[96] Reflecting on this work, Peter C. Perdue has drawn a fruitful comparison of the similar effects of the frontier experience on both the Qing and the Ottoman empires, in particular their response to the needs and demands of peoples in the borderlands as opposed to the traditional emphasis on centralization as the basis for state-building.[97]

In analyzing the variety of Chinese frontiers, S. A. M. Adshead has portrayed them as constituting a "vast three-quarters of a circle around the rim of the Chinese heartland of the lower Hung-ho and Yangtse." In Kansu Chinghai and parts of Xinjiang the frontiers were pastoral; in Kirin, Kwangsei, and Taiwan they were mining frontiers; in Xinjiang and Siking they were military. Agreeing with Lattimore and Skinner, he further notes that these frontiers were turbulent and inward looking: "the mid-century rebellions are best understood as an inversion of the frontier, attempts by

---

[94] For suggestive evidence, see Jonathan Spence, *The Search for Modern China*, 2nd edn (New York: W. W. Norton, 1999), pp. 174 (Taiping rebellion), 183 (Nian rebellion), 188 (Muslim rebellion).

[95] Pamela Kyle Crossley, *The Manchus* (Oxford University Press, 1997); Pamela Kyle Crossley, *A Translucent Mirror. History and Identity in Qing Imperial Ideology* (Berkeley, CA: University of California Press, 1999); Evelyn S. Rawski, *The Last Emperors. A Social History of Qing Institutions* (Berkeley, CA: University of California Press, 1998); James A. Millward, *Beyond the Pass. Economy, Ethnicity and Empire in Qing Trans Caspia, 1759–1864* (Stanford University Press, 1998).

[96] Mote, *Imperial China*, pp. 376, 393–97, 405, 457, 559, 605–8, 844–50, 867–69, 874–75; Crossley, *The Manchus*; Rawski, *The Last Emperors*, esp. chs. 1 and 2.

[97] Peter C. Perdue, "Empire and Nation in Comparative Perspective. Frontier Administration in Eighteenth Century China," *Journal of Early Modern History* 4 (2001): 283–88, 293. This comparison can also be extended to other Eurasian empires.

the backcountry to conquer the heartlands."[98] They were also inhabited by a mix of ethnolinguistic groups penetrated by Han colonization only late in Qing history. These new interpretations have stimulated a debate over the concept of Sinicization.[99] One attempt to synthesize the divergent points of view on the relationship between the Manchu and the Han has suggested that the policy of co-opting military elites through the banner system gradually led to the reverse effect of facilitating the acculturation of the Manchu into the Chinese way of life.[100] These interpretations help to illuminate how Chinese colonization contributed to the shifting populations of the shatter zones in the Inner Asian borderlands.

In the early period of Qing rule, the central Manchu authorities sought to prevent Han Chinese settlements in their original homeland. Their policy was undermined by a combination of population pressure in north China and the reluctance of local officials to stem the tide of potentially productive and revenue-producing colonists. The government undercut its own policy by sending tens of thousands of exiles into the northeast provinces. By the late nineteenth century, the Manchu had given up their attempt to prevent their tribal lands from being swamped by Chinese (Han). The convict population was swelled by woodsmen, gold miners, ginseng diggers, pearl fishers, brigands, and, finally, illegal peasant settlers. By the early twentieth century the Chinese greatly outnumbered the Manchu.[101] A similar change was taking place in Inner Mongolia. In both frontier regions the "New Administration" of the post-Boxer Rebellion era sought to protect the border against foreign, mainly Russian, intervention by developing the economy and opening grazing lands to Chinese settlement.[102]

In Xinjiang, colonization began even before the completion of the conquest. The Qing sought to make the new borderland self-sufficient, to raise a buffer against Kazakh and Russian pressure, and to create a nucleus of loyal Han Chinese to balance the multicultures of the region.

---

[98] S. A. M. Adshead, *China in World History*, 3rd edn (New York: St. Martin's Press, 2000), pp. 320–21.

[99] See, for example, Evelyn S. Rawski, "Presidential Address. Reenvisioning the Qing: The Significance of the Qing Period in Chinese History," *Journal of Asian Studies* 55(4) (November 1996): 829–50; Ping-Ti Ho, "In Defense of Sinicization: A Rebuttal of Evelyn Rawski's 'Reenvisioning the Qing,'" *Journal of Asian Studies* 57(1) (February 1998): 123–55.

[100] Marc C. Elliott, *The Manchu Way. The Eight Banners and Ethnic Identity in Late Imperial China* (Stanford University Press, 2001).

[101] Lee, *The Manchurian Frontier*, esp. ch. 5.

[102] Mei-hua Lan, "China's 'New Administration' in Mongolia," in Stephen Kotkin and Bruce A. Elleman (eds.), *Mongolia in the Twentieth Century. Landlocked Cosmopolitan* (Armonk, NY: M. E. Sharpe, 2000), pp. 39–45.

Settlements were concentrated north of the Tianshan Range, where the abundance of arable land and the partial depopulation caused by the prolonged Qing–Dzhungar wars created favorable conditions. The Qing garrison forces, including Manchu and Mongols, tribal groups from Mongolia and Manchuria, and regular Han army units, added to the rich ethnic mix of the borderland. In addition to civilian and military colonists, smaller groups of "trouble-makers" and criminals were exiled to Xinjiang, as in Manchuria.[103] In the south, more heavily populated by organized Turkic Muslim communities, the Qing authorities refrained from actively pursuing colonizing policies until the nineteenth century. In the 1830s, in response to a serious regional revolt, the Qing increased their military presence and initiated a policy of settling military and civilian colonists south of the Tianshan. But they did not seek to Sinicize the region.[104] The government allowed Chinese Muslim merchants from the neighboring provinces of Gansu to set up shop in the oases. But as in Mongolia the local population regarded the Han middlemen as exploiters, leading to internal disturbances.[105] By the end of the century the Qing was encouraging immigration of the Han population and the conversion of pasture land into settled colonies. These were not entirely successful. Sinicization came too late. The integration of the "new frontier" depended on stability and strength at the imperial power center. When in the mid-nineteenth century decline set in, the ties with Xinjiang and the Mongol borderlands frayed to breaking point. Russia was waiting in the wings.

West Eurasia

In west Eurasia, the brief but destructive Mongol impact accelerated the movement of German colonists from west to east. In the twelfth century, the Teutonic Order, initially inspired by the early successes of the Crusades in the Holy Land and then tempted by the opportunities for landed wealth, conquered and colonized the poorly organized and sparsely inhabited territories of the Baltic region. They converted and absorbed the pagan Baltic Prus until they were checked by the Lithuanians.[106] During the

---

[103] Joanna Waley-Cohen, *Exile in Mid-Qing China. Banishment to Xinjiang (1758–1820)* (New Haven, CT: Yale University Press, 1991), pp. 23–29.

[104] L. J. Newby, "The Begs of Xinjiang: Between Two Worlds," *Bulletin of the School of Oriental and African Studies* 61(2) (1998): 296.

[105] Fletcher, "Ch'ing Inner Asia," pp. 36–41, 48, 65; Perdue, *China Marches West*, ch. 9.

[106] Paul W. Knol, "The Most Unique Crusader State. The Teutonic Order in the Development of the Political Culture of Northeastern Europe during the Middle Ages," in Charles W. Ingrao and Franz A. J. Szabo (eds.), *The Germans and the East*

following centuries German settlement (*Ostsiedlung*) in the Slavic lands continued along more pacific lines. However, beginning as early as the mid-nineteenth century, Czech, Polish, and Russian historians reversed the picture, portraying the German colonists as the cutting-edge of an aggressive *deutsche Drang nach Osten*.[107] The character of the ancient frontier between "Teuton and Slav" was actually a more complex process combining conquest and peaceful settlement.[108]

It would be a mistake to portray the interaction of Germans and Slavs as one driven by a conscious, unmediated ethnic or proto-national antagonism. The colonization of the east over a period of many centuries was not exclusively "German," but multinational. It was more often peaceful than warlike, by invitation rather than by right of conquest, followed by integration if not assimilation into the local body politic.[109] It is just as important, however, not to ignore the tension that sprang up between the Germans, who settled mainly in the towns, and the Polish rural population. Moreover, a prolonged political conflict simmered between the east German Marks (Brandenburg and Pomerania) as well as the Teutonic Knights in the Baltikum and the Poles over their frontier. The supreme political propagandist of his day, Frederick II, was one of the first to promote the idea of Prussia's eastern borders as the line between civilization and barbarism. On the eve of the partitions he posted his scurrilously satirical poem on Poland to Voltaire; the Poles, he quipped, were "the last people in Europe."[110]

From the twelfth to the late fourteenth century the medieval rulers of Bohemia, Poland, and Hungary invited German colonists as skilled cultivators, mining engineers, and craftsmen. In Poland, the earliest colonists arrived in Silesia according to a regular plan of colonization. It has been

(West Lafayette, IN: Purdue University Press, 2008), pp. 37–48; Raisa Mazeika, "An Amicable Enmity. Some Peculiarities in Teutonic–Balt Relations in the Chronicles of the Baltic Crusades," in Ingrao and Szabo (eds.), *The Germans and the East*, pp. 49–63.

[107] Wolfgang Wipperman, *Der "Deutsche Drang nach Osten." Ideologie und Wirklichkeit eines politischen Schlagworts* (Darmstadt: Wissenschaftliche Buchgesellschaft, 1981); Franz A. J. Szabo and Charles Ingrao, "Introduction," in Ingrao and Szabo (eds.), *The Germans and the East*, pp. 3–5.

[108] Alexander Demandt (ed.), *Deutschlands Grenzen in der Geschichte* (Munich: Beck, 1990); see also essays in Ingrao and Szabo, *The Germans and the East*, especially Jan M. Piskorski, "Medieval Colonization in East Central Europe," pp. 27–36.

[109] Martin Rady, "The German Settlement in Central and Eastern Europe during the High Middle Ages," in Roger Bartlett and Karen Schonwalder (eds.), *The German Lands and Eastern Europe. Essays on the History of their Social, Cultural and Political Relations* (Basingstoke: Macmillan, 1999), pp. 11–47; Karin Friedrich, "Cives Patriae: 'German' Burghers in the Polish–Lithuanian Commonwealth," in Bartlett and Schonwalder (eds.), *German Lands and Eastern Europe*, pp. 48–71.

[110] Cited in Larry Wolff, *Inventing Eastern Europe. The Map of Civilization on the Mind of the Enlightenment* (Stanford University Press, 1994), pp. 65–66, 186–89, 307, 335, 340–41.

estimated that approximately 250,000 German settlers arrived in the Polish lands where the indigenous population did not exceed 1.5 million. The contribution of these settlers to the economic and cultural development of Poland became a much disputed subject among German and Polish nationalist historians right down to the Second World War.[111] The major controversy centered on the importance of the Magdeburg Law, a collection of legal instruments dealing with civil law, public administration, and social relations that evolved from Italian urban codes and was first applied by the German emperor, Otto the Great, in the Saxon and east Elbian province, from whence they were introduced into Poland. The question of whether colonization beyond the Elbe involved mainly foreigners, and how many were Poles who were granted "charter under German law" of Silesia, remains in dispute. In any case, the transfer in the late fourteenth century of Magdeburg Law into the eastern Galician–Russian borderlands after their incorporation into the Polish–Lithuanian Commonwealth was regarded by the Polish rulers as a means of polonization. The local town councils (*rada*) became a battleground between Catholic Poles and Orthodox Russians over religious questions, which led on occasion to the creation of two separate councils.[112] Thus, ironically, the transfer of Germanic law created an arena for the long Polish–Russian cultural struggle over the borderlands.

In the medieval period, the interaction of the Germans and Poles combined elements of cooperation and friendship with resentment and even hatred, though little violence. Having escaped the destructive impact of the Mongols, the Polish noble landlords had welcomed a large-scale migration of German, Flemish, and Walloon colonists. They had helped to revitalize agriculture and develop new centers of urban life, sparking what one Polish historian has called the "Thirteenth Century Breakthrough."[113]

By the end of the fourteenth century the borderlands of the Kingdom of Poland formed a personal union with the Lithuanian state to form the Polish–Lithuanian Commonwealth. The Poles checked the advance of the Teutonic Order (but did not expel the German knights from the Baltic). They penetrated deeply into the forests of what is today Belorus

---

[111] Paul Knoll, "The Polish–German Frontier," in Robert Bartlett and Angus MacKay (eds.), *Medieval Frontier Societies* (Oxford: Clarendon Press, 1989), pp. 159–62.

[112] N. Vasilenko, "Pravo Magdeburgskoe," in F.A. Brokgaus and I.A. Efron (eds.), *Entsiklopedicheskii slovar'* (St. Petersburg: I.A. Efron, 1898), vol. XXXXVIII, pp. 893–96.

[113] Benedykt Zientara, "Melioratio terrae: The Thirteenth Century Breakthrough in Polish History," in J.K. Fedorowicz (ed.), *A Republic of Nobles. Studies in Polish History to 1864* (Cambridge University Press, 1982), pp. 34–35.

and advanced toward the southwest into the Pontic steppe. They brought under their control the Orthodox population of the ancient Russian principalities in Galicia. They incorporated the right bank of the Dnieper, including Kiev "the mother of Russian cities." The Russians living under Mongol authority considered these territories as a lost part of their patrimony. By the late sixteenth century the Polish nobles and the Catholic Church were competing with the Muslim Ottomans to the south and the Orthodox Russians to the northeast for political and cultural hegemony over the entire Pontic steppe. During the succeeding 200 years, these territories would become a vast shatter zone where a multisided struggle raged among Poles, Russians, Crimean Tatars, and the Cossack brotherhoods. The lines of demarcation would be drawn and redrawn; key strategic points would be won and lost; colonization, resettlement, and deportation of the increasingly mixed population would continue into the mid-twentieth century.

In Hungary, even before the devastation of the Mongol invasion, German peasants from the Rhineland (called Saxons by the Hungarians) settled in Transylvania and the northern Hungarian plain. German miners came in to work the silver and copper mines of Transylvania and the Carpathians. In Transylvania they became the third *natio*, with a fixed territory and enjoying civic rights which they defended repeatedly in the following centuries. In the early thirteenth century, Germans were settled in the royal manors of the north and granted privileges in order to help to re-populate the land after the Mongol devastation. South German traders and entrepreneurs began to dominate external trade and competed with Italians and Hungarians. For several centuries thereafter, Buda and most of the towns in the Hungarian plain were "dominated by powerful German elements."[114] However, the Germans did not develop a strong separatist, still less a nationalist, movement in Hungary. Nor were they encouraged to do so by Count Metternich despite his concern over the rise of Magyar nationalism in the post-Napoleonic period. Nationalism of any sort was abhorrent to him. Still, the Germans in Budapest sought to bridge the gap between the two cultures by portraying themselves as German-speaking Hungarian patriots. But in 1848 a *Deutschmagyar* identity was not acceptable in the eyes of Hungarian revolutionaries. In the wake of the repression of the revolution, Vienna re-imposed German as the language of administration. The attempt to keep alive an imperial language steadily waned in the face

---

[114] Martyn C. Rady, *Medieval Buda. A Study of Municipal Government and Jurisdiction in the Kingdom of Hungary* (Boulder, CO: East European Monographs, 1985), pp. 106–7, 162–64.

of strong Hungarian opposition, although German remained a second language in the capital down to the end of the Second World War.[115]

In Bohemia, as in Poland and Hungary, German colonists had begun in the twelfth century and increasingly in the thirteenth century to migrate into the frontier zones (*Rand-Gebieten*) of Bohemia. Early contacts between Czechs and Germans promised a fusion, or at least a symbiotic relationship. But the socioeconomic tensions turned into a cultural and then a destructive armed conflict when the Hussite reform movement in the church turned against the German clergy and townsmen. In the nineteenth and early twentieth centuries, Czech and German nationalist historians lined up on opposite sides over responsibilities and consequences of the Hussite wars. But the tendency of the historiography of the 1930s to cast these tensions in nationalist terms seems now to be anachronistic. A fresh wave of German immigrants at the end of the fifteenth century settled in the depopulated villages, and relations with the Czechs briefly improved as the Germans became Protestants. But a conflict broke out in 1618, when a Czech and German Protestant oligarchy refused to accept the election of an absolutist, religiously intolerant Habsburg candidate to the throne. Their defeat and the confiscation of their estates enabled the Emperor Ferdinand to grant new patents of nobility and to bring in more German colonists from Austria, Bavaria, and Swabia. However, the process of integration of the newcomers with the local nobility who had remained loyal to the Monarchy appears to have continued peaceably.[116] The German-speaking population gradually expanded during the rest of the seventeenth century all along the peripheral lands, setting the language frontier for the next 200 years.[117]

In the west Balkans and Danubian frontier, German colonization was an instrument of Habsburg imperial frontier policy aimed at checking the expansion of the Ottomans. The Military Frontier (*Militärgrenze*) was first established by Habsburg Archduke Ferdinand I in 1521 as a buffer against Islam. It gradually acquired new features. The government in Vienna promoted colonization, established a quarantine against the spread of disease, and erected an economic barrier to protect trade against

---

[115] Robert Nemes, *The Once and Future Budapest* (De Kalb, IL: Northern Illinois University Press, 2005), pp. 71–76, 177–78.

[116] Tomáš Knoz, "Die Konfiskationen nach 1620 in (erb)länderübergreifender Perspektive. Thesen zu Wirkungen, Aspekten und Prinzipien des Konfiskationprozesses," in Petr Mat'a and Thomas Winkelbauer (eds.), *Die Habsburgermonarchie 1620 bis 1740* (Stuttgart: Franz Steiner, 2006), esp. pp. 112–14 and 124–26.

[117] Elizabeth Wiskemann, *Czechs and Germans. A Study of the Struggle in the Historic Provinces of Bohemia and Moravia* (Oxford University Press, 1938), pp. 4–10.

Ottoman competition.[118] It took advantage of the opportunities offered by the Great Serbian Migration of 1691 to colonize the Military Frontier with loyal settlers. It granted extensive privileges to the Rascians, as the Serbs were then called after the medieval Serbian Kingdom of Raska, exempted them from manorial dues, and, most importantly, placed them under the direct authority of the Hofkammer or local Austrian military authorities. After the Treaty of Karlowitz in 1699, Vienna extended the Military Frontier from the Triplex Confinium east to the new borders in Slavonia and along the Theiss (Tisza) and Marosch (Mureš) rivers. The soldiers, mainly Serbs, who had served there during the war received tax-free farm plots as frontier colonists. Their dual function was to protect the border against the Turks, on the one hand, and hem in the Hungarians, on the other hand. In the early eighteenth century friction developed between the Austrian frontier officials, the Hungarian chancellery, and the Serbs over questions of jurisdiction and taxes. The Austrians attempted to separate the civil (tax-paying) and military (tax-exempt) elements among the Serbs – like similar attempts by Poles and Russians to regulate and control the Cossacks – with similar results. Disillusioned, large numbers of demobilized Serbs left for Russia. A few decades later the remnants of the Zaporozhian Cossacks reacted in a similar way to the final abolition of their autonomy by leaving Russia to seek refuge and accept Habsburg service on the Military Frontier.[119]

The most ambitious Habsburg colonization project followed their last great military conquest at the juncture of the Triplex and the Danubian frontier. By the Treaty of Passarowitz in 1718 the Habsburgs acquired the left bank of the Danube, the Banat of Temesvár, West or Little Wallachia, and the great prize of Belgrade, which the Ottomans called "the Lock." This was the high watermark of Habsburg success in bringing the west Balkan and Danubian borderlands under their control. The centerpiece of the new policy was the attempt to make Belgrade a German city. A law of 1720 decreed that all the inhabitants of the newly liberated city must be German by ethnic origin and Roman Catholic in religion. The Serb and Orthodox inhabitants were rounded up and resettled outside the city limits. The German residents were allowed to elect their own municipal officials, levy taxes, and set their cultural imprimatur on the city. The reconstruction of its fortifications turned the city into a frontier bastion of

---

[118] William O'Reilly, "The Historiography of the Military Frontier, 1521–1881," in Ellis and Esser, *Frontiers*, pp. 229–44.

[119] Wynar Lubomyr (ed. and intro.), *Habsburgs and Zaporozhian Cossacks. The Diary of Erich Lassota von Steblau, 1594* (Littleton, CT: Ukrainian Historical Association, 1975), pp. 41–46; Volodimir Mil'chev, *Zaporozhtsi na Viis'komu Kordoni Avstriis'koi imperii, 1785–1790 (dosidzheniia ta materiali)* (Zaporozhe: Tandem-U, 2007).

Habsburg defense against the Turks.[120] After much hesitation and despite the great difficulties involved, the government decided on an extremely complicated frontier policy designed to keep the Hungarians in check, satisfy the Serbs, and defend against an Ottoman reconquest. There were two keys to the double doors facing south against the Ottomans and north against the Hungarians. The first opened the way to a colonization of the Banat under imperial rule; the second locked in place the old Theiss–Marosch frontier institutions.[121]

In order to integrate the Banat into the imperial system Vienna sought to combine the old frontier strategy of settling Serbian military colonists along the new Ottoman border with a new approach. Under the enlightened stewardship of General Claudio Florimond Mersia a policy of economic development was launched. His aim was to shift the semi-nomadic, stock-rearing economy to intensive cultivation by promoting land reclamation and planned immigration. A scheme to attract peasants and craftsmen from as far away as the Rhineland brought in about 15,000 German colonists by the 1720s. Others followed, including Bulgarians, Armenians, and in the 1740s, for the first time, the Hungarians. Their new villages were named after members of the royal dynasty as integrating symbols of imperial rule. Between 1748 and 1753 another wave of Germans settled in the region. A Colonization Patent in 1763 and the creation of a Colonization Commission in 1766 consolidated a state system of privileges and financial support for colonists, not only Germans but also foreigners from Western Europe. Only Hungarians were excluded.[122] Soon afterwards, a mass immigration of Romanians escaping Ottoman repression in the neighboring Orsova district stirred the ethnic mix once again. By 1780, the Romanians constituted more than half the population of the Banat.[123]

The liberation of Belgrade and the Banat had brought the majority of Serbs under the imperial flag. Twenty years later a revitalized Ottoman

[120] Karl A. Roider, *The Reluctant Ally. Austria's Policy in the Austro-Turkish War, 1737–1739* (Baton Rouge, LA: Louisiana State University Press, 1972), pp. 6–7, based on Theodore von Stefanovic-Volovsky, *Belgrad unter der Regierung Kaiser Karls VI, 1717–1739* (Vienna: Holzheusen, 1908), pp. 23–30.

[121] The maintenance of the Theiss–Marosch frontier was bitterly resented by the Hungarians and caused the Imperial authorities endless problems with the Serbian Grenzers until Maria Theresa finally abolished it as a concession to the Hungarians during the War of the Austrian Succession. Kurt Wesseley, "The Development of the Hungarian Military Frontier until the Middle of the Eighteenth Century," *Austrian History Yearbook* 9/10 (1973/4): 70–80, 100–1.

[122] Iu. V. Kostiashov, *Serby v avstriiskoi monarkhii v XVIII veke* (Kaliningrad: Kaliningradskii gosudarstvennyi universitet, 1997), pp. 26–36.

[123] Thomas Cohen, "The Anatomy of a Colonization Frontier in the Banat of Temesvar," *Austrian History Yearbook* 19/20(2) (1983/4): 10–11; Wesseley, "The Development,"

Empire drove them back north of the Sava and reoccupied Belgrade, touching off another mass Serbian migration into the Habsburg Empire. The migratory flow continued throughout the eighteenth century. The prospect of an overwhelmingly preponderant Serbian population along the Ottoman frontier aroused concern among the Habsburg leadership. The imperial authorities wavered between placating the Hungarians and supporting the Serbians. Under Maria Theresa, from 1741 to 1749, the Theiss–Marosch military frontier was gradually abolished in the face of bitter Serbian resistance; the lands passed under Hungarian administration. About 3,000 Serbs then emigrated to Russia. Maria Theresa's infringement on the autonomy of the Serbian Orthodox Church also antagonized her Serbian subjects. But they celebrated Joseph II's decision to postpone the transfer of the Banat to Hungarian administration and the promulgation of his Toleration Patent. Their hopes for a grant of a unified territorial autonomy were dashed after Joseph II's death when the Hungarian county system was extended throughout most of the Banat. With the expiration of many of the colonists' economic privileges, the Hungarian magnates were able to impose a seigniorial system on the land.[124] Once again numbers of Serbian Grenzers and colonists reacted by migrating to Russia. The failure of the policies of colonization to achieve complete assimilation on the frontier was one of the main reasons that the Austrian "mission in the East" lapsed into an ambiguous state.

In the eighteenth century the enlightened rulers of the Habsburg and Russian empires sponsored another wave of German immigration, by the end of which there were islands of German-speaking settlers in the Baltic, Volynia, Transylvania, the Danube Basin, Dobrudja, Bessarabia, the Habsburg Military Frontier, Voevodina, and the central Volga. The consequences of their dispersed pattern of colonization haunted the Germans for another hundred years. Throughout the nineteenth century, the question of how to encompass *Deutschtom* emerged as a persistent theme in a set of larger concerns of Germans who were seeking to define their cultural identity and construct a unified state. Was the goal to create an ethnically homogeneous national state on the French (Jacobin) model or to bring as many Germans as possible under one flag? It became clear at the Frankfurt Assembly in 1848, when the debate over unification of the Germans had its first airing, that neither alternative was ideal. However,

pp. 95–98, but see also the most comprehensive treatment in N. L. Gaćesa, *Agrarna reforma i kolonizacija u Bačkoj, 1918–1941* (Novi Sad: Matica srpska, Odeljanye za društvene nauke, 1968), pp. 7–28.
[124] Ernest Schimsche, *Technik und Methoden der Theresianischen Besiedlung des Banats* (Baden bei Wien: Rohrer, 1939); Sonja Jordan, *Die Kaiserliche Wirtschaftspolitik im Banat in 18. Jahrhundert* (Munich: Oldenbourg, 1967); Karl A. Roider, *Austria's Eastern Question, 1700–1790* (Princeton University Press, 1982).

throughout much of 1848, a majority, including not only democrats and Catholics but liberals as well, favored the incorporation of the German-speaking Habsburg lands into a greater Reich. They were inspired by great power ambitions and fear of the Slavs. As one speaker put it: "Only when we have Austria which is now educating the Slavs through its free constitution and which draws them to German freedom and education will we neutralize the dangers which pan-Slavism threatens us."[125] The most widely cited text among the nationalists in 1848 was the German poet Arndt's lied, *Das Deutsch Vaterland*, written in 1813 at the height of the German War of Liberation against Napoleon. Each stanza expanded German territory from Preussenland to Austria with a coda that the fatherland should extend "As far as the German tongue is spoken."[126] A *kleindeutsch* solution would leave too many Germans outside the nation-state and the *grossdeutsch* solution would bring too many non-Germans, Poles, and Danes, perhaps Czechs as well, into what would become a multinational empire. The Bismarckian compromise fell somewhere between these two solutions.[127]

The Russian Empire

The migration of the east Slavic tribes, like the Germanic *Völkerwanderung*, began very early in the history of Eurasia around the fifth and sixth centuries, moving in three directions, to the north, south, and east. Natural obstacles such as swamps and thick forests broke up the land of west Eurasia into different ecological niches, which meant that the colonizing process was not carried out by large masses of the population, but in a dispersed manner. Slavic tribes migrating out of the region watered by the upper reaches of the western Dvina, Dniester, and Dnieper merged peaceably with the Finnish tribes in the northern forests. To the south, the advance took place behind the "shield" provided by the Khazar khanate on the steppe. When that shield collapsed under the pressure of the nomadic Polovtsy and the Arab-Islamic expansion, the settlers were forced back into the forest margins of the steppe, though hardy hunters and fishers strayed south along the rivers, the forerunners of the Cossacks. A pattern

---

[125] Günter Wollstein, *"Das Grossdeutschland" der Paulskirke Nationale Zielein der bürgerlichen Revolution, 1848–49* (Dusseldorf: Droste, 1977), pp. 266–335, quotation on p. 304.

[126] Mack Hewitson, *Nationalism in Germany, 1848–1866* (London: Palgrave Macmillan, 2010), p. 60.

[127] For a convincing argument that the Second Reich was in fact an empire, see Philip Ther, "Imperial instead of National History: Positioning Modern German History on the Map of European Empires," in Alexei Miller and Alfred J. Rieber (eds.), *Imperial Rule* (Budapest: CEU Press, 2004), pp. 47–68.

had been established of advance and retreat reflecting the fluctuations of steppe politics. Settlers fleeing the Mongols migrated into the heavily forested area to the north or into the foothills of the Carpathians where the principalities of Galicia and Volynia took shape; this was the origin of a distinctive branch of the Slavic language and ethnicity subsequently called Little Russian and then Ukrainian. But the Russians did not disappear from the margins of the steppe.[128]

Extensive cultivation of the land and the desire to escape the obligations of serfdom spurred peasant colonization. The ruling elite took an ambivalent attitude toward these population movements. On the one hand, the landowners in the core provinces of Muscovy sought to stem the flight of peasant migrants seeking to escape from the heavy burdens of taxation. On the other hand, servicemen on the frontier were eager to increase the labor force on their estates. The tug of war was legally resolved when the Law Code (*Ulozhenie*) of 1649 imposed serfdom on a peasantry that was already economically bound to the landlord. But the drain of manpower from the center continued. In the long run government policy contributed to the success of the peasants in consolidating Russian control over the Pontic steppe and south Caucasus. In contrast to the Ottoman and Iranian treatment of the nomads, Moscow confiscated much of their pasture and distributed it to servicemen, who were then able to settle peasant migrant agriculturalists on the rich Black Earth lands of the Pontic frontier.[129]

There was always an unresolved set of tensions in the migration of the Russians between state-sponsored colonization and spontaneous movement of people, between the colonists and the indigenous people, between the nomadic and settled concepts of sovereignty and property. But there were two shared and distinctive features of Russian colonization. First, the terms colonization (*kolonizatsiia*) and resettlement (*pereselenie*) were linked in Russian usage and reflected a social reality, namely, that they were virtually indistinguishable from one another. Russians migrated internally, while west Europeans settled overseas.[130]

---

[128] A. Ia. Degtiarev, Iu.F. Ivanov, and D.V. Karev, "Akademik M.K. Liubavskii i ego nasledie," in M.K. Liubavskii (ed.), *Obzor istorii russkoi kolonizatsii s drevneishikh vremen i do XX veka* (Moscow: Izd. Moskovskogo universiteta, 1996), pp. 42–43. This fundamental work was written in the early 1930s, but never published during the Soviet period.

[129] David Moon, "Peasant Migration and the Settlement of Russia's Frontiers, 1550–1897," *Historical Journal* 40(4) (December 1997): 883–84.

[130] Willard Sunderland, "The 'Colonization Question.' Visions of Colonization in Late Imperial Russia," *Jahrbücher für Geschichte Osteuropas* 48 (2000): 22–31; Boris Mironov, *Sotsial'naia istoriia Rossii period imperii (XVII–nachalo XX v.) Genezis lichnosti, demokraticheskoi semi, grazhdanskogo obshchestva i pravovogo gosudarstva*, 2 vols. (St. Petersburg: Dmitrii Bulanin, 1999), vol. I, p. 23, demonstrates the uneven and regional distribution of colonization.

Second, Russian colonization proceeded in irregular spurts over time and concentrated on certain frontiers, producing an uneven distribution of Russians and Ukrainian migrants throughout the empire. Third, colonization provided the empire with a flexible framework which held up under the pressure of internal rebellions and external wars to the end of the Soviet period. But it was never sufficient to swamp the indigenous people by sheer numbers. This helps to explain why the government failed in its sporadic efforts to integrate the non-Russians into an imperial order. In the long run, the tensions between the colonists and the indigenous peoples created problems of internal stability and external security that placed a heavy strain on the resources of the state whatever its constitutional form.[131]

The Russian migration into Siberia began in the twelfth century, when fur traders from the merchant city of Novgorod followed the Kama River and its tributaries and then crossed "the Rock" that is the Ural Mountains. After the Mongols had crushed the Russian principalities to the south, the Novgorod merchants expanded their northern colonies, raiding as far as the Volga. The conquest of the vast forest zone of Siberia took another century. The Moscow principality gradually emerged as the chief commercial rival of Novgorod in the fur trade, employing missionaries to convert the indigenous tribes and consolidate their interests. By the end of the fifteenth century, Moscow had succeeded in gathering the Russian lands clustered around the headwaters of the Volga, Dnieper, and western Dvina rivers, and had broken the power of Novgorod. Moscow incorporated Novgorod's colonies, including the vast province of Viatka, the gateway to Siberia. But colonization was hampered by the severe climate

Number of colonists settling in regions in thousands

Region	1678–1740	1740–1782	1782–1858	1870–1896	1897–1915	Total
Center	260	370	–			630
Siberia	90	–	517	926	3,520	5,053
New Russia	–	135	1,510	1,045	333	3,023
Volga–Ural	–	270	968	358	80	1,676
North Caucasus	–	–	565	1,687	296	2,448
Total	350	775	3,560	4,016	4,229	12,830

[131] "Russian Colonization. An Introduction," in Nicholas B. Breyfogle, Abby Schrader, and Willard Sunderland (eds.), *Peopling the Russian Periphery. Borderland Colonization in Eurasian History* (London: Routledge, 2007), pp. 1–18.

and the need to import grain from Moscow. Relations with the indigenous tribes revolved around cycles of trade and raid that characterized similar relations between the semi-nomadic or nomadic and sedentary populations of the Eurasian periphery.[132]

Over the following century small bands of Cossacks and trappers pushed deeper into Siberia, gradually bringing that immense area under the nominal sovereignty of Muscovy. Furs fueled the engine of Russian expansion into eastern Siberia, accounting for approximately 10 percent of the income of Muscovy in the mid-seventeenth century. The Russians employed different methods of obtaining furs, extracting tribute (*iasak*) from the Siberian tribes and Russian merchant entrepreneurs (*promyshlenniks*), and purchasing in a controlled market. That private entrepreneurs were equally involved with state servitors in the race for profits eased their initial contacts with representatives of the Qing Empire in establishing commercial relations.[133]

The Orthodox Church continued to play an important role in expansion. Kiprian, the first archbishop of the new eparchy of Tobolsk in western Siberia, developed a myth of Siberian conquest. A dynamic figure, this former monk from Novgorod who had supported Moscow against the Swedes in the Time of Troubles, embarked on a program of conversion, land acquisition, construction of monasteries, and improvement of the material life of the Cossack frontiersmen. Intent on endowing his eparchy with a spiritual distinction to match those of the settled lands, he used a local Cossack chronicle to cast an aureole of martyrdom around the dead Cossacks of Ermak's Siberian expedition of the 1590s, stopping just short of canonizing them.

In Siberia the state did not always side with the Russian settlers in ethnic conflicts; there was much competitive bargaining between the Russians and nomads for support by government officials.[134] From the earliest conquests the interests of the government and the private traders clashed. Muscovite officials were cautious in preparing their expansion and sought to take the indigenous tribes under their protection in return for the tribute. The traders were less scrupulous. Muscovite servicemen followed in the footsteps of the traders, competing and often clashing with them

[132] S. V. Bakhrushin, *Ocherki po istorii kolonizatsii Sibiri v XVI i XVII vv.* (Moscow: M. & S. Sabashnikovy, 1928).

[133] Raymond H. Fisher, *The Russian Fur Trade, 1550–1700* (Berkeley, CA: University of California Press, 1943); Richard Pierce, *Siberia in the Seventeenth Century. A Study in Colonial Administration* (Berkeley, CA: University of California Press, 1943).

[134] Willard Sunderland, "Peasants on the Move. State Peasant Resettlement in Imperial Russia, 1805–1830s," *Russian Review* 52 (1993): 472–84.

and one another in the style of Spanish conquistadores. The forts (*ostrogs*) and fortified lines facing south were the fore posts of advance from the forest zone into the Siberian steppe. Colonization was slow and the number of settlers was small.[135]

The law of 1822, drafted by Mikhail Speranskii, aimed at regulating colonization in Siberia and limiting it to authorized groups of state peasants. But the legislation touched off a mass exodus, which in Orenburg Province "reduced the local officials to impotence." The government was concerned about possible clashes between unregulated migrants and the Kirghiz nomads. But it was never able to exercise complete control over the flow. After the emancipation of the serfs and the expiration of the twenty-year temporary obligation period, new legislation in the 1880s and 1890s opened Siberia to large-scale migration. By 1914, the population had increased to 10 percent of the total and it was almost exclusively Russian and Ukrainian.[136]

Four geocultural factors help to explain why the Russians and not the Chinese or Turkmens conquered Siberia. The Russians of the forest zone had direct access to the Siberian taiga and did not first have to subdue powerful nomadic confederations on the steppe; the elaborate longitudinal river system provided a safer alternative mode of transportation than movement across the steppe, enabling small bands rather than large military expeditions to penetrate the taiga; the social organization and economic activity of the Russians was more favorable to settlement in the forest zone and the margins of the steppe where peasants practiced a combination of cattle raising and agriculture with its slash and burn techniques that encouraged a forward-moving colonization, while Cossacks and freebooters operated independently over great distances without state control and guidance; yet the whole enterprise was backed up by a centralized state that gradually asserted its control.

In comparing the different Siberian and southern frontiers of Russian expansion, Michael Khodarkovsky demonstrates that the conquest of the southern steppe was more gradual, slower, and more costly, accomplished against greater resistance by the nomads, consolidated mainly by military

[135] Bakhrushin, *Ocherki*; George Lantzeff and Richard A. Pierce, *Eastward to Empire. Exploration and Conquest in the Russian Open Frontier to 1750* (Montreal: McGill and Queens University Press, 1973); Valerie Kivelson, *Cartographies of Tsardom. The Land and its Meanings in Seventeenth Century Russia* (Ithaca, NY: Cornell University Press, 2006); Anatolii Remnev, "Rossiiskaia vlast' v Sibir i na dal'nom vostoke," in *Imperium inter pares: Rol' transferov v istorii Rossiiskoi imperii (1700–1917)* (Moscow: Novoe literaturnoe obozrenie, 2010), pp. 150–81.
[136] François-Xavier Coquin, *La Sibérie. Peuplement et immigration paysanne en XIXe siècle* (Paris: Institut d'études slaves, 1969), p. 77.

means, yet more systematic, persistent, and successful than that of the Ottoman or Iranian empires because of the particular process of on-going colonization. Different characteristics also marked the statist western boundaries with Poland–Lithuania, which were demarcated, negotiated, and confirmed in written treaties and *de facto* frontier pacts with the nomads in the south and east where there were "few common references and fixed definitions."[137]

The breakthrough to the south was made possible by the conquest of the khanate of Kazan by Ivan IV in 1555. Russian military servitors colonized the city and the neighboring lands. Attracted by the rich soil and fisheries on both banks of the Volga, servicemen and boiars with their peasants moved ever southward under the protection of government-built forts and walls.[138] In Astrakhan, colonization proceeded more slowly because of its exposure to nomadic raids. Farther west, the advance across the steppe to the mouth of the Dnieper was a more prolonged process that was not completed until the reign of Catherine the Great at the end of the eighteenth century. The three-way competition was complicated by the presence of powerful nomadic federations in the steppe, first the Nogai and then in the 1630s the even more formidable Kalmyks. The Muscovites employed a variety of tactics to manage the Nogai, none of them particularly successful. They offered payments and presents; they manipulated factions within the Horde; they demanded hostages and oaths of allegiance; they played the role of intermediary between the Nogai and the more warlike Kalmyks. But well into the seventeenth century the one thing the Russian government would not do was to assume responsibility for protecting the Nogai Hordes against other nomads migrating from the east. The Nogai themselves were astute steppe politicians, accepting presents from both the Poles and the Russians, allying themselves first with one then another of its neighbors, Muscovy, the Commonwealth, and the Crimean Tatars. But they were increasingly unable to defend themselves against the superior firepower of their enemies to the west or the attacks of Kalmyk horsemen to the east. Pressed from all directions, they suffered the fate of many steppe people. In the 1630s the tribal confederation broke up. The remnants drifted westward into the Bujak (Bessarabia) along the Ottoman–Polish frontier. They were replaced on the Pontic steppe by the Kalmyks, with whom the

---

[137] Michael Khodarkovsky, "From Frontier to Empire. The Concept of the Frontier in Russia, Sixteenth–Eighteenth Centuries," *Russian History* 1–4 (1992): 115–28; Michael Khodarkovsky, *Russia's Steppe Frontier. The Making of a Colonial Empire, 1500–1800* (Bloomington, IN: Indiana University Press, 2002).
[138] Liubavskii, *Obzor istorii*, pp. 547–50.

Russians were forced to deal on a similar basis for the following century and a half.[139]

In their new location the Nogai continued to be a turbulent element on the frontier. Converts to Islam, they like their Tatar neighbors and allies in the Crimea kept alive the *gazi* frontier tradition of permanent raiding into Christian lands. They ignored the provisions of the Treaty of Karlowitz that had established for the first time a permanent boundary between the Ottoman Empire and the Christian powers. They rebelled against Ottoman sovereignty, and in 1702 entered into an alliance with the Crimean Tatars to abrogate the treaties and keep alive the *gazi* tradition. The sultan disavowed the rebels and forced their compliance. But the frontier was not so easily tamed. In Istanbul, military and religious sympathizers with the old frontier tradition overthrew the sultan, accusing him of betraying the faith and the state.[140] The incident illustrates once again that the struggle over the borderlands could not always be settled by the imperial powers imposing their will on the indigenous populations.

In the Pontic steppe, as elsewhere on the Russian frontiers, colonization was both state-directed and spontaneous. The government's most innovative step was taken in 1752 when Empress Elizabeth endorsed the idea of a Serbian captain in Russian service of establishing military colonies on the Polish–Russian frontier. Based on the model of the Habsburg Military Frontier, the territories of New Serbia and Slavanovo-Serbia were settled by Serbian colonists who enjoyed special privileges in Russia's service. Later St. Petersburg also welcomed Bulgarians and Wallachians fleeing Ottoman rule. Occupying space between the hetmanate, Zaporozhian, and Don Cossacks, the colonists effectively separated the three fractious polities. In their relations with the Crimean Tatars, they rapidly assumed the role of a frontier people; in peacetime, they engaged in trade; in wartime, they served as the avant-garde of the Russian army.

Colonization of the Dnieper–Dniester steppe proceeded less systematically and more spontaneously. Colonists filtering in from Poland and the hetmanate settled in the villages created by the Serbs rather than on separate plots set aside for them. Once the Zaporozhian Cossacks had

---

[139] Michael Khodarkovsky, *Where Two Worlds Met. The Russian State and the Kalmyk Nomads, 1600–1771* (Ithaca, NY: Cornell University Press, 1992); Khodarkovsky, *Russia's Steppe Frontier*, pp. 8–11 and throughout. The subsequent history of the Nogai further illustrates their complex and prolonged struggle to survive. The repeated attempts of the Imperial Russian government to turn them into agriculturists failed. In three waves of migration in the nineteenth century they left Russia for the Ottoman Empire. N. V. "Nagai," *Entsiklopedicheskii slovar'* (St. Petersburg, 1897), vol. XXXIX, pp. 421–22.

[140] Abou-el-Haj, "Formal Closure," pp. 474–75.

been re-admitted to Russian territory, they launched a three-pronged colonization drive toward Azov and the southeast along the Dnieper tributaries and east into Slobodskaia Ukraine, which created problems with their neighbors. During the rest of the eighteenth century, colonization followed an irregular course as Russia expanded its control over the entire Pontic frontier. In the Bug–Dniester area, for example, colonists ignored the best-laid plans of the governor and settled where they pleased, wandering a great deal from place to place.[141]

The systematic colonization of the Pontic steppe proceeded rapidly under Catherine II, with the energetic leadership of two of her favorites, Grigorii Orlov and Prince Grigorii Potemkin, and inspired by the Enlightenment belief in a vigorous population policy. Catherine was the first Russian ruler who planned to use colonization not just to occupy land, but to create model communities in the spirit of the Enlightenment. Equating power and wealth with territorial expansion and population growth, she imported foreigners to instruct the Russian peasant by example in the virtues of social self-discipline and modern agricultural techniques. Thus, plans for colonization were integrated with administrative and social reforms. A large influx of foreigners, lured by free land and privileges, settled along the Volga and in New Russia along the southern frontier between the Bug and Dniester. Russian nobles were granted large estates and peasants were promised personal freedom; runaway serfs were offered amnesty. When the Crimea was annexed in 1783, landowners and officials rushed in as the majority of the Muslim Tatar population departed for the Ottoman Empire. Potemkin once again attracted a variety of colonists, mainly state peasants, ex-soldiers, and Old Believers.[142]

Almost half a million people moved to the steppe during Catherine's reign in what was increasingly a much more highly organized campaign of resettlement of "empty lands" based on the concept of "utility," that is, usefulness to the state and the colonists.[143] With the strategic aim of rapidly consolidating the new territories, Catherine promoted policies that created a new social structure of land-holding peasants who were

---

[141] Boris Nolde, *La formation de l'empire russe. Études, notes et documents*, 2 vols. (Paris: Institut des études slaves, 1952), vol. I, p. 230.

[142] Roger Bartlett, *Human Capital. The Settlement of Foreigners in Russia, 1762–1804* (Cambridge University Press, 1979), pp. 81 ff, 126 ff; Isabel de Madariaga, *Russia in the Age of Catherine the Great* (New Haven, CT: Yale University Press, 1981), pp. 361–66; Marc Raeff, "The Style of Russia's Imperial Policy and Prince G. A. Potemkin," in Gerald N. Grob (ed.), *Statesmen and Statecraft of the Modern West. Essays in Honor of Dwight E. Lee and H. Donaldson Jordan* (Barre, MA: Barre Publishing, 1967), pp. 1–51.

[143] Willard Sunderland, *Taming the Wild Field. Colonization and Empire on the Russian Steppe* (Ithaca, NY: Cornell University Press, 2004), ch. 2.

different in fundamental ways from those of the central provinces.[144] Colonization led to an ecological transformation of the steppe. Cultivation of the rich black earth ploughed up the virgin grasslands that had supported the great nomadic flocks. This meant greater social stability. In the long run these social characteristics strengthened the regional distinctiveness that contributed to the rise of Ukrainian separatism in the twentieth century. In the short run, colonization continued to be a disorderly and confusing process, despite the best efforts of the government bureaucracy to control and direct the movement of peoples into the steppe.[145]

During the early stages of the Russian–Ottoman War of 1806–1812, illegal settlers in larger numbers began to filter into the lands between the Dniester and Pruth, even before the Russian army had driven out the Ottomans. After the annexation of Bessarabia in 1815, the Russian government faced a familiar dilemma and resolved it in a familiar way. They discouraged but did not block migration. About 9,000 Romanians crossed into the province, offsetting the flight of local peasants going the other way in order to escape the heavy exactions of the boiar landlords. Meanwhile, an even larger number of Bulgarians crossed the frontier, seeking refuge from Ottoman rule with the encouragement of Alexander I who granted them extensive privileges. The boiars resented and opposed this policy, but the Bulgarian colonists prevailed. By the time of the Crimean War, the number of immigrants totaled 75,000, contributing to what was rapidly becoming another vast shatter zone.[146]

In the north Caucasus peasant colonists from the center played a relatively minor role in comparison with the Cossacks and the army. As early as 1711/12, Peter the Great had ordered the colonization of the frontier with the Ottomans and Crimean Tatars by settling Cossacks on the left bank of the Terek. Throughout the eighteenth century they were periodically reinforced with additional Cossack colonists who, under Catherine II, began the construction of fortresses and the Caucasus military line. Throughout the nineteenth century about 100,000 Little Russian Cossacks were settled on the lands of the Black Sea Cossacks. Peasant colonization followed, briefly accelerating after the Treaty of

[144] Sunderland, *Taming the Wild Field*, p. 365; de Madariaga, *Russia in the Age of Catherine*, pp. 363–67; Khodarkovsky, *Russia's Steppe Frontier*, pp. 172, 216–17.

[145] Khodarkovsky, *Russia's Steppe Frontier*, pp. 131–34.

[146] George F. Jewsbury, *The Russian Annexation of Bessarabia, 1774–1828* (Boulder, CO: East European Monographs, 1976), pp. 66–73; Detlef Brandes, *Von den Zaren adoptiert. Die deutschen Kolonisten und die Balkansiedler in Neurussland und Bessarabien 1751–1914* (Munich: R. Oldenbourg, 1993), pp. 114–20, 129–33.

Kuchuk Kainardji, but Catherine's plans to duplicate the pattern of New Russia were disrupted by clashes with the mountaineers and ended in failure.[147]

In Trans Caspia, the late colonization policy of the central government was riddled with inconsistencies.[148] Russian peasants began to arrive in the steppe in the1860s despite government opposition. They were forced to rent lands from the Cossacks. Up to 1899, St. Petersburg repeatedly changed its policy toward peasant settlements as it kept shifting the steppe region from one administrative authority to another. In the Syr Daria region there was no Cossack colonization. Peasant colonists had to contend with the official governmental protection of the Kirghiz grazing lands. In Turkestan, colonization was associated with irrigation involving the settlement of both native and Russian workers on the new lands. After the famine of 1891, a large peasant migration into Turkestan brought sectarians and Mennonites into the Hunger Steppe looking for work on irrigation. But these projects were badly planned and failed. Overall the process of colonization was characterized by a lack of organization and proper arrangements for transportation or building materials for new homes. The influx of poor peasants created fresh problems for the administration. The majority crowded into Tashkent, where local officials blamed their lack of basic sanitary procedures for the cholera epidemic in 1892. In 1897, Governor General A. B. Vrevskii banned all colonization. But Minister of War A. N. Kuropatkin persuaded the tsar to undertake construction of a direct rail line from Moscow to Tashkent in order to prevent the penetration of any potential Chinese or British influence. This introduced over 5,000 Russian railroad workers, who were later to be the source of labor disturbances. In the countryside, Russian migrants also led to rural violence. But the central government remained undaunted and continued to promote settlements. By 1911 Russians, numbering over 2 million, constituted 40 percent of the population of the eastern steppe, providing a firm foundation for Russian (Bolshevik) control over eastern Siberia during the Civil War and Intervention.

---

[147] I. L. Babich *et al.*, "Kavkazskie gortsy i kazaki na granitsakh imperii," in V. O. Bobrovnikov and I. L. Babich (eds.), *Severny Kavkaz v sostave Rossiiskoi imperii* (Moscow: Novoe literaturnoe obozrenie, 2007), pp. 70–76.

[148] The following is based on V. V. Bartol'd, *Izucheniia vostoka v Evrope i Rossii* (Leningrad: Leningradskii vostochnyi institut, 1925), pp. 150–69, and Jeff Sahadeo, *Russian Colonial Society in Tashkent, 1825–1923* (Bloomington, IN: Indiana University Press, 2007), especially chs. 2 and 4.

Borderlands

Like frontier, the term borderlands signifies the fluidity of geographical concepts in Eurasian imperial space. It is used in the following pages to describe territories on the periphery of the multicultural states that were carved out of the shifting frontiers and incorporated into the imperial system as separate administrative units, sometimes with autonomous institutions, reflecting their distinctive political and cultural features. Their status and relationship with the center of imperial power could change over time. Examples at different periods in history would be Manchuria, Mongolia, and Xinjiang in the Qing Empire; Azerbaijan in the Qajar Empire; the Crimean khanate, the Danubian principalities, and Bosnia in the Ottoman Empire; Galicia, Royal Hungary, and the Banat in the Habsburg Monarchy; and the Grand Duchy of Finland and the Kingdom of Poland in the Russian Empire.

The incorporation of a borderland into a multicultural state did not mean the end of the struggle over its political or cultural identity. Instead, it continued to be the object of struggles played out on two levels: externally among competing imperial states, and internally between the centers of power and the conquered peoples. Thus, borderlands faced frontiers in two directions: an inner cultural frontier turned toward the center of state power; and an outer, inherently unstable military frontier facing territories contested by rival powers.[149] The web of relationships between borderlands and the core was highly complex and underwent extensive changes over time. If the Eurasian empires were the objects of an Orientalist gaze from the west, then it is also true that the Eurasian multicultural states shared an Orientalist (or "barbarian") perception of their own borderlands as culturally inferior or incapable of governing themselves.[150]

Logically, the term borderland implies the existence of a core. Paradoxically, it is more difficult to arrive at a satisfactory spatial definition of core than it is of borderlands. In line with the geocultural approach, this study defines the core as a place shaped by the exercise and symbolic display of power. Its main components were the ruler, the court, the army command, the administrative offices, and the main residences of the

---

[149] Alexei Miller, "The Empire and the Nation in the Imagination of Russian Nationalism," in Miller and Rieber (eds.), *Imperial Rule*, pp. 9–26.

[150] Cf. Ussama Makdisi, "Ottoman Orientalism," *American Historical Review* 107(3) (June 2002): 1–32; David Schimmelpennick van der Oye, *Russian Orientalism. Asia in the Russian Mind from Peter the Great to the Emigration* (New Haven, CT: Yale University Press, 2010); Mary Ferenczy, "Chinese Historiographers' Views on Barbarian–Chinese Relations (14–16th Centuries)," *Acta Orientalia Academiae Scientarum Hungaricae* 21(3) (1968): 353–62.

ruling elite. Nothing illustrates the difficulty of locating the core than the phenomenon of moveable capitals, the most visible symbol of imperial rule. The Habsburgs moved early from Prague to Vienna, and would have had to change again had the Ottomans succeeded in either of their two sieges of Vienna. The shift in China from Nanking to Beijing (and back and forth again in the twentieth century) was a defensive response to the threat from the northern frontier. The change from Moscow to St. Petersburg (and back again in the twentieth century) was also a response to a frontier in a different direction for a different purpose. The Ottomans moved their capital from Bursa and Adrianople (Edirne) to Constantinople and again back to Edirne under Mehmed IV, which was perceived as the *gazi* center for jihad in Europe. In Iran, the shifts were more frequent than anywhere else until the twentieth century because of the enormous threats to the stability of the center from external enemies and provincial and tribal groups. In all these cases, the location and fortification of the capital city reflected to a greater or lesser extent the nature of the external threat and the proximity of the frontier.[151]

In the early years of imperial state formation, the centers of power tended to be more or less culturally and ethnolinguistically homogeneous. But as the empires expanded and became increasingly multicultural, the imperial capitals – Vienna, St. Petersburg, Constantinople-Istanbul, Tehran, and Beijing – became more cosmopolitan. Moreover, anomalies developed as the imperial capitals lost some of their symbolic centrality or monopoly of power. In the Habsburg Monarchy the settlement of 1867 split the center of power between the Austrian (Cisleithenian) and Hungarian (Transleithenian) lands. Budapest could claim to be as much a center of power as Vienna. Although Istanbul was incontestably the center of Ottoman power from the fifteenth century, its hinterland shifted from Rumelia to Anatolia as military defeats forced it to surrender territories in the Balkans. In Imperial Russia, the removal of the capital from Moscow to St. Petersburg generated a cultural rivalry over which center embodied the true spirit of Russia. In Iran, cultural tension continued to exist between two centers in Turkic Azerbaijan (Tabriz) and on the Persian plateau (Isfahan and then Tehran). Under the Qing dynasty the Manchu sought to maintain two distinctive centers of power, one in their

---

[151] For insights into moving capitals see Edward L. Farmer, *Early Ming Government. The Evolution of Dual Capitals* (Cambridge, MA: Harvard University Press, 1968); Eckart Ehlers, "Capitals and Spatial Organization in Iran. Esfahan, Shiraz, Teheran," in C. Adle and B. Hourcade (eds.), *Teheran. Capitale bicentenaire* (Paris: Institut français de recherche en Iran, 1992), pp. 155–61. For the tension between Constantinople and Edirne, see Kafadar, *Between Two Worlds*, pp. 148–50.

homeland of Manchuria and the other in the ancient provinces of the Han Chinese with Beijing as the hinge.

Within the capitals and the peripheries group identities were also fluid. The shaping and reshaping of primary loyalties and allegiances, whether social, cultural, or political, continued into the nineteenth century and in many places down to the present. Identification with nation, still less with a nation-state was a relatively late phenomenon in Eurasia compared with Western Europe, and in many cases had not been completed at the turn of the twenty-first century. The problem of naming these social collectivities has continued to divide scholars. Although no vocabulary has been generally accepted, ethnolinguistic communities, while awkward, is preferable to pre-modern nations.[152] Their emergence on the historical stage – ethnogenesis – has given rise to much debate among anthropologists. At every stage in the debate, the theoretical analysis of the process became more complex.[153]

The historian seeking guidance on controversies over group identification in Eurasian history ends up confronting three approaches: the situational, which stresses the interaction of populations living within different ecological niches; the primordial, which deals with culturally essential characteristics; and the experiential, which explores the commonality of shared experience.[154] These approaches do not exhaust the problem of identification, nor are they exclusive. Some communities underwent a process of dissolution or amalgamation (can this be called ethnoterminus?). Shifting and multiple terminologies are often used to designate one and the same ethnic community either by the group itself or by outsiders; these may also change over time. For example, there is very little consistency in naming tribal groups in Trans Caspia either by the tribal

[152] Anthony D. Smith, *The Ethnic Origin of Nations* (Oxford University Press, 1986). Cf. John Armstrong, *Nations Before Nationalism* (Chapel Hill, NC: University of North Carolina Press, 1984). For a critique of Smith, see John Breuilly, "Approaches to Nationalism," in Gopal Balakrishnan (ed.), *Mapping the Nation* (London: Verso, 1996), pp. 146–74, and Smith's response in *Nationalism and Modernism. A Critical Survey of Recent Theories of Nations and Nationalism* (London: Routledge, 1998), esp. pp. 170–98.

[153] Key texts are Charles F. Keyes (ed.), *Ethnic Change* (Seattle, WA: University of Washington Press, 1981); C. Carter Bentley, "Theoretical Perspectives on Ethnicity and Nationality," *Sage Race Relations Abstracts* 8(2) (1983): 1–53; C. Carter Bentley, "Ethnicity and Practice," *Comparative Studies in Society and History* 29 (1987): 24–55; T. Hyland Eriksen, *Ethnicity and Nationalism. Anthropological Perspectives* (London: Pluto, 1993); Walter Connors, *Ethnonationalism. The Quest for Understanding* (Princeton University Press, 1994).

[154] A useful summary of these approaches as they apply to the Trans Caspian borderlands is Jo-Ann Gross (ed.), "Introduction: Approaches to the Problem of Identity Formation," in *Muslims in Trans Caspia. Expressions of Identity and Change* (Durham, NC: Duke University Press, 1992), pp. 1–26.

members themselves or outside observers. Much the same is true of settled agriculturists in many areas of Eurasia. In extreme cases taken from the recent history of Belorus at one end and Xinjiang at the other end of Eurasia, indigenous cultivators of the land when asked to identify themselves responded that they were "locals." In Macedonia, up to the nineteenth century, as contemporary observers noted, the population could have been transformed into Bulgarians or Serbs, possibly into Greeks, if they had been brought under prolonged and direct control of either one of the ethnically secure core lands. Finally, even self-conscious ethnic communities do not necessarily evolve into nations. They may or they may not; much depends on whether they are drawn into the nexus of literacy and intergroup communication, or undergo the influence of intellectuals and mass education, conditions that were not found every-where until the mid-twentieth century, by which time many ethnic com-munities had simply vanished.[155]

The great variety of borderlands and the mix of populations obliged the ruling elites of multicultural states to devise different administrative sol-utions to govern them. These generally aimed at taking into consideration historical and cultural factors. But the ruling elites and the conquered people did not often interpret these factors in the same way. Moreover, imperial rule frequently imposed changes in the organization or status of a borderland depending upon the exigencies of internal stability and exter-nal security.[156] In their attempts to strengthen the attachment of border-lands to the centers of power, imperial ruling elites periodically introduced reforms that affected imperial rule as a whole. These were most often prompted by defeat in frontier wars and the loss of territories or perceived threats to the integrity of the state.

The problem of defining a borderland is not simply an academic exer-cise; it has become absorbed into major political controversies, not least of which has been the polemics of the Cold War. Historians of societies that have found themselves reduced on occasion from an independent state to a borderland partitioned among competing multicultural states have devised an interpretation of their historical condition in civilizational terms. Such efforts are of long standing and enjoyed a revival during the Cold War. Polish and Hungarian historians have been over-represented in

---

[155] Breuilly, "Approaches."

[156] Gabor Agoston, "A Flexible Empire. Authority and its Limits on the Ottoman Frontiers," in Kemal Karpat with Robert W. Zens (eds.), *Ottoman Borderlands. Issues, Personalities and Political Changes* (Madison, WI: University of Wisconsin Press, 2003), pp. 15–32; Nicola di Cosmo, "Qing Colonial Administration in Inner Asia," *International History Review* 20(2) (June 1998): 287–309.

this group.[157] Summing up a tradition in Polish historiography, Oscar Halecki defined East Central Europe as "borderlands of Western Civilization." Their destiny was to resist both German and Russian imperial expansion. Dismissing both a geographic and a racial determinism, he stressed the historical process that gave these lands without "permanent boundaries" their particular features that distinguished them from Eastern and Western Europe.[158] Similarly, the Hungarian historians István Bibó and Jenö Szücs identified three historical regions of Europe. Szücs also used the term East Central Europe and summarized its defining features as varieties of "western structures in East European conditions." By "western structures" he meant a set of institutions evolving from the feudal system and the absolutist state: the dual society of Church and state, the acceptance of Roman law, the growth of urban autonomy, the recognition of human dignity. Bibó called these "the plurality of small spheres of freedom." Eastern European conditions were the expansion of the two imperial autocracies, Russian and Ottoman, and the formation of a hybrid variant of west and east under Habsburg rule. The combination of these external penetrations with the weakly developed "western structures" in Hungary and Poland created societies where the nobilities struggled to preserve the liberties of their medieval estates, yet upheld the institution or defended serfdom and excluded the urban estates from the political nation.[159] By contrast, Soviet historians sought to justify the incorporation of borderlands into the Russian Empire as the "lesser evil" in comparison with the fate in store for them had they fallen under the imperial expansion of other multicultural states.[160] Quite the reverse spin has characterized many nationalist histories in the successor states of the former Soviet Union, Czechoslovakia, and Yugoslavia.

[157] Among the most influential purveyors of this myth were three great Polish poets, Adam Mickiewicz, Juljusz Slowacki, and Zygmunt Krasinski, and the romantic historian, Joachim Lelewel, who claimed that the Slavic principles of freedom (*wolnosc*) and citizenship (*obywatelstwo*) were most fully developed under the Poles. Manfred Kridl, *A Survey of Polish Literature* (New York: Columbia University Press, 1956), ch. 8; Joan S. Skurnowicz, *Romantic Nationalism and Liberalism. Joachim Lelewel and the Polish National Idea* (New York: East European Monographs, 1981), esp. ch. 7.
[158] Oscar Halecki, *Borderlands of Western Civilization. A History of East Central Europe* (New York: Ronald Press, 1952).
[159] István Bibó, *A kelet-európai kisállamok nyomorúsága* (Budapest: Argumentum, [1946] 2011), unfortunately never translated into English, and Jenö Szücs, "The Three Historical Regions of Europe. An Outline," *Acta Historica Academiae Scientiarum Hungaricae* 29(2–4) (1983): 131–84.
[160] Lowell Tillet, *The Great Friendship. Soviet Historians on the Non-Russian Nationalities* (Chapel Hill, NC: University of North Carolina Press, 1969).

Once a borderland was incorporated into a multicultural state the struggle over control shifted to the relations between the subjugated population and the center of imperial power. David Slater expresses this as the "imbrication of geopolitics and social movements," a relationship which I would modify by substituting geoculture for geopolitics, and thus narrowing the distinction between the two while preserving the dynamic he proposes between "the territoriality of politics ... as well as the transnational flows and penetrations of different kinds of power."[161] These reactions ranged along a wide spectrum from accommodation to resistance, terms that should not be regarded here as either fixed or essentialist. In the complex world of social realities they were flexible and not easily disentangled. Moreover, the responses were formulated within different contexts and were inextricably intertwined with the nature of imperial rule.[162]

There was no discernible pattern of reaction to imperial rule within the borderlands. From the earliest conquests to the mid-twentieth century, individuals and whole social groups passed from accommodation to resistance and back again, oscillating between resignation and defiance as psychological moods, social conditions, and political pressures altered. Because the language and practices of accommodation and resistance followed different contours within separate cultures, they were often misinterpreted or misunderstood by the conquerors and the conquered, being fraught with psychological ambiguity and social complexity. The line between the two extremes, like that between imperial frontiers, was blurred and often crossed.[163]

An analysis of these relationships must take into account a variety of historical circumstances. Much depended upon the nature and duration of the conquest; the extent to which an ethnic group was divided by a military frontier; the cultural distance separating the periphery from the core with respect to language, ethnicity, religion, and social organization; the nature of external pressure or intervention by foreign powers; the influence of the diasporas of the conquered people; the levels of collective consciousness arising from previous statist traditions; and, finally, the cultural policies of the ruling elites.

---

[161] David Slater, "Spatial Politics/Social Movements. Questions of (B)orders and Resistance in Global Times," in Steve Pile and Michael Keith (eds.), *Geographies of Resistance* (London: Routledge, 1997), pp. 259–60.

[162] Cf. Frederick Cooper and Ann L. Stoler, "Tensions of Empire: Colonial Control and Visions of Rule," *American Ethnologist* 16 (1989): 608–10.

[163] Sherry Ortner, "Resistance and the Problem of Ethnographic Refusal," *Journal of Comparative Studies of Society and History* 10 (2005): 175.

Accommodation

Accommodation included many kinds of behavior ranging from passive acceptance of external authority to active political cooperation and complete identification with the hegemonic power of the imperial center. Accommodation is a complex phenomenon not only because of the variety of its forms. As many theorists have pointed out, accommodation may, under certain circumstances, be more apparent than real, subversive rather than supportive of the structures of power.[164] In Islam, this is expressed by the technical term *taqīyya* or religious dissimulation. Accommodation can also be both voluntary and forced. Its fluid nature cautions against rigid categories. For heuristic purposes, a rough hierarchy of beliefs and practices would begin with simple compliance with the laws, regulations, and obligations of imperial rule to the point of performing specific functions in commerce, local government, and frontier defense, while at the same time preserving a distinctive cultural identity. Acculturation would signify adopting the external cultural norms of the state-supported culture, speaking its language (at least in public), converting to the state religion or embracing the state ideology (even if observing it only indifferently), and following social practices. This final step toward assimilation would involve internalizing all aspects of, or fusing with, the dominant culture. A complete change in identity was rare in the borderlands because of the ethnoterritorial pattern of settlement and, particularly in the twentieth century, the persistence of primordial theories of classification whether racial or class based. Assimilation required a receptive environment on the part of both the ruling elites and social groups.[165] Common to all was a basic loyalty, whether genuine or opportunistic, to the dominant political order. Moreover, accommodation of any type required the connivance of the ruling power and the subject. The state had to provide opportunities and

---

[164] James C. Scott, *Weapons of the Weak. Everyday Forms of Peasant Resistance* (New Haven, CT: Yale University Press, 1985), pp. 24–26, 246–47, 324–25; Michel de Certeau, *The Practice of Everyday Life* (Berkeley, CA: University of California Press, 1984), pp. xiii, 31–32, refers to indigenous people who "remained other within the system which they assimilated and which assimilated them externally." See also Michel Foucault, *Discipline and Punish* (New York: Pantheon, 1977).

[165] Much of the literature on assimilation in the Habsburg monarchy is devoted to the Jewish population. See, for example, the useful analyses by Marsha I. Rozenblit, *The Jews of Vienna, 1867–1914. Assimilation and Identity* (Albany, NY: State University of New York Press, 1983), pp. 3–12 and *passim*; Peter Hanak, "Problems of Jewish Assimilation in Austria Hungary," in P. Thane *et al.* (eds.), *The Power of the Past* (Cambridge University Press, 1984); William O. McCagg, *A History of Habsburg Jews, 1670–1918* (Bloomington, IN: Indiana University Press, 1992).

rewards for those seeking to accommodate, and the subject had to perform his or her duties consistently without relapse or reversal.

Under imperial rule the most widely practiced and mutually beneficial forms of accommodation were the social co-optation of elites through issuing patents of nobility or recognizing previous titles and ranks as a means of eliminating potential leaders of resistance. The Habsburgs granted patents of nobility to Hungarians, Poles, Croats, and others. The Russians were particularly active in opening the imperial nobility to such groups as the Baltic barons, the Ukrainian *starshina*, Muslim *murzas*, Polish *szlachta*, Georgian princes, and some tribal leaders from Trans Caspia.[166] The Ottomans confirmed the authority of religious leaders of Christian and Jewish communities; they granted titles to Christian converts to Islam who entered their service and often rose to the highest military and administrative positions in the empire. The Manchu ruling elite sought to maintain a degree of cultural distance from their Chinese and Mongol subjects, but at the same time they retained the Confucian tradition and examination system that opened a path, however narrow, to membership of the ruling elite. The Iranians ennobled tribal leaders, particularly among the Turkic people of the northern frontier.

The conquered elites of the imperial borderlands were motivated not only by the promise of privilege and the advancement of careers, but also by the belief that the alternative to working within the system would be a weak state that could easily fall under the domination of another, possibly harsher, master. This may help to explain why as late as the eve of the First World War there was little active sentiment for outright independence among most of the local elites in the borderlands of the multicultural empires.

A second attraction for collaborators was through service in the military or civilian bureaucracies. In both the Habsburg and Russian empires, for example, frontier guards like the Croats and Cossacks ranked among the most reliable troops in the imperial armies. In Iran, it was the Georgian slave armies, and in China the Manchu and Mongol bannermen who were among the elite formations. The janissaries in the Ottoman Empire were a unique case of recruiting and converting Christian children from the periphery, although the Porte also employed Kurdish auxiliaries. The Ottomans made extensive use of converted Christians, especially

[166] Alfred J. Rieber, "Sotsial'naia identifikatsiia i politicheskaia voliia: russkoe dvorianstvo ot Petra i do 1861 g.," in *P.A. Zaionchkovskii, 1904–1983 gg. Stat'i, publikatsii i vospominania o nem* (Moscow: Rosspen, 1998), pp. 273–314; Khodarkovsky, *Russia's Steppe Frontier*, pp. 202–6.

Armenians and Greeks, who played important roles as administrators and reformers, and Albanians as army officers and soldiers. Representatives from the borderlands often staffed bureaucracies. In Russia, there were a large number of Poles up to 1863, and always a small, but highly visible, representation from among the Baltic Germans, the Georgians, and Armenians. Tribal elements, like the Bashkirs, formed units of the Imperial cavalry. In the early years, the Qing dynasty heavily recruited officials among the Mongols. In Iran, the central bureaucracies remained dominated by Persians, but provincial governments were largely in the hands of local tribal elites.

Attempts to co-opt elites did not always win over their intended targets. Obstacles arose in cultures at opposite ends of the spectrum of social cohesion and political consciousness. At one extreme in the Russian Empire, the Polish nobles cultivated feelings of superiority toward their conquerors and retained a collective memory of a glorious, pre-conquest, state tradition that nourished a spirit of independence expressed periodically in open rebellion.[167] At another extreme among Caucasian mountaineers, the process of co-optation broke down in the face of social and political fragmentation that frustrated the application of a uniform policy.[168] One of the most ambitious and, until recently, neglected aspects of the many Russian policies aimed at assimilating the *inorodtsy* of the eastern borderlands was the introduction of the concept of citizenship (*grazhdanstvennost'*) as a means of transforming the local, customary social and juridical norms. But once again, the Russian bureaucrats found that "instead they had to share power with networks of native leaders and contend with pervasive resistance."[169]

A different problem arose when new indigenous elites sought accommodation with imperial rule, but only on their own terms. Such was the Jadid movements in Muslim borderlands of the Russian Empire. One of their major aims "involved an attempt to overcome the split between the Russian and native publics through an entry of Muslims into the Russian

---

[167] L. E. Gorizontov, *Paradoksy imperskoi politiki: Poliaki v Rossii i russkie v Pol'she* (Moscow: Indrik, 1999), esp. Pt. 1, ch. 1 and Pt. 2, ch. 2.

[168] Chantal Lemercier-Quelquejay, "Cooptation of Elites of Kabarda and Daghestan in the Sixteenth Century," in Marie Bennigson Broxop (ed.), *The North Caucasus Barrier. The Russia Advance Toward the Muslim World* (New York: St. Martin's Press, 1992), pp. 18–44.

[169] Dov B. Yarshevskii, "Empire and Citizenship," in Daniel R. Brower and Edward J. Lazzerini (eds.), *The Russian Orient. Imperial Borderlands and Peoples, 1750–1917* (Bloomington, IN: Indiana University Press, 1997), pp. 58–79; Michael Stanislawski, *Tsar Nicholas I and the Jews. The Transformation of Jewish Society in Russia, 1825–1855* (Philadelphia, PA: Jewish Publication Society of America, 1983), pp. 13–42.

sphere."[170] For the economic elites of the borderlands accommodation often offered tangible material rewards. These included special privileges, especially in developing commercial links with foreigners. For example, in the Russian Empire local administrators in the borderlands regarded the indigenous merchants as more enterprising and successful than the Russians and promoted their interests actively, especially in St. Petersburg and ports such as Riga and Odessa. In the Ottoman Empire, non-Muslim merchants benefited from the government's policy of concessions to foreign traders to become intermediaries in the export trade and then to push out their erstwhile foreign patrons. By the late nineteenth century, Jews, Armenians, and Greeks on the periphery dominated trade with Europe. In Qing China, the government gave extensive privileges to the Mongol traders along the northern frontier and to Muslims in the west. It also allowed Chinese traders to operate beyond the otherwise closed frontier of Manchuria. These concessions often caused ethnic tensions, even violence, between the dominant and subordinate ethnic groups. But these were not generally directed against the government. Exceptional was the case of the revolt in Iran against the tobacco monopoly, when concessions granted to foreigners were perceived to be excessive by the indigenous merchants. The advantages accrued by the merchant ethnic minorities of the borderlands rendered them as a social group among the most passive and loyal subjects of the multicultural states.[171]

In religious affairs accommodation was very much a two-way street. Voluntary conversion to the state religion was, along with mastering the dominant language, the highest form of integration into the multicultural state in the pre-nationalist era. At least this was true in the Romanov, Habsburg, and Ottoman empires, whereas in Iran there is little evidence of it and in China no compelling reason for it. Where it was practiced the motivation appears to have been improvement in life chances, especially in fields like commerce and the arts or high government service. Up to the end of the nineteenth century, imperial governments were willing, as a rule, to welcome converts, acknowledging that their action erased any stain of ethnic difference. But they were not consistent in their efforts to

---

[170] Adeeb Khalid, *The Politics of Muslim Cultural Reform. Jadidism in Central Asia* (Berkeley, CA: University of California Press, 1998), p. 235 and throughout.

[171] Alfred J. Rieber, *Merchants and Entrepreneurs in Imperial Russia* (Chapel Hill, NC: University of North Carolina Press, 1982), pp. 52–73; Halil Inalcik with Donald Quataert (eds.), *An Economic and Social History of the Ottoman Empire, vol. 2: 1600–1914* (Cambridge University Press, 1994), pp. 518–19, 705, 837–41; Josef Mentsel and Gustav Otruba, *Österreichische Industrielle und Bankiers* (Vienna: Bergland Verlag, 1965). But cf. David Good, "National Bias in the Austrian Capital Market before World War I," *Explorations in Entrepreneurial History* 14 (1977): 141–66.

carry out policies of forced conversion or, alternatively, to win support from religious minorities in the borderlands, especially in those cases where they identified religious belief with political opposition.

On occasion, the Habsburgs and Romanovs were willing to grant privileged status to certain sects and religious leaders who were willing to accept or preach obedience and loyalty to the ruling house.[172] At times the Russian government practiced toleration in dealing with the Muslim population. But it was hostile to Roman Catholicism after the Polish revolt of 1863. Its policy toward the Jews was more complex, alternating between assimilation without acculturation to discrimination and repression.[173]

In the Polish–Lithuanian Commonwealth during the Counter Reformation, an attempt was made to create a half-way house for the Orthodox Church to accommodate Latin Christianity through the medium of the Uniat Church. Initially successful, during the period of Russian imperial rule it became the object of a fierce struggle between the official Orthodox hierarchy backed by the state and the Catholic hierarchy backed by the Papal See. Ottoman toleration of Christians and Jews was broad and generous in the early period, but dissipated when churches became identified with national liberation movements.[174] The Habsburg Monarchy proved to be the most enlightened in its treatment of the Jews, but was less well disposed toward the Orthodox population for the same reason as the Ottomans. The Chinese were tolerant of all religions until they became associated with rebellion, as during the Christian Taiping or Muslim revolts in Xinjiang. By contrast, in Iran the Sunni minority was persecuted as a dangerous ally of co-religionists across the Ottoman and Uzbek frontiers, and conversion to Shi'ism was forcible.

Resistance

Resistance to the conquest and incorporation of the borderlands, like accommodation, took many forms over time and in different regions. At

[172] See, for example, Drago Roksandic, "Religious Tolerance and Division in the Krajina. The Croatian Serbs of the Habsburg Military Border," *Christianity and Islam in Southeastern Europe, Occasional Papers* (Washington, DC: Woodrow Wilson Center, East European Studies, 1997), p. 47; Robert Crews, "Empire and the Confessional State. Islam and Religious Politics in Nineteenth Century Russia," *American Historical Review* 108(1) (February 2003): 50–83.
[173] John Klier, *Russia Gathers Her Jews. The Origins of the Jewish Question in Russia, 1772–1825* (De Kalb, IL: Northern Illinois University Press, 1986); John Klier, *Imperial Russia's Jewish Question, 1855–1881* (Cambridge University Press, 1995).
[174] Selim Deringil, "Redefining Identities in the Late Ottoman Empire. Policies of Conversion and Apostasy," in Miller and Rieber (eds.), *Imperial Rule*, pp. 107–32.

the micro-level, small acts of everyday resistance, the "unwritten texts" of James Scott, went largely unrecorded in the early periods of conquest and domination.[175] But the mere preservation of distinctive cultural identity, what Fredrik Barth has called boundary maintenance, could be by itself a form of resistance that enabled a conquered population to survive despite its inferior status in an imperial system.[176] In opting for one or another form of protest movement, the peoples of the borderlands were often governed by expectations about the level of repression their actions would incite.[177]

Armed resistance to imperial rule in the form of rebellion was the most extreme form and differed in one important way from most rebellions in Western Europe over the same period. In the west, with the exception of the Celtic fringe (Brittany and Ireland), revolution was a state-building process; in the Eurasian borderlands, it was motivated by the opposite impulse, to oppose incorporation into an imperial multicultural state or to break away. On occasion, however, rebellion on the frontier like defeat in war could stimulate reforms at the center of power.[178]

In borderlands with a statist tradition and strong landowning nobilities like Poland, Hungary, and Georgia, rebellions and anti-imperial conspiracies were led by the old elites. Among these were the three major Hungarian anti-Habsburg uprisings – the Bocskai in the first years of the seventeenth century, the Thökököy rebellion in the 1670s, and the great Rákóczi rebellion in the early eighteenth century (1703–1711) – and the three major Polish rebellions against the Russians in 1791, led by Kosciusko, 1830, and 1863. In Georgia, nobles participated in the numerous uprisings against Russian rule in the first third of the nineteenth century culminating in the great conspiracy of 1832 inspired by the Polish insurrection. In all three cases, the rebellious nobles considered themselves to be the embodiment of the nation and disregarded the interests of the peasantry. What distinguished the Hungarian and Polish rebels was their invention of a tradition of resistance expressed in a new political language. The Hungarian tradition took as its points of departure the "resistance clause" of the Golden Bull granted by King Andrew II in

---

[175] Scott, *Weapons of the Weak*, esp. pp. 29, 37–41, 289–300.
[176] Fredrik Barth (ed.), *Ethnic Groups and Boundaries. The Social Organization of Cultural Difference* (London: Allen Unwin, 1969), pp. 14–15. Cf. Guy Herau, *L'Europe des ethnies* (Paris: Presses d'Europe, 1963), p. 58.
[177] James de Nardo, *Power in Numbers. The Political Strategy of Protest Rebellion* (Princeton University Press, 1985).
[178] For the effect of the "rebellious seventeenth century" in Muscovy on sparking a "cultural revolution," see A. M. Panchenko, "Buntashnyi vek," in *Iz Istorii russkoi kul'tury, 3. XVII–nachalo XVIII veka* (Moscow: Iazyki russkoi kul'tury, 2000), pp. 11–24.

1222, and the related concept of dualism between king and estates as expressed in the *Gesta Hungarorum* (Deeds of the Hungarians) dating from the early 1280s, where the definition of the military nobility was linked to the nomadic Huns.[179] It was further developed by the humanists in the fifteenth and sixteenth centuries, and the polemicists of the Reformation for whom the right of resistance was upheld in the face of religious persecution. Following the Ottoman invasion, the old multi-cultural Hungarian monarchy fell into three borderlands: Royal Hungary incorporated into the Habsburg Empire; the southern districts incorporated into the Ottoman Empire; and the principality of Transylvania sought to maintain a precarious independence between the contesting imperial powers. Resistance to both Ottoman and Habsburg domination continued to be justified in the name of the ancient liberties and corporate dualism.[180]

In the Polish lands after the partitions there were many accents in the language of resistance. By the time of the uprising of 1831 they had formed a messianic chorus. In the Kingdom of Poland under Russian domination the language of resistance drew upon two not altogether compatible traditions: Sarmatianism (or Sarmatism); and the Enlightenment representing, respectively, the old szlachta way of life and the new thought from France. However, the neat distinction between the two, like that of Slavophilism and Westernism in Russia, can be exaggerated. Both traditions were of recent vintage in the early nineteenth century, although they harkened back to ancient myths. Polish Sarmatianism most probably influenced another mythical tradition that forged a link between the Ukrainian Cossacks and the Khazars, a steppe people of pre-Mongol Eurasia. Inserted into the *Pacta et Conditiones* of 1710 by Cossack officers in exile who elected a hetman committed to independence from Russia, it created a new genealogy that justified the existence of a Cossack nation separate from both Poland and Muscovy.[181] In common with the invented traditions of the Hungarians and Poles, the Cossack myth celebrated a warrior culture and ancient liberties. For the beleaguered gentry of the western borderlands, the combination epitomized the historical basis for their resistance to foreign domination and the establishment or reestablishment of an independent state. The

---

[179] Simon Kézai *et al.* (eds.), *Gesta Hungarorum (The Deeds of the Hungarians)*, ed. and trans. László Veszprémy and Frank Schaer (Budapest: CEU Press, 1999), especially the critical essay by Jenö Szücs.
[180] László Kontler and Balázs Trencsényi, "Introduction," in *Hungary. De-Composing the Political Community* (Budapest: CEU Press, 2007).
[181] Serhii Plohii, *The Origins of the Slavic Nations. Premodern Identities in Russia, Ukraine and Belarus* (Cambridge University Press, 2006), pp. 339–443.

penetration of the ideas of the Enlightenment would invert the tradition. Ancient liberties would henceforth be identified with those of the west, not the east.

In the case of the nomadic peoples, a legitimizing political discourse of resistance was less clearly articulated, but was not completely absent. It merely took a different form of expression. The steppe peoples' definition of what constituted submission differed from that of Moscow. While Moscow required an oath of allegiance (*sert'*), the surrender of hostages from important families (*amanat*), and the payment of a tax, normally in furs (*iasak*), the nomads regarded oaths as non-binding, resented the demands for hostages, and interpreted the gifts from the Russians as part of an exchange for furs. When conflicts arising from these misunderstandings are placed within the context of the nomads' traditional frontier warfare culture, it is hard to resist the conclusion of Michael Khodarkovsky that "peace was impossible" between the sedentary peoples and the steppe nomads.[182] Such was the case, for example, with the four Bashkir uprisings against the Russians over the course of a century from 1662 to 1774. In the first three, the causes, though not altogether clear, appeared to have centered on resistance to paying certain taxes, including the fur tax; the behavior of Russian agents; and, more obscurely, the spontaneous outbreak of raiding Russian settlements for booty. In the great Pugachev rebellion of the eighteenth century, nomads joined Cossacks and peasants, but its leaders did not accept the authority of the "pretender" to the Romanov throne and went their own way.[183]

Among peoples without a statist tradition, violent resistance to imperial rule mainly took the form of banditry and peasant risings, or *jacquerie* during the first imperial phase of the struggle over the borderlands. Heavy taxation and discriminatory land policies were the main economic source of grievances among the conquered population, and were a cause for resistance that they often shared with the peasantry of the core lands. In the Balkan borderlands, from the Adriatic to the north Caucasus, the Danube to the Aegean, the Caucasian isthmus and the Pontic steppe, resistance had deep roots in the social phenomenon of banditry, military brotherhoods, and local militias for self-protection. They flourished at the peripheries of imperial power, along frontiers or in mountainous regions.

---

[182] Khodarkovsky, *Russia's Steppe Frontier*, esp. ch. 2. At least in the very long run. In Siberia, as elsewhere along the Eurasian frontiers, trade often mitigated conflict. See, for example, Yurii Malikov, *Tsar, Cossacks and Nomads. The Formation of a Borderland Culture in Northern Kazakhstan in the Eighteenth and Nineteenth Centuries* (Berlin: Klaus Schwarz Verlag, 2011).

[183] Nolde, *La formation*, pp. 208–35. Muslim clergy were involved, but it is unclear as to what extent.

They were variously called *uskoks*, *armatolas*, *haiduks*, and *klephts* in the Balkans; Cossacks along the river valleys of the Pontic steppe from the Zaporozhians on the Dnieper to the Don, Kuban, and Iaik (Ural); and mountaineers (Chechens) in the north Caucasus. Empire-builders often hired them as mercenaries, but when they were dismissed from service they frequently turned to plundering and raiding. The Venetians employed the Uskok pirates and revived the use of Greek militias (*armatolas*), originally formed under Byzantine rule, against the Turks. Selim I (1512–1520) adopted the name for internal security forces to be employed against Greek bandits (*klephts*). But the militiamen often went over to the other side and played an active role in the Greek Revolution of the early nineteenth century. The term *haiduk* (Hungarian for cattle drivers) was originally applied in the sixteenth century to Magyar, Serb, and Vlach pastoralists who fled the Ottoman occupation into the forests and mountains where they conducted a partisan war against their oppressors. Some of them were enrolled as irregular troops in the Habsburg army. Others were recruited by István Bocskai, a Calvinist magnate, later elected prince of Transylvania, when he revolted against the Habsburgs in alliance with the Turks.

During the seventeenth century in the Danubian provinces and Greek archipelago, the terms *haiduks, klephts,* and *armatolas* appear more frequently in the sources. Their increased activity was largely a product of intermittent warfare and the breakdown of public order. Their plundering and raiding did not endear them to the local peasant population, whether Christian or Muslim.[184] But gradually, and especially in the south Slavic lands, the haiduks acquired a mythopoeic quality as the heroic bandit. Celebrated in the folk epos, their deeds, dress, and conduct were minutely described. Among Serbians, Montenegrins, Bulgarians, and Greeks, in the nineteenth century the haiduks and klephts were cast in the role of protonational opponents of the Turkish domination.[185] These

[184] Dmitrije Djordjevic and Stephen Fischer-Galati, *The Balkan Revolutionary Tradition* (New York: Columbia University Press, 1981), pp. 31–32, 42. Called *hajdús* in Hungary, they were roaming bands of Protestant garrison soldiers. Pál Fodor, "The Ottomans and their Christians in Hungary," in Andor and Tóth (eds.), *Frontiers of Faith*, p. 146.

[185] Eric Hobsbawm, *Primitive Rebels* (New York: Norton, 1959), but cf. Anton Blok, "The Peasant and the Brigand. Social Banditry Reconsidered," *Comparative Studies in Society and History* 14(4) (September 1972): 494–503; Bistra Cvetkova, "Mouvements anti-féodaux dans les terres bulgares sous domination ottomane du XVIe au XVIIIe siècles," *Études historiques* 2 (1965): 146–68; Dennis N. Skiotis, "Greek Mountain Warriors and the Greek Revolution," in Vernon J. Perry and Malcolm E. Yapp (eds.), *War, Technology and Society in the Middle East* (London: Oxford University Press, 1976), pp. 308–29; Christopher Boehm, *Montenegrin Social Organization and Values. Political Ethnography of a Refuge Area Tribal Adaptation* (New York: AMS Press, 1983), pp. 132–33.

traditions were revived in modern form during the twentieth century, and were particularly strong in the Greek and Yugoslav resistance movements during the Second World War.

The Cossack communities originated as freebooters on the frontiers outside the control of state authority. Although nominally Orthodox, they raided and plundered the lands of Turkic Muslims, and Russian and Polish Christians with equal enthusiasm. In the seventeenth century, the Polish kings occasionally enrolled a specific number of "registered" Cossacks as auxiliaries, as did the tsar. But these arrangements often broke down and led to rebellions. The Zaporozhian and Don Cossacks constituted the main leadership of the great peasant rebellions of the seventeenth century. Although the Cossacks' autonomy, and hence their resistance, was finally broken under Catherine II, their exploits were enshrined in chronicles and *belles lettres* that became the founding myth of Ukrainian nationalism. As the Russians advanced into the Caucasus, Trans Caspia, and Inner Asia, they resettled Cossacks along their porous frontiers to ensure the security of the colonists. On the north Caucasus frontier they played a major role in subjugating the mountaineers. Here too, however, they sometimes changed sides or else, like some Uskoks, swore oaths of blood brotherhood with their Muslim counterparts. In the long run, the Habsburg and Russian empires were more successful than the Ottomans, if not completely so, in bringing the rebellious elements of the populations under imperial authority. Along the fringes of Eurasian Islam, from the Caucasian isthmus to the fringes of Inner Asia, the Sufi sects, especially the Naqshbandi in the nineteenth century, were often the sources of rebellions. "When these movements spilled over the porous frontiers and joined forces with their equivalents in neighboring regions they became particularly serious liabilities for the Ottomans."[186] In the struggle over the borderlands between the Ottoman and Safavid empires, certain Shi'ia orders of Alevi Turkmens were among those who defected to Iran, earning for the entire tribe the reputation of rebels and traitors.

Flight and migration were another form of resistance in the Eurasian borderlands. Examples abound: the Great Migration of the Serbs fleeing Ottoman occupation at the end of the seventeenth century; the flight of the Zaporozhian Cossacks from Russian to Habsburg lands at the end of the eighteenth century; the emigration of the Crimean Tatars following Russian occupation of their homeland in 1783; the great Kazakh migration of the eighteenth century; the flight of the Oirat Mongols from Qing power in the eighteenth century; the departure in 1859 of Muslim

---

[186] Hobsbawm, *Primitive Rebels*, p. 35.

mountain tribes from the Russian to the Ottoman Empire. The emigration of Polish participants in the rebellion of 1863 created an important center of resistance in exile. The flight of the Armenians from Turkish rule at the end of the nineteenth century was more a matter of survival, but it also contributed to a form of diaspora in resistance that exercised widespread influence in Western Europe and the United States directed against the Ottoman Empire.

The diaspora of unsuccessful rebels, Poles, Hungarians, Armenians foremost among the peoples of the borderlands, devoted themselves wholeheartedly to conspiracies, publication and dissemination of illegal propaganda, and even participation in the armed forces of the enemies of their enemy; the Polish Legionnaire tradition being the most active and persistent of these. They set a precedent for the activities of the various governments, committees, and parties in exile that were to play an important part in the resistance and struggle over the borderlands during the First and Second World Wars. In time of war the central state power often anticipated or reacted to the defection of peoples of the borderlands by executing its own repressive population transfers. Extreme measures of ethnic cleansing were aimed at allegedly hostile or inassimilable elements in the population, a form of state-sponsored civil war with repression anticipating resistance.[187]

Resistance by Christian peasants under Ottoman rule increased throughout the eighteenth century largely as the result of economic exploitation by local Muslim elites (*ayans*) and the declining authority of the central government.[188] In the borderlands of the Qing, mixed economic and religious conflicts provoked the Muslim rebellions in Gansu in the northwest, and the Uighur–Mongol–Han rebellions in western Turkestan (Xinjiang). But caution should be exercised in equating these rebellions with modern ethnic and national types.[189]

In Iran, tribal revolts were not confined to the borderlands. However, from time immemorial they flourished in the Kurdish regions and especially in Azerbaijan, which became notorious in Iranian history as a rebellious province like Xinjiang later became in Chinese

---

[187] Alfred J. Rieber (ed.), "Repressive Population Transfers in Central, Eastern and Southeastern Europe. A Historical Overview," in *Forced Migration in Central and Eastern Europe, 1939–1950* (London: Frank Cass, 2000), pp. 1–27; Nick Baron and Peter Gatrell, "Population Displacement, State-Building and Social Identity in the Lands of the Former Russian Empire, 1917–23," *Kritika* 4(1) (Winter 2003): 51–101.

[188] Barbara Jelavich, *History of the Balkans. Eighteenth and Nineteenth Centuries* (Cambridge University Press, 1983), remains the standard survey. See also Djordjevich and Fischer-Galati, *The Balkan Revolutionary Tradition.*

[189] Jonathan N. Lipman, *Familiar Strangers. A History of Muslims in Northwest China* (Seattle, WA: University of Washington Press, 1997).

history.[190] Under different circumstances these two provinces would become centers of rebellions during and after the Second World War, leading to Soviet intervention and tensions with the governments of Iran, and both Nationalists and Communists in China as well as the United States and Great Britain.

In the nineteenth century, growing nationalist sentiment among peoples of the borderlands gradually transformed the nature of banditry and peasant wars.[191] If *jacqueries* had erupted mainly from economic grievances in the seventeenth and eighteenth centuries, by the nineteenth and early twentieth centuries they increasingly took on the trappings of nationalist rebellions. Long-standing economic, ethnic, and religious grievances in the countryside were re-directed by the emerging civil and military intelligentsia, occasionally supported by clerics, and fused with workers' strike movements and student protests that also contained national and class components. The timing, social composition, and leadership of peasant-centered national liberation movements differed widely among the borderlands of the multicultural empires, reflecting local geocultural conditions. The earliest broke out in the western Balkans. Rural rebellions on the frontiers became recurrent during the retreat of the Ottoman Empire from southeast Europe.[192] By the early years of the twentieth century, the rising curve of peasant disorders combined with urban protests created highly volatile social conditions in the Russian Empire, which culminated in the revolution of 1905 when some of the most intense fighting occurred in the imperial borderlands.[193] The rebellions that weakened and then brought down the Qajar dynasty originated in Iranian Azerbaijan. In the Qing Empire the great uprisings of the nineteenth century were not typical peasant rebellions. They occurred mainly in frontier regions either on the outer perimeters like Xinjiang, "the most rebellious" of the provinces, or else in the border areas between provinces

---

[190] Frye, *The Golden Age of Persia*, pp. 112–15, 119.
[191] John Walton and Geza Seddon, *Free Markets and Food Riots. The Politics of Global Adjustment* (Oxford University Press, 1994), ch. 2; James Hughes, "Re-evaluating Stalin's Peasant Policy in 1928–30," in Judith Pallot (ed.), *Transforming Peasants. Society, State and Peasantry, 1861–1930* (London: St. Martin's Press, 1998), pp. 238–42. Cf. Leslie Anderson, *The Political Ecology of the Modern Peasant. Calculation and Community* (Baltimore, MD: Johns Hopkins University Press, 1994), pp. 5–18.
[192] Quataert, "The Age of Reforms," pp. 876–83.
[193] Teodor Shanin, *Russia 1905–07. The Revolution as a Moment of Truth*, 2 vols. (New Haven, CT: Yale University Press, 1986), vol. II, pp. 66–70; Abraham Ascher, *The Revolution of 1905*, 2 vols. (Stanford University Press, 1988), vol. I, pp. 152–60. See also L. M. Ivanov, A. M. Pankratova, and A. L. Sidorov (eds.), *Revoliutsiia 1905–1907 gg. v natsional'nykh raionakh Rossii* (Moscow: Gosudarstvennoe izdatel'stvo politicheskoi literatury, 1955).

where ethnic and religious minorities were strong.[194] The persistent threat on the northern frontier led to a "militarization" of Chinese society, that is, the formation of self-defense groups, providing a large reservoir for rebellion.[195]

Rebellions haunted the multicultural states by raising the specter of foreign intervention. They were a constant reminder of the fragility of imperial rule over the borderlands. Russia was particularly vulnerable to the double threat of rebellion and foreign intervention, beginning with the Time of Troubles (1603–1613). In the eighteenth century, the central government feared that the Bashkir uprisings might trigger Ottoman intervention, or, in the nineteenth century, that the two Polish rebellions might entail European intervention. The nightmare became reality during the period of the Russian Civil War and Intervention, creating a psychology of fear and suspicion of internal enemies that gripped Soviet policy makers during and after the Second World War.

The Ottoman Empire confronted an equally threatening situation in its borderlands where the Russians repeatedly sought to intervene by demanding reforms that would promote the interests of the Christian population. The sultans occasionally sought to reverse the tactic by inciting the Muslim tribesmen in the Caucasus, but more tentatively and with much less success. The Russians also exploited Muslim rebellions against the Qing in western Turkestan in the nineteenth century. During the sixteenth and seventeenth centuries, the Ottomans supported Hungarian rebels against the Habsburgs in their struggle to gain control of the Danubian borderlands. The links between rebellions and foreign intervention would multiply during the two world wars in the twentieth century and played an important role in the coming of the Cold War.

Closely related to the danger that rebellions could spark foreign intervention or that foreign wars could ignite internal rebellions was the nightmare of dismemberment. Rulers and ruling elites often feared that the combination of defeat in a foreign war connected to a domestic rebellion could spread from one region to the entire periphery, creating conditions for multiple wars of succession or national liberation. In acute form the Habsburgs faced that prospect in 1848, the Russians in 1855 and 1918, the Ottomans in 1878, the Iranians in 1908, and the Chinese in 1911.

---

[194] Sue Naquin and Evelyn Rawski, *Chinese Society in the Eighteenth Century* (New Haven, CT: Yale University Press, 1987), see esp. the chart on p. 228.
[195] Philip Kuhn, *Rebellion and its Enemies in Late Imperial China. Militarization and Social Structure, 1796–1864* (Cambridge, MA: Harvard University Press, 1970), esp. pp. 6–15, 29–30, 88.

An arc of flash points

In the course of state-building the multicultural conquest empires of
Eurasia were drawn into a struggle over the borderlands all along a great
continuum of contested frontiers extending from the Baltic to the Sea of
Japan. Within this space mass population movements and the shifting
fortunes of war produced a string of unstable shatter zones, kaleidoscopes
of peoples of different ethnolinguistic and religious groups. As the struggle intensified, these trouble spots assumed greater importance for the
external security and internal stability of imperial rule. To anticipate the
following narrative, they became the sites of small and large wars, and
many of the major rebellions of Eurasia from the sixteenth century to the
First World War. The postwar reconstruction did not eliminate them
from the territories of the successor states: the governments of Poland,
Hungary, Czechoslovakia, Yugoslavia, Bulgaria, Greece, Turkey, Iran,
and China. To understand how the struggle over the territories and
peoples of the borderlands affected the domestic and foreign affairs of
the imperial multicultural states and, by implication and extension, their
twentieth-century successors, it will be necessary to turn to the peculiarities of the continuous process of state-building in Eurasia that unfolded
from the sixteenth and seventeenth centuries and that was still incomplete
at the collapse of empire. The following two chapters will explore the
attempts by the ruling elites to invent an imperial ideology or political
theology to function as a legitimizing force in welding together disparate
cultural traditions and social groups, and to erect the institutional framework within which to exercise their political and military control over the
borderlands.

2 Imperial ideologies: cultural practices

In their struggle for hegemony over the Eurasian borderlands, the rulers and ruling elites of the multicultural states – the Habsburg, Ottoman, Romanov, Safavid–Qajar, and Qing empires – sought to fashion an overarching ideology and a set of cultural practices aimed at binding together peoples of different ethnic, religious, and regional loyalties. In the twentieth century this search for a principle of authority became as persistent an imperative for the fascist and communist leaders of multinational states as it had been for the dynasts of the imperial period. In both cases, legitimacy was not easily established in the tumultuous process of state-building accompanied by the rapid expansion or contraction of frontiers, and the incorporation and loss of large populations in the borderlands.

In the imperial period the four ideological mainstays of imperial rule were: (1) a divinely inspired dynastic succession, although inconsistently followed; (2) a founding myth based in part on ancient chronicles and epic poetry, and in part on the invention of intellectuals in service of the state; (3) a set of cultural practices designed to glorify the ruler's authority, project his power, and intimidate his subjects and foreign rivals; (4) a symbolic imagining of borderlands as an intrinsic manifestation of imperial power. The amalgam of these four real and symbolic representations of power constituted an imperial cultural system.

The hereditary dynastic idea was enveloped in a quasi-divine and sacerdotal aura, and fashioned into a political theology by Christian and Muslim clerics or Confucian scholars. Here political theology is taken to mean the symbolic transfer of ecclesiastical tropes and images to their monarchical equivalents.[1] Despite its longevity, the dynastic idea was not

---

[1] The major theorists of political theology have concentrated on the application of religious symbolism to twentieth-century authoritarian or liberal-ethical movements. Cf. Carl Schmitt, *Political Theology. Four Chapters on the Concept of Sovereignty*, trans. George D. Schwab (University of Chicago Press, [1922] 2005); Eric Voegelin, "The Political Religious," in *Modernity without Restraint*, in *Collected Works of Eric Voegelin*, 34 vols. (Columbia, MO: University of Missouri Press, 1999), vol. V, pp. 27–71; Langdon Gilkey, "The Political Dimensions of Theology," *Journal of Religion* 59(3) (1979): 154–68.

always a source of stability. Biologically, it rested on the vagaries of human fertility and mortality. Childlessness, the lack of a male issue, premature, accidental, or violent death of the ruler or his designated heir could, and all too frequently did, lead to a succession crisis. For example, in the Ottoman Empire for centuries there was no succession law. Following an ancient Turkic tradition sovereign authority was determined by divine fortune. This meant that whoever among the sons of the sultan succeeded in taking power, often as the result of a factional struggle, gained legitimacy. Once on the throne, the sultan was justified in eliminating his brothers. The principle of the oldest male member as the legitimate heir apparent was formally adopted only in 1617. An attempt to establish primogeniture came only in the mid-nineteenth century. In the Russian Empire, there was no established principle of succession until Paul I established one at the end of the eighteenth century.[2] In the Habsburg Empire, the prospective end of the male line in the early eighteenth century led to a series of internal concessions and international agreements that secured the throne for Maria Theresa, but at the cost of sparking the War of the Austrian Succession. In China, external signs that the Mandate of Heaven had been withdrawn could lead to the disposition of the ruler. Under the Qajars, the shah could designate his successor, but at his death a struggle for power could, and did, occur.

Politically, the theoretical absolutism of the dynastic ruler was also tempered in these societies by custom. Recourse to assassination or palace coups, which increased in frequency in the eighteenth and nineteenth centuries, was often justified by appeals to a higher principle of justice. Given the divine sanction of imperial rule, dynastic crises could only be attributed to the deity's mysterious purposes. There were times when those purposes stretched the credulity of men.[3]

The imperial culture systems of the Eurasian multicultural states drew inspiration from a common source of myths embedded in the two great traditions of the ancient world: the Roman–Byzantine and the

---

[2] For the Ottoman succession, see Hakan T. Karateke, "Who is the Next Ottoman Sultan? Attempts to Change the Rule of Succession during the Nineteenth Century," in Itzchak Weismann and Fruma Zachs (eds.), *Ottoman Reform and Muslim Regeneration. Studies in Honour of Butrus Abu-Manneh* (London: Tauris, 2005), pp. 37–53.

[3] David Cannadine, "Introduction: Divine Rites of Kings," in David Cannadine and S. Price (eds.), *Ritual of Royalty. Power and Ceremonial in Traditional Societies* (Cambridge University Press, 1987), pp. 1–19; Geoffrey Hosking and George Schöpflin (eds.), *Myths and Nationhood* (London: Routledge, 1997), especially the articles by George Schöpflin, "The Function of Myth and a Taxonomy of Myths," pp. 19–35, and Anthony D. Smith, "The Golden Age and National Renewal," pp. 36–59. See also Ernst Kantorowicz, *The King's Two Bodies. A Study of Medieval Political Theology* (Princeton University Press, 1959), for similar views of royalty in western Europe.

Achaemenian–Sasanian, overlaid by Christian and Islamic accretions. Symbols and images drawn from the same sources embellished the discursive and material artifacts of imperial rule. China was something of a special case. However, the Qing dynasty also based its claim for legitimacy in terms of *translatio imperii*, the continuation of an ancient, continuous tradition enshrined in Confucian thought.

The main symbolic forms of cultural practices were the performance of state functions and the organization of imperial space designed to impress and overawe the elites, the general public, and visiting foreign dignitaries. The court provided a semi-public setting, regulated by strict protocol, for attaching the elite to the person of the ruler and inculcating habits of deference, although it could also isolate him or her from the rest of society.[4] Public ceremonials and rituals and well-orchestrated visits of the ruler and his or her entourage outside the capital served to make the ruler visible to the ruled and to lessen the distance between throne and village. For a ruler, perhaps the most dramatic public appearances were at coronations, great religious ceremonies, and military reviews, requiring elaborate panoplies of uniforms or regalia.[5] The commissioning of works of art and the construction of palaces, even the urban design of capital cities, contributed to defining and enhancing the ruler's absolute power to control public space.[6] Multiple titles were employed by rulers not only to enhance their glory, but also to suggest the variety of peoples and traditions they represented. Imperial policies of assimilation also varied over time and place between the coercive and the enlightened. Forced conversion and the imposition of linguistic uniformity alternated with toleration, co-optation of elites, and acceptance of cultural diversity as long as it did not lead to disruptive proselytizing. To a considerable degree

---

[4] Norbert Elias, *The Civilizing Process. Sociogenetic and Psychogenetic Investigations*, revised edn (Oxford: Blackwell, 2000), esp. pp. 389–97. For criticism of Elias that gives greater emphasis to the process of negotiation between the ruler and elites, see Jeroen Duindam, *Myths of Power. Norbert Elias and the Early Modern European Court* (Amsterdam University Press, 1990); John Adamson (ed.), *The Princely Courts of Europe. Ritual, Politics and Culture under the Ancient Regime, 1500–1750* (London: Weidenfeld & Nicolson, 1998).

[5] Richard Wortman, *Scenarios of Power, Myth and Ceremony in the Russian Monarchy*, 2 vols. (Princeton University Press, 1995, 2000); J. P. Bled, *Franz Joseph* (Oxford: Blackwell, 1992), pp. 220–21, based on P. Promintzer, "Die Reisen Kaiser Franz Joseph (1848–1867)," PhD dissertation, University of Vienna, 1967.

[6] Hugh Murry Baillie, "Etiquette and Planning of State Apartments in Baroque Palaces," *Archéologie* 101 (1967): 169–89; Felix Driver and David Gilbert (eds.), *Imperial Cities. Landscape Display and Identity* (Manchester University Press, 1999). See also Randolph Starns, "Seeing Culture in a Room for a Renaissance Prince," in Lynn Hunt (ed.), *The New Cultural History* (Berkeley, CA: University of California Press, 1989), pp. 205–32.

flexibility became a part of the ideology itself.[7] Shifting emphases within imperial ideology and cultural practices also contributed to tensions between advocates of secular versus divine attributes of a ruler, between bureaucratic and ecclesiastical authority, and between real and symbolic power.

The most corrosive solvents of the dynastic idea were rational-scientific reasoning and nationalist-patriotic feelings. These were modern ideas in the chronology of the Western European intellectual tradition, and they did not represent a coherent body of thought any more than the principles of imperial ideology that they challenged. Rational-scientific thought cultivated by intellectuals and dispersed through an educational system attempted to bring institutions and practices in line with certain universal principles. As applied by the imperial ruling elites, these ideas contributed to the establishment of professional bureaucracies and professional armies, hierarchical in structure but based on merit and predictable rules; on economic systems that combined state and public interests; on cultural practices that established a dominant value system, but made room for alternative, if not subversive, beliefs. At the same time, they posed a potential challenge to imperial rule by threatening to de-sacralize the founding myths and weakening the legitimacy of the ruler.

National feelings might represent imagined communities elsewhere, but in Eurasia there were formidable difficulties in imagining let alone creating a strong sense of secular unity among the populations under imperial rule. When in the wake of the French Revolution, Napoleonic imperialism, and the earliest appearance of local secular ideologues outside the confines of the ruling elite, national sentiment filtered into the multicultural empires, stimulating a flexible if inconsistent counterpoint. Imperial rulers began to add nationalizing ideas to their store of political theologies by introducing an official language in their bureaucracies, schools, and armies, and inventing new rituals, visible symbols, and institutions that stimulated strong feelings for the homeland (*Heimat*, *rodina*, etc.). This interaction between rising nationalist sentiment in the borderlands and nationalizing movements at the power center was often transferred across porous frontiers, especially where two adjacent empires contained border populations that claimed the same ethnolinguistic identity.[8]

---

[7] From a different perspective, imperial cultures can be portrayed as differentiated, contested, weakly bound, and vulnerable to change. Cf. William H. Sewell Jr., "The Concepts of Culture," in Victoria E. Bonnell and Lynn Hunt (eds.), *Beyond the Cultural Turn* (Berkeley, CA: University of California Press, 1999), pp. 51–55.

[8] Alexei Miller, "The Romanov Empire and the Russian Nation," in Alexei Miller *et al.* (eds.), *Internal Colonization. Russia's Imperial Experience* (Cambridge: Polity Press, 2011).

Nationalist ideologues among the conquered peoples under imperial rule were already hard at work in the early nineteenth century, seeking at first to gain varying degrees of autonomy. In the borderlands they were largely confined to small groups of intellectuals. Among the notable exceptions were the Polish and Hungarian nobilities, who cherished memories of their own participation as conquest states in the struggle over the borderlands; the Serbs, where the Orthodox Church kept alive a tradition of resistance to alien rule whether Catholic Habsburg or Muslim Ottoman; the Georgian nobles, who had for centuries resisted the crushing encirclement of Islam; and the Mongol nobles, who could look back to the greatest empire of all. Not until defeat in the wars of the late nineteenth or early twentieth centuries undermined imperial authority did most national movements assume mass proportions, resorting to revolutionary action and demanding independence from imperial rule. By this time the tension between the alternative sources of legitimizing power had increased to the point where they could not be easily reconciled, contributing to the internal weakness and collapse of the empires. But the dialectical outcome of this process had taken several centuries to mature.

The Habsburg Empire

The centrality of the dynastic idea in the ideology of the Habsburg Empire derived from a set of marital and contractual relationships that led to the union of the hereditary Austrian lands with the Bohemian, Hungarian, and Croatian crown lands in the early part of the sixteenth century.[9] Given the legal and political complexities of these arrangements, which preserved the rights and privileges of local elites, the monarchs and their closest servitors gave special prominence to dynastic continuity in the institutional triad of imperial ideology, the army, and the bureaucracy. The Austrian Habsburgs inherited from Philip II of Spain the mythical link to the Byzantine emperors with their quasi-sacerdotal powers. These were institutionalized in the ceremonies of the Eucharistic miracle introduced by Rudolph I and the Order of the Golden Fleece.[10]

---

[9] Andrew Wheatcroft, *The Habsburgs. Embodying Empire* (New York: Viking, 1995).

[10] M. Tanner, *The Last Descendent of Aeneas. The Habsburgs and the Mythic Image of the Emperor* (New Haven, CT: Yale University Press, 1993). Although the coronation ceremony continued to impress observers like Goethe, for example, it was regarded as anachronistic by the "enlightened despot" Joseph II; an early indication of the problem for Austrian emperors of defining their imperial persona in a consistent manner. See D. Beales, *Joseph II. In the Shadow of Maria Theresa, 1741–1780*, 2 vols. (Cambridge University Press, 1987), vol. I, pp. 111–15.

By the time of the Renaissance, the Habsburgs had evolved an elaborate imperial imagery combining pagan, ancient Hebrew, and Christian motifs in their bid to fuse secular power and priestly functions. Writers and artists under the direction and control of the imperial courts employed a new literary-historical discourse in fashioning a prophetic-eschatological ideology.[11] Throughout the life of the Monarchy the rulers sought to embellish dynastic traditions and values by creating a pantheon of heroes. Beginning with the founder of the dynasty in Austria, Rudolph I, the line of ascent included Maximilian, whose marriage policy had created the Central European core of the empire; Leopold I; Joseph I; Charles VI, who had valiantly fought the Turks throughout the sixteenth and seventeenth centuries; and Maria Theresa, "the mother of all her people." Joseph II was too controversial to include, and Franz Joseph only gained admission in the second half of his reign. Outstanding military commanders filled secondary roles, especially Prince Eugène of Savoy, Duke Charles of Lorraine, and Count Raimondo Montecuccoli, significantly all foreigners ennobled by the dynasts for their military achievements.[12]

In the sixteenth and seventeenth centuries, the Austrian Habsburgs continued to promote a Catholic culture and used the Church as an instrument of social discipline, persuading some historians to baptize the Monarchy as a species of "confessional absolutism."[13] After the end of the Thirty Years War in 1648, the Catholic Church took over the entire spiritual administration of Bohemia. Catholic religious orders enjoyed a boom. The official mission of the Church was to convert all the inhabitants of the Bohemian crown lands. A second wave of re-Catholicization began in mid-century focusing on the peasantry. By the end of the century

---

[11] F. A. Yates, "Charles Quint et l'idée d'empire. Fêtes et cérémonies au temps de Charles Quint," *11e congrès des historiens de la Renaissance* (Paris, 1960); John M. Headley, "The Habsburg World Empire and the Revival of Ghibellinism," *Medieval and Renaissance Studies* 7 (1978): 93–127.

[12] Peter Urbanitsch, "Pluralist Myth and Nationalist Realities. The Dynastic Myth of the Habsburg Monarchy: A Futile Exercise in the Creation of Identity?" *Austrian History Yearbook* 35 (2004): 109–11.

[13] Robert Bireley, SJ, "Confessional Absolutism in the Habsburg Lands in the Seventeenth Century," in Charles Ingrao (ed.), *State and Society in Early Modern Austria* (West Lafayette, IN: Purdue University Press, 1994), pp. 36–43; Karl Vocelka, "Public Opinion and the Phenomenon of Sozialdisziplinierung," in Ingrao (ed.), *State and Society*, pp. 119–40, emphasizes the role of Jesuit schooling, sermons, and oral communication, as well as Polizeiordnungen regulating morality and patterns of behavior. For the confessionalization of court patronage and land grants to Catholic high nobles in Bohemia, see Karin J. MacHardy, *War, Religion and Court Patronage in Habsburg Austria. The Social and Cultural Dimensions of Political Interaction, 1521–1622* (Basingstoke: Palgrave Macmillan, 2003).

conversion was completed, although the search for secret non-Catholics continued.[14] Emperor Leopold I (1657–1705) was renowned for his piety and zealous pursuit of the "re-Catholicization" of the hereditary Habsburg lands. As symbols of his opposition to the Protestants he exalted the cult of the Virgin Mary, together with the miracle of the Holy Sacrament. He dedicated over 800 parish churches to the Virgin, as well as the lands of Hungary recovered from the Turks. He even named the Virgin generalissimo of the Austrian armies. He popularized the cult of local saints such as St. Wenceslas in Bohemia and St. Stephen in Hungary in order to win the loyalty of the recently converted and wavering Catholics. He relied heavily on the Jesuits not only because of their vigorous missionary and educational activities, but also because of the decline in the number of parish priests during the Reformation. His personal piety and the strict morality of his court were in sharp contrast to the monarchs of other Catholic courts, and won him widespread approval. Under his patronage and with the support of the Jesuits, popular religious manifestations such as pilgrimages, religious processions, and theatrical presentations reinforced popular piety.[15] Policies of cultural and social assimilation reached their high point in the Catholic Baroque.

On the other hand, the Austrian Habsburgs had given up the idea of a universal monarchy, an idea that had become moot once the empire of Charles V was divided in 1526 between its Spanish and Austrian parts. Until the eighteenth century, the Austrian monarchy retained elements of the Spanish court protocol, generally regarded as the strictest and most elaborate in Europe.[16] Yet during the reign of Leopold I the focus of imperial ideology was beginning to shift from the dynasty to the ruler. Sanctified by the Church, the emperor was glorified by the secular culture of the elites. The court theater, poetry, and panegyrics, as well as sermons, celebrated his manliness and soldierly qualities.[17] This created problems for Maria Theresa, who found herself burdened by a unique gender role in the Habsburg dynastic succession. She responded by representing herself to her court and country as an empress, mother, wife, and widow by reshaping both her public image and her private space. She undertook a

---

[14] Jiří Mikube, "Baroque Absolutism (1620–1740)," in Jaroslav Pánek *et al.* (eds.), *A History of the Czech Lands* (Prague: Karolinium Press, 2009), pp. 240–42.

[15] Jean Berenger, *Léopold Ier (1640–1705). Fondateur de la puissance autrichienne* (Paris: Presses universitaires de France, 2004), pp. 116–26.

[16] Christian Hoffmann, *Das Spanische Hofzeremoniell von 1500–1700* (Frankfurt: Peter Lang, 1985). For the use of architecture to structure absolutist power in the early modern Habsburg monarchy, see Hubert Ch. Erhalt, *Ausdrucksformen absolutischen Herrschaft. Der Wiener Hof in 17. und 18. Jahrhundert* (Munich: R. Oldenbourg, 1980).

[17] Maria Goloubeva, *The Glorification of Emperor Leopold I in Image, Spectacle and Text* (Mainz: Verlag Philipp von Zahern, 2000).

renovation of Schönbrünn Palace that increased her privacy, but kept her imperial dignity. Her arrangements "prefigured modern ways of organizing domestic space," while her hybrid identity as a maternal and imperial figure enabled her to exercise her power in various ways. Her son Joseph II, reflecting his Enlightenment ideas of rulership, disliked Schönbrünn, preferring the Hofburg, and there he occupied only a plainly furnished room unadorned by allegorical and mythical figures.[18]

As with other Eurasian empires, the geocultural location of the Habsburg Monarchy created a duality in its external mission to which historians have often given a symbolic representation in the crest of the double black eagle looking west and east. To the west, from the mid-sixteenth century, its policy was to defeat the Reformation. Thereafter, until the mid-nineteenth century, it sought to maintain its hegemony over a mosaic of small German states by securing the recurrent election of an Austrian Habsburg as Holy Roman Emperor. In the Italian peninsula, they inherited the Ghibellin idea of restricting the pope to his pastoral role and situating the Italian states under imperial control. Their main rival was the French monarchy, which also sought to dominate a fragmented Germany and Italy. To the east it long retained its role as Christian defender of the faith against the Muslim Turks, known as "Austria's eastern mission."[19]

In his famous essay "The Dynasty and the Imperial Idea," Robert A. Kann follows the major Austrian historians in arguing that the Habsburg rulers were concerned mainly with preserving the strength of the western German part of their domains despite the fact that "geographic contiguity and economic interests and defense needs increased the ties of the hereditary lands with the East rather than those of the western lands."[20] This contradiction was never resolved. It involved fighting five major wars against the Ottoman Empire in the seventeenth and eighteenth centuries. When in the mid-nineteenth century the Habsburgs were expelled from the Italian peninsula and the German Confederation in the wars of unification, the black eagle had nowhere to look but to the east. Making peace with the Hungarians in the *Ausgleich* of 1867, Habsburg foreign policy

---

[18] Michael E. Yonan, "Modesty and Monarchy. Rethinking Empress Maria Theresa at Schonbrunn," *Austrian History Yearbook* 35 (2004): 25–47, quotation on p. 43. Skillfully managed these representations strongly appealed, for example, to the gallantry of the Hungarian nobility.

[19] Hans Sturmberger, "Turkengefahr und Osterreichische Staatlichkeit," *Sudostdeutsches Arkhiv* 10 (1967): 139. See Headley, "The Habsburg World Empire," p. 66, for the origins of a holy war against the Turks in the work of Mercurino de Gattinara, advisor to Charles V.

[20] Robert A. Kann, "The Dynasty and the Imperial Idea," in *A Study in Austrian Intellectual History from Late Baroque to Romanticism* (New York: Praeger, 1960), p. 49.

became one of maintaining the territorial status quo in the Balkans. It could no longer raise the banner of Christian liberation without benefiting Serbian nationalists backed by Russian pan-Slavs. A partial substitute was its policy of economic penetration. But the Austrians had lost their ideological justification. The occupation of Bosnia and Hercegovina in 1876, and its belated and fateful annexation in 1908, merely confirmed the bankruptcy of the Austrian mission.

The French Revolutionary Wars, the dissolution of the Holy Roman Empire, and the coronation of the first "Austrian Emperor" in 1804 marked the final shift, underway since the mid-eighteenth century, away from emulating cultural standards set by French, Spanish, and Italian influence toward embracing German courtly culture. After 1848, the monarchy, shaken by revolution, engaged in a desperate search for a principle of authority and a mission. Constitutional experiments succeeded one another with great rapidity. Even after the creation of the Dual Monarchy in 1867, according to the Hungarian historian Peter Hanák, six major political concepts competed with one another for supremacy as the guiding ideology of the empire.[21] Despite these constitutional crises the world view of Franz Joseph hardly changed. He adhered to the idea of a *Rechsstaat*, exhibiting a broad toleration of all the nationalities or at least displaying no favorites, while remaining deeply attached to Roman Catholicism, and performing rituals of piety and humility throughout his reign.[22]

By the time Franz Joseph ascended the throne in 1848, the idea of a confessional state was undergoing a double transformation. The widespread revival of religious feelings opened "a second confessional age"; the confessional state was giving way to "a certain confessional pluralism."[23] Greater toleration could, and did, cut two ways. For the Czechs, it meant a reinforcement of their national traditions, providing ammunition for anti-German sentiment associated with the Counter Reformation and the loss of Czech sovereignty. For the Jews, the reaction was quite the opposite. In contrast to what was happening in the Russian Empire, where integration was highly selective, the Jews in the Habsburg Empire appreciated the opportunity to retain their identification as Jews, whether secular or religious, yet share in the riches of German, Hungarian, or

---

[21] Peter Hanak, "Problem der Krise de Dualismus," in V. Sandor and Peter Hanak (eds.), *Studien zum Geschichte der öesterreichisch-ungarnischen Monarchie* (Budapest: Akadémiai Kiadó, 1961), pp. 338–85.

[22] A. Novotny, "Der Monarch und seine Ratgeber," in A. Wanbruszka and P. Urbanitsch (eds.), *Die Habsburgermonarchie, 1848–1918. Verwaltung und Rechtswesen* (Vienna: Österreichische Akademie der Wissenschaften, 1975), vol. II, pp. 64–65.

[23] Urbanitsch, "Pluralist Myth," pp. 107–8.

Polish culture.[24] It is only a slightly tarnished truism that of all the peoples of the Habsburg Monarchy the Jews were the most *Kaisertreu*.

Looked at from a different perspective, the changing concept of the imperial ideal in the Habsburg Monarchy suggests a remarkable flexibility on the part of the rulers and their advisors in response to the tides of cultural and intellectual fashions that engulfed the social and political elites of Europe in the eighteenth and nineteenth centuries. The Monarchy never abandoned its close association with the Catholic Church even in the years of the high Enlightenment. But the de-sacralization of European monarchy embodied in the image of the rational, dispassionate ruler – the enlightened despot – created a wholly new utilitarian set of principles for the exercise of absolute power. These principles found their most ardent champion in Joseph II, whose reputation as an enlightened despot has, however, been challenged.[25] In the Habsburg Empire, as in the smaller German states, the cameralist variation of the Enlightenment (*Aufklärung*) owed more to Italian and German than to French inspiration. The key idea, growing out of German natural law, was that the firmest foundation for a wealthy and strong state was a happy and prosperous population. In return for obedience and loyalty the state would protect the people's material interests by the rule of law and guarantee their religious beliefs by a policy of toleration.[26]

The first generation of cameralists in the Habsburg lands constituted a small group of advisors at the court of Leopold I. Educated in the universities of Western Europe, and experienced in setting up small manufactures, they criticized not only the traditional orders or *Stände*, which they perceived as obstacles to innovation, but also the unproductive luxury-loving ways of the aristocracy. Their most influential representative,

---

[24] Marsha L. Rozenblit, *Reconstructing a National Identity. The Jews of Habsburg Austria during World War I* (Oxford University Press, 2001), pp. 23, 28–31; Robert S. Wistrich, *The Jews of Vienna in the Age of Franz Joseph* (Oxford University Press, 1989), pp. 175–81. For comparisons with Russia, see Benjamin Nathans, *Beyond the Pale. The Jewish Encounter with Late Imperial Russia* (Berkeley, CA: University of California Press, 2002), pp. 371–73.

[25] H. Dollinger, "Das Leitbild des Burgerkonigtums in der europaischen Monarchie des 19. Jahrhunderts," in K. F. Werner (ed.), *Hof, Kultur, und Politik im 19. Jahrhundert* (Bonn: L. Röhrscheid, 1985), pp. 337–43. For the debate over whether Joseph II was in fact enlightened, see D. Beales, "Was Joseph II an Enlightened Despot?" in R. Robertson and E. Timms (eds.), *The Austrian Enlightenment and its Aftermath* (Edinburgh University Press, 1991), pp. 1–21. Beales locates Joseph II squarely in the tradition of enlightened despotism of the cameralist variety while noting his increasingly despotic inclinations.

[26] H. M. Scott (ed.), "The Problem of Enlightened Absolutism," in *Enlightened Absolutism. Reform and Reformers in Later Eighteenth Century Europe* (Basingstoke: Palgrave Macmillan, 1990), pp. 18–19; Marc Raeff, *The Well-Ordered Police State. Social and Intellectual Change through Law in the Germanies and Russia, 1600–1800* (New Haven, CT: Yale University Press, 1983).

Johann Joachim Becher, extolled the virtues of a large, active population, well nourished and gainfully employed. He proposed to limit the export of raw materials in favor of producing finished goods to compete with the French imports with their snobbish appeal. He further advocated the establishment of new forms of credit and the creation of a central bank. The cameralists found an advocate in the inner circle of government in the person of Count Georg-Louis Sinzendorf, although his influence was cut short by a scandal that forced him to resign. Leopold gave the cameralists a sympathetic hearing, but mercantilist ideas encountered numerous structural obstacles: the opposition of the traditional orders; the lack of a customs union; the feeble endorsement of the court; and, perhaps most formidable of all, the War of the Spanish Succession beginning in 1700.[27]

The cameralist ideas were revived, embellished, and synthesized under the reigns of Maria Theresa and Joseph II into a more comprehensive administrative model of the well-ordered police state (*Politzeiwissenshaft*). The leading Austrian theorists of the well-ordered police state, Joseph von Sonnenfels and J. H. G. Justi, wrote and lectured at the Theresianum and the University of Vienna during the reign of Maria Theresa. Their work encompassed virtually every aspect of public policy from health and population to wealth and poverty. At the heart of Justi's economic policy was his belief that the state should be the main regulator of the economy. His proposals to encourage private initiative included freeing commerce from feudal regulations, reducing financial burdens on the peasantry, and freeing them from personal serfdom. He urged Maria Theresa to establish a "police agency" that would serve to advance by indirect means what would be called today a welfare state.[28]

Justi's contribution to the ideology of empire was to combine elements of the German cameralists and the French *philosophes*, primarily Montesquieu. His synthesis was a characteristic feature of the transfer of ideas from France and the German states to the Austrian and Russian autocracies. He fully endorsed Montesquieu's ideas on despotism, but differed from him on how its most harmful aspects could be eliminated. He criticized Peter the Great for failing to see that "despotism was by far

[27] Berenger, *Léopold Ier*, pp. 180–89; Kann, *A Study in Austrian Intellectual History*, pp. 174–87.

[28] The most comprehensive study of the Austrian cameralists is Louise Sommer, *Die österreichischer Kameralisten in dogmengeschichtler Darstellung*, 2 vols. (Vienna: C. Konegen, [1920–26] 1967). See also Gunther Chaloupek, "Justi in Austria. His Writings in the Context of Economic and Industrial Policies of the Habsburg Empire in the Eighteenth Century," in J. G. Backhaus (ed.), *The Beginnings of Political Economy. Johann Heinrich Gottlob von Justi* (New York: Springer, 2009), pp. 147–56.

the greatest obstacle to commerce." But he also opposed Montesquieu's corporate model of governing. For him the landowning nobility was just as formidable an obstacle to commerce as the tsar's despotism. He cited the Ottoman Empire and China as examples of effective imperial rule without a constitutionally established hereditary monarchy. He proposed creating a personal, lifetime nobility based on merit to encourage enterprise and to act as a moral check on the power of the monarch to prevent despotism.[29] Like many contemporary French writers, he accepted the Jesuits' idealized version of Chinese imperial rule in order to preach the virtues of moral constraint to the ruler, the absence of hereditary nobility, and the establishment of a professional bureaucracy based on a conciliar rather than hierarchical ministerial structure.[30]

Joseph von Sonnenfels popularized Justi's ideas a decade later. In 1771, he argued that the idea of patriotism or "love of fatherland," as he entitled an influential book, could be generated by a *Rechtsstaat* providing freedom, security, and material well-being. Following Justi, he made the amelioration of the condition of the peasantry a key component in his definition of the good ruler.[31] As we shall see, the "enlightened despot," Joseph II, only adopted these theoretical ideas piecemeal, although with important consequences in agriculture, without embracing the rational order that lay at their foundations.

In a prenationalist world, the monarchy embraced two unifying ideas that would, subsequently, contribute to the dissolution of the monarchy. The first was the use of a vernacular language. The second related idea was a dual concept of citizenship that established a common, empire-wide *Landespatriotismus*, allowing for a local patriotism based on the "nation" in the sense of a distinctive ethno-religiolinguistic group identity.[32] In the long aftermath of the French Revolution, this "hybrid" form of legitimization came under attack. The local vernaculars and ethnolinguistic loyalties found a more appealing lodging in the exclusivist concepts of the

---

[29] Ulrich Adam, *The Political Economy of J. H. G. Justi* (Bern: Peter Lang, 2006), pp. 107–17, 135–38.

[30] Adam, *Political Economy of J. H. G. Justi*, pp. 138–41; Walter W. Davis, "China, the Confucian Ideal and the European Age of Enlightenment," *Journal of the History of Ideas* 44 (1983): 523–48.

[31] Ernst Wangermann, "Joseph von Sonnenfels und die Vaterlandsliebe der Aufklärung," in Helmut Reinalter (ed.), *Joseph von Sonnenfels* (Vienna: Österreichische Akademie der Wissenschaften, 1988), pp. 157–69.

[32] R. J. W. Evans, "Joseph II and Nationality. The Habsburg Lands," in Scott (ed.), *Enlightened Absolutism*, pp. 210–18. Maciej Janowski, "Justifying Political Power in 19th Century Europe. The Habsburg Monarchy and Beyond," in Miller and Rieber (eds.), *Imperial Rule*, pp. 69–82, makes the important point that imperial legitimization was a fusion of the modern and traditional elements that encompassed divine right and popular sovereignty, diversity, and centralization.

nation-state and popular sovereignty, thus undermining the ideological foundations of imperial rule.

Up to the period of *Aufklärung*, multilingualism was part of the Habsburg tradition.[33] German was in practice the common tongue. Other vernaculars were in use at the local level for educational purposes on the assumption that the key to culture was a national language. The rulers themselves were educated to be multilingual, although most of their training was in the languages of Western Europe: German, French, Spanish, and Italian. Czech and Hungarian were occasional acquisitions. But German gradually assumed a dominant position, although the Counter Reformation and the special position of Hungary preserved Latin until the late eighteenth century. The politicization of language gained momentum under Maria Theresa and especially under Joseph II, whose language decree of 1784 established German as the administrative language of the realm. The Hungarians reacted and resisted by promoting Magyar to replace Latin, a process that was completed in 1844 with the requirement of its use in sessions of the diet. This gave rise to what Robert Evans has called "portentous ideological issues."[34] A debate ensued over the "Asiatic" origins of the Magyars. The Hungarian specialists who expressed pride in their ties with the traditions of the steppe nomads founded a counter myth of Hunnic origins. Together the two concepts laid the foundation for a romantic Magyar nationalism that reinforced traditional resistance to centralized imperial rule.[35]

The last attempt of the monarchy to impose German on its subjects was part of the constitutional experiment of the 1850s called neo-absolutism. The only attempt to rule all the Habsburg lands with a single language, it established German as the language of administration, the law courts, and higher education. In the face of resistance the monarchy soon retreated. Nevertheless, German continued to be the dominant language of the bureaucracy, army, and commercial life; German-speaking regions enjoyed the highest standard of living in the Monarchy. Consequently, up to the 1880s the German-speaking population felt no compulsion to create an organization to defend their nationality or to oppose that of others. A regional consciousness (*Landesbewusssein*) for those living in Bohemia, Moravia, Styria, Carinthia, etc. prevailed until the last decades of the nineteenth century. But the external shock of German unification

---

[33] The following is based on R. J. W. Evans, "Language and State Building. The Case of the Habsburg Monarchy," *Austrian History Yearbook* 35 (2004): 1–24.

[34] Evans, "Language and State Building," p. 9.

[35] Gábor Klaniczay, "Le myth d'origine scythique et le culte d'Attilla du 19e siècle." I am grateful to the author for supplying me with a pre-publication version of his article.

under Prussia and the internal pressures of the growing national move-
ments stirred the embers of German–Austrian national consciousness.
The opening salvo was fired by a disparate group of intellectuals, who in
1882 proclaimed the Linz Program. It proposed a democratic Austro-
German nation-state shorn of its Slavic provinces and committed to an
uncompromising nationalization of provinces of mixed nationality, like
Bohemia. Three years later a German member of parliament, Georg von
Schönerer, supplemented Linz with a pan-German, anti-Semitic, anti-
Catholic program. Although this never gained a mass following in Austria,
it did influence the young Adolph Hitler. In its wake other German
nationalist organizations sprang into action. None of them mustered
many votes, but they helped to poison the political atmosphere at the
end of the nineteenth century.[36]

The real breakdown in attempts to consolidate an imperial ideology
came with the compromise with the Hungarians. This, too, was an outcome of military defeats in 1859 and 1866, the exclusion of the Habsburgs
from Italy and the German confederation, and the resistance of the
Hungarians to the centralizing politics of neo-absolutism. During the
late nineteenth century Hungarian legalists invented a new tradition of
the Holy Crown which served as an alternative imperial ideology. The
crown of St. Stephen, the patron saint of Hungary, was represented as a
corporate political concept comprising the king and the nobility, but
reversing the centuries-old bipolarity between royal power and the
ország (country or nation) in favor of the latter. As the hereditary possession of an alien dynasty, the crown was transformed to represent the
sovereignty of the Hungarian nation.[37]

The free use of the Magyar language, sanctioned by the Ausgleich in
1867, further supported claims for sovereignty in the realm of cultural
practice. All the citizens of the Austrian half of the monarchy (sometimes
called Cisleithenia) were also granted equality of language use in schools,
offices, and public life. The Hungarians were satisfied, but only because
the right to use their own language was part of a general settlement which
gave them real autonomy. Their status had changed from an imperial
borderland to co-rulers of the empire. They rapidly proceeded to impose
an official language on the citizens of its half of the Monarchy through the
introduction of universal schooling. At the same time, the Hungarian

---

[36] Arnold Suppan, "'Germans' in the Habsburg Empire. Language, Imperial Ideology,
National Identity and Assimilation," in Charles W. Ingrao and Franz A. J. Szabo (eds.),
The Germans and the East (West Lafayette, IN: Purdue University Press, 2008),
pp. 147–90.

[37] László Peter, "The Holy Crown of Hungary, Visible and Invisible," *Slavonic and East
European Review* 81(3) (July 2003): 421–507.

parliament passed a nationality law stating that "all Hungarian citizens constitute a nation in the political sense, the one and indivisible Hungarian nation."[38] These two cultural practices were the driving force behind Magyarization and the attempt to create a nation-state out of Greater Hungary. It set Hungary on a different course than the Austrian half of the Monarchy. In the decades preceding the outbreak of war Magyarization intensified. The social and economic pressures to become Magyars were more indirect than direct, though no less powerful. And the government used administrative and judicial instruments to curb the activities of the non-Magyars in the borderlands of Hungary.

For the Slavic peoples linguistic rights proved to be insufficient to satisfy their aspirations. Like toleration, linguistic equality came late in the political life of the monarchy, when religious and language issues were inevitably drawn into the conflict between the center and the borderlands.

The fierce controversy between Czech- and German-speaking Austrians at the end of the century provides a classic case of the boomerang effect of linguistic politics in the borderlands. Once the Hungarians had achieved equal rights for their language, the Czechs pressed for the same recognition. In the 1890s, successive Habsburg governments were willing to accede. This touched off a firestorm among German speakers not only in Austria, but in Germany as well. The Austrian reaction revealed a deep insecurity about the purity of their speech, raising the level of their opposition to a frenzy and igniting a defensive reaction based on a racist exploitation of language.[39] All this contributed to a virtual paralysis of normal parliamentary life in the Austrian half of the monarchy with all its debilitating effects on imperial rule.

In the final analysis the imperial idea was to a large extent embodied in the persona of Franz Joseph. Emerging from the trauma of 1848, and surviving the military defeats in Italy in 1859 and Germany in 1866, he gradually gained enormous popularity, acquiring the status of a myth. In part this was the result of an official campaign to bolster and disseminate the dynastic myth. This was accomplished by reviving the glamor of the court, orchestrating the performance of imperial ceremonies, and multiplying the number of public symbols, particularly by erecting monuments. Celebrations of the emperor's birthday, the Corpus Christi procession, and the emperor's performance of the foot-washing ceremony became

---

[38] László Kontler, *Millennium in Central Europe. A History of Hungary* (Budapest: Atlantisz, 1999), pp. 285–90; Tibor Frank, "Hungary and the Dual Monarchy, 1867–1890," in Peter Sugar, Péter Hanák, and Tibor Frank (eds.), *A History of Hungary* (Bloomington, IN: Indiana University Press, 1994), pp. 254–58.

[39] Evans, "Language and State Building," pp. 15–16, 21.

part of the yearly imperial calendar marked by public observance and participation. Imperial inspection tours brought the emperor into personal contact with the population and gave him the opportunity to attend religious rituals of all the major faiths represented in the monarchy – Roman Catholic, Greek Catholic, Eastern Orthodox, Protestant, Jewish, and even Muslim – emphasizing his personal, and also the Monarchy's, endorsement of piety as a universalist ideal.[40] At the same time the Roman Catholic hierarchy undertook a quiet campaign to transform Franz Joseph's image from the Christ-anointed to the Christ-like in an attempt to revive the medieval identification of the ruler with the Savior. In part, this was a reaction to ideological threats from the right by Schönerer's pan-German, crypto-Protestant movement with its slogan of "Los von Rom"; from the left by the Christian Socialists; and from the Czech and Hungarian nationalists reacting to the language decrees.[41]

The construction of monuments and the organization of ceremonies also centered on the emperor cult. The earliest of the post-1848 imperial monuments was the Votivkirche constructed in 1853 as the official church for the garrison in Vienna and serving as a kind of Austrian Westminster Abbey. The great Kaiserforum project with its monument to Maria Theresa and its historical statuary paid tribute to the imperial dynasty. The construction of the Ringstrasse was embellished with numerous tributes to Franz Joseph, including the sculpture in front of parliament depicting him as a Roman emperor granting his lands a constitution. Another imperial symbol, a full-sized monument of the emperor, was raised in front of a military establishment in Vienna-Breitensee.[42] By the end of his life the cult of the monarch assumed extraordinary proportions. His portrait was everywhere; large-scale demonstrations testified to his popularity. His many journeys to the provinces, organized carefully to be sure, were nonetheless highly successful in bringing the living image of the emperor to his people. The spectacular jubilee celebrations of 1898 featured a parade of 2,000 representing all the nationalities (except the recalcitrant Czechs) in their colorful national costumes.[43] The construction of Franz Joseph as pious hero, combining the two most powerful elements of charisma, was not enough to create what Durkheim called an overarching symbol of consensus. That the imperial idea had shrunk to

---

[40] Daniel Unkowsky, "Reasserting Empire. Habsburg Imperial Celebrations after the Revolutions of 1848–1849," in Maria Bucur and Nancy M. Wingfield (eds.), *Staging the Past. The Politics of Commemoration in Habsburg Central Europe, 1848 to the Present* (West Lafayette, IN: Purdue University Press, 2001), pp. 13–45.

[41] James Shedel, "Emperor, Church and People. Religion and Dynastic Loyalty during the Golden Jubilee of Franz Joseph," *Catholic Historical Review* 76(1) (1990): 71–92.

[42] Urbanitsch, "Pluralist Myth," pp. 118–21.   [43] Bled, *Franz Joseph*, pp. 220–21.

one aging and frail man demonstrated the fragility of an empire that had weathered many storms at the cost of losing much of its raison d'être.

The Russian Empire

From the sixteenth century, the Russian tsar ruled as the direct representative of God on earth, and at times claimed or enjoyed a semi-divine status. The rulers and their image makers from the so-called Moscow bookmen to Over Procurators of the Holy Synod melded aspects of the Byzantine Basileus, the Mongol–Tatar khan, the Renaissance prince, and the Western absolutist monarch with the Russian Orthodox and indigenous traditions going back to the Grand Prince of Kievan Rus'.[44] The changing title of the Russian ruler – five times in the half millennium following the thirteenth century – was accompanied by revised enumerations of territories added to the crown reflecting the extent to which imperial expansion shaped the image of the *gospodar–tsar–imperator*, and proclaimed to his subjects and the external world his rule over a multicultural society.[45] In seeking divine legitimation for their rule, the Russian tsars were never entirely successful in establishing a clear-cut and stable relationship between their secular and spiritual persona and their imperial and ecumenical mission.

Between the fall of Constantinople in 1453 to the Ottoman Turks and the conquest of the Muslim khanates of Kazan and Astrakhan by Ivan IV, "the Terrible," in the 1550s, Orthodox clergymen and the Moscow bookmen sought to create a political theology that would establish Muscovy as the true defender of Orthodoxy. The most important and disputed text in this tradition was the so-called doctrine of the third Rome. The invention of a monk, Filofei, in the early sixteenth century, it proclaimed Muscovy as the imperial heir to the two preceding Romes with a warning that a lapse into heresy would bring the end of the world "for a fourth Rome there

---

[44] Michael Cherniavsky, "Khan or Basileus. An Aspect of Russian Medieval Political Theory," *Journal of the History of Ideas* 20 (1959): 459–76; Michael Cherniavsky, "Ivan the Terrible as Renaissance Prince," *Slavic Review* 27 (1968): 195–211; I. Shevchenko, "Muscovy's Conquest of Kazan. Two Views Reconciled," *Slavic Review* 4 (1967): 541–47; E. Keenan, "Royal Russian Behavior. Style and Self-Image," in Edward Allworth (ed.), *Ethnic Russia: The USSR. The Decline of Dominance* (New York: Pergamon Press, 1980), pp. 1–16.

[45] Marc Szeftel, "The Title of the Muscovite Monarch up to the End of the Seventeenth Century," *Canadian–American Slavic Studies* 13 (1979): 59–81. The use of the term "white tsar" for the Russian ruler by the Nogai Horde in the sixteenth century strongly suggests that they regarded Moscow as one of the heirs of the Golden Horde. Michael Khodarkovsky, *Russia's Steppe Frontier. The Making of a Colonial Empire 1500–1800* (Bloomington, IN: Indiana University Press, 2002), p. 44 and the literature cited.

would not be." The idea had some currency among clerics, but ironically it was most enthusiastically embraced by the Old Believers who accepted its apocalyptic implications.[46] The Moscow princes hesitated to claim that *translatio imperii* from the Byzantine Empire to Muscovy had occurred, for this would have involved them in a moral obligation to wrest the second Rome, Byzantium, from the infidel Turks, committing them to a crusade that they simply lacked the power to conduct. By the time that Moscow had acquired sufficient military strength to conquer the neighboring khanates of Kazan and Astrakhan in the 1550s, the idea of a crusade ran counter to the idea of peacefully assimilating the large Muslim population of these khanates into the empire.

A second complexity arose from the reluctance of the princes to base their legitimacy solely on the foundations of the Orthodox Church. To have done so would have meant subordinating their ambitions to the moral authority of the Church. On the other hand, the Church had been a steady supporter of the power of the Moscow princes in their struggle to "gather the Russian land," and a valued partner in maintaining their drive to consolidate an absolutist rule. Thus, from the emergence of a unified Russian state, ambivalence characterized Russian political theology and created a tension in church–state relations that was never completely resolved.[47]

The difficulties facing the Church as a unifying political theology and a weapon in the struggle over the borderlands erupted in the spiritual crisis of the seventeenth century leading to the great schism. The schism was the culmination of a long debate over reform within the Church that exhibited some similarities to the Protestant movements in Central Europe a century earlier. It was also part of a larger cultural conflict in the western borderlands, where Calvinism and more radical brotherhoods battled the Counter Reformation led by the Jesuits. Both contestants competed to win over the Orthodox laity and churchmen overwhelmed by the disasters of the Time of Troubles in the early seventeenth century when belief in the

---

[46] For recent reconsiderations of the Third Rome, see especially Peter Nitsche, "Translatio imperii? Beobachtungen zum historischen Selbstverständnis im Moskauer Zartum um die Mitte des 16 Jahrhunderts," *Jahrbücher für Geschichte Osteuropas* 35 (1987): 321–38; Daniel Rowland, "Moscow. Third Rome or New Israel?" *Russian Review* 55 (1996): 59–88; Daniel Ostrowsky, *Muscovy and the Mongols. Cross-Cultural Influences on the Steppe Frontier, 1304–1589* (Cambridge University Press, 1998), ch. 10.

[47] In Russian history the concept of political theology was first explored by Michael Cherniavsky, *Tsar and People. Studies in Russian Myths* (New Haven, CT: Yale University Press, 1961). A recent reevaluation is V. M. Zhivkov, *Razyskaniia v oblasti i predistorii russkoi kul'tury* (Moscow: Iazyki slavianskoi kul'tury, 2002).

Russian Church as the defender of the purity of Orthodoxy was severely shaken.[48]

In the mid-seventeenth century, two currents of thought, one internal and the other external, combined to challenge the dominant view in the Church hierarchy that the Russian liturgy and theological texts possessed the only true road to salvation.[49] A group of clerics known as Zealots of Piety criticized a number of practices in the performance of church services and popular rituals and celebrations of religious feasts. The dispute spread to the meaning of the liturgy and the relative importance of the parish clergy and the episcopate. The newly appointed Patriarch Nikon was originally associated with the Zealots, but he also fell under the influence of the Greek clerics who sought refuge from Ottoman rule, and new careers and opportunities in Muscovy. By virtue of their learning, they gradually influenced Russian clerics in the direction of correcting abuses that had crept into the ritual and texts over the previous century. Among them Paisios, Patriarch of Jerusalem, conducted a one-man campaign to persuade Tsar Aleksei Mikhailovich (1645–1676) to accept the leadership of the Orthodox world against the Catholic Poles and the Muslim Ottomans. He supported petitions to the tsar from the Cossack insurgent leader, Bogdan Khmel'nits'ky, seeking aid in his rebellion against the Poles. He also overcame Moscow's initial resistance to the idea of war with the Poles over Ukraine. He helped to smooth relations between Khmel'nits'ky and the tsar, leading to the Treaty of Pereiaslavl in 1654 which brought the left bank Ukraine into the Muscovite state. Together with other leading clerics in the Balkans and the Near East, he preached the need for Khmel'nits'ky and the Muscovites to join in a war to liberate the Slavs from the Turkish yoke. Nikon was sympathetic. As Metropolitan of Novgorod he had opposed the government's policy of returning Orthodox refugees from Swedish rule in the Karelian borderlands and supported the idea of freeing his co-religionists from the heretical Swedes.[50] But pious as he was, Aleksei Mikhailovich would not embark on crusades.

[48] Sergei Zenkovskii, *Russkoe staroobriadchestvo. Dukhovnye dvizheniia semnadtsatogo veka* (Munich: Fink, 1970), pp. 50–58. The competition between the two western churches to capture Orthodoxy reached as far as Constantinople, where with the help of the Ottomans their representatives manipulated the appointment and dismissal of patriarchs more than forty times in the period from 1595 to 1657. *Ibid.*, p. 57.
[49] Paul Bushkovitch, *Religion and Society in Russia. The Sixteenth and Seventeenth Centuries* (Oxford University Press, 1992), stresses the internal causes. Cf. N. F. Kapterev, *Kharakter otnoshenii Rossii k pravoslavnomu vostoku v XVI–XVII stoletiiakh* (The Hague: Mouton, [1914] 1968), for the external influences.
[50] Zenkovskii, *Russkoe staroobriadchestvo*, pp. 197–202. To what extent the idea of a pan-Orthodox empire influenced Nikon's reforms is still unclear.

By the end of the century influential Orthodox churchmen in the Balkans pressed harder for Muscovy's intervention and liberation of the Slavs. The Russians responded under the regency of Peter's sister, Sophia, by launching two Crimean campaigns. Although they failed, a precedent had been set. Russia's role as protector of the spiritual interests of the Orthodox gradually acquired a political cast.[51] Russian rulers would not proclaim a religious war in their struggle over the borderlands; this would open the way for the Ottomans to reciprocate in kind. Both empires contained too many co-religionists of the other to risk a "total holy war" of this kind. But the Russians would henceforth appeal for the assistance of the Slavic population in the name of Orthodox solidarity whenever a war with the Ottomans broke out for other reasons.

The ambivalence of Russia's rulers toward Orthodoxy as the ideological basis for imperial rule also characterized their disparate views of conversion as a cultural policy. Conversion to Orthodoxy was in the interests of both church and state. But their perception of its importance in the hierarchy of imperial aims did not always coincide. Even after Peter's abolition of the patriarchate, the church was not simply an arm of the state.[52] Rather, their relations were interactive and changed over time. Conversion was never a systematic policy of either church or state. There were periods when conversion as a general policy was more actively pursued as opposed to periods of greater passivity or even tolerance of non-Orthodox religions prevailed. To be sure, religious tolerance (*veroterpimost'*) in the Russian Empire did not carry the meaning that it has acquired in contemporary Western societies. It was not based on ideas of civil or human rights. The government only granted legal sanction to freedom of conscience in 1905. Even then the Orthodox Church delayed its implementation by opposing enabling legislation in the state Duma.[53] Toleration in Russia was, like its putative opposite, conversion, an instrument of imperial rule. That is, the state assumed the role of the protector of the Orthodox, here meaning mainstream confessions, with their well-established hierarchies, rules, and dogmas. The aim was to prevent disruptive schisms and heresies from rending the social fabric of imperial

---

[51] Kapterev, *Rossiia i vostok*, pp. 368–82.

[52] Gregory Freeze, "Handmaiden of the State? The Church in Imperial Russia Reconsidered," *Journal of Ecclesiastical History* 36(1) (1985): 82–102.

[53] Peter Waldron, "Religious Toleration in Late Imperial Russia," in Olga Crisp and Linda Edmunson (eds.), *Civil Rights in Imperial Russia* (Oxford: Clarendon Press, 1989), pp. 103–19; Raymond Pearson, "Privileges, Rights and Russification," in Crisp and Edmunson (eds.), *Civil Rights in Imperial Russia*, pp. 85–102.

society. Some would go as far as to call the Russian Empire "a confessional state" in much the same way that the Ottoman Empire or the Habsburg Monarchy could claim to be.[54] But even here there were important exceptions and ambiguities in the state policy of opposing deviant movements splitting away from established confessions. In certain cases, where religious dissenters accepted their civic obligations and demonstrated their obedience to authority and devotion to fatherland, the state was willing to tolerate their existence.[55]

The first period of intensive conversion was launched by Ivan IV after his conquest of the khanate of Kazan. There is disagreement over how many of the conversions were forced. In any case, they were accompanied by large deportations of Muslims and the colonization of their land by Russians.[56] Employed in tandem these two elements were powerful instruments of integration of the borderlands. But the tsar was more circumspect in pressing for conversion after his conquest of Astrakhan in 1556 and Russia's first penetration into the north Caucasus following warnings from the sultan, Selim III, that these borderlands were traditional Ottoman spheres.[57] The missionary spirit withered during the great crisis of the seventeenth century, but revived under Peter the Great. For all his reputation as an irreligious ruler, he undertook a systematic and ruthless policy of conversion. He was motivated in part by strategic concerns related to the struggle over the southern borderlands, "the constant fear of a hostile Islamic axis – a united front of various Muslim peoples under the Ottoman umbrella."[58] The high tide of state involvement in conversion followed Peter's death, with the creation in 1740 of an Agency of Convert Affairs to operate mainly in the internal provinces with Muslim populations. Missionaries reported mass conversions in the Volga–Kama

---

[54] Robert Crews, "Empire and the Confessional State. Islam and Religious Politics in Nineteenth Century Russia," *American Historical Review* 108(1) (February 2003): 55–83.

[55] Paul Werth, "Schism Once Removed: Brotherhoods, State Authority, and Meanings of Religious Toleration in Imperial Russia," in Miller and Rieber (eds.), *Imperial Rule*, pp. 83–105.

[56] A. N. Grigor'ev, "Khristianizatsiia nerusskikh narodnostei kak odin iz metodov natsional'noi kolonial'noi politiki tsarizma v Tatarii," in *Materialy po istorii Tatarii* (Kazan: Tatgosizdat, 1948), pp. 226–28, emphasized the coercion, reflecting perhaps the brief reappearance in Soviet historiography of the anti-imperialist theme. See also Chantal Lemercier-Quelquejay, "Les Missions orthodoxes en pays musulmans de moyenne-et basse-Volga," *Cahiers du monde russe et sovietique* 8 (July–September 1967): 380–81.

[57] Michael Khodarkovsky, "The Conversion of non-Christians in Early Modern Russia," in Robert P. Geraci and Khodarkovsky (eds.), *Of Religion and Empire. Missions, Conversions and Tolerance in Tsarist Russia* (Ithaca, NY: Cornell University Press, 2001), p. 121.

[58] Michael Khodarkovsky, *Russia's Steppe Frontier. The Making of a Colonial Empire, 1500–1800* (Bloomington, IN: Indiana University Press, 2002), pp. 192–93; Michael Khodarkovsky, *Where Two Worlds Met. The Russian State and the Kalmyk Nomads, 1600–1771* (Ithaca, NY: Cornell University Press, 1992), pp. 98, 145–46.

region, with estimates as high as 400,000 non-Christians having been baptized.[59]

Catherine the Great, inspired by Western models of toleration, abolished the Agency of Convert Affairs and sought the collaboration of non-Christian religious leaders, especially among Muslim Tatars. With her the "confessional state" appears to have earned its sobriquet. She recognized the value of stable religious hierarchies in regulating confessional beliefs and practices, preventing schisms and brotherhoods which created disorder and undermined the authority of the state.[60] Her policy was successful in certain interior provinces, but posed problems for authorities dealing with ethnic groups in the borderlands who were divided on confessional lines. For example, in the western borderlands the Belorussian people who inhabited a long-disputed cultural and political borderland between Poles and Russians were split among adherents of the Orthodox, Catholic, and Uniat faiths. Similar confessional splits existed in other borderlands as well.[61]

Despite her confessional tolerance, Catherine granted the Orthodox Church the exclusive right to proselytize, and forbade apostasy from Orthodoxy. Her concept of the enlightened and well-governed state also guided her policy of toleration toward the Jewish population in the western borderlands acquired in the First Partition of Poland. When the Second Partition brought in large numbers of Jews, pragmatic concerns gained the upper hand. Her legislative decree of 1791 restricted their place of settlement and commercial activity in response to complaints by Russian merchants, laying the foundations for the establishment of the Pale of Settlement.[62] There was no attempt to embark on a campaign to convert the Jews. Nevertheless, the territorial confinement of the Jews, supplemented by additional discriminatory legislation throughout the nineteenth century, effectively turned the Pale of Settlement into an inner borderland. It became a serious obstacle to assimilation and contributed to widespread disaffection among the Jewish population. This helps to explain the disproportionate number of Jews in the leadership of

---

[59] Paul Werth, *At the Margins of Orthodoxy. Mission, Governance and Confessional Politics in Russia's Volga–Kama Region, 1827–1905* (Ithaca, NY: Cornell University Press, 2002), p. 22. Many of these converts were pagan; the conversions were not sincere and subsequently repudiated. Khodarkovsky, *Russia's Steppe Frontier*, pp. 194–96.

[60] Crews, "Empire and the Confessional State," pp. 50–83.

[61] Theodore Weeks, "Religion and Russification. Russian Language and the Catholic Churches of the 'Northwest Provinces' after 1862," *Kritika* 2(1) (Winter 2001): 87–110; Werth, "Schism Once Removed," pp. 85–108.

[62] John Doyle Klier, *Russia Gathers Her Jews. The Origins of the "Jewish Question" in Russia, 1772–1825* (De Kalb, IL: Northern Illinois University Press, 1986), p. 75.

socialist movements at the end of the century and the appearance in Russia of the first proponents of Zionism.[63]

Throughout the nineteenth century official policies toward Orthodoxy continued to reflect the personal preferences of the rulers, and oscillated between conversion and toleration without settling on a clear-cut course of action. Alexander I, psychologically the most complex tsar, presided over a society undergoing a religious revival. His heterodox religious outlook was shaped in part by Pietism following his own spiritual conversion during the fire that consumed Moscow during Napoleon's occupation. He also founded the Society of Israelite Christians, more as a vehicle of personal redemption than raison d'état – though with Alexander it is hard to separate the two. Its ostensible purpose was to support and sustain Jewish converts to Christianity. It was characteristic of Alexander's ambivalent attitude toward the Orthodox Church that recruits to the Society could be drawn from any Christian confession.[64] In a far more radical deviation from the official position of the Church, Alexander approved the creation of the Imperial Russian Bible Society and the fusion of the Holy Synod with the Ministry of Education. The practical effect was to reduce the Orthodox Church to equal status with other confessions, to enforce toleration, and to forbid proselytizing among churches.[65] Not surprisingly, the translation of the Holy Scripture from Church Slavonic to vernacular Russian under the auspices of the Bible Society aroused the ire of leading Orthodox churchmen for "degrading the word of God."[66] The project was not completed for half a century, disrupting the progress toward the Petrine goal of a Russian "reformation" that would place the political theology of empire on the same intellectual level as the competing religions of the book. In general, Alexander's policy of conversion might be called one of benign neglect seasoned with contradictory elements of mysticism and rationality.

[63] Some historians place emphasis on the pogroms of 1881 as the decisive event in impelling Russian Jews to take the leap into revolutionary action. But other historians have pointed to the emergence of Jewish resistance before the pogroms. For the longer tradition, see Erich Haberer, *Jews and Revolution in Nineteenth Century Russia* (Cambridge University Press, 1995). See also the discussion in Nathans, *Beyond the Pale*, pp. 6–11.

[64] John Doyle Klier, "State Policy and Conversion of the Jews in Imperial Russia," in Geraci and Khodarkovsky (eds.), *Of Religion and Empire*, pp. 95–96.

[65] Alexander Martin, *Romantics, Reformers, Reactionaries. Russian Conservative Thought and Politics in the Reign of Alexander I* (De Kalb, IL: Northern Illinois University Press, 1997), pp. 185–86.

[66] Stephen K. Batalden, "Printing the Bible in the Reign of Alexander I. Toward a Reinterpretation of the Imperial Russian Bible Society," in Geoffrey Hosking (ed.), *Church, Nation and State in Russia and Ukraine* (London: St. Martin's Press, 1991), pp. 65–78.

Nicholas I took steps to restore the primacy of Orthodoxy. He enthusiastically endorsed the formula Orthodoxy, Autocracy, and Nationality (*narodnost'*) designed by his Minister of Education, Count Sergei Uvarov, to serve as a set of principles to guide "the education of the people."[67] Uvarov was hardly a religious fanatic, and he never resorted to coercive methods to convert the non-Orthodox. His main concern was to defend the Church against the twin evils of rationalism on the left and mysticism on the right.[68]

Even Nicholas adopted different tactics in his efforts to solidify the links between religion and "Russianness." He abolished the Society of Israelite Christians. Viewing Jews as a parasitic element in the population, he sought to weaken their religious community (*kahal*) through taxes and carry out their conversion through the imposition of military recruitment. Regarding the Uniat Church as an instrument of polonization, he decreed its abolition in 1839, restoring 1.5 million people to Orthodoxy. A rare case of forced conversion, it backfired when during the Polish revolt of 1863 Uniats joined Catholics in battling imperial rule. In the Volga region attempts to convert Muslims were not successful, leading to a movement of mass apostasy in 1866.[69] The government continued to be frustrated by its own inability to reconcile the concept of religious toleration and the political theology of empire.

In the Caucasian borderlands, the process of converting the Muslim population was, like that of the western borderlands, closely tied to security. Islam supplied the staying power of the resistance to imperial rule by the north Caucasus tribes. It took twenty years for the Russian army to subdue the mountaineers. But there were those like Field Marshal Prince Michael Vorontsov, the Viceroy of the Caucasus from 1843 to 1856, who brought an enlightened view of imperial rule to the Caucasian borderlands. The son of a grandee of Catherine's era, educated in

---

[67] Nicholas V. Riasanovsky, *Nicholas I and Official Nationality in Russia, 1825–1855* (Berkeley, CA: University of California Press, 1952); Nicholas V. Riasanovsky, *A Parting of Ways. Government and the Educated Public in Russia, 1801–1855* (Oxford University Press, 1976), pp. 103–47, are the standard treatments. The designation of this triad of principles as "Official Nationality" was coined by a latter-day liberal critic. Riasanovsky, *A Parting of Ways*, p. 105. Cf. Cynthia A. Whittaker, *The Origins of Modern Russian Education. An Intellectual Biography of Count Sergei Uvarov* (De Kalb, IL: Northern Illinois University Press, 1984), who presents Uvarov as a moderate motivated by practical concerns.

[68] Andrei Zorin, *Kormia dvuglavnogo orla. Literaturaia i gosudarstvennaia ideologiia v Rossii v poslednei treti XVIII–pervoi treti XIX veka* (Moscow: Novoe literaturnoe obozrenie, 2001).

[69] For the Jews, see Klier, "State Policy," pp. 96–102; for the Uniats, see Theodore R. Weeks, "Between Rome and Tsargrad. The Uniate Church in Imperial Russia," in Geraci and Khodarkovsky (eds.), *Of Religion and Empire*, pp. 74–84; for the Volga Muslims, see Werth, *At the Margins of Orthodoxy*, ch. 6.

England, a veteran of all Russia's wars in the first half of the century, he expanded Catherine's policies of toleration by allowing the ulama to continue to run elementary schools and operate their own *Shari'a* (Islamic law) religious courts in the belief that the local Muslim elites could be won over as allies against the rebellious mountaineers. His successor, Field Marshal A.I. Bariatinskii, took a different, perhaps no less "enlightened," view. Like Vorontsov, however, he had come to the conclusion, as he stated in memos to Alexander II, that Russia had become for Asia what Europe had represented for so long in Russia: the source and bearer of the world's most advanced civilization. But he doubted the effectiveness of Vorontsov's policy of toleration and feared that persistent resistance to Russian rule in the form of Muridism, a fiercely egalitarian Naqshbandi Sufi brotherhood, would cripple the Caucasian army in the event of a foreign war. He intended to blunt its appeal by reestablishing the force of customary law (*adat*) and restoring the prestige of the local nobles. By reducing the authority of the mullahs, he hoped to make clear to the Muslims the difference between civil and religious life, and gradually introduce Russian civil law. At the same time, he sought "to resurrect Orthodoxy in this region." Alexander II approved his proposal to form a Society for the Restoration of Orthodox Christianity, and placed it under the patronage of Empress Maria Alexandrovna. The aim was not to antagonize the mountaineers by active proselytizing, but rather to restore the faith where it had existed from ancient times to the sixteenth century when the Ottomans and Persians conquered the region. Foreshadowing the policies of N. I. Il'minskii in Siberia, he advocated the opening of seminaries where local languages would be taught and Christian religious texts translated.[70]

The Society's proselytizing activities were a mixed success, but its main achievements in Abkhazia were due to conditions and circumstances that were almost precisely the opposite of those prevailing in the Volga–Kama area or other regions of the Caucasus. The Society was well organized and well funded, it had the backing of successive viceroys and their staffs, and many of the missionaries were Georgians with knowledge of local conditions and languages. Moreover, the Abkhasians still retained some vestiges of Christian belief in their syncretic religious life. But the favorable outlook for conversion dimmed toward the end of the nineteenth

[70] Alfred J. Rieber (ed.), "The Politics of Imperialism," in *The Politics of Autocracy. Letters of Alexander II to Prince A. I. Bariatinskii 1857–1864* (The Hague: Mouton, 1966), pp. 69, 71; Firouzeh Mostashari, "Colonial Dilemmas. Russian Politics in the Muslim Caucasus," in Geraci and Khodarkovsky (eds.), *Of Religion and Empire*, pp. 234–38.

century when the Ottoman Empire under Sultan Abdülhamid revived the older militant tradition and began to send mullahs educated in Istanbul into the Caucasus. Under the last rulers of both the Russian and Ottoman empires, imperial authorities sought to fuse religious belief and loyalty to the nationalizing state in a new form of political theology. That the Russian Church steadily lost ground to Islam in the Caucasus was testimony to the growing resistance of the local population to Russian rule as well as to the traditional weaknesses of the Orthodox missionary enterprise.[71]

In the era of the Great Reforms (1861–1881) policies of conversion became more complex and contradictory. Differences multiplied within the state administration, and between the central and peripheral authorities. In the borderlands of the Baltic provinces, the Caucasus, and Central Asia the Russian proconsuls experimented with a variety of means to gain the loyalty of the local population, alternating between greater and lesser toleration of non-Orthodox faiths. Robert Geraci has demonstrated the formidable problems facing even the most dedicated and intelligent missionaries in Siberia. Men like N. I. Il'minskii encountered obstacles within the Church and among more aggressive Russifiers in his campaign to spread Orthodoxy through the use of native languages. Ultimately, the problem came down to the fact that many Russian missionaries, bureaucrats, and publicists exhibited a profound ambivalence toward the process of conversion as the best means to assimilate the Muslim and pagan peoples of the east.[72]

All these efforts suffered from the failure of the Orthodox Church to undertake much needed internal reform and to provide strong intellectual leadership. During the Great Reforms there was an exodus of the sons of priests (*popovichi*) from the clerical estate, including many of the best and the brightest. Although they continued to serve as "useful agents of cultural russification" especially in the southwest borderlands, they could no longer be counted on as staunch monarchists. Their political views were either ambivalent or anti-authoritarian.[73] By the end of the century the Church faced a general crisis in corporate self-identity. Many aspects of ecclesiastical life remained contentious, dividing not only the

[71] Manana Gnolidze-Swanson, "Activity of the Russian Orthodox Church among the Muslim Natives of the Caucasus in Imperial Russia," *Caucasus and Central Asia Newsletter* 4 (Summer 2003): 9–19.

[72] Robert P. Geraci, *Window on the East. National and Imperial Identities in Late Tsarist Russia* (Ithaca, NY: Cornell University Press, 2001).

[73] Laurie Manchester, *Holy Fathers, Secular Sons. Clergy Intelligentsia and the Modern Self in Revolutionary Russia* (Ithaca, NY: Cornell University Press, 2008), pp. 156–61.

clergy and laity, but churchmen as well.[74] The most innovative theologians of the second half of the nineteenth century were laymen, Konstantin Leontiev, Vladimir Solov'ev, and Leo Tolstoy, and they were frequently at odds with the official hierarchy. In the 1905 debates over Church reform, well-known secular writers such as V.V. Rozanov, Dimitri Merezhkovskii, and V.A. Ternavtsev, the so-called maximalists, vainly sought the reconciliation of Orthodoxy and the intelligentsia over such issues as private property, and a synthesis of God's justice and the justice of humanity.[75] The Church was further weakened by its inability to end the schism and bring the Old Believers back into the fold. There are no agreed figures for the number of Old Believers at the end of the empire, but estimates range from a quarter to a third of the Great Russian peasantry. This meant, in effect, that a substantial proportion of the population in the central provinces did not believe that their government was legitimate.[76] When Nicholas II was forced by the revolution of 1905 to issue an edict of toleration, there were mass defections from Orthodoxy and re-conversions to Roman Catholicism by former Uniats in the western borderlands, and to Islam by Tatars, Buriat Mongols, and others in Siberia. This amounted to nothing less than a renunciation of being Russian.

Perhaps the most serious damage to the religious foundations of imperial rule was inflicted by the imperial family. Nicholas II and his wife Alexandra attempted to create a new historicoreligious myth by fusing two older traditions of rulership: on the one hand, the resplendent Muscovite tsar surrounded by the hieratic Byzantine ritual and, on the other hand, the Russian pilgrim-holy man in the humble service of the people. The effect was inherently contradictory, confusing, and divisive. It led to controversies over canonization that opened up another fissure between the common people and the official hierarchy of the Holy Synod. At the same time, the tsar's misguided enthusiasm for creating new objects of religious piety offended high church officials, who believed that they alone had the right to define sainthood.[77] The imperial couple

---

[74] Vera Shevzov, *Russian Orthodoxy on the Eve of Revolution* (Oxford University Press, 2004), pp. 258–59.
[75] V.A. Tvardovskaia, "Tsarstvovanie Aleksandra III," in V. Ia. Grosul (ed.), *Russkii konservatizm XIX stoletii. Ideologiia i praktika* (Moscow: Progress-Traditsiia, 2000), pp. 331–39; Paul R. Valliere, "The Idea of a Council in Russian Orthodoxy in 1905," in Robert L. Nicholas and Theofanis George Stavrou (eds.), *Russian Orthodoxy under the Old Regime* (Minneapolis, MN: University of Minnesota Press, 1978), pp. 192–93.
[76] Zenkovskii, *Russkoe staroobriadchestvo*, p. 15.
[77] Wortman, *Scenarios of Power*, vol. II, pp. 384–90; Gregory Freeze, "Tserkov', religiia, i politicheskaia kul'tura na zakate starogo rezhima," in D. Geiger and V.S. Diakin (eds.), *Reformy ili revoliutsiia? Rossiia, 1861–1917* (St. Petersburg: Nauka, 1992), pp. 31–42.

were desperate to sustain the illusion that their power derived from God and also rested upon a mystic bond with the people. This opened the way for "the dark forces" to penetrate the citadel of autocracy. Both Nicholas and Alexandra were drawn to Rasputin in part because they took him to be the embodiment of the national popular idea.[78]

In the end the political theology of empire became increasingly splintered; conversion was proven to be a dull instrument of imperial rule. The idea that Orthodoxy could serve as the foundation on which an imperial ideology could be constructed was not consistently endorsed by the rulers or governing elites. The Church lacked the cultural resources to complete a mass conversion of the population in the borderlands. Yet a consistent policy of toleration in a multicultural empire could only nourish sentiments of greater autonomy in all spheres of public life, including national aspirations. The dilemma was never resolved in the Russian Empire.

The contradictions in imperial ideology were replicated in the secular sphere following successive waves of transfer of Western ideas into Russia that provided alternative principles of authority and legitimacy. The Ukrainian borderland was the filter through which the first currents of Western thought penetrated into the center of Russian imperial power. The key figure in this process was Peter Mohyla, of noble Moldovan–Ukrainian origin, educated in Paris in the Latin tradition, and then at the Kievan Monastery of the Caves, rising to become Archimandrite and Metropolitan of Kiev. Founding a printing press and reforming church schools, he turned the Kiev Theological Academy into the major dissemination point for all eastern Europe of learning that combined the greatest classical Latin and Greek authors. Graduates of the Academy founded other centers of learning such as the Kharkov Collegium (later Kharkov University). Under the leadership of Stefan Prokopovich, Peter the Great's most trusted churchman and the principal ecclesiastical ideologue of autocracy, the Ukrainian Church provided the majority of bishops occupying sees in the Russian Empire from 1700 to 1762. Prokopovich, himself a graduate of the Kievan Academy who had studied in Rome, championed post-Aristotelian learning. He preached and wrote on the need for the Church to fill practical as well as spiritual functions in promoting imperial rule.[79]

---

[78] For Nicholas' and Alexandra's "populism," see Dominic Lieven, *Nicholas II. Emperor of all the Russias* (London: John Murray, 1993), pp. 32–34, 127–28, 152–53, 164–67, although he downplays Rasputin's pernicious influence. This view gains some support from V. I. Gurko, *Features and Figures of the Past. Government and Opinion in the Reign of Nicholas II* (Stanford University Press, 1939), pp. 551, 560, but cf. p. 579.

[79] Eduard Winter, *Byzanz und Rom im Kampf um die Ukraine, 955–1939* (Leipzig: Otto Harrassowitz, 1942), pp. 85–90; Paul Bushkovitch, *Peter the Great. The Struggle for Power,*

Under Peter the Great and his successors the Church continued to play a role in defining imperial power, but it had to share the stage with secular themes of legitimacy. Refusing to appoint a patriarch after the death of Adrian in 1700, Peter abolished the office in 1721, replacing it with the Holy Synod, a department of the state bureaucracy. The "reform" was pursued in accord with the principles of Pietism. Nothing could symbolize more dramatically his determination to subordinate the Church to the state and to terminate the claims of the church hierarchs to share power with the tsar.[80] As Richard Wortman has written: "By the end of the seventeenth century the forms of Christian Empire and the Christian emperor no longer fit the needs of an autonomous, dynamic, monarchical rule."[81] Peter expanded on the idea embraced by previous tsars of identifying empire with territorial expansion, by grounding the authority of the ruler on his exploits in war. In ritual, ceremony, and imperial propaganda the image of the tsar underwent a transformation. Themes of ancient Rome encroached on religious symbolism. Official spokesmen like Feofan Prokopovich and Peter Shafirov reinforced the ideological foundations of imperial rule by invoking west European norms of governance drawn from the writings of Hugo Grotius, Samuel Pufendorf, Gottfried Leibniz, and other advocates of natural law and cameralist thought. In his own pragmatic way, Peter endorsed by his actions the ideals of the neo-Stoic ruler who regarded the increase in wealth and power of the empire as the basis for the welfare of its people.[82] He believed in the creative power of science and technology to provide the knowledge and skills necessary to carry out these aims. The ideas that guided Peter's educational policies centered on a technical education that was "narrowly utilitarian, highly specialized and tied to military requirements." Similarly, his sponsorship of geographic expeditions and large-scale map-making projects not only emulated Western models of increasing knowledge about the physical world, but aimed at establishing and expanding the frontiers of empire.[83]

Peter's decision to shift the capital from the center of his realm to the northwestern periphery (even before the ground had been officially ceded

1671–1725 (Cambridge University Press, 2001), pp. 435–37; statistics from K. V. Kharlampovich, *Malorossiiskoe vlianie na velikorusskuiu tserkovnuiu zhizn'* (The Hague: Mouton, [1914] 1968), vol. I, pp. 459–60, 636.

[80] The most complete study is James Cracraft, *The Church Reform of Peter the Great* (Stanford University Press, 1971).

[81] Wortman, *Scenarios of Power*, vol. I, p. 41.

[82] Raeff, *The Well-Ordered Police State*, pp. 206–7; Lindsey Hughes, *Russia in the Age of Peter the Great* (New Haven, CT: Yale University Press, 1998), pp. 94–98, 145; Bushkovitch, *Peter the Great*, pp. 440–41.

[83] Alfred J. Rieber, "Politics and Technology in Eighteenth Century Russia," *Science in Context* 8(2) (Summer 1995): 345–49, quotation on p. 345; Hughes, *Russia in the Age of Peter the Great*, pp. 309–12.

to Russia by Sweden) was in many ways his most dramatic ideological statement. It was a close cultural fit with his reform of the Church and the imposition of Western models of dress and deportment, at least at court. Moscow represented a different image of empire. Foreigners called it medieval or Asiatic. The city retained strong physical and symbolic reminders of the past: its narrow streets and wooden buildings were dominated by great churches in the Byzantine-Kievan style, and the Kremlin walls, though built by Italians on the Renaissance model of the Palazzo Sforzesco in Milan, were intended to defend against Tatar and Polish raids. The urban design of St. Petersburg was to be rational with rectilinear streets and canals, huge squares and no walls, triumphal arches, based on Swedish and Dutch models, built by foreigners, overwhelmingly dominated by secular buildings, palaces, and government offices. Four buildings in particular encompassed Peter's concept of the new monarchy. The Admiralty symbolized Russia as a major maritime power, its spire the focal point of "a unique and vast system of inter-brotherhooding spaces ... that would define the harmony of Petersburg's urban plan for the next century"; the Peter and Paul Fortress exemplified the fusion of church and state, with Peter's dominant statue holding the keys to heaven and hell; the Kunstkammer, with its severe classical design and central tower culminating in a polygonal lantern and globe, housing Russia's first observatory and anatomy theater, represented Peter's commitment to science; and the building of the Twelve Colleges defined imperial space for the Petrine bureaucracy, the modern principle of organization as recommended by Leibniz.[84] The ensemble provided Peter with a spatial field in which to display his power through triumphal rituals. His plans, largely unfinished in his lifetime, underwent stylistic modifications, but the original concept, assuming even more grandiose proportions as it was enlarged and embellished by Peter's successors, projected imperial power facing west on the water, if not yet on the open sea.[85]

There is some debate over whether Peter regarded the state as the reflection of his personal power or as a separate, immortal entity. Much depends upon interpretations of such political acts as the succession. When his only son, Alexei, died under obscure circumstances following his torture, trial, and death sentence, Peter declared that he would name his successor. He died without doing so. This left the succession up for

---

[84] William Craft Brumfield, *A History of Russian Architecture* (Cambridge University Press, 1993), pp. 209–10, 213–15, 227, quotation on p. 227.

[85] James Cracraft, *The Petrine Revolution in Russian Architecture* (University of Chicago Press, 1988); James Cracraft, *The Petrine Revolution in Russian Imagery* (University of Chicago Press, 1997), esp. pp. 136–47, 194–200; Wortman, *Scenarios of Power*, vol. I, pp. 6–7, 25, 42–51, 53.

grabs. Factional fights brought to the throne his wife, Catherine I, inaugurating an almost unbroken succession of women over the following
seventy-five years.

It was only at the end of the century that Paul I sought to regularize the
succession by placing it on an hereditary basis and, to spite his mother,
Catherine II, the usurper, excluded women from the line. Even then, his
childless son, Alexander I, reordered the line of succession to pass from
his next oldest brother, Konstantin, to the youngest brother, Nicholas, in
a secret family compact as though the state was his private possession.[86]
The shaky tradition of dynastic succession may have had something to do
with the counter-tradition of the pretender or *samozvanets* (the self-styled
tsar) that haunted legitimate imperial rule from the late sixteenth to the
early nineteenth century.[87]

More than any other Russian ruler, Catherine II attempted to envelop
autocratic power in full-blown secular ideology. She was an avid reader of
the literature of the political philosophy of the eighteenth century, particularly the works of the French *philosophes*, Montesquieu heading the list,
and the German cameralists, including J. H. G. Justi and J. F. Bielfeld. In
her Instructions (*Nakaz*) to the delegates of the consultative Legislative
Assembly she summoned in 1767, she borrowed and mixed ingredients
from representatives of both points of view.[88] What resonated for her was
Justi's conclusion that countries like Poland and Hungary where the
feudal tradition was strongest were subject to the worst form of petty
tyranny by local nobles. Instead of relying on the privileges of corporate
estates to check tyranny, Justi favored consultative assemblies, like the one
Catherine called into existence, and the exercise of moral restraint. Here,
we should recall, Justi invoked the case of Qing China, which he considered the most efficient form of government known to men.[89]

The attempt to synthesize the secular and religious aspects of imperial
rule emerged most clearly in the way the tsars represented themselves in
the major ceremonial occasions, and in their attitude and policies toward

[86] Wortman, *Scenarios of Power*, vol. I, pp. 65–75, 405–6; Bushkovitch, *Peter the Great*,
pp. 432–34; Hughes, *Russia in the Age of Peter the Great*, pp. 184–202, 398.
[87] K. V. Chistov, *Russkie narodnye sotsial'no-utopicheskie legendy XVII–XIX vv.* (Moscow:
Nauka, 1967).
[88] N. D. Chechulin (ed.), "Nakaz Imperatritsy Ekateriny II, dannyi Kommissii o sochinenii
proekta novogo ulozheniia," in *Pamiatniki russkogo zakonodatel'stva 1649–1832 gg* (St.
Petersburg, 1907), pp. cxxix–cxl; Ia.Ia. Zutis, *Ostzeiskii vopros v XVIII veka* (Riga: n.p.,
1946), pp. 288–97. Justi's work on the commercial nobility had already been translated
into Russian by Denis Fonvizin as *Torguiushchee dvorianstvo protivu polozhenoe dvorianstvo
voenomu* (St. Petersburg, 1766).
[89] Ulrich Adam, *The Political Economy of J. H. G. Justi* (Bern: Peter Land, 2006), pp. 128–41.

the whole Orthodox community (*oikumene*). To bind the new nobility more closely to the throne, Peter had invented a new symbolic order. By staging elaborate rituals and ceremonies for the ruling elite he gave his imperial authority a powerful publicly visible dimension that the tsars of Muscovy lacked. Even before Peter I the image of the tsar as a Christian ruler was increasingly diluted by secular themes. Peter completed the process of creating an *imperator* that placed the Russian ruler in a lineal descent from the ancient pagan, that is, Roman, rather than the Byzantine line. The new image of ruler was as a conqueror and reformer. The coronation of his empress, Catherine I, and Peter's own funeral displayed religious symbolism in order to sanction Western concepts of secular power. The traditional symbols of Orthodox Christianity were not wholly abandoned. But they were supplemented and largely overshadowed by references to classical mythology and historical legends that identified the Russian tsar with the European concepts of kingship.[90]

Peter's successors refined and elaborated the imperial myth and symbols. Each succeeding ruler refashioned the image of the ruler in order to suit his or her own needs without surrendering the central concept of absolute power. Richard Wortman calls these changing symbolic representations of the Russian monarchy "scenarios of power." Beginning with Catherine II, the two most visible symbolic representations of empire were the coronations and the journeys of the ruler outside the two capitals.[91] As the empire expanded, the participation of exotic representatives of the different national and ethnic groups at the coronation increased. These were most colorful and impressive under Alexander III and Nicholas II, yet it was they who increasingly emphasized the Russian (*russkoe*) as opposed to all-Russian (*rossiiskoe*) character of the empire.[92] This apparent contradiction reveals a basic problem in the political-ideological construction of Romanov dynastic rule.

The most powerful ingredient of the secular trends was the attempt to incorporate the new European idea of nationalizing dynastic rule into the imperial Russian political theology through the instrument of

---

[90] Wortman, *Scenarios of Power*, vol. I, pp. 41, 63, 71, 80–83.

[91] Wortman, *Scenarios of Power*. For the journeys, see Catherine II, vol. I, pp. 139–42; Alexander I, vol. I, pp. 239–41; Alexander II, vol. I, pp. 362–69; Nicholas I, vol. I, pp. 306–8; Alexander III, vol. II, pp. 173, 282–83 (the only trip of a reigning tsar to the Caucasus); Nicholas II, vol. II, pp. 323–31 (the only trip of a reigning tsar to the Russian Far East). For the coronations: Catherine II, vol. I, pp. 114–16; Alexander II, vol. II, pp. 35–37; Alexander III, vol. II, pp. 215–17; Nicholas II, vol. II, pp. 351–52.

[92] Richard Wortman, "Symvoly imperii: ekzoticheskie narody v Rossiiskoi imperii: ot etnicheskogo k prostranstvennomu podkhodu," in I. Gerasimov *et al.* (eds.), *Novaia imperskaia istoriia postsovetskogog prostranstva* (Kazan: Tsentr issledovaniii natsionalizma i imperii, 2004), pp. 409–26.

Russification. The term Russification itself has been used in many contexts to mean different things, ranging from acculturation to assimilation.[93] Broadly speaking, there was a distinction between cultural and administrative Russification. But as it was applied differently to different borderlands, the plural Russifications seems more appropriate.[94] An unofficial aspect of Russification deserving closer attention was the role of Russian literature in performing an integrative function.[95]

Since Catherine the Great's time Russian officials had used the intransitive verb *obruset'* to mean "to become Russian" in the sense of being assimilated gradually into a centralized imperial administrative structure. Administrative Russification was not pursued consistently by Alexander I, but was taken up again by Nicholas I in the aftermath of the Polish revolt of 1830.[96] Under his reign, the ruling elites, who had had earlier regarded Orthodoxy as the essential quality of being Russian, were beginning to place language in the same category. As cultural practices of integration they often, but not always, appeared in combination with one another. Yet there is something to be gained by analyzing them separately as a way of emphasizing the absence of a comprehensive strategy of imperial rule in contrast to the greater cohesive vision and coercive practices of the Communist Party in its renewed struggle over governing the borderlands of the Soviet national republics.

The evolution of a modern Russian language was a lengthy process that began even before Peter's reforms. By the turn of the nineteenth century, it had achieved a high level of refinement. But debates over the extent to which the language should retain or reject elements from Church Slavonic and the use of foreign words took on an almost eschatological tone, as had the changes in the Orthodox liturgy a century and a half earlier.[97] Under

[93] See, for example, Andreas Kappeler, "The Ambiguities of Russification," *Kritika* 5(2) (Spring 2004): 291–98, and articles by Mikhail Dobilov, "Russification and the Bureaucratic Mind in the Russian Empire's Northwestern Region in the 1860s," *Kritika* 5(2) (Spring 2004): 245–72; Darius Staliūnas, "Did the Government Seek to Russify Lithuanians and Poles in the Northwest Territory after the Uprising of 1863–64?" *Kritika* 5(2) (Spring 2004): 273–90.
[94] Alexei Miller, *The Ukrainian Question. The Russian Empire and Nationalism in the Nineteenth Century* (Budapest: CEU Press, 2003), pp. 19–48; Alexei Miller, "Russification or Russifications?" in *The Romanov Empire and Nationalism* (Budapest: CEU Press, 2008), pp. 45–66.
[95] Alexander Etkind, *Internal Colonization. Russia's Imperial Experience* (Cambridge: Polity, 2011), esp. ch. 8; Olga Maiorova, *From the Shadow of Empire. Defining the Russian Nation through Cultural Mythology, 1855–1870* (Madison, WI: University of Wisconsin Press, 2010), pp. 26–52, 128–54.
[96] Edward Thaden (ed.), "Introduction," in *Russification in the Baltic Provinces and Finland, 1855–1914* (Princeton University Press, 1981), pp. 7–9.
[97] Martin, *Romantics*, pp. 25–38.

Nicholas I enthusiasm for things Russian inspired the tsar to order that Russian be spoken at court functions and insist upon the use of Russian in official reports.[98] A more active policy of cultural Russification was introduced into the western provinces with special efforts to Russify law and education, by replacing Polish with Russian as the language of instruction in state-supported primary and secondary schools. Russian was also made obligatory for all official business in the Baltic provinces.

As we have seen, Nicholas' Minister of Education, Count Sergei Uvarov, sponsored the teaching of Russian throughout the imperial educational system, but opposed coercive measures. On a broader scale, his famous formulation of "Orthodoxy, Autocracy and Nationality" (*Narodnost'*) introduced the innovative and subtle cultural concept that in order to modernize, that is, to become more European, the empire would have to use a peculiar form of Russian nationalism as "the source of its legitimacy and an instrument of mobilization."[99] Uvarov's promotion of Russian culture in the borderlands challenged Polish influence in Belorus and Ukraine, and also encouraged scholarly work on the unity of the Slavic peoples. But here he recognized the need to move cautiously. He took some tentative steps to encourage the education of Poles whom he thought might enter imperial service and perhaps even counter the influence of extremists. But his policy was not consistent nor did it appear to be very effective.[100]

Uvarov also advocated a revival of interest in the language and history of that part of Ukraine called Little Russia. He sought out intellectuals who sympathized with these ideas, the so-called Ukrainophils, to combat Polish cultural influence in St. Vladimir University in Kiev and in a few secondary schools. Like other attempts at toleration of local cultures under a Great Russian umbrella, this backfired. The government reacted strongly when a few Ukrainian university students and young intellectuals founded the Cyril and Methodius Society in 1846 in order to forge a Slavic alliance in which Ukrainians would find their place side by side with the Poles and Russians. Tsar Nicholas was convinced that the society was linked to Polish emigration and ordered its members arrested.

A more virulent phase in the cultural struggle erupted, ironically, during the period of the Great Reforms. Under Alexander II the relaxation of censorship and other restrictive measures once again allowed small

---

[98]   Riasanovsky, *A Parting of Ways*, p. 128.

[99]   Alexei Miller, "'Official Nationality'? A Reassessment of Count Sergei Uvarov's Triad in the Context of Nationalism Politics," in *The Romanov Empire*, p. 153.

[100] James T. Flynn, "Uvarov and the 'Western Provinces': A Study of Russia's Polish Problem," *Slavic and East European Review* 64(2) (April 1986): 212–36.

Ukrainophil groups to organize and publish in the capital and in Kiev. Their views aroused the ire of Russian nationalists, who denied the possibility of Ukrainian as a separate language, and they tarred the Ukrainophils with the brush of Polish-sponsored separatism. Russian officials in the western provinces were also increasingly concerned over the spread of separatist tendencies among Ukrainian intellectuals. In 1863, their concern turned to fear that the Polish rebels would champion Ukrainian separatism as a weapon in their campaign. They even hesitated to use Little Russian Cossack regiments against the rebels.[101] The government issued the so-called Valuev Circular, which suspended the publication in Ukrainian of all books for popular consumption except for *belles lettres*. The author, Minister of the Interior P. A. Valuev, intended the measure to be temporary, hoping to gain time and resources to deal with the problem of assimilation in the borderlands. "What tools do we need," he asked the Russian nationalist press lord M. N. Katkov, "with the center and peripheries we possess, to generate centripetal not centrifugal forces?"[102]

Typically, government officials were not in agreement over the circular, the Minister of Education, A. V. Golovnin, being a particularly strong opponent. But even supporters of the measure failed in the subsequent years to follow up the logic of Valuev's position and develop a primary school system in Russian that would guarantee loyalty to the imperial regime. Instead, in 1876, the government imposed an even more restrictive language policy on Ukraine by dictating the Ems Edict, which remained in force until 1905, though it was only weakly enforced. The best that can be said about the effectiveness of the government's half-hearted policy of assimilation is, in the words of Alexei Miller, that it "considerably slowed down the process of the development of a Ukrainian national movement." The absence of a positive program of assimilation as opposed to a negative one doomed "the All-Russian nation building project the goal for which their creators were aiming."[103]

Cultural Russification followed a different trajectory in the Baltic littoral, where there could be even less doubt about the loyalty of the dominant German-speaking nobility than that of intellectuals in Ukraine or surely of the szlachta in Poland. Still, the Baltic nobles were just as determined to resist the imposition of Russian as the official language of administration, to say nothing of education and everyday speech. By

---

[101] Miller, *The Ukrainian Question*, p. 109.
[102] Letter Valuev to Katkov, July 16, 1864 as cited in Miller, *The Ukrainian Question*, p. 111.
[103] Miller, *The Ukrainian Question*, p. 257.

virtue of their strong representation at the highest levels of government they were in a better position to mount resistance. But their local cultural hegemony was both vulnerable in the face of a large non-German peasant population and potentially subversive in the eyes of Russian nationalists because of their ties with Prussia and, after 1871, with the German Empire across the border.

From Catherine the Great to the mid-nineteenth century, Russia's rulers exerted gentle pressure on the Baltic Germans to learn Russian. Even after Nicholas I approved a law in 1850 requiring the use of Russian in all internal correspondence in the Baltic provinces, resistance in high places blocked its implementation. In 1869, under Alexander II, a language edict reaffirmed the law. As usual legislation of this sort had less impact than intended because the government did not follow it with a vigorous program of Russian education. The local nobles financed most elementary and secondary schools, which were steeped in German culture. Dorpat University long remained a bastion of German culture; the establishment of the Riga Institute of Technology became one from its founding in 1861.[104] The real push for cultural Russification in the Baltic littoral came, as elsewhere, only with the accession of Alexander III, as we shall see in Chapter 5.

In the Caucasian and Trans Caspian borderlands, Russification took on a different cast. The question was how a Europeanizing Russia could integrate a large Islamic population whose socioeconomic life was organized for the most part along tribal, clan, and semi-nomadic lines. It had been a different matter in the sixteenth century with the conquest of Kazan and Astrakhan when religion constituted the main difference between the two civilizations. By the nineteenth century, the imperial elites considered themselves to be the bearers of a secularized civilizing mission that required more than conversion as a measure of true assimilation. Hegelian notions of stages of social evolution, combined with the practical experience of Russian proconsuls on the Caucasian frontier, gave rise to a Russian discourse of Orientalism that provided an ideological justification for that mission.[105]

While Viceroy Vorontsov's policy of pacification reflected the strategic imperatives of securing the Caucasian borderlands as a military frontier with the Ottoman Empire and Iran, consolidation of imperial rule meant

---

[104] Michael H. Haltzel, "Quarrels and Accommodations with Russian Officialdom," in Thaden, *Russification*, pp. 138–45.

[105] For a survey of some aspects of these perceptions throughout the history of the empire, see David Schimmelpennick van der Oye, *Russian Orientalism. Asia in the Russian Mind from Peter the Great to the Emigration* (New Haven, CT: Yale University Press, 2010); Vera Tolz, "Ex Tempore: Orientalism and Russia," *Kritika* 1(4) (2000): 691–727.

introducing the advantages of civilization. Although Vorontsov did not use the term "civilizing mission" in his correspondence, it was clear enough from a letter to his father, written in 1826, that this is what he had in mind:

> The administration of Russia must be as large as its territory. In this spiritual and physical immensity, measures based on the rules of Asian cities are both absurd and fatal ... The admirable system of Peter the Great combined forces with the enlightenment surpassing in its age in true liberality and in education, encouraging commerce, industry, all crafts, not by minute regulations, prohibitions and obstacles, but by facilitating everything.[106]

These were the principles which guided his thirty-three-year rule as Governor General of South Russia, and which he then applied as Viceroy of the Caucasus from 1846 to 1854. Having obtained full freedom of action from the Petersburg ministries, he restored traditional ethnic groupings of the population, but imposed a Russian organization of provinces. He perceived the indigenous Christian population as the principal regional vehicle for this transformation. He co-opted their elites by recruiting educated Georgians and Armenians to staff the lower and middle ranks of his administration, and even more successfully to serve as army officers. He vastly improved the educational system and opened Caucasian branches of the Imperial Geographical and Imperial Agricultural societies. He left his imprint on the urban character of Tiflis, beginning the process of turning it into a European city. His economic activities were equally inspired by the goal of attaching the Caucasus not only to the Russian center, but to Europe: the establishment of steamship communication across the Black Sea; the creation of a tax-free status for many items of the transit trade, exploring the region's great mineral wealth; the development of modern agriculture, including inaugurating cotton, tea, and silk cultivation.[107] Many of his initiatives only bore fruit later under his successors, Field Marshal A.I. Bariatinskii, Grand Duke Mikhail Nikolaevich, and Prince A.M. Dondukov-Korsakov.

The civilizing mission could also take on new meaning as an expression of Russia's generous treatment of its defeated foes. It was a stroke of public relations genius for the conqueror of the Caucasus, Prince Bariatinskii, to have advertised his great victory over the mountaineers by making a celebrity of Shamil, the legendary leader of the Murid uprising who had surrendered after years of resistance. Through his dispatches as reported

---

[106] Anthony L. H. Rhinelander, *Prince Michael Vorontsov, Viceroy to the Tsar* (Montreal: McGill and Queens University Press, 1990), p. iii.

[107] Rhinelander, *Prince Michael Vorontsov*, pp. 169–84.

by the newspapers and his staging of Shamil's trip into honorable captivity in Russia, Bariatinskii orchestrated a tumultuous public reception. The honorable surrender of Shamil and his generous treatment shed reflected glory on the noble victor. The Russians were eager to contrast their behavior with that of the British in India during the Mutiny. The whole episode inaugurated a new phase in public interest in the region, and an affirmation of Russia's imperial rule as a kinder, gentler form of imperialism.[108]

The celebration of noble adversaries to the Russian civilizing mission could also give rise to ambiguity about the enterprise, especially among the creative intelligentsia. From Pushkin's invention of the Caucasus in his poem "The Captive of the Caucasus" to Tolstoy's Hadji Murad at the end of the century, the literary encounters of Russia writers with native peoples were replete with contradictions. Pushkin, Lermontov, Tolstoy, and Bestuzhev-Marlinskii, all having experienced the Caucasus first-hand, tapped into a vein of anti-imperialism. In their works, the figure of the mountaineer challenged or replaced the Cossack as the model of the heroic frontiersman. As noble savage he represented the free spirit that could exist only on the edge of civilization that claimed to be European, but fell short of its ideal.[109] Although it is difficult to discern the precise effects of these contradictory currents on policy makers, it cannot be denied that Russia's pro-consuls in the Caucasian and Trans Caspian borderlands showed greater signs of tolerance and a willingness to cooperate with the indigenous peoples compared with the white Americans toward the Native Americans.

"Orientalism" in music expressed some of the same tendencies to contrast, but not to diminish, the appeal of the exotic when disciplined by a more orderly Europeanizing structure.[110] By inventing melodic and harmonic "codes" Russian composers sought to convey the sounds and images of the exotic and mysterious East. The occasional use of authentic melodies was less important than musical devices that represented the East

---

[108] Thomas M. Barrett, "The Remaking of the Lion of Daghestan. Shamil in Captivity," *Russian Review* 53(3) (July 1994): 353–66; Alfred J. Rieber, "Russian Imperialism. Popular, Emblematic, Ambiguous," *Russian Review* 53(3) (July 1994): 334.

[109] Susan Layton, "Nineteenth Century Russian Mythologies of Caucasian Savagery," in Daniel Brower and Edward J. Lazzerini (eds.), *Russia's Orient. Imperial Borderlands and Peoples, 1700–1917* (Bloomington, IN: Indiana University Press, 1997), and more generally, Susan Layton, *Russian Literature and Empire. Conquest of the Caucasus from Pushkin to Tolstoy* (Cambridge University Press, 1994). Cf. Katya Hokanson, "Literary Imperialism, *Narodnost'* and Pushkin's Invention of the Caucasus," *Russian Review* 53(3) (July 1994): 336–52, which emphasizes more strongly Pushkin's ambivalent attitude toward the Russian conquest.

[110] Based mainly on Francis Maes, *A History of Russian Music. From Kamarinskaya to Babi Yar* (Berkeley, CA: University of California Press, 2002), pp. 80–83, 193; Schimmelpennick van der Oye, *Russian Orientalism*, pp. 203–11.

as hedonistic and sensual. Stereotypical in their own way, they strongly suggested that the music of the native peoples could be appreciated by Russians (or Europeans) only if they were filtered through the screen of Western rules of composition.[111] Mily Balakirev, who visited the Caucasus in 1862 and 1863, used Circassian tunes in his works, wrote a popular *Georgian Song* with Pushkin's lyrics, and an orchestral work, *Tamara* (first draft 1869), based on Lermontov's poem of a Georgian princess who seduced and murdered passing travelers. His most famous piece, still played by those who can, the fiendishly difficult *Islamey, An Oriental Fantasy* (1869), bristles with obsessive rhythms and accelerating tempi to convey the impression of unbridled religious ecstasy. At the same time, Alexander Borodin completed the first version of *Prince Igor* (1869), the quintessentially orientalist opera contrasting the erotic Polovtsian dancing girls and the upright, vigorous Russian warrior prince.[112] Commissioned to compose a work for the twenty-fifth anniversary of the reign of Alexander II, he chose to celebrate Russia's imperial advance with *In the Steppes of Central Asia* (1880). Even the irascible Modest Mussorgsky, writing for the same occasion, produced *The Capture of Kars* with its alternation of martial pomp and oriental sensuality. Mikhail Ippolitov-Ivanov, for many years director of the Tiflis Conservatory and conductor of the city orchestra, composed *Caucasian Sketches* and three operas on orientalist themes; the last, *Izmena* (1908/9), is set in sixteenth-century Georgia during the struggle between the Christians and Iranian Muslims.

Defining Russia's relations with the peoples of the borderlands became a vast cultural enterprise that built upon a scientific as well as an imaginative ontology. In the process, the imperial idea became popularized and emblematic of Russians' self-perception. Ever since Peter the Great founded the Academy of Sciences and sent off Vitus Bering to explore the Pacific coasts of Siberia, the acquisition and publication of geographical and ethnographic knowledge had been part of the imperial enterprise. These efforts remained limited until Nicholas I dispatched Alexander von Humboldt on his famous exploration of Siberia, and then in 1845 founded the Imperial Russian Geographical Society. The explorers and both major scientific institutions were still dominated by foreigners who were not attached to the ideas of publicizing, promoting, and justifying Russia's imperial expansion. It was only after the Crimean War that the

---

[111] The same assumptions were made when composers, beginning with Glinka, began to incorporate Russian folk music into their formal compositions. Pure folk music, like pure native music, was regarded as ethnographical material well into the twentieth century.

[112] "'Entailing the Falconet': Russian Musical Orientalism in Context," *Cambridge Opera Journal* 4 (1992): 253–80.

enlargement of the public sphere in Russia through a mass press and increased literacy made possible the popularization of Russia's expansion into the Caucasian, Trans Caspian, and Inner Asian borderlands.

The post-Romantic era ethnographers produced their own justification of imperial rule by combining Orientalist perceptions and scientific methods to count, label, and historicize the peoples of Caucasian borderlands. Once again, the effects were unintended and paradoxical, for they succeeded also in stamping peoples with an identity that would later blossom into national sentiments counterpoised to imperial rule.[113] The angle of perception and the audience shifted markedly on the Trans Caspian frontier where the native population was perceived to be more savage than noble. Russia began to produce its own intrepid explorers and unblemished warriors celebrated in the mass press for an enlarged educated public hungry for heroes.

Two of Russia's most famous explorers used the celebrity they acquired from the coverage of their exploits in the mass press to preach the doctrine of Russia's civilizing mission in Trans Caspia. Petr Semenov acquired the addition to his surname of Tian-shanskii, in the style of victorious Russian military commanders, to commemorate his expedition to the Tianshan Mountains in the 1850s. He celebrated Russia's explorations of the borderlands "as Providence itself has ordained, in the general interest of humanity: the civilizing of Asia." But Russia's mission was unique, in his view, because of its special location between Europe and Asia, and its more humane treatment of the Asian peoples. This refrain would become familiar throughout the late tsarist and the entire Soviet period, always tempered by a defensive tone. The West may have perceived the Russians as standing "on a low level of civilization," he wrote, but their achievements already destined them for a higher level "in view of the rapid pace characterizing the history of our development." As Mark Bassin points out, "In a word, by civilizing Asia the Russians obviously believed they could and would civilize themselves."[114] Serving for decades as president of the Imperial Geographical Society, Semenov was an ardent propagandist for Russia's imperial destiny in the borderlands of Trans Caspia and Inner Asia.

---

[113] Austin Jersild, *Orientalism and Empire. North Caucasus Mountain Peoples and the Georgian Frontier, 1845–1917* (Montreal: McGill and Queens University Press, 2002), ch. 4. This tradition, with similar outcomes, was continued by Soviet ethnographers. See Francine Hirsch, *Empire of Nations. Ethnographic Knowledge and the Making of the Soviet Union* (Ithaca, NY: Cornell University Press, 2005). See also Vera Tolz, "European, National and (Anti-)Imperial. The Formation of Academic Oriental Studies in Late Tsarist and Early Soviet Russia," *Kritika* 9(1) (2008): 53–81.

[114] Mark Bassin, *Imperial Visions. Nationalist Imagination and Geographical Expansion in the Russian Far East, 1840–1865* (Cambridge University Press, 1999), pp. 203–4.

The second famous explorer, Nikolai Przheval'skii, struck the same chords in representing his exploits, for which the public and the press raised him to the rank of national hero. His expedition to Inner Asia in 1870–1874 turned into an adventure story. It brought him to the edge of the Qing Empire, where he found reason to warn of a future conflict with Britain "in China and the depths of Asia." Here his views dovetailed with those of the Minister of War, Dmitri Miliutin, and the Governor General of Turkestan, K. P. von Kaufman. He was riding the crest of a great wave of public interest in the East. The first Ethnographic Exhibition in Moscow in 1867 was followed in 1874 by the Polytechnic Exhibition with its many artifacts from the East. Two year later, the first exhibit of the paintings of Vasily Vereshchagin's Turkestan Series complemented the purely scientific with the imaginary in his portrayal of the encounter between Russians and the indigenous population. The artist had already made a name with his Caucasian Sketches when he accompanied von Kaufman to Turkestan as his official artist-ethnographer. Thousands attended the exhibition, including von Kaufman who had nothing but praise for the paintings.[115]

Similar in many ways to the West European concept of Orientalism, the Russian variation differed by resisting the inclusion of Russia in the Western definition of the Orient. As we have seen, one method was defensive, namely, to adopt the European discourse with appropriate variations that would portray Russia as a more humane civilizing force. The other method was to take the offensive by claiming that Russian civilization represented an alternative to Western civilization, as defined primarily in its Germanic form. With its origins in the Slavophil thinkers of the 1840s, this perspective evolved into the more aggressive ideology of pan-Slavism in the 1860s and 1870s. Although neither Slavophil nor pan-Slavic ideas were admitted into the canon of imperial ideology, they made subtle inroads into the thinking of the last three Romanovs and members of the ruling elite, though their traces are not always easy to uncover. Rulers like Peter the Great and Catherine the Great had manipulated the idea of Slavic unity or, more precisely, the common bond of Orthodoxy to advance their interests in the struggle over the Balkan borderlands.[116] But for them Russia was part of European civilization, not an alternative.

---

[115] Daniel R. Brower, "Imperial Russia and its Orient. The Renown of Nikolai Przhevalsky," *Russian Review* 53(3) (July 1994): 367–81; Daniel R. Brower, *Turkestan and the Fate of the Russian Empire* (London: Routledge-Curzon, 2003), pp. 49–51. Vereshchagin was himself a soldier who won the coveted St. George's Cross in fighting against the emir of Bukhara.

[116] This did not prevent the periodic ringing of alarm bells in Western Europe. As early as 1841 the well-known Russian editor N. Nadezhdin wrote from Berlin about the "fears, rumors, suspicion, alarms against some terrible thing called by the mystical name of

Like "Russification," pan-Slavism was mainly reactive, confronting a perceived external, ideological threat, in this case German culture and the imperial policies of the Habsburgs and Hohenzollerns. In its original form pan-Slavism was the invention of a small group of Czech intellectuals, subsequently embraced and adapted by a similarly small group of Russian intellectuals.[117] For Russia's rulers the doctrine posed several problems. Uvarov was sensitive to these, and limited his support to the promotion of cultural unity among the Slavs. Full-blown pan-Slavism was both too inclusive and too exclusive. It required equal treatment of the Catholic Poles and recognition of Ukrainians as a separate people. But it could not encompass the many non-Slavic peoples of the multicultural empire. Moreover, it contained an implicitly revolutionary message, calling upon the Balkan Slavs to rise up against their Ottoman masters. Not only was revolt against established authority abhorrent to a Russian autocrat, but it threatened the European balance and could involve the intervention of the Great Powers.

Pan-Slav publicists and literary figures exercised a persistent, if subrosa, influence on imperial elites. The line was often blurred between Russian nationalism and pan-Slavism in the minds of Russian conservative intellectuals and policy makers. It disappeared completely in 1875–1878 when pan-Slav sentiment played a major part in precipitating the war against the Ottoman Empire in 1877. And what a chorus of voices it was: Fedor Dostoevsky, Fedor Tiuchev, Mikhail Katkov, Ivan Aksakov, and Konstantin Pobedonostsev in solo roles.[118] The passing of that generation and the inherent revolutionary dangers of the doctrine weakened its appeal to the rulers. But ardent adherents continued to occupy important positions in the Russian government, men like Prince S.V. Shakhovskii, Governor General of Lifland from 1885 to 1894, and Count Nikolai Ignat'ev, Minister of the Interior from 1881 to 1882, and president of the Slavic Benevolent Society from 1888 to his death. Even Pobedonostsev, who recoiled in horror before his earlier enthusiasm for a political pan-Slav program, endorsed a cultural version of the doctrine to

---

Panslavism." *Letter to Moskvitianin*, No. 6 (1841): 515–25, cited in Nikolai P. Barsukov, *Zhizn' i trudy M. P. Pogodina*, 22 vols. (St. Petersburg: M. M. Stasiulevich, 1892), vol. VI, p. 139.

[117] The standard work remains Hans Kohn, *Pan-Slavism. Its History and Ideology* (South Bend, IN: Notre Dame University Press, 1953), which is hostile to Russia. More balanced is Michael Boro Petrovich, *The Emergence of Russian Panslavism 1856–1870* (New York: Columbia University Press, 1956).

[118] Robert Byrnes, *Pobedonostsev. His Life and Thought* (Bloomington, IN: Indiana University Press, 1968), esp. ch. 6.

strengthen Russian influence among Orthodox Slavs. The organization of the Orthodox Palestine Society in 1882 was its most visible manifestation. As Pobedonostsev's brain child, its ostensible purpose was to collect and distribute in Russia information about the Holy Land, but in the 1890s it acquired a political tone. By this time, Alexander III and the imperial family had become members and its activities were supported by Russian diplomats in the Ottoman Empire. This naturally aroused the suspicion of the Ottoman government. At the same time, Pobedonostsev cultivated Orthodox churchmen in Serbia, Montenegro, and Bulgaria, extended financial aid, often through the Slavic Benevolent Society, and recruited students for training in Russian seminaries. Particularly irritating for Vienna was his financial and moral support for the embattled Uniat and Orthodox Church in Austrian Galicia. After a twenty-year hiatus, his cultural pan-Slav efforts were revived in 1913 with the establishment of the Galician Benevolent Society.[119]

The continuous but quiet activity of the Slavic benevolent societies is an unwritten page in the history of Russian pan-Slavism.[120] The reemergence of Slavic solidarity as an active political doctrine surfaced almost simultaneously at the end of the nineteenth century in Prague and Russia. In their conflict with the German Austrians, some Czechs turned once again to Russia as a source of moral and diplomatic support. Their aim was to reorient Habsburg domestic policy by reviving the ideas of Austro-Slavism as the basis for a federative solution to the nationalities problem. In foreign policy they sought to pry Vienna away from Berlin and attach it to St. Petersburg. Toward these ends they took the lead in what became known as the neo-Slav Movement.[121] Official Russia was slow to react, but public opinion was more responsive. An active interest in a Slavic movement revived even before the Austrian annexation of Bosnia and Hercegovina in 1907 sparked a strong reaction in Russia. The Russian

[119] Byrnes, *Pobedonostsev*, pp. 220–24.

[120] Continuous, as exemplified by the activity of N. V. Ignat'ev, who pursued his pan-Slav agenda behind the screen of the Slavic Benevolent Society; so quiet that some scholars dubbed pan-Slavism a "phantom." S. Harrison Thomson, "A Century of a Phantom. Pan Slavism and the Western Slavs," *Journal of Central European Affairs* 11 (1951): 57–77. Reinforcing this view were the reports of the Habsburg diplomats from St. Petersburg. They expressed annoyance, relayed to the Russian government by Vienna, when individual Russians expressed pan-Slav sentiments aimed against the Monarchy. But they were reassured by the Russian Foreign Ministry that these were personal opinions not shared by the government. Eduard Winter, *Der Panslawismus nach den Berichten der österreichisch-ungarischen Botshafter in St. Petersburg* (Prague: Dt. Akademie der Wissenschaften, 1944), pp. 16, 21–22, 60–63, 88–90.

[121] Paul Vyšný, *Neo-Slavism and the Czechs, 1898–1914* (Cambridge University Press, 1977).

press began to take a more lively interest in the south Slavs, especially the conservative organ *Novoe vremia*.[122] The quiescent benevolent societies stirred from their slumbers, while new societies for the promotion of Slavic culture were created. It might appear paradoxical that the leading members of the new societies came from the center of the political spectrum, the Octobrist and Kadet parties and the Polish Kolo. But Russia's liberals perceived that a democratically inclined Slav movement could help to solve the Polish problem. Although they sought to distance themselves from the older aggressive pan-Slavism, they reused many of its ideas in their program of liberal imperialism.[123] Even the Polish Kolo led by Dmowski endorsed the idea as the best defense against German imperialism – the greater evil – and the firmest foundation for the economic and cultural flowering of Poland within the Russian Empire – the lesser evil. For them neo-Slavism fitted well into the concept of organic work. But the great expectations of its supporters, primarily the Czechs, were bound to be disappointed by the conflicting views of neo-Slavism among the people of the borderlands and the Russians. After the neo-Slav Congress of 1908 the movement declined.[124]

Two years later another neo-Slav congress in Sofia revealed the deep splits among the Slav representatives, and the shift to the right among Russian delegates who reverted to the old pan-Slav line. Once again the potential for a unifying imperial ideology evaporated.[125] Yet Slavophil sentiments were widely distributed throughout Russian society from the imperial family through the spectrum of public opinion expressed in the press, and in the Duma from the center to the extreme right.[126] Moreover, the Russian Foreign Ministry, especially its Asiatic Department concerned with the Balkans, displayed a strong, if not unified, commitment to promoting ties with the Slavic peoples. The official line of the Russian government right up to the July Crisis in 1914 was to avoid contamination with pan-Slavism, fearing that would compromise its already shaky

---

[122] Louise McReynolds, *The News under Russia's Old Regime* (Princeton University Press, 1991), pp. 74–78.

[123] Few, perhaps, went as far as P. B. Struve, who attended the pan-Slav Conference of 1908 and repeatedly defended pan-Slav aspirations in the Balkans during the First World War. His views found a sympathetic response in the journal *Slovo*. Richard Pipes, *Struve. Liberal on the Right, 1905–1944* (Cambridge, MA: Harvard University Press, 1980), pp. 92, 170, 180, 210. The progressive wing of the Moscow merchants and founders of the Moderate Progressive Party also strongly supported pan-Slav views in their paper *Utro Rossii* during the Balkan wars and the First World War. Rieber, *Merchants*, pp. 297, 318–19.

[124] Vyšný, *Neo-Slavism*, ch. 5.   [125] Vyšný, *Neo-Slavism*, pp. 187–88.

[126] David M. McDonald, *United Government and Foreign Policy in Russia, 1900–1914* (Cambridge, MA: Harvard University Press, 1992), pp. 122, 127, 147–48.

relations with the Habsburg Monarchy. In promoting Russian interests in the Balkans, it was guided mainly by strategic considerations, but underlying these was a long history of cultural affinities. Once the war broke out, the government wrestled with the problem of how to reconstruct East Central Europe without reaching any clear-cut conclusions. But there were strong sentiments for a solution tinged with pan-Slav overtones.[127]

Unlike the Habsburgs, the Russian rulers fiercely resisted constitutional experiments as a threat to imperial ideology as well as to the institutions of autocracy until the early twentieth century. At the same time, the Russian "scenario of power" under the reigns of Alexander III and Nicholas II underwent a radical shift away from the secular and cosmopolitan image of empire to a more constricted national-religious myth.[128] This meant that when a representative assembly – the State Duma – was finally wrested from the monarchy by the revolution of 1905, the ideological gap between ruler and ruled had widened. No wonder then that Tsar Nicholas II denied that the "Fundamental Laws," creating the new representative institutions, set limits on his autocratic power, while some of his own advisors and the mass of the population thought otherwise. No wonder, too, that the imperial couple, Nicholas and Alexandra, slipped deeper into a mystical religious faith that further alienated them from both the official Church and the Westernized elite.[129]

The Ottoman Empire

Despite their very different origins, the Ottoman rulers, like their counterparts in other multicultural states, also drew upon a variety of earlier traditions in shaping their image and defining their power. They also exhibited similar problems in establishing a clearly defined and stable relationship between their terrestrial and divine identities and missions. The complex frontier environment between the Seljuk and Byzantine

---

[127] This was, of course, pan-Slavism in its Russian guise. See the essays in *Russian Diplomacy and Eastern Europe, 1914–1917* (New York: King's Crown Press, 1963); A. Iu. Bakhturina, *Okrainy rossiiskoi imperii. Gosudarstvennoe upravlenie i national'naia politika v gody pervoi mirovoi voiny (1914–1917)* (Moscow: Rosspen, 2004), and Chapter 6 below.

[128] Wortman calls this "the synchronic mode" in order to demonstrate the attempt to break with the official time frame in which the ruler was the maker of history in favor of a mythical past, the seventeenth century, when tsar and people were allegedly spiritually united. *Scenarios*, vol. II, pp. 235–36.

[129] G. Freeze, "Subversive Piety. Religion and the Political Crisis in Late Imperial Russia," *Journal of Modern History* 3 (June 1996): 312–28; G. Friz [G. Freeze], "Tserkov', religiia i politicheskaia kultura na zakate starogo rezhima," in Geiger and Diakin (eds.), *Reformy ili revoliutsiia?*, pp. 31–42.

empires in the fourteenth century was the meeting place of three traditions. First, the Turkmen nomads from Central Asia who migrated and
settled this region embodied the ideal of a military regime based on the
Turko-Mongolian concept of kingship. The Ottomans later adopted the
secular title of sultan first brought into Anatolia by the nomadic Seljuk
Turks in the eleventh century.[130] Second, conversion to Islam provided
them with a new set of stable cultural and political institutions. It shaped
their vision of the external world along fluid and syncretic lines. On the
one hand, they viewed the "lands of unbelief" beyond their military
frontier as *dar al-harb*, the abode of war, with which they were in legal
theory, if not always in practice, in a state of permanent conflict. On the
other hand, their treatment of non-Muslims within their lands, the *dar al-
Islam*, was marked by varying degrees of tolerance.[131] Third, the
Ottomans inherited the Byzantine imperial tradition symbolized by their
conquest of the great city of Constantinople, the second Rome.

Mehmed the Conqueror may be regarded as the last representative of
the Islamo-Christian syncretism of the early Ottoman state. He was by all
accounts not consistently a good Muslim, as his commission of a portrait
by the Italian artist Bellini testifies. He was attracted to an eclectic religion
blending elements of the Jewish kabala, Christianity, and other mystical
brotherhoods. He was the embodiment of a nomadic Turkic leader, a
believer in Islam who claimed the legacy of the Byzantine Empire. The
decision to keep Constantinople as the capital confronted the Ottoman
rulers with the peculiar problem of how to compete visually with the
powerful symbols of a Christian empire. They responded by converting
the churches into mosques, whitewashing the great mosaics, constructing
equally imposing religious structures like the Blue Mosque, and building
secular palaces, most notably the Topkapi Sarayi. Mehmed regarded
the Armenians, Jews, and Greek Orthodox as people of the book. By

[130] Joseph Fletcher, "The Turko-Mongolian Monarchic Tradition in the Ottoman
Empire," *Harvard Ukrainian Studies* 3/4 (1979/80): 236–51. The Mongol and
Ottoman frontier policies were similar in weaning the tribal populations away from
their old loyalties, and maintaining a balance between the steppe tradition of sharing
power and the sedentary tradition of centralizing it. But the Ottomans were more
successful in transforming the idea of a "world order" into reality by embracing Islam
and thus minimizing the tension between the two traditions. Isenbike Togan, "Ottoman
History by Inner Asian Norms," in Halil Berktay and Suraiya Faroqui (eds.), *New
Approaches to State and Peasant in Ottoman History* (London: Frank Cass, 1992),
pp. 185–210.

[131] For a discussion of tolerance in the Ottoman Empire, see Benjamin Braude and Bernard
Lewis, "Introduction," in *Christians and Jews in the Ottoman Empire. The Functioning of a
Plural Society. The Central Lands* (London: Holmes & Meier, 1982), vol. I, pp. 6–9, and
especially Selim Deringil, *Conversion and Apostasy in the Late Ottoman Empire*
(Cambridge University Press, 2012).

welcoming Jews fleeing the Inquisition in Spain, he gained a highly productive population that contributed to the financial and commercial vigor of the empire. Overall, his policies of religious toleration created an atmosphere in which Muslims and non-Muslims could live together in peace. In order to integrate the Christian population into the empire, he organized them into separate religious communities, in contemporary terms *tâ'ife* (congregation) and *cemaat* (community). This met with the stipulation of Islamic law concerning non-Muslims who submitted to conquest without resistance.[132]

By promoting Istanbul as the center of Eastern Orthodoxy, he sought to bring the Church more easily under his control and to reinforce the Ottoman claim to universal empire. He continued the Ottoman policy of co-opting Orthodox subjects in all spheres of public life outside the army from the church to commerce and administration in order to broaden the base of imperial rule. Later, during a period of decentralized rule in the seventeenth century, the Ottomans applied the term *millet* to a new organization of the religious communities that gave greater authority to the Orthodox Ecumenical patriarch and the Apostolic Armenian patriarch in Istanbul. Millets were more of a series of ad hoc arrangements than a system. The degree of legal autonomy and the authority of their spiritual leaders varied over time and within different regions of the empire. But the object remained the same, to ease the integration of the Jewish and Christian communities into the Ottoman world.

Gradually, over the next century the religious hegemony of the two patriarchs was employed by the churches to impose linguistic conformity, endowing them with a political as well as cultural function. They advanced the fallacious claim of having been granted spiritual leadership as well as administrative authority by Mehmed II. In part, they were prompted by the growing pressure from Latin missionaries, mainly Franciscans from the Habsburg lands, who were proselytizing among Christians more vigorously and creating Uniat churches in the Balkans and elsewhere in the Ottoman Empire similar to those in the Polish–Ukrainian borderlands. In these cultural struggles, the sultan sided with the Orthodox, perceiving the Catholics as security risks because of the papal denunciations of Islam and the frequent frontier wars with Catholic powers, the Habsburg Empire and Venetian Republic. The prohibition against the construction of new religious buildings was more strictly

[132] Halil İnalcik, "The Status of the Greek Orthodox Patriarch under the Ottomans," in *Essays in Ottoman History* (Istanbul: Eren, 1998), pp. 196–97.

applied to them than to the Orthodox. As a result, many Catholics converted to Orthodoxy in Bosnia.[133]

The Ottoman rulers did not enforce unity among the religious communities, but allowed them to break up along linguistic and doctrinal lines. The granting of privileges and the appointment of religious leaders took on a more and more ad hoc character. Before the nineteenth century these communities were not unified under a single head. They were only given constitutional sanction during the Tanzimat.[134] By this time, however, resistance to the authority of the patriarch, as well as Greek influence, was on the rise among autonomous centers of religious life in Serbia and Bulgaria, emerging gradually as the foundations of national movements.

In the secular sphere, Mehmed II created a set of symbolic representations that incorporated the great regional imperial traditions of the past – the Byzantine, Turkic, and Mongol.[135] He completed the process of transforming the image of a ruler from a Turkic nomadic tribal leader, who had adopted elements of Persian kingship, to an heir of the imperial Byzantine tradition. Among the titles he assumed was that of Roman Caesar (*kayseri-i-rūm*). He surrounded himself with non-Muslims and non-Turks as advisors. He had the lives of Alexander the Great, Hannibal, and Caesar read to him daily by a Greek and Latin reader.[136] Mehmed retained the Roman name of the imperial city, Constantinople, on all official documents and coins. He rebuilt the great Byzantine walls.

---

[133] Bruce Masters, "Christians in a Changing World," in Suraiya N. Faroqui (ed.), *The Cambridge History of Turkey, vol. 3: The Later Ottoman Empire, 1603–1839* (Cambridge University Press, 2006), pp. 186–208.

[134] Kemal Karpat, *An Inquiry into the Social Foundations of Nationalism in the Ottoman State. From Social Estates to Classes, From Millets to Nations* (Princeton University Press, 1973), pp. 88–91; Paraskevas Konortas, "From Tâ'ife to Millet. Ottoman Terms for the Ottoman Greek Orthodox Community," in Dmitri Gondicas and Charles P. Issawi (eds.), *Ottoman Greeks in the Age of Nationalism. Politics, Economy and Society in the Nineteenth Century* (Princeton, NJ: Darwin Press, 1999), pp. 169–79.

[135] Albert Hourani, *A History of the Arab Peoples* (Cambridge, MA: Harvard University Press, 1991), pp. 142–44, 220–21. Halil İnalcik, "Comments on 'Sultanism.' Max Weber's Typification of the Ottoman Polity," in *Princeton Papers in Near Eastern Studies* (1992): 49–72. The author notes that: "The Iranian state tradition was transmitted to the Ottomans through native bureaucrats and the literary activity of the Iranian converts who translated Sasanian advice literature into Arabic." A debate continues over the respective weight of these three traditions in the Ottoman Empire, mainly because they shifted over time. Nicholas Iorga demonstrated how the Ottoman Empire served as a filter for the transmission of Byzantine practices to the principalities of Moldavia and Wallachia. See his *Byzantium after Byzantium* (Iași/Portland: Center for Romanian Studies, 2000) (introduction by Virgil Cândea and translated by Laura Treptov from the original French published in Paris, 1935), esp. pp. 89–90, 106–8, 138–40.

[136] Gülru Necipoğlu, *Architecture, Ceremonial and Power. The Topkapi Palace in the Fifteenth and Sixteenth Centuries* (Cambridge, MA: Harvard University Press, 1991), p. 248.

To restore the splendor of the city, he employed Italian architects, like his Muscovite contemporaries, to construct new palaces and mosques. He also inquired about Arab and Iranian models before ordering the construction of the Topkapi Palace.

The opulent court ceremonial was also an eclectic concoction designed to impress and even to intimidate foreign dignitaries of both Europe and Asia who were engaged in diplomatic negotiations. Both Habsburg and Persian representatives testified to the stunning impression left by the display of massed janissaries and the "ornament, luster and magnificence" of the Council Hall. There were elements of the court ceremony resembling those in the tenth-century Byzantine *Book of Ceremonies* compiled for Emperor Constantine VII Porphyrogenitus. In the planning of the internal space and gardens of the palace, diverse stylistic units represented the Greek, Persian, and Ottoman kingdoms, while certain ceremonies, such as cutting the ropes of a tent belonging to a disgraced official, recalled the Turko-Mongol heritage.[137] By virtue of its symbolic and strategic significance Constantinople-Istanbul remained, with one significant exception, the power center of the empire until its demise. Early in his reign, Sultan Mehmed IV (1648–1687) shifted the court and the main royal residence to the city of Edirne, "the hearth of the *ghazi*," serving both as the launching pad for war on the Habsburg frontier and as the headquarters of his legendary hunting expeditions, also in the warrior tradition.[138]

In a letter to Mehmed II in 1466, the Greek Christian scholar, George of Trebizond, wrote: "No one doubts you are the emperor of the Romans. Whoever holds by right [of conquest?] the center of the Empire is emperor as the center of the Roman Empire is Constantinople."[139] The city was literally situated at one of the great crossroads of Eurasia linking along vertical lines the two Ottoman seas, the Black and the Mediterranean, on the one hand, and along horizontal lines the land masses of the Balkans (Rum) and Anatolia, with their European and Asian frontiers, respectively, on the other. If Mehmed's original concept was to create an imperial city where all religions and races could mix freely, the ideal was never quite achieved, and it eroded over time. With the exception of the well-to-do of different ethnic and religious communities who built villas along the Bosporus in the eighteenth century, neighborhoods became

---

[137] Necipoğlu, *Architecture, Ceremonial and Power*, pp. 15, 68, 245.
[138] The symbolism of an alternative capital remained alive long after, mainly as a way of connecting with the great, if long moribund, tradition of the *gazi*, eventuating in the shift of Constantinople to Ankara under the Turkish republic. Cemal Kafadar, *Between Two Worlds. The Construction of the Ottoman State* (Berkeley, CA: University of California Press, 1995), pp. 148–49.
[139] Cited in Necipoğlu, *Architecture, Ceremonial and Power*, p. 12.

increasingly compartmentalized. This pattern of settlement became pronounced in the nineteenth century as national identities solidified. The cosmopolitanism of Istanbul may have been a myth, but its distinctive cultural neighborhoods translated into a "plurality of nations."[140] The city remained a meeting place of Western and Islamic cultures. The court, army, and bureaucracy were never exclusively Turkish, but rather integrated many ethnic groups on condition of conversion to Islam.

Like Peter the Great two and a half centuries later, Mehmed encouraged, albeit more gently, the new ruling elite drawn from Byzantine aristocratic families to build and patronize construction in the capital. The plans were designed, however, not along rectilinear lines like St. Petersburg in a later age, but favoring the privilege of view in order to give visual prominence to the new architecture in its competition with the Byzantine structures.[141] The layout of the palace duplicated the organization of an Ottoman encampment blended with Roman–Byzantine elements, borrowed in particular from the Great Palace of Constantine near the Hippodrome. This was another symbolic statement that power no longer rested on a nomadic tribal federation. It had been transferred to a sedentary empire run by a centralized bureaucracy spatially located in an urban setting.

The seclusion of the ruler gradually increased in the sixteenth century. Ceremonies in the four courtyards of the Great Palace were hidden from the mass of the population. Each court represented a different function, with the sultans increasingly concentrating their attention on the harem and the third court as opposed to the second court occupied by the high officials, including the grand vizier.[142] The sultans engaged in public display mainly through hunting and lavish entertainment for the elite in the kiosks, which were small elegant garden structures, and summer palaces. Hunting became the mark of manhood and martial skills. A sultan who participated in military campaigns gained in prestige, celebrated in triumphal parades, but there was always the risk of defeat that could undermine his legitimacy.[143] After the great territorial losses in the

---

[140] Edhem Eldem, "Istanbul," in Edhem Eldem, Daniel Goffman, and Bruce Masters, *The Ottoman City between East and West, Aleppo, Izmir and Istanbul* (Cambridge University Press, 1999).

[141] Çiğiten Kafescioğlu, *Constantinopolis/Istanbul. Cultural Encounter, Imperial Vision and the Construction of the Ottoman Capital* (University Park, PA: Penn State University Press, 2009), pp. 128–29.

[142] Necipoğlu, *Architecture, Ceremonial and Power*, pp. 91–93.

[143] Suraiya Faroqhi, "Crisis and Change, 1590–1699," in Suraiya Faroqhi et al. (eds.), *An Economic and Social History of the Ottoman Empire, vol. 2: 1600–1914* (Cambridge University Press, 1994), pp. 609–20; Marc David Baer, *Honored by the Glory of Islam. Conversion and Conquest in Ottoman Europe* (Oxford University Press, 2008), pp. 25–31,

long war with the Habsburgs at the end of the seventeenth century, the sultans no longer led their armies into the field.

For all his personal eclecticism, Mehmed understood the importance of consolidating Sunni Islam as the state ideology. Islam had endowed the rule with divine legitimacy and provided a means of governing. Mehmed infused his new administrative and judicial institutions with the Islamic spirit. This placed the ulama in a unique position to share in the interpretation of Islam. There were four sources of interpreting Islam: the state, the ulama, the mystical Sufi brotherhoods, and the folk tradition. The first two were centered in Istanbul; the latter two were heterodox and flourished mainly in the borderlands where the Sufi circles often transformed social protest into millenarian movements.[144] In 1516, following the conquest of Egypt, Selim I laid claim to the caliphate, transferring its seat from Cairo to Istanbul. By this time, however, the caliphate had been emptied of all but symbolic content. Since its establishment in the early days of the Arab conquests, the caliphate inextricably combined politics and religion, reflecting the influence of the Sasanian (Persian) kingship upon the founders of the first Arab empires. Its meaning had undergone several changes over time, although it was gradually identified more with the spiritual rather than with the coercive side of the Islamic state.[145]

The most complete expression of the messianic spirit in the political theology of the Ottoman imperial rule has been associated with the reign of Suleiman II (1520–1566). His titles and attributes combined the Islamic and Turko-Persian traditions: the sultan as the "shadow of God" and as his "deputy on earth." Known to the Ottomans as "the Lawgiver," Suleiman embodied the Islamic ideal of the just ruler who followed the principles and traditions of the Shari'a (the law), which combined the teachings of the schools of Sunni jurisprudence with imperial decrees and local custom.[146] Under Suleiman, the traditional claims to universality assumed practical significance in his military campaigns

---

180–203, comparing the morally negligent behavior of Sultan Ibrahim that led to his overthrow and the manly pursuits and hunting for animals and converts of his successor Mehmed IV.

[144] Ahmet Yaşar Ocak, "Islam in the Ottoman Empire. A Sociological Framework for a New Interpretation," in Kemal Karpat with Robert W. Zens, *Ottoman Borderlands. Issues, Personalities and Political Changes* (Madison, WI: University of Wisconsin Press, 2003), pp. 187–94.

[145] D. Sourdel, "Khalifa," *Encyclopedia of Islam*, new edn (Leiden: Brill, 1986), vol. IV/2, pp. 946–50; Colin Inber, *The Ottoman Empire, 1300–1650* (London: Palgrave, 2002), pp. 116, 125–27; Sir Thomas Walker Arnold, *The Caliphate* (New York: Barnes & Noble, 1965), pp. 120–26.

[146] Christine Woodhead, "Perspectives on Süleynab," in Metin Kunt and Christine Woodhead (eds.), *Süleyman the Magnificent and His Age. The Ottoman Empire in the Early Modern World* (London: Longman, 1995), pp. 164–67.

against the Habsburg and Safavid empires. To the Habsburg emperors he justified these claims, in terms familiar to them, as "master of the lands of the Roman Caesars and Alexander the Great." To the Islamic rulers, he asserted his primacy by adopting the title of "Caliph of all Muslims in the world" and "the Servitor of the two Holy Sanctuaries" (Mecca and Medina). In practice, he assumed the defense of the pilgrimage routes against the threats of Christian Europe. His deeds evoked a response from as far distant as the Uzbek khans of Trans Caspia, who appealed to the sultan to restore the safety of their pilgrims in the face of Muscovite expansion. In order to justify his campaigns against the Safavids, he obtained a legal opinion from the ulama (fatwa) obliging him to overthrow heresy (Shi'ia), although the main reason may have been a desire to overthrow the Iranian dynasty and acquire the silk-producing borderlands of Azerbaijan, Shirvan, and Gilan.[147]

As the defender of the Abode of Islam against heretics and schismatics, he issued decrees condemning heterodox traditions that antagonized the Turkmen pastoral tribes along the frontiers of eastern Anatolia, particularly the popular religious brotherhoods, such as the Bektaşi, with their cult of saints and heterodox beliefs. As they bore a close resemblance to Shi'ism, they constituted a security risk to the Ottomans on the frontier with Safavid Iran, where Shah Ismail I (1501–1524) had assumed spiritual authority over them.

With the decline of Ottoman power after the long war against Russia at the end of the eighteenth century, the attenuated gazi tradition and the idea of the sultan as the protector of Muslims throughout the world steadily diminished. During negotiations over the Treaty of Kuchuk Kainardji in 1774, the Ottoman statesmen encountered for the first time a similar Russian idea of extending extraterritorial protection over co-religionists embodied in the concept of oikoumene. Up to this point, the sultan had enjoyed the distinction among Western diplomats of possessing the authority of the caliphate. In the treaty, the sultan was still called "the imam of the Believers and the caliph of those who profess the divine unity," which appeared in the French version as "le Souverain calife de la religion mahometane." But the treaty changed the significance of the title in international diplomacy by separating the sultan's religious authority from his political authority. This had particular significance for relations with the Crimean khanate, which lost its status as vassal of the Ottoman Empire, but was allowed to maintain its religious ties. The Russians then felt free to annex the khanate in 1783 without fear of another war

---

[147] Halil İnalcik, "Suleiman the Lawgiver and Ottoman Law," *Archivum Ottomanicum* 1 (1969): 105–38.

with the Ottoman Empire. However, the religious connection helped to keep alive the Ottoman hope of reconquering the khanate during the reign of Selim III (1789–1807). It also served as a precedent for maintaining religious ties with Muslims in the borderlands lost during the wars of the nineteenth century.[148]

There is still confusion over the terms of the Treaty of Kuchuk Kainardji dealing with the religious question. Roderic Davison has demonstrated persuasively that Russia obtained only a limited right to make representations to the Porte on behalf of the Christian population of Moldavia and Wallachia, and a single Russian (not Greek) Orthodox Church in Istanbul.[149] But his research has not put to rest the interpretation that the Russians intended to use the ambiguity of the clauses to claim the right to intervene in defense of Christian rights throughout the Balkans.[150] A further "misunderstanding" of the Treaty arose over the right of the Crimean Tatars to submit petitions (*mahzars*) to the Ottoman Porte, acknowledging the sultan as "the supreme caliph of the Muslim religion," and to receive his benediction. In a supplemental convention to the treaty, Russia promised not to interfere with anything that was absolutely necessary for the unity of Islam. But the sultan promised not to interfere in any way under any pretext of spiritual concern with the civil authority of the Crimean khan.[151] To be sure, the attempt to draw a clearcut line between religious and civil authority in the Islamic religion was as naive – or cynical – as the Russian promise not to intervene in the defense of the religious rights of the Christians in the Danubian principalities except in cases where those religious rights were violated! Over the following half century Russian policy makers continued to dispute the wisdom of these clauses. More cautious statesmen denounced them as "one of the most frequent causes of our successive complications with Turkey."[152]

---

[148] Ş. Tufan Buzpınar, "The Question of the Caliphate under the Last Ottoman Sultans," in Weismann and Zachs, *Ottoman Reform*, pp. 18–19 and n. 6, p. 31.

[149] Roderic H. Davison, "'Russian Skill and Turkish Imbecility.' The Treaty of Kuchuk-Kainardji Reconsidered," *Slavic Review* 35(3) (September 1976): 463–83. Davison bases his analysis on the Italian-language version of the treaty, which was recognized by both sides as the official text.

[150] See, for example, John LeDonne, *The Russian Empire and the World, 1700–1917. The Geopolitics of Expansionism and Containment* (Oxford University Press, 1997), p. 107.

[151] The convention also specified that the sultan would withdraw all Zaporozhian Cossacks who refused to accept the empress' amnesty to lands beyond the Danube as far as possible from the Black Sea. Gabriel Noradoughian (ed.), *Recueil d'actes internationaux de l'empire Ottoman* (Paris: Pichon, 1897), pp. 338–44.

[152] This was the opinion of Baron Brunnow in his extensive review of Russian foreign policy for the future Nicholas I. "Aperçu des transactions politiques du Cabinet de Russie," *Sbornik imperatorskogo russkogo istoricheskogo obshchestva* 31 (1880): 210. Brunnow

Contrary to later interpretations by the Russians, the treaty only acknowledged the tsar's right to protect the Orthodox population of Constantinople, and not the entire Ottoman Empire, and to make representations to the sultan concerning their welfare.[153] The Russians were quick to reject the reciprocal authority of the sultan-caliph within the Russian Empire. Similarly, the Ottoman sultans sought to refute the Russians' broad interpretation of the treaty which claimed to extend their protection and right of intervention to the entire Orthodox population of the Ottoman Empire. The mutual claims by the Russian and Ottoman empires of extraterritorial spiritual authority added another level of conflict to their prolonged rivalry over the borderlands. Ottoman rulers continued throughout the first half of the nineteenth century to interpret Russian representations on behalf of the Slavic Christians as a wedge driven into their body politic. Their resistance in 1853 to Russian pressure on this issue was the main cause of the Crimean War.[154]

The outcome of the Crimean War profoundly affected the Ottoman ideology of imperial rule over the borderlands. Under Western pressure, the Reform Edict of 1856 expanded the rights of religious minorities in the empire. It was essentially the handiwork of Stratford Canning, the British minister in Istanbul. Since the 1840s, the British statesman George Canning had pursued with fanatical zeal the idea of applying the liberal principle of *laisser-passer* embodied in the Ottoman Commercial Code of 1838 to religious affairs. In 1847, he achieved one aim by obtaining the formal repeal of the decree on apostasy. But he continued to press for complete freedom of religion guaranteed by international sanction. This principle was enshrined in the Reform Edict.[155] The success of Ottoman resistance to Russian intervention in the empire's religious affairs had

concluded that "for a treaty to be truly a work of peace, it ought to resolve as much as possible past disputes that caused the rupture between belligerent states but not open intentionally the door to future complications between the contracting parties."

[153] Roderic H. Davison, "The Treaty of Kuchuk Kaynardja. A Note on its Italian Text," *International History Review* 10(4) (November 1988): 611–21. For a Russian interpretation, see E. I. Druzhinina, *Kiuchuk-Kainardzhiiskii mir 1774 goda. Ego podgotovka i zakliuchenie* (Moscow: Nauka, 1955), pp. 278–307.

[154] For the debate over interpretations of the disputed passages leading to the Crimean War, see David Goldfrank, "Policy Traditions and the Menshikov Mission of 1853," in Hugh Ragsdale (ed.), *Imperial Russian Foreign Policy* (Washington and Cambridge: Woodrow Wilson Center and Cambridge University Press, 1993), pp. 119–58; V. N. Vinogradov, "Personal Responsibility of Emperor Nicholas I for the Coming of the Crimean War. An Episode in the Diplomatic Struggle in the Eastern Question," in Ragsdale (ed.), *Imperial Russian Foreign Policy*, pp. 159–72.

[155] Roderic H. Davison, *Reform in the Ottoman Empire, 1856–1876* (Princeton University Press, 1963), pp. 52–55; Niyazi Berkes, *The Development of Secularism in Turkey* (Montreal: McGill University Press, 1964), pp. 148–53.

been bought at the cost of submission to British intervention in the same sphere.

In the post-Crimean period the Ottoman reformers aimed at rebuilding the state by separating the temporal and spiritual realms, and at the same time creating a new form of patriotism by inventing the concept of Ottomanism (*Osmanlılık*) that would apply to the peoples of all religious communities. This represented an important shift in the reforming process from the rescript of Gülhane in 1839, which had inaugurated the great period reform, the Tanzimat. Permeated with the spirit of Islam, it was intended to restore the trust and confidence of the Muslim population that had been antagonized by the overly zealous and brutal reforms of Mahmud II. Contrary to accepted wisdom, it did not promise legal equality, but only that all subjects had the right to be treated in accordance with the law.[156]

By contrast, the post-Crimean reformers sought to remove all judicial and civic privileges from the religious communities and transfer them to the state in the form of full and equal rights of all citizens. This meant abolishing the Shari'a as the basic law of the empire and treating it as the private law of the Muslims. The problem was that, having eliminated Islam as the ideological foundation of the state, the reformers failed to provide a substitute. "The Tanzimat regime lacked both the traditional pillars of Ottoman sovereignty and a constitutional doctrine which would base legislation and government on the will of the people."[157] Moreover, the leaders of the religious communities in the Ottoman Empire opposed the reform because it deprived them of the right to exercise control over many secular activities of their flock. It weakened the authority of the Greek patriarch, opening the way for Bulgarian churchmen to demand a separate hierarchy in the form of an exarchate, which served as the rallying point for a national movement. For similar reasons, the Russian government opposed the reorganization of the religious communities as a step toward eliminating the components of sovereignty, which could be used to pressure the Porte to grant greater autonomy to the borderlands and, if conditions were ripe, even the independence of the Balkan Christians. The Russians soon discovered, however, that the Bulgarian agitation for an exarchate sharpened the inherent contradiction between the ideals of pan-Slavism and pan-Orthodoxy. No less a figure than the ardent pan-Slav Count Nikolai Ignat'ev found himself caught between contradictory

---

[156] Frederick Anscombe, "Islam and the Age of Ottoman Reform," *Past and Present* 208 (August 2010): 183–85.

[157] Berkes, *The Development of Secularism*, p. 201.

claims in his attempt to mediate the quarrel between the Bulgarians and the Orthodox Patriarch of Constantinople.[158]

Disparate voices were also raised among Ottoman critics of the Reform Edict, stemming from the same ideological grounds but for opposite reasons. The so-called Young Ottomans focused on the apparent capitulation of the reformers to Western secular ideas that undermined the Islamic foundations of the Ottoman state. They confronted an ideological dilemma that persisted to the end of the empire: how to reconcile certain superior Western innovations in technology and education with the cultural and, above all, legal foundations of the Shari'a. The effort to resolve the dilemma was to inspire a constitutional movement. Galvanized by the mounting crisis in the Balkans, a group of high-ranking Ottoman officials removed Sultan Abdülaziz in 1876 by a coup d'état and virtually imposed a constitution on his successor, Murad V. A landmark, it was the first written constitution adopted by any multicultural Eurasian state.[159]

The constitution contained many of the same contradictions that ran like a thread through the history of the Tanzimat. Islam was proclaimed as the religion of the state, but freedom of religion was also guaranteed. The empire was defined as indivisible. This meant that the privileged status of provinces like the principalities was abolished, while provincial decentralization was introduced throughout the empire. The upper house of parliament was to be appointed, the lower house elected. But the sultan retained considerable, but not always well-defined, powers. He was caliph, not responsible for his acts, and a sacred person. It has been described by one authority as "a limited autocracy."[160] The confusion bears a striking resemblance to that pervading the Fundamental Laws promulgated by Nicholas II in 1905.

Following the disastrous war of 1877/8, the new sultan, Abdülhamid II, rejected the secular ideas implicit in the constitution and sought to restore the tradition of an Islamic state as the foundation of imperial rule. A counter trend toward secularism had already begun under Sultan Abdülaziz. It gained momentum when military operations and the large territorial losses imposed by the Treaty of Berlin caused hundreds of thousands of Muslims to flee the Balkan borderlands, vastly increasing the percentage of Muslims and sharply reducing the numbers of

---

[158] Thomas A. Meininger, *Ignatiev and the Establishment of the Bulgarian Exarchate, 1864–1872. A Study in Personal Diplomacy* (Madison, WI: University of Wisconsin Press, 1970).

[159] Berkes, *The Development of Secularism*, pp. 208–22, who presents Nemık Kemal as the key figure in these debates; see also Şerif Mardin, *The Genesis of Young Ottoman Thought. A Study in the Modernization of Turkish Political Ideas* (Princeton University Press, 1962).

[160] Davison, *Reform in the Ottoman Empire*, p. 387.

Christians in the empire. By adopting a new Ottomanist policy, Abdülhamid identified himself as the secular and religious embodiment of an Islamic nation, undermining the tradition of tolerance and making religion the psychological basis for nationality.[161]

At the same time, Abdülhamid endorsed certain precepts of pan-Islamism in order to bolster his domestic position and to advance his own foreign policies. Pan-Islamism, like pan-Slavism, was an amalgam of ideas lacking a formal ideological structure, developed in different directions by Muslim intellectuals throughout the nineteenth century both within and outside the Ottoman Empire. For Abdülhamid, it appealed as a way of underlining the Christian threat to the internal stability of the empire and rallying Muslims outside the empire as a defensive measure to restrain imperial powers with large Muslim minorities like the British and Russians from advocating or planning its dismemberment.

As part of his campaign to revitalize the Islamic component of the Ottoman political theology, Abdülhamid forged new relations with representatives of the mystical Sufi order, the Naqshbandi (Nakşbandi). Its Turkish origins inclined its members to take a passive and loyal attitude toward the Ottoman state, while opposing European-inspired reforms and influence. It underwent a change in the second half of the nineteenth century, mainly under the impact of the massive influx of immigrants from the Caucasus following the defeat of Shamil. Abdülhamid welcomed the militant and fiercely anti-Russian newcomers, and settled them in Anatolia where they helped to re-Islamize the local population. In the short run, their galvanized faith strengthened the position of the sultan, but "their teachings not only helped strengthen society's Islamic consciousness but also increased its awareness of their material backwardness and the government's inability to cope with it."[162]

The final key element in Abdülhamid's strategy was to revive the Ottoman claim on the caliphate. His personal devotion to the title and its symbolic significance to Muslims outside the Ottoman Empire were intended not only to bolster his prestige, but also to counter the threat of an alternative Arab caliphate backed by the British.[163] In fostering his aims, he often operated in the shadows. This not only makes it difficult to follow his traces. In empires with Muslim minorities like the British,

---

[161] Kemal Karpat, "The Social and Political Foundations of Nationalism in South East Europe After 1878," in *Studies on Ottoman Social and Political History. Selected Articles and Essays* (Leiden: Brill, 2002), pp. 352–84.

[162] Kemal Karpat, *The Politicization of Islam. Reconstructing Identity, State, Faith and Community in the Late Ottoman State* (Oxford University Press, 2001), pp. 107–13, quotation on p. 111.

[163] Buzpınar, "The Question of the Caliphate," pp. 26–30.

alarmists fed fears of a vast underground conspiracy, while in all probability only small groups of pan-Islamist activists existed.[164] The Russians
were particularly sensitive to the activities of his agents in the Central
Asian borderlands, where, in 1895, they accused them of fomenting
revolt.[165]

Like Nicholas II, Sultan Abdülhamid II sought to revive and to bring
under his control the spiritual element by harkening back to his dynastic
ancestors of the early Ottoman period, that is, before Mahmud II. Both
autocrats turned to the past in reaction to the idea of constitutional reform
aimed at establishing an equality of all citizens within the empire. In the
Ottoman case, this was the doctrine of Osmanlılık, or "fusion," to be
considered in greater detail in the following chapter on bureaucracy.
Abdülhamid never sincerely embraced this doctrine. Instead, he
employed a traditional religious discourse and complementary motifs
(both literary and visual) in order to reconcile the institutions of the
modern secular state and the founding Islamic myths of the empire. His
pan-Islamic tendencies manifested themselves in four forms: public symbols; official iconography; personal manifestation of royal favor; and
symbolic language.[166] His activities ranged from repairing the tombs of
the Prophet's family to attempting to bring the Shi'ites of Iran and other
marginal Islamic groups back into the fold of the Orthodox Sunni faith.[167]

Simultaneously, he implemented measures to counter the spread of
Shi'ism, which he considered to be particularly dangerous because it
claimed the loyalty of much of the population of the frontier provinces
with Iran: Baghdad, Basra, and Mosul. He was concerned about the
activities of Christian missionaries in the borderland between the empire
and Iran, and gave orders to chase them away. Similarly, he appointed an
advisory commission to bring the heretical sect of the Yezids back to
Sunni Orthodoxy so that they would be suitable for military service.[168]

---

[164] Jacob M. Landau, *The Politics of Pan-Islam. Ideology and Organization* (Oxford University
Press, 1990), esp. pp. 13–72.
[165] E. D. Sokol, *The Revolt of 1916 in Russian Central Asia* (Baltimore, MD: Johns Hopkins
University Press, 1954), pp. 59–64. Senator K. K. Pahlen, reporting on the situation in
Turkestan in 1909, identified small clandestine circles of pan-Islamic propaganda set up
by Abdülhamid's agents. *Mission to Turkestan, 1908–09. Being the Memoirs of K. K.
Pahlen*, ed. Richard A. Pierce (London: Oxford University Press, 1964), pp. 46–52.
The Okhrana continued to monitor allegedly pan-Islamic activities right up to the end of
the Romanov Empire. Sokol, *The Revolt of 1916*, pp. 74–77.
[166] Selim Deringil, *The Well-Protected Domains. Ideology and the Legitimization of Power in the
Ottoman Empire, 1876–1909* (London: Tauris, 1998), pp. 17–42.
[167] Karpat, *The Politicization of Islam*, pp. 199–205.
[168] Selim Deringil, "Legitimacy Structures in the Ottoman State. The Reign of Abdülhamid
II (1876–1909)," in *The Ottomans, the Turks and World Power Politics* (Istanbul: Isis Press,
2000), pp. 86–87. For Abdülhamid's promotion of active proselytizing against other

The overall aim of his eclectic political theology was, once again, similar to the ideological turn of Nicholas II: to employ traditional elements in modern form in order to renew or restore bonds with the older dominant culture of the empire, while at the same time projecting a strong image of imperial rule abroad. The difference between them was also significant. While Nicholas continued to foster Russification, Abdülhamid did not support Turkification, its nationalizing counterpart, for his realm.

The Iranian empires

The Iranian empires under the Safavid and Qajar dynasties were heirs to the ancient kingship traditions of the Sasanian Empire, with a heavy overlay of Islamic religious beliefs, and nomadic and Turkmen tribal customs. A thousand years before the Arab conquest, the concept of Iranshahr as the domain of the *Shahanshah* (king of kings) was well established, although its boundaries were amorphous. Originally, it appears to have signified an area where the Persian language and culture were dominant.[169] The Sasanian kings ruled by divine right, but they were not themselves divine figures like the Roman emperors, and their power was limited by traditions and respect for the privileges of the nobility and clergy (Zoroastrian) which became increasingly strong in late antiquity. The ruler was regarded both as a heroic and knightly figure and as a protector and impartial judge of his people; access to the throne by the poor and helpless was a hallowed tradition.[170]

Major changes in the concept of rulership came with the Arab conquest in the mid-seventh century, and the periodic waves of nomadic conquests of Iran beginning with the Mongols and continuing down to the foundation of the Safavid dynasty in the early sixteenth century. The twin problems of legitimacy and succession had their roots in the pre-Islamic period, but became more acute thereafter. Under Islam the ideal concept of the Just Ruler was based on his ability to maintain the stability and security of the state and the welfare of the population, although these conditions were defined more by tradition than by law; his legitimacy was embodied in the titles the Shadow of God and the Pivot of the Universe. If a ruler appeared to violate these norms, then he was deemed to have lost the divine Grace that gave him legitimacy. This exposed him to legitimate rebellion. As in

religious minorities, see Selim Deringil, "The Transformation of the Public Image of the State in the Hamidian Period. Ideological Challenges and Responses (1876–1908)," in *The Ottomans, the Turks*, pp. 147–64.

[169] Richard N. Frye, *The Golden Age of Persia* (London: Phoenix Press, 2000), pp. 8–9, 13–15.

[170] Richard N. Frye, "The Political History of Iran under the Sasanians," in *The Cambridge History of Iran* (Cambridge University Press, 1983), vol. 3, pp. 136–48.

the Ottoman Empire there was no law of succession. The man who won the struggle for power at the death of the shah, or in a rebellion against an unjust ruler, inherited the divine Grace as the result of his success.[171] The growth in the authority of the ulama and the power of the tribal aristocracies also continued to exercise a restraining influence upon the ruling dynasts who had been nomadic chieftains themselves.

The Safavid dynasty emerged from a popular rebellion by Turkic tribes from Azerbaijan dubbed *qizilbashi* (redheads), according to legend, for the twelve red folds on their turbans in honor of the twelve imams of the Shi'ites. Their leaders belonged to a Sufi-dervish religious order from the Safavid clan that had been linked, as early as the Mongol period, with the tradition of popular rebellion.[172] Under this leadership they formed a virtual independent state in the southeast of the province from which they launched attacks aimed at unifying Azerbaijan and then all of Iran.[173] In 1501, they raised to the throne of Iran Shah Ismail Safavid (1501–1524), the founder of a new dynasty built on theocratic principles with himself as heir to the chiliastic traditions of the Shi'ia. Originally, the tribal leaders regarded Ismail as a god. He claimed to possess esoteric knowledge and represented himself as the reincarnation of Iranian heroes of the past. He adopted the Persian title of shah as the political leader of Iran. The qizilbashi regarded the frontier province of Azerbaijan as the ideal Turkic state where syncretic religious practices prevailed, blending pre-Islamic with shamanist beliefs from the steppe under a thin veneer of Shi'ite Islam.[174]

Under the Safavids the most powerful integrative element in society was a form of Imami or Twelver Shi'ism. The Shi'ia (or "partisans") were members of the Islamic community who believed that the leadership of that community had been passed from the Prophet Mohammed to his

---

[171] Homa Katouzian, *Iranian History and Politics. The Dialectic of State and Society* (London: Routledge Curzon, 2003), especially the essay on "Arbitrary Rule. A Comparative Theory of State, Politics and Society in Iran."

[172] The view that the qizilbashi were part of a syncretic religious culture coming out of Trans Caspia linking older millenarian themes with Shi'ia symbols developed by Mehmed Fuad Köprülü, *Islam after the Turkish Invasion (Prolegomena)*, trans. and ed. Gary Leiser (Salt Lake City, UT: Brigham Young University Press, 1993), has been challenged by Ahmet T. Karamustafa, *God's Unruly Friends. Dervish Groups in the Islamic Later Middle Period, 1200–1550* (Salt Lake City, UT: Brigham Young University Press, 1994).

[173] I. P. Petrushevskii, "Gosudarstva Azerbaizhana v XV v," in *Sbornik statei po istorii Azerbaizhana* (Baku: Akademiia Nauk Azerbaizhanskoi SSR 1949), vol. I, pp. 197–210.

[174] J. Aubin, "Études Safavides. Shah Isma'il et les notables de l'Iraq persan," *Journal of the Economic and Social History of the Orient* 2(1) (January 1959): 37–81; J. Aubin, "Études Safavides. L'avénement des Safavides reconsideré," *Moyen Orient et Océan Indien* 5 (1988): 1–130.

son-in-law, Ali, and his descendants called imams. The line of descent was clear until the Twelfth Imam disappeared, but was still living (occluded) in 873 without issue. Thereafter, the Shi'ia anticipated his return in order to establish the perfect Islamic political community on earth. Over time additional philosophical and legal differences surfaced to divide them further from the Sunni, who did not accept the hereditary principle of succession and who formed the majority of Muslims. Until the establishment of the Safavid dynasty Shi'ism was a minority faith even in Iran. Beginning with Shah Ismail, it provided the Iranians with the outlines of a unifying political theology in their internal struggle to convert the Sunnis in Iran, and in their external struggle against the surrounding Sunni powers of the Ottomans, the Afghans, and the Mughal Empire located on their western, northern, and eastern frontiers.[175] Yet in the Safavid–Ottoman struggle over the borderland of Iraq, or "Iraq-i'Arab" as the Iranian sources called it, strategic considerations initially took precedence over the control of the holy cities of Najab, Karbala, and Sammara, the site of the disappearance of the Twelfth Imam. It was only after Shah Ismail approached Baghdad that contemporary chronicles endowed his expedition with a religious significance that later accounts embellished. Claims of authority over the holy places became part of the official ideology, but never determined the Iranian struggle with the militarily superior Ottomans.[176]

Safavids founded numerous schools (*madreseh*), although it took time before the Shi'ia ulama outside Iran were willing to accept their authority. The buildings of these schools were decorated with "an outward finish of gloriously colored tiles with arabesque designs [that] gave an impression of continuity and harmony of architectural and painted space unrivaled anywhere else in the world."[177] Gradually, then, Shi'ism served a double function as a messianic justification of royal authority and as a religious frontier for "the soil of Iran."

But it also introduced an ambivalent attitude toward government on the part of the ulama. First of all, the Safavids belonged to a Sufi brotherhood, a mystical order that claimed spiritual authority on the basis of ascetic

---

[175] It took some time to eliminate the Sufi brotherhoods like the Naqshbandi who were associated with the Sunni Ottomans. Dina Le Gall, *A Culture of Sufism. Naqshebandi in the Ottoman World, 1450–1700* (Albany, NY: State University of New York, 2005), pp. 24–26, 131, 133.

[176] Rudi Matthee, "The Safavid–Ottoman Frontier: Iraq-i Arab as Seen by the Safavids," in Kemal Karpat with Robert W. Zens (eds.), *Ottoman Borderlands. Issues, Personalities and Political Changes* (Madison, WI: University of Wisconsin Press, 2003), pp. 157–66.

[177] Roy Mottahedeh, *The Mantle of the Prophet. Religion and Politics in Iran*, new edn (Oxford University Press, 2000), p. 97.

devotions, whereas the Shi'ia ulama insisted upon the acquisition of knowledge through formal study. Second, as long as the Twelfth Imam remained hidden, despite Ismail's claims to the contrary, all governments were makeshift and questionable even if based on Shi'ism, although under certain conditions cooperation was acceptable. Third, the ulama gradually reinterpreted the coming of Ismail as prefiguring the appearance of the *mahdī* rather than embodying him, thus stripping the shah of all spiritual dominion. This led to the decline of *qizilbashi* influence at court. By the seventeenth century, the ulama qualified to interpret the law secured the right to sanction royal authority.[178] These shifts in religious ideology engendered a "general reluctance to accept both moral and political responsibility" among both the religious classes and the population. As Anne Lambton has remarked, it complicated the rulers' task of centralizing the state institutions.[179] This was the opposite of what was happening in Muscovy even before the accession of Peter the Great.

But the effects of these changes were slow in coming and rulers resorted to other devices to enhance their authority. Pilgrimages by the shah to the two centers of legitimacy for the dynasty gave a symbolic but visible form to the intense interplay of religion and rulership. Mashad, the shrine of Imam Riza, and Ardabil, the dynastic family shrine, both also enjoyed the patronage of the Safavids. An extraordinary moment in these devotions came in 1601 when Shah Abbas undertook his unprecedented march on foot to Mashad. The city had long been contested on the frontier with the Uzbeks. Abbas made his frequent visits in the course of military expeditions to the northeast to Herat, Balkh, and Qandahar, and once for spiritual support of his projected campaign in Azerbaijan at the other end of the empire. Although none of his successors demonstrated the same degree of spirituality, they too occasionally made a pilgrimage to one or the other shrine. Mashad continued to attract pilgrims throughout the seventeenth and into the eighteenth century, particularly when Ottoman–Iran wars made the journey to Mecca problematic.[180]

---

[178] Kathryn Babayan, "Sufis, Dervishes and Mullas. The Controversy over Spiritual and Temporal Dominion in Seventeenth Century Iran," *Pembroke Papers* 4 (1996): 117–19. The author also makes clear that neither the *qizilbashi* nor the traditional ulama were unified in their beliefs, but that the differences between them were more significant.

[179] Ann K. S. Lambton, "Social Change in Persia in the Nineteenth Century," in *Qajar Persia. Eleven Studies* (Austin, TX: University of Texas Press, 1987), pp. 194–95.

[180] Charles Melville, "The Pilgrimage to Mashad in 1601," in *Safavid Persia. The History and Politics of an Islamic Society* (London: Tauris, 1996), pp. 192–99, 218–20. Another unifying ceremony embraced by the Safavid dynasts was the commemoration of the martyrdom of the Imam Hosein with its processions of flagellants that survived in popular folklore and "are only a step away from the full-blown modern Shiah theater of martyrdom." Mottahedeh, *The Mantle of the Prophet*, p. 175.

The enlargement of imperial cultural space in Safavid Iran was reflected in the design and construction of a new capital, Isfahan, adjacent to a medieval Seljuk city in the first half of the seventeenth century. Up to this time the Safavids had ruled from several seats of power, first Tabriz and then Qazvin. Places of temporary residence of the shah, they reflected the tribal concept of governance linked to the alliance of the dynasty with the qizilbashi. This itinerant concept was dramatically altered by the construction of Isfahan, which centralized imperial rule symbolically and geographically. Isfahan occupied a strategic position approximately midway between the eastern and western frontiers. Its construction followed a central plan designed by Shah Abbas to express a wholly new concept for Iran of an imperial capital. "Half the world is Isfahan," its inhabitants were soon able to boast. Its magnificent royal gardens and palace represented an allegoric and symbolic order reproducing the concentric circles of imperial space from imperial center to the borderlands. As an expression of power, it combined the metaphysical image of paradise with an assertion of political sovereignty, of divine kingship, and Shi'ite legitimacy.[181]

The spatial design symbolized his desire to subordinate the politics, commerce, and culture of the country to the ruling dynasty. However, the Safavid palaces allowed greater access to the ruler than did the Ottoman palaces, who, according to the Venetian ambassador, "constantly stayed in public," in contrast to the sultan who, in the words of the same source, "did not speak to anyone and was rarely visible."[182] The focal point of the planned city was the great square (*maydan*) known as the Image of the World. Its four sides unified the commercial, religious, and administrative functions of the empire. The square became the stage for court-sponsored rituals and display that provided a link between imperial power and the public. The architectural design also attracted the patronage of the three major sources of Abbas' new polity: the Georgian slave (*ghulam*) administrators; the protected Armenian merchant community; and the ulama. Like Mehmed the Conqueror before him and Peter the Great a century later, Shah Abbas commanded the court and slave administrative elite to build their stately homes along the great promenade leading to the center of the city, creating the impression of its social solidarity.[183]

---

[181] Heidi A. Walcher, "Between Paradise and Political Capital. The Semiotics of Safavid Isfahan," *Middle Eastern Natural Environments. Lessons and Legacies*, Bulletin 103 (1998): 330–45.

[182] Necipoğlu, *Architecture, Ceremonial and Power*, pp. 253–56.

[183] Sussan Babaie, "Launching from Isfahan. Slaves and the Construction of the Empire," in Sussan Babaie et al. (eds.), *Slaves of the Shah. New Elites of Safavid Iran* (London: Tauris, 2004), pp. 80–88.

In an effort to extend his authority over the south of the country, Abbas appointed loyal members of his household as governors who followed their imperial master in designing imperial space befitting a representative of the central power, albeit a subordinate. The *maydan* of the city of Kirman, for example, may have lacked imperial grandeur; that would have been presumptuous. But it expressed in a restrained and modest fashion the same functions as its inspiration in Isfahan. Similar construction was carried out in other cities, including restoration of the famous Shi'ia shrine of the Imam Ali in Najaf and projects in several towns in the province of Mazanderan, the shah's matrilineal homeland. There on the northwestern frontiers of his realm, Abbas commanded the resettlement of 15,000 mainly Armenian families to stimulate trade and the silk manufacturing industry.[184]

Despite the inspired efforts of Shah Abbas, by the end of the seventeenth century the theocratic basis of imperial authority had eroded. He had sought to centralize the state and place his authority on the more traditional foundations of absolutism, even though he remained head of a Sufi order and was venerated by his subjects as possessing supernatural powers. But a centralized monarchy was not typical of post-Mongol Iran. The imperial ideology did not overcome the claims of the ulama or tribal and clan loyalties. Under weak rulers seduced by the harem atmosphere and plagued by tribal revolts, banditry became endemic. Even a religious revival at the end of the seventeenth century could not restore the authority of the shah. Its target was the Sunnis within the country, rather than the Ottomans, who were the main external enemy. Thus, it antagonized some of the most warlike tribal elements and contributed to further internal dissolution.

During Iran's long period of troubles in the eighteenth century, the dynastic concept faded into little more than a shadow. Power fell into the hands of charismatic tribal warriors; men like Nadir Shah (1736–1747), whose outstanding military gifts won him great victories, which he failed to translate into dynastic authority. His was the last vain attempt to broaden the political theology of Iran by introducing radical changes in Shi'ism. Himself a Sunni, Nadir Shah sought in this way to maintain the loyalty of the majority of his troops recruited from the Sunni borderlands of Iran. But the Ottoman sultan, fearing the universalist implication of his claims, rejected his appeal to accept the reforms as a fifth school of the Sunni, and the Iranian ulama responded typically with "prudent

---

[184] Babaie, "Launching from Isfahan," pp. 95–99.

dissimulation" (*taqīyya*).[185] The founder of the new dynasty, Aga Muhammed Khan, was another Turkic tribal chieftain of the Qajar clan, "lords of the marches in the zone between Turkmen nomadic pastoralism and Iranian sedentary agriculture [who] maintained an uneasy balance between the traditions of the Iranian plateau and those of the steppes."[186] In 1789, after almost a decade of continuous fighting to reunite the country, he took the title shah in a coronation ceremony that followed the Safavid model. It blended Sufi religious symbolism and pilgrimage to holy shrines with the glitter of the old court. Beyond the trappings, however, there was no real attempt to restore the substance of a centralized theocratic monarchy.

When the Qajars came to power, they had no claim to religious legitimacy through alleged descent from the imams. They relied instead on the early Persian concept of kingship that portrayed the shah as "God's shadow on earth." Although this concept enjoyed some support from interpreters of the Koran, there was another tradition that introduced reservations. According to the Imam Muhammed Ghazali (d. 1111), the shah was the shadow of God on earth only if he was just: "the unjust sultan is ill-starred and will have no endurance." Subsequent sources make a distinction between the man and the office. The attempts of the Qajar rulers to strengthen their rule over the periphery by raising taxes for military purposes encountered charges of injustice. So too did any attempt to alter the balance among the four basic status groups upholding social stability: the men of the pen or jurists; the men of the sword or soldiers; the men of commerce or merchants; and the men of husbandry of the earth or peasants. This set limits on innovation and implied fear of change. Qajar rulers who violated these ideals were vulnerable to attack. Of the six shahs who ruled Iran from the mid-nineteenth century only one escaped exile or death by assassination.[187]

Throughout their rule, the Qajar sought to maintain an uneasy truce with the ulama who had adopted an ambiguous stance toward the monarchy, considering it as basically illegitimate in the absence of the hidden Twelfth Imam of Shi'ite tradition.[188] In the course of the eighteenth

[185] Hamid Algar, "Religious Forces in Eighteenth and Nineteenth Century Iran," in *Cambridge History of Iran*, vol. 7, pp. 708–9.
[186] G. Hambly, "Aga Muhammad Khan and the Establishment of the Qajar Dynasty," in *Cambridge History of Iran*, vol. 7, p. 107.
[187] A. Reza Sheikholeslami, *The Structure of Central Authority in Qajar Iran, 1871–1896* (Atlanta, GA: Scholars Press, 1997), pp. 1–8, quotation on p. 3.
[188] E. Abrahamian, "Oriental Despotism. The Case of Qajar Iran," *International Journal of Middle East Studies* 5 (1974): 3–31; Hamid Algar, *Religion and State in Iran, 1785–1806. The Role of the Ulama in the Qajar Period* (Berkeley, CA: University of California Press, 1969).

century the Shi'ia evolved farther and farther from the Sunni. During the intra-dynastic period, teaching at the Shi'ia schools widened doctrinal differences with the state. A great debate raged from the eighteenth into the nineteenth century between the strict interpreters of the traditions (*hadith*) and those who argued that they had the right to interpret the will of God and of the Twelfth Imam through the exercise of reason; the latter won out. This gave them a special position of religious authority in the community to which even the ruler was subject. Moreover, they performed a whole range of social and economic functions, having control over the collection of religious taxes, unlike the Sunni ulama in the Ottoman Empire. Furthermore, a number of leading clerics lived abroad in the holy cities of Ottoman Iraq from where they were outside the control of Qajar rule.[189] Their concern over the legitimacy of the ruler did not, however, prevent them from preaching obedience as a protection against disorder.[190]

Although the ulama were never a monolithic group, their cohesion began to erode dramatically in the nineteenth century with the revival of mystical and speculative elements that became increasingly secular by the end of the century. Among the dissident sects, Babism represented the most radical trend. In 1844, a young merchant proclaimed himself the *bab*, that is, "the gate" to the Hidden Imam, which was tantamount to claiming to be the *mahdī*. He founded a movement directed against the Sh'ia hierarchy and the state with the aim of establishing a theocracy in the tradition of Shi'ia messianism. He was brought to trial in Tabriz, where the young shah, Nasir al-Din (1848–1896), presided over the tribunal, found guilty of heresy and executed. Nasir al-Din later reminded a leading Shi'ia cleric of the dependence of religious authority on the power of the state: "Do you know that if, God forbid, there was no government, those same Babis would cut off your heads."[191] With the death of the Bab, his movement split: one branch established the syncretic Bahai religion, which aspired to universalism but was politically neutral; and the Azalis, whose secret opposition to the state was masked by the practice of *taqīyya*. Their opposition to the ruling power fed on the shifting ideological

---

[189] Malise Ruthven, *Islam in the World* (London: Oxford University Press, 1984), pp. 221–26; Nikki R. Keddie (ed.), *Scholars, Saints and Sufis. Muslim Religious Institutions since 1500* (Berkeley, CA: University of California Press, 1972), argues that a kind of church–state dichotomy similar to that in Medieval Europe emerged in nineteenth-century Iran, with the religious authorities asserting and often maintaining superior claims to those of the state.

[190] Lambton, "Social Change," p. 197.

[191] Mangol Bayat, *Iran's First Revolution. Shi'ism and the Constitutional Revolution of 1905–1909* (New York: Oxford University Press, 1991), p. 21.

preferences of Nasir al-Din, a pious Muslim, who was increasingly attracted to Western models of imperial rule.[192] When, in 1891, he granted an unprecedented monopoly over the sale of tobacco to a foreign (British) subject, the ulama issued a fatwa prohibiting smoking. Faced with mass demonstrations and a total boycott of tobacco, the shah was forced to withdraw the concession. By the early twentieth century, the tension between the secular authority of the shah and the dissidents had increased to the point where a significant part of the ulama took part in the Constitutional Revolution of 1907. Thus, in Iran, as in the Ottoman Empire, the internal frontiers of political theology like the external geographical frontiers were contested and shifted. Yet they remained an important dimension of imperial rule.

In the late nineteenth century, Nasir al-Din made a belated attempt to bridge the gap between the remote, quasi-divine, imperial persona and the people of Iran. Similar to rulers of the Habsburg Monarchy, Russia, and the early Qing Empire, he sought to represent the imperial idea by displaying his person in official journeys throughout the country. At best he succeeded in stimulating public interest in the frontier provinces as an integral part of the realm.[193]

In order to overcome the fissiparous tendencies in Iranian society, the Qajar dynasty sought to create a new royal nobility. The paradoxical effect was to weaken further the ability of the shah to reform the army and bureaucracy, and at the same time to transform the Qajar tribe "from a diffuse oligarchy with shaky loyalties into a closely knit patrimony." Through multiple marriages designed to extend the royal family, Fath Ali Shah (1797–1834) brought almost a thousand wives of different tribal and social origins into his royal harem and fathered sixty sons and forty daughters; equally prolific, they had produced thousands of offspring by the time of his death in 1834.[194] On a more sober note, Fath Ali also patronized a literary revival that glorified the traditional values of the Persian monarchy. Raised in the ancient Persian model of conduct to pursue the glories of feasting and hunting, his great-grandson and future shah, Nasir al-Din, emulated and even surpassed these sensual and symbolic exploits. The sumptuous and ostentatious display and ritual, the large harem, and the patronage of poets contributed to the image of the

[192] Algar, "Religious Forces," pp. 710–15; Mehrdad Kia, "Inside the Court of Naser od-Din Qajar, 1881–1896. The Life and Diary of Mohammad Hasan Khan E'temad os-Saltaneh (Iran)," *Middle Eastern Studies* 37(1) (January 2001): 14.
[193] Kashani-Sabet, *Frontier Fictions*, pp. 62–63.
[194] Abbas Amanat, *Pivot of the Universe. Nasir Al-Din Shah and the Iranian Monarchy, 1831–1896* (Berkeley, CA: University of California Press, 1997), pp. 19–20.

shah's glory and power among his servitors, but struck Europeans as the mark of a corrupt and sensual "Oriental."[195]

The Qing Empire

The Chinese case was exceptional on several counts. First, the concept of rulership was entirely autochthonous and remarkably uniform over very long periods of time. Second, the ideology of empire-building was shared by both indigenous and conquest dynasties. The difference between them was that the conquest dynasties, Yuan (Mongol) and Qing (Manchu), sought to use China as a vast resource from which to expand their power over the Inner Asian steppe from whence they originated. The longevity of the Chinese empire was due in large measure to the combination of a high level of cultural uniformity reinforced by a powerful integrative mechanism, together with a flexibility of response and a toleration of alien traditions. A holistic cosmology rooted in the tradition of the divinity of the emperor was linked to a highly developed moral-ethical system (Confucianism), embodied in ritual codes that defined the functions of the bureaucracy and the commitments of the emperor. When the Manchu emperors acquired an Inner Asian empire in the eighteenth century they sought to integrate non-Chinese religious legitimizations of their power. To Mongols and Tibetans, the emperor was "a living incarnation of the gods" in the form of a reincarnation of the Buddhist Bodhisattva of wisdom.[196]

The emperor was the supreme law-giver, judge, and executive. His power was absolute in theory, but constrained in different ways to that of the Russian tsar, Ottoman sultan, Iranian shah, or Habsburg monarch. The emperor's authority could be challenged, although it took a brave man, on matters of ethics as defined by the scholars relying on their interpretation of the past. Accumulated precedents drawn from the acts of previous rulers possessed great moral force. It was possible for the emperor to proclaim "new beginnings," but for the most part these did not substantially change the "ancient" institutions, such as the examination system or the following of prescribed rituals.[197]

Evidence of the political importance of ritual abounds in Chinese history, and reveals the inherent problem of reconciling conflicting ethical

---

[195] Amanat, *Pivot of the Universe*, pp. 64–70.

[196] D. M. Farquhar, "Emperor as Bodhisattva in the Governance of the Ch'ing Empire," *Harvard Journal of Asiatic Studies* 1 (June 1978): 5–34.

[197] F. W. Mote, *Imperial China, 900–1800* (Cambridge, MA: Harvard University Press, 1999), pp. 98–99, 296.

norms. In the famous "rites controversy" of 1524, the Emperor Shizong sought to raise his parents posthumously to the imperial rank as a sign of filial piety, one of the highest virtues of the Confucian ethic. But this act contradicted historical precedence and ritual correctness stemming from the same source. The conflict between family and state values led to a clash between the emperor and the majority of the scholar-officials. It was resolved by the emperor replacing the officials, whose only recourse was to submit or suffer for adherence to their ethical ideals.[198]

The Chinese emperor was not a public figure, more like the Iranian shah or Ottoman sultan than the Romanov or Habsburg dynasts. The early emperors were notable exceptions. Endowed with military skills, the Kangxi emperor actually took the field with his troops, as did the first Ming emperor Zhu Yuanzhang. He also revived the tradition of the imperial tour as a means of redefining imperial space as a mobile center. The tours were highly stylized and afforded little opportunity for real contact with the population.[199] Nevertheless, the organization of magnificent tours of the south and shorter visits to other regions stimulated the construction of temporary palaces and left behind a visible symbol of imperial power.[200] In Beijing, the real center, the construction of garden complexes was designed to emphasize the cultural diversity of the empire. The architecture drew on southern residential models, Inner Asian pleasure palaces, and Tibetan religious buildings. These structures may not have been visible to the mass of the population, but their intended audience was high officials and visiting delegations from the borderlands who were drawn into the symbolic multicultural space of the Qing.[201]

The most visible visual symbols of imperial rule were the walled cities, especially Beijing. But even before the Qing, the city symbolized the geographical center of the world, a fifth symbolic direction, the other four – east, west, north, and south – defined in terms of non-civilized people, for example, northern barbarians (beidi) and southern barbarians (nanman). The walls, the great squares, and the imperial palaces of the

---

[198] Mote, *Imperial China*, p. 644. During the civil war of 1399–1402 that preceded the founding of the Ming dynasty, the future Emperor Chengzu attempted to justify his usurpation of the throne from the legitimate ruler, his nephew, with the statement "This is my family matter," claiming in effect that the dynasty was not a matter of state. Those who opposed this interpretation were mercilessly killed. *Ibid.*, p. 589.

[199] Mote, *Imperial China*, pp. 867–88, 916.

[200] Jonathan Spence, *Ts'ao Yin and the K'ang-hsi Emperor* (New Haven, CT: Yale University Press, 1966); Silas H. L. Wu, *Passage to Power. K'ang-hsi and His Heir Apparent* (Cambridge, MA: Harvard University Press, 1979).

[201] Jonathan Hay, "The Diachronics of Early Qing Visual and Material Culture," in Lynn Struve (ed.), *The Qing Formation in World Historical Time* (Cambridge, MA: Harvard University Press, 2004), pp. 310–16.

capital were aligned on a longitudinal axis that represented the "imperial processional path."[202] The quadripartite walled segmentation of Beijing symbolized the hierarchical order of imperial rule. The Forbidden City housed the emperor and his court; the Imperial City included government buildings and domiciles of many officials; the Inner City was populated mainly by Manchu, Mongol, and Chinese bannermen and their families. The majority of the urban population lived in the Outer City in ethnically mixed neighborhoods.[203]

As a small minority ruling over a vast Chinese-speaking Han population, the Manchu rulers opted for a policy of cultural pluralism. The Qianlong emperor identified himself as the ruler of five peoples: the Manchus, Mongols, Tibetans, Uighurs, and Chinese, and learned their languages.[204] But the rulers took care to preserve their own language as a symbol of their identity as conquerors, just as they protected their homelands against Sinicization. They eliminated local variations in Manchu and established a standard speech, which was then used as the language of instruction for Mongols and other northeast Asian peoples enrolled in banner schools. They did not seek to replace Chinese as the official language, making it instead one of the two languages of government. The dynasty fostered the development of cultural traditions and the translation of Chinese classics into the languages of the peoples of the borderlands, especially the Mongols and Tibetans.[205] Thus, the "barbarian" conquerors not only co-opted local elites, but also trained new generations of literati and administrators from the borderlands as well as the majority Han population to accept their benevolent imperial rule.

The most ancient and persistent component of the imperial ideal was the Mandate of Heaven, which had its origin in the first millennium BCE. It established an ethical principle of right conduct as the basis for the emperor's legitimacy. For the emperor to fail to meet the standards of right conduct meant that the Mandate of Heaven had been withdrawn. Natural disasters and foreign invasions or other kinds of systemic crises could seriously undermine the moral authority of the emperor, and help to

---

[202] Ronald G. Knapp, *China's Walled Cities* (Oxford University Press, 2000), pp. 2, 9, 54–66.

[203] Alison Dray-Novey, "Spatial Order and Police in Imperial Beijing," *Journal of Asian Studies* 52(4) (November 1993): 890–91; Susan Naquin, *Peking. Temples and City Life, 1400–1900* (Berkeley, CA: University of California Press, 2001).

[204] Pamela K. Crossley, "An Introduction to the Qing Foundation Myth," *Late Imperial China* 14(1) (1985): 13–36.

[205] Pamela K. Crossley and Evelyn S. Rawski, "A Profile of the Manchu Language in Ch'ing History," *Harvard Journal of Asiatic Studies* 53(1) (1993): 63–102; Evelyn S. Rawski, "The Qing Formation in the Early-Modern Period," in Struve (ed.), *The Qing Formation*, pp. 226–32.

justify rebellion or massive defection of officials and soldiers from the reigning dynasty. This established a method of bringing about violent change while guaranteeing the new rulers the renewal of divine sanction. But any alternative to the emperor's absolute authority was inconceivable until the twentieth century. At times, however, a real tension developed over the relationship between the Confucian tradition and the Mandate of Heaven. For example, under the early Manchus there were disagreements over whether the legitimacy of the new dynasty rested upon its absorption of the ethical standards of the Chinese civilization or upon "unique and inherent favor by Heaven" that preceded the conquest.[206]

The Confucian tradition provided a detailed and elaborate set of ethical ideals and an administrative framework by which they could be transmitted to the population. Confucian thought had never been a monolithic or static set of principles. Although Confucianism lacked any sense of the transcendental – there was no priestly hierarchy – it did not reject alternative belief systems like Buddhism and Taoism. Without being mutually exclusive, the three teachings competed with one another for the patronage of the emperor and for government resources. The system was uniform but not static. Each successive dynasty produced its own ritual codes. Confucianism proved to be responsive to certain kinds of change. For example, in the Sung dynasty there was a noticeable shift toward a broader, less court-centered intellectual community. Perspectives on mankind became more universal, with an emphasis on self-cultivation and the quest for sagehood matched by a decline in court ritual.[207] Ever since the Southern Song (twelfth century) there had been a tension within the Confucian tradition between reason, or "evidential research," and idealism, or innate knowledge. The controversy between advocates of each school testified to the vitality of the tradition. As conditions changed and new problems arose, scholars explored new approaches to the ancient texts. As the neo-Confucian synthesis of the Sung, the school of reason, became more highly stylized and dogmatic over the following centuries, it came under sharp criticism in the sixteenth century by Wang Yang Ming who attempted to reinvigorate the tradition of the unity of thought and action.[208]

Under the Qing it underwent further modification. Kangxi (1654–1722), the second Manchu emperor, addressed the complex legacy of

[206] Pamela Kyle Crossley, *A Translucent Mirror. History and Identity in Qing Imperial Ideology* (Berkeley, CA: University of California Press, 1999), pp. 256–59.
[207] D. McMullen, "Bureaucrats and Cosmology. The Ritual Code of T'ang China," in Cannadine and Price (eds.), *Rituals of Royalty*, pp. 181–236.
[208] Mote, *Imperial China*, pp. 144–49, 679–81, 931–35.

Confucianism as a means of consolidating his rule and winning over a large body of Chinese scholars who retained a lingering loyalty for the preceding Ming dynasty. Kangxi ordered a new compilation of Confucian moral precepts embodied in a series of sixteen maxims, known as the Sacred Edict. The neo-Confucianism that he sponsored was socially and politically more prescriptive than earlier interpretations. It emphasized hierarchical social relations, obedience, and hard work, but also the segregation of the sexes and absolute loyalty to the ruler no matter what his personal shortcomings might be.[209] The emperor himself participated in the discussions with court scholars and ordered the wide dissemination of the Sacred Edict in colloquial style to the literate population.

Painting and calligraphy had always been part of the Confucian system. Kangxi actively sought to co-opt scholars, poets, and artists to the court in order to celebrate the glories of his reign and to illustrate the moral failure of the preceding dynasty which doomed it to collapse. This work of moral indoctrination intensified under the reign of his son Yongzheng (1723–1735), and became in the words of Jonathan Spence, "a recurrent theme in later Chinese history, both after the great rebellions of the mid-nineteenth century and under the successive governments of the Chinese Nationalists and the Chinese Communists."[210] Sun Yat-sen incorporated many precepts of neo-Confucianism in his eclectic work, *The Three Principles of the People*, and Chiang Kai-shek drew on the same sources for his more authoritarian doctrine, the New Life Movement.[211]

The Manchu endorsement, and indeed exaltation, of Confucian values and the Chinese literary tradition not only enabled the dynasty to win the loyalty of the scholar-officials, but also the broader strata of the Chinese population. The early Qing emperors sought to formalize the old Manchu folk culture in order to bring it into line with the classical Chinese tradition. At the same time, the Qing emperors were sensitive to the need to maintain the warrior traditions among its banner forces in the newly acquired borderlands to the northwest. Despite his fascination with

---

[209] Arthur T. Wright (ed.), *The Confucian Persuasion* (Stanford University Press, 1962); Thomas A. Metzger, *Escape from Predicament. Neo-Confucianism and China's Evolving Political Culture* (New York: Columbia University Press, 1977); Jonathan Spence, *Emperor of China. Self-Portrait of K'ang-hsi* (New York: Vintage Books, 1974).

[210] Jonathan Spence, *The Search for Modern China*, 2nd edn (New York: W. W. Norton, 1999), pp. 60–65, and quote on p. 92. See also Mary C. Wright, *The Last Stand of Chinese Conservatism. The T'ung Chich Restoration, 1862–1874* (Stanford University Press, 1957), ch. 12; K-W. Chow, *The Rise of Confucian Ritualism in Late Imperial China. Ethics, Classics and Lineage* (Stanford University Press, 1994).

[211] Marie-Claire Bergère, *Sun Yat-sen*, trans. Janet Lloyd (Stanford University Press, 1998), pp. 392, 410; Spence, *The Search*, pp. 356–57.

Confucian scholarship, the Qianlong emperor (1736–1799) was concerned over the decline of the warrior traditions of the Manchus and
especially of the banner men on the frontiers. His revival of shamanism
and his romanticization of the manly strength of frontier culture prominent in his own compositions demonstrate both the broadly syncretic
ideology of the Qing and a recurrent influence of the frontier on the
culture of the imperial center.[212] In reshaping the imperial myth, the
Qianlong period represented the most ambitious attempt to create what
Pamela Kyle Crossley has called "multiple imperial personae." The religious representation of the emperor was universalized through a process
of ideological abstraction. Portrayed as embracing multiple traditions and
value systems, the emperor could appeal to a variety of constituents who
were able to locate in his mythical status their own aspirations.[213]

However tolerant the Qing Empire was of other cultural traditions,
Confucian ethics continued to occupy the central place in its imperial
ideology. Its place in the reforming impulse of the nineteenth century, the
so-called Qing restoration following the great internal rebellions, is a
matter of scholarly debate. One point emerges clearly, however. The
reformers divided into two camps. The conservatives sought to restore
the old order by borrowing some elements of Western technology and
diplomacy. The other group among the Confucian literati and scholars
aimed for a revitalization of an eclectic approach that stressed self-sacrifice
in serving the state, pragmatic solutions to current problems, and legalist
concepts. They formed the early foundations of the School of Practical
Statecraft that emerged full-blown at the end of the nineteenth century.
Among the key policy changes introduced by this lengthy process of
ideological renewal was an endorsement of the economic principle of
profitability for the general public and an active policy of colonization,
especially for the border provinces.[214]

---

[212] Pamela Kyle Crossley, "Manzhou Yuanli Kao and Formalization of the Manchu
Heritage," *Journal of Asian Studies* 46(4) (1987): 761–90; Caroline Humphrey,
"Shamanic Practices and the State in Northern Asia. Views from the Center and
Periphery," in Nicholas Thomas and Caroline Humphrey (eds.), *Shamanism, History
and the State* (Ann Arbor, MI: University of Michigan Press, 1996), pp. 191–228.

[213] Crossley, *A Translucent Mirror*, pp. 41–44, notes a similar analysis of the Russian tsar by
Cherniavsky in *Tsar and People*, pp. 80–81, 93, and 99.

[214] The conservative elements were the main focus of Wright, *The Last Stand*. For the
revisionists, see, *inter alia*, Hao Chan, *Liang Ch'i-ch'ao and Intellectual Transition in
China, 1890–1907* (Cambridge, MA: Harvard University Press, 1971), pp. 7–34; Shen
Chen Han-yin, "Tseng Kuo-fan in Peking, 1840–1852. His Ideas on Statecraft and
Reform," *Journal of Asian Studies* 27(1) (November 1967): 61–80; Peter Mitchell,
"The Limits of Reformism. Wei Yüan's Reaction to Western Intrusion," *Modern Asian
Studies* 6(2) (April 1972): 175–204.

The Chinese defeat in the Sino-Japanese War of 1894/5 inspired the most ambitious efforts to demonstrate that Confucian thought had not been opposed to social change or progress. The intellectual leaders of the reform movement called the "Hundred Days" sometimes employed "a transcendental language derived from New Text Confucianism that posited progressive forces in the cosmos." Although there were contradictions and ambiguities in their reasoning, the reformers sought to reconcile the traditional idea of the emperor as divinely inspired sage and, therefore, as an absolute and active monarch with the role of the non-official literati as the commoner sage in the mold of Confucius who "had understood the need to save the world from chaos and clarify universal principles."[215] These liberal interpretations of the classics aroused the interest of the young emperor Guangxu (1871–1908), who issued the famous edicts that launched the period of the "Hundred Days" Reforms. These touched many Chinese institutions; a subject to be taken up in the next chapter.

Among the four basic reforms the emperor ordered a drastic revision of the examination system, including the abolition of its highly stylized format and the introduction of more questions dealing with practical questions of administration and finances. He also welcomed petitions from the scholar-reformists, including a particularly instructive work of historical analysis by one of its major proponents, Kang Youwei, on the fate of Poland.[216] The mounting pressure for educational reform from the young scholars, many of whom were seeking education abroad, finally led to the abolition of the examination system in 1904. However, new civil service examinations were introduced two years later. Their aim was to combine the traditional literary and philosophical texts on personal morality and talent with a more modern curriculum. These ideas were central to the last decade of reform, the *xinzheng* period from 1902 to 1911. The majority of the ruling elite were products of the traditional Confucian education. They opposed or retarded the process of reform until moderate solutions, including the retention of the dynasty, were no longer viable options for the new power elites in the army. It is still a matter of dispute how deeply or widely Confucian values were distributed throughout society or the extent to which they survived the fall of the dynasty, the establishment of republican government, and the triumph of communism. However, it has been argued, there was little difference between

---

[215] Peter Zarrow, "The Reform Movement, the Monarchy and Political Modernity," in Rebecca E. Karl and Peter Zarrow (eds.), *Rethinking the 1898 Reform Period. Political and Cultural Change in Late Qing China* (Cambridge, MA: Harvard University Press, 2002), pp. 20–21, 44.
[216] Spence, *The Search*, p. 228.

the questions on the various *xinzheng* exams and those given to upper civil servants in the 1930s.[217] Moreover, American sociologists conducting interviews in the 1960s in China concluded that "values inculcated as part of the 'great tradition' spread beyond those who received formal training in the Confucian classics."[218]

The universalizing ideology of the Qing rulers broke down when challenged from within by the Taiping rebels. Up to the mid-nineteenth century rebellions in China were more the result of economic grievances than ethnic conflict, as in the Muslim rebellions in the western borderlands. The Taiping rebels drew a sharp distinction between themselves as the people of God and the ethnoreligiously alien Manchu–Mongol peoples as the spawn of the devil. Following the suppression of the rebellion, the targeted communities absorbed the terms of identification wielded by their enemies. The Boxer Rebellion at the end of the century completed the long march toward nationalist feelings not only by the politically dominant non-Han peoples (Manchu–Mongol), but also, in a perversely reversed order, by the subjected majority of Chinese. The Chinese nationalist ideologues borrowed two fundamental ideas from the vocabulary of the Qing. First, they embraced the concept of a territorial China within the frontiers established by the military conquests of the dynasty, including the dynastic homeland of Manchuria. Second, they adopted the genealogical taxonomy of the peoples of the empire as developed by the Qing rulers. This dual heritage posed a dilemma for them not unlike that faced by contemporary Russian revolutionaries. How was it possible to construct a successor state to empire, ruled by a single figure claiming a supernational legitimacy that reconciled the idea of a theoretically pure and indivisible national ideal with the existence of multinational borderlands? Was there a choice between the perils of imposing cultural assimilation or allowing secession of the borderlands as possibly hostile states occupying strategic space on what would have to be contested frontiers?[219]

[217] Julia C. Strauss, "Creating Virtuous and Talented Officials for the Twentieth Century. Discourse and Practice in Xinzheng China," *Modern Asian Studies* 37(4) (2003): 834–37, 848–49.

[218] R. Solomon, *Mao's Revolution and Chinese Political Culture* (Berkeley, CA: University of California Press, 1970), p. 92. A substantial part of this volume is devoted to uncovering evidence of the persistence of pre-communist cultural linkages between the elites and peasants. *Ibid.*, pp. 99–159.

[219] See the discussion in Crossley, *A Translucent Mirror*, pp. 342–52 ff; Pamela Kyle Crossley, *Orphan Warriors. Three Manchu Generations and the End of the Qing World* (Princeton University Press, 1990); Michael Gasster, *Chinese Intellectuals and the Revolution of 1911. The Birth of Chinese Radicalism* (Seattle, WA: University of Washington Press, 1969).

Polish–Lithuanian Commonwealth

In contrast to the other multicultural states, the dominant political ideology of the Polish–Lithuanian Commonwealth did not center on the ruler, but on the ruling szlachta. A survey of its principles helps to clarify the reasons for the early failure of the Commonwealth to stay the course in the struggle over the borderlands. The attempts of Poland's kings to envelop royal authority in a myth of legitimacy and the symbolic practices to sustain it were weak and ineffective, primarily, if not solely, due to the countervailing force of the elective principle so stubbornly defended by the szlachta. The closest Polish royal authority came to inventing a mission was a legacy of the rule of Casimir the Great in the fifteenth century. The first of the Jagiellonians, he appears to have envisaged the organization of East Central Europe in the form of a loose federation under Polish–Lithuanian rule. Although he never articulated a plan for creating such a system, his initiatives have been interpreted as aiming for this goal. As it emerged, it had the potential for challenging the Habsburg dynastic policies in the west and the Muscovite in the east. In other words, it engaged Poland–Lithuania in a struggle over the borderlands between the imperial centers of Vienna and Moscow. At its height in the 1490s the Jagiellonian system included dynastic ties with Bohemia and Hungary, and the establishment of vassal states in Moldavia and East Prussia under the Teutonic Knights. A complementary element in the scheme was the defense of Christianity in its Latin form against the infidel Turks and the schismatic Orthodox Russians.

In his attempt to strengthen his position, Sigismund I continued the cultural policies of his predecessors by seeking to establish a new symbolic center of royal authority. From the early years of the six-teenth century the Jagiellonian rulers had aspired to make Cracow the capital of a Renaissance monarchy. Sigismund I was a great patron of the arts, especially of architecture. The reconstruction of the Royal Palace on Wawel Hill, blending Renaissance and Gothic elements, served as a model for magnates all over Poland to emulate. His marriage to Bona Sforza brought in additional Italian painters, sculptors, and architects appointed to adorn the capital. While the king presided over the opening of the "golden age" in Polish culture, he did not attempt to harness the humanistic spirit in literature to serve the needs of the monarchy. Although the University of Cracow had long been an intellectual center, humanism flourished outside its walls, spreading widely throughout the country. Its representatives were concerned more with extolling republican liberties than with justifying royal authority.[220]

The last systematic attempt to construct a royal ideology supported by a symbolic system of royal power came under the Vasa kings, Sigmund III, Wladyslaw IV, and John Casimir, who together ruled for eighty-one years from 1587 to 1668. Claimants to the Swedish throne, they were also connected to the Jagiellons, and championed the principle of hereditary rights not only to the Swedish but also to the crown of the Commonwealth. Masters of propaganda glorifying the dynasty, they sought to make the new capital of Warsaw, to which Sigismund III had gradually transferred the court, a center of power both in the geographical and political sense. Located in the heart of the solidly Catholic Mazovian plain, where the provincial szlachta was loyal to the crown, it stood on lands owned mainly by the king. The royal castle was a public building, the seat of the Polish Sejm (parliament), endowed with a magnificent Marble Room containing battle scenes of great Polish victories, and portraits of the kings and queens of Poland going back to the founder of the Jagiellonian dynasty and including those of blood relatives among the Habsburgs. Staunch Catholics, the Vasas identified their rule with the patron saints of Poland and the canonization of St. Casimir. They mapped out a processional route from Cracow to Warsaw to celebrate the military triumphs of the Vasas over the Muscovites. They sought to circumvent the magnates in the Sejm by appealing to the patriotism of the szlachta in their provincial diets (*Sejmiks*) in order to raise local units for the army. But as Frost concludes in his survey of their work, "the last of the Vasas was also the last of the Jagiellons," and the Polish–Lithuanian monarchy then entered a new and harsher age.[221]

In opposition to the centralization of royal power, the szlachta culti-vated a "Sarmatian myth," a widely held belief that the nobles all shared a common descent from the legendary brave and free horsemen of the

---

[220] The relevant chapters by Oscar Halecki, A. Bruckner, and W. Tatarkiewiez in *The Cambridge History of Poland to 1696* remain useful surveys. But cf. Andrzej Wyrobisz, "The Arts and Social Prestige in Poland between the Sixteenth and Eighteenth Centuries," in J. K. Fedorowicz (ed.), *A Republic of Nobles. Studies in Polish History to 1864* (Cambridge University Press, 1982), pp. 153–78, who argues that as a result of the spread of humanist ideas the szlachta looked to the Roman Republic for models of civic virtue, even as they began to trace their ancestry to the Sarmatians who were never conquered by the Romans. Such contradictions did not seem to bother them.

[221] Robert I. Frost, "Obsequious Disrespect. The Problem of Royal Power in the Polish–Lithuanian Commonwealth under the Vasas, 1587–1668," in Richard Butterwick (ed.), *The Polish–Lithuanian Monarchy in European Context c. 1500–1795* (New York: Palgrave, 2001), pp. 159–68, quotations on pp. 167 and 168.

steppe and constituted a unique civilization.[222] Sarmatianism took its name from the Latin term for Poland, Sarmatia. The myth that the szlachta had descended from the nomadic Sarmatian tribes of the second century was similar to that of the Hunnic heritage invoked by the Magyar nobles.[223] In the age of romantic nationalism they claimed to be the only true representatives of the nation. The Sarmatian idea rested on three tenets: the szlachta as the warders of "the granary of Europe"; the garrison of "the bulwark of Christianity"; and the embodiment of the "golden liberty" that made Poland superior to the rest of Europe.[224]

Sarmatianism was really a product of the Polish Baroque, together with institutions of resistance to royal power in Poland like the confederation and the liberum veto.[225] Under Russian occupation these appeals to "ancient" privileges were strengthened and diluted by the revival of Occidentalism, that is, the use of the language of the Enlightenment to argue for a Polish mission to spread civilization to the east. Its advocates perceived first Napoleon and then Alexander I as the instruments of this mission. In both cases disillusionment came quickly and the inherent tension between Polish values (Sarmatianism) and foreign influences (the Enlightenment) came to the surface. During the uprising of 1831 voices on the left found a dialectical synthesis in the clash of traditions by proclaiming: "as to liberal principles and institutions, we were ahead of all

---

[222] As there is no agreed corpus of Sarmatian ideology, interpretations differ over its significance in Polish history. One representative of its all-compassing and powerful influence can be found in the work of Maria Boguska, especially *The Lost World of the "Sarmatians." Custom as the Regulation of Polish Social Life in the Early Modern Times* (Warsaw: Academy of Sciences, Institute of History, 1996). For Andrzej Walicki, Polish freedoms of the sixteenth century were of the ancient republican tradition of collective decision making and not the modern freedoms of private rights. "The Political Heritage of the Sixteenth Century and its Influence on the Nation-Building Ideologies of the Polish Enlightenment and Romanticism," in Samuel Fiszman (ed.), *The Polish Renaissance in its European Context* (Bloomington, IN: Indiana University Press, 1988), pp. 34–38. The key to him was the "moral unity" of the szlachta, which enables him to give a spirited defense of the liberum veto.

[223] Stanisław Cynarski, "The Shape of Sarmatian Ideology in Poland," *Acta Poloniae Historica* 9 (1968): 5–17, provides a balanced view of the problem.

[224] Jerzy Michalski, "Le Sarmatisme et le problème d'Europésation de la Pologne," in Vera Zimányi (ed.), *La Pologne et la Hongrie* (Budapest: Akadémiai Kiadó, 1981), pp. 113–20; Andrzej Walicki, *Poland between East and West. The Controversies over Self-Definition and Modernization in Partitioned Poland* (Cambridge, MA: Harvard University Press, 1994), pp. 9–11.

[225] Confederacies were originally based on royal authority, but by the sixteenth century they were being formed by szlachta and clergy in defense of their privileges. In the eighteenth century, they proved to be vulnerable to outside influence and were exploited by the Russians to keep Poland weak. But the Confederation of the Bar in 1768–1772 served just the opposite function, that is, to oppose foreign domination. Michal Wielhorski, *Sur la restoration du gouvernement* (Paris, 1775). The use of the liberum veto underwent a similar evolution.

the nations of Europe." The myth of Poland's moral superiority had been born.[226] The Polish diaspora, inspired by the uprising, preached a new revolutionary messianism that combined an idealization of the gentry republic with a cult of martyrdom and resurrection that was all the more powerful for being articulated by great poets and intellectuals such as Adam Mickiewicz, Juliusz Slowacki, and Zygmunt Krasinski.[227]

The idea that the szlachta state represented an island of liberty amid the authoritarian empires, like the Muscovite and Ottoman, and the bureaucratic absolutism of the West, particularly the Habsburg Monarchy, was disseminated in hundreds of publications throughout the sixteenth and seventeenth centuries. According to one Utopian version by the Jesuit priest Walenty Peşki, the free, Polish way was "not a human but a heavenly way of life."[228]

The Sarmatian myth, like the "missions" of other multicultural states, contained the potential for promoting an outer as well as an inner messianic message couched in both cultural and political terms. Throughout the sixteenth century and into the seventeenth century eloquent advocates preached the Polish way to the East, especially among the Ruthenians. A Slavic-speaking people of the borderland between the Polish and Great Russian core areas, the Ruthenians were ideal subjects, having not yet developed a distinctive ethnolinguistic identity. In the mid-sixteenth century the pamphleteering priest and noble, Stanisław Orzechowski, proposed a formula, *"gente Ruthenus, natione Polonus,"* subsequently much cited, for those Ruthenians like himself who were devoted to the Latin civilization in its Polish version. In an earlier pamphlet, *Turcyki,* he also strongly supported the idea of a religious war against the Turks.[229] Along different lines, Polish cultural imperialism reached its climax during the Counter Reformation spearheaded by the Jesuits.

---

[226] Jerzy Jedlicki, *A Suburb of Europe. Nineteenth Century Approaches to Western Civilization* (Budapest: CEU Press, 1999), ch. 1, quotation on p. 33.
[227] Andrzej Walicki, *Philosophy and Romantic Nationalism. The Case of Poland* (Oxford University Press, 1982), especially Pt. 3, chs. 2 and 3. Walicki clearly distinguishes among the many voices of messianism.
[228] Andrzej Nowak, "Between Imperial Temptations and Anti-imperial Function in Eastern European Politics. Poland from the Eighteenth to the Twenty-First Century," in Kimitaka Matsuzato (ed.), *Emerging Meso-Areas in the Former Socialist Countries. Histories Revived or Improvised?* (Sapporo: Slavic Research Center, Hokkaido University, 2005), p. 250.
[229] Orzechowski linked the Sarmatian myth to Polish success in the borderlands in the following way: "Could Poland have conquered the ancient and more numerous peoples, such as the Rus', otherwise than by these liberties?" *Ibid.* citing Stanislaw Orzechowski, *Wybor pism,* ed. J. Starnawski (Wroclaw: Zakład Narodwy im. Ossolińskich, 1972), pp. 99–114.

The Sarmatian myth, with its corresponding institutional enshrinement of szlachta liberties, was a powerful ideology for spreading Polish influence to the east. But its success depended on a parallel process of "latinization" of Orthodoxy. In other words, the cultural integration of the state meant both the polonization of the Lithuanian nobility and its conversion to Catholicism. This required a reversal of the federalist idea that had bound together the two parts of the Commonwealth since the fourteenth century and had culminated in the Union of Brest. Thus, at the same time the Polish szlachta engaged in its on and off conflict with royal power, it also sought an alliance with the Church to foster its own integrationist ideology.

The Counter Reformation in the Commonwealth completed the identification of szlachta and the Roman Catholic Church. Although the Protestants were the main target of the Counter Reformation in Poland, the Jesuit Order also launched a campaign to revive the spirit of the Union of Florence and restore the schism with Orthodoxy. Among their chief spokesmen was the fiery Piotr Skarga, first rector of the University of Wilno in the northeast borderlands and an advisor to the king. Skarga was the author of "On the Unity of the Church of God and on the Greek Deviation from that Unity," published in 1577. His tract defined Orthodoxy as a heresy and outlined conditions for unity with Catholicism that amounted to complete absorption rather than any real compromise. His plan represented an effort to integrate the eastern borderlands by reviving the idea of a union between the Latin and Greek Orthodox hierarchies that would bring the Ruthenian population under the authority of the Roman pontiff. But there were other plans proposed by members of the Catholic hierarchy that foreshadowed a union based on acceptance by the Orthodox of the spiritual authority of the pope and theological uniformity in return for recognition of Slavonic rites of the Ruthenian Church. From among the szlachta came a third variant of unity contained in "utopian" proposals to reunite Christianity by recognizing the essential similarity of the two faiths and the need to combine them on an equal basis. But this was very much a minority position.[230]

At the same time as these plans were being proposed, the Church mounted a vigorous educational and propaganda campaign to convert the Orthodox in the eastern borderlands of the Commonwealth. Its missionary work could not always count on the direct support of the state, but by the 1590s royal policy was moving away from its previous policy of toleration toward a more "confessional" stance. This may have been in

---

[230] M. V. Dmitriev, *Mezhdu Rimom i Tsargradom. Gnezis Brestskoi tserkovnoi unii* (Moscow: Izd. Moskovskogo Universiteta, 2003), pp. 265–73.

part a reaction to the reestablishment in 1589 of the Moscow patriarchate, which claimed jurisdiction over the Orthodox clergy of Lithuania and Ukraine. But the decisive initiative leading to the Union of Brest was taken by the Orthodox bishops of the eastern borderlands of the Commonwealth. By the 1590s the Orthodox hierarchy in Ukraine was embattled. Their dilemma was a classic case of elites in a contested borderland. Pressed hard by Polish Catholic proselytizing, on the one hand, and pressure from the Moscow patriarch, on the other, they also faced an internal challenge to their spiritual leadership from the Orthodox lay brotherhoods and rampant heresies within their own church. They took the dramatic step of seeking reconciliation with the Catholic Church that would preserve their liturgy and customs in return for recognizing the authority of the Roman pontiff. But, in the words of Mikhail Dmitriev, "the history of the Union of Brest was the history of illusions," built upon a mutual miscomprehension of Catholics and Orthodox churchmen.[231]

The reconciliation and assimilation of the Orthodox was only partially successful. Initially, the movement won support among the Orthodox hierarchy (from szlachta families) and lay magnates who saw it as a means of reforming corruption and abuses in their Church. Acceptance of the Uniat Church by some Lithuanian nobles signified another step in their polonization. Resistance quickly surfaced among the Ruthenian Orthodox lay brotherhoods in the towns. They regarded the Union as another example of szlachta arrogance and the loss of local control over the appointment of clerics. Even before, but especially after the Union of Brest, a fierce propaganda war broke out between Catholics and Orthodox. The Polish government denounced the Orthodox spokesmen as fanatical heretics and opposition to the Uniat Church as criminal. The hybrid church never penetrated into the mass of the peasant population of the borderlands and was fiercely rejected by the Cossacks.[232]

The polonization of the Ruthenian nobles, integrated into the Commonwealth by the Union of Lublin in 1569, had been far-reaching but was not complete by the mid-seventeenth century. Inhabiting the eastern marches of the Grand Duchy of Lithuania (Volynia and Kiev), they retained their own language and Orthodox religion even as they accepted the szlachta mental universe based on the Sarmatian myth. They differed from the Polish nobles in several significant ways. They

---

[231] Dmitriev, *Mezhdu Rimom i Tsargradom*, p. 283.

[232] Serhii Plokhy, *The Cossacks and Religion in Early Modern Ukraine* (Oxford University Press, 2001). It was not until the second decade of the seventeenth century that the Cossacks actively intervened in the religious struggle on the side of the Orthodox, *ibid.*, pp. 100–13.

cooperated with townsmen through the lay brotherhoods and with the clergy through the tradition of an active laity. Their location on the frontier of the Pontic steppe forced them to become more active in military life and even at times to conduct their own foreign policy with neighboring powers, the Russians, Tatars, and Turks. The impact of their contacts with nomadic societies and Islam on their lifestyle and outlook may well be insufficiently appreciated.[233] It would be anachronistic to speak of a nationalist or even protonationalist feeling among them. But like the Uniat Church and the Cossack brotherhoods, the Ruthenian nobility contributed to a complex regional identity that the Commonwealth failed either to assimilate or to integrate as a distinctive culture in the body politic.[234]

Opposed by the bulk of the Orthodox but never entirely accepted by the Catholic population, the Uniat Church survived mainly in Galicia after the partitions of Poland. There it subsequently became one of the cultural foundations of Ukrainian nationalism in the nineteenth century and the movement for independence in the twentieth century.

The Union of Lublin and then the Union of Brest created new possibilities for Polish economic and cultural expansion in Lithuania. Some historians regard it as the last great achievement of the Jagiellonian spirit of federalism as well as the high point of humanistic culture of the Renaissance, which attained its farthest penetration of the East. After the Union of Lublin in 1569, the Polish magnates were able rapidly to expand their holdings in the rich agricultural regions of the Lithuanian realm, that is, Ukraine, and to impose serfdom on what had been a free population, which reached its full expression by the 1640s.[235] At the same time, deteriorating conditions in the center led to the flight of peasants and the urban lower classes to the same region, adding to the socioeconomic discontent. The growing influence of the Catholic Polish magnates created resentment among the local Orthodox elites and the peasantry,

---

[233] Frank Sysyn, "The Problem of Nobilities in the Ukrainian Past. The Polish Period, 1569–1648," in Ivan L. Rudnytsky (ed.), *Rethinking Ukrainian History* (Edmonton: Canadian Institute of Ukrainian Studies, University of Alberta, 1981), pp. 36–41, 52–59, 63.

[234] Traditionally, Polish and Russian historians have differed, as might be expected, over a wide range of issues connected with the creation of the Uniat Church. Representative defenders of the two positions can be found in the older accounts of S. M. Solov'ev, *Istoriia Rossii s drevneishikh vremen* (Moscow, n.d.), vol. X, pp. 1408–409; and Oscar Halecki, *Borderlands of Western Civilization. A History of East Central Europe* (New York: Ronald Press, 1952), pp. 181–85. Cf. Dmitriev, *Mezhdu Rimom i Tsargradom*, pp. 7–29, for a comprehensive review of the literature.

[235] Robert I. Frost, *After the Deluge. Poland–Lithuania and the Second Northern War 1655–1660* (Cambridge University Press, 1993), p. 7.

who looked to the Cossacks for leadership in a massive uprising that shook the foundations of the Commonwealth. It was here that the szlachta failed to develop a borderlands policy that might have secured its position in Ukraine, a tantalizing possibility more fully explored in Chapter 4.[236] The szlachta defense of its feudal liberties sapped royal power when, in the eighteenth century, the rulers of predatory neighbors were increasing theirs. The failure to combine noble and royal power in the Commonwealth was fatal.

Comparisons and contrasts

In designing imperial ideologies and cultural practices in the multicultural states, rulers and their advisors showed a surprising flexibility in adapting to changing circumstances engendered by the struggle over the borderlands. Traditions and myths were frequently invented or reinterpreted, and then transmitted to the ruling elite and the rest of society through new rituals, ceremonies, monuments, and historical narratives. During certain periods in the course of empire-building, the rulers displayed a willingness to extend toleration to heterodox beliefs and ideologies that arose on the peripheries of the centers of power. Long before the French and the Industrial revolutions, the Eurasian empires were receptive to external cultural influences. Even when faced with the potentially destructive impact of the dual revolutions, individual rulers and groups within the ruling elites made efforts to incorporate or synthesize new currents of thought into the hegemonic culture.

Yet the ruling elites never freed themselves completely from the ideological bedrock of the dynastic idea, the founding myths, and their adherence, if only formally, to a mission or a destiny. Myths functioned to provide legitimacy and the basis for social solidarity among the elites. They generally embodied a universalist theology that could be variously interpreted. The Russian tsars posed as the champions of Orthodoxy wherever it existed, but avoided crusading on its behalf; the Habsburg emperors gradually gave up their idea of achieving a universal empire and settled for a more modest Austrian mission in the Balkans; the Ottoman sultans and the Iranian rulers embraced exclusivist messianic variations of Islam and then abandoned them in practice; and the Chinese emperors embraced the idea of the Middle Kingdom or Celestial Empire as the sole legitimate polity, but in practice they repeatedly settled for

---

[236] A discussion of these reformist impulses belongs more properly to the following chapter on imperial institutions.

compromise of their universalist claims. In the nineteenth century secular trends engendered by the dual revolutions in the west eroded the religious foundations of imperial rule. Representatives among the ruling elites perceived the advantages of incorporating nationalizing elements into the imperial ideology, but the mixture was not a good fit.

In the Habsburg, Romanov, and Ottoman empires the decline of religious fervor, if not religious imagery, as a spiritual mainstay of empires, inspired attempts by officials and loyal intellectuals to devise supranational ideologies in order to combat the rising tide of nationalist agitation. The origins of the pan movements illustrate how the transfer of ideas among intellectuals of the multicultural empires became increasingly common in the nineteenth century. Pan-Germanism, pan-Slavism, and pan-Islamism or pan-Turkism were not officially embraced by any of the rulers of the three empires, yet they exercised a greater or lesser degree of influence within the ruling circles and at times were a decisive factor in determining policy. There have been attempts to portray one or more of these pan movements as protonationalist.[237] While there is some truth in this, it is important to make a crucial distinction among them on the basis of their religious and racial components. The idea of pan-Germanism as preached by Georg Ritter von Schönerer was predominantly racial and anti-Semitic. It had its origins in the Habsburg Monarchy, not Germany, and had little appeal even among the German-speaking population. Its main influence came after its dissolution and the rise of National Socialism.[238] Pan-Slavism had its origins in the Habsburg Monarchy. Its Russian advocates mixed religious (Orthodox), national (Great Russian), and racial (Slavic) elements in various combinations. While it was never officially adopted by the imperial government, its proponents exercised an intermittently strong influence on foreign policy, particularly in 1877 and after 1910.[239] Throughout the nineteenth century, the phantoms of pan-Germanism and pan-Slavism continued to inhabit imperial space by frightening one another.

Of the three transcendent ideologies, pan-Islamism had the strongest religious component and came closest to official recognition by a ruler, Sultan Abdülhamid II, who revived the office of the caliphate in the

---

[237] See, for example, N. R. Keddie, "Pan-Islam as Proto-Nationalism," *Journal of Modern History* 1 (March 1969): 17–28.

[238] Andrew Whiteside, *The Socialism of Fools. Georg Ritter von Schönerer and Austrian Pan-Germanism* (Berkeley, CA: University of California Press, 1975).

[239] B. H. Sumner, *Russia and the Balkans, 1870–1880* (Hamden, CT: Archon Books, 1962), ch. 2; David MacKenzie, *The Serbs and Russian Pan-Slavism, 1875–1878* (Ithaca, NY: Cornell University Press, 1967).

Ottoman constitution of 1876 (only implemented in 1908).[240]
Paradoxically, pan-Turkism, in both its cultural and political manifestations, originated with the ideas of Western Turkologists, especially the
Hungarian Armenius Vámbéry, and the Russian Turks, especially the
Crimean Tatar Ismail Gasprinskii.[241] As a representative of the accommodationist or collaborator tendency among Muslims in the Russian
Empire, Gasprinskii preached the message popularly known as jadīdism
(the new method). It was a form of Turkic cultural nationalism that
reinterpreted Islam along rational lines that would grant autonomy and
tolerance to science and philosophy; reform education along more practical and productive lines by teaching a simplified Turkish, adding
Russian while retaining Arabic; empowering women by eliminating accretion of customs such as veiling not sanctioned by the Koran; and stressing
the need for economic initiatives and technological progress.[242] Jadīdism
never evolved into a unified cultural or political movement: "there were
many Jadīdisms in the Russian empire, each with its own concerns rooted
in local social struggles."[243] Pan-Turkism reached the peak of its influence in the Russian Empire during the 1905 revolution and thereafter
declined under tsarist pressure. In the Ottoman Empire, pan-Turkism

[240] A highly amorphous idea, pan-Islamism differed in important ways from other pan
movements in the Ottoman Empire, including Ottomanism and pan-Turkism, which
were not free from an ethical-religious substratum, but gave more prominence to secular
reform. See Landau, *The Politics of Pan-Islam*, esp. ch. 1, and Mardin, *The Genesis of
Young Ottoman Thought*.
[241] Armenius Vámbéry, *Travels in Central Asia. Being an Account of a Journey from Teheran
Across the Turkomen Desert at the Eastern Shore of the Caspian to Khiva, Bokhara and
Samarkand Performed in the Year 1863* (New York: Praeger, [1864] 1970), pp. 435–36,
declared that the Ottoman Empire had missed its chance to become the dominant power
in the borderlands of the Caucasus and Central Asia: "In its character of Turkish
dynasty, the house of Osman might, out of the different kindred elements with which it
is connected by the bond of common language, religion and history, have found an
empire extending from the shores of the Adriatic far into China, an empire mightier than
that which the great Romanoff [sic] was obliged to employ not only force but cunning to
put together out of the most disconnected materials. Anatolians, Azerbaizhani,
Turkmens, Özbegs [Uzbeks], Kirghiz and Tatars are the respective members out of
which a mighty Turkish Colossus might have risen, certainly better capable of measuring
itself with its northern competitor than Turkey as we see it in the present days." Could
Enver Pasha have said it better?
[242] Landau, *The Politics of Pan-Islam*, pp. 146–56; Edward Lazzerini, "The Jādid Response
to Pressure for Change in the Modern Age," in Jo-Ann Gross (ed.), *Muslims in Central
Asia. Expressions of Identity and Change* (Durham, NC: Duke University Press, 1992),
pp. 151–66.
[243] Adeeb Khalid, *The Politics of Muslim Cultural Reform. Jadidism in Central Asia* (Berkeley,
CA: University of California Press, 1998), p. 93. The most successful moment in the
jadīd strategy of accommodation came in the 1920s under Soviet power as part of the
general trend toward indigenation, but was then just as quickly snuffed out by Stalin.
Ibid., pp. 297–300.

and pan-Islamism were rivals, and the latter-day influence of pan-Turanianism, despite its endorsement by Enver Pasha, was much exaggerated by Western commentators.[244]

None of these supranational ideas gained a mass following under imperial rule. The reasons are clear enough. Although they too embraced "imagined communities," they could not compete with the emotional and psychological appeals of nationalism as a state-building ideology; for the imperial elites they represented potentially disruptive rather than unifying ideologies in multicultural societies; and they carried dangerously explosive implications for foreign policy. After the collapse of empires, however, the pan movements were revived, revised, and manipulated through propaganda as another weapon in the struggle over the borderlands. Hitler acknowledged his debt to Schönerer; Stalin more than once appealed to Slavic unity against the Germans during the Second World War. The brief and farcical adventure by Enver Pasha in the chaos of the post-First World War Caucasus and Central Asia did not put an end to pan-Turanian aspirations, which continued to exist quietly in Turkey despite government opposition throughout the Second World War.

At the end of the nineteenth century, the rulers of the multicultural empires reacted against secular trends by reviving older religious or ethical traditions. These efforts split the new reforming elites educated in the values of rationality, science, and technology as the preferred means of solving contemporary problems. Moreover, neither the old myths nor their embellishment with a national gloss could satisfy the aspirations or secure the loyalty of the peoples of the borderlands. Demands for autonomy increased as the dynastic ties frayed and the countervailing nationalizing pressures built in the borderlands. The survival of the empires increasingly rested upon *force majeure*. The danger increased of a major war in defense of the imperial idea that would end in the destruction of the imperial state.

The defeat and disintegration of the Eurasian empires represented in many ways a radical break with the past. New men, rising from obscure backgrounds, organizing mass parties, and unfurling new ideological banners, were state-builders on the ruins of empire. Yet the period after the fall represented a *translatio imperii* similar to that which over a much longer time span followed the collapse of the Roman, Byzantine, Sasanian, Mongol, and Ming empires. To be sure, the dynastic idea was dead, except in Iran where it briefly revived in the form of a national monarchy.

---

[244] Michael Reynolds, "Buffers, not Brethren. Young Turk Military Policy in the First World War and the Myth of Panturanism," *Past and Present* 203 (May 2009): 137–79.

Elsewhere, it was supplanted by the idea of a secular ruler, often bearing the title of leader (*führer, vozhd, gazi,* or simply chairman), whose legitimacy and authoritarian power derived from a newly invented political theology and personal charisma broadcast by technologies of communication and techniques of mobilization. Nevertheless, the different ideological foundations of these regimes had roots in the imperial past. The lineage was not direct, but well within the tradition of coping with the demographic challenge of state-building in a multicultural milieu that required that the ideal type of nation-state as approximated in the West be transcended. This did not mean a denial of the national idea. Rather, these new rulers adopted some of the same techniques of nationalizing their rule over multiethnic populations as their imperial predecessors.

The transfer of de-sacralized imperial ideologies was surprisingly direct, although the inspiration came from a deviant tradition. Such was the case with Hitler's racial theories with their links to the pan-German ideas originating in the Habsburg Monarchy; or with Stalin's ideas of "nationalist in form but socialist in content," reflecting his debt to the Austro-Marxists; or with Sun Yat-sen's three principles of "nationalism, democracy and socialism," modified by Chiang Kai-shek along neo-Confucian lines. The szlachta–Sarmatian myth that nourished Polish romantic nationalism together with the federal idea still inspired Polish elites in the twentieth century. In reconstructing Poland after the First World War, Marshal Piłsudski, himself a man of the Lithuanian borderlands, sought to restore a Jagiellonian-type, multicultural state under a republican form of government. Stalin's rule represented a new response to the persistent problems that confronted the tsarist multicultural empire which drew on earlier traditions. If ideology was the scaffolding of the multicultural empires, the military and civil bureaucracies constituted the supporting walls and protective roofs. This is the subject of the following chapter.

3   Imperial institutions: armies, bureaucracies, and elites

If the struggle over the borderlands profoundly affected state-building in the multicultural societies of Eurasia, the reverse was also true. The two processes interacted with one another not only in shaping imperial ideologies, but also in constructing political and socioeconomic institutions. Three key elements in the evolving structures of empire were the army, the bureaucracy, and the ruling elites. This chapter deals with the ways in which these institutions and groups reflected the particular needs of a multicultural state in expanding and defending its military frontiers and imposing order in the borderlands.

The exercise of power in the multicultural states of Eurasia combined in different proportions elements of what Max Weber identified as charismatic, patriarchal, and bureaucratic forms of authority. As he noted, "the majority of all great continental empires had a fairly strong patrimonial character until and even after the beginning of modern times."[1] But pure patriarchalism probably never existed. In its most arbitrary forms it gradually diminished without entirely disappearing under the increasing need of the ruler for a more reliable system of raising revenue and a greater functional specialization in administration. In an imperial, multicultural system the personal authority of the ruler depended heavily on his ability to project charisma through myths, symbols, rituals, and ceremonies of power that had meaning for peoples of different cultures. But charisma, as Weber and others also remind us, is unstable.

No matter how universal the appeal of a transcendent ideology, the personal failings of an individual ruler could erode his legitimacy. To guard against the dangers of their empires dissolving into its component parts, the patrimonial rulers of multicultural states needed to transfer and

---

[1] Max Weber, *Economy and Society. An Outline of Interpretive Sociology*, eds. Guenther Roth and Claus Wittich, 2 vols. (Berkeley, CA: University of California Press, 1978), vol. II, p. 1007, quotation on p. 1013.

transform part of their personal charisma into permanent institutions.[2] Because the Eurasian empires were conquest states with shifting, military frontiers and incompletely assimilated borderlands, the army proved time and time again to be the glue of imperial rule. At the same time, prolonged frontier warfare also played its role in affecting the structure of the armed forces and in driving the periodic need for military reforms. The demands of building and holding together a multicultural state continued to shape the character of the armed forces until the collapse of the empires. In the end, the collapse came about when the loyalty and cohesion of the army began to dissolve. Long serving as the glue of imperial rule, the army ultimately became its solvent.

The second institutional bulwark of imperial rule was the centralized professional bureaucracy. It performed a dual function: first, mobilizing human and financial resources for the support of the armed forces; and, second, devising administrative policies along a wide spectrum ranging from assimilation to autonomy aimed at securing the acceptance of imperial rule by the diverse populations of the conquered borderlands who were accustomed to different cultural practices. The bureaucracies imposed additional, if informal, restraints upon the ruler and weakened some of the older interests that asserted rival claims to the resources of the country.[3] The bureaucrats were not free-floating actors, but were rooted in the social structures of the multicultural states. Their outlook and behavior was always modified by special economic and social interests organized in a variety of institutional forms, depending on whether they drew their power from traditional intermediary bodies such as households, clans, tribes and estates, or the court. The growth of professional armies and bureaucracies ran along roughly parallel lines. The top civil and military ranks, together with religious leaders of the dominant faith, the upper reaches of the nobility, the leading merchants, and entrepreneurs formed the ruling elites, or what Norbert Elias called "the core group" of imperial rule.[4] Their ethnic composition also reflected the multicultural character of imperial rule. The membership was cosmopolitan and was augmented by the co-optation of local elites from the conquered borderlands as a means of guaranteeing order, integrating the economy, and weakening potential opposition to imperial rule.

---

[2] Cf. Edward Shils, "Charisma, Order and Status," *American Sociological Review* 30 (April 1965): 201.
[3] Weber, *Economy and Society*, vol. I, pp. 223, 229; vol. II, pp. 1006–13, 1028, 1112–121, 1136, 1149.
[4] Norbert Elias, *The Court Society* (Oxford University Press, 1983), pp. 117–29.

In the Eurasian empires the process of creating a professional bureaucracy was prolonged and, within individual states, uneven. It was only in the mid-nineteenth century that a third layer of institutional structures was introduced, that is, a empire-wide elected parliament and a constitution: first, in the Habsburg Monarchy and Ottoman Empire, where it was aborted; then, in the early twentieth century, again in the Ottoman and for the first time in the Russian, Iranian, and Qing empires. These changes further impinged upon patriarchal authority but, to repeat, did not entirely eliminate it.

The key to state-building cannot always be found in centralizing policies, which were often unevenly and only partially applied. The sheer size and diversity of the empires and the persistent challenge of maintaining the military frontiers frequently forced rulers to grant administrative autonomy to regional or provincial elites. For example, the Habsburg Empire displayed a veritable patchwork of administrative units, with Bohemia, Galicia, and Hungary having their own representative estates, while crown lands like Bukovina were ruled directly from Vienna. In the early nineteenth century Russia's western borderlands, Finland, the Baltic provinces, and the Kingdom of Poland, were granted representative institutions denied to the Great Russian core provinces. The Ottoman Empire had a long history of extending different forms of autonomy to Hungary, the Crimean khanate, the Danubian principalities, Egypt, and the Arab provinces. At times, the Qing dynasts extended different types of provincial rule to Xinjiang, Mongolia, and Manchuria. In Qajar Iran the province of Azerbaijan enjoyed long periods of autonomy. Adaptations to local conditions and cultures explain in part the longevity of empires, despite their location in a highly competitive Eurasian world. Bargaining with local elites was often the most effective means of ensuring stability in the borderlands; a measure of the underestimated flexibility of imperial rule. In certain cases, like the Ottoman and the Iranian, the recourse to devolution may have helped to prolong the longevity of empires, while it may also have contributed to the loss of refractory borderlands by encouraging separatism.

In the struggle over the borderlands, however, the comparatively greater institutional centralization and rationalization in the Russian Empire by the end of the eighteenth century was beginning to provide the resources necessary to gain a critical advantage in the wars with its rivals along the complex frontiers of Eurasia. This is often forgotten in the tendency of historians to employ another standard of comparison with the Western powers in order to conclude that the process of rationalization in Russia had not gone far enough.

It is also well to remember that the relationships between the centers of power and the borderlands were dynamic and interactive. The aim of this chapter is to give equal emphasis to contrasting tendencies in the evolution of imperial rule: bargaining and concessions alternating with coercion and repression; and reactions by groups in the borderlands ranging from armed resistance through passive acceptance to active cooperation with the imperial authorities.

Military revolutions

From the inception of their struggle over the borderlands, the Eurasian conquest empires faced a common challenge arising from the changing nature of warfare. From the sixteenth to the nineteenth centuries three major transformations or revolutions took place in the conduct of warfare, all of which originated in the states of Western Europe and were only subsequently adopted or imitated elsewhere. Like most so-called revolutions, they were really a series of uneven changes spread over decades, although their long-term effects were in fact revolutionary. Technology transfer and tactical innovations constituted only a small part of the military revolutions, the nature of modern warfare, and hence the outcome of subsequent phases of the struggle over the borderlands. During the development of each one of these transformations, the costs of manufacturing of new, more complex weaponry, organizing the supply, recruitment, and training of professional armies, and constructing fortresses not only required greater centralization, but also provided the driving force behind financial and administrative reforms that promoted political and economic convergence within Eurasia during the early modern period.[5]

The first, or "gunpowder," revolution began with the earliest use of gunpowder in the thirteenth century, leading to the development of firearms, handguns, muskets, and cannon. The Eurasian "gunpowder empires" of the Ottoman, Safavid, and Mughal dynasties, as Marshall G. S. Hodgson called them, gained multiple advantages in their struggle with the nomadic societies by borrowing the new technology from Europe and employing it in the process of building an empire. In addition, they developed a superior administrative organization based on a rich resource base of surplus food production and precious metals which they obtained through both plundering and taxation.[6] They were slower to introduce the

---

[5] Victor Lieberman (ed.), "Transcending East–West Dichotomies. State and Culture Formation in Six Ostensibly Disparate Areas," in *Beyond Binary Histories. Re-Imagining Eurasia to c. 1830* (Ann Arbor, MI: University of Michigan Press, 1999), pp. 71–75.

[6] Marshall G. S. Hodgson, *The Venture of Islam*, 3 vols. (University of Chicago Press, 1974), vol. III, pp. 13, 18, 25–26. For the Ottoman case, see Rhoades Murphey, *Ottoman Warfare 1500–1700* (New Brunswick, NJ: Rutgers University Press, 1999); for the Qing, see Nicola

changes in training and tactics initiated in the West during the second, so-called "military revolution." The main problem here was the resistance of tribal, private, or privileged military formations to the creation of a centralized, professional standing army.

The dating and character of the second "military revolution" remains disputed. Michael Roberts originally proposed it as a radical change in linear infantry tactics devised by Maurice of Nassau in the late sixteenth century and refined by the Swedes under Gustavus Adolphus in the Thirty Years War. Geoffrey Parker correctly noted that there were parallel and independent innovations in the French, Dutch, and Habsburg armies. In his view, the three interrelated elements of a military revolution were the invention of the Italian bastion trace, the spread of firearms on a large scale with greater reliance on artillery, and a large increase in the number of armed forces. He located these developments in the latter half of the sixteenth century.[7] Jeremy Black argued for a later dating at the end of the seventeenth and beginning of the eighteenth centuries when the imposition of greater administrative order and the introduction of new financial instruments enabled the absolutist monarchies to field truly massive armies.[8] The development of a modern, professional army was

di Cosmo, "Did Guns Matter? Firearms and the Qing Formation," in Lynn A. Struve (ed.), *The Qing Formation in World Historical Time* (Cambridge, MA: Harvard East Asian Center, 2004), pp. 121–44.

[7] Geoffrey Parker, "The Military Revolution 1560–1600. A Myth?" *Journal of Modern History* 48 (1976): 195–214; Geoffrey Parker, *The Military Revolution. Military Innovation and the Rise of the West, 1500–1800* (Cambridge University Press, 1988).

[8] For a review of the debate see T. F. Arnold, "War in 16th Century Europe. Revolution and Renaissance," in Jeremy Black (ed.), *European Warfare, 1453–1815* (New York: St. Martin's Press, 1999), pp. 23–44. For critics of the concept altogether, see John Childe, *Warfare in the 17th Century* (London: Cassell, 2001). As to whether the changes gave an advantage to the Habsburg over the Ottoman armies, see Parker, *The Military Revolution*, who claims it did, and Murphey, *Ottoman Warfare*, who argues there were no major differences before 1680. Jeremy Black, "Military Organizations and Military Change in Historical Perspective," *Journal of Military History* 62 (October 1998): 871–93. Cf. Paul Kennedy, *The Rise and Fall of the Great Powers* (New York: Random House, 1987), ch. 1; William Hardy McNeill, *The Pursuit of Power. Technology, Armed Forces and Society since A.D. 1000* (University of Chicago Press, 1982), ch. 4. It is more likely that the different nature of warfare in Europe with its sieges and reliance on infantry tactics as opposed to the war of movement in the Eurasian steppe was a more important factor in the technological "lag." See V. J. Parry, "La manière de combattre," in V. J. Parry and M. E. Yapp (eds.), *War, Technology and Society in the Middle East* (London: Oxford University Press, 1975), pp. 218–56; Colin Imber, "Ibrahim Pecevi on War. A Note on the European Military Revolution," in Colin Imber *et al.* (eds.), *Frontiers of Ottoman Studies. State, Provinces and the West* (London: Tauris, 2005), vol. II, pp. 7–22, stresses the superiority of Austrian defensive infantry tactics over Ottoman cavalry, a legacy of steppe warfare. But cf. Michael Hochedlinger, *Austria's Wars of Emergence. War State and Society in the Habsburg Monarchy, 1683–1797* (London: Pearson Education, 2003), p. 127, who notes that the Ottoman army, at least the janissaries, adopted the superior flintlock muskets earlier than the Habsburgs, although this did not help them much in the war of 1683–1699.

the result of what William H. McNeill has called a managerial and a psychological transformation. Logistics, mapping, standardization of equipment, a rational hierarchy of command, strict discipline, and even different concepts of what constituted honorable combat all meant radical alterations in the administrative structures of the state and the behavioral patterns of its servitors.[9]

The rising costs of war in the late sixteenth century and throughout the seventeenth century due to the large increase in the size of armies, the construction of more elaborate fortresses, and the production of more technically refined weapons occurred during a period when the destabilizing effects of silver bullion flows from the New World created severe financial problems for the Eurasian as well as the European economies, although there is much dispute over the nature and extent of the "seventeenth century crisis."[10] Pre-imperial Muscovy was spared the most debilitating economic effects due to its relatively autonomous, inner-directed economy and the weak commercial ties to the West.[11] The formal institution of serfdom in 1649 further insulated the economy from outside influences, while at the same time creating the potential basis for a stable tax-paying population and a source of recruits that would enable Peter the Great to construct his centralized militarized state as a powerful competitor in the struggle over the borderlands in the eighteenth century.

The third transformation, which began in the mid-nineteenth century, reached a climax on the eve of the First World War. Its two key components were the mechanization of warfare and conscription. From the early eighteenth to the mid-nineteenth centuries the technology of weaponry had remained more or less the same and officers had required little specialized education.[12] The application of steam-driven power and mechanized production to the mass production of small arms, artillery,

[9] McNeill, *The Pursuit of Power*, pp. 158–84.
[10] For the Ottoman Empire, see Halil Inalcik with Donald Quataert (eds.), *An Economic and Social History of the Ottoman Empire*, 2 vols. (Cambridge University Press, 1994), vol. II, pp. 525–26, 531–42, 572–73; for the Chinese (Ming) Empire, see Frederic Wakeman, Jr., "China in the Seventeenth Century Crisis," *Late Imperial China* 7 (1986): 1–26; Evelyn S. Rawski, "Was the Early Qing 'Early Modern'?" in Struve (ed.), *The Qing Formation*, pp. 211–13. For Hungary, see Vera Zimanyi, *Economy and Society in Sixteenth and Seventeenth Century Hungary (1526–1650)* (Budapest: Akadémiai Kiadó, 1987), pp. 27–37, 77–85.
[11] Fernand Braudel, *Civilization and Capitalism, 15–18th Century, vol. III: The Perspective of the World* (New York: Harper & Row, 1984), pp. 441–55.
[12] Walter Pintner, "The Burden of Defense in Imperial Russia, 1725–1914," *Russian Review* 43 (1984): 15–35; Walter Pintner, "The Nobility and the Officer Corps in the Nineteenth Century," in Eric Lohr and Marshall Poe (eds.), *The Military and Society in Russia, 1450–1917* (Leiden: Brill, 2002), pp. 243–45.

and naval vessels, the construction of strategic railroads, and the use of the telegraph forced major changes in financing, organizing, and training armies.[13] Conscription was a practical realization of the idea of the nation-in-arms. Originally, the concept of the nation-in-arms may have been a myth propagandized by the leaders of the First French Republic and enshrined by Napoleon, but it was close enough to reality to inspire others to seek an equivalent. Not until the wars of German unification, however, did the idea of mass armies based on conscription become a common feature of the army reforms in all the Eurasian empires except for Iran. Even then, the multicultural profile of these states prevented the universal application of conscription.[14]

The Polish–Lithuanian Commonwealth

The Polish Commonwealth may serve as an example of a multicultural conquest state that peaked early in the struggle over the borderlands, and then faded rapidly because it failed to develop the twin pillars of power – a professional army and a bureaucracy – which enabled its competitors to stay the course and in the process to reduce the once largest state in Europe to a set of borderlands lodged between the German (Prussian and Habsburg), Russian, and Ottoman powers. At its height in the fifteenth and early sixteenth centuries, the Polish–Lithuanian Commonwealth possessed a sizable population and adequate resources for imperial ambitions. Although not an empire in the strictest sense of the term, the Commonwealth was a multicultural, expansionist state engaged in the struggle over the borderlands with the neighboring Russian, Ottoman, and Habsburg empires. The major missing ingredient in its institutions was strong royal authority. The kingship was elective rather than hereditary, lacking in a sacral myth, and confronted by an alternative ideology of legitimacy embodied in the traditional "liberties" of the Polish nobility (*szlachta*). Although challenges to centralizing policies existed among social or regional elites in all the Eurasian empires, they were fatally successful in the case of the Commonwealth. To be sure, the interpretation that royal authority steadily eroded from the fifteenth century under pressure from the szlachta has been disputed.[15] Like the idea of

---

[13] McNeill, *The Pursuit of Power*, pp. 223–61.

[14] Jörn Leonhard and Ulrike von Hirschhausen (eds.), "Multiethnic Empires and the Military. Conscription in Europe between Integration and Disintegration, 1860–1918," in *Comparing Empires. Encounters and Transfers in the Long Nineteenth Century* (Göttingen: Candenhoeck & Ruprecht, 2011).

[15] See especially Andrzej Wyczanski, "The Problem of Authority in Sixteenth Century Poland. An Essay in Reinterpretation," in J. K. Fedorowicz (ed. and trans.), *A Republic*

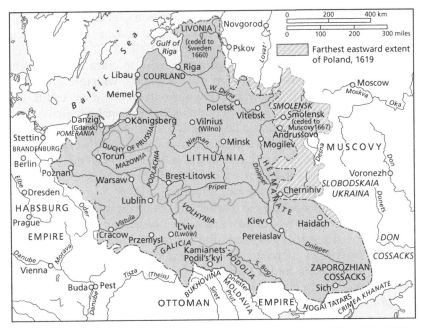

Map 3.1 Poland–Lithuanian Commonwealth at its height, 1660–1667

a prolonged Ottoman "decline," it oversimplifies a complex process, and ignores or denies possibilities for a different outcome. The szlachta sought relentlessly to impose restrictions on the power of the kings in the name of preserving traditional liberties.[16] But the contest was not one-sided. The szlachta was not unified in its defense of its collective political liberties. That it was divided into factions over the means of achieving its ends, and socially split between the upper level of magnates and the middle and lesser strata, enabled the kings to negotiate and to play one group against another.

Under the last two kings of the Jagiellonian dynasty in the sixteenth and early seventeenth centuries, a concerted effort was launched to strengthen the prestige and power of the central government. Although the Polish crown had been elective since the fourteenth century, the szlachta

of Nobles. Studies in Polish History to 1864 (Cambridge University Press, 1982), pp. 91–108; Robert I. Frost, After the Deluge. Poland–Lithuania and the Second Northern War 1655–1660 (Cambridge University Press, 1993).

[16] For a summary of their efforts, see Jerzy Lukowski, Liberty's Folly. The Polish–Lithuanian Commonwealth in the Eighteenth Century (London: Routledge, 1991), esp. pp. 9–25, 86–109.

assembled in the Sejm had traditionally elected a member of the Jagiellon family. In return they extracted various concessions, including tax exemptions, personal inviolability, and a decisive vote in making laws. From time to time the royal power sought to reverse the trend. Early in his reign Sigismund I (1506–1548) appealed to the Sejm to grant him sufficient revenue to maintain a standing army in order to cope with rebellion in the southeast (Ukrainian) borderland. He was only partially successful. His only clear victory was in gaining control over Episcopal nominations. A political movement by the middle range of the szlachta called "the execution of the laws" actually strengthened royal power by weakening the influence of the magnates. The result was an improved and more efficient central bureaucracy and a return of lands alienated from the crown to royal authority, increasing the king's revenue.[17]

Authorities differ as to exactly when the contest was lost for the royal cause. For the purposes of advancing the borderland thesis, a critical moment occurred in 1569 when the Union of Lublin completed the lengthy process of merging the Kingdom of Poland and the Grand Duchy of Lithuania into a single state with a common monarch and parliament.[18] In the election of 1573, the szlachta secured recognition of the principle of *viritim* whereby every noble in the realm was granted the right to participate in the election of the king. This had the effect of further restricting the influence of the magnates, but also of transforming the voting into something resembling an auction. The highest bidder was Henry of Valois, who accepted a whole series of concessions (the Henrician articles), virtually reducing the king to a figurehead. The next election of the Transylvanian prince Stefan Batory as king in 1576 checked the downward slide briefly. He won respect from the szlachta by his energy and military skills without resorting to institutional reforms. Batory was not only something of a military genius, he also recognized the need for a standing army. He created the first regular infantry units and enrolled 500 Cossacks as part of a paid cavalry force, thus lessening his dependence on the szlachta levée. An expansion and consolidation of these forces depended on financial approval by the Sejm, which was dominated by the szlachta. When Sigismund II Augustus (Zygmunt

[17] Wyczanski, "The Problem of Authority," pp. 98–100; Antoni Maczak, "The Structure of Power in the Commonwealth of the Sixteenth and Seventeenth Centuries," in Fedorowicz (ed.), *A Republic of Nobles*, pp. 118–19.
[18] Cf. Almut Blues, "The Formation of the Polish–Lithuanian Monarchy in the Sixteenth Century," in Richard Butterwick (ed.), *The Polish–Lithuanian Monarchy in European Context c. 1500–1795* (New York: Palgrave, 2001), pp. 63–67; Harry E. Dembkowski, *The Union of Lublin. Polish Federalism in the Golden Age* (Boulder, CO: East European Monographs, 1982), pp. 213–20.

August) (1587–1632) demanded a permanent yearly subsidy for the army to be approved by a majority vote, he ran into strong opposition. The szlachta interpreted this as a challenge to their traditional liberties, rightly suspecting him of autocratic, centralizing pretensions in order to promote his claims to the Swedish throne where there were fewer restraints on royal power. A brief civil war was repressed by the royal army, but the cause of constitutional reform was dead.

Another warrior king, Jan Sobieski, could still write a glorious page in Polish military history by helping to raise the Ottoman siege of Vienna in 1683. Thereafter, however, the history of the army is one of almost continuous decline in numbers and financing. The Sejm of 1699 reduced the army from 38,000 to 24,000. There was a brief expansion during the Great Northern War to 90,000, but the "Silent Sejm" of 1717 cut it back to its prewar levels and drastically reduced its tax base. Polish military expenditures that year represented only a fraction of those of the surrounding imperial rivals: about 43 percent of the Prussian, 27 percent of the Russian, and 16 percent of the Habsburg. By mid-century the Prussian army numbered 80,000, the Russian 200,000, and the Austrian 67,000. The actual military strength of the Polish Royal Army was about 16,000.[19]

The szlachta mentality also penetrated deeply into the tactical military sphere. Their "equophilia," as Norman Davies calls it, led to "an exaggerated dependence on the cavalry arm," an obsession the Poles found hard to shake even in the twentieth century. They affected a public display of chivalric attitudes that became increasingly divorced from reality as Poland sank into anarchy.[20] More than half a century before the First Partition, the surrounding powers perceived that the way to control Poland was to preserve its traditional liberties which guaranteed its military weakness. This was the turning point when Poland had *de facto* lost its independence.

The Habsburg Monarchy

The Habsburg rulers faced many of the same daunting problems in state-building as the Polish kings, but were more successful in solving them, or at least postponing their long-term destructive effects. Centralization of

[19] Lukowski, *Liberty's Folly*, pp. 109–13.
[20] Norman Davies, "The Military Tradition of the Polish Szlachta, 1700–1864," in Béla Király and Gunther E. Rothenberg (eds.), *War and Society in East Central Europe, vol. I: Special Topics and Generalizations on the 18th and 19th Centuries* (New York: Brooklyn College Press, 1979), pp. 41–44.

administrative authority and the raising of a professional army in the Habsburg Empire were achieved more by skillful bargaining and negotiation than by coercion. From the separation of the Austrian from the Spanish branch of the Habsburgs in 1521 until 1740, the growth of central institutions was an irregular and haphazard process. To put it even more forcefully, in the words of Robert Kann: "for the most part of the period between the time of the union of Hungary, Croatia and Bohemia with the hereditary Habsburg lands in 1526–1527 and the dissolution of the monarchy in 1918 the very concept of a Habsburg Empire as a constitutional entity was heavily contested."[21] As a result, Charles Ingrao has concluded, the Monarchy passed through eight major crises over three centuries that shook its very foundations and threatened dismemberment: in 1618–1620, 1683, 1704–1705, 1740–1741, 1790, 1809–1810, 1848–1849, and 1916–1918.[22] From the beginning the Monarchy was actually a *Hofstaat*, which administered a collectivity of territories assembled not by conquest, but through marriage and inheritance, bound together by medieval contracts and allegiances. Vienna was involved in endless "bargaining" with local vested interests.[23] The process became a recurrent feature of Habsburg history, and it enabled the empire to weather the storms of war and rebellion for almost five centuries.

As early as the reign of Ferdinand II (1619–1637), often considered the first absolutist, the dynasty anchored its authority on the twin principles of primogeniture and heredity, established its sole right to keep troops under arms, and subordinated the estates to the sovereignty of the ruler. It undertook to create a "Habsburg nobility" by distributing lands throughout the Monarchy (always excepting Hungary) in return for absolute loyalty to the throne with the object of weakening regional ties. Policies of cultural and social assimilation, which reached their high point in the Catholic Baroque, had no exact counterpart in the administrative realm. The two major central institutions for financing and maintaining the army in the long wars with the Turks over the borderlands were the *Hofkriegsrat* and the *Hofkammer*. Both were collegial bodies with overlapping functions. Contributions for the upkeep of the army came from a complex process of bargaining with the provincial *landtag* of the hereditary lands (*Erblande*). Consequently, there was no way of telling how much revenue would be available from year to year. When necessary the government had

---

[21] Robert A. Kann, "The Dynasty and the Imperial Idea," in *Dynasty, Politics and Culture. Selected Essays* (Boulder, CO: East European Monographs, 1991), p. 50.

[22] Charles W. Ingrao, *The Habsburg Monarchy, 1618–1825* (Cambridge University Press, 1994), p. 21.

[23] R. J. W. Evans, "Introduction," in Charles Ingrao (ed.), *State and Society in Early Modern Austria* (West Lafayette, IN: Purdue University Press, 1994), Pt. 1, p. 3.

to seek supplemental funding from foreign loans and subsidies (mainly Spanish for most of the sixteenth and seventeenth centuries and then British) and voluntary donations from the Church and the great noble families.

A regular Habsburg army began to emerge from the destructive military excesses of the Thirty Years War. Its prototype was created by Ferdinand III in 1649 when he refused to disband the imperial forces. In this way he sought to circumvent the resistance of the traditional estates represented in the provincial *landtag* to furnishing recruits. His initiatives weakened the authority of mercenary colonels whose private armies were the scourge of Central Europe. Thereafter, the emperors were also able at times of crisis to raise contingents from other states in the Holy Roman Empire.[24] Unlike the Russians, his successors were not able to centralize financing, supply, and recruitment, which remained mainly in the hands of the hereditary lands until the mid-eighteenth century.[25] Still, the ability to raise a powerful army was in striking contrast to what was happening across the frontiers in the Polish–Lithuanian Commonwealth.

Under the military entrepreneur system, mercenary colonels raised their own forces and hired the commanders of smaller units irrespective of origin or status. This long affected the ethnic and social structure of the Habsburg officer corps. The majority of colonels who owned regiments in the seventeenth century were foreign mercenaries, mainly Italians and Germans from the Holy Roman Empire, with a scattering of representatives of other national groups.[26] Leopold I (1657–1705) recognized that the army was the only institution apart from the court that was subject to his personal authority without the need to rely on the local elites and their elective institutions. His policy of recruiting foreigners independent of local diets to positions of command and then ennobling them was another method of assuring loyalty of the army. Changes began to take place only in the eighteenth century when, unlike the Prussian and Russian armies where nobleman and officer were virtually synonymous, the Habsburg army was increasingly officered by commoners except for the highest ranks and the elite guard and cavalry regiments.[27]

---

[24] Karl A. Roider, *The Reluctant Ally. Austria's Policy in the Austro-Turkish War, 1737–1739* (Baton Rouge, LA: Louisiana State University Press, 1972); John A. Mears, "The Thirty Years War and the Origins of a Standing Army in the Habsburg Monarchy," *Central European History* 21 (1988): 125–39.

[25] Hochedlinger, *Austria's Wars*, pp. 98–111.

[26] Thomas M. Barker, "Absolutism and Military Entrepreneurship. Habsburg Models," in *Army, Aristocracy, Monarchy. Essays on War, Society and Government in Austria, 1618–1780* (New York: Social Science Monographs, 1982), pp. 14–17.

[27] Fritz Redlich, "The German Military Enterprise and Work Force," *Vierteljahrsschrift für Sozial-und-Weltgeschichte* 47 (1964).

Throughout the seventeenth century, the army absorbed approximately 80 percent of the budget. By this time the Habsburg army had become a match for that of the Ottomans, their main rival in the struggle over the Balkan borderlands. In the early eighteenth century, it was able to fight on both ends of the double frontier against the Hungarian rebellion in the east (Kuruc War, 1703–1711) and to the west in the War of the Spanish Succession (1700–1714). A large part of the credit belongs to a trio of brilliant foreign military organizers and commanders: Raimondo Montecuccoli, Duke Charles of Lorraine, and Prince Eugène of Savoy. As president of the *Hofkriegsrat* from 1668 to 1681 and commander-in-chief, Montecuccoli unified civil and military control of the army. He reorganized the Austrian infantry, increasing its mobility and firepower. Having learned his lessons like so many others from the Swedish army in the Thirty Years War, he introduced light artillery and turned the cavalry into a more versatile force. Responding to the challenge of Ottoman warfare, he employed Croat horsemen as hussars and irregular infantry, an innovation among western armies. Key to the Austrian success on the battlefield was a reliance on constant drill and iron discipline in order to maintain a fire line in the face of the mass rushes of the Ottoman troops. A man of the Renaissance and a Renaissance man, he was one of the first commanders to develop a general theory of war.[28] That the commanders were also military planners who organized finances, constructed arsenals, and improved logistical support contributed to the establishment of a standing army of 100,000 that ranked with the best in Europe.[29]

The main shortcoming of the army continued to be its recurrent reliance on local diets to provide recruits and finances; a problem that was never entirely overcome especially in Hungary. Under Maria Theresa alternative proposals to solve the problem reflected the different combat conditions on the double frontiers. The advocates of a Prussian-style conscription supported by Joseph II and leading military figures were responding to the challenge of Frederick the Great on the northern frontier. Count Kaunitz advocated a strict separation of the army and society by proposing the highly militarized Military Border facing the Ottoman as a viable model. The "military party" won over Maria Theresa and her advisors. Conscription was introduced first into the Austrian–Bohemian provinces and then to Hungary. Recruitment of

---

[28] Azar Gat, *The Origins of Military Thought from the Enlightenment to Clausewitz* (Oxford University Press, 1989), pp. 13–24; Derek McKay, *Prince Eugène of Savoy* (London: Thames & Hudson, 1977).

[29] Jean Berenger, *Léopold Ier (1640–1705). Fondateur de la puissance autrichienne* (Paris: Presses universitaires de France, 2004), ch. 10.

foreign mercenaries was extended; a furlough system eased the lifelong service which was only abolished in 1802; regular regiments were formed; German became the language of command; and a whole set of improvements were introduced in the training and education of officers. The overall effect was to increase vastly the control of the sovereign over her subjects. By the end of her reign the army, now called "imperial-royal (*kaiserlich-und-königliche* or *k-u-k*), numbered 200,000 men.[30] The revitalized army had not been able to prevent Frederick II from seizing and holding Silesia, but it did help to preserve the Monarchy during one of its many moments of crisis.

These reforms were supplemented by equally far-reaching changes on the Military Border with the Ottoman Empire. It was turned into a reservoir of manpower for the regular armed forces. Joseph II sought to reduce expenditures by encouraging troops stationed more or less permanently on the Military Frontier to undertake some kind of gainful employment in peacetime.[31] There was even an "enlightened" aspect to these measures, for Joseph believed that these activities would contribute to the welfare and happiness of the soldiers.[32]

Of all the European armies, the Habsburg army was ethnically the most highly diversified. Recruited from all corners of the empire and beyond, its soldiers spoke a dozen languages, although the language of drill and commands remained German. During the Napoleonic Wars, reforms were introduced by Archduke Charles, the brother of the emperor and the most able general in the army. But there was no attempt to emulate the French or the Prussians in creating a truly national army. Charles strongly opposed a mass army on the French model, arguing that "such a mobilization would ruin industry and national prosperity, and disrupt the established order, including the system of government." He even distrusted the citizen militia (*Landwehr*), which was inspired by local patriotic motives.[33]

[30] Christopher Duffy, *The Army of Maria Theresa. The Armed Forces of Imperial Austria, 1740–1780* (North Pomfret, VT: David Charles, 1977), pp. 43, 46, 208–9, 218; Hochedlinger, *Austria's Wars*, pp. 303–16.

[31] Herman Freudenberger, "Introduction," in Charles Ingrao (ed.), *State and Society in Early Modern Austria* (West Lafayette, IN: Purdue University Press, 1994), Pt. 3, pp. 141–45; P. G. M. Dickson, *Finance and Government under Maria Theresa, 1740–1780*, 2 vols. (Oxford University Press, 1987), vol. II, p. 117.

[32] J. C. Allmayer-Beck, "Das Heerwesen unter Joseph II," in Karl Gutkas (ed.), *Österreich zur Zeit Kaiser Josephs II. Mitregent Kaiserin Maria Theresias, Kaiser und Landesfürst* (Vienna: Niederösterreichische Landesausstellung, 1980), pp. 42–43.

[33] Gunther E. Rothenberg, "Archduke Charles and the 'New' Army," in Béla Király and Albert Nofi (eds.), *East Central War Leaders. Civilian and Military* (Boulder, CO: Atlantic Research and Publishing, 1988), pp. 187–95, quotation from Charles' memorandum of 1804 on p. 191.

The performance of the Habsburg army in the Napoleonic Wars was mixed; it lost more battles than it won. Yet it was a key component of all the coalitions. Its mere staying power greatly assisted Metternich in gaining for the monarchy a leading role in European politics down to the revolutions of 1848. The main problem confronting the makers of military policy in Vienna was the dissatisfaction of the Hungarian elites with their role in the army. The Hungarians persistently opposed Vienna's control over the Military Border, although they continued to supply light cavalry units for the army. When the chips were down, the Hungarians rallied around the dynasty to resist Napoleon, unlike their Polish counterparts who supported him. Up to 1848 the Hungarians constituted 68 percent of the infantry stationed in Hungary and 43 percent of the army as a whole.[34] But ever since 1790 the Hungarian diet had repeatedly demanded the establishment of national units composed of Magyar-speaking officers and soldiers. Growing nationalist sentiments produced similar, if less sharply defined, friction between the German command and Czech, Italian, and even Polish troops. Vienna's response was twofold. The predominantly aristocratic officer corps and long-term recruitment for soldiers (up to the 1840s) was complemented by the well-known policy of stationing troops of one nationality in the territory of another – which paid off in the revolutions of 1848/9.[35]

The supreme test for the army came in 1848/9. Rebellions throughout the monarchy, both in the center and in the borderlands, appeared to presage the disintegration of the state. But the army did not disintegrate into its national components. Regional commands in Bohemia, Lombardy-Venetia, and Croatia rallied to the dynasty. In Lombardy-Venetia, half to two-thirds of the troops remained loyal.[36] Although the fighting in Hungary took on some aspects of a national uprising, it also resembled a civil war. The loyal units of the "imperial and royal" army were a mix of all the nationalities, including Hungarians. The rebellious Hungarian army included Slovaks and Germans in its ranks. Individual soldiers were often confused, switching sides or deserting according to circumstances. To be sure, under the leadership of Lajos Kossuth the Hungarian diet declared independence. But the greater Hungarian state he envisaged was like the monarchy, multinational with its own

[34] Alan Sked, *The Survival of the Habsburg Monarchy. Radetzky, the Imperial Army and the Class War, 1848* (London: Longman, 1979), p. 49. The main problem for the army was insufficient funding. *Ibid.*, Pt. 1.
[35] Gunther E. Rothenberg, "The Habsburg Army and the Nationality Problem in the Nineteenth Century, 1815–1914," *Austrian History Yearbook* 3(1) (1967): 71–73.
[36] Lawrence Sondhaus, *In the Service of the Emperor. Italians in the Austrian Armed Forces, 1814–1918* (Boulder, CO: East European Monographs, 1990), p. 42.

borderlands in Slovakia, Transylvania, the Banat, and Croatia; this was a surefire recipe for generating opposition in these regions.

Although the loyal Austrian forces were gaining the upper hand, the young emperor, Franz Joseph (1848–1916), appealed for Russian aid in a moment of panic. Nicholas I, worried about the spread of revolution to Poland, was only too happy to respond. For the Russians the appearance of József Bem, a Polish general and exiled revolutionary, as commander of the successful Hungarian campaign in Transylvania was an ominous sign.[37] The Russian intervention earned them the undying enmity of the Hungarians, periodically reinforced over the following hundred years.

The unsteady loyalty of the polyethnic army contributed to the defeats in the wars of Italian and German national unification against France and Piedmont in 1859, and against Prussia in 1866. Desertions of Hungarian regiments at the battle of Solferino led to the withdrawal of the Hungarian corps from military operations. In 1866, two Italian regiments defected to the Prussians, and Hungarian prisoners of war formed an anti-Habsburg legion. These defeats persuaded Vienna of the necessity for reforms in the army and a political settlement with Hungary in 1867 that effectively divided the monarchy into two separate parts, linked by common foreign, financial, and military institutions. The terms of the economic compromise had to be renegotiated every ten years, giving rise to periodic conflicts over the size and apportionment of the military budget. The military provisions of the compromise provided for the common imperial-royal army, with dynastic insignia and German remaining as the language of command, two sources of resentment among Hungarians. In addition two militias were created: the *honvéd* for Hungary and the *landwehr* for Austria. The *honvéd* (defenders of the fatherland) had first been raised in 1848 as the core of the Hungarian national revolutionary army, and its re-creation was clearly a concession to Hungarian national sentiment.[38]

The reorganization of the armed forces, entrusted to the head of the Austrian military chancellery, Friedrich Beck, offered something to everyone, but satisfied no one.[39] He followed the Prussian model by creating a general staff to replace the system of ministerial domination and requiring

[37] István Deak, *The Lawful Revolution. Louis Kossuth and the Hungarians, 1848–1849* (New York: Columbia University Press, 1979). But cf. László Péter, "Old Hats and Closet Revisionists. Reflections on Domokos Kosáry's Latest Work on the 1848 Hungarian Revolution," *Slavic and East European Review* 80(2) (April 2002): 296–319.

[38] László Kontler, *Millennium in Central Europe. A History of Hungary* (Budapest: Atlantisz, 1999), pp. 251, 279, 290, 295, 300; István Deak, *Beyond Nationalism. A Social and Political History of the Habsburg Officer Corps, 1848–1918* (New York: Oxford University Press, 1990), p. 55.

[39] Scott W. Lackey, *The Rebirth of the Habsburg Army. Friedrich Beck and the Rise of the General Staff* (Westport, CT: Greenwood Press, 1995).

the completion of courses at the *Kriegsschule* for entrance into its membership. This preserved German domination of the officer corps. The two militias were intended for home defense, but the Hungarians were determined to transform the *honvéd* into something resembling a national army with Hungarian as the language of command.[40] There was no comparable movement by the Germans with respect to the *landwehr*, and it never evolved in the direction of an Austro-German national army. But Beck sought to integrate the *landwehr* and *honvéd* into the regular army and substitute a new levy called *landsturm* for home defense.

The imperial and royal army was never turned into a national force, although it was dominated by Germans through the language of command and the preponderance of Germans on the general staff (60 percent to 18 percent Slavs and only 4.5 percent Hungarians at the end of the nineteenth century) and the officer corps in general.[41] The monarch Franz Joseph retained his role as supreme commander, and was perfectly confident in using the *honvéd* to support Hungarian landowners in repressing agrarian disorder by their discontented peasants.[42]

Efforts to instill a supranational, dynastic loyalty in the army reached a peacetime climax during the celebrations of the imperial jubilee in 1898. Franz Joseph had adopted a military way of life as if to signal that the army (along with the Church) was the strongest guarantor of state unity; in this he was like the other rulers of the Eurasian empires. The symbolic fusion of the military and the Church, the two supranational pillars of the empire, infused the ceremonies throughout the jubilee year. The massive awarding of medals to the troops was accompanied by the distribution of a thirteen-page *Commemorative Pamphlet for the Soldiers on the Occasion of the Fiftieth Jubilee of His Majesty Franz Joseph I*. It was "in effect, an attempt to immunize the joint Army against the threat of radical nationalism."[43]

By this time the implementation of mass conscription had produced an army whose ethnic composition closely corresponded to that of the empire as a whole. Correspondingly, a regimental language was

---

[40] Rothenberg, "The Habsburg Army," pp. 77–78.

[41] Between 1895 and 1910 the percentage of German officers in the joint army was between 77 and 80 percent according to the calculations of Tibor Hajdu, *Tisztikar és középosztály 1850–1914. Ferenc József Magyar tisztjei* (Budapest: MTA Történettudományi Intézet, 1999), quoted in Gergely Romsics, *Myth and Remembrance. The Dissolution of the Habsburg Empire in the Memoir Literature of the Austro-Hungarian Political Elite* (Boulder, CO: Social Science Monographs, 2006), p. 216, n. 3.

[42] Péter Hanák, "Hungary in the Austro-Hungarian Monarchy: Preponderancy or Dependency?" in *Austrian History Yearbook* 3(1) (1967): 296–98.

[43] Daniel L. Unowsky, *The Pomp and Politics of Patriotism. Imperial Celebrations in Habsburg Austria, 1848–1916* (West Lafayette, IN: Purdue University Press, 2005), pp. 97–104, quotation on p. 99.

introduced, chosen on the basis of the unit's ethnic composition; if at least 20 percent of the regiment's soldiers spoke a native (non-German) language, then the officers had to learn and speak it as well. But attempts to achieve integration through a manipulation of imperial symbols and concessions to local nationalist sentiments fell short of creating a truly integrated army representing society as a whole. Only around 20 percent of those youths liable for military service were actually called to the colors, and the number who failed to muster kept increasing up to 1910 when it reached a figure of 22 percent.[44]

The Austro-Hungarian armed forces were designed not to fight a major war, but to maintain the delicate balance between the major components of the empire. Measured by the size of the defense budget and the percentage of the population annually conscripted, the Austro-Hungarian forces lagged behind the major European powers. In 1914, the army fielded fewer infantry battalions than in 1866.[45] Piecemeal reforms were introduced to improve the condition of the soldiers and the education of the officers. But there was no unified command or concentration of authority in the War Ministry, as was the case in the reformed Russian army. Franz Joseph, who fancied himself a soldier until 1859 when his failings were highlighted, played arbiter among the factions and rival departments with disastrous results in the First World War. By this time, the high command was in the hands of Conrad von Hötzendorf, the talented, modernizing chief-of-staff, who was committed to the idea of a preventative war, but pessimistic about the chances of the monarchy surviving it. The officer corps was socially isolated from the rank-and-file as well as the civilian population; first, by its oath to the emperor and direct subordination to him and, second, paradoxically, by its cultivation of a form of prestige based on an artificial, caste-like, social distinction between non-noble officers and the rest of society, and not on the hereditary privilege that bred a natural *noblesse oblige*. The result was a "bureaucratic army" ill-suited to fight wars in the nationalist era.[46]

The performance of the army in the First World War may seem to have refuted such a pessimistic conclusion. Aside from a few exaggerated incidents of unit mutiny or desertion, the army maintained its cohesion

---

[44] Christa Hämmerle, "Die Allgemeine Wehrpflicht in der multiethnischen Armee der Habsburgermonarchie," *Journal of Modern European History* 5(2) (September 2007): 227–35.

[45] Holger H. Herwig, *The First World War. Germany and Austria-Hungary, 1914–1918* (London: Arnold, 1997), pp. 12–13.

[46] Robert Kann, "The Social Prestige of the Officer Corps in the Habsburg Empire from the Eighteenth Century to 1918," in Király and Rothenberg (eds.), *War and Society*, pp. 113–37.

in the face of severe battlefield losses to the Russians in 1915. However, by the spring of 1918 the warning issued by Count Kasimir Badeni in 1895 was turning out to be correct: "a state of nationalities can make no war without danger to itself."[47] It might have been more correct to have said: "a state of nationalities can suffer *no general defeat* without *mortal* danger to itself." Once the compromise with Hungary had been sealed, the monarchy had two options in reorganizing the army in Cisleithenia. It could have permitted the formation of national units comparable to the Hungarian. This is what the Czechs advocated in their petitions to create a Czech national guard. Or it could have embarked on a program of Germanization of the army. Both options were fraught with political dangers. The monarchy reacted, as it often did, by pursuing neither course. The fragile compromise ensured only a modicum of loyalty to the dynasty.

The memoirs of former high-ranking officers, both German and Hungarian, reveal their belief that during the First World War the army, even including the Czech frontline units, were loyal to the end.[48] However, even before 1914 two different attitudes toward the primacy of imperial or national tendencies had already begun to show up among German-speaking officers. Those who called themselves Old Austrians identified with the dynasty and imperial rule. Another group, who perceived the process of nationalizing the empire as having advanced much farther, considered themselves to be primarily Germans or Austro-Germans. A similar line dividing Hungarian officers is more difficult to draw because of their more highly developed identification with Hungarian nationalism, and their ambivalence toward the imperial idea both as a protective cover for their national aspirations and a brake on the further development of those aspirations.[49] Underneath the surface, the rank-and-file were vulnerable to nationalist propaganda. In a time of a long and hard war this loyalty would become increasingly frayed.

In the first half of 1918, the Austro-Hungarian army was sorely tried by internal disturbances. In January, a mass strike movement with radical social and economic demands began in Vienna, spread to the Austrian provinces, then to Brno and Budapest where soviets were formed for the first time. With the Bolsheviks negotiating for peace, the government was able to move seven full-strength divisions from the Russian front to check the disorders. But fresh outbreaks occurred in the mining districts of Moravia. Again the army was forced to intervene. In early spring mutinies

[47] Cited in Rothenberg, "The Habsburg Army," p. 79.
[48] Romsics, *Myth and Remembrance*, pp. 14–15, 24, 27–29, 36–39.
[49] Romsics, *Myth and Remembrance*, pp. 51–58, 101–10.

broke out among Slovene, Ruthene, and Serb regiments, followed by the Czechs. Loyal units of the army suppressed them. But this was not 1848. In the view of Z. A. B. Zeman, the army had become "a blunt instrument; it eventually failed the Habsburg dynasty in its hour of need." By repressing the mass strikes, it enabled the nationalist leaders inside and outside the country to rally support without splitting the revolutionary movements into their potentially antagonistic national and social currents.[50] By August 1918, the Habsburg army was disintegrating into its component ethnic parts, beginning with the mass defection of the Croatian regiments. The new emperor, Charles, refused to use the army to check the national councils in the imperial borderlands that were organizing the dissolution of the empire.[51]

As the imperial army disintegrated, its officers and men attempted to reach their homelands, which were in the process of forming new states under national banners. But the tasks of defining and defending new boundaries along ethnolinguistic lines were formidable given the highly mixed populations in the imperial borderlands. While the Great Powers in Paris sought from afar to trace new boundaries for successor states by balancing the principle of national self-determination with economic and strategic requirements, local nationalist forces fought one another over disputed ground. Polish units made up of former soldiers of the Russian and Habsburg armies and General Haller's regiments from France were engaged at one time or another on three fronts, against the Germans, the Bolsheviks, and the Hungarians. The Czech units battled at home against the Hungarians and abroad against the Bolsheviks in Siberia as a way of winning Allied support for an economic and strategically viable, but multinational, Czechoslovak state that they would dominate. The Hungarians, though a defeated power, still fought under both a liberal and soviet government against the Romanians, Serbs, and Czechs. The k-u-k army had finally given birth to a set of quarreling national offspring.

The bureaucratic web

The attempts to bring together the disparate parts of the Monarchy through the creation of central bureaucratic institutions faced problems similar to those confronting the organization of a modernized, unified military. Although the largely German-speaking bureaucracy of the

[50] Z. A. B. Zeman, *The Breakup of the Habsburg Empire, 1914–1918. A Study in National and Social Revolution* (Oxford University Press, 1962), pp. 134–35, 139, 140, 143, 146, quotation on p. 219.
[51] Herwig, *The First World War*, pp. 436–37.

Habsburg Monarchy most nearly approached the Weberian ideal type, it too passed through a series of historical changes that altered its relationship to other corporate bodies in society and to the ruler as well. It is possible to discern four major periods in its evolution. During the seventeenth century, it took shape in reaction to threats to the integrity of the Monarchy from the Ottoman Turks and the Protestants. In alliance with the Catholic Church and the army as the three bulwarks of the empire, the bureaucracy fitted easily into the hierarchical Baroque model of government with its emphasis on conformity, rank, formal interpersonal exchanges, submissiveness to authority, and the theatricality of public occasions.

The coming of Maria Theresa to the throne in 1740 opened a new phase in the Habsburg campaign to reconcile conflicting local interests while promoting its policies of centralization and assimilation. The older picture of an increasingly rational and secular Austrian absolutism under Maria Theresa and Joseph II has undergone modification. What remains undeniable is the strong commitment of the army and the bureaucracy to a policy of centralization in order to cope with the demands of foreign policy, especially the Silesian wars against Prussia, and also the costs of frontier maintenance against the Turks. But in other areas resistance and countervailing pressures from the Church and the Hungarians forced them to act cautiously, to bargain, and to accept compromise. Throughout the period from 1740 to 1780 reforms at both the central and regional level established firm foundations for a modern administrative and financial structure. All the Weberian markers of bureaucratic practice were gradually, albeit tentatively, introduced: functional differentiation, regular salaries, clear-cut hierarchies of command.[52]

As was so often the case with the multicultural empires, military defeat was the most powerful incentive for financial as well as military reforms. When Maria Theresa, under attack by Frederick the Great, faced an empty treasury she turned to Count Wilhelm Haugwitz to introduce a new financial and administrative system throughout the empire. A scion of the cameralist school, Haugwitz was the driving force behind a project of administrative reform based on a union of the Bohemian and Austrian chancelleries. Subsequently, this institution became the embodiment of what Richard Evans calls an "oligarchy from Bohemia" in the bureaucratic governance of the Monarchy over the following half century. Whatever their ethnic origins, they shared a Germanized culture, were strong advocates of Josephinian reforms, and opposed Hungarian autonomy. Their loyalty to the Monarchy was most dramatically

---

[52] Dickson, *Finance and Government*, vol. I, chs. 9–10 are comprehensive.

personified in "the saviors of Austria in 1848, two Bohemian generals and a Bohemian statesman": Field Marshal Prince Alfred Windischgrätz, Field Marshal Josef Wenzel Radetzky (Radecký), and Prince Felix Schwarzenberg.[53]

Haugwitz also understood the necessity of turning the Theresianum Academy, founded by the Jesuits for the education of the sons of Hungarian aristocrats, into a secularized institution with instruction in German on public finance and economics. Although the plan to make German the language of the imperial bureaucracy proved premature, this was a first step.

It was not until Joseph II assumed full powers as emperor that a systematic effort was launched to create a new elite. Civil servants were given privileges unusual for the time, including regular income, regulated working hours, provisions for pensions, as well as the traditional rewards of titles and decorations. But there were obligations too. In order to obtain a high official post it was necessary to receive legal training, and bureaucrats were expected to begin their service in the provinces at the lowest level to gain practical experience.[54] Under Joseph II the old aristocracy dominated the high bureaucratic ranks, while the lower ranks became a place of employment and refuge for writers, poets, and scholars committed to progressive, rationalist reform until a reversal set in as a reaction to the French Revolution. The Josephinian reforms brought about immediate and direct improvements in the life of the serfs, prompting the origins of the *Führermythos*, the almost religious trust of the peasantry in the higher authority represented by the emperor.[55]

The new upwardly mobile groups in the bureaucracy steadily eroded the position of the aristocracy. Between 1840 and 1867 they gradually came to occupy two-thirds of the top positions. This new service nobility was composed of members of the urban, German-speaking middle classes, educated in the legal faculties of the universities. They developed a distinctive lifestyle ensconced under the name of *Biedermeier kultur*, which gave them a solid standing and high status in society from which,

---

[53] R. J. W. Evans, "The Habsburg Monarchy and Bohemia," in *Austria, Hungary and the Habsburgs. Essays on Central Europe, c. 1683–1867* (Oxford University Press, 2006), pp. 94–97.

[54] Waltraud Heindl, "Bureaucracy, Officials, and the State in the Austrian Monarchy. Stages of Change since the Eighteenth Century," *Austrian History Yearbook* 37 (2006): 35–57, who calls Joseph II "the founder of professional officialdom," at p. 39.

[55] E. Hanisch, *Österreichische Geschichte, 1890–1990. Der lange Schatten des Staates: Östereichische Gesellschaftsgeschichte im zwanzigsten Jahrhundert* (Vienna: Uberreuter, 1994), pp. 30–41.

if necessary, to challenge the hegemony of the nobility.[56] Despite the predominance of Germans in the bureaucracy, the official doctrine was to maintain strict ethnic neutrality, nourishing a perception by the bureaucrats that their loyalty was to the dynasty and not to the state.[57] With their concern for equality under the law derived from their professional training, the new elites sought to reduce the arbitrary and unpredictable character of the absolutist state. But they were hampered by the rules and regulations that blocked them from playing a major role in introducing major reforms. Thus, they were caught in a tension between obedience and innovation, which was broken briefly, if dramatically, by the revolution of 1848. But this merely reproduced the dilemma as a choice between order and chaos.

After 1848, the bureaucracy provided the state, shaken by revolution, with a stabilizing force that gave cohesion to the empire. In reaction to the centrifugal forces unleashed by the revolutions, a renewed effort was undertaken at the center to reform and standardize bureaucratic structures throughout the empire, including Hungary. The administrative style of the so-called neo-absolutist regime continued to influence Habsburg imperial rule until the end, despite the radical changes in the political relations between the center and peripheries. After 1867, it more and more assumed the role of creating a welfare state earlier than almost anywhere else in Europe. The bureaucracy emerged from the constitutional experiments of the 1850s and 1860s as a new three-dimensional, state-centralized administration in which a powerful étatist tradition coexisted with a politically influential system of local and regional corporate bodies (parties and interest groups), and a liberal constitutional ethos that emphasized individual political rights.[58]

The Hungarian borderland

The major problem facing the periodic centralizing tendencies of the Habsburg dynasty arose in the Hungarian borderland. Following the expulsion of the Ottoman forces from Hungary and the suppression by the Habsburg forces of the Hungarian *kuruc* (popular) in the war for independence, Emperor Joseph I (1705–1711) acknowledged the need for a compromise with the rebellious Magyar nobility. By the Treaty of

---

[56] Waltraud Heindl, "Beamtenum, Elitenbildung und Wissenschaftspolitik im Vormärz," in Hanna Schedl (ed.), *Vormärz. Wendepunkt und Herausforderung* (Vienna: Chölzl, 1983), pp. 56–60.

[57] Waltraud Heindl, *Gehorsame Rebellen. Bürokratie und Beamte in Österreich 1780 bis 1848* (Vienna: Böhlau, 1991), pp. 84–87.

[58] J. W. Boyer, "Freud, Marriage and Late Viennese Liberalism. A Commentary from 1905," *Journal of Modern History* 2 (March 1978): 72–74.

Szatmár in 1711 he agreed to observe their traditional liberties and to govern together with the diet in accordance with the laws of the country. The nobility who declared their allegiance to the emperor retained their landed estates, tax exempt status, and absolute authority over their serfs. In return the nobility reaffirmed their acceptance of hereditary Habsburg rule and their renunciation of the legal right to resist the central authority of the state as guaranteed by the Golden Bull of 1222. The conditions of the kuruc surrender were so mild in the eyes of the loyalist magnates that they complained about the arrogance of the rebel leaders "as if they had triumphed over the emperor."[59] Once the Ottoman threat had been repulsed, the main value of Hungary was to serve as a pacific borderland in the Habsburg rear while it pursued an ambitious dynastic foreign policy in Central Europe and the Netherlands.

Under Maria Theresa and Joseph II steps taken to co-opt the top stratum of the Hungarian nobility met with some measure of success. The lure of Vienna drew a number of aristocrats to build palaces in the Austrian capital rather than reside on their country estates. The loyalists were rewarded with high rank, decorations, and places in the civil and military bureaucracy. Among the most prominent examples of integration were family members of the old aristocracy, the Batthyánys, Zichys, Esterházys, and even the Pálffys and Károlyis, who were amnestied kuruc insurrectionists; Rákóczi's former general Sándor Károlyi even became a Knight of the Golden Fleece, Field Marshal, and guardian to the heir Joseph. The monarchy made a special effort to create magnates in Transylvania. In the complex world of intermarriages and personal networks the process of integration proceeded most strongly in the west of Hungary. Here the predominantly Catholic gentry who had remained loyal during the Rákóczi rebellion were increasingly drawn into the cultural and official life of Vienna. The two institutions which facilitated their integration were the Theresianum as a school for young Hungarian aristocrats and the army through the Royal Hungarian Bodyguard. By 1840 there were 4,300 appointed officials in Hungary. Most were trained in Hungarian law, but not all were Magyar speakers.[60]

But there were increasing signs of ambivalence toward the central administration even among some of the most ardent Hungarian loyalists. The Hungarian elite were shocked by the administrative restructuring of the empire and the proclamation of the German language edict under

[59] Kontler, *Millennium*, p. 189.
[60] Éva H. Balázs, *Hungary and the Habsburgs, 1765–1800* (Budapest: CEU Press, 1997), pp. 100–15; R. J. W. Evans, "The Habsburgs and the Hungarian Problem, 1790–1848," in *Austria, Hungary*, pp. 177–81.

Joseph II. Not only did his reforms tighten central control over the borderlands, including Hungary, but he ordered the removal of the crown of
St. Stephen from the country. "More than a symbol, it was of immense
political value in its own right; the whole exercise of royal authority was
intrinsic to it and its ownership."[61] The life and careers of two prominent
figures stand out in particular. Ferenc Széchény and József Podmaniczky
supported the idea of enlightened absolutist administration in the early
years of Joseph II, but turned against the social engineering of the latter
part of the reign as a threat to their particularist views and class position.[62]
Perhaps the most powerful countervailing factor in alienating Hungarian
nobles was the failure of the central administration to improve substantially the economic conditions in Hungary.

Hungary not only remained an overwhelmingly agrarian country well
into the nineteenth century, but it was also a relatively backward one. The
"agricultural revolution" in Western and Central Europe hardly reached
the Hungarian lands in the eighteenth century. Nearly a quarter of the
lowland areas was marshland or flooded for most of the year. The primitive two-field system and the lack of selective breeding of the abundant
livestock predominated everywhere outside a few estates of the magnates.
The peasantry was burdened by an increasingly heavy war tax, the quar-
tering of troops, and the obligation to provide transport and labor for the
army stationed on the volatile frontier with the Ottoman Empire.[63]

During the reigns of Maria Theresa and Joseph II the Hungarian nobles
entertained high hopes for a revival of the economy. But commerce
remained stagnant and the fragmentation of manorial land in the absence
of primogeniture reduced their income. Vienna adopted a policy of favoring one kind of urban conglomeration, the royal boroughs, over another,
the market towns, in order to strengthen its representation in the
Hungarian diet and gain the support of the German-speaking townsmen
against the Magyar clergy and nobility. But this tactic failed to expand the
burgher class and, where it did not antagonize the landed nobles, it proved
to be a disappointment.[64]

The two most severe blows sustained by the Hungarian economy in the
eighteenth century came as a result of Maria Theresa's need for money to
fight her wars. The Hungarian diet resisted her request to increase the war
tax and to exchange the general levy for a fixed cash payment. In retaliation she imposed a discriminatory custom reform in 1754 that raised

[61] Henrik Marczali, *Magyarország története II. József korában* (Budapest: Pfeifer F. Kiadása,
    1885–1888), vol. II, p. 364, cited in Evans, "The Habsburgs," in *Austria, Hungary*, p. 205.
[62] Evans, "The Habsburgs," in *Austria, Hungary*, pp. 204–11.
[63] Kontler, *Millennium*, p. 210.   [64] Kontler, *Millennium*, pp. 123–27.

duties on Hungarian exports to non-Habsburg lands and on Hungarian manufactured goods sold in Austria and Bohemia. Over the following twenty years, tough bargaining over the war tax persuaded her to impose another protectionist tariff in 1775 in favor of Austrian and Bohemian enterprises and non-Hungarian agricultural goods. She then prorogued the Hungarian diet, which did not meet again for thirty years.[65]

Conditions were particularly unstable in Transylvania where a major Romanian peasant rebellion broke out in 1784. It was sparked by Joseph's decision to carry out a trial census in the border villages preliminary to reinforcing the frontier guards. A rumor circulated that volunteering for military service in the militia would liberate them from the burdens of serfdom. The rebellion spread rapidly with the tacit and often open support from Orthodox priests and even Romanian gentry. The imperial command was reluctant to come to the aid of the Hungarian landlords and Joseph rebuked the landlords for organizing self-defense. Vienna finally ordered imperial troops to intervene. The repression was brutal, but was followed almost immediately by Joseph's Patent concerning serfs in Hungary. The minor concessions to the peasantry did not satisfy them, while at the same time antagonizing the Hungarian nobles who remained impervious to any fundamental social changes in the countryside.[66]

The immediate causes of the collapse of the Josephinian system within Hungary were a combination of external difficulties and internal resistance. The war against the Ottoman Empire was militarily successful but financially draining. Both a revolt of the estates in the Austrian Netherlands and the French Revolution reverberated in Hungary, where resistance to recruitment had briefly unified all elements of society. On the eve of his death Joseph revoked all his reforms and restored the Hungarian laws and institutions he had previously replaced. When the Hungarian Diet finally met again in 1790–1791, the nobility demanded a restoration of its traditional liberties. Inspired by the revolutions in America and France, they demanded further concessions to protect themselves against arbitrary rule by Vienna. At the same time, they also proposed administrative, judicial, and education reforms that would, nevertheless, preserve their dominant position in Hungarian society. It was a feudal reaction in modern dress. In the see-saw struggle between center and borderland, Joseph's successor, Leopold II (1790–1792), resorted to a time-honored Habsburg tactic of seeking to balance the Magyars by cultivating elements

[65] Horst Haselsteiner, "Cooperation and Confrontation between Rulers and the Noble Estates, 1711–1790," in Peter Sugar, Péter Hanák, and Tibor Frank (eds.), *A History of Hungary* (Bloomington, IN: Indiana University Press, 1994), pp. 149–51.
[66] Balázs, *Hungary*, pp. 222–32.

among the Orthodox population of Hungary and even among the peasantry. Resentful of the centralizing policies of Vienna and concerned over challenges to their cultural and socioeconomic dominance, the majority of magnates resorted to their traditional tactic of supporting the dynasty as the best method of ensuring their privileges, while agitating for the replacement of Latin and German in the public sphere by Magyar.[67] But a split was opening up in the ranks of the nobility, foreshadowing the deep division of the 1840s.

During the period of the French Revolution, according to Ernst Wangermann, "the democratic groups [in Hungary] were more numerous than anywhere else in the Habsburg dominions." They included lawyers, intellectuals, and civil servants in Pest and the provinces.[68] Two secret societies formed, but were ignorant of one another's existence. Like the Decembrist conspiracy in Russia a generation later, they differed over basic constitutional issues. The Society of Reformers proposed the establishment of a republic dominated by nobles. The serfs would be liberated but without property. The Society of Liberty and Equality stood for a popular and egalitarian republic. Betrayed by their amateurish activities, the so-called Hungarian "Jacobin" conspiracy ended in the arrest, imprisonment, and, in a few cases, the execution of its members under the repressive regime of Francis I (1792–1835). A generation of Hungarian literati was virtually snuffed out.[69]

In Vienna a few officials also recognized the need to respond to the enormous increase in state power organized by the French revolutionaries and Napoleon which enabled the Habsburgs' traditional enemy to mobilize unprecedented aggregates of human and productive resources for expansionist aims. Among them Count Clemens Metternich took the lead in proposing to recast the institutions of the Habsburg Monarchy. From the earliest years of his career he planned to create a "well-organized Council of State" as a means of strengthening the central power. To be appointed by the emperor, it would represent all the Habsburg lands including Hungary. It would serve as an advisory body, coexisting with a conference of ministers to coordinate the operations of the bureaucracy. But Francis II was suspicious of any apparent attempt to limit his power.

---

[67] George Barany, "The Age of Royal Absolutism, 1790–1848," in Sugar *et al.* (eds.), *A History of Hungary*, pp. 175–79.

[68] Ernst Wangermann, *From Joseph II to the Jacobin Trials. Government Policy and Public Opinion in the Habsburg Dominions in the Period of the French Revolution* (Oxford University Press, 1959), p. 138.

[69] Kontler, *Millennium*, pp. 220–22.

He not only refused to appoint a prime minister, but insisted on meeting with his ministers separately in what became known in Austria as *Kabinettsweg*.[70] Outside Vienna the most serious challenge to the centralization of the Monarchy continued to come from Hungary.

At the end of the eighteenth century the Hungarian lands were a mirror image of the Polish–Lithuanian Commonwealth. The two nobilities shared similar myths, cherished their ancient constitutional liberties, and claimed to represent their nation as a whole. But they were evolving in different directions: the Poles were about to lose their statehood and undergo incorporation into the three partitioning empires; while the Hungarians were on their way to restoring most of the attributes of statehood, culminating in the settlement of 1867.

Under the influence of post-Napoleonic ideas of romantic nationalism filtering in from the German states, a campaign gathered momentum among the Hungarian nobility at the Diet of 1825 to demand the substitution of Magyar for Latin as the official language of their deliberations. The idea began to stir powerful emotions that would transform the nobility's defense of its traditional privileges into a national movement. Additional demands to introduce Magyar as the dominant language of Hungarian schools and the administration steadily gained ground. By the 1840s, the noble elite linked the language issue to a series of political demands. At the same time, the earlier split in its ranks began to widen between those who sought a more moderate accommodation with Vienna and those prepared to pursue a more radical form of resistance, although in the eyes of Metternich they were all culpable of engaging in opposition to imperial rule.

At one end of the national movement, Count István Széchenyi sought to promote a set of cultural institutions that would fulfill his project of civilizing the nobility, a process of humanistic Magyarization that would transform what he called "an Asiatic colony in the heart of Europe."[71] He played a leading role in a number of ventures to achieve this goal, including establishing the Academy of Sciences, the National Casino – modeled on the English club – the Danube Steamship Navigation Company, horse breeding and racing, constructing the Chain Bridge linking Buda and Pest, and promoting public health. A believer in working within the imperial system, he conducted a lengthy epistolary exchange with

---

[70] Alan Sked, *Metternich and Austria. An Evaluation* (Basingstoke: Palgrave Macmillan, 2008), pp. 107–19.
[71] George Barany, *Stephen Széchenyi and the Awakening of Hungarian Nationalism, 1791–1841* (Princeton University Press, 1968), p. 223.

Metternich in the hope of persuading him to accept a gradual expansion of Hungarian control over their own affairs.[72]

At the other end of the national movement, Lajos Kossuth, representing a younger generation and the Protestant nobles, propounded Magyarization as part of a greater mission directed against the twin evils of *Deutschtom* and Slavdom, pressing in on the Hungarian borderland from two sides, and urged the creation of a Greater Hungary that would include unification with Transylvania, which was ruled directly from Vienna. He and Széchenyi crossed swords. In an 1841 pamphlet the elder statesman denounced Kossuth as a fanatic whose actions would lead to revolution and chaos. As "a people of the Orient," he reiterated, the Hungarians had to be transformed into a people of reason before they could assimilate the other nationalities.[73]

Maneuvered between these extremes, Hungarian politicians began to coalesce around two political poles. The neo-conservatives favored working closely with the Habsburg center in pursuit of a policy of "deliberate progress," which resembled the program of organic work in the Kingdom of Poland. The liberals, or radicals, took a firm stand against the Habsburg absolutism and demanded constitutional institutions for all the provinces within a unified kingdom. Their program became the basis for the sweeping reforms introduced in the first phase of the "lawful revolution" of 1848; lawful because it hearkened back to the program of the Diet of 1790; "lawful" too because its aspirations proved to be the basis for the peaceful compromise settlement of 1867 that created the Dual Monarchy.[74] In 1848/9, the "lawful revolution" quickly blossomed into a war of national liberation in which Kossuth and the radicals rapidly eclipsed the neo-conservatives. The repression of the uprising by the Habsburg imperial forces and the Russian army seemed to justify Kossuth's fears of *Deutschtom* and Slavdom as Hungary's greatest enemies.

The reaction of Vienna to the revolutions of 1848 that had shaken the Monarchy throughout its borderlands was to experiment with a series of constitutional and bureaucratic reforms aimed at reconstructing imperial rule on a more highly centralized foundation. These experiments failed largely because the Monarchy lost two wars against France with its Piedmont ally in 1859 and Prussia in 1866, leading to a result feared by the Habsburgs ever since the outbreak of the French Revolution, namely,

---

[72] Barany, *Stephen Széchenyi*, pp. 124–33; George Barany, "The Széchenyi Problem," *Journal of Central European Affairs*, 20 (1960): 258. See also Kontler, *Millennium*, pp. 232–40.

[73] Barany, *Stephen Széchenyi*, pp. 388, 404–6.

[74] Barany, "Age of Royal Absolutism," pp. 202–5, 211–17.

the effective expulsion of the Monarchy from its dominant position in Central Europe and the unification of the Italian and German states.

Following the defeat by Prussia, the Vienna government confronted three institutional alternatives: to continue the centralizing policies, which had little appeal outside the court, army, and bureaucracy; to introduce a federative policy, which the Slav politicians favored but the Hungarians opposed; or to strike a compromise with Hungary alone, which the spokesmen for the other nationalities opposed. The latter sentiment found a sympathetic response among the conservative and moderate liberal Hungarian politicians who had been only temporarily brushed aside in the revolutionary atmosphere of 1848. The young emperor Franz Joseph accepted the arguments of his foreign minister, Count Friedrich Beust, that: "We must stand, first of all, on solid ground ... This solid ground, as things stand at present, is the cooperation of the German and Hungarian elements in opposition to Panslavism." As early as the Crimean War, the emperor had considered reformulating the Austrian mission "to be the bearer of civilization in the lands newly won for Europe," that is, the Balkans.[75] Reaching out to one another, Austrian and Hungarian leaders were groping their way toward a new role in the struggle over the borderlands. They began to embrace the idea of Palmerston and other British statesmen that a dual monarchy would serve as a bulwark against Russian expansion and at the same time provide them with the solid ground, as Beust would have it, for a forward policy in southeastern Europe if it proved to be necessary to check the aspirations of Russia's client states in the region.

Most historians recognize that both the Austrian and Hungarian sides made concessions in 1867, but there is disagreement over which side gained the most. The compromise, or settlement as historians now prefer to call it, assured the monarchy of a degree of institutional stability for almost two generations. But its complicated institutional arrangements and procedures revealed its fundamental fragility.[76] The Czechs, Serbs,

---

[75] Eva Somogyi, "The Age of Neo-Absolutism 1849–1867," in Sugar *et al.* (eds.), *A History of Hungary*, pp. 235–51, with the quotation by Beust on p. 249; Evans, "The Habsburgs and the Hungarian Problem," pp. 173–92; Evans, "From Confederation to Compromise. The Austrian Experiment, 1848–1867," in *Austria, Hungary and the Habsburgs*, pp. 266–90, quotation from Franz Joseph on p. 290; R. J. W. Evans, "The Habsburg Monarchy and Bohemia," in *Austria, Hungary and the Habsburgs. Essays on Central Europe, c. 1683–1867.*

[76] The classic statement of Louis Eisenmann, *Le compromis austro-hongrois de 1867. Étude sur le Dualisme* (Paris: Société nouvelle librairie et d'édition, 1904), remains fundamental. But cf. Lázsló Péter, "The Dualist Character of the 1867 Hungarian Settlement," in György Ránki (ed.), *Hungarian History–World History* (Budapest: Akadémiai Kiadó, 1984), pp. 85–164.

and Romanians were excluded, and reacted bitterly, but even the Hungarians were not entirely satisfied. Their ruling elites continued to maneuver between a policy of accommodation on the surface and a sub rosa resistance. Their relationship with their king, also the Habsburg emperor, Franz Joseph, whom they despised, was marked by what András Gerö has called "a substantial measure of self-deception and lies."[77] Respectful on the surface, they continued to press for more advantages during the renegotiation of the compromise in 1897 and beyond. As George Barany pointed out, they were trapped by "the incompatibility of the two most cherished national goals, namely Hungary's 'complete' independence and the preservation or repossession of her 'thousand-year-old' territorial integrity."[78]

The settlement with Hungary made possible other institutional arrangements with the borderlands, most notably the *Nadgodba*, or little *Ausgleich*, between Hungary and Croatia, and the establishment of the formerly Polish province of Galicia as a crown land under Austrian administration. Galicia may serve as an instructive comparative example of how this policy worked.

The Galician borderland

The Habsburg policy of integrating Galicia – the Austrian share of partitioned Poland – resembled in some ways that of Russia in the Kingdom of Poland. Although the rhythm was different, there was a similar oscillation between granting greater or lesser degrees of autonomy. Austrian bureaucrats, like their Russian counterparts, played the ethnic card in attempting to divide and rule the Poles and Ukrainians. And in both regions the Polish response also alternated between collaboration and resistance, with, however, a stronger commitment in Galicia to the former. After 1867, the Austrian government had resorted to its traditional policies of bargaining with the most vocal and best organized local elites in the hope of winning them over to a peaceful competition within the constitutional system of the dual monarchy.[79] Bargaining and making concessions to

---

[77] András Gerö, *Emperor Francis Joseph, King of the Hungarians* (Wayne, NJ: Center for Hungarian Studies and Publications, 2001), p. 167.

[78] George Barany, "Hungary. The Uncompromising Compromise," *Austrian History Yearbook* 2 (1966): 234.

[79] For much of the following, see Ivan Rudnytsky, "The Ukrainians in Galicia under Austrian Rule," in Andrei S. Markovits and Frank Sysyn (eds.), *Nation Building and the Politics of Nationalism. Essays on Austrian Galicia* (Cambridge, MA: Harvard University Press, 1982), pp. 24–69; Piotr S. Wandycz, "The Poles in the Habsburg Monarchy," in Markovits and Sysyn (eds.), *Nation Building and the Politics of Nationalism*, pp. 69–92.

one national group, particularly on the language question, tended to incite a violent reaction on the part of another linguistic group within the same borderland. This is what happened in the Hungarian part of the Monarchy, as well as those regions where concessions were less freely distributed. In the crown land of Galicia the policy of co-optation and compromise worked well in the short term, but led in the long run to divisive consequences.

The reforms of Maria Theresa and Joseph II had directly challenged Polish hegemony over the two social groups that retained elements of a Ruthenian (Ukrainian) identity, the peasantry, and the Uniat Church. In the opinion of Joseph, who made three trips to Galicia, the province was steeped in barbarism and the work of civilizing it was "immense."[80] His agrarian reform limited the labor obligations of the peasantry and gave them *de facto* possession of the land. Even though much of his work was repealed shortly after his death, and many peasants were forced to sell their farms over the following decades, they venerated his name down to 1914.

With the growth of a Polish national movement in Galicia in the 1840s, the Austrian bureaucrats were handed a golden opportunity to split the peasants from their Polish landlords. In 1846, Poles in the free city of Krakow revolted under the banner of reestablishing pre-partition Poland. They attempted to rally the peasantry to their cause, but they refused to recognize the demands of Ruthenian intellectuals for political equality for all citizens. Local Austrian officials incited the peasants to launch deadly attacks on their Polish landlords, while the police and army stood aside. Across the frontier, Nicholas I reacted to the Galician massacres by issuing a proclamation restricting the authority of Polish landlords over their peasants. The incongruous alliance between imperial bureaucrats and Polish peasants doomed the revolution in Krakow and helped to forestall a general rising of the Poles against both the Habsburg and Russian empires. "The year 1846 [also] made a laughing stock of the Poles in the eyes of the Ruthenian peasants."[81]

At the same time, the Austrian bureaucrats had begun to take a positive interest in the idea of a Ukrainian national movement as a counterweight to the dangers of both Polish and Russian (pan-Slav) cultural influences in the Habsburg borderlands. On the eve of the revolution of 1848, the

---

[80] Larry Wolff, *The Idea of Galicia. History and Fantasy in Habsburg Political Culture* (Stanford University Press, 2010), pp. 14–19.

[81] Jan Kozik, *The Ukrainian National Movement in Galicia, 1815–1849* (Edmonton: Canadian Institute of Ukrainian Studies, University of Alberta, 1986), p. 162, citing a contemporary Ruthenian intellectual.

governor of Galicia, Count Franz Stadion, preempted the Polish landlords and forestalled peasant revolutionary agitation by proclaiming the
abolition of the *robot*, the feudal dues, with indemnification. But the
government reneged on its promises to settle the question of demarcating
the manorial and peasant holdings. Once the revolutionary agitation had
died down, it was more appealing for Vienna to win back the support of
the Polish landlords.[82]

Vienna's religious policy proved to be more successful. By renaming the
Uniat Church as the Greek Catholic Church and granting it equal status
with Roman Catholicism, the Monarchy transformed it from an instrument of Polish domination to an embryo of the Ukrainian National
Church that emerged full-blown after 1848. Decrees of Maria Theresa
and Joseph II had raised the status of the Greek Catholic seminaries to
institutions of higher education. In 1848, young Ruthenian graduates
became the first leaders of the Ruthenian national movement. Their
children formed the core of the secular intelligentsia that led the movement to 1918 and beyond. A second reform upgraded the hierarchy and
administrative staff, restored the Metropolitan of Halych, and established
a cathedral chapter for the bishops of Przemysl and Lemberg (L'viv).
These innovations too were long lasting, remaining in place to 1946.[83]
But it took another half a century before the Ruthenians could emerge as a
counterweight to the Polish economic and cultural domination of Galicia.
And then the results were not what Vienna anticipated. An alternative
strategy of encouraging German colonists to settle in the province as a
counterweight to Polish dominance fell short of expectations. The small
number of settlers who responded was quickly assimilated into the dominant Polish culture. Viennese officials grudgingly reached the conclusion, after a series of shocks forced their hand, that the only alternative was
to reach an accommodation with Poles who were willing to serve the
Monarchy loyally.

After the partitions of Poland, accommodation with Austrian rule in
Galicia had been limited to the upper ranks of the szlachta. Widespread
resistance among the lesser gentry and former Polish army officers
reached a peak in 1809 with Napoleon's occupation of Vienna.
Conspiracies were hatched in 1830, but, unlike what happened in the
Kingdom of Poland, they were snuffed out by the Austrian police before
they flared into rebellion. On the eve of 1848, the Polish leaders in the

---

[82] Kozik, *Ukrainian National Movement*, pp. 20–22, 164–65, 184–88.
[83] John Paul Himka, *Religion and Nationality in Western Ukraine. The Greek Catholic Church
and the Ruthenian National Movement in Galicia, 1867–1900* (Montreal: McGill and
Queens University Press, 1999), pp. 6–8, 11.

Habsburg Monarchy were divided over a strategy of liberation. Some favored an uprising in all three parts of partitioned Poland; others sought to promote a general European war against Russia from bases in Galicia and the Grand Duchy of Posen in Prussia.[84] The revolutions of 1848 broke out even before Vienna abolished labor services on private estates, thus depriving the szlachta of support from their peasants. In the end, they joined the Hungarians in the hope that by acting together they could reestablish their historic boundaries in the lands between their twin enemies, the Austro-Germans and the Russians. The military recovery of the Habsburgs and the massive invasion by the Russian army in 1849 crushed the revolutions in Galicia and Hungary and restored the status quo. But the Habsburg leaders extracted a different lesson from the debacle than the Russians. Henceforth, they would reverse their policy in Galicia and seek a settlement with those Poles who were willing to collaborate.

In 1867, the settlement with the Galician Poles enabled them to join the Germans and Magyars as one of the three master races in the Habsburg Empire, although the road to accommodation was a rocky one. After 1848, Polish aristocrats had worked to extract autonomy from Vienna in exchange for unswerving loyalty as a counterweight to the Hungarians. Step by step they won further concessions: first, the establishment of an elective Sejm; then, the elevation of Polish to the same level as German in official business. These were followed by the opening of Jagiellonian University with Polish as the language of instruction, the creation in 1871 of a Ministry of Galician Affairs in Vienna, and the establishment in 1873 of a Polish Academy of Sciences. The position of viceroy was held by a Pole, Agenor Gołuchowskli, for sixteen out of the twenty-five years between 1850 and 1875. But autonomy meant the rule of the Polish landlords – only 10 percent of the population could vote – over the Ruthenian peasantry. The Monarchy rewarded their desire to collaborate by making the viceroyalty of Galicia a Polish monopoly and appointing a Polish *Landesmeister* for Galicia as a permanent fixture of every Austrian cabinet. Two Polish aristocrats, Count Alfred Potocki and Count Kazimierz Badeni, became the only non-German prime ministers of the Dual Monarchy. For the rest of the century, Poles were more prominent in the central ministries than were any other of the non-German nationalities.[85]

---

[84] Benjamin Goriely, "Poland in 1848," in Francois Fejto, *The Opening of an Era. 1848* (New York: Grosset & Dunlop, 1948), pp. 372–75.

[85] James Shedel, "Austria and its Polish Subjects, 1866–1914. A Relationship of Interests," *Austrian History Yearbook* 19/20(2) (1983/4): 23–42; Wolff, *The Idea of Galicia*, pp. 200–2, 227–28.

By the last decades of the Monarchy, the Habsburg bureaucracy engaged the corporate bodies of the borderlands in an almost continuous process of bargaining in order to circumvent the deadlock in parliament produced by the conflict between the nationalities. After 1897, ministerial appointments were made increasingly from the higher levels of the civil service. The bureaucracy retained, and in some cases even strengthened, its control over a mass of internal administrative matters from regulating trade and industry, sanitation, and primary school education to criminal justice. Yet the bureaucracy, like the army, failed to provide the integrating function necessary to reconcile the competing interests of the borderlands and the center. Bureaucrats remained divided over their duty to the emperor and the state, and unnerved by the struggle between the center and the nationalities into which they were reluctantly drawn.[86]

The entangled relations with the political parties further reduced the effectiveness of the Habsburg bureaucracy as the elected representatives of the nationalities sought to use the powerful administrative state to their own advantage.[87] This process survived the collapse of the Monarchy. The elites of the successor states, many of them tempered in the Habsburg political arena, continued to rule by combining a powerful centralized bureaucracy with an elected parliament. But the differences were striking. Unlike the discarded imperial model, parliaments were controlled by the dominant ethnic group in the country without the mediating presence of the emperor. There was little bargaining with minorities. It was a formula that easily gave way to authoritarian rule.

The Russian Empire

In the struggle over the borderlands Russia began to lengthen its lead over its rivals under Peter I, "the Great." Although he had no grand design, his policies aimed at centralizing the administrative, financial, and military institutions of the empire, eliminating internal opposition, and incorporating and assimilating Eurasian borderlands from the Baltic to the frontiers of China. His decision to build a new capital on the extreme northwestern periphery of his empire was, perhaps, the boldest attempt to reconfigure the symbolic role of the imperial city. The move, imposed by force on a recalcitrant population, advertised his aspiration to reorder the priorities of Russian foreign policy and cultural orientation. By

---

[86] Heindl, "Bureaucracy, Officials," p. 48.
[87] Hanisch, Öesterreichische Geschichte, p. 232; for a case study of bargaining, see G. B. Cohen, Education and Middle Class Society in Imperial Austria, 1848–1918 (West Lafayette, IN: Purdue University Press, 1996), pp. 108–26.

disdaining to encircle his new city with walls, despite the fact that it was being constructed on land that still belonged to Sweden, he declared his intention to continue the war to victory no matter what the cost, and to begin the task of breaking through the barrier states blocking Russia's direct access to Europe. Without exaggeration, it can be said that this decision set the course of Russian policy over the following century of acquiring the western borderlands in the struggle with, and at the expense of, Sweden, the Polish–Lithuanian Commonwealth, and the Ottoman Empire. But neither Peter nor his successors could ignore Russia's old capital and second city, Moscow, as the jump-off point for expansion along the southern frontiers. Indeed, Russia continued to have "two hearts"; each one served as a site for imperial rituals and ceremonies as well as a symbol of Russia's imperial destiny.[88]

The army and reform

As with other conquest states, the foundation of Peter's state-building was the army. Like many of his other reforms, the creation of a professional, European-style army had its origins in the Muscovite period.[89] Peter's innovations were to replace the archaic chain of command and outmoded battlefield tactics of the old Muscovite army, and to destroy its most inefficient, conservative, and rebellious military formation – the musketeers (strel'tsy). In their place, he rapidly adopted the advances of the Western military revolution and created Russia's first naval arm.

The nucleus of the new army was the Guards regiments. In his adolescence Peter had gathered around him the sons of boiars and organized them into two regiments of boys who fought mock battles under his command. He named them the Preobrazhenskii and Semeonovskii Guards after the suburbs of Moscow where they originated. They became the model for the later European-style formations that constituted the fighting core of his army. During his reign, he hand-picked the Guards

---

[88] Richard Wortman, "Moscow and Petersburg. The Problem of Imperial Center in Tsarist Russia, 1881–1914," in Sean Wilentz (ed.), *Rites of Power. Symbolism, Ritual and Politics Since the Middle Ages* (Philadelphia, PA: University of Pennsylvania Press, 1985), pp. 244–71; James Cracraft, *The Petrine Revolution in Russian Architecture* (University of Chicago Press, 1988).

[89] Richard Hellie, "The Petrine Army. Continuity, Change and Impact," *Canadian–American Slavic Studies* 8(2) (Summer 1974): 237–52; Richard Hellie, "Warfare, Changing Military Technology and the Evolution of Muscovite Society," in John A. Lynn (ed.), *Tools of War. Instruments, Ideas and Institutions of Warfare* (Urbana, IL: University of Illinois Press, 1990), pp. 74–99; and especially Marshall Poe, "The Consequences of the Military Revolution in Muscovy. A Comparative Perspective," *Comparative Studies in Society and History* 38(4) (October 1996): 603–18.

officers and entrusted them with important administrative as well as military assignments. He had hoped to force all noble sons into their ranks. Although this effort failed, the Guards continued to retain their high status and attracted recruits mainly from the nobility. The equivalent of a Praetorian Guard, the Preobrazhenskii Guards provided crucial support for the dynasty during critical moments of internal rebellion down to the revolution of 1905.[90]

Until the nineteenth century, in comparison with the armies of Western Europe and Eurasia, the Russian army was unique in many ways. Unlike the armies of Western Europe, it was not composed mainly of mercenaries. Unlike the armies of the Ottoman Empire and Iran, its elite formations were not composed of slaves. It was an army made up primarily of Russian peasants, though all social strata were required to serve, commanded by Russian nobles and a few foreigners. Most of the rank-and-file had been serfs, but they lost that status when they enlisted. To be sure, they were obliged to serve for life, a term reduced to twenty-five years at the end of the eighteenth century. But they were paid, if miserably and not always on time, and provided with uniforms. They could be promoted and decorated if they performed courageously under fire. Under the husk of harsh discipline they were able to organize themselves into small working collectives, *artels*, in order to provide many of their daily necessities, including boot making, tailoring, and growing food to supplement their often meager rations. *Artels* could even serve as primitive savings deposits for pooling their meager salaries. The homogeneity and social bonds must have contributed to the high level of unit cohesion and discipline that was noticed even by their opponents.[91] Was this what drove Frederick the Great to exclaim: "It is easier to kill these Russians than to defeat them"?[92]

With the aim of mobilizing the human and material resources required for his armies, Peter the Great undertook a massive reorganization of the economy and society. Did he create a "garrison state"? The term is provocative and has been challenged.[93] Whatever terms are used, there can be no doubt that Peter's reorganization of finances and the tax system,

[90] On the Guards, see John L. H. Keep, *The Soldiers of the Tsar. Army and Society in Russia, 1462–1874* (Oxford University Press, 1985), pp. 96, 98, 121–22; Dietrich Beyrau, *Militär und Gesellschaft im vorrevolutionären Russland* (Cologne: Böhlau, 1984), pp. 190–93.

[91] Keep, *Soldiers of the Tsar*, Pt. 2; Elise Kimerling Wirtshafter, *From Serf to Russian Soldier* (Princeton University Press, 1990), ch. 5; John Bushnell, "Peasants in Uniform. The Tsarist Army as a Peasant Society," *Journal of Social History* 13 (1979/80): 565–76.

[92] Walter M. Pintner, "Russia's Military Style, Russian Society, and Russian Power in the Eighteenth Century," in A. G. Cross (ed.), *Russia and the West in the Eighteenth Century* (Newtonville, MA: Oriental Research Partners, 1983), p. 265.

[93] Richard Hellie, *The Economy and Material Culture of Russia, 1600–1725* (University of Chicago Press, 1999), p. 536; John L. H. Keep, "The Origins of Russian Militarism,"

and the administrative subdivision of the country into *gubernii* (provinces) and districts were initially designed to provide the necessary revenue and recruits to fight the Great Northern War (1700–1721). His mercantilist industrial policies established state monopolies and encouraged private entrepreneurs in key defense sectors by attaching state peasants to private factories and mines producing uniforms, equipment, and firearms. By the end of his reign, the Russian armaments industry was largely self-sufficient and was producing a sufficient surplus of iron to become a net exporter. By mid-century, the army could boast of an artillery train second to none, including such innovative weapons as the Shuvalov howitzer.[94]

Throughout the eighteenth century the Russian army acquired a European reputation through participation in wars against the Swedes, Prussians, and French. The steadfast behavior of the infantry under fire and the power of its artillery were generally recognized as the equal, if not the superior, of the other European armies.[95] Military service became the preferred profession for ambitious and talented nobles. It offered the best opportunity for social advancement and political influence at court, and in the higher offices of the bureaucracy which were predominantly staffed by military officers until the mid-nineteenth century. The creation of the first Cadet Corps in 1732 and the expansion under the direction of a palace favorite, Count Peter Shuvalov, laid the foundations for a military and general education that greatly enhanced the prestige of its noble graduates and even its drop outs.[96] By the end of the eighteenth century a military intelligentsia had begun to emerge. The penetration of Western ideas into the cultural life of the upper classes promoted ethical ideals tinged with Stoicism; virtue, bravery, and the attainment of rank were identified with personal merit rather than with birth, although the nobility monopolized all avenues leading to that goal. The attitudes and values of what Marc

Cahiers du monde russe et soviétiques 26 (1985): 5–20. The challenge has come from William C. Fuller, Jr., *Civil–Military Conflict in Imperial Russia, 1881–1914* (Princeton University Press, 1985). See especially the discussion on pp. xix–xxii for the later period and Janet M. Hartley, *Russia, 1762–1825. Military Power, the State, and the People* (Westport, CT: Praeger, 2008), pp. 4–5.

[94] Arcadius Kahan, *The Plow, the Hammer and the Knout. An Economic History of Eighteenth Century Russia* (University of Chicago Press, 1985), pp. 96–99, 111–12; Pintner, "The Burden of Defense," pp. 231–35.

[95] Christopher Duffy, *Russia's Military Way to the West. Origins and Nature of Russian Military Power 1700–1800* (London: Routledge & Kegan Paul, 1981).

[96] L. G. Beskrovnyi, "Voennye shkoly v pervoi polovine XVIII v.," *Istoricheskie zapiski* 42 (1953): 285–300; Max J. Okenfuss, "Education and Empire. School Reform in Enlightened Russia," *Jahrbücher für Geschichte Osteuropas* 27 (1979): 59, is critical of the quality of instruction given in the Cadet Corps.

Raeff has called the "military ethos" left a strong imprint on the institutions of imperial rule.[97]

Up to the mid-nineteenth century the Russian army had fulfilled the imperial dreams of Peter the Great. It had advanced the Russian frontiers deep into Europe, securing a position as the ultimate mediator in the Prussian–Habsburg rivalry. It had cleared the Ottoman Turks from the northern shores of the Black Sea, and had established a Russian presence on the Danube from which it could dominate the principalities and invade the Balkans at will. It had also expelled both Ottoman and Iranian power from the south Caucasus. As a participant in the major European wars, it had followed up its victory over Charles XI by defeating Frederick the Great and Napoleon, the three outstanding military geniuses of their time. It had raised its standards over Berlin and Paris. Paul I, Alexander I, Nicholas I, and his heir, the future Alexander II, had increasingly identified imperial rule with the success of their armies. No wonder then that defeat in the Crimean War on Russian soil and the humiliating Treaty of Paris in 1856, imposing demilitarization of the Black Sea littoral, administered a terrible psychological blow to the new emperor, Alexander II, and the ruling elite.

In the wake of defeat, the tsar and his closest advisors recognized that Russia's Great Power standing could be restored only by reforming an outmoded army and rebuilding the empire's financial stability which had been shaken by the costs of war. In the winter of 1855/6, Alexander's military advisors had warned that the army was in no state to continue to fight and that the crushing burden of military operations threatened to exhaust Russia's dwindling financial resources.[98]

Serfdom stood in the path of creating a more efficient army with a large ready reserve and the construction of a modern fiscal system with a European-style budget. The first steps were taken in 1855; serfdom was abolished in 1861, but the long process of planning and carrying out a comprehensive military reform took another thirteen years.[99] Under the

[97] Marc Raeff, "L'état, le gouvernement et la tradition politique en Russie impériale avant 1861," *Revue d'histoire moderne et contemporaine* 9 (October–December 1962): 302; Marc Raeff, *The Origins of the Russian Intelligentsia. The Eighteenth Century Nobility* (New York: Harcourt, Brace & World, 1966), pp. 48–50; Keep, *The Soldiers of the Tsar*, pp. 239–45. Cf. Iurii Lotman, "Dekabrist v poslevoenoi zhizni: bytovoe povedenie kak istoriko-psikhologicheskaia kategoriia," in V. G. Bazonov and V. E. Vatsuro (eds.), *Literaturnye nasledie dekabristov* (Leningrad: Nauka, 1975), pp. 25–74.

[98] "Ob opastnosti v 1856 g. voennykh deistvii," *Istoricheskii arkhiv* 1 (January–February 1959): 206–8, and discussion in Alfred J. Rieber (ed.), *The Politics of Autocracy. Letters of Alexander II to Prince A. I. Bariatinski, 1857–1864* (Paris: Mouton, 1966), pp. 23–40, 59–60.

[99] Alfred J. Rieber, "Alexander II. A Revisionist View," *Journal of Modern History* 43(1) (March 1971): 42–58, and discussion in Rieber, *The Politics of Autocracy*, pp. 18–19.

leadership of the Minister for War Dmitri Miliutin, a veteran of the
Caucasus wars, the reform of 1874 created a conscript army, equipped
with modern rifled weapons, organized into military districts, led by
officers professionally trained in military academies, with the elite being
selected for the general staff. He vigorously championed the construction
of strategic railroads. An activist in bureaucratic politics, he was an ardent
advocate of rational and centralized imperial rule. He was also an advocate
of a repressive regime in Warsaw, with a forward policy in the Caucasus
and Trans Caspia, helping to bring the last of the borderlands under
Russian control.[100]

After Miliutin left office in 1881, according to William C. Fuller
military professionalism in the Russian army steadily declined to a low
level in comparison with the great European armies. Conflict with the civil
authorities over financing and the role of the army further eroded
Miliutin's program.[101] Although the Russian army continued to be the
largest in Europe, it counted fewer troops per capita than France or
Germany and not many more than Austria-Hungary. Because of the
spatial location of the borderlands, Russia concentrated more of its forces
there than the overseas empires stationed in their colonies. Military
spending was also on a lower level per soldier than its neighbors. It
could not afford to call up annually more than 35 percent of the eligible
male population, and it trained a smaller proportion of its men than any
other European country.[102] It was only during the First World War that
the last obstacles to a citizen-soldier were swept away under the pressure
of replacing large losses. By this time, too, a new spirit of comradeship and
enhanced feelings of masculine pride developing out of the reforms of
1908 was building toward a full "nationalization of the army."[103]

Although the military reforms were incomplete by the time of the
Russo-Turkish War in 1877/8, the army was successful in overcoming
the stiff resistance of the Ottoman forces, which were also undergoing
modernization. The Russian army would have completely dominated Iran
if it had not been for the British counterweight. To be sure, in the Russo-
Japanese War, the Russian armed forces on land and sea performed badly
due mainly to poor leadership and severe logistical problems. But if the

[100] P. A. Zaionchkovskii, *Voennye reformy 1860–1870 gg. v Rossii* (Moscow: Izd. Moskovskogo universiteta, 1952). See also Forrestt A. Miller, *Dimitri Miliutin and the Reform Era in Russia* (Nashville, TN: Vanderbilt University Press, 1968).
[101] Fuller, *Civil–Military Conflict*, p. 32.
[102] Stephen Velychenko, "The Size of the Imperial Russian Bureaucracy and Army in Comparative Perspective," *Jahrbücher für Geschichte Osteuropas* 49(3) (2001): 357–59.
[103] Joshua A. Sanborn, *Drafting the Russian Nation. Military Conscription, Total War and Mass Politics* (DeKalb, IL: Northern Illinois University Press, 2003).

revolution at home had not forced Russia to sue for peace, the Far Eastern Army, heavily reinforced from Europe, would probably have overwhelmed the exhausted Japanese forces.

From 1914 to 1916, the army repeatedly defeated the Habsburg forces in Galicia. In the final analysis, it was only outmatched by the best army in Europe, surrendering less territory than the Red Army in 1941/2. However, in 1917, Russia lost the war on the home front. During the critical days of February 1917 the army command played a key role in orchestrating attempts to limit the power of the tsar and then to force his abdication. Their overriding concern was to win the war and preserve the social order. If this meant cooperating with the republican Provisional Government then the army command was "willing to accept the revolution in order to contain it."[104] The glue that held the Russian Empire together had come unstuck.

The bureaucratic web

From the outset of his reign, Peter the Great selected his advisors, military commanders, and diplomats from a wide range of social origins: the sons of boiars, clerics, and petty urban classes. What counted was talent and loyalty. He formalized his policy of recruiting on the basis of merit only at the end of his reign when he created the Table of Ranks. It embodied his ideal of service to the state as the measure of all things. His insistence on transforming the appearance of his servitors – shaving beards and abolishing the traditional dress – was simply the external expression of his desire to transform the inner man into a rational and efficient cog in the machinery of government.

Peter's reforms of the central institutions of state, especially the creation of the senate and the administrative departments, or colleges, owed much to the political ideology of German cameralism and the vision of a well-ordered police state.[105] In practice, his bureaucratic devices served to concentrate his power, assign responsibility, and, rather less successfully, diminish corruption and favoritism. The instructions guiding the work of the colleges best expressed the enlarged functions of government he

---

[104] George Katkov, *Russia, 1917. The February Revolution* (New York: Harper & Row, 1967), pp. 306–58; Tsuyoshi Hasegawa, *The February Revolution. Petrograd, 1917* (Seattle, WA: University of Washington Press, 1981), pp. 487–507.

[105] Marc Raeff, *The Well-Ordered Police State. Social and Institutional Change through Law in the Germanies and Russia, 1600–1800* (New Haven, CT: Yale University Press, 1983), esp. pp. 181–218; E. V. Anisimov, *The Reforms of Peter the Great. Progress through Coercion in Russia*, trans. and introduction John T. Alexander (Armonk, NY: M. E. Sharpe, 1993), pp. 217–43.

envisioned. They prescribed the rational management of revenues, encouragement of trade, handicrafts, and manufactures, and mining of minerals. Often impatient with procedures that he had introduced, he relied heavily on officers of his Guards regiments as his personal representatives with plenipotentiary powers to intervene arbitrarily in the administrative mechanism of government at the central and provincial level. In the absence of sufficient trained personnel to administer the countryside, he was obliged to use troops billeted in the provinces in order to collect taxes and enforce the law.[106]

Peter's administrative organization of the country into eight gigantic *gubernii* in 1708 was a direct consequence of his requirements in fighting the Great Northern War against Sweden. The term first appeared in Russian legislation in 1701 when he launched his first attempt to mobilize resources for the war. The administration of a *guberniia* was divided into a civil section, designed to conduct the census and collect taxes, and the military section. The subdivision of the *guberniia* into *okrug* (regions) was, like many of his reforms, not original but followed the practice of the first three Romanovs who had introduced "unified frontier districts in large military regions." Peter appointed leading nobles or his close associates in the military command to serve as governors. Their powers and functions were gradually extended to encompass judicial, financial, and police affairs.

The structure was highly militarized. Instructions from the center outlined the necessary resources for the army, including forage, horses, equipment, and, above all, recruits. Failure to provide recruits was deemed to be treasonable and punished accordingly. As was so often the case in Russia, decrees from above, no matter how severe the punishment for evasion, lost much of their force in the hands of inexperienced, untrained, overly burdened, often corrupt officials scattered thinly over the vast territories of the empire.[107] Nevertheless, by ruthlessly subordinating the administrative, economic, and social life of the country to the needs of the armed forces, Peter established the precedents for future reforms, enabling the Russian Empire to outmatch its rivals in the struggle

---

[106] B. V. Anan'ich *et al.* (eds.), *Vlast' i reformy ot samoderzhavnoi k sovetskoi Rossii* (St. Petersburg: Dmitrii Bulanin, 1996), pp. 120–51. This section was written by E. V. Anisimov.

[107] See in particular V. V. Cherkesov *et al.* (eds.), *Institut general-gubernatorstva i namestnichestva v Rossiiskoi imperii* (St. Petersburg: Izd. St. Peterburgskogo Universiteta, 2001), pp. 11–16, 25, citing with approval the magisterial work of Paul Miliukov, *Khozaistvo Rossii v pervoi chetverti XVIII stoletiia i reforma Petra Velikogo* (St. Petersburg: M. M. Stasiulevich, 1905).

over the borderlands throughout the eighteenth and much of the nineteenth centuries.

By introducing the Table of Ranks, Peter I created the framework for incorporating the nobility into the military and civil bureaucracy. But this too did not mark a radical break with the past. Among the strong elements of continuity with the previous century were the importance of merit as well as birth, remuneration in salaries instead of land, a fusion of the low born and the high born, and the strong presence of the intellectual elite in government offices.[108] Peter's reforms did introduce uniform ranking and a clear definition of career development for the elite that only gradually replaced the clan and family basis for advancement in office.[109] But the higher nobles continued to dominate the top ranks well into the nineteenth century.

In building his state, Peter tolerated no opposition. Here, too, he was pragmatic, resorting to a range of repressive measures from studied neglect to ruthless suppression. He did not abolish the Boiar Duma, but allowed it to wither away. He waited twenty years after the death of the last patriarch before replacing his office with the Holy Synod. He openly persecuted schismatics, especially the Old Believers who regarded him as the personification of anti-Christ. When he encountered opposition from his own son, he sacrificed him and thereby jeopardized his own succession. Peter's policy of destroying real and potential opposition while introducing a new concept of loyalty to the state was the major reason that Russia did not pass through another time of troubles after his death. This aspect of his reign undoubtedly had a particular appeal to Stalin.

Under Peter, instability was limited to the court intrigues and dynastic squabbles, but did not jeopardize the central institutions of power. United by a common interest and the privileges of a Westernized lifestyle, Peter's ruling elite combined the old boiar aristocracy with new men. His "eagles," as Pushkin called them, maintained and built upon his legacy. With their support the institutional foundations he had laid down proved to be resilient enough to survive forty years of dynastic turmoil over the succession to the throne, the so-called era of palace revolutions from 1724 to 1762.

---

[108] B. Plavsic, "Seventeenth Century Chanceries and their Staffs," in W. M. Pintner and D. K. Rowney (eds.), *Russian Officialdom. The Bureaucratization of Russian History from the Seventeenth to the Twentieth Century* (Chapel Hill, NC: University of North Carolina Press, 1980), pp. 19–45.

[109] Nancy S. Kollmann, *Kinship and Politics. The Making of the Muscovite Political System, 1345–1547* (Stanford University Press, 1987), pp. 14–19. Cf. Paul Bushkovich, *Peter the Great. The Struggle for Power, 1671–1725* (Cambridge University Press, 2001).

Catherine II took up the threads of Peter's centralizing administrative policies by borrowing freely from the administrative practices advocated by the German cameralists and the French *philosophes*. She completed the process of transforming the country into a major player in the European state system and securing Russia's ascendancy in the struggle over the borderlands. Her major reform of the provinces was a response to the last great rebellion led by Cossacks on the Russian frontier (1773–1775). The leader, Emilian Pugachev, a renegade Cossack of the Don, was also the last major rebel in the tradition of the *samozvanets*, the pretender to the throne who claimed to be the true tsar, in this case the deposed and murdered husband of Catherine, Peter III. Pugachev's rebellion appealed to a variety of volatile elements on Russia's southern and southeastern frontiers ranging from the Yaik Cossacks, Tatar, and Kalmyk nomads to Old Believer settlers and discontented serfs. In his half-literate manifestos, Pugachev promised freedom from state interference and the restoration of the old liberties. A powerful element in his appeal was peasant monarchism, that is, the popular belief that injustice in the realm could only be explained by the presence of a usurper on the throne (which Catherine was) while the true tsar sought his rightful throne among the loyal mass of his people. This opposition from below stood in contrast to the potential opposition from above in the form of a palace revolution, ever present since the death of Peter the Great, which had brought Catherine to power. Thus, her institutional reforms moved in two directions. She aimed both to increase central authority over the peasantry and the Cossacks, especially on the frontier, and to placate the nobility, enlisting them to help carry out the functions of imperial rule in the provinces.

The reorganizing of the provincial administration in 1775 reproduced the structure of the Governing Senate created by Peter and provided the local nobles with salaried offices. Her Charter of the Nobility in 1785 granted them corporate privileges.[110] The attempts to attract nobles into provincial service and settle them on their country estates were not very successful. The lure of the imperial court and the more promising career opportunities in the army and civil bureaucracy were stronger magnets. Provincial Russia remained "under governed" in the oft repeated phrase of S. Frederick Starr.[111] But this also meant that, unlike the ayans in the Ottoman Empire, the Hungarian nobility, the tribal chiefs in Iran, or the

---

[110] George Yaney, *The Systematization of Russian Government. Social Evolution in the Domestic Administration of Imperial Russia, 1711–1905* (Urbana, IL: University of Illinois Press, 1973); Robert E. Jones, *The Emancipation of the Russian Nobility, 1762–85* (Princeton University Press, 1973).

[111] S. Frederick Starr, *Decentralization and Self-Government in Russia, 1830–1870* (Princeton University Press, 1972).

local gentry in the Qing, the provincial nobles in Russia never challenged the authority of the center. This did not mean the absence of politics. Rationalization and centralization were tempered by favoritism and court intrigues, including conspiracies to depose unpopular rulers.[112]

Given Catherine's views on the nature of the well-governed state, it is not surprising that she attempted to impose institutional uniformity on the borderlands.[113] After she created the post of governor general, it was frequently employed to designate a special administrative unit, *okrain*, or borderland. Over time, it was expected that the administrator of the okrain, either a governor general or viceroy, would be replaced in official documents and administrative practice by a provincial governor signifying the integration of the borderland into the regular institutional structure of the empire. By the end of the empire, however, the process had not been completed for all the borderlands, another indication that imperial state-building remained unfinished business.[114]

By introducing the Charter of Nobility into Livonia, Catherine deprived the German Baltic barons of Estland and Livonia of the special privileges acquired under Swedish rule and confirmed by Peter the Great. She also whittled away the separate military organization of the Ukrainian Cossacks and began the process of selective incorporation of their chiefs (*starshina*) into the Russian nobility. By introducing the poll tax into the provinces of Little Russia, the Slobodskaia Ukraine, the Baltic provinces, and the newly acquired Polish provinces she further reduced the legal mobility of Cossacks and peasants on the frontier.[115] Conforming to the old pattern of resistance, numbers of discontented serfs and Cossacks continued to opt for flight across the porous borders into Poland, Moldavia, and the Ottoman Empire. As Robert E. Jones has suggested, the problem of runaway serfs provided one of the major incentives for

---

[112] John P. LeDonne, *Ruling Russia. Politics and Administration in the Age of Absolutism, 1762–1796* (Princeton University Press, 1984), pp. 4–6 and *passim*; David Ransel, *The Politics of Catherinian Russia. The Panin Party* (New Haven, CT: Yale University Press, 1975).

[113] Marc Raeff, "Uniformity, Diversity and the Imperial Administration in the Reign of Catherine I," *Osteuropa in Geschichte und Gegenwart, Festschrift für Gunther Stokl zum 60. Geburtstag* (Cologne: Böhlau, 1977), pp. 97–113; LeDonne, *Ruling Russia*, esp. Pt. 5.

[114] The term *okrain* was first used in the Slavophil polemics of Iuri Samarin to single out the peculiarities of the Baltic (*Ostzei*) provinces, but later incorporated into official discourse. Cherkesov, *Institut general-gubernatorstva*, vol. I, pp. 186–87.

[115] Isabel de Madariaga, *Russia in the Age of Catherine the Great* (New Haven, CT: Yale University Press, 1981), pp. 308–24; Zenon Kohut, *Russian Centralism and Ukrainian Autonomy. Imperial Absorption in the Hetmanate, 1760s–1830s* (Cambridge University Press, 1988).

Catherine's government to participate in the First Partition of Poland in 1772 and delimit new more regularly policed borders on the frontiers.[116]

Alexander I continued the reforming tradition. Following the direction of his grandmother, he completed the transition from the collegial to the ministerial form of administration. But he stopped short of creating a cabinet system, reserving the right of the autocrat to deal separately with his ministers and thus more easily control them. Just as seriously, the reform sharpened the difference between what John LeDonne has called the "territorial," represented by the governors general, and the "functional," represented by the ministries. The bureaucratic dichotomy further complicated the coordination of policy in the borderlands, particularly because both sets of officials were personal representatives of the tsar and could claim to be the embodiment of his will even when they disagreed with one another.[117]

During the Great Reforms of the 1860s and 1870s, the central Russian bureaucracy developed more fully along the functional and professional lines of the Weberian ideal type. A new generation of enlightened bureaucrats graduating from the universities and the Imperial Lycée began to replace the free-floating bureaucrats, who were mainly military appointees without specialized training.[118] The new men pursued bureaucratic politics through informal ministerial interest groups, which were attached to a set of aims and aspirations that went beyond the personality and tenure of a single minister.[119] Within their own spheres these interest groups were able to bring about significant changes in the social and economic life of the empire; they were the architects of the great reforms. But Alexander II remained too strongly attached to his autocratic power to allow the

[116] Robert E. Jones, "Runaway Peasants and Russian Motives for the Partitions of Poland," in Hugh Ragsdale (ed.), *Imperial Russian Foreign Policy* (Washington and Cambridge: Woodrow Wilson Center and Cambridge University Press, 1993), pp. 103–16.
[117] John LeDonne, "Frontier Governors General, 1772–1825," *Jahrbücher für Geschichte Osteuropas*, New Series, 1 (1999): 56–81; 2 (1999): 161–83; 3 (1999): 321–40; John LeDonne, "Russian Governors General 1775–1825. Territorial or Functional Administration?" *Cahiers du monde russe* 42(1) (2001): 5–30; M. D. Dolbilov, "Rozhdenie imperatoskikh reshenii. Monarkh, sovetnik i 'Vysochaishaia Volia' v Rossii XIX v.," *Istoricheskie zapiski* 9(127) (2006): 5–48.
[118] Dmitri Kobeko, *Imperatorskii Tsarskosel'skii Litsei. Nastavniki i potomtsy, 1811–1843* (St. Petersburg: Tip. V. F. Kirshbauma, 1911), pp. 71–72, 80–81, 100–1.
[119] Walter Pintner, "Civil Officialdom and the Nobility in the 1850s," in Pintner and Rowney (eds.), *Russian Officialdom*, pp. 227–49; Bruce Lincoln, *In the Vanguard of Reform. Russia's Enlightened Bureaucrats, 1825–1861* (De Kalb, IL: Northern Illinois University Press, 1982); Alfred J. Rieber, "Interest Group Politics in the Era of the Great Reforms," in Ben Eklof et al. (eds.), *Russia's Great Reforms* (Bloomington, IN: Indiana University Press, 1994), pp. 58–83.

formation of a united government, that is, a homogeneous ministry of like-minded reformers, even one under his own chairmanship. Instead, he preferred the role of the "managerial tsar," the mediator among the conflicting interest groups and ministers.[120] This strategy was pursued by his successors. As a result the reforming process continued to be guided by the bureaucracy, but along uneven and uncoordinated lines with often counterproductive results.

By the end of the nineteenth century, Russian officials were increasingly concerned over their role in governing the empire and its borderlands. One of their internal debates questioned the size of the bureaucracy. Within the borderlands, the two provinces with the largest number of administrators per capita were Warsaw and Tiflis, which might be considered the most likely centers of resistance. The staffing levels in the central provinces and the borderlands were comparable to those in the major European colonies, although the percentages were higher for Trans Caspia than for British India or the French African colonies. In terms of its size and population distribution, the empire appeared to be governed by a bureaucracy that was still thin on the ground.[121]

The central bureaucracies also became increasingly split over the question of how to integrate the disparate parts of the empire. Within the bureaucracy on the eve of the First World War a few voices were raised in favor of a more flexible policy toward the national question in the borderlands, arguing that extreme Russian nationalism could only result in inciting "treason and revolution," and proposing closer relations with the representatives of the local elites who accepted the "imperial idea."[122] Constituting the second generation of enlightened bureaucrats, they perceived themselves as heirs to the unfinished business of the Great Reforms. They were responsible for launching the industrial development of the 1890s and drafting the Stolypin reforms that aimed at creating a landed peasant class loyal to the autocracy.[123]

Western scholars continue to disagree over the effectiveness and efficiency of the late imperial bureaucracy. In one camp there are those who stress the evidence of higher levels of education, growing professionalization of outlook, and a stronger commitment to legality, although they

---

[120] Rieber, "Interest Group Politics," pp. 78–79.
[121] Velychenko, "The Size of the Imperial Russian Bureaucracy," pp. 354–56.
[122] B. V. Anan'ich and R. Sh. Ganelin, *Sergei Iul'evich Vitte i ego vremia* (St. Petersburg: Dmitrii Bulanin, 1999), p. 572, citing contemporary newspapers.
[123] D. A. J. Macey, *Government and Peasant in Russia, 1861–1906. The Prehistory of the Stolypin Reforms* (De Kalb, IL: Northern Illinois University Press, 1987), pp. 44–68.

recognize that the process was uneven in different ministries and between the center and the provinces.[124] Those populating another camp emphasize the persistence of patron–client relationships, the absence of a unified bureaucratic system, and the failure to create a genuine rule of law (*Rechsstaat*).[125] A variation on this interpretation points up the tension between the tsar's unconstrained power and the legal foundations of Russian institutions.[126] There is general agreement, however, that the bureaucracy was divided into warring factions.[127]

There is also general agreement that in the reign of Nicholas II the bureaucracy became increasingly isolated from society and detached from the person of the tsar. The bureaucracy had functioned as the main arena of politics where conflicting points of view could be advanced, debated, and, in theory, be resolved. But Nicholas II was unable to manage the system. He had little confidence in his own abilities. He seemed incapable of maintaining a consistent position on any major question except the preservation of his autocratic rule. His hesitations, abrupt reversals, and susceptibility to persuasion by favorites and adventurers proved to be disastrous at moments of crisis. His predecessors had been largely successful, for the most part, in retaining bureaucratic servitors of differing opinions by reserving the right to choose one policy over another and to pursue it consistently. But Nicholas became muddled by conflicting opinions among his top officials and the court circles. He not only failed to coordinate the activities of his ministers, but also circumvented and undermined their authority by giving full rein to personal favorites and

---

[124] For example, Yaney, *The Systematization*; Dominic Lieven, *Russia's Rulers under the Old Regime* (New Haven, CT: Yale University Press, 1987).

[125] For example, Raeff, "The Bureaucratic Phenomenon"; Andrew M. Verner, *The Crisis of Russian Autocracy. Nicholas II and the 1905 Revolution* (Princeton University Press, 1990), pp. 52–55; Pintner and Rowney, "Officialdom and Bureaucratization. Conclusion," in Pintner and Rowney (eds.), *Russian Officialdom*, p. 379.

[126] For example, A. V. Remnev, *Samoderzhavnoe pravitel'stvo. Komitet ministrov v sisteme vysshego upravleniia Rossiiskoi imperii (vtoraia polovina XIX–nachalo XX veka)* (Moscow: Rosspen, 2010). Cf. Mikhail Dobilov, "The Political Mythology of Autocracy. Scenarios of Power and the Role of the Autocrat," *Kritika* 2(4) (Fall 2001): 773–95, for a reflection on the political space of autocracy.

[127] Rieber, "Interest Group Politics," pp. 44–72; Alfred J. Rieber, "Patronage and Professionalism. The Witte System," in B. V. Anan'ich *et al.* (eds.), *Problemy vsemirnoi istorii. Sbornik statei v chest' Aleksandra Aleksandrovicha Fursenko* (St. Petersburg: Dmitrii Bulanin, 2000), pp. 286–97; David M. McDonald, "United Government and the Crisis of Autocracy, 1905–1914," in Theodore Taranovskii (ed.), *Reform in Modern Russian History. Progress or Cycle?* (Washington, DC and Cambridge: Woodrow Wilson Center Press and Cambridge University Press, 1995), pp. 208–12; Verner, *Russian Autocracy*, ch. 2.

occasionally to adventurers.[128] The astute diarist and member of the State Council, A. A. Polovtsov, noted in 1901 that:

in no area of policy is there a principled, well considered and firmly implemented course of action. Everything is done hastily, haphazardly, under the influence of the moment, in response to the demands of this or that person and interventions from various sources. The young Tsar harbors more and more contempt for the organs of his own power and begins to believe in the advantageous strength of his own autocracy which he expresses sporadically without preliminary discussion and without any link to the overall course of policy.[129]

Throughout the nineteenth century the administrative practices of imperial rule over both the central provinces and the borderlands suffered from debilitating dualities. Should the nobility or the bureaucracy be the main social basis for the autocracy? Was reform from above or the status quo the firmest foundation of imperial rule?[130] This debate haunted the corridors of power during the Great Reforms of the 1860s and 1870s and the Counter Reforms of the 1880s and 1890s. Nobles and bureaucrats, centralizers and decentralizers could be found on both sides of the argument. This is one good reason to be wary of attaching terms like liberal and conservative to Russian political thinkers and actors, although it is done all the time.[131] In a second duality, advocates of the "nationalist-chauvinist" doctrine were caught in a basic contradiction between a commitment to the autocratic principle and hostility toward the bureaucracy.[132] A third duality, as we have seen, was the ideological conflict between the believers in the Orthodox Church as an independent spiritual force and the advocates of the subordination of the Church to the superior authority of the state. That the bureaucrats lacked a common ethos and

[128] Igor V. Lukoianov, "The Bezobrazovtsy," in John W. Steinberg et al. (eds.), The Russia Japanese War in Global Perspective. World War Zero (Leiden: Brill, 2005), pp. 78–83; David Schimmelpenninck, "The Immediate Causes of the War," in Steinberg et al. (eds.), The Russia Japanese War in Global Perspective, pp. 31–41.

[129] "Iz dnevnika A. A. Polovtsov," Krasnyi arkhiv 3 (1923): 99, quoted in Dominic Lieven, Nicholas II. Emperor of All the Russias (London: BCA, 1994), p. 109.

[130] Don Karl Rowney, "Structure, Class and Career. The Problem of Bureaucracy and Society in Russia, 1801–1917," Social Science History 6(1) (Winter 1982): 87–109.

[131] Cf. Rieber, "Alexander II," pp. 42–58; Alfred J. Rieber, "Bureaucratic Politics in Imperial Russia," Social Science History 2 (Summer 1978): 399–413; Alfred J. Rieber, "The Reforming Tradition in Russian and Soviet History. A Commentary," in Taranovskii (ed.), Reform in Modern Russian History, pp. 237–43; Daniel Orlovsky, The Limits of Reform. The Ministry of Internal Affairs in Imperial Russia, 1802–1881 (Cambridge, MA: Harvard University Press, 1981).

[132] Valentina G. Cherukha and Boris V. Anan'ich, "Russia Falls Back, Russia Catches Up. Three Generations of Russian Reformers," in Taranovskii (ed.), Reform in Modern Russian History, pp. 55–96; Daniel Field, "Reforms and Political Culture in Prerevolutionary Russia. Commentary," in Taranovskii (ed.), Reform in Modern Russian History, pp. 125–36.

were split into so many factions without firm leadership from the top crippled their ability to deal with the fissiparous tendencies in the borderlands. Following the creation of a State Duma in 1906 and the growing hostility of the tsar to any sign of opposition to his autocratic beliefs, whether on the floor of the Duma or within the imperial chancelleries, the bureaucracy lost its main function as the link between the autocrat and the people.

The militarization and centralization of Russian imperial rule had enabled a small ruling elite to expand and maintain control over a vast empire. But the cultural disparity between the borderlands and the central provinces increased as the empire expanded to the west during the Napoleonic Wars, creating a radically new situation. The elites of the newly acquired regions, the Polish and Swedish–Finnish nobles, and the Bessarabian boiars and Georgian princes had long historical ties to different multicultural states. The Poles, Swedish-Finns, and Georgians cherished traditions of self-governance that deviated sharply from the experience of the Russian provincial nobility, and they considered themselves culturally superior. Conquest of the borderlands had been a long and costly process, but administering and assimilating them proved to be even more difficult and costly. An exception to this pattern was the Russian governance of the Baltic borderlands.

The Baltic provinces and the Grand Duchy of Finland

Russian success in integrating the Baltic borderlands was due in large measure to a policy of confirming and even extending the local privileges and language rights of the German landowners and offering them an unusually privileged access to the ruling elite. At the end of the Great Northern War, Peter restored all the estates that had been confiscated by the Swedish government, virtually handing over the peasantry to the tender mercies of the nobility. The Baltic German nobility became "the real Mamelukes of the tsar."[133] The social organization and legal structure of the German noble corporation remained intact, attracting Peter's interest as a model for the empire as a whole. According to Edward Thaden, Peter was willing to confirm most, if not all, of the special privileges of the Baltic Germans because he admired their institutions of local self-government. He welcomed the European training and expertise of their officials and military officers, who constituted about a quarter of the Russian officer corps by the 1730s. He also needed the support of the

---

[133] Ia. Ia. Zutis, *Politika tsarizma v Pribaltike v pervoi polovine XVIII v.* (Moscow: Gosudarstvenoe sotsial'no-ekonomicheskoe izd., 1937), p. 18.

Baltic Germans to protect his one direct access to the west and to advance his diplomacy in the region.

Catherine continued and expanded Peter's policy toward the Baltic Germans. Besides recruiting talents from their ranks to serve in important diplomatic posts and in the mid-level bureaucracy, she used the Baltic borderlands as a field for experimentation in governance. Improvements were introduced in the status of the peasantry, anticipating their emancipation under Alexander I, and in improving provincial finances and provincial administration. Through the influence of Pietism the provinces had become the bridge between the *Aufklärung* and the Russian Enlightenment, and infused its administrators with the spirit of rationality, efficiency, and honesty.[134] The embodiment of these talents, and one of Catherine's favorite administrators, Count Jacob Sievers, "turned out to be the perfect lieutenant of enlightened despotism working tirelessly on the problems of internal administration such as water communication, urban planning, road construction, forest management, the promotion of commerce and the building of schools."[135] But there were too few like him. The Russian provincial nobility failed to fulfill Catherine's expectations. They were in general poorly educated, impoverished, and immersed in local quarrels. Acknowledging the problem, Alexander considered the possibility that the elites of the borderlands rather than those of the center might serve as the model for reconstructing the empire. Under his reign imperial rule began to be organized along asymmetrical lines, reflecting national and historical differences.

In the Baltic provinces Alexander reconfirmed the rights of the local elites of Estland, Livland, and Riga restored by Paul after Catherine had abrogated them, but only "insofar as they are in agreement with the general decrees and laws of our state." He granted the serfs personal freedom, but left them economically dependent on the German landlords.[136] In drafting plans for the governance of the Baltikum, Alexander selected advisors from a mix of Russian and local elites. As men of a transitional era, they shared with him a set of principles drawn from the rational bureaucratic absolutism of the Enlightenment and the emerging historicism of the Romantic era. The attempt to reconcile the universalist and the particularistic generated institutions that contained inherently contradictory properties. The emperor and the imperial elites

---

[134] Claus Scharf, *Katharina II, Deutschland und die deutschen* (Mainz: Philip von Zabern, 1995), pp. 167–77.

[135] Jones, *The Emancipation of the Russian Nobility*, pp. 177–78, 191–95, quotation on p. 178.

[136] Edward C. Thaden, *Russia's Western Borderlands, 1710–1870* (Princeton University Press, 1984), pp. 98–99, 231.

found it increasingly difficult to maintain the delicate balance between the two principles in day-to-day governance. Local elites were able to find ample justification in the dual system for both accommodation and resistance.

Throughout most of the nineteenth century the Baltic German landlords were able to maintain their favored position. But the growing economic discontent of the Estonian and Latvian peasantry, the emergence of a local nationalist intelligentsia, and attacks from Russifying intellectuals and imperial bureaucrats threatened to undermine their dominant position.[137] By 1905, as we shall see, the Baltic barons were fighting for their lives.

The incorporation of Finland into the Russian Empire as a grand duchy was facilitated by a small group of Finnish intelligentsia and Swedish–Finnish military and civil officials who had become disillusioned with rule from Stockholm. They began to listen to the siren calls of Russian diplomats. In 1808, discontented over the lost wars and their devastating effects on the country, they rallied to the idea of an autonomous Finland within the Russian Empire.[138] But the incorporation of Finland into the Russian Empire did not proceed smoothly and remained to the end juridically ambiguous.

Originally based on three separate documents lacking internal consistency, the constitutional structure of the Grand Duchy of Finland rested on two contradictory principles: local autonomy (*bytie politicheskoe*) and political integration (*derzhavnoe obladanie*). They were never reconciled. Alexander I accepted the proposals of the local elites to place Finnish affairs directly under the scepter of the tsar, a formula that lacked clarity. He confirmed and even broadened the rights and privileges the Finns had enjoyed under Swedish rule. Following the advice of Mikhail Speranskii, he enlarged the territory of the grand duchy by reuniting it with Old Finland (the districts of Karelia and Vyborg) annexed by Elizabeth Petrovna. This was all in line with the tsar's desire "that the affairs concerning the administration of the newly acquired Finland which are submitted for My decision be first examined and considered on those very principles and laws which are peculiar to that country and have been confirmed by Us." At the same time, he accepted Speranskii's counsel by refusing to introduce any constitutional and representative features that would place these particularistic rights and privileges on a firmly legal basis. Once created, the Finnish Sejm did not

---

[137] Thaden, *Russia's Western Borderlands*, pp. 5–12, chs. 6 and 9.
[138] Thaden, *Russia's Western Borderlands*, pp. 83–85.

meet from 1809 to 1864.[139] As Marc Raeff has suggested, their ultimate aim was "to bring about a structural identity between the Russian and Finnish administrations," although only gradually.[140] If so, a century proved to be not time enough.

Bessarabia and the principalities

At the southern end of Russia's western frontier a similar pattern of adjustment to imperial rule was negotiated by another of Alexander's foreign-born advisors, Ioan Capo d'Istria, who entered Russian service in 1808 and rose to the rank of Foreign Minister. He was already involved in planning Russia's support for Greek independence when he was assigned the task of drafting "The Rules for the Temporary Government of Bessarabia." They incorporated Alexander's promise to respect local laws and customs when in 1806, during the war against the Ottoman Empire, the Russians occupied the Danubian principalities. But Capo d'Istria also saw the possibility of using the province of Bessarabia, annexed by Russia in 1812 after a six-year war with the Ottoman Empire, as a "promised land for the Greeks." He was instrumental in having a prominent Moldavian boiar and personal friend, Scarlat Sturdza, appointed the first governor and in drafting instructions to him. The aim was to eliminate local "vices" and introduce rational, enlightened legislation.

As in Finland and later Poland, Russian policy reflected two contradictory elements, although they took slightly different forms. On the one hand, the Moldavian boiars were confirmed in their historical rights. On the other hand, a project was launched in the spirit of Catherine II to colonize the "empty spaces," which the Moldavian boiars subsequently claimed belonged to them on historicist grounds. That the bulk of the colonists were Bulgarian peasants who had fled the rule of Ottoman officials and landlords in order to seek Russian protection complicated social relations in the region. The boiars claimed seigniorial rights over the peasants. The latter resisted mainly by fleeing across the Pruth into Ukraine, further disrupting the inchoate process of colonization.[141] In

---

[139] A.Iu. Bakhturnina, *Okrainy rossiiskoi imperii. Gosudarstvennoe upravlenie i natsional'naia politika v gody pervoi mirovoi voiny (1914–1917 gg.)* (Moscow: Rosspen, 2004), pp. 226–27, 232–81.

[140] Marc Raeff, *Michael Speransky. Statesman of Imperial Russia, 1772–1839*, 2nd edn. (The Hague: Mouton, 1969), pp. 71–75, quotation on pp. 73–74. See also Thaden, *Russia's Western Borderlands*, pp. 68–76.

[141] Victor Taki, "Between *Politzeistaat* and *Cordon Sanitaire*. Epidemics and Police Reform during the Russian Occupation of Moldavia and Wallachia, 1828–1834," *Ab Imperio* 4 (2008): 82–89. Sturdza, one of the boiar landlords, was the governor.

his attempt to sort things out, Alexander reiterated his twofold desire to maintain local laws, mores, and customs, and to organize the territory in accord with policies already adopted in Finland and the Kingdom of Poland. The Bessarabian Statute of 1818 embodied these principles. Its implementation proved to be fraught with difficulties.

The first difficulty stemmed from a general systemic problem that serves as a leitmotif in this study, namely, the tension in the state-building of a multicultural empire between local traditions and centralizing practices. The second difficulty, also systemic but peculiar to the Russian Empire, was the multiple sources of institutional authority. As we have also seen, the ministerial reforms of Alexander I increased the number of competing forms of imperial rule without rationalizing the lines of command.

In the early 1820s, the newly appointed Governor General of New Russia and Viceroy of Bessarabia, M. S. Vorontsov, and the civil governor of Bessarabia, F. F. Vigel', were appalled by the chaotic conditions in the province and the depraved morals of the local boiars whom they perceived through an Orientalist lens. They undertook sweeping changes in the local administration. Vorontsov vigorously pursued a policy of colonization of the southern part of the province by Serbs, Cossacks, and state peasants, giving preference to their interests over those of the local boiars. He worked with the Ministry of the Interior to replace the Statute of 1818, to sharply curtail the autonomous institutions of the province, and to promote the incorporation of the boiars into the Russian nobility.[142]

During this period, the Russian administration of the principalities under the enlightened rule of Count Pavel Kiselev replaced the model of Ottoman imperial rule. Kiselev belonged to that brilliant generation of Russian army officers, veterans of the Napoleonic campaigns, who subsequently diverged into two political currents: one leading to the Decembrist uprising and the other to administrative reform. Kiselev was closely associated with the future Decembrist leaders and shared their humanitarian and rational views toward governing, but not their revolutionary outlook or their conspiratorial plans. His postwar reform of the disorganized Second Army on the southwest frontier won him the approval of Alexander. His able command of the occupation forces in the principalities during the Russo-Turkish War of 1828/9 convinced Nicholas to appoint him president plenipotentiary of the principalities,

---

[142] Anthony Rhinelander, *Prince Michael Vorontsov, Viceroy to the Tsar* (Montreal: McGill and Queens University Press, 1990), pp. 67–93.

with full civil and military authority, a position he occupied for six years.[143]

Kiselev was responsible for introducing a series of reforms that combined the administrative and welfare functions of a well-ordered police state (*Politzeistaat*) with the establishment of new political institutions. The Organic Statutes of 1829 provided for an elective assembly dominated by the big boiars, which would in turn elect the two princes of Moldavia and Wallachia for life and share power with them.[144] Kiselev inaugurated a rule of law and order with the help of a Russian-trained police force. He replaced archaic rules governing trade and taxation, and encouraged trade and industry. The Statute also regulated relations between boiars and their peasants, and served as a model for his reforms of the Russian state peasantry in the following decade.

Russian policy further aimed at defining more sharply the frontier between the principalities and the Ottoman "Orient" by imposing a quarantine line on the Danube. According to official instructions, the quarantine would serve not only to control the spread of plague, but also to hamper communications between the Ottoman Empire and the principalities.[145] Although the Ottoman sultan retained nominal sovereignty over the principalities, they became in fact a joint Ottoman–Russian condominium. The presence of Russian advisors, the existence of a Russian party among the boiars, and the Russian guarantees of the political order set the tone for life in the principalities for the following twenty years until the European-wide revolutions of 1848 reached the Danube.

In form and function Kiselev's policies continued and expanded the Russian administrative experiments introduced by Alexander I throughout the western borderlands. But disagreements soon emerged within the Russian ruling elites over the long-term aims of Russian policy in the principalities, fueling the general debate over imperial strategy in the borderlands. Nicholas I and his advisors pursued two aims. First, they sought to guarantee future Russian influence by offering the local boiar elites privileges that they did not enjoy under the Ottomans. Second, they maintained a balance between the authority of the princes (*hospodars*) and that of the boiars, enabling the Russians through the agency of their

---

[143] A. P. Zablotskii-Desiatovskii, *Graf P. D. Kiselev i ego vremia. Materialy dlia istorii imperatorov Aleksandra I, Nikolaia I, Aleksandra II*, 4 vols. (St. Petersburg: M. M. Stasiulevich, 1882), vol. I, pp. 348–57; N. M. Druzhinin, *Gosudarstvennye krest'iane i reformy*, 2 vols. (Moscow: Izd. Akademiia nauka SSSR, 1946), vol. I, pp. 257–63.

[144] Taki, "Between *Politzeistaat*," pp. 74–101. Cf. Alexander Bitis, *Russia and the Eastern Question. Army, Government and Society, 1815–1833* (Oxford University Press, 2006).

[145] Taki, "Between *Politzeistaat*," p. 99.

consuls to intervene in local politics. The language of the reforms was designed to represent Russia's European face and to reassure the Great Powers that Russian administrators were the *kulturträgers* of enlightened government in its cameralist form. But Kiselev had more ambitious ends in mind. Here he parted company with the Russian Foreign Minister Count Nesselrode.

For Kiselev, the Organic Statutes were a form of tutelary authority built on the assumptions that the populations of the principalities and particularly the boiars were not ready to govern the country by themselves, and that in the long run the principalities would become an integral part of the Russian Empire. "I consider the Danube as the frontier of the Empire," he wrote to his friend Prince Orlov in 1833, "and in spite of Nesselrode and all our politicians in Petersburg the force of circumstances will triumph over fixed plans and we will end up being there where we ought to be." Consequently, he favored a long-term military occupation even after the introduction of the internal reforms, arguing that "by prolonging the occupation, opinion (*les esprits*) will become accustomed to seeing us there and incorporation will become easier."[146] But Nesselrode and Nicholas were determined to adhere to the policy articulated in 1829, embracing a purely legitimist approach.

The Kingdom of Poland

In the years after the Napoleonic Wars, Alexander was eager to enhance his European influence by playing the role of an enlightened promoter of liberal ideas before fears of internal subversion and Metternich's influence altered his course. But his attempts to adapt the constitutional reforms he supported in France under the Bourbon restoration to Russian conditions, particularly the creation of ministries and four new universities on the European model, raised fresh questions among Alexander's advisors over what this meant for the governance of the western borderlands. The tsar finally embraced the ideas of his Polish advisors, such as Prince Adam Czartoryski and Count Seweryn Potocki, who advocated the restoration of a Polish state against the advice of some of his Russian advisors and the

---

[146] Kiselev to Orlov, June 18, 1833 in Zablotskii-Desiatovskii, *Graf P. D. Kiselev*, vol. IV, p. 111. Kiselev recognized that in the struggle over the principalities, the Porte sought to delay approving the Statutes until the date set for the evacuation of the Russian army. Vienna opposed the Statutes, first, because they provided commercial freedom and political advantages that would weaken its influence and, second, because by improving the lot of the Romanian peasantry they would eliminate the causes for emigration from Wallachia to Austria and would promote immigration from Transylvania and Bukovina. Kiselev to Nesselrode, March 8, 1832, *ibid.*, vol. IV, pp. 69–71.

opposition of the Great Powers at the Congress of Vienna. The Polish Constitutional Charter of 1815 created a Kingdom of Poland linked to the empire by a personal union. Crafted by a group of Polish and Russian officials, it adopted some of the principles introduced by the Polish constitution of 1791 and the Napoleonic constitution for the Grand Duchy of Warsaw in 1807. Equality before the law, personal liberty for the peasants, and basic civil rights were confirmed. Legislative power was shared by the tsar-king and the legislature (Sejm), a bicameral legislature; the Senate was to be appointed; and the Lower House was to be elected on the basis of property qualifications. The tsar-king had the power of an absolute veto. It was a remarkable document, and it granted the Poles far more personal rights and a more active participation in political life than Alexander's Russian subjects.[147] In a famous speech delivered in French to the Sejm in 1818, Alexander called upon the Polish representatives "to give a great example to Europe which is turning its eyes on you." He strongly implied that the institutions of the kingdom were to be an experiment that, if successful, could be a model for the empire as a whole. "The organization that previously existed in your country has enabled me to introduce immediately what I have given you, putting into practice the principles of those liberal institutions that have been my constant concern and whose salutary influence I hope, with the help of God, to extend to all the lands Providence has entrusted to my care."[148]

But from the outset the great expectations and, it is tempting to say, illusions of cooperation between the Russians and the Poles were based on different assumptions. In a speech to the Sejm, the eloquent deputy, Dominik Krysiński, seemed to echo Alexander's words: "Europe is looking at us. Yes, Europe may admire us but it will also judge us . . . the degree of our participation in the hierarchy of civilized nations depends on our statute on national representation."[149] It quickly became evident that both the Poles and the Russians were divided among themselves and were not always clear in their own minds as to what the kingdom was to represent. For several years after the Congress of Vienna the Polish intellectual elite of Warsaw and Wilno continued to consider themselves to be an integral part of Europe. But in a revival of "Occidentalism" they debated whether Poland should wholly embrace the values of the Enlightenment as a universal norm or preserve its own traditions, partly

---

[147] Thaden, *Russia's Western Borderlands*, pp. 83–85.

[148] N. S. Shil'der, *Imperator Aleksandr Pervyi. Ego zhizn' i tsarstvovanie*, 4 vols., 2nd edn (St. Petersburg: A. S. Suvorin, 1905), vol. IV, pp. 86–87.

[149] Cited in Jerzy Jedlicki, *A Suburb of Europe. Nineteenth-Century Polish Approaches to Western Civilization* (Budapest: CEU Press, 1999), p. 16.

mythical, of ancient republican liberties that predated the evolution of civic rights in the West. Did Poland as the most western of Slavic nations have a mission to pass on the values of Western civilization to the East?[150] Beyond that there was the political question for the Poles of whether to serve the imperial Russian government without question or to defend the most liberal interpretation of the rights granted by the Constitutional Charter even if this threatened to oppose the will of the tsar. The elite continued to be split over the institutional structure of the country and their own political and social roles within it.[151]

This was part of the larger problem of how to deal with the loss of their national independence. The Poles faced two options: they could accept the framework of the Russian Empire as a peaceful arena for competing with the Russians and promoting their own national development; or they could strive to restore their independence and their multicultural state by force of arms if necessary. Accommodation or resistance – assimilation was never an option – such were the two extremes between which the pendulum of Polish attitudes toward Russia was henceforth to swing until 1989 when it finally came to rest. The Russian response was either to compromise or to repress, but never to grant real independence. Debate and disagreement over the proper course of action to take divided the elites of both countries over the following two centuries.

The insurrectionist tradition in Polish history took many turns. Before the Second Partition, the resort to "legal rebellion" (*roskosz*) of the szlachta had been directed against what was perceived as an abuse of power by the king. In 1793, it was led by a revolutionary democrat, Tadeusz Kościuszko, against the partitioning powers in the name of Polish independence and personal freedom for the peasants. From that time forward it flowed like an underground stream, occasionally breaking to the surface in 1806, 1830, 1846, 1863, 1905, 1918, and 1944, bearing old myths and fed by new currents. Within the insurrectionist tradition the legions, in form if not yet in name, occupied an honored place. Composed of exiles, the first of them appeared as émigré units in Lombardy in 1797 during Napoleon's Italian campaign. A fighting protest against the partitions, they provided both military training and a

---

[150] Jedlicki, *A Suburb of Europe*, pp. 13–16.

[151] Norman Davies makes the valuable distinction in Polish politics among three types of reaction to Russian rule which he calls loyalism (*Lojalizm*), insurrection (*Poswstanie*), and conciliation (*Ugoda*) taken from contemporary Polish discourse and inseparable from their specific Polish context. He further notes that leading Polish figures moved from one posture to another depending upon circumstances. See Norman Davies, *God's Playground. A History of Poland, vol. I: The Origins to 1795* (Oxford University Press, 1981), pp. 30–60.

political school for the officers and soldiers. The Poles continued to serve in Napoleon's armies, playing a large role in the defeat of Prussia in 1806. Napoleon rewarded them by creating the Grand Duchy of Warsaw out of the Prussian share of the partitions. Most of the Austrian share was added in 1809. The rump state was manipulated by Napoleon as a pressure point against Alexander. A French-inspired constitution restored the dynastic rule of the king of Saxony, but only with the reduced title of grand duke. The Polish forces were placed under the command of Prince Joseph Poniatowski, who led over 100,000 men in Napoleon's Russian campaign of 1812. Loyal to the end, Poniatowski died at the head of his Polish lancers in the battle of Leipzig. The cult of Napoleon was born in Poland, pinning hopes for freedom on intervention by France.

In virtually every European upheaval in the nineteenth century, exiled Poles formed armed groups on the model of the original units in expectation of fighting the partitioning powers once again on Polish soil. Among these were the poet Adam Mickiewicz's attempt to form a legion in Italy in 1848; the volunteers that fought under General Józef Bem with the Hungarians in 1849; the "Ottoman Cossacks" organized during the Crimean War; volunteer units from Prussian Posen (Poznan) and Austrian Galicia in the insurrection of 1863; and Piłsudski's abortive attempt to create a legion in Japan during the Russo-Japanese War. More successful in 1912, he formed the Riflemen's Union in Galicia, which he then led into the war against Russia in 1914, proclaiming it in grandiose style as the "advanced column of the Polish Army setting out to fight for the liberation of the Fatherland." It was the first of two legions sponsored by the Austrian High Command on the Eastern front. Although the term "legion" was not used to designate the Polish forces in exile during the Second World War, that is what they were. Formed in both the Soviet Union and Great Britain, Polish units fought for the freedom of Poland from Nazism, but each for a different kind of Poland.[152]

The Poles who accepted Russian rule devolved from a tradition going back into the eighteenth century, and was marked, as we have seen, by the periodic appearance in Warsaw of a Russian party prepared to serve Moscow's interests in Central Europe. Its first post-partition manifestation was not very edifying. A number of the great szlachta families, the magnates, like the Magyar magnates, accepted the new rulers and were rewarded with the estates confiscated from their peers who had supported Kościuszko. Others sought to ingratiate themselves, pursued titles, and

---

[152] Piotr Wandycz, *The Lands of Partitioned Poland, 1795–1918* (Seattle, WA: University of Washington Press, 1974), pp. 28–33.

plunged, if only briefly, into a riotous social life that Piotr Wandycz has called a *"danse macabre."*[153] Over time, however, those who rejected the idea of resistance, whatever their motives, devoted themselves to reconstructing Polish economic and cultural life, or even cooperating with one of the partitioning powers against the others in the hope of reconstituting Poland in one form or another.

In the early history of collaboration under Alexander I some of the most distinguished szlachta families were represented. Among them the most prominent was Prince Adam Jerzy Czartoryski. His youth was spent at the court of Catherine the Great as a hostage for the good behavior of his family, which had taken a leading part in resistance to Russian domination and the partitions. Taking hostages from the families of conquered elites was a familiar strategy for the Russians in dealing with the steppe borderlands dating back to the sixteenth century. Czartoryski's youthful friendship with Alexander was based on their common enthusiasm for the liberating ideals of the Enlightenment. Once Alexander became tsar, he included him as a member of the four-man Unofficial Committee known as "the tsar's young friends."

As deputy (but in fact real) minister of foreign affairs from 1804 to 1806, Czartoryski worked closely with other members of the Unofficial Committee, V. P. Kochubei, N. N. Novosil'tsev, and P. A. Stroganov, to redirect Russian foreign policy by forging an alliance with Britain against Napoleonic France, and projecting Russian power deeper into Europe by reshaping the configuration of the western and southeastern borderlands.[154] The "young friends" understood the necessity of combating the French liberation ideology by countering it with one of their own. They envisaged a reconstruction of Eastern Europe that would establish a number of satellite states along Russia's frontiers linking Russian policy in Poland with the Balkans, a recurrent theme of Russian foreign policy from the eighteenth to the mid-twentieth centuries. Supported by his friends on the Unofficial Committee, Czartoryski devised grandiose plans for carving out, with the help of local liberation movements, a number of autonomous states in the Balkans that would remain under the suzerainty of the Porte, but would be placed under Russian protection. He urged Alexander to annex Moldavia, Wallachia, and Bessarabia. The tsar reacted cautiously at the time, limiting his ambition to the annexation

[153] Wandycz, *The Lands*, pp. 22–23.
[154] A. M. Stanislavskaia, *Russko-angliskie otnosheniia i problemy sredizemnomor'ia, 1798–1807* (Moscow: Izd. Akademiia nauka SSSR, 1962), pp. 335–38, which also reviews critically Russian and Western historiography of Czartoryski. She correctly points out that Russian policy making at the time was a collective enterprise and not simply a product of Czartoryski's personal views.

of Bessarabia in 1812.[155] Czartoryski's idea of reconstituting Poland by uniting the Prussian and Russian shares of partitioned Poland in a personal union with Russia under the scepter of the tsar won over Alexander. But when the tsar introduced the idea at the Congress of Vienna, he was violently opposed by the British and Austrians, provoking a crisis that almost broke up the Congress. Czartoryski had to be satisfied with a smaller Kingdom of Poland. He continued in Russian service, serving as curator of the University of Wilno (Vilnius). Gradually becoming disillusioned with his role as a collaborator, he was forced into exile by the revolt of 1830.

That Czartoryski also envisioned Poland as a model for the cultural transformation of Russia suggests that he might have had in mind the possibility of emulating a role some Greeks thought they might play in the Roman Empire.[156] Czartoryski and Count Stanisław Potocki were mainly responsible for drafting the university reform of 1802 based on the work of the Polish Commission of National Education created in 1773. Their activities in the field of education reached their peak in the decade after the Congress of Vienna when Czartoryski seized upon Alexander's promise to treat the Russian provinces of partitioned Poland as a cultural whole. Potocki had been one of the supporters of the liberal constitution of 1791 that brought down the wrath of Catherine II. He fled to Austria after the Russian intervention and Third Partition, but returned with the Napoleonic armies to become president of the Educational Department in the Grand Duchy of Warsaw. As a gesture of reconciliation, Alexander I appointed him Minister of Instruction and Enlightenment. A steadfast liberal and freemason, he played a prominent role in founding the University of Warsaw, a number of higher technical schools designed to train a new professional elite, and over a thousand secular primary schools. Satirizing the Church and ridiculing the Sarmatian mentality of the szlachta earned him the hostility of powerful enemies and he was forced to resign.[157] Acting more prudently, Czartoryski, as curator of the University of Wilno until 1823, brought the entire school system of

---

[155] Stanislavskaia, *Russko-angliskie,* pp. 412–20. There were several variants of Czartoryski's plan, all supported by his friends on the Unofficial Committee. Alexander took a more cautious view at the time, but later adopted aspects of them, for example, in the annexation of Bessarabia in 1812 and the creation of the Kingdom of Poland in 1815.

[156] Marian Kukiel, *Czartoryski and the Unity of Europe, 1770–1861* (Princeton University Press, 1955); Patricia Grimstead, *The Foreign Ministers of Alexander I* (Berkeley, CA: University of California Press, 1969).

[157] Davies, *God's Playground,* vol. II, p. 310; Frank W. Thackeray, *Antecedents of Revolution. Alexander I and the Polish Kingdom, 1815–1825* (Boulder, CO: East European Monographs, 1980), pp. 40–41, 99–100. The Potocki family, like other aristocrats, divided their loyalties. Among the loyalists were Stanisław-Feliks Potocki, the marshal

all the western *gubernii* under his authority. During the golden years before the uprising of 1830 most of the important literary figures of Polish Romanticism graduated from Polish schools under his supervision.[158]

Playing a similar role in accommodating imperial rule, F-S. Drucki-Lubecki, the Minister of Finance of the kingdom from 1821 to 1831, envisioned the industrialization of the Kingdom of Poland as the motor driving the economic transformation of the Russian Empire.[159] Accumulating a small capital reserve, he built up a textile industry that successfully challenged its Russian counterpart. He revived the languishing Polish mining industry and established a Polish State Bank in 1828 more than thirty years before a comparable institution was founded for the Russian Empire as a whole. He was ably seconded by Stanisław Staszic, a geologist, industrialist, and pamphleteer, perhaps the original pan-Slav. After the fall of Napoleon he urged the Poles to accept the leadership of Russia in a political union of all Slavs. Appointed director of the Commission on Industry and Crafts, he was the first to survey Poland's mineral deposits, founded a modern metallurgical industry, built bridges and roads, and opened a number of technical schools.[160] Even after the Polish revolt of 1830, Lubecki continued to develop the Polish economy, helping to finance the first railroad company in the kingdom linking Warsaw with Vienna.[161] At the outset of the insurrection of 1830, both Czartoryski and Lubecki sought to adhere to constitutional principles and guide the events along a peaceful path. Their failure forced them to quit Poland. While Czartoryski became the symbol of resistance in "the Great Emigration," he remained a strict constitutionalist. He criticized the radical Polish republicans and condemned the Russians for illegally abrogating the constitution of the kingdom. He urged the continuation of what

of the Targowica Confederation, a theoretician of *mozhnovladstva* of the Polish–Lithuanian Commonwealth, who served as a general in the Russian Army; Jan Potocki, who began on the other side as a member of the Fourth of May Sejm, but then like Stanisław switched allegiance to serve in the Imperial Russian Foreign Ministry, and who published more than twenty books of history and ethnography (F. A. Brokgaus and I. A. Efron (eds.), *Entsiklopedicheskii slovar'* (St. Petersburg: I. A. Efron, 1898), vol. XXXXVIII, p. 739); and Stanisław-Szczęsny Potocki, another confederate of Targowica, who declared, "Poles should abandon all memory of their fatherland. I myself am a Russian forever" (Davies, *God's Playground*, vol. II, p. 30).

[158] Irena Roseveare, "Wielopolski's Reforms and their Failure before the Uprising of 1867," *Antemurale*, 15 (Rome 1971): 114–15.

[159] Jerzy Edlicki, "Industrial State Economy of Poland in the 19th Century," *Acta Poloniae Historica* 18 (1968): 221–37; Natalia Gasiorowska, "Les origines de la grande industrie polonaise au XIX siècle," in *La Pologne au VIe Congrès Internationale des Sciences Historiques* (Warsaw: Société polonaise d'histoire, 1930).

[160] Davies, *God's Playground*, p. 169; *Entsiklopedicheskii slovar'*, vol. LXII, p. 536.

[161] Alfred J. Rieber, *Merchants and Entrepreneurs in Imperial Russia* (Chapel Hill, NC: University of North Carolina Press, 1982), pp. 62–65.

later became known as organic work in preparation for the day when changes in the international situation, which he hoped to bring about, would force a restoration of the Kingdom of Poland.

From the Polish nationalist perspective the most notorious of the collaborators was General Jóseph Zajączek. A fervid Jacobin and veteran fighter against the Russians in the 1790s, a legionnaire and officer in Napoleon's armies, he went over to the Russians in 1812. Alexander surprised the Poles by appointing him Viceroy of the Kingdom, a position that he filled with complete loyalty, even subservience, until his death in 1826.[162] The revolt of 1830 set back the cause of accommodation by a whole generation.

Many high-ranking Russian statesmen feared the spread of the ideas of the French Revolution to the lands of partitioned Poland. Referring to the formation of Polish legions and the flow of Polish émigrés into Moldavia, Bulgaria, and Bosnia in the 1790s, Chancellor Alexander Bezborodko put it most starkly:

I fear that Poland is rising up and by an act of insurgency in Moldavia once again is proposing on the basis of equality and French ideas to decide who will be entrusted (I have in mind the petty bourgeoisie and mob and partly the petty gentry) with the task of attaching which of our borderlands (*porubezhnie provintsii*) to it. That will be the end of everything![163]

This opinion was widely shared. Alexander's decision to resurrect Poland met with almost universal opposition among the Russian elites, including all his advisors in foreign affairs at the Congress of Vienna, Capo d'Istria, Karl Nesselrode, and Pozzo di Borgo. They argued that a restored Poland would recreate the old *barrière de l'est*, plunge Russia into barbarism, and convert it into an Asiatic state. They insinuated that the institutions of a constitutional Poland and an autocratic Russia would be incompatible with one another. Alexander's speech to the Sejm in 1818 agitated the top Russian generals, Count Osterman-Tolstoi, A. P. Ermolov, A. A. Zakrevskii, and even Count P. D. Kiselev; even the court historian Nikolai Karamzin joined the chorus.[164] Alexander disregarded their advice and ignored the opposition, but he was not indifferent to the problem of reconciling the inherent contradictions in his institutional

---

[162] Thackeray, *Antecedents*, pp. 25–26, 86–88, 116–19.

[163] Bezborodko to Vorontsov, 2/13 July 1798, *Arkhiv kniazia Vorontsova*, 40 vols. (Moscow: A. I. Mamontova, 1870–1895), vol. XIII, p. 401.

[164] Thackeray, *Antecedents*, pp. 7–12, 47–48. Speransky was concerned over the form and timing of the declaration. Even a few of the future Decembrists were unhappy with it. *Ibid.*, pp. 34–35, 49.

arrangements. His solution was to retract in content what he had granted in form.

Alexander was not content to rely on the provisions of the Charter to secure his personal authority in the kingdom. He appointed his brother, Grand Duke Konstantin Pavlovich, as commander of the Polish army, though the Poles would have preferred Kościuszko. He named Novosil'tsev as a Russian commissioner, a post not provided for in the Constitutional Charter. Once again, the tsar resorted to a number of ad hoc arrangements that subverted both principles of autonomous rule and bureaucratic rationalism upon which the organization of the kingdom had been constructed. Both the viceroy and the commissioner acquired a reputation among the Poles for arbitrariness and brutality. Ironically, after 1820, Konstantin became more favorably disposed toward the Poles, due in part to his marriage to a Polish noblewoman and in part to his command of the Lithuanian Army Corps, which inclined him to support the idea of unifying congress Poland with Lithuania. This would have restored Poland to its approximate boundaries before the Third Partition. Until his death, Alexander skillfully, if somewhat deceitfully, kept alive this tantalizing possibility as a means of binding the Poles to his imperial rule.

After Alexander, the supreme juggler, died in 1825, the relations between Russia and its Polish borderland rapidly deteriorated. The causes of friction remained the same, but the two sides were less inclined to compromise. Nicholas I dispelled the illusions cultivated by his brothers and cherished by the Poles that Russia might detach Lithuania from the central administration and attach it to the kingdom. He opposed the idea because it would "infringe upon the territorial integrity of the empire."[165] Nicholas proceeded to Russify the Lithuanian Army Corps, purge Poles from the civil administration, and strip the Wilno Educational District of its authority over schools in the Mogilev, Vitebsk, and Minsk provinces. He also launched a campaign to absorb the Uniats into the official Orthodox Church. The contested territory of the old Grand Duchy of Lithuania (called the *Kresy* by the Poles) would remain a bone of contention between Poles and Russians for more than a century.

The second major issue driving the two sides apart was the rise of secret societies and jurisdiction over trials of political cases. On his succession to the throne, Nicholas demanded an investigation of the underground Polish Patriotic Society, which had been partly suppressed in the last years of Alexander's reign, but had maintained secret ties with

---

[165] Nicholas I to Konstantin Pavlovich, November 5 and 24, 1827, in "Imperator Nikolai I i Pol'sha v 1825–1831 gg.," ed. N. K. Shilder, *Russkaia starina* 101 (1900): 302.

Decembrists. The mild verdicts handed down by the Polish authorities in their public trials provoked a prolonged legal wrangle. The tsar finally intervened, reprimanding the Senate, and ordering a retrial for several of the defendants in a Russian court. Despite these and other tensions, neither Nicholas nor his brother, Konstantin Pavlovich, showed any intention of abolishing the Kingdom of Poland or destroying its principal governing institutions. Nor did leading Polish advocates of conciliation, such as Czartoryski, Lubecki, most of the officials in the government, and representatives in the Sejm, nourish revolutionary aspirations. But for good reason each suspected the other of seeking in different ways to modify the governing institutions in the direction of greater or lesser autonomy. When a small group of conspirators resorted to violence, the gulf separating the responsible leaders of the Polish and Russian governments proved too great to bridge by conciliatory measures. Most of the Polish nobility joined the radicals in the revolt of 1830.[166]

Following the repression of the insurrection in 1832, Nicholas imposed the kind of regime he probably favored even before it broke out. The kingdom retained its title, but little else of Alexander's design survived. An Organic Statute replaced the constitutional instruments, but even its provisions were never fully carried out. The kingdom was subdivided into Russian provinces, with the administrative structure being reduced to a shell. The real ruler was Field Marshal I. F. Paskevich, familiarly known to the Poles as "the Hound of Mogilev." The Polish army was disbanded and its soldiers incorporated into Russian regiments serving in the Caucasus. Perhaps as many as 10 percent of landed estates were confiscated; 80,000 Poles were deported to Siberia; another 10,000 fled abroad to join "the Great Migration."

In the aftermath, the Russian bureaucracy attempted to weaken the absolute power of the noble landlords over the Ruthenian peasantry and to snuff out any spark of Polish cultural resurgence in Ukraine. Under the paternalistic administration of Governor General D. G. Bibikov (1838–1852), the Inventory Laws (1847) minutely regulated the duties and obligations of both landlords and peasants. At the time it represented an extraordinarily bold and innovative step by bureaucratizing agrarian relations and setting a precedent for state intervention on an all-empire scale. Improving the peasants' lot in the borderlands as a gambit in the

---

[166] Cf. Thackeray, *Antecedents*, pp. 132–44, and Kukiel, *Czartoryski*, pp. 140–50, who are most critical of the Russians; R. F. Leslie, "Polish Political Divisions and the Struggle for Power at the Beginning of the Insurrection of November 1830," *Slavonic and East European Review* 31(76) (December 1952): 113–32, who warns against too hasty a conclusion that the revolt was the result of Russian mismanagement.

struggle for control helped to set the stage for the abolition of serfdom a decade later. Bibikov also launched an assault upon the social status of the szlachta by stripping 340,000 landless nobles of their titles. He confiscated the property of the great Catholic monasteries and coerced 130,000 Uniats to return to Orthodoxy. He capped his centralizing policies in education and religious affairs by forcing the biggest landlords to enroll their sons in imperial service.[167]

The Poles continued to compete with the Russians in the one area where they still retained an advantage, higher education. Polish students flocked to the newly established St. Vladimir University in Kiev, and also enrolled in proportionately large numbers in Moscow University. Steering a cautious course, the Russian Minister of Enlightenment, Count Uvarov, took some tentative steps to promote the education of Poles whom he thought might enter imperial service and perhaps even counter the influence of extremists. But his policy was not consistent nor did it appear very effective.[168]

The Polish struggle to regain cultural control over Ukraine was doomed by what Daniel Beauvois has called "a double paralysis." The Sarmatian mentality of the wealthiest Polish nobles imprisoned them in an archaic society based upon their exploitation of the peasants. They were hostile to all reform in the countryside, and even reacted tardily to the creation of Orthodox parish schools in 1859/60. When they did, the tsarist police cracked down on them. In any case, it was too late for the Poles to win over the Ukrainian masses, one of the major reasons their second great insurrection failed in 1863. Polish romantic writers and poets masked the harsh social reality of agrarian relations in their sentimental and heroic celebrations of an idyllic past, when frontier knights and warrior monks roamed the Pontic steppe. These fantasies had no effect upon the peasantry. But future generations of Poles kept alive the ideal of a Polish Ukraine, inspiring Piłsudski's legions in 1920 to march on Kiev. The hollowness of the Ukrainian idyll was quickly exposed, although Polish nationalists clung to the tattered shreds of this tradition until the Polish–Ukrainian conflict broke out again at the very end of the Second World War.

Following the death of Nicholas I in 1855, the autocracy sought once again to reach an accommodation with the Polish elite. Alexander II, the first tsar to speak Polish, immediately granted moderate concessions, declaring an amnesty for Polish exiles in Siberia, reopening the Polish

---

[167] Daniel Beauvois, *Le noble, le serf et le révizor* (Paris: Éditions archives contemporaines, 1984), p. 262.

[168] James T. Flynn, "Uvarov and the 'Western Provinces.' A Study of Russia's Polish Problem," *Slavic and East European Review* 64(2) (April 1986): 212–36.

Medical Academy, and inviting Polish landlords to participate in the debate on emancipating the serfs. However, he warned the Poles, "no daydreaming gentlemen." But as Norman Davies has remarked, "He gave an inch and his Polish subjects immediately thought of taking a mile."[169]

The chief Polish architect of a new era of collaboration, the Marquis Alexander Wielopolski, was a veteran of the insurrection of 1830 who had come round in exile to working with the Russians. In an open letter to Prince Metternich in 1846, Wielopolski counseled the Poles to abandon the past and seek the protection of Nicholas I as "the most generous of our enemies" in contrast to "the eternal hatred of our Slav race by the Germans."[170] When Alexander's initial gestures to relax Russian rule were met by patriotic demonstrations, he turned to Wielopolski to help to restore order. Wielopolski's program of reform to ease the condition of the peasantry, emancipate the Jews, and polonize the administration, all within the framework of the Organic Statute, failed to win the respect of the moderates, satisfy the insurrectionists, or gain the confidence of the Russian bureaucrats. The moderates gathered in the Agricultural Society were only willing to give lip service to their cooperation with Wielopolski. They sought to extract broad concessions that would have restored Polish autonomy and extend the frontiers once again into the eastern marches.[171]

Alexander II was prepared to grant concessions, but not autonomy. Following the disorders in 1861, he appointed his brother, Konstantin Nikolaevich, who still enjoyed a reputation as a reformer, to be the new viceroy and Wielopolski to be the head of the civilian administration. Alexander's instructions to Konstantin reveal how little his ideas differed from his father's on ruling the Poles, although he was temperamentally better disposed toward them. He wrote that his main aim was to restore the legal order established by the Organic Statute. He warned against courting popularity or yielding to demands of the extreme patriotic party which would never be satisfied by concessions. He reminded his brother never to forget that "*the Kingdom of Poland in its present boundaries ought to remain forever the possession (dostoianie) of Russia.*" To avoid the errors of the past, Alexander continued, there could be no talk of a constitution or a national army. "To agree to these would mean to renounce Poland and recognize its independence with all the ruinous results for Russia, that is,

---

[169] Davies, *God's Playground*, vol. I, p. 348; R. F. Leslie, *Reform and Insurrection in Russian Poland, 1856–1865* (London: Athlone Press, 1963), pp. 49–50.

[170] Roseveare, "Wielopolski's Reforms," p. 105.

[171] Leslie, *Reform and Insurrection*, pp. 116–25, 132, 139–44; *Vospominaniia generala-fel'd-marshala grafa Dmitriia Aleksandrovicha Miliutina 1860–1862*, introduction L. G. Zakharova (Moscow: Studiia TRITE, RIO Rossiiskii arkhiv, 1999), pp. 81–110, 175.

the loss of everything that had been ever conquered by Poland and that Polish patriots considered their rightful possession." He also warned Konstantin against the seductions of pan-Slavism. It was a utopia that could only endanger Russia's unity and lead to the dissolution of the empire into separate republics. The Catholic Church was to be respected, Alexander noted, but prevented from entering politics. It was important to win over women, who were overwhelmingly hostile to Russia, through cultural and philanthropic activities. Alexander characterized Wielopolski as a useful, if stubborn, subordinate who had to be kept well in hand.[172]

Alexander was counting on a combination of firmness and benevolence on the part of the Russian representatives in Warsaw, and compliance by the Polish elite to stabilize the kingdom. He was disappointed on both counts. When Wielopolski attempted to revive his program of reform, his administration crumbled in the face of the insurrection of 1863. When the fighting broke out, once again as in 1830, the Polish moderates were split, but did not oppose the insurrection. Wielopolski's main rival, Andrzej Zamoyski, was both more conservative than Wielopolski and more reluctant to work with the Russians. Isolated, Wielopolski was discredited.[173]

If the Polish advocates of accommodation were unwilling to support the Russian government, the insurrectionists were unwilling to cooperate with their Russian counterparts. The bone of contention was the borderland of the Kresy. On the eve of the 1863 uprising, negotiations between members of the Russian Land and Freedom (*Zemlia i Volia*) and representatives of the Polish radical groups ended in a deadlock. The Poles refused to ratify an agreement worked out with Alexander Herzen in London that would have provided for a plebiscite in the western *gubernii* (Lithuania, Belorus, and Ukraine) and reaffirmed their commitment to restore the frontiers of 1771.[174]

The Poles were only partially successful in winning support from the other ethnic groups in the borderlands. The leaders of the insurrection appealed to the Jews and Ruthenians, and won over some elements in the Lithuanian and Belorussian peasantry. But in the southwest region their efforts met with disaster when the Ruthenian peasantry, nurturing old

[172] Alexander II to Konstantin Nikolaevich, June 18/30, 1862, in "Perepiska Imperatora Aleksandra II-go s velikim kniazem Konstantinom Nikolaevichem za vremia prebyvaniia ego v dolzhnosti Namestnika Tsarstva Pol'skogo v 1862–1863 gg.," ed. A. A. Sivers, *Dela i Dni* 1 (1920): 123–24 (italics in original).
[173] Wandycz, *The Lands*, p. 159.
[174] See Andrzej Walicki, "Alexander Herzen's 'Russian Socialism' as a Response to Polish Revolutionary Slavophilism," in *Russia, Poland and Universal Regeneration. Studies in Russian and Polish Thought of the Romantic Epoch* (South Bend, IN: University of Notre Dame Press, 1991), pp. 1–72.

suspicions of the Polish szlachta, massacred their envoys. The suspicions and violent incidents lived on in the memory of both sides and poisoned relations between Poles and Ukrainians.

The Polish insurrection also left scars on the Russian body politic, inflaming public opinion and reversing the course of institutional reform. Although Grand Duke Konstantin gallantly defended conciliation even after an attempt on his life and the outbreak of fighting in Warsaw, he resigned in despair once his brother, the tsar, had taken the decision to impose a military dictatorship on the kingdom. Alexander's policy then proceeded along three lines. First, a flurry of diplomatic activity turned aside the attempts of France, Britain, and the Habsburg Monarchy to intervene on the basis of the Treaty of Vienna of 1815. Second, fresh military commanders, including the feared veteran of the 1830 repression, M. N. Murev'ev, were dispatched together with a massive infusion of troops to crush the insurrection. Third, and most important for the future of Russia in its western borderlands, the tsar called back into service the leading figure in drafting the emancipation of the Russian serfs, Nikolai Miliutin, as the architect of a new agrarian policy aimed at neutralizing the Polish peasantry and luring it away from the szlachta insurrectionists. This firm Russian policy received powerful endorsement from the moment the insurrection broke out from the influential newspaper editor Mikhail Katkov. His passionate editorials in *Moskovskie vedimosti* rallied the educated classes around a banner of Russian nationalism that became a permanent feature of Russian public life.

The bureaucratic partisans of reconstructing the imperial center and its relationship with the borderlands joined with Miliutin; his closest collaborators were Prince V. A. Cherkasskii, Iuri Samarin of the populist-Slavophile wing of the agrarian reformers and his brother Dmitri, the Minister of War. Their broad program of reform from above featured the elimination of class privileges of the nobility whether Russian, Polish, Swedish–Finnish, or Baltic German; economic and social freedom for the peasantry; the rule of an enlightened bureaucracy; and the drastic reduction of the number of Catholic monasteries. While the Miliutin brothers accepted the necessity of uncompromising repression, Murev'ev reversed his position on the peasantry and accepted their proposals. Their odd alliance encountered opposition within the ministries. The Minister of the Interior, P. A. Valuev, the Chief of the Gendarmes V. A. Dolgorukov, and Foreign Minister Gorchakov favored alliances with the local szlachta as the best way of ensuring Russian control over the borderlands and, in the case of Gorchakov, of reassuring the rest of Europe.[175] But their views failed to persuade the tsar.

[175] Miliutin, *Vospominaniia, 1863–1864*, pp. 266–68, 304–9, 328–29, 404, 416–21, 502–3; *Dnevnik D. A. Miliutina, 1873–1875*, ed. P. A. Zaionchkovskii (Moscow: Biblioteka

Alexander endorsed most of the Miliutin plan. The agrarian reform in the kingdom and western provinces was more generous than those in the Polish provinces of Prussia or Austria, and simpler to implement than in Russia. Dmitri Miliutin summed up the views of his group. No matter what the reasons for the partitions had been, he wrote, Russia had the responsibility of ensuring the order and prosperity of the majority of the Polish population:

This does not mean that one nationality should swallow another; it would be against universal norms of justice [*obshchechelovechskaia spravedlivost'*] to demand that a conquered people be denied their own language, their own faith, their customs ... let the Poles speak in the Sejm and with their fellow men in Polish as the Riga Germans do in German, side by side with Estonians speaking Estonian; let them love their national literature, their folk songs; but when it comes to administration, courts and government institutions there should be no place for nationality; here what is necessary is the greatest possible unity and fusion [*sliianie*] between the [different] parts of a single government.[176]

By "an entire system of secret instructions" as Gorizontov defined it, the government sought to weaken the influence of Poles throughout the empire, discriminating everywhere on the basis of religion and proper names.[177] Once the insurrection had been suppressed, the Russian government moved to eliminate the Kingdom of Poland from the map, replacing it with the administrative designation of *Privislinskii krai* (the Vistula region), subordinating it to an all-powerful governor general, and depriving it of the institutions of local self-government (the *zemstvos*) and municipal councils (*dumas*) granted to the rest of European Russia in 1864. Even the Catholic Church was administratively attached to a Catholic College in St. Petersburg. The introduction of Russian into the educational system from elementary schools to university failed to promote assimilation and only resulted in a decline in standards. Poles abandoned the University of Warsaw to the Russians and other nationalities and flocked to the University of Cracow in Austrian Galicia or to west European universities.

In the decade after the uprising Russian officials and publicists often acted at cross-purposes in promoting Russification. They also disagreed over its potential in converting peoples of the Kresy (northwest province). Poles were hopeless and should be driven out; Belorussians were wayward

---

imeni V. I. Lenina, 1947), pp. 6–8, 233–34; *Dnevnik P. A. Valueva Ministra Vnutrennikh Del, 1861–1864*, ed. P. A. Zaionchkovskii (Moscow: Izd. Akademiia nauk SSSR, 1961), vol. I, pp. 23, 29–30, 336–42.

[176] Miliutin, *Vospominaniia, 1863–1864*, pp. 505–6.

[177] L. E. Gorizontov, *Paradoksy imperskoi politiki. Poliaki v Rossii i russkie v Pol'she* (Moscow: Indrik, 1999), p. 63; Patrice M. Dabrowski, "Russian–Polish Relations Revisited, or the ABC's of 'Treason' under Tsarist Rule," *Kritika* 4(1) (Winter 2003): 177–99.

and could be assimilated; Lithuanians could be depolonized by granting them more freedom in the use of their language; and Jews could only be isolated and segregated.[178] The confusion was characteristic of a general failure to master, let alone to understand, the complexities of governing such a diverse empire in competition with both internal and external rivals for cultural hegemony.

With the execution of their leaders, the deportation and flight abroad of many insurrectionists, and the gradual incorporation of the kingdom into the administrative structure of the Russian provinces, the Polish intelligentsia took refuge in "organic work." Many of the original leaders were disillusioned insurrectionists. They became the main advocates of raising the educational level of the population. Engaging in productive work was central to the program of the Warsaw positivists. But their attempts to accommodate the new regime created fresh difficulties. The new generation found itself caught in what Jedlicki has called a set of vicious circles. Secondary education did not prepare them for practical life; there was an overproduction of university graduates given their limited opportunities in the world of the liberal professions; and the economy did not grow fast enough to absorb those educated for technical or industrial jobs. The intelligentsia vainly attempted to integrate the romantic tradition stripped of its messianic spirit and its nostalgia for the old values of the szlachta with the prosaic demands of pursuing a career and achieving some measure of "internal self-dependence."[179]

The Pale of Settlement

With the entry of over half a million Jews into the Russian Empire as a result of the partitions of Poland, Catherine the Great laid down the first interior lines for a unique borderland called the Pale of Settlement. She restricted the residence of Jews to a number of western provinces, an area subsequently enlarged to include the Kingdom of Poland and seventeen provinces, except for a few cities like Kiev and Sevastopol, and Cossack villages in Poltava. She appears to have been motivated by a concern over

---

[178] Darius Staliūnas, "Between Russification and Divide and Rule. Russian Nationality Policy in the Western Borderlands in mid-19th Century," *Jahrbücher für Geschichte Osteuropas*, New series, 55(3) (2007): 357–73, and more generally, Darius Staliūnas, *Making Russians. Meaning and Practices of Russification in Lithuania and Belarus after 1863* (Amsterdam: Rodopi, 2007).

[179] Jedlicki, *A Suburb of Europe*, esp. pp. 175–200. See also Maciej Janowski, *Polish Liberal Thought Before 1918* (Budapest: CEU Press, 2004), esp. pp. 147–88; Miliutin, *Vospominaniia*, pp. 505–6.

the potential conflict between the Jewish population, especially its commercial element, with the Russian peasantry and merchantry.

A vast cultural divide separated the Jews from the Russians. An equally formidable obstacle to integration was the complex social relationship in the western borderlands between the Jewish population and dominant class of szlachta, whose suspicion and dislike of the Jews had been on the increase after a long period of toleration had given way to the anti-Semitism of the Counter Reformation led by the Jesuits. In response to the problems raised by these circumstances, imperial rule oscillated between attempts to integrate the Jews into the Russian estate system by transforming them into model citizens, while placating the szlachta and the Russian merchantry by imposing restrictions on the Jews. As Polish prejudices seeped deeper into Russian official thinking, a series of abortive reforms in the first third of the nineteenth century moved toward rendering the Jews "harmless" politically, socially, and especially economically.[180]

During the reigns of Alexander I and Nicholas I, Jews were saddled with various, often vaguely designed, special obligations and restrictions that further set them apart from the rest of the population. Under Nicholas I a two-pronged policy of Russification and discrimination abolished the Jewish self-governing institution (the *kahal*), imposed military service, and required conversion for Jews to enter government service. Legislation also forbade Jews from settling within thirty miles of the frontier, to prevent smuggling.[181]

The Great Reforms relaxed some of the restrictions on the rights of Jews to settle near the frontier or outside the Pale. Opportunities for education in Russian schools improved. But the attempts to introduce modern, secular schools into the Jewish communities produced ambivalent results. Assimilation was the primary aim. But as a German Jewish observer noted, "As long as the state does not grant the right of citizenship to the Jews, education will only be a disaster."[182] In 1862, Wielopolski issued a decree extending emancipation to the Jews in the hope of winning them over to a policy of polonization, and thus placating the szlachta who

[180] John Doyle Klier, *Russia Gathers Her Jews. The Origins of the "Jewish Question" in Russia, 1772–1825* (De Kalb, IL: Northern Illinois University Press, 1986), esp. pp. 60, 75–76, 140, 143.
[181] Salo W. Baron, *The Russian Jew under Tsars and Soviets*, 2nd edn (New York: Macmillan, 1976), pp. 18, 32, 40, 68; Michael Stanislawski, *Tsar Nicholas I and the Jews. The Transformation of Jewish Society in Russia, 1825–1855* (Philadelphia, PA: Jewish Publications Society, 1983).
[182] Heinz-Dietrich Löwe, *The Tsars and the Jews. Reform, Reaction and Anti-Semitism in Imperial Russia, 1772–1917* (Chur: Harwood Academic Publishers, 1993), p. 39.

regarded assimilation as the only acceptable course for the Jewish population. The decree was not rescinded after the suppression of the Polish uprising. Yet emancipation remained elusive in the post-Polish insurrectionist atmosphere of heightened Russian nationalism. In 1864, Jews were forbidden from acquiring land in the six western *gubernii* (the former Kingdom of Poland). A few highly placed representatives within the Jewish community, including religious leaders, first guild merchants, and entrepreneurs like Peter Steinkeller, accepted conversion to Catholicism as the only road to accommodation with their Polish neighbors. The Jewish intelligentsia continued to support the idea until it was undermined by the influx into the western *gubernii* and the Vistula region of Jews who had been secularized and partly assimilated to Russian culture; anti-Semitism among the Poles grew exponentially.[183] The assimilated Jews had no desire to be instruments of Russification. Yet they found themselves trapped between Russian and Polish pressures to adopt the language and religion of the two cultures struggling to gain hegemony over the Kresy. They reacted to pressure from both sides by finding new voices of protest and resistance in socialism and Zionism. Neither choice endeared them to Polish and Russian nationalists.

The Caucasian isthmus

In the Caucasus, Nicholas I launched another experiment in administering a borderland. After a visit to the region in 1837 he decided that the complex of problems facing Russian administrators could be solved only by concentrating authority in the hands of his personal representative, a viceroy. Yet, at the same time, he created a Caucasian Committee to exercise general supervision and to review the work of the viceroy. This body was superseded under Bariatinskii, who concentrated virtually all administrative powers in his own hands. At the end of the war against Muridism, Bariatinskii and his deputy, future Minister of War Dmitri Miliutin, introduced reforms that became known as the "military–popular" (*voenno-narodnyi*) system. It combined two methods of governing. Administrative affairs remained in the hands of military officers, but the courts were to be based on customary law (*adat*). As the previous chapter showed, this was intended to reduce the authority of the mullahs.

---

[183] Theodore R. Weeks, *From Assimilation to Antisemitism. The Polish Question in Poland 1850–1914* (DeKalb, IL: Northern Illinois University Press, 2006); Anthony Polonsky, "The New Jewish Politics and its Discontents," in Zvi Gitelman (ed.), *Modern Jewish Politics. Bundism and Zionism in Eastern Europe* (Pittsburgh, PA: University of Pittsburgh Press, 2003), pp. 40–41.

It was expanded and introduced into the provinces of Baku and Kars after their conquest and incorporation into the empire as a result of the Russo-Turkish War of 1877–78. In its revised form, reflecting borrowings from the Ottoman experience, the model was copied in organizing the Viceroyalty of Turkestan.[184] The first Viceroy of Turkestan, General Konstantin von Kaufman, had served fifteen years in the Caucasus under Vorontsov. There he became a protégé of Miliutin, who recommended him as an administrator for the western borderlands after the Polish uprising and then as governor general in Turkestan. He represented another link in the network of military administrators in the borderlands during this period.

The Ottoman Empire

With the conquest of Constantinople in 1452, the Ottomans succeeded in reconstituting the territorial integrity of the Eastern Roman (Byzantine) Empire at its maximum extent. Yet the institutions of the new empire still bore the strong imprint of its nomadic origins. In order to consolidate his conquests, Sultan Mehmed "the Conqueror" needed to complete the transition already under way to a centralized administrative and financial system. To state the problem in terms of Ottoman historiography: how was it possible to repair the rupture between the *gazi*–dervish tradition and the aspirations of the House of Osman to create a sedentary bureaucratic state, a rupture which had produced what Cemal Kafadar has called "a schizoid mental topography in Ottoman political imagination in the same old pattern that divides the land between a core area and an *uc* [frontier]."[185] The origins of this dichotomy have been sought as far back as the reign of Murad I in the fourteenth century, especially the 1360s and 1370s when chiefs (*begs*) of the *gazis* in Thrace were appointed by the sultan as governors of the frontier. In the growing tension between the vision of constant warfare and unlimited expansion, on the one hand, and permanent institutions, on the other hand, the *gazi* tradition gradually weakened. Under Mehmed the Conqueror the marginalization of the *gazis* increased dramatically.

---

[184] B. O. Bobrovnikov and I. L. Babich (eds.), *Severny Kavkaz v sostave Rossiiskoi imperii* (Moscow: Novoe literaturnoe obozrenie, 2007), pp. 189–94, 204–5; Daniel Brower, *Turkestan and the Fate of the Russian Empire* (London: Routledge Curzon, 2003), pp. 10–14, 32.
[185] Cemal Kafadar, *Between Two Worlds. The Construction of the Ottoman State* (Berkeley, CA: University of California Press, 1995), p. 143.

The army, administration, and reform

The Ottoman armed forces evolved from frontier raiders in the *gazi* tradition on the frontiers of Byzantium in the fourteenth century to one of the most formidable regular armies in Europe in the sixteenth century. The key to their early successes lay primarily in their ability to combine their own innovative practices of the gunpowder and military revolutions with the new technologies and tactics borrowed from their Christian opponents. In many ways the growth of their military prowess was similar to that of the Jürchen–Manchu nomads in their warfare with the Ming Empire in China. As early as the late fourteenth century, the Ottoman rulers demonstrated their mastery of both siege warfare against Byzantine fortresses and battlefield tactics. At the same time, they completed the reorganization of their military forces through the establishment of land for service (*timars*) that provided cavalrymen (*sipahi*) and the *devşirme* system of recruiting young Christian boys to serve as slaves in elite infantry units, or janissaries. At the height of Ottoman military power in the fifteenth and sixteenth centuries, the army was built around these two formations. The origins of both exemplified the adaptation of the nomadic society to Ottoman state-building in order to maintain a permanent army in a pre-capitalist economy.

The timar was not unlike the Russian *pomestie*. It was not a hereditary fief, but held only as long as the *sipahi* fulfilled his military obligations. He was authorized to collect taxes from the peasant cultivators on his land, who were not serfs but enjoyed a kind of permanent tenure, in order to support himself and his retainers. Through conquest and confiscation of Christian secular estates and monastic lands, the state disposed of almost all arable lands outside those granted to religious foundations. As long as new territories were conquered, the timar system and the cavalry arm it supported could be constantly expanded. As long as the state exercised its authority, the *sipahi* was bound to the center and not to personal or local interests. When those two conditions changed the foundation of state power was seriously weakened.[186]

The Janissary Corps derived from a tradition of recruiting slaves for military service from the Turkic peoples of Trans Caspia, which the Ottomans adopted for their own needs, and represented the "syncretic mood of a frontier zone."[187] It was formed by selecting outstanding

---

[186] Halil Inalcik, *The Ottoman State, Economy and Society, 1300–1600* (Cambridge University Press, 1994), pp. 305–7.

[187] I. Metin Kunt, *The Sultan's Servants. The Transformation of Ottoman Provincial Government* (New York: Columbia University Press, 1983), pp. 7, 32.

physical types from annual levies of Christian boys in Balkan villages, who were then obliged to convert to Islam. Trained as an elite military unit, they developed a legendary esprit de corps and were supplied with the most modern weapons as a sign of their status. The dual aim, originally introduced by the founder of the Ottoman dynasty, Orkhan, was to create an absolutely loyal body of servitors who would have no other ties except to the person of the sultan and to prevent the development of a genealogical nobility. It has been estimated that when the system was at its height in the fifteenth and sixteenth centuries as many as 200,000 Christian youths were impressed into the Janissary Corps. In principle, slavery is contrary to Islamic law. But the janissaries were in fact privileged and became a reservoir of administrative as well as military talent. Many of them rose to high rank in Turkish service as pashas and viziers, although they retained ties with their families and continued to speak Slavonic at the sultan's court. The system worked well until the janissaries began to lose their exclusive military character and to act as an interest group in defense of their own privileges against military reforms, contributing to the inner decay of the empire.[188]

In the Hungarian wars of the 1440s the Ottomans learned quickly from their enemies to adopt the mobile fortress of cannon mounted on carts (*wagonburg*) and field artillery. In their first siege of Constantinople in 1422, they employed siege artillery, forged by Hungarians; armed with muskets they won a decisive victory at Varna in 1444 over a combined Hungarian–Wallachian army, opening the way to their conquest of the Balkans and Constantinople. Mehmed rapidly freed himself from dependence on foreign experts and created a Corps of Gunners manned by growing numbers of Muslims. He introduced the process of manufacturing cannon from gun metal and scrap during sieges and set up permanent gun foundries.[189] During their final siege of Constantinople in 1454 the Ottoman army employed a monster cannon to breach the walls of "the strongest fortification of the Middle Ages."[190] Even more astonishing, these steppe warriors adapted to naval warfare and were able to challenge the great maritime power of Venice.

---

[188] Stanford Shaw, "The Ottoman View of the Balkans," in Charles Jelavich and Barbara Jelavich (eds.), *The Balkans in Transition. Essays in the Development of Balkan Life and Politics Since the Eighteenth Century* (Berkeley, CA: University of California Press, 1963), pp. 69–70; C. Fleischer, *Bureaucrat and Intellectual in the Ottoman Empire* (Princeton University Press, 1986); Albert Hourani, *A History of the Arab Peoples* (Cambridge, MA: Harvard University Press, 1991), pp. 214–22.

[189] Colin Imber, *The Ottoman Empire, 1300–1650. The Structure of Power*, 2nd edn (Basingstoke: Palgrave Macmillan, 2002), pp. 252–86.

[190] Halil Inalcik, *The Ottoman Empire. The Classic Age, 1300–1600* (London: Phoenix, 1994), pp. 7–8, 21, 23.

After his occupation of Constantinople, Mehmed took his first important steps in co-opting local elites. He expanded the well-established devşirme system by reserving the key positions in the government for slaves taken from among the old feudal Christian families that were willing to convert in order to accommodate to imperial rule.[191] He won over many well-established Christian landowners by granting them timars on the frontiers for military service without requiring them to convert. His aim was to form a body of absolutely loyal servitors as a counterweight to the Turkish tribal aristocracy. At the same time he created a number of central government offices headed by the grand vizier, who embodied the sultan's full authority, and which included the chief judge, chief treasurer, and chief scribe. Continuity of administration was provided by the Corps of Scribes. "A permanent substructure of career bureaucrats," in the words of Stanford Shaw, they carried on their work irrespective of the changes at the top of the Ottoman ruling class.[192]

Mehmed recognized the ecclesiastical authority of religious leaders in exchange for using their hierarchies to collect taxes and to administer justice through religious courts. He created the infrastructure for social services such as education and welfare that became one of the mainstays of Ottoman society at the local level.

As a colonizer, in order to consolidate his hold on newly conquered provinces, Mehmed increased and systematized Turkish migration that had for centuries periodically swept into the Balkans. He repopulated Constantinople with Muslims and Christians from the Balkans and Anatolia. He shifted Muslims from Anatolia to the Balkans as a means of breaking up the old Turkmen dynasties, providing a refuge for the qizilbashi emigrating from Iran, and strengthening the military frontier. Deportation from Anatolia (*sürgün*) and voluntary migration reached its peak in the seventeenth century. The influx filled out the lands in Western Rumelia (present-day Bulgaria) depopulated by war. By the mid-sixteenth century the majority of the inhabitants in the region were Turkish-Muslim, who adopted a sedentary way of life but served as frontier troops. In Sofia they constituted 80 percent of the population. As the Ottomans advanced to the north, frontier fortress towns like

---

[191] Bruce Masters, *Christians and Jews in the Ottoman Arab World* (Cambridge University Press, 2000), p. 61.
[192] Stanford Shaw, *History of the Ottoman Empire and Turkey, vol. I: Empire of the Gazis. The Rise and Decline of the Ottoman Empire, 1280–1808*, 2 vols. (Cambridge University Press, 1976), p. 280.

Silistria on the Danube acquired the features of a typical Turkish-Islamic city.[193]

In order to support his conquests, Mehmed pursued a deliberate policy of developing major centers of manufacturing and gaining access to trade routes in the borderlands. For more than a century the Ottoman–Iranian struggle over the Caucasus centered on control over the lucrative silk route. The high point of Ottoman success came after the peace of 1590 that extended Ottoman sovereignty over the silk-producing regions of Ganya and Shirvan in the Caucasian borderlands north of the Kura River. In the sixteenth century, the Ottoman policy of granting privileges to traders from Western Europe – the "capitulations" – opened Ottoman markets to high-quality cloth, English tin and steel, and especially bullion. In the long run, however, Ottoman statesmen resisted the evolution of the economy along capitalist lines. They were satisfied to increase their resources while maintaining the members of each class in place and guaranteeing their property. By the late sixteenth and early seventeenth centuries, the wars had exhausted traditional revenues, and inflation, fueled by the importation of foreign bullion, began to sap the vitals of the economy. Similar to the seventeenth-century crisis affecting other European and Eurasian states, the Ottoman Empire suffered an economic contraction due to the increased pressure of the central administration on the agricultural sector to provide revenue for the growing military and civilian bureaucracy.[194] The state had no other recourse but to increase taxes and duties. The result was to drive prices higher. The effect on international trade was to induce British and Dutch traders to divert their trading activities to a direct all-water route to the Indies.[195] In the economic sphere centralization had become a scourge.

The centralizing policies of Mehmed reached an apogee under Suleiman "the Magnificent," during the so-called classic age of the Ottoman Empire. Known in Turkish as the law-giver (kanuni), he attempted to introduce more regular procedures in making appointments and creating the rudiments of a functional bureaucracy. The idea that Suleiman was the embodiment of a patrimonial ruler wielding despotic

[193] Ilhan Şahin, Feridun M. Emecen, and Yusuf Halaçoğlu, "Turkish Settlements in Rumelia (Bulgaria) in the 15th and 16th Centuries. Town and Village Population," *International Journal of Turkish Studies* 4(2) (Fall/Winter 1989): 23–37.
[194] Suraiya Faroqui, *Making a Living in the Ottoman Lands, 1480–1820* (Istanbul: Isis, 1995), pp. 275–90.
[195] Halil Inalcik, "The Ottoman Economic Mind and Aspects of the Ottoman Economy," in M. A. Cook (ed.), *Studies in the Economic History of the Middle East from the Rise of Islam to the Present Day* (New York: Oxford University Press, 1970), pp. 207–18.

power has been demolished.[196] His absolutism was tempered by the practical necessity of acting through and even negotiating with the three major social groups of the ruling elite: the soldiers, ulama, and bureaucrats.[197] Together they constituted the non-tax-paying population or *askeri*. A military term, askeri expressed the origins of the empire and the commitment to a continual state of war.[198] Belonging to the askeri, the provincial notables (*ayan*) were also essential elements in the traditional Ottoman system. No sultan, however powerful and determined, conceived of sweeping them away until the early nineteenth century. Standing at the head of the askeri, the sultan "whose moral obligation as a just and pious ruler, drawing his authority from Islamic law (Shari'a) and sultanic prerogative (*kanun*) was to secure the financial and political stability of the state."[199] Absolute in theory, the sultan's power was hedged in by traditional interests during his lifetime and evaporated at his death. As Inalcik has pointed out, "every new succession in Ottoman history represented a revolution" that wiped out all his decrees, appointments, and disposition of landed property.[200]

The success of a sultan as a ruler depended to a large extent on his ability to maintain a harmonious balance among the interests represented by individuals he had appointed to positions of influence. Decisions were most often taken after consultation, a practice recommended by the Koran. The practice received institutional form in the nineteenth century with the creation of the state consultative council. To offset the bureaucracy, the sultan might consult his personal companion, "a pre-Islamic Iranian institution, as an alternative source of advice."[201] Policies of centralization followed a pattern of cyclical reform within the traditional

---

[196] Gilles Veinstein, "La voix du maître à travers les firmans de Soliman le Magnifique," in *Soliman le Magnifique et son temps* (Paris: La documentation française, 1992), pp. 127–44; Halil Inalcik, "Decision Making in the Ottoman State," in C. E. Farah (ed.), *Decision Making and Change in the Ottoman Empire* (Kirksville, MO: Thomas Jefferson University Press, 1993), pp. 9–18.

[197] Kafadar, *Between Two Worlds*; Serif Mardin, "Power, Civil Society and Culture in the Ottoman Empire," *Comparative Studies in Society and History* 11 (1969): 258–81; Kunt, *The Sultan's Servants*, pp. 7–9, 32–36.

[198] It is clear, however, from the work of Caroline Finkel that the Ottoman army through to the end of the seventeenth century was composed of a great variety of troops financed by different sources in what appears to be a highly improvisational manner. The increased monetarization of the costs of war meant higher taxes on the subject population and greater prominence of the financial bureaucracy over the military. Caroline Finkel, *The Administration of Warfare. The Ottoman Military Campaigns in Hungary, 1593–1606* (Vienna: VWGÖ, 1988), pp. 30 and *passim*.

[199] Virginia Aksan, *An Ottoman Statesman in War and Peace. Ahmed Resmi Efendi, 1700–1783* (Leiden: Brill, 1995), p. xi.

[200] Inalcik, "Decision Making in the Ottoman State," p. 11.

[201] Inalcik, "Decision Making in the Ottoman State," pp. 14–15.

structure of the empire. Whenever a crisis arose, the result of a military setback, a succession struggle, or the reign of a weak and incompetent ruler, the reformers drawn from the devşirme elements in the government restored stability by reorganizing the janissaries, reviving the timar system, eliminating corruption, reestablishing a sound currency, and returning to a fair distribution of taxes. Here again the Ottoman rulers displayed the pragmatic and flexible side to their politics.[202] But the enormous cost of almost constant warfare on the far-flung frontiers and the inadequate financial instruments, as well as the opposition of interest groups threatened by the reforms started a new cycle. One of the reasons that there is much debate over the beginning of a "decline" of the Ottoman Empire is that every reforming movement carried within itself the seeds of its own decay and appeared to announce the beginning of the end.[203]

The problem of decline

The question of the decline of the Ottoman Empire remains a central concern for historians of the post-classical period. The Ottoman literature of advice for kings written by the scribal class for the edification of the sultan shaped the concept of rulership by creating the metaphoric polarities of rise and decline, order and disorder, ruler and subject, which then characterized the meta-narrative of subsequent historians.[204] Yet, as Albert Hourani long ago stated, "the idea of decline is a difficult one to use."[205] Recently, a revisionist school has taken issue with "the myth of decline."[206] As a substitute it has unveiled a more nuanced picture of

[202] Şevket Pamuk, "Institutional Change and the Longevity of the Ottoman Empire, 1500–1800," *Journal of Interdisciplinary History* 35(2) (Autumn 2004): 225–47.

[203] Another source of the myth of decline was the political literature of the seventeenth century that deplored the vanishing "Golden Age" of Suleiman's reign. See the debate over this issue between Rhoads Murphey, "Review Article: Mustafa Ali and the Politics of Cultural Despair," *International Journal of Middle East Studies* 21(2) (1989): 243–45, and Cornell H. Fleischer, "Response to Rhoads Murphey's 'Review Article' of Bureaucrat and Intellectual in the Ottoman Empire. The Historian Mustafa Ali, 1541–1600," *International Journal of Middle East Studies* 22 (1990): 127–28.

[204] Douglas A. Howard, "Genre and Myth in the Ottoman Advice for Kings Literature," in Virginia H. Aksan and Daniel Goffman (eds.), *The Early Modern Ottomans* (Cambridge University Press, 2007), pp. 137–66, reviews the literature. See in particular Aziz Al-Azmeh, *Muslim Kingship. Power and the Sacred in Muslim, Christian and Pagan Polities* (London: Tauris, 1997).

[205] Hourani, *A History of the Arab Peoples*, p. 249. See also Fernand Braudel, *Civilization and Capitalism, 15th–18th Century, vol. III: The Perspective of the World* (New York: Harper & Row, 1984), p. 482.

[206] Earlier criticisms of the thesis of decline include Albert Hourani, "Ottoman Reform and the Politics of Notables," in W. R. Polk and R. L. Chambers (eds.), *Beginning of Modernization in the Middle East* (University of Chicago Press, 1968), and Roger

imperial rule. The emphasis in these studies falls on institutional change that shifted administrative authority to local elites and reorganized the financial structures to meet the crisis of the seventeenth century.[207] The problem for historians remains one of striking a balance between the flexibility of response by the ruling elites of the center and periphery, on the one hand, and the loss of territory in the struggle over the borderlands, on the other hand.

What Halil Inalcik calls the beginnings of the ruination of the Ottoman state in the 1570s coincided with the end of one long frontier war and the beginning of another. The connection was not, however, entirely fortuitous. Inalcik points to a number of structural problems within Ottoman government and society, some related to the nomadic origins of the dynasty, others to the burden of external conflict.[208] As was the case with its rivals, the most important challenges facing Ottoman imperial rule were maintaining a balance between the power center and the local elites, and sustaining a permanent armed force to conduct the struggle over the borderlands. Due to the special geocultural configuration of the empire and its multiple frontiers, the Ottoman ruling elite was obliged to adopt a strategy combining centralizing and decentralizing policies in pursuing both these goals.

By the early seventeenth century the shift from the Turkic nomadic style of rulership, essentially from the saddle and tent to the luxurious court atmosphere, began to have a corrupting effect on the ruler and his household. Princes were raised in the imperial harem and not allowed to father children until they attained the throne. Politics centered on the imperial household where factions formed around powerful family figures. At the same time, elite households outside the palace also gained power, creating a state-as-household. The shift from "warrior-ruler to symbolic sultan," in the phrase of Carter Findley, also affected the administration of justice.

Owen, "Introduction," in Thomas Naff and Roger Owen (eds.), *Studies in Eighteenth Century Islamic History* (Carbondale, IL: Southern Illinois University Press, 1977), Pt. II, pp. 133–51.

[207] Linda Darling, *Revenue-Raising and Legitimacy. Tax Collection and Finance Administration in the Ottoman Empire, 1560–1660* (Leiden: Brill, 1996), reviews the historiography in her introduction titled "The Myth of Decline," pp. 1–21. In conclusion she states: "Through regularization and bureaucratization of provincial and local government and the provision of justice for the subjects of the empire, finance department procedures contributed to internal stability." *Ibid.*, pp. 303–4. See also Dina Rizk Khoury, *State and Provincial Society in the Ottoman Empire. Mosul, 1540–1834* (Cambridge University Press, 1997).

[208] Halil Inalcik, "The Ottoman Decline and Its Effects upon the Reaya," *Actes du IIe congrès internationale des études de sud-est européen* (Athens: n.p., 1978), vol. III (*Histoire*), pp. 73–90.

Patronage played an increasingly large role in applying the law and supporting cultural institutions.[209]

Palace favorites began to dispose of timar lands so reducing the land fund available for *sipahis*. As a measure of compensation there was increased recruitment of janissaries, who were not permitted to hold land and could be supported only by increased taxation. Increasingly attracted to the pleasures of life in the towns, sipahis became absentee landlords who irregularly performed their service obligations. After the 1580s the influx of silver and the price revolution began a long spiral of economic crises.[210] Inflation and the circulation of counterfeit money particularly affected fixed income groups like the janissaries, who responded by rioting, and the timar holders, who resorted to squeezing more out of the peasants. Central institutions steadily lost the ability to protect the tax-paying population of peasants, artisans, and merchants (*reaya*), whether Christian or Muslim, from the depredations of local officials and wandering bands of soldiers. Various kinds of adventurers, rural bandits, and deserters who were themselves a product of the economic crisis and gradual disappearance of timar holders in the countryside, seized land and offered protection to the peasants from the depredations of others. The timar was gradually converted into a hereditary manor (*çiftlik*) with a powerful overseer imposing a second level of economic exploitation on the peasantry.[211]

The weakening of central authority and the growth of insecurity in the countryside throughout the seventeenth century gave rise to various forms of peasant resistance, ranging from falsification of feudal documents and refusal to pay taxes, to mass flight and brigandage. The traditional division between the askeri and reaya began to break down. The separation had

---

[209] Carter Vaughn Findley, "Political Culture and the Great Households," in Suraiya N. Faroqui (ed.), *The Cambridge History of Turkey. The Later Ottoman Empire 1603–1839* (Cambridge University Press, 2006), vol. III, pp. 66–68; Jane Hathaway, *The Politics of Households in Ottoman Egypt. The Rise of the Qazdağlıs* (Cambridge University Press, 1997).

[210] Halil Inalcik, "Bursa and the Commerce of the Levant," *Journal of Economic and Social History of the Orient* 3(2) (1960): 131–47; Robert Mantran, "L'empire Ottoman et le commerce asiatique au XVIe et au XVIIe siècle," in D. S. Richards (ed.), *Islam and the Trade of Asia* (Philadelphia, PA: University of Pennsylvania Press, 1970), pp. 169–80. In the long run this may have been less serious than the inability of the Ottoman economic system, rooted in Islamic law, to secure new economic resources or accumulating capital for major infrastructural improvements, including, in the eighteenth century, industrialization. Halil Inalcik, "Capital Formation in the Ottoman Empire," *Journal of Economic History* 29(1) (March 1969): 97–140.

[211] Kunt, *The Sultan's Servants*, pp. 80–85; Bernard Lewis, "Some Reflections on the Decline of the Ottoman Empire," *Studia Islamica* 9 (1958): 111–27, and more generally Bernard Lewis, *The Emergence of Modern Turkey* (London: Oxford University Press, 1961).

never been rigid, but by the early seventeenth century the government increasingly turned a blind eye to the flow of non-timar holders into the armed forces. Volunteers were drawn from a variety of social categories. By the end of the sixteenth century they may already have constituted as much as 20 percent of the armed forces. Tapping new sources of manpower revealed the inadequacy of the timar–janissary structure to provide enough men to defend or advance the frontiers. The government's ambivalence toward diluting the social core of the army antagonized some observers at court, one of whom protested: "The *reaya* are prohibited to gird themselves with a sword and mount a horse."[212] The use of volunteers created other problems. The failure to meet promises of rewards in the form of prebends (*timars*) in the fierce competition for limited resources and demobilization after military campaigns created bitterness, and frequently led to the formation of armed bands of experienced soldiers that roamed the countryside.

An early account in 1636 records the flight of peasants from the district of Bitolja into the mountains to join the bandit gangs (*haiduks*), who supported their refusal to furnish provisions for the Ottoman army in Hungary.[213] The haiduks existed at all stages of Ottoman rule, but by the seventeenth century the bands were spread wide throughout the Balkans, although they clustered in regions like Macedonia where the terrain and the prevalence of large çiftliks provided suitable conditions. In years of Ottoman military activity when the tax burden was increased and local garrisons were dispatched to the front, their activities multiplied in reaction to centralization. Haiduks often collaborated with foreign armies, especially during the Habsburg–Ottoman wars (1586–1606 and 1683–1699) when their harassment of supply lines and attacks on isolated Ottoman posts took on the character of a full-scale guerrilla war. Mass outbreaks of violence and insurrections aimed at overthrowing Ottoman power occurred more rarely, and failed because of lack of arms, experience, and organization.[214]

---

[212] Pál Fodor, "Volunteers in the Ottoman Army," in Géza Dávid and Pál Fodor (eds.), *Ottomans, Hungarians and Habsburgs in Central Europe. The Military Confines in the Era of Ottoman Conquest* (Leiden: Brill, 2000), pp. 229–55, quotation on pp. 239–40.

[213] Bistra Cvetkova, "Mouvements antiféodaux dans les terres bulgares sous domination ottomane du XVIe au XVIIIe siècle," *Études historiques à l'occasion du XIIe congrès internationale des sciences historiques*, Vienne, August/September 1965, vol. II, p. 153.

[214] Karen Barkey, *Bandits and Bureaucrats. The Ottoman Route to State Centralization* (Ithaca, NY: Cornell University Press, 1994). See also Karen Barkey, "In Different Times. Scheduling and Control in the Ottoman Empire, 1550–1659," *Comparative Studies in Society and History* 38 (1996): 460–83; Fikret Adanir, "Heiduckentum und Osmanische Herrschaft. Sozialgeschichtliche Aspekte der Diskussinon um das früneuzeitliche Räuberwesen in Südosteuropa," *Südost-Forschungen* 41 (1982): 43–116.

The Ottoman retreat along the northern frontiers left a more lasting legacy of conflict and violence than, say, the Arab expulsion from the Iberian Peninsula. The differences lay in the relatively late chronology, its attenuated and uneven pace, and the incomplete nature of the retreat. During the early to mid-nineteenth century, the traditional forms of social resistance and protest – peasant rebellions, religious clashes, mass flight – gradually evolved into national independence movements. They spread partly under Western influence and partly in recognition by local intellectuals of their effectiveness in mobilizing the population against foreign oppression. A word of caution is in order here. Nationalist historians of the successor states have a tendency to predate and exaggerate the scale of these movements, often perceiving striving for autonomy as declarations of independence.

The apparent decline of the power center was offset to a degree by what Albert Hourani has called "the politics of notables."[215] With the decay of the timar system and the emergence of a subsistence economy in the mid- to late seventeenth century, a major change took place in the fiscal and administrative foundations of the Ottoman state. A monetary system gradually replaced it. The collection of taxes was farmed out to local notables, including former sipahis who had settled in towns, ulama, merchants, and moneylenders. Local elites holding land in hereditary tenure (çiftliks) emerged as a parallel locus of power responsible for recruiting, training, and socializing manpower for state service. Organized into households, they created patronage networks which promoted advancement in the state bureaucracy. The two groups found common ground in supporting one another and gradually merged.[216]

In the different provinces of the multicultural Ottoman Empire the defining characteristics of the notables differed. For example, in the autonomous principalities of Moldavia and Wallachia, the Phanariotes, a Hellenized Orthodox Christian elite with roots in the Phanar district of Istanbul, served as the governing elite from the late seventeenth century to the Greek revolt in 1821. Locally, they maintained their position by marrying into the Romanian boiar families, and in Istanbul by insinuating themselves into patronage networks based on the institution of the

---

[215] Hourani, "Ottoman Reform," pp. 41–68.

[216] Bruce McGowan, "The Age of the Ayans," in Halil Inalcik and Donald Quataert (eds.), *An Economic and Social History of the Ottoman Empire, vol. 1: 1600–1914* (Cambridge University Press, 1994), pp. 661–63; Rifaat Ali Abou-El-Haj, *Formation of the Modern State. The Ottoman Empire, Sixteenth to Eighteenth Centuries* (Albany, NY: State University of New York Press, 1991), pp. 18–52; Hathaway, *Politics of Households*; Ariel Salzmann, *Tocqueville in the Ottoman Empire* (Leiden: Brill, 2007), pp. 105–10.

dragoman (intermediaries with the European powers and the military institutions).[217]

In the Arab provinces, the local ulama, commanders of local garrisons, and secular figures or families who wielded influence growing from their administrative responsibilities or traditional standing in society formed the core of the notables. In the cities of Syria and Hejaz an urban elite of great families restrained the power of the local governor. In Egypt, it was the hereditary Mameluke households descended from an earlier ruling elite who gained control of tax farms and local bureaucratic offices. In Hourani's opinion, Istanbul tolerated these households because of their locations on the frontier and the need to maintain loyal armed forces and tax collectors.[218] In Karen Barkey's view the stability of the Ottoman Empire up to the nineteenth century rested upon an attitude of the central authorities toward ayans in the provinces which she defines as "the pragmatic and flexible management of diversity, with boundaries as mobile markers of difference."[219] During times of external threat or reigns of weak sultans, the ayan could provide a stabilizing force in the provinces. For example, in 1737, in Bosnia, the Ottoman governor relied on a locally raised militia made up of different groups in Bosnian society in order to defeat the Austrian invasion of the province. Financed by mutual agreements between the Ottoman authorities and the local population, this "gave the Bosnians a shared set of interests with the central government."[220]

Alliances and arrangements with ayans also displayed a darker side. Building their influence on their functions as tax collectors and recruitment officers, the ayans infiltrated the provincial administrative offices, undermining the authority of officials appointed from the center. They also formed alliances at the local level with the tribal leaders at a time when nomadism was on the rise.[221] At the end of the eighteenth and beginning of the nineteenth centuries, defeats in wars against their Russian rival in

---

[217] Christine M. Philliou, *Biography of an Empire. Governing Ottomans in an Age of Revolution* (Berkeley, CA: University of California Press, 2011), pp. 5–37.

[218] Philliou, *Biography of an Empire*, p. 51.

[219] Karen Barkey, *Empire of Difference. The Ottomans in Comparative Perspective* (Cambridge University Press, 2008), p. 277.

[220] Michael R. Hickok, *Ottoman Military Administration in Eighteenth Century Bosnia* (Leiden: Brill, 1997), p. 79. Hickok argues that the system broke down in the late eighteenth century, with disastrous results in the nineteenth century when Istanbul introduced a middleman between the provincial administration and the central government, *ibid.*, p. 98.

[221] For this section I have relied on Reşet Kasaba, *A Moveable Empire. Ottoman Nomads, Migrants and Refugees* (Seattle, WA: University of Washington Press, 2009), esp. pp. 85–122.

Map 3.2 Height of Ottoman expansion in Europe, 1674

the struggle over the borderlands led to a series of large-scale migrations of
Muslim refugees from territories on the periphery lost to the Ottomans.
As the government strove to settle the displaced populations, the tribes
took advantage of disturbed local conditions to increase their freedom
from state control. At the same time, ayans saw an opportunity to gain
access to fresh sources of manpower and animals. Powerful families allied
with tribal confederations extended their influence and power over whole
provinces, defying efforts by the ruling elites at the center from implementing reforms. The government responded with military force, organizing campaigns in the 1830s, 1840s, and 1850s against the
predominantly Muslim borderlands of the east and south. It also sought
to survey and count the nomadic population as the prelude to breaking up
tribal communities and reducing the power of the ayans. After the
Crimean War the massive influx of Muslim refugees, with estimates
running as high as 900,000, forced the government to bargain with the
tribal leaders in order to obtain their cooperation in the process of resettlement. The government was beginning to make headway in reducing
nomadism and settling the refugee population when the Russo-Turkish
War of 1877/8 administered what Reşat Kasaba has called "a decisive

blow to the order established earlier in the nineteenth century."[222] Ottoman officials were forced to rely on people they were trying to bring under their control. The price of holding the empire together was a policy of concessions that helped to undermine it.

If not a precipitous or steady decline, then gradual erosion, occasionally checked, sapped imperial power in the borderlands. The territorial retreat of the Ottoman power from its high watermark was neither uniform nor rapid. It was interrupted by bursts of the old conquest zeal, such as the periods of vigorous revival, if brief, in the mid-seventeenth century. Under the Köprülü viziers they regained half of the south Caucasus and part of Ukraine, retained Transylvania as a vassal, and conquered Crete. But the army was once again checked at Vienna in 1683, and thereafter lost most of Hungary and all of Ukraine for good.

During the eighteenth century, dark patches began to spread in the general picture of stability and prosperity. There were ominous signs of linkages between the breakdown of internal order, financial weakness, and the heavy demands of defense along the overstretched frontier lines of the northwestern, northern, and eastern borderlands. After their reconquest of Belgrade in 1739, the Ottoman armies failed to win any major war against its Habsburg or Russian rivals (unless the Crimean War is counted where the British and French did most of the fighting). The factors leading to military decline and the consequences of a steady loss of territory have been hotly debated. Literature based on Ottoman sources has replaced the interpretation that blamed Islamic conservatism as an obstacle to technological innovation. Instead a more complex picture has emerged.

The relative decline of the armed forces, like other institutional changes in the Ottoman Empire, followed a long and irregular trajectory. In the late sixteenth century, the evolution of the Janissary Corps from an elite unit of the sultan's army into an unreliable, often disorderly force opposed to military reforms was already noticeable. One of its most important functions had been to garrison frontier fortresses. Between 30 and 60 percent of the janissaries served on the frontier. The remainder were stationed in Istanbul. Although their number increased throughout the seventeenth century, they provided fewer combat troops, and their fighting capabilities declined.[223] In regions remote from the capital they gradually acquired a corporate identity separating them from the local population. Once they were allowed to marry, opportunities opened up for their sons to inherit their functions. The pressing need for more troops

---

[222] Kasaba, *A Moveable Empire*, p. 118.
[223] Gábor Ágoston, "Military Transformation in the Ottoman Empire and Russia, 1500–1800," *Kritika* 12(2) (Spring 2011): 303–8.

to fight wars on several frontiers and to match the large Austrian armies forced the government to open recruitment to non-Christians and enroll volunteers from the flotsam and jetsam of Christian society. Inflationary pressures caused by the influx of silver obliged the janissaries to seek supplementary employment in artisanal or commercial enterprises. In the provinces, many of them renounced their military profession and became agriculturalists. Acquiring small properties, they resisted paying taxes, considering themselves by virtue of their previous military service to be members of the ruling, non-tax-paying population. They used their military training in order to coerce and intimidate the local tradesmen, who began to shower the capital with complaints of unfair competition. The demilitarization of the janissaries contributed to social discontent, reduced their military effectiveness, and increased their resistance to any form of innovation in the army.[224] Even their loyalty to the sultan eroded over time; they became a law unto themselves and their conduct in battle was often unpredictable.[225] What effect did their resistance to change have on Ottoman military success or failure? Were the costs of war too heavy a burden on the population?

An Ottoman observer in the early eighteenth century commented that "The enemy has begun to get the upper hand through the use of certain war materials, new kinds of weapon and cannon, which our soldiers have delayed in introducing."[226] Up to that time, as one authority has recently argued, the Ottoman army had kept pace with advances in military technology and the financial administration was still solvent.[227] But all this was soon to change.

There was no lack of attempts to overcome the weaknesses in the Ottoman armed forces that its most perceptive critics had identified. Up to the end of the seventeenth century proponents of Ottoman military reforms had mainly resorted to what Avigdor Levy has called "restorative measures." That is, they argued for the return of the Ottoman institutions that had fallen into decay. This strategy gave them protective cover to

---

[224] Halil Inalcik, "Military and Fiscal Transformation in the Ottoman Empire, 1600–1700," *Archivum Ottomanicum* 6 (1980); V. J. Parry, "La manière de combattre," in Perry and Yapp (eds.), *War, Technology and Society*, pp. 218–56; I. E. Petrosian, "Ianicharskie garnizony v provintsiiakh osmanskoi imperii v XVI–XVII vv.," in G. G. Litavrin (ed.), *Osmanskaia imperiia i strany tsentral'noi, vostochnoi i iugo-vostochnoi Evropy v XVII v. Glavnye tendentsii politicheskikh zaimootnoshenii* (Moscow: Pamiatniki istoricheskoi mysli, 1998), Pt. 1.
[225] Viginia Aksan, *Ottoman Wars, 1700–1870. An Empire Besieged* (Edinburgh: Longman, 2007), pp. 38–40, 53, 117.
[226] Parry, "La manière," p. 241; see also Imber, *The Ottoman Empire*, pp. 285–86, for the tax-paying population.
[227] Murphey, *Ottoman Warfare*, pp. 50 and *passim*.

introduce technological innovations in weaponry borrowed from the infidels, but it also imposed limitations on the extent of the borrowing.[228] Two big defeats at the hands of the Habsburgs forced a reconsideration of the type and pace of reform. At the negotiations culminating in the Treaty of Karlowitz in 1699, the sultan was obliged for the first time to enter the European state system and to accept a new legal concept of the frontier, one based on negotiation rather than conquest. Diplomacy required trained personnel who could deal with their European counterparts as equals, thus opening a path for the penetration of European ideas of statecraft.[229] Reacting to a second defeat in 1716/17 and the surrender of Belgrade, the Ottoman ruling elite broadened its interest in European culture from growing tulips to instituting far-reaching military reforms. The more serious aspect of the so-called Tulip Era was the dispatch by Grand Vizier Damad Ibrahim Pasha of five missions to Vienna, Moscow, Poland, and Paris with instructions to report on military and technological matters in particular. This foreshadowed the first of three spurts of military reform in the eighteenth century.[230]

Renewing the reformist impulse

Sultan Mahmud I (1730–1754) and his advisors took the first tentative steps to introduce the latest Western techniques by engaging a converted French officer, the Comte de Bonneval, to reorganize the entire military. The janissaries once again blocked all the major changes. Another convert, a Hungarian known only as Ibrahim Müteferrika, was one of the first to advocate publicly the virtue of absorbing the lessons of defeat by the Christians. In 1731 he founded the first Muslim printing press in the empire. All of the first sixteen books printed by his press dealt with political-military matters. Citing the reforms of Peter the Great, he declared that adopting the new military techniques of the enemy could restore Ottoman greatness because the Ottomans possessed the moral superiority of the Shari'a and the jihad.[231] But the pressure for military reform lifted, ironically, as a result of their last successful campaign

---

[228] Avigdor Levy, "Military Reform and the Problem of Centralization in the Eighteenth Century," *Middle Eastern Studies* 18(3) (July 1982): 229–30.

[229] Rifa'at 'Ali Abou-El-Haj, "Ottoman Attitudes towards Peace Making. The Karlowitz Case," *Der Islam* 51 (1974): 131–37; Secil Akgun, "European Influence on the Development of Social and Cultural Life of the Ottoman Empire in the Eighteenth Century," *Revue des études sud-est européenes* 21 (1983): 92.

[230] Levy, "Military Reform," pp. 231–32. Damad Pasha had no time to implement any new ideas before he was overthrown in 1730 by a janissary-led revolt sparked by economic causes, and the defeat in a war against Iran, but cloaked in anti-European terms.

[231] Aksan, *An Ottoman Statesman*, pp. 186–88.

against the Habsburgs in the war of 1738/9 when they won back Bosnia and Serbia, including Belgrade. Thirty years of peace followed, apparently lulling them into a false sense of security. The outbreak of a new war with Russia in 1768 jogged Sultan Mustafa III (1757–1774) out of complacency.

Responding positively to the crushing defeat at the hands of the Russians in the war of 1768–1774, Mustafa's successor, Abdülhamid I (1768–1789), recruited his top advisors from the professionally trained and salaried bureaucracy which had gradually been evolving along European lines. Virginia Aksan has shown that the influence of French technical specialists has been exaggerated in the casting of artillery, the recruiting and training of new units of field artillery, and other technological innovations that the Habsburg and Russian armies had acquired during the Seven Years War.[232] The new Ottoman officials purchased military equipment from Europe, purged the Janissary Corps of the most disorderly elements, and introduced improvements in the navy. They sought to curb the power of the provincial notables and introduced more efficient methods into the central administration. Their efforts fell short of a radical transformation of the army and bureaucracy due mainly to growing financial constraints, the cost of the war, and growing opposition within the empire. The latter arose not so much from religious conservatism, as from opposition by the entrenched interests in the army and ulama to what they perceived as threats to their preeminent position as the traditional ruling elite.[233]

The third reforming spurt came under the reign of Selim III (1789–1807), once again under pressure from an unsuccessful war against an alliance of the Habsburg and Russian empires.[234] One of the most ambitious reformers among the Ottoman sultans, he was strongly influenced by events in France during the first years of the revolution, but the urgency came once again from the 1787–1792 war with Russia ending with the Treaty of Iaşi. Even before the defeat was registered, he solicited reforming proposals from his closest advisors. Most of these dealt with the need for military reform, taking Russia as the example of what could be

---

[232] Virginia Aksan, "Breaking the Spell of the Baron de Tott. Reframing the Question of Military Reform in the Ottoman Empire, 1760–1830," *International History Review* 24(2) (June 2002): 258–63.

[233] Levy, "Military Reform," pp. 235–38; Aksan, *Ottoman Wars*, pp. 198–202.

[234] The older account of the reign by Stanford J. Shaw, *Between Old and New. The Ottoman Empire under Sultan Selim III (1789–1807)* (Cambridge, MA: Harvard University Press, 1973), has been superseded in many ways by Aksan, *Ottoman Warfare*, which is the main source for the following account of military reform.

done, but France as the model of how to do it. In the vanguard of reforming bureaucrats, Ahmed Resmi provided the intellectual inspiration. A seasoned diplomat, he was second in command to the grand vizier for much of the Russo-Turkish War. His comprehensive report on the reasons for defeat outlined ten major shortcomings of the Ottoman army, including its organization, tactics, and provisioning. He was also one of the earliest and most profound Ottoman analysts of the struggle over the borderlands. He warned against the dangers of imperial overextension into borderlands that could not be easily defended, citing the examples of Chingghis Khan and Suleiman I. He prophesized the same fate for the Russian Empire. An advocate of settling disputes by negotiation, he rejected the concept of limitless frontiers of the Dar-al-Islam in favor of Ottoman integration into a European state system as the best guarantee of stable borders.[235] But his ideas were still straws in the wind, and the wind of the provincial notables still gusted powerfully.

As Virginia Aksan has argued, Selim's military reforms must be placed within the context of "the climate and articulation of reform within Ottoman society." The new triad of imperial power linked those reforms to the bureaucratization, the incorporation of new elites into the center of power, and reformulating dynastic and religious ideology.[236] Faced with the lack of order and discipline among the sipahis and janissaries under combat conditions, Selim created an entirely new force known as the "New Order Army." Trained in the European manner with an independent financial base, recruited from Turkish boys from Anatolia, it was to be officered by graduates of the new technical schools he established. Special attention continued to focus on the development of the artillery arm. But Selim lacked the ruthlessness of Peter the Great. He failed to crush his opponents in the old army or the ayans in the Balkans, who opposed conscription into the New Order Army as a threat to their entrenched interests, or to overcome the resistance of the ulama, who condemned his consorting with the infidel. His only allies were drawn from the non-Muslim population. There were other problems as well: the lack of a technical vocabulary to facilitate technology transfer, and the

---

[235] Aksan, *An Ottoman Statesman*, pp. 196–98, who notes that his advocacy of negotiation was "a bit equivocal" given the fact that the Ottomans started the war, but his deeper convictions were reinforced by his own humiliating role in signing the Treaty of Kuchuk-Kainardji. *Ibid.*, p. 204.

[236] Aksan, *Ottoman Warfare*, pp. 180–81. The author points out the similarity with the pattern of military reform in Muscovy as suggested by Marshall Poe, "The Consequences of Military Revolution in Muscovy in Comparative Perspective," *Comparative Studies in Society and History* 38 (1996): 603–18.

unfamiliarity of the ruling elite, except for non-Muslim minorities, with Western ideas.[237]

Under the reign of Selim internal reforms became entangled in the dense web of international relations formed by the shifting alliances in the era of Napoleonic imperialism. Selim maneuvered among the Great Powers, aligning himself alternately with the British and French in order to ward off the Russians, and to obtain military advisors and transfers of technology. But he finally fell victim to an internal revolt against his policy of conscription. Deposed in 1808, his reforms were aborted.

The revolt that brought Mahmud II (1808–1839) to the throne was sealed by a Deed of Agreement between him and the provincial notables. Sometimes called the Ottoman magna carta, it established the foundation of public law in the empire. It also committed the provincial notables to providing troops for the defense of the empire, and provided the financial guarantees by reaffirming the tax farming system. The agreement freed the hands of the sultan and his advisors to revive the reforming process and, of the greatest importance, to break with the traditional mold of reform in 1826 by destroying for the first time an established institution – the Janissary Corps – rather than as in the past tinkering with its leadership and organization. He relied on remnants of the disbanded New Order Army, the soldiers forced out of the ceded territories, and the flotsam and jetsam of the "masterless men" in the provinces. An official proclamation accused the janissaries of being polluted by infidels. The reformers, with the help of the Sunni ulama, then turned against the Bektaşi brotherhood that had traditionally provided the janissaries with spiritual support. Their leaders were executed and their property confiscated, although it took time to eliminate the janissaries in the frontier provinces.[238]

The parallel has often been drawn between the destruction of the janissaries and Peter the Great's repression of the musketeers (strel'tsy) backed by the schismatic Old Believers. But there were important differences. Ottoman society was more complex than that of Muscovy. Peter was able to create a new army by reorganizing and Westernizing the ruling noble

[237] Shaw, *History of the Ottoman Empire*, vol. I, pp. 261–66; Aksan, *Ottoman Wars*, pp. 202–6 and ch. 6; Levy, "Military Reform," pp. 239–41. Aksan, *An Ottoman Statesman*, pp. 201–3, notes that many of Ahmed Resmi's ideas had become part of the reforming discourse by this time. For an analysis of the expanded role of the ulama in government and diplomacy in the eighteenth century, see Madeline C. Zilfi, "The Ottoman Ulama," in Suraiya N. Faroqui (ed.), *The Cambridge History of Turkey, vol. 3: The Later Ottoman Empire, 1603–1839* (Cambridge University Press, 2006), pp. 223–25.
[238] Aksan, *Ottoman Warfare*, pp. 261–65; Uriel Heyd, "The Ottoman Ulama and Westernization at the Time of Selim III and Mahmud II," reprinted from *Studies in Islamic History and Civilization*, in *Scripta Hierusoly Mitana* IX (Jerusalem 1961).

elite, separating Church and state, and abolishing the patriarchate as an alternative source of authority. There were no powerful urban elites or independent local notables to challenge him. In Peter's empire the population was still overwhelmingly Russian and Orthodox, and the Muslim Tatars were concentrated in the interior provinces far from the volatile frontiers. These conditions favorable to greater centralization were absent in the Ottoman state where the non-Muslims, who constituted about half the population, were located in borderlands.

Nonetheless, Mahmud's reforms may be seen as the first major step in the direction of nationalizing the empire and the army by creating "an Ottoman absolutism based on a more rigorously defined (Turkish and Muslim) citizenship."[239] The term "Turk" gradually assumed an ideological content for the Ottoman rulers, particularly in the army where it first began to replace the traditional meaning of "hick" or "rube" which long survived outside the military sphere. In part this was a result of the difficulty encountered by army recruiters in enrolling recruits from the borderlands where the local notables controlled their own militias. Instead, they had to rely increasingly on the "Turkic" peasantry of Anatolia, from the districts near the capital in the Balkans and on the Caucasus frontier. In part, too, it was a response to the growing nationalist agitation among the non-Muslim population and the pressure from Western Europe in support of rights previously guaranteed by the Ottoman government. The value of the "Turkic" soldiers was recognized by the governor of Egypt, Mehmed Ali, who was carrying out a major economic and military transformation of his province, by his son, Ibrahim Pasha who commanded his army, and by Ottoman commanders in the frontier fortresses on the Danubian frontier fighting the Greek rebels.[240]

The two major obstacles to a comprehensive and effective reconstruction of the Ottoman army and administration reflected the deep structural faults within imperial rule. First, there was a recurrence of a financial crisis, but this time in the form of runaway inflation unprecedented in scope.[241] Second, the prevalence of the patriarchal system beginning with the sultan and distributed through favoritism and factional rivalry fostered

---

[239] Aksan, "Military Reform," p. 258 for quotation, and p. 274.

[240] Virginia H. Aksan, "The Ottoman Military and State Transformation in a Globalizing World," *Comparative Studies of South Asia, Africa and the Middle East* 27(2) (2007): 257–70; Hakan Erdem, "Recruitment of the 'Victorious Soldiers of Muhammad' in the Arab Provinces, 1826–1828," in Israel Gershoni, Hakan Erdem, and Ursula Wokök (eds.), *Histories of the Modern Middle East. New Directions* (Boulder, CO: Lynne Rienner, 2002), pp. 198–200.

[241] Mehemet Genç, "L'economie ottoman et la guerre au XVIIIe siècle," *Turcica* 27 (1995): 177–96, and especially Şevket Pamuk, "Prices in the Ottoman Empire, 1469–1914," *International Journal of Middle East Studies* 36 (2004): 463.

corruption and intrigue within the ruling elites. To be sure, fresh talent
continued to filter into the bureaucracy; new regiments were created to
replace the janissaries.[242] But Christians were surely alienated by the
name of the new formations, the "Trained Victorious Muslim Army,"
and by the new taxes imposed to support them. Moreover, the frontiers
continued to be defended by militias under the command of local notables. The greatest weakness of the new army was the junior officer ranks.
Mahmud did not create an officers' training school until 1834, more than
a century after the Russian Cadet Corps.[243] Mahmud's war with Russia in
1827 under the banner of jihad revealed improvements in the fighting
capacity of the army, yet familiar weaknesses remained in military organization and strategic planning.[244] The next important step in reconstituting the army was the creation in 1834 of a militia based on the Prussian
Landwehr, designed to maintain order in the countryside during peacetime and to act as a reserve for the regular army in wartime. But the
introduction of universal conscription was delayed until the introduction
of comprehensive reform.

The Tanzimat

The renewal of the reforming impulse under the name of Tanzimat or
"Auspicious Reorderings" (1839–1876) by Mahmud II's successors was
largely the work of a small number of Europeanized officials. Its defining
aim during the reigns of Abdülmecid (1839–1861) and Abdülaziz
(1861–1876) was to create an Ottoman citizenship with equal rights and
responsibilities for all subjects, and to create an imperial army based upon
this new foundation. A key figure in the early phase was Mustafa Reşit
Paşa, an official who came up through the ranks of the government
bureaucracy, but who enjoyed high patronage. A student of English and
French, he gained much from his travels in Europe. As early as 1839 he
persuaded the new sultan to issue the Gülhane *hatt-i humayun* (imperial
rescript) that promised the establishment of new institutions in order to
guarantee his subjects security of life, honor, and property, and a regular
tax system under the banner of Islam. The third basic principle of the
rescript was the introduction of "an equally regular system for the conscription of requisite troops and the duration of service," it being "the

---

[242] Aksan, *Ottoman Warfare*, pp. 328–36.
[243] Avigdor Levy, "The Officer Corps in Sultan Mahmud's New Ottoman Army, 1826–39," *International Journal of Middle East Studies* 2 (1971): 21–39.
[244] Erik Jan Zürcher, "The Ottoman Conscription System, 1844–1914," *International Review of Social History* 43 (1998): 436–37.

inescapable duty of all the people to provide soldiers for the defense of the fatherland."[245] For the next thirty years the government struggled to realize the concept of Ottomanism, defined as a citizenry enjoying equal rights while recognizing the supremacy of Islam. Guided by the principle of centralization and rationalization, the reformers set up functional equivalents of ministries to replace the multiplicity of overlapping jurisdictions. Officialdom was reorganized, bringing the Ottoman bureaucracy closer to a European model without eliminating its arbitrary and autocratic character.[246]

The key figure in the second phase of reforms was Midhat Pasha, the statesman who implemented the constitutional ideas of the Young Ottomans. He had gained his experience as an Ottoman official in the borderlands of the empire. His early service was in the Asian provinces. He then became a troubleshooter in Damascus and Aleppo, but his career blossomed on the Danubian frontier. As governor of the unruly province of Niš, he cooperated with both Muslim and Christian local notables in order to check the spread of Bulgarian nationalist sentiment, nourished by groups infiltrating across the porous inner frontiers with the autonomous Serbian and Romanian provinces of the empire. Inspired by the principle of equality among the sultan's subjects (Osmanlılık), he attempted to introduce a mixed school system that would attract both Muslim and Christian Bulgarians with instruction on a bilingual basis. But he ran afoul of both Orthodox clerics and Bulgarian nationalists, who insisted that education was the prerogative of the religious community (millet).[247]

Midhat also helped to draft a new administrative reform that introduced representation by Muslims and non-Muslims in local elected bodies. But here, too, his efforts fell short of success. Implementing this reform in the enlarged Danubian (Tuna) vilayet in 1864, he faced similar problems that were further complicated by the problem of integrating the thousands of Tatars and Circassian refugees from the Crimean War who were resettled there to defend the frontier against the Serbs and possibly to serve as a counterweight to Bulgarian agitation. He worked as energetically to unify the population of the empire as the Russian ambassador in

---

[245] J. C. Hurewitz, *The Middle East and North Africa in World Politics*, 2nd edn, 2 vols. (New Haven, CT: Yale University Press, 1975), vol. I, p. 270.

[246] Shaw, *History of the Ottoman Empire*, vol. II, pp. 69 ff; Hourani, "Ottoman Reform," pp. 36–66; Aksan, *Ottoman Warfare*, pp. 402–16; Carter V. Findley, *Bureaucratic Reform in the Ottoman Empire, 1789–1922* (Princeton University Press, 1980), pp. 16–87; Carter V. Findley, "The Legacy of Tradition to Reform. Origins of the Ottoman Foreign Ministry," *International Journal of Middle Eastern Studies* 1 (1970): 335–38.

[247] Fikret Adanir and Hilmar Kaiser, "Migration, Deportation and Nation Building. The Case of the Ottoman Empire," in René Laboutte (ed.), *Migration et migrants dans une perspective historique. Permanences et innovations* (Bruxelles: Peter Lang, 2000), p. 277.

Istanbul, Count Ignat'ev, his bête noire, worked to break it up. His next assignment in Baghdad plunged him into another turbulent frontier province, where once again he introduced civic improvements and helped to settle some of the Bedouin nomads. He was recalled to the capital and made grand vizier at a time when the empire was entering a period of great turmoil.

Midhat was battling against heavy odds. The higher Ottoman bureaucracy was divided by warring factions, while Ignat'ev was actively conspiring against him. Nevertheless, he succeeded in deposing two incompetent sultans in one year, bringing Abdülhamid to the throne. He was then in a position to draft a constitution, a project he had been mulling over for some years. The drafting went forward, despite the ominous war clouds, with the participation of Namık Kemal, other members of the Young Ottomans, and a small group of Christians. Among the latter was an Armenian advisor to Midhat, one of the authors of the Armenian millet constitution.[248] Once in power, however, Abdülhamid was determined to defend the prerogatives of the sultanate. Shortly after the promulgation of the constitution, he launched a coup against the reformers. In 1876, he dismissed Midhat Pasha. By the end of the Russo-Turkish War he had suspended the constitution without formally abolishing it. His rule then became personal and authoritarian.

During the Tanzimat, military reforms were aimed at correcting the major shortcomings in the chain of command and financial support that had led to earlier defeats. Under Abdülaziz, who was particularly interested in the army, the Minister of War, Hüseyin Avni, undertook the first major military reform since the 1830s. A veteran of the conquest of Crete, he adopted the Prussian model, reducing the length of service and creating an active reserve. Modern weapons acquired abroad increased combat efficiency. The Ottoman soldier, in the eyes of Foreign Minister Fuad Pasha, was to lead by example. In 1860, he had exhorted the troops sent to repress sectarian violence in Syria to become, in the words of a modern historian, "the vanguard of Ottoman modernity, rationality and nationalism."[249] Although the army was defeated in the Russo-Turkish War, it performed reasonably well even in the eyes of Count Ignat'ev.[250]

---

[248] Roderic H. Davison, *Reform in the Ottoman Empire, 1856–1876* (Princeton University Press, 1963), pp. 151–58, 160–64, for Midhat's provincial career, and pp. 367–78 for a detailed account of the drafting process of the constitution. Maria Todorova, "Midhat Pasha's Governorship of the Danube Province," in Farah (ed.), *Decision Making and Change*, pp. 115–28, is more critical.

[249] Ussama Makdisi, "Ottoman Orientalism," *American Historical Review* 107(3) (June 2002): 12.

[250] Davison, *Reform in the Ottoman Empire*, pp. 264–66.

Gradual and cautious though it was, the reforming process ran into the familiar structural obstacles and political opposition that ultimately brought it to a crashing end and doomed its architects. There was growing resentment within the army against working with "infidel" advisors, and protests by the ulama against the idea of civic equality for non-Muslims. By the early 1870s, a new wave of Muslim revivalism broke over the reformers. It was generated in part by the legendary Iranian-born preacher of pan-Islamism, Jamal al-Din Al-Afgani, who carried his powerful, if obscure, message of Islamic modernism throughout Europe and the Muslim world.[251] Attacks against Western influence were nourished by stories of Russian atrocities against the Turks in their conquest of Trans Caspia, and news of the great Muslim uprising of Ya'qub Beg in the Chinese province of Xinjiang, followed by the arrival in the Ottoman lands of refugees from these embattled borderlands.[252]

A second obstacle to the creation of a truly imperial army was the large proportion of the population exempted from military service. Non-Muslims were not registered for the draft until 1856, and in practice they were not conscripted until 1909; the nomadic tribes were also exempt in practice. Other groups exempt from service were religious functionaries and students in religious schools, most professions, and even the lower ranks of civil servants, at least in peacetime. There were also a mass of individual exemptions regulated by family relationships and payment of a fee. This meant that the Ottoman army was composed overwhelmingly of peasants from the countryside until the Young Turk revolution; it was also a much smaller army both relative to the population and in absolute terms than the Habsburg or Russian armies.[253] Funding the reforms was a third major stumbling block.

The economic balance sheet

The fate of the Tanzimat depended, as in the past, on a stronger performance by the Ottoman economy. The vitality of Ottoman trade well into the eighteenth century also appeared to belie the picture of decline. The great age of Ottoman expansion created an immense and secure trading area stretching from the Euphrates to the Danube and the Crimea to Tunisia. More important than foreign trade, the domestic market produced a dazzling variety of goods. Turks controlled the chartering of ships, but

---

[251] Nikki R. Keddie, *Sayyid Jamal al-Din 'al-Afghani. A Political Biography* (Berkeley, CA: University of California Press, 1972).
[252] Shaw, *History of the Ottoman Empire*, vol. II, p. 157.
[253] Zürcher, "Ottoman Conscription," pp. 455–56.

the Greeks and Armenians gradually assumed a more important position in trade with Europe.[254]

The Ottomans were also successful in adapting to new patterns of international trade, which for two centuries enabled them to play the role of intermediary in the east–west exchange of goods between Europe and Iran, to develop a north–south trade with Russia, and to compete with the west Europeans in the Indies. Up to the eighteenth century, their strong naval presence in the eastern Mediterranean, the Black Sea, Red Sea, and Persian Gulf, as well as their control over the traditional overland routes through central Anatolia and Mesopotamia, placed them in a unique position. By dominating the Black Sea, the Ottomans also opened up direct trade relations with the Pontic steppe and farther to the north with Muscovy.[255] Despite the penetration of Western European trading vessels and ships of war in the Indian Ocean, as Neils Steengaard has shown, the Ottomans, along with the Safavid and Mughal empires, maintained their control over the Asian trade until the eighteenth century.[256] In addition to benefiting from integration into an international system, the economic elites of the conquered territories also gained advantages from Ottoman domestic policies. For several centuries, the extension of religious toleration and the encouragement of traders of all ethnic and religious groups within the empire proved to be judicious, profitable, and effective in preventing west European merchants from taking over. The alliance of interests among the central government, provincial officials, and local elites, including ulama and merchants, guaranteed social stability and a high level of agricultural production. The state protected the urban guilds, stimulating handicraft production. All-embracing state regulation of the economy was one of the characteristic features of Ottoman policy designed to strengthen ties between the center and the periphery. The government was particularly sensitive to the control over the sale, distribution, and storage of food in order to prevent high prices and shortages.[257]

---

[254] Daniel Panzac, *Commerce et navigation dans l'Empire Ottoman au XVIIIe siècle* (Istanbul: Isis, 1996), pp. vii–viii, 212–14.

[255] Inalcik, *The Ottoman Empire*, ch. 14.

[256] Neils Steengaard, "The Indian Ocean Network and the Emerging World Economy *c.* 1500–1750," in Satish Chandra (ed.), *The Indian Ocean. Explorations in History, Commerce and Politics* (New Delhi: Sage, 1987), pp. 125–50. See also Neils Steengaard, *Carracks, Caravans and Companies. The Structural Crisis in European–Asian Trade in the Early 17th Century* (Lund: Studentenliteratur, 1973).

[257] Nikolai Todorov, *The Balkan City, 1400–1900* (Seattle, WA: University of Washington Press, 1983), pp. 59–60, 107, 123, 183. Cf. Ira M. Lapidus, *Muslim Cities in the Later Middle Ages* (Cambridge University Press, 1967), who argues that Muslim societies did not allow for autonomous cities, thus hampering the development of capitalism.

Yet once again there was a darker side to the picture. The hidden cost of the policies of social stability was the lack of incentives for Ottoman entrepreneurs and obstacles to developing modern corporate organizations that could compete with foreign capitalists. Operating under a number of handicaps from state controls to Islamic inheritance laws, Ottoman merchants were forced to limit their activities to local markets or become protégés of foreign powers. By the end of the eighteenth century, major ports such as Istanbul, Saloniki, and Izmir had become "a subservient part of the European-dominated world economy." Foreign powers, especially Britain and Russia, used commercial treaties and the privileged position of their consuls to intervene in Ottoman domestic politics.[258] The prospects were not encouraging.

Tax farming, introduced at the end of the seventeenth century, had run its course by the end of the eighteenth century. Attempts to replace the tax farmers faltered in the absence of trained officials. But the long-term structural problems proved to be more serious. Turkish landlords had been slow to adapt to market conditions and convert their estates to capitalist enterprises, and the state failed to invest its surplus in productive activities. The effects of these changes were not immediately visible. Trade still flourished and the internal market remained strong. But by the end of the eighteenth century the need for greater revenue had driven the Ottoman elites to turn over more and more commercial enterprises to Western merchants, a harbinger of greater dependence to come.

In the nineteenth century, attempts to redress the trade imbalances by limiting imports were frustrated by the practice of granting capitulations to foreign governments and firms. By the early years of the Tanzimat, foreign merchants were arriving in large numbers, competing with and forcing out the under-capitalized Ottomans. The heavy expenditures on lost wars, beginning with the large indemnity to Russia in 1775 and continuing throughout the Napoleonic period, forced the government to increase the tax burden, assume a large internal debt. and to borrow abroad. The costs of maintaining the bureaucracy and the armed forces, and the lavish style of the court, swallowed up the greater part of the budget.[259]

The obstacles to the transformation of a basic agricultural economy to a more balanced, not to say industrial, one ran head on into the opposition

---

[258] Suraiya Faroqui and Gilles Veinstein, "Introduction," in Suraiya Faroqui and Gilles Veinstein (eds.), *Merchants in the Ottoman Empire* (Louvain: Peeters, 2008), pp. xvi–xxiv, quotation on p. xix; and Murat Çizakçka and Macit Kenanoğlu, "Ottoman Merchants and the Jurisprudential Shift Hypothesis," in *ibid.*, pp. 195–213.

[259] M. Şükrü Hanioğlu, *A Brief History of the Late Ottoman Empire* (Princeton University Press, 2008), pp. 19–24.

of the Western maritime powers. Selim III had taken an interest in improving the domestic production of military equipment and weaponry,[260] but most of the manufactures were still imported. In 1838, under British pressure, the Ottoman government signed a Commercial Convention which forced it to abandon most state monopolies and import–export controls.[261] In economic terms this was part of the global surge of Britain's indirect imperialism. Simultaneously, the British were knocking down the tariff barriers in the southern coastal cities of Qing China. Politically, the British aim was twofold: first, to weaken the power of the sultan's rebellious vassal, Mehmed Ali Pasha of Egypt, who was supported by France; and, second, to deny Russia an excuse for a unilateral intervention to shore up the sultan's authority. The Commercial Convention came just as the government launched a major effort to industrialize, a logical but monumentally ill-timed extension of the Tanzimat into the military sphere. Most of the manufactures of the 1840s were consumed by the army and the palace. But structural obstacles slowed the pace, and the Crimean War with its large European loans and growing Ottoman indebtedness brought an end to the program.[262] The men of the Tanzimat were not sophisticated in financial matters, and they encountered the classic dilemma of having to extract funding for expensive reforms from a population already overburdened by taxes, or else to borrow from abroad and repay loans at exorbitant rates of interest that cut deeper into the money available for current needs. These dilemmas were never resolved. As a consequence, although the reforming impulse did not die in the latter decades of the nineteenth century, it repeatedly fell short of fulfilling its highest goals.

Iran

As participants in the struggle over the borderlands, Iranian rulers, like their counterparts in the Ottoman and Russian empires, confronted a number of persistent factors that can be interpreted as three paradoxes linked by a common thread. First, as a continuous civilization Iran has existed for more than 2,000 years, longer than any of the Eurasian empires

---

[260] Shaw, *Between Old and New*, pp. 138–44.
[261] J. C. Hurewitz, *Diplomacy in the Near and Middle East* (Princeton University Press, 1956), vol. I, pp. 110–11, for the full text of the Balta Liman Convention.
[262] Edward C. Clark, "The Ottoman Industrial Revolution," *Journal of Middle East Studies* 5 (1974): 65–76; Çağlar Keyder, "Creation and Destruction of Forms of Manufacturing. The Ottoman Example," in Jean Batou (ed.), *Between Development and Underdevelopment. The Precocious Attempts at Industrialization of the Periphery, 1800–1870* (Geneva: Droz, 1991), pp. 157–79.

except the Chinese; yet from the earliest times, under the Achaemenid dynasty of the first millennium, the great Iranian plateau has been inhabited by a multiplicity of peoples and cultures. Consequently, the concept of a centralized state has always been problematic, challenged by regional entities whether defined as satraps, provinces, tribal areas, or borderlands.[263] Powerful centrifugal forces have threatened to overwhelm the centripetal pull from time to time, yet the Persian idea of kingship (*Shahanshah*) survived well into the twentieth century. Second, the most densely populated and economically productive lands of Iran were located in the highlands of the periphery, leaving the geographical center of the country, with the exception of the one-time capital of Isfahan, under-populated and relatively barren.[264] Third, from the earliest times the administrative structure of the state rested upon the orderly functioning of a well-trained bureaucratic elite similar to that in China. Successive Turkic and Arab conquerors incorporated the Persian bureaucratic organization and methods into their imperial rule.[265] Yet the Safavids and their Qajar successors were no more successful than the Seljuks had been in completing the transition to a bureaucratic system that could transform the nomadic way of life and overcome the resistance of the tribal confederations to a centralized state. The common thread providing continuity throughout Iranian history was, then, the tension between the elements of unity and diversity characteristic of the geocultural founda-tions of Eurasia.

The Safavid reformers

The founder of the Safavid dynasty, Shah Ismail (1501–1524), achieved his reputation as a state-builder by combining the cultures of the Turkic nomadic warrior elite with that of the Persian administrators who pro-vided the bureaucratic know-how distilled from long experience.[266] His most illustrious successor, Shah Abbas (1587–1629), launched the most ambitious and ingenious attempt by a Safavid shah to centralize imperial

---

[263] Under the Achaemenids the army, as well as administrative divisions, was organized along regional lines. A. T. Olmstead, *History of the Persian Empire* (University of Chicago Press, 1948), pp. 219–24, 239–47.

[264] W. B. Fisher, "The Land of Iran," in *The Cambridge History of Iran* (Cambridge University Press, 1968), vol. 1, pp. 734–35; Richard N. Frye, *The Golden Age of Persia* (London: Phoenix Press, 2000), pp. 8–14.

[265] Frey, *The Golden Age of Persia*, pp. 5, 17, 34–35, 62–64.

[266] Jean Aubin, "Études Safavides. I. Shah Isma'il et les notables de l'Iraq persan," *Journal of the Economic and Social History of the Orient* 2(1) (January 1959): 37–81; Jean Aubin, "Études Safavides. III. L'avénement des Safavides reconsidéré," *Moyen Orient et Océan Indien* 5 (1988): 1–30.

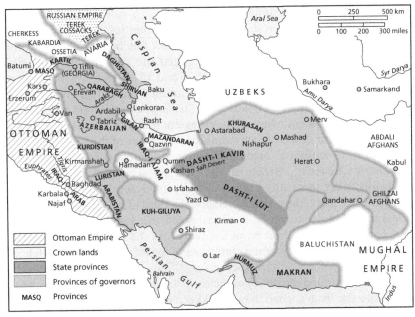

Map 3.3 The Safavid Empire at its height, 1660

rule. Like his near contemporary the Russia tsar, Ivan IV, Abbas virtually divided the state into two realms, building up his power on the basis of the urban and settled agricultural populations, while allowing the tribal elements to fend for themselves in order to reduce their power. Frustrated by his failure he is said to have exclaimed: "Governing Persians is not only impossible, it is ridiculous."[267]

Abbas' decision to relocate the capital was part of his centralizing strategy. Previously, several cities had served as the mobile capital of the shah. The multiplicity of centers reflected the traditional decentralized tribal system inherited from the nomadic past. But Tabriz was too vulnerable to Ottoman thrusts from the west, and Qazvin was exposed to nomads from the north. By shifting his center of power to the restored city of Isfahan, he located the capital as far as possible from the traditional qizilbashi tribal areas.

---

[267] Pierre Oberling, *The Qashqā'i Nomads of Fārs* (The Hague: Mouton, 1974), p. 113.

Having been instrumental in establishing the Safavid dynasty, the qizil-bashi had gradually assumed the functions of a ruling elite governing Iran's pastoral, agricultural, and urban communities according to their tribal and religious principles. But they did not bring stability to the country. Highly volatile, they had plunged the country into two civil wars in the previous century (1524–1536 and 1571–1590), which almost destroyed Safavid rule. Abbas fully institutionalized military and civilian slavery by appointing Georgian slaves (*ghulam*) as governors and admin-istrators of clerical endowments to the extent that they may have occupied up to 20 percent of the higher administrative ranks of the state.[268] At the same time, he sought to break the qizilbashi monopoly over the army by recruiting Circassian, Armenian, and Georgian slaves converted to Islam, and organizing them into special cavalry, musketeer, and artillery regi-ments. Ultimately, they constituted about a third of his armed forces. The Georgian slaves became the mainstay of the Iranian army, earning the reputation of the bravest of the brave. As the Persian adage had it: "The Persians are but women compared to the Afghans, and the Afghans but women compared to the Georgians."[269]

Abbas continued the policy of the early Safavid rulers by soliciting arms and expertise from abroad in order to keep pace with the military changes taking place in the Ottoman Empire, and seeking by diplomatic means to win over anti-Ottoman allies in Europe. In the 1590s, the Russians, harassed by Istanbul's Crimean Tatar allies, often served as intermedia-ries or direct suppliers of arms to Iranian embassies. Ironically, the Iranians obtained most of their firearms from the Ottomans through defections, the caravan trade, and smuggling across the porous frontiers.[270]

To cover the costs of the new army, Abbas imposed a state monopoly on the silk trade, and converted a number of provinces administered by qizilbashi governors to crown provinces administered by the converted Georgian slaves. He changed the policy of apportioning lands in order to reduce the properties of the feudal notables and increase the holdings of the state, crown, and religious trusts (*waqf*). His economic policy has been called patrimonial state capitalism because of the government's control over commerce and industry, including the construction of roads, organ-ization of the postal service, and maintenance of caravanserai. Similarly,

---

[268] Sussan Babaie *et al.* (eds.), *Slaves of the Shah. New Elites of Safavid Iran* (London: Tauris, 2004), pp. 6–7.

[269] Lawrence Lockhart, *The Fall of the Safavid Dynasty and the Afghan Occupation of Persia* (Cambridge University Press, 1958), p. 146.

[270] Halil Inalcik, "The Socio-political Effects of the Diffusion of Firearms in the Middle East," in Parry and Yapp (eds.), *War, Technology and Society*, pp. 207–8.

he sought to control foreign trade by reopening the east–west routes through Iran, and by encouraging Europe to buy Iranian goods and raw materials. Under his reign the old urban centers, Isfahan, Tabriz, and Kashan, recovered some of their former wealth. Following the centralizing trend, the trades and crafts were subject to state control like the old Byzantine guilds, and the merchants functioned as the Shah's semi-bureaucratic agents.[271] Abbas was able to institute the reforms despite the opposition of the qizilbashi, but he was not able to dispense with their services. They still provided both the spiritual foundations for the state order and what Savory calls "the fighting élan, based on a strong tribal esprit de corps, which made [them] the only troops in the Middle East to win the grudging respect of the Ottoman Janissaries."[272]

Despite his long reign, Shah Abbas was not able to complete the transformation of Iran into a centralized bureaucratic state. In addition to the persistent tensions between the old and new elements in the army and in the administration of the provinces, the Iranian economy began to show signs of structural weakness. The frontier wars in the south Caucasus and Trans Caspia drained the treasury. He was unable to restore urban centers like Derbent in Azerbaijan. His attempts, with the cooperation of Armenian merchants, to impose the same kind of quasi-state monopolies on trade that worked in the central provinces, and his imposition of heavy taxes to pay for the occupation of the borderlands, sparked resistance under his successors and open revolts among the tribes on the periphery. By the mid-seventeenth century economic recovery, thanks to a long period of peace, began to give way to a major financial crisis.

Part of the problem lay with over-reliance on the silk trade and part with the inflationary effects connected to the worldwide seventeenth-century crisis. The major source of hard currency came from the export of silk to Europe. By the 1660s, however, production had peaked and had begun to decline. Moreover, the profits from a favorable balance of trade with the West were drained away by the importation of cotton, spices, and drugs from the Dutch and English colonies in the east. The overland silk trade with the Ottoman Empire exposed Iran to inflationary pressures that were part of a worldwide trend. In the second half of the seventeenth century spending on the royal harem grew exponentially. According to one chronicler, in 1694 Sultan Husain's harem numbered 500 wives and daughters in the imperial family and 4,500 slave girls. His extravagant

---

[271] Ahmad Ashraf, "Historical Obstacles to the Development of a Bourgeoisie in Iran," in Cook (ed.), *Studies in the Economic History*, pp. 308–18.
[272] Savory, *Iran under the Safavids*, p. 81.

penchant for constructing pleasure gardens, palaces, and mosques exhausted the Treasury.[273]

The government resorted to short-term expedients that further diminished the authority of the shah and the ruling elite. The sale of offices became scandalous; tax farming led to widespread corruption; the conversion of state lands administered by qizilbashi tribal chiefs to crown lands administered by imperial bureaucrats, often Georgian slaves who sought to recover the expense of having bought their appointment, led to corruption and exploitation of the local population. Although the shah increased his income, the provincial armies lost the major source of their income. In 1722, they did not come to the aid of the capital besieged by Afghan tribesmen.

To compensate for the declining numbers of qizilbashi tribal levies, the new army of Shah Abbas I required a level of expenditure by the state treasury and close supervision by the ruling elite that the center of power could not maintain. The court and the harem viewed the army as a source of savings. The rulers allowed the army to deteriorate, with the exception of Shah Abbas II (1642–1667), who briefly restored its fighting ability and seized Qandahar on the northeastern frontier for the last time. H. R. Roemer summed up a common view that "it was quite useful for military parades but no use at all for war."[274]

For over two hundred years the dynasty's efforts to build a strong, centralized administrative and financial system had failed to overcome factional rivalries. "Tribal feudalism," the ambivalence of the ulama, and regional interests on the frontiers had all contributed to the collapse of the Safavid Empire. The Safavids, like the Ottomans, laid claim to ownership of all the land. But they were not able to enforce their authority over either the tribes, which continued to occupy a quasi-autonomous position in Iranian society, or the urban notables, particularly in Azerbaijan. The army was split between qizilbashi, Georgian, and Iranian elements; the Persian bureaucracy was not strong enough to balance these regional forces and the state was obliged to negotiate with its powerful feudatories

---

[273] John Foran, "The Long Fall of the Safavid Dynasty. Moving Beyond the Standard Views," *International Journal of Middle East Studies* 24 (1992): 282–86. In 1706–1708 in his pilgrimage to Meshed, Husain dragged along the entire harem and 60,000 retainers, "which not only compleately drein'd his Exchequer but also ruin'd all the Provinces through which he pass'd." Father Judasz Tadeusz Krusinski, *The History of the Late Revolutions of Persia* (London: J. Ostborne, 1740), as quoted by Foran in *ibid.*, p. 286.

[274] H. R. Roemer, "The Safavid Period," in *The Cambridge History of Iran* (Cambridge University Press, 1986), vol. 6, p. 291.

rather than compelling them to contribute to the maintenance of state institutions.

The ambitious Safavid imperial policies, fueled in large part by Shi'ia messianism, encountered equally passionate Sunni opposition along the western and eastern frontiers and led to wars over the borderlands that ultimately destroyed the empire. To be sure, in the twilight of Safavid power in the early eighteenth century, the central government formed tribal clusters under petty khans in order to prevent the formation of local tribal coalitions and confederacies that threatened its existence.[275] But this was a poor substitute for integrating them into a stable sedentary community.

Richard Tapper has noted that in Iran "tribal organization and nomadism may be seen as political and social responses to a condition of alienation from and opposition to the state, as much as economic or ecological adaptation." Although the Safavid rulers had success in subjugating some tribes to serve the state, the submission was voluntary and often conditional. Despite the efforts of Shah Abbas and others to strengthen the urban networks, the cities remained islands within a semi-nomadic society. Imperial Iran under both the Safavids and Qajars never succeeded in overcoming the condition of a hybrid state, reflected also in the nature of the army.[276] Well into the eighteenth century Iranian dynasties continued to face the persistent threat of nomadic incursions along the open frontiers to the north and northeast. Neglecting to transform cities into walled fortresses armed with artillery, the dynasty continued to rely on its mobile forces to fight frontier wars. Disaster overtook the dynasty when it overreached itself in its last successful campaign in the east to subdue the even more truculent Afghan tribes.

Defeat and retreat

By the early eighteenth century the cracks in the state edifice had widened as a series of tribal revolts, always the bane of Iranian governments, broke out among the Sunni Ghilzai (Afghans) in 1716/17, and the Kurds and Lezgis in 1719/20. Pirates in the Gulf and Baluchi raiders plunged the south and southeast into chaos. Then in 1722 the northeast frontier burst

---

[275] Richard Tapper, *Frontier Nomads of Iran. A Political and Social History of the Shahsevan* (Cambridge University Press, 1997), p. 144. See also Ann K. S. Lambton, "The Tribal Resurgence and the Decline of Bureaucracy in the 18th Century," in Naff and Owens (eds.), *Studies*, pp. 108–32.

[276] Richard Tapper (ed.), "Introduction," in *The Conflict of Tribe and State in Iran and Afghanistan* (New York: St. Martin's Press, 1983), pp. 9–10, 45, quotation on p. 53, and throughout.

open flooding the country with Afghan tribes who besieged and sacked Isfahan. The great city never fully recovered its external brilliance and economic importance. After the decline of Isfahan and the end of the dynasty, Iran only sporadically recovered its military power. The capital was shifted once again to safer ground in the northwest. The choice of Tehran as the new capital was dictated in part by its proximity to the home region of the new Qajar dynasty in Gurgon and to the frontier province of Azerbaijan, which had provided the Iranians with their most reliable military forces since the advent of the Safavids in the early sixteenth century. These were the years when Russia, under Peter the Great, first occupied the northern Iranian provinces of Azerbaijan and Gilan, where they would return three more times in the twentieth century when Iran was again weak.

Assailed on all sides, Safavid rule finally collapsed. Over the following five years Iran came under Afghan and Turkish occupation. Iran enjoyed a brief recovery under the charismatic leadership of warrior rulers like Nadir Shah and Ahmad Shah Durrani. After fourteen years of anarchy, Nadir Shah attempted to restore an Iranian empire by fusing disparate elements of the Safavid army – Georgian slaves, qizilbashi, and Persian royal troops. Nadir Shah was from a Turkic tribal background, and the bulk of his army was drawn from the tribes whom he rallied by appointing local khans and forming confederacies. His extraordinary military exploits expanded Iranshahr to its greatest territorial extent, driving the Ottomans out of the south Caucasus, clearing Iran of the Afghans, sacking Delhi, defeating the Uzbeks, and forcing them to accept the Amu Darya as the southern boundary of the khanate of Bukhara with Iran.

Nadir Shah faced more complex problems in restoring an effective administrative infrastructure. A large part of the Iranian financial records had been destroyed in the Afghan invasion, the sacking of Isfahan, and subsequent warfare. The old Persian bureaucracy clung to their posts, serving usurpers like Nadir Shah as best they could. But in the absence of any further institutional reforms his empire collapsed at his death in 1747. Only another exceptional leader could pull together the large and powerful tribal groups that he had forged into a great confederacy. Such was Ahmad Shah Durrani, the last of the charismatic empire-builders in the region. An Afghan tribal leader, he had served Nadir Shah before going on to forge the last great tribal state between Iran and India, which again fell apart under his less talented successor. With the passing of such men, the glorious days of the tribal armies was over.[277] By the end of the eighteenth

[277] James J. Reid, "Rebellion and Social Change in Astarabad, 1537–1744," *International Journal of Middle East Studies* 13(1) (February 1981): 47–49, compares Nadir Shah to a

century the resurgence of the tribes had further eroded the urban foundations of Iranian society. Contemporary chronicles recorded the devastation of major cities such as Isfahan, Qazvin, Shiraz, and Yazd, which lost two-thirds of their populations.[278] The twin tasks of military conquest and state-building in the ethnically heterogeneous and religiously splintered Trans Caspian borderlands remained too great for any one leader to bridge, no matter how much of a military genius.

An uncertain political stability returned to Iran with the founding of the Qajar dynasty, whose rulers reigned, even if they did not always rule, from 1794 to 1926. During the previous period of internal struggle that lasted from 1726 to 1779, the Qajars had formed part of the armies of Nadir Shah. Under the leadership of Aga Muhammed Khan, the leading Qajar clans terminated their internal rivalry, enabling him to defeat or win over their major tribal rivals. His success depended on his skillful military organization – his reign appearing little more than a string of engagements – and ruthless policies of repression. Using Treasury funds to pay his soldiers, he was able by the turn of the nineteenth century to field an army of 35,000 cavalry, 15,000 infantry, and effective artillery manned by Georgian and Armenian gunners. But he realized that his forces were still no match for the Russians in close combat because of, in his words, "their formidable firepower and unyielding ranks."[279] His successors failed to appreciate the wisdom of his insights.

Beyond the trappings of kingship borrowed from the Safavids, neither Aga Muhammed Khan nor his successors made any real attempt to restore the substance of a centralized bureaucratic monarchy. Instead, the Qajar dynasty relied on managing tribal politics and maintaining an uneasy truce with the ulama, who questioned the legitimacy of the state in the absence of the hidden (osculated) imam of Shi'ite tradition.[280] The process of negotiation implied a value system derived from Islamic law and traditional customs. As we have seen, the responsibility of the shah was to defend Shi'ia Islam, to be its "Guardian" (*Shahanshah Islam Panah*). If he failed to meet his obligations he would lose his legitimacy

---

Cossack-type frontier rebel like Pugachev. The armies of Ahmed Shah were made up of a similar tribal mix with Afghan (Abdali) cavalry. Ganda Singh, *Ahmad Shah Durrani. Father of Modern Afghanistan* (New Delhi: Asia Publishing House, 1959).

[278] Said Amir Arjomand, *The Turban for the Crown. The Islamic Revolution in Iran* (Oxford University Press, 1988), p. 19.

[279] Arjomand, *The Turban for the Crown*, p. 136.

[280] Edvard Abrahamian, "Oriental Despotism. The Case of Qajar Iran," *International Journal of Middle East Studies* 5 (1974): 3–31; Hamid Algar, *Religion and the State in Iran, 1785–1806. The Role of the Ulama in the Qajar Period* (Berkeley, CA: University of California Press, 1969). For a local study of hierarchy and community factionalism, see Mary Jo del Vecchio Good, "Social Hierarchy in Provincial Iran. The Case of Qajar Maragheh," *Iranian Studies* 10 (1977): 129–63.

and could be challenged. The two most powerful means of protest were admonishments from the pulpit of the mosque or by closure of the bazaar, a form of boycotting the state.[281] In Iran internal stability, like external security, rested on a razor's edge.

Reformers under the Qajars

The Qajar power rested primarily on their own clan and secondarily on the Turkish tribes of Azerbaijan. Unlike the Safavids, the Qajars were no longer able to draw on a reservoir of Georgian slaves once the Georgian borderland had fallen under Russian control. The Qajar army was made up of a small detachment of the shah's personal cavalry, which in the 1820s was still composed of veteran Georgian slaves officered by Iranian nobles, irregular cavalry levies supplied by tribal leaders but not always dependable, and local militias maintained by the cities and villages. Clearly, they were no match for a military force like the Russian army. To overcome the weakness of the Iranian army was the main object of reformers in the nineteenth century.[282]

At the center of imperial rule – the court, the army, and the bureaucracy – would-be reformers were hampered, frustrated, and ultimately destroyed by three interrelated problems: a weak economy, increasingly dominated by foreign interests; family and factional strife; and the intervention in state affairs by two great power rivals, Britain and Russia, who reduced Iran from being a competitor in the struggle over the borderlands to a state of virtual dependency. Throughout the nineteenth century, state revenues fell off in real terms. The government was often faced with insolvency. Tax farming and the sale of offices and corruption continued to drain the financial resources of the country. Attempts to increase revenue by raising taxes invariably incurred opposition by the local notables. As a result of the Treaty of Turkmanchai (1828), which ended the second Russo-Iranian War, Iran was saddled with a crushing burden of reparations and capitulary rights for Russian merchants that were subsequently extended to Britain and other European powers.[283] By the end of the century, as we shall see in Chapter 5, concessions to foreign interests had

---

[281] Vanessa Martin, *The Qajar Pact. Bargaining, Protest and the State in Nineteenth Century Persia* (London: Tauris, 2005), pp. 183–87, succinctly summarizes the rules of the game with additional detail on the weapons of the weak.

[282] Gavin Hambly, "Iran During the Reigns of Fath' Ali Shah and Muhammed Shah," in *Cambridge History of Iran*, vol. 7, pp. 158–60.

[283] Hurewitz, *Diplomacy in the Near and Middle East*, pp. 96–102 for the peace and commercial Treaty of Turkmanchai, and pp. 123–24 for the Treaty of Commerce, October 1841, between the United Kingdom and Persia.

outraged the public and the ulama, leading to violence and culminating in the Constitutional Revolution.

In the long nineteenth century, reformers launched three major attempts to recover from the devastating psychological and financial results of the defeats in the two wars with Russia, and the incapacity of the rulers to resist Anglo-Russian intervention in Iranian politics. During the reign of Fath Ali Shah (1797–1834), the shah's most energetic son, Crown Prince Abbās Mīrzā, the governor of Tabriz, chose to learn from his defeat at the hands of the Russians during the first war (1805–1813) when Iran ceded its valuable silk-producing borderlands in the south Caucasus. Seeking to modernize the army, he emulated the Ottoman example. While adopting European models, he sought justification for his reforms in the history of Islam. He engaged foreign instructors, initially Russian deserters and then French officers. British advisors provided a subsidy enabling him to buy modern arms and to field a respectable force (*Nizam Jadid*, the New Army) of 12,000 infantry recruited from Azerbaijan. However, his more ambitious campaign to introduce conscription had by 1830 fallen far short of expectations.

A man of vision, Abbās Mīrzā was the first Iranian leader to send students abroad to learn European techniques. Although few in number, they returned to forge weapons, found Iran's first printing press, translate works including a history of Peter the Great, introduce the cabinet system into Iranian government, and to teach children of the nobility technology and foreign languages.[284] The opposition to his reforms by his fraternal rivals, who raised religious objections to the influence of infidels, forced him to engage in a war of words over the interpretation of the Koran, with both sides bidding for the support of the ulama.[285] After his death the army reverted to the traditional pattern. None of the intermittent efforts at modernizing had taken hold. Tribal authorities restored their control over the New Army; loyalty to the chieftain replaced unit discipline.[286]

A second major attempt at reform was undertaken in the early years of the new ruler, Nadir al-Din Shah (1848–1896), by another military chief of the Azerbaijan army, best known under the title Amir Kabir. Taking full control of the European-trained New Army, he virtually ruled the country from 1848 to 1852. His reforming initiatives were inspired by an earlier visit to Russia and a three-year sojourn in the Ottoman Empire. Unlike his successors, who tried to bring about change from the top down, he

---

[284] Hafez Farman Farmayan, "The Forces of Modernization in Nineteenth Century Iran. A Historical Survey," in R. Polk (ed.), *The Beginnings of Modernization in the Middle East* (University of Chicago Press, 1968), pp. 121–22.
[285] Algar, *Religion and the State*, pp. 73–79.   [286] Martin, *The Qajar Pact*, pp. 134–35.

grasped the importance of a European-style education as practiced by Muhammed Ali in Egypt. The Polytechnic College in Tehran, which he founded in 1851 and staffed with instructors from France, Italy, and Austria, provided the country with some of its leading figures over the following half century. Amir Kabir also sent students to Russia for technical training. He set up the first manufactures for small arms, textiles, and glass. At his orders the courts were reformed and began to extend protection to religious minorities. He established Iran's first newspaper. But, like others who followed in his footsteps, he fell victim to the machinations of court rivals who preyed on the shah's fear of his immense authority.[287]

A third attempt at reform was led by Mirza Husein Khan (given the title Moshiral-Daula), the son of a high-ranking bureaucrat who was among the first Iranian students to be sent abroad. Like Amir Kabir, he was deeply influenced by his service abroad, first in Russia, where he spent three years as a diplomat, and then for twelve years as minister and ambassador at the Porte during the period of the Tanzimat. He persuaded the shah to visit Ottoman Iraq, then administered by one of the leading Ottoman reformers, his friend Midhat Pasha. Called to Tehran as grand vizier, he introduced some of the administrative reforms he had observed in the Ottoman Empire, establishing a high court and introducing a cabinet system. He sought to separate religious and secular courts.[288] He arranged for the shah to make the first of three trips to Europe despite the protests of the ulama. In 1872, he overreached himself by granting an extraordinary set of economic concessions to Baron de Reuter, possibly the most extensive ever made to a foreigner by any sovereign state, including a monopoly on building railroads, exploiting mines, and setting up a national banking system. The Russians expressed their strong opposition, and a powerful domestic coalition of the ulama and the court harem forced Nadir al-Din to dismiss him as grand vizier. He soon recovered to become Minister of War and commander of the army, hiring instructors from Austria to reorganize the army and drafting legislation separating the provincial administration from military authority.[289]

---

[287] Abbas Amanat, *Pivot of the Universe. Nasir Al-Din Shah and the Iranian Monarchy, 1831–1896* (Berkeley, CA: University of California Press, 1997); Nikki Keddie, "Iran under the Later Qajars, 1848–1922," in *Cambridge History of Iran*, vol. 7, pp. 174–77.

[288] Mangol Bayat, *Iran's First Revolution. Shi'ism and the Constitutional Revolution of 1905–1909* (New York: Oxford University Press, 1991), pp. 36–39. For reforming initiatives from below, such as the new school movement which began in the early years of Mirza Husein Khan's administration, see Monica M. Ringer, *Education, Religion and the Discourse of Cultural Reform in Qajar Iran* (Costa Mesa, CA: Mazda Publications, 2001), ch. 5.

[289] Keddie, "Iran," pp. 183–92; Farmayan, "The Forces of Modernization," pp. 129–32.

Up to the late nineteenth century the reformers were largely isolated and easily defeated by entrenched interests. But a new generation of Iranian intellectuals came to maturity under Nadir al-Din's reign. They often gained their knowledge of reformist ideas and constitutionalism through government service that took them abroad to Europe, the Ottoman Empire, and Russia. The growth of a mass press of opinion enabled "turbaned" men of the pen, mullahs who adapted to the "peculiar socioreligious climate then prevailing in Iran," to envelop their calls for change in Islamic rhetoric. These were the figures who became the leaders of constitutional revolution in 1906.[290]

Contemporary observers and historians have been deeply divided in their overall assessment of institutional change under Nadir al-Din. Given the formidable structural obstacles to forging a modern, centralized bureaucratic state, his greatest accomplishment may have been to hold the country together and to preserve its independence without any further loss of territory. In the eyes of contemporary European diplomats and military men, his bureaucrats were venal, his army a shambles, and the shah a poorly educated and vainglorious ruler.

These Orientalist views propagated by Western travelers and diplomats have undergone revision. The Persian bureaucratic tradition, however attenuated, going back at least to the Seljuk period deserves some credit for preserving the integrity of the state. The lasting success of the bureaucracy was in reaching accommodation with the factions among the tribes and the ulama through a process of bargaining. The practice of settling political questions by negotiation penetrated all levels of Iranian society and contributed to the stability of the regime. The central authorities wielded little power in areas of commerce, education, health, and welfare; these functions were regulated by the communities.[291] As long as the government, and especially the shah, could demonstrate a modicum of piety, it could avoid a direct confrontation with the ulama. The more formidable task facing the bureaucracy was the growing influence of Russia and Great Britain over the Iranian economy, which peaked in the late nineteenth and early twentieth centuries.

Perhaps the single most important innovation in binding the country together was the installation of the telegraph and postal systems in the early years of Nadir al-Din's reign. By the end of his reign all the cities and major towns were linked by telegraph. The system served the shah as a

---

[290] Bayat, *Iran's First Revolution*, pp. 40–44.
[291] Martin, *The Qajar Pact*. For a case study of the complex interaction of social groups at the provincial level, see del Vecchio Good, "Social Hierarchy in Provincial Iran," pp. 129–63.

reliable means of communication and control. But, like education, it too became a two-edged sword. In 1907, during the constitutional movement, it fell into the hands of rebellious subjects who used it to disseminate the revolutionary message.[292]

As a reformer Nadir al-Din Shah compares unfavorably to his contemporaries, Franz Joseph, Alexander II, and Abdülhamid. If there was any consistency to his policies, it was in encouraging reform of the army and bureaucracy to the point where he encountered opposition that appeared to threaten his personal rule. This might have come either from the Russians or the British, on the one hand, and local notables and the ulama, on the other. Given the fact that he was not a courageous man, the threshold of opposition did not have to be very high to be effective. Beyond that, he skillfully maintained the patriarchal nature of his power. He viewed his office as a private possession and exercised iron rule over state officials. In his relations with the local notables he also recognized their patriarchal authority. His administrative style was increasingly marked by bargaining with the local notables and tribal leaders whose support he needed to stabilize his dynastic rule. This translated into a diminution of his power on the periphery.[293] Toward the end of his reign he became increasingly conservative, subject to harem intrigues, and preoccupied with childish hobbies.[294]

The second most serious weakness of his rule was the lack of financial resources to carry out the few reforming projects he did endorse. Before the discovery of great oil resources, Iran was a poor state. The economy under the Qajars continued to be based on a policy of patrimonial state capitalism. Most manufacturing was in the hands of the state, including a monopoly over the profitable silk trade. Prosperous traders acquired wealth as the shah's semi-bureaucratic agents. But the economic penetration of Iranian markets by the Russians and the British destroyed Iranian manufactures and contributed to the decay of the cities and the shrinking tax base.[295]

The state institution that suffered the most from the opposition of tribal chiefs and the shortage of capital was the army. But the connivance of the

---

[292] Farmayan, "The Forces of Modernization," pp. 150–51.

[293] See in particular the insights of A. Reza Sheikholeslami, *The Structure of Central Authority in Qajar Iran, 1871–1896* (Atlanta, GA: Scholars Press, 1997), pp. 7–13, 21–24, 107 ff, 209–13.

[294] An intimate portrait of the shah by an insider is provided by the unique diary of one of his high officials, Mehdrad Kia, "Inside the Court of Naser od-Din Shah Qajar, 1881–1896. The Life and Diary of Mohammed Hasan Khan E'temad os-Saltaneh (Iran)," *Middle Eastern Studies* 37(1) (January 2001), esp. pp. 101–17.

[295] Ahmad Ashraf, "Historical Obstacles to the Development of a Bourgeoisie in Iran," in Cook, *Studies in the Economic History*, pp. 318–25.

British and Russian rivals at Iran's expense proved to be decisive in crippling attempts to reform the Iranian army. The Russians took advantage of Nasir al-Din's fascination with the Cossacks he had seen on his second European trip in 1879, offering to provide him with a military mission and a small force of Cossacks, which later became known as the Cossack Brigade. It was commanded by Russian officers and wholly under the control of the Russian ambassador. It was the most professional armed force in Iran for the next generation. The British, fearing the influence of Russia, turned to the tribes as a counterforce. Signing treaties with the Bakhtiari and Lur tribes and furnishing them with modern weapons, the British ensured that southern Iran was fast becoming a British protectorate. This left the Iranian army at the mercy of the whims of the shah and the depredations of corrupt viziers, ministers, and senior officers. The result was a ragtag force, under-manned, badly trained (if at all), ill paid (when paid at all), equipped with outmoded weapons, and lacking ammunition.[296]

During the rise of the constitutional movement on the eve of the Russian–British partition of Iran into spheres of influence, the sorry state of Iran's finances forced the government to suspend payment to the army and even to the Cossack Brigade, which had become, ironically, the defender of all foreign interests. The disintegration of the army during the disorders led to mass defections: "the very tool designed to enforce the authority of the government had turned sharply against it."[297] By this time Iran had long since lost the power to take an active part in the struggle over the borderlands.

Qing China

The Manchu conquest and consolidation of power under the Qing dynasty inaugurated a new phase in China's struggle over the Inner Asian borderlands. In the words of Nicola Di Cosmo: "Both the territorial expansion and bureaucratic rule of Qing rule in Inner Asia had no precedent in Chinese history." The military and civil institutions of the entire imperial state-building project were profoundly influenced by the conquest and incorporation of the borderlands.[298]

---

[296] Reza Ra'iss Tousi, "The Persian Army, 1880–1907," *Middle Eastern Studies* 24(2) (April 1988): 206–29, gives a devastating account based on reports of French and British observers. See also Firouzeh Kazemzadeh, "The Origin and Early Development of the Persian Cossack Brigade," *American Slavic and East European Review* 15(3) (October 1956): 351–63.
[297] Tousi, "The Persian Army," p. 226.
[298] Nicola Di Cosmo, "Qing Colonial Administration in Inner Asia," *International History Review* 20(2) (June 1998): 287–309, quotation on p. 288.

The army

The founder of the dynasty, Nurhaci, was a charismatic young noble of a Jürchen tribe from the northeast border region, who succeeded, like Chinggis Khan, in welding together a great tribal federation. Although he adopted the title khan, he does not seem to have cultivated imperial ambitions. It was his son, Hong Taiji, who proclaimed a new dynasty to be called Qing (pure or clear) and changed the name of his followers from Jürchen to Manchu. The unique military organization created by Nurhaci, called the Eight Banners, became the basis for the Manchu state. Identified by different colors, the banners were lineage groups of warriors and their families performing military, social, and administrative functions. The commanders were military officers and clan leaders. It appears Nurhaci's aim was to erase tribal loyalties without destroying the traditional clan structure of Jürchen society. In their early battles against the troops of the Ming emperors, he and his commanders exhibited great flexibility in combining the tactics of their own military organization with the new technologies of the military revolution. Like other semi-nomadic invaders from the steppe, the Manchus displayed great valor and a high degree of mobility, but initially they suffered from a marked inferiority in siege warfare. They were unable to compete with the advanced weaponry of the Ming armies, which as early as the late sixteenth century had acquired artillery and muskets from the Ottoman Empire and the West, mainly the Portuguese. In the 1620s, they used them in defending their walled cities with deadly effect on the waves of attacking Manchu archers and swordsmen. Within a decade Hong Taiji had begun manufacturing siege guns based on captured European models and had developed new tactics to match.[299]

In the course of his military campaigns, Nurhaci expanded the banner system in order to incorporate the military elites of the Mongols and Han Chinese. Ming troops of mixed ancestry in the northeast border regions were organized into new units called Chinese-martial banners.[300] Under his son and successor, Hong Taiji, a plan was devised to educate the banner nobles as the future administrators of the empire. Up until the eighteenth century they were used by the emperors as a check on the civil service, to sit on the Deliberative Council, the major policy-making body

---

[299] Di Cosmo, "Did Guns Matter?" pp. 121–66.
[300] Robert H. G. Lee, *The Manchurian Frontier in Ch'ing History* (Cambridge University Press, 1970), pp. 34–41; Mark C. Elliott, *The Manchu Way. The Eight Banners and Ethnic Identity in Late Imperial China* (Stanford University Press, 2001), pp. 29–31, 58.

of imperial rule, and to fill administrative posts in the borderlands.[301] As stalwarts of frontier defense, the banners combined personal and institutional features of the frontier into a structure that kept the conquest elite in a state of continued mobilization and, unlike the Ottoman or Iranian armies, independent of the influence of local notables.[302] In comparative terms, they functioned like the janissaries and Russian Guards officers in the early Ottoman and Petrine periods.

When in the eighteenth century the Qing emperors launched their conquest of the northwest borderlands, they were forced to deal with an age-old problem that had in the past hampered such expeditions: how to overcome the logistics of supplying and feeding a large enough army over great distances of arid or semi-arid terrain with widely scattered oases for a long enough time to defeat the nomads who always had the option of withdrawing farther into the steppe. The local populations were too poor to provide sufficient food. The Qing answer was to stockpile supplies in a chain of military magazines linked by protected supply lines. As Peter Perdue states: "only the commercialization of the eighteenth century economy as a whole enabled the Qing officials to purchase large supplies on the open markets of northwest China and ship them out to Xinjiang." Like the Russian army about the same time, these expedients proved to be decisive in organizing deep expeditions into the steppe, enabling the Qing to break the power of the last great semi-nomadic empire of the Dzhungars.[303] By the mid-eighteenth century the banner armies with their highly developed military technology and well-organized logistics had enabled the Qing to expand imperial rule to the borderlands, subsequently recognized by both their republican and communist successors as constituting the sovereign territory of China.

Bureaucracy

Not surprisingly, China, as the oldest continuous empire in Eurasia, was the first to develop the principles of bureaucratic government. What is surprising is the stability of the original design over a period of almost 2,000 years. Although pre-Confucian in its origins, the Chinese bureaucracy was consolidated by the examination system based upon mastery of

[301] Evelyn S. Rawski, "Presidential Address. Reenvisioning the Qing. The Significance of the Qing Period in Chinese History," *Journal of Asian Studies* 55(4) (November 1996): 832.

[302] Roberto M. Unger, *Plasticity and Power. Comparative-Historical Studies on the Institutional Conditions of Economic and Military Power* (Cambridge University Press, 1987), p. 59.

[303] Peter C. Perdue, *China Marches West. The Qing Conquest of Central Eurasia* (Cambridge, MA: Belknap Press, 2005), pp. 238, 522–23, see also pp. 397–400.

Confucian texts. At the top of the pyramid of power, the emperor person-ally made all appointments. Rationalistic, hierarchical, mobile with built-in control mechanisms, the bureaucracy was able to govern an enormous population with surprisingly few numbers; by the nineteenth century 30,000 to 40,000 officials of all ranks administered a country of about 400 million inhabitants.[304]

The authority of the bureaucrats (sometimes called scholar-officials) derived from two complementary sources. First, officials were governed by administrative regulations and precedents that were minutely detailed. Second, its moral strength from a set of ethical precepts, allowed it to claim an autonomous position in relation to the emperor and a mediating position between the emperor and people. Propriety, wisdom, righteous-ness, and truthfulness were values embedded in the classical texts and widely spread throughout rural China and the market towns by local officials, literati, and traders more by example and oral transmission than by written communication. Inculcated with a sense of responsibility for popular well-being and domestic order, they were primed to respond to periodic appeals by emperors for new ideas, claiming for themselves "the voice of the people on behalf of heaven." They cherished a belief in the power of the will of the individual to uphold the high ethical ideals of the society even in the face of pressure or persecution by an unjust ruler.[305] The moral code of the bureaucrats was not an iron-clad guaran-tee against corruption or the amassing of great wealth. The main problem that complicated the role of the scholar-official was his dual loyalty; on the one hand, to his regional base and bureaucratic ethos and, on the other hand, to the emperor, who all too often made demands upon them that could not be squared with their conscience.[306]

If the scholar-officials could not conceive of a state without an emperor with absolute powers, so the emperors could not govern without the scholar-officials. This lesson was brought home with particular force

[304] For the originality of the system, see H. G. Creel, *The Origins of Statecraft in China. The Western Chou Empire* (University of Chicago Press, 1970); and at its height, T. Metzger, *The Internal Organization of Ch'ing Bureaucracy. Legal, Normative and Communications Aspects* (Cambridge, MA: Harvard University Press, 1974). The myth of the examination system as a source of social mobility and egalitarianism has been exploded in Benjamin A. Elman, "Political, Social and Cultural Reproduction via Civil Service Examinations in Late Imperial China," *Journal of Asian Studies* 50(1) (February 1991): 17–19.

[305] T. Wei-ming, "The Enlightenment Mentality and the Chinese Intellectual Dilemma," in Kenneth Lieberthal et al. (eds.), *Perspectives on Modern China. Four Anniversaries* (Armonk, NY: M. E. Sharpe, 1991), pp. 109–12.

[306] V. Shue, *The Reach of the State. Sketches of the Chinese Body Politic* (Stanford University Press, 1988), p. 87.

whenever a nomadic conquest dynasty seized power in China. The Mongols and Manchus were not numerous nor experienced enough to administer a vast and populous sedentary society without assistance from the Chinese bureaucrats.[307] To be sure, the new rulers like Kublai Khan (1271–1294) sought to staff the government offices insofar as possible with Mongols and western Asians, but even they had to be literate and have some knowledge of Chinese bureaucratic methods. Kublai Khan was himself a great admirer of Confucian principles. Throughout the history of imperial China there were periods of tinkering with the central institutions of rule; there were also cases of vast purges of officials, burning of texts, and re-editing of the classics. But the main supports of the structure remained unchanged, as did the examination system, providing continuity in imperial rule.

In the early years of the Manchu dynasty, tension existed between the Chinese scholar-officials and Manchu nobles, who were granted extensive lands by the Qing emperors, but the administrative role of the Manchu bannermen gradually declined throughout the eighteenth century. The central Qing bureaucracy gradually reasserted its traditional control.[308] In seeking to cope with the complex regional structures of Chinese society, the Qing developed a bifurcated imperial rule. An overarching superstructure rested upon a "matrix of diverse governing units," which differed from region to region. The success of the system relied upon the mutual cooperation of local economic and power groups with the central administration. These local groups existed outside the formal bureaucratic structure. Informal arrangements enabled the dynasty to draw on a pool of local experts to solve problems relating to food supply and water conservation quickly and efficiently. To be sure, local groups outside the commercialized urban centers, particularly in the borderlands, did not always accommodate readily to the larger needs of the state. Recognizing this, the central administration continued to experiment with different forms of indirect rule in the borderlands. But when accommodation broke

---

[307] Scholars have long recognized that employing ethnic terms like Manchu, Mongol, and Chinese (Han) to social groups in seventeenth-century China greatly simplifies complex cultural identities, particularly within the Inner Asian borderlands. But these designations suited the purposes of the Qing empire-builders who needed to name and categorize the various "constituencies," as Pamela Kyle Crossley chooses to call them, in order to govern effectively. Pamela Kyle Crossley, *A Translucent Mirror. History and Identity in Qing Imperial Ideology* (Berkeley, CA: University of California Press, 1999), pp. 43–52.

[308] F. W. Mote, *Imperial China, 900–1800* (Cambridge, MA: Harvard University Press, 1999), pp. 489–94, 892–96.

down, the center resorted to harsh repressive measures, which in turn could spark large-scale resistance.[309]

The Qing maintained separate administrations between the "inner" Han provinces, Manchuria, and the "outer" Inner Asian borderlands. The emperors were successful in preserving the administrative autonomy of the northeastern provinces (Manchuria) and maintaining the original military organization that brought them to power. Experience on the Manchurian frontier with Russian territory influenced the administrative practices elsewhere in Inner Asia. In the two northeastern provinces, control was vested in the hands of a military governor, while a virtual secondary capital at Shenyang administered the southern-most province of Liaodung.[310]

The Qing created a central bureaucratic organ, the Lifan Yuan, sometimes translated as colonial office, but more properly in the words of Di Cosmo as a "court for the administration of the outer provinces," in order to establish order and co-opt the local elites.[311] Composed exclusively of Manchu and Mongol officials and excluding the Han Chinese, its rules and functions gradually increased as the Qing expanded deeper into Inner Asia. Functioning as a second tier of administration at the local level, imperial residents, often soldiers, were appointed to manage civic as well as military affairs. Over time, another layer of "frontier specialists" was added. Within this system, the administrative structures of Mongolia and Xinjiang differed, reflecting the relationship of the local elites to the center of power.

The Mongols had been allies of the Manchus even before the conquest and voluntarily submitted to their imperial rule. Consequently, the Qing did not establish a military occupation in Mongolia, but allowed a measure of self-government to the clans and tribes under the loose supervision of Chinese officials. Hereditary princes ruled the Mongolian banners. They swore oaths of fealty to the dynasty in return for land grants and subsidies from Beijing. The Qing emperors conferred titles on members of the Mongol nomadic nobility. Taxes were moderate and levied in

---

[309] Robert J. Anthony and Jane Kate Leonard (eds.), "Introduction," *Dragons, Tigers and Dogs. Qing Crisis Management and the Boundaries of State Power in Late Imperial China* (Ithaca, NY: East Asian Program, Cornell University, 2002), pp. 16–19.

[310] Lee, *The Manchurian Frontier*, pp. 59–77.

[311] di Cosmo, "Qing Colonial Administration," p. 294. The following draws heavily on this article, as well as Evelyn S. Rawski, "The Qing Formation in the Early Modern Period," in Struve (ed.), *The Qing Formation*, pp. 223–26; and L.J. Newby, "The Begs of Xinjiang. Between Two Worlds," *Bulletin of the School of Oriental and African Studies* 2 (1998): 278–97.

kind.[312] The Qing codified Mongol customary law into a Mongol statute book, but then brought it into line with the standardized and bureaucratic practices of Chinese legal institutions.[313]

After the conquest of Xinjiang the role of the military varied according to regional patterns of settlement. The Qing also altered the traditional lifestyles of pastoral peoples in the borderlands. They recruited hunting and fishing peoples of the north into banners to man garrisons defending the northeast against the Russians. They assigned pasture lands to tribes and organized them into banners.[314]

The Qing elites recognized the need to reorganize the imperial finances and increase revenues in light of their belief that the Ming dynasty had been weakened by economic shortcomings that crippled its military effort to suppress domestic rebellion and repulse invasions from Inner Asia.[315] The Qing administrators centralized tax-collecting, tightened tax regulations, tapped the Privy Purse, and imposed imperial monopolies on items of mass consumption such as salt and on expensive items such as ginseng and jewelry.[316] Without these resources the great territorial expansion of the state would have been impossible. Even so, borderlands like Xinjiang were a drain on imperial resources despite the best efforts of the government to encourage trade as the basis for its self-sufficiency.[317] Clearly, the main aim of the Qing in the outer territories was strategic not economic.

The problem of decline

In retrospect, the decline of Qing power from its peak at the end of the eighteenth century appears precipitous. Several explanations have been proposed for the failure of the Qing to resist Western penetration during the mid-century crisis beginning with the Opium Wars. John K. Fairbank and his school have attributed this failure to the rigidity of Confucian ideologists, who placed China at the center of the world order and devised the tribute system as the principal strategy for dealing with barbarians. Greater emphasis is now given to the devastating effects of large-scale internal rebellions, especially the White Lotus in the 1770s and the first of

---

[312] Joseph Fletcher, "Ch'ing Inner Asia c. 1800," in *Cambridge History of China*, vol. 10, pp. 48–58; Thomas E. Ewing, *Between the Hammer and the Anvil? Chinese and Russian Policies in Outer Mongolia* (Bloomington, IN: Indiana University Press, 1980), pp. 8–9.

[313] Dorothy Heuschert, "Legal Pluralism in the Qing Empire. Manchu Legislation for the Mongols," *International History Review* 20(2) (June 1998): 310–24.

[314] Rawski, "Presidential Address," p. 836.

[315] Frederic Wakeman, Jr., "China and the Seventeenth Century Crisis," *Late Imperial China* 7(1) (1986): 1–26.

[316] Rawski, "The Qing Formation," pp. 213–18.

[317] Millward, *Beyond the Pass*, pp. 45–49, 59–66; Perdue, *China Marches West*, pp. 392–400.

many Muslim revolts in the 1780s. In the first half of the nineteenth century, four great uprisings shook the dynasty; two of them, the Taiping (1851–1864) and Nian (1851–1868), threatened to overthrow it. Although social unrest has been attributed to many causes, the rebellions in China were often distinguished from those in the Habsburg, Ottoman, Russian, and Iran empires by virtue of their millenarian character.[318] The growing difficulty of the ruling elite to cope with the rapidly expanding population and social malcontents was magnified by the problem of opium addiction and the pressure of the British to protect the opium trade. In China's first clash with the West, it suffered a humiliating defeat by the British in the Opium War of 1839–1842.

Frederic Wakeman, Jr. has argued that the prolonged and costly Taiping rebellion in particular undermined the foundations of imperial rule, and forced the center to rely for allies on local elites whose xenophobia led to clashes with militarily superior British forces.[319] Peter Perdue has identified four factors that contributed to the Qing setbacks. All of them demonstrate how the policies successfully applied to managing security on the frontiers of the Inner Asian borderlands were adopted with disastrous results to different conditions on the coastal frontiers. First, the Qing, having just defeated the formidable Dzhungars in the northwest, made the serious mistake of underestimating the threat of British penetration on their coastal frontier. Their victory reinforced the belief acquired over centuries of experience that the northern barbarians constituted the greatest danger to imperial rule. Second, officials who had gained their military experience on the Inner Asian frontier failed to adapt their strategies in fighting nomads to repelling a major maritime power such as Britain. Third, the time-honored tactics of negotiating and bargaining with local elites rather than strengthening the central bureaucracy worked well in dividing barbarians in the north, but proved to be ineffective in dealing with the maritime powers, all of whom accepted British

---

[318] See, for example, Susan Naquin, *Millenarian Rebellion in China. The Eight Trigrams Uprising of 1813* (New Haven, CT: Yale University Press, 1976); Susan Naquin, *Shantung Rebellion. The Wang Lun Uprising of 1774* (New Haven, CT: Yale University Press, 1981); Jonathan Spence, *God's Chinese Son. The Taiping Heavenly Kingdom of Hong Xiuquan* (New York: W. W. Norton, 1996).

[319] John K. Fairbank (ed.), *The Chinese World Order. Traditional China's Foreign Relations* (Cambridge, MA: Harvard University Press, 1968); Frederic Wakeman, Jr., *Strangers at the Gate. Social Disorder in South China, 1839–1861* (Berkeley, CA: University of California Press, 1966). For a critique of these views, see James M. Polacher, *The Inner Opium War* (Cambridge, MA: Harvard University Press, 1992), who takes the position that bureaucratic interest group politics, particularly the role played by a small subgroup of literati, was the determining factor in the shaping of Qing foreign policy and not ideology or local politics.

leadership. Finally, the growth of commercialization in the coastal cities weakened the ties between them and the imperial center, enabling the Western maritime powers to forge alliances with local mercantile interests.[320]

Qing officials responded to the multiple crises that shook the dynasty in mid-century by undertaking institutional reforms which they called "the restoration," a term borrowed from similar periods of change under earlier dynasties. Another term that became popular among the reforming literati was "self-strengthening." It was coined in the 1860s by a scholar-general, Zeng Guofan, who propounded an eclectic form of Confucianism. He believed that the empire needed to launch a techno-logical revolution in China, although his educational reform proposed nothing more than reinstituting a strict Confucian curriculum. In many ways his initiatives corresponded to the Great Reforms in Russia, the Tanzimat in the Ottoman Empire, and the *Ausgleich* in the Habsburg Monarchy, although the pace, depth, and success of these reform move-ments obviously varied greatly.

Following a series of crises marked by defeats in the Opium Wars and the Taiping Rebellion, China passed through three periods of reform. The first, lasting from the early nineteenth century to a dynastic restoration in the 1870s, concentrated on bringing the armed forces up to competitive levels with the Western powers and accepting certain Western diplomatic techniques. Yet in most cases the changes remained imbued with the Confucian world view. Moreover, the effective military response to the Taiping Rebellion was organized by provincial, not central, forces. As an administrator of Hunan Province, Zheng Guofan raised an army of 120,000, inspired his troops with his modern adaptation of Confucian ethics, and recruited his officers from the young scholars of the prov-ince.[321] Similarly, the establishment of the Zongli Yamen, the Chinese equivalent of a foreign ministry, and a Navy Board was largely the work of individual scholar-officials gaining legitimacy by reinterpreting traditional Confucian principles. By contrast, the central government lacked the vision or the will to support a comprehensive and integrated program of reforms, or to provide the necessary financial underpinnings for the new institutions.[322]

[320] Perdue, *China Marches West*, pp. 552–65.

[321] David B. Ralston, *Importing the European Army. The Introduction of European Military Techniques and Institutions into the Extra-European World, 1600–1914* (Chicago University Press, 1990), pp. 111–12.

[322] David Pong, *Shen Pao Chen and China's Modernization in the Nineteenth Century* (Cambridge University Press, 1994), esp. pp. 315–37.

The more conservative officials who opposed functional specialization and changes that threatened their privileges found powerful backing from the dowager empress, Cixi. An ambitious, talented, and authoritarian figure, she served as regent from 1861 until 1908, first, for her son, the last legitimate emperor, Tongzhi, and then for her nephew who she appointed to the throne in violation of a fundamental law of succession. She was instrumental in cutting short the second, much briefer period of reforms called the Hundred Days. It was launched in reaction to China's humiliating defeat at the hands of the Japanese in the war of 1894/5, and the renewed pressure in 1898 from the Western powers for economic and residence rights leading to "the scramble for concessions." The emerging mass press in China echoed the voices of the reformer literati in warning of the fate of Poland and the Ottoman Empire, and in extolling the examples of Peter the Great and the Meiji emperor of Japan in instituting fundamental changes.[323] The young emperor Guangxu, struggling to free himself of Cixi's influence, issued four important edicts on education, the economy, the military, and the bureaucracy. These echoed the earlier recommendations of the self-strengthening reformers. But a palace coup by Cixi placed the emperor under palace detention and she executed several of his advisors. It required another great shock to the system in the form of the Boxer Rebellion in 1900 to shake the dowager empress' confidence in the old system.

The last reforming efforts

The last series of major reforms in Qing China, the New Policy (*xinzheng*), was the culmination of almost a century of efforts to rationalize imperial rule. Similar to the pattern of reform in the Ottoman Empire, the structural changes in China had often been a response to Western pressure legitimized by the dominant ideology and adapted to the interests of the ruling elite. The New Policy was no exception. The first step was to reorganize the Zongli Yamen to complete its transformation into a Western-style Ministry of Foreign Affairs. In a move reminiscent of Russian and Ottoman reformers, a Reform Commission was then dispatched abroad to Western Europe, Russia, and Japan to examine alternative forms of government. It returned with a recommendation to reject the Russian autocratic system in favor of the Japanese constitutional system. Many of its ideas reflected, once again, the proposals of earlier reformers, most prominently those of Kang Youwei.

---

[323] Jonathan Spence, *The Search for Modern China*, 2nd edn (New York: W. W. Norton, 1999), p. 227.

At the turn of the century, Kang Youwei had drawn on his classical training to argue, as had others before him, that Confucius did not deny the advantages of social change or the idea of progress. His arguments would have been familiar *mutatis mutandis* to the preaching of Jamal Al-Afgani on the compatibility of Islam and rational progressive change. Kang helped to coordinate a long memorial to the throne drafted by fellow scholars in 1895 that urged a comprehensive program of reform, beginning with a Western-style army and the widespread adoption of technological innovations in industry and agriculture. Among his many proposals, he advocated a vast resettlement program to assist the rural poor by colonizing the frontier regions. He had been appointed secretary in the Grand Council, which allowed him to memorialize the throne. His two works of historical analysis examined the fate of Poland as a warning and the Meiji reforms in Japan as an inspiration. Forced into exile by the coup of the dowager empress, he continued to agitate for the transformation of the Qing into a constitutional monarchy under the Emperor Guangxu. He represented the voice of moderate reform that was gradually supplanted among the critics of the government by nationalist and republican platforms personified by Sun Yat-sen.[324]

In a last ditch attempt to save the dynasty, the dowager empress issued an edict in 1906 reorganizing the central bureaucratic institutions based on West European models. Distinctions between positions for Manchu and Han officials were abolished. Two notable omissions were the absence of a cabinet system and the failure to curb the authority of provincial officials.[325] The plan was ambitious, but appeared too late and was too dependent on foreign assistance. Despite a reorganization of the central ministries and preparations for a derogation of power to the provinces, the reforming impulse proved to be too feeble in the face of mounting pressure by advocates of radical change. The traditional bureaucracy was incapable of controlling the transition to a constitutional government. As in other multicultural states, the reforms sowed the seeds of destruction of dynastic rule.

---

[324] Jonathan Spence, *The Gate of Heavenly Peace. The Chinese and their Revolution, 1895–1980* (New York: Viking Press, 1981), pp. 32–56, 108–19.

[325] Richard S. Horowitz, "Breaking the Bonds of Precedent. The 1905–6 Government Reform Commission and the Remaking of the Qing Central State," *Modern Asian Studies* 37(4) (2003): 775–97. The reforms also rationalized the recruitment, payment, and promotion practices in the lower levels of the bureaucracy. Luca Gabbiani, "The Xinzheng Reforms and the Transformation of the Status of Lower Level Central Administration," *Modern Asian Studies* 37(4) (2003): 827–29.

Comparisons and conclusion

Imperial institutions, like imperial ideologies, evolved in the process of multicultural state-building through the conquest and incorporation of the borderlands. Displaying a mix of patriarchal, bureaucratic, and charismatic elements, imperial rule proved to be surprisingly flexible in meeting repeated challenges to internal order and external security arising from the struggle over the borderlands. Reforms from above, bargains with local elites, and toleration alternated with coercion and cultural assimilation. The ruling elites experimented with various centralizing and decentralizing practices, but were never entirely successful in eliminating domestic resistance or stabilizing the frontiers. Periodically, rebellions in the borderlands threatened to bring foreign intervention in their wake; frontier wars threatened to touch off domestic uprisings. So it was in the early period of state-building and reconstruction as the sedentary, agricultural-based states began to overcome the long military hegemony of the pastoral nomads and encounter one another. So it would continue, as we shall see, to the end of imperial rule and beyond.

The responses of imperial bureaucracies to external threats and internal crises demonstrate the fallacy of most theories of decline. Periods of crisis and renewal alternated throughout the long history of the Eurasian empires. The so-called revolutions in military technology and organization were actually spurts in a continuous process of adjusting to the needs of warfare on the frontiers. The similarity among the armies of the Eurasian multicultural states lessened over time as changes in weaponry, recruitment, training, and tactics required corresponding changes in social, cultural, and financial structures. In the sixteenth and seventeenth centuries, however, armies still rested upon an agrarian or semi-nomadic base and a rigid caste system that separated the solider from the rest of society. In tracing the sources of technical and tactical innovations in Eurasian armies, direct borrowing from the West may well be exaggerated. Transfers frequently took place among the rival Eurasian states, with the Russian and the Ottoman empires serving as filters.

In the eighteenth century a pronounced shift took place in the relative strength of the competing states. The Habsburg and Russian armies introduced greater centralization of command and tactical innovations based on stricter discipline. The first mass citizen armies emerged from the wars of the French Revolution, but the model of the nation-in-arms was abandoned in the post-1815 period by conservative governments who preferred long-term professional armies. The Habsburg and Russian empires led the parade toward conscript armies, the former after 1867 and the latter in 1874. They also were in advance of other Eurasian empires in creating a domestic armaments industry. By comparison with the Russian army, the Ottoman army entered a period of "military devolution" to compensate for the growing limitation of its fiscal resources and the growth in the local power of the ayans.[326] The technological and organizational transformation of the Ottoman and Chinese armies lagged behind them until the end of the century. The Iranian army never built a professional army trained in modern warfare or a mass citizen militia.

Although the bureaucratic functions and procedures of imperial rule were routinized in the Weberian sense, the bureaucrats shared with intellectuals, literati, and religious thinkers the same educational system that imbued them with ethical sources of governance, whether ancient concepts of kingship, the Koran, Confucian Analects, Christian theologies, or the secular humanism of the Enlightenment. But they were also guided by the practical necessities of governing multicultural societies. However, when enlightened government officials generated programs of political reform they encountered powerful opposition from others who feared tampering with the basic institutions of imperial rule that guaranteed their status and power. Centralizing reforms from above had to contend with restive constituencies organized at the local and provincial level or around alternative sources of authority, whether landed estates in the Habsburg Monarchy, Cossack hosts and szlachta in the Russian Empire, ayans and ulama in the Ottoman Empire, tribal confederacies in Iran, or regional movements in China. Although none of these was capable of paralyzing the government and hastening its dismemberment (with the exception of the szlachta in pre-partition Poland), they often hampered or crippled the work of the military reformers.

Underlying the problem of administrative and military reform was the pressure to mobilize new financial resources. Predominantly agrarian societies with islands of industry scattered over the rural landscape, the Eurasian states remained relatively backward in comparison with Western Europe. The Habsburg and Russian empires were relatively more advanced in industrial development than the other three empires, and more successful than the other three in creating financial institutions to support the administration and the army.

The challenge to imperial rule posed by Western ideas was of a wholly different magnitude. It posed the problem of how to justify change that

---

[326] Ágoston, "Military Transformation," pp. 281–320.

appeared to be culturally subversive. Although there were numerous attempts within the imperial bureaucracies to reconcile the contradiction, none of them succeeded. It had been considerably easier to adjust to or absorb the invasive steppe cultures, which had comparatively few well-established institutions, than to incorporate the complex cultures of the West.

4   Imperial frontier encounters

The rise and expansion of the multicultural conquest states changed one important feature of the Eurasian frontiers and inaugurated an era of struggle over the Eurasian borderlands. The frontier became less a zone of encounter between nomadic and sedentary societies and more a zone of encounters between organized state systems based on agricultural communities and urban centers, ruled (mainly) by hereditary monarchs or emperors wielding great, if not always absolute, power legitimized by various political theologies; they were governed with the assistance of civil and military elites drawn up in hierarchical orders and occupying the central institutions of the state. These frontier encounters also involved the indigenous populations that inhabited the contested territories. New types of frontier communities sprang up, some organized by the central state, others resisting that authority. Different sections of the Eurasian frontiers began to take on distinctive geocultural profiles. Henceforth in this narrative these sections will be called complex frontiers; complexity in this case signifying the number of state systems and social groups engaged in violent and peaceful intercourse within a broadly conceived geographical space that set restraints and opened possibilities for human action. On this basis, seven complex frontiers will serve as the matrix for this chapter: the Baltic littoral, the western Balkans (Triplex Confinium), Danubian frontier, Pontic steppe, Caucasian isthmus, Trans Caspia, and Inner Asia. As frontiers they cannot be sharply delimited; they are blurred and porous at the margins. Encounters in one section often spilled over into others. As the conquest states carved out territories within these frontiers, annexed and incorporated them, these borderlands did not cease to become sites of external and internal conflicts.

The chronology of the prolonged frontier wars and cross-cultural encounters, which in the long term determined the relative power positions of the multicultural states in their struggle over the borderlands, divides into two periods. From the sixteenth to the mid- to late eighteenth century the major multicultural states, Muscovy-Russia, the Polish–Lithuanian Commonwealth, Sweden, the Habsburg, Ottoman, Safavid, and Qing empires were all players in the game. They still competed on more or less equal terms and continued to enjoy moments of revival and expansion. Thereafter, the balance began to tilt. The Polish–Lithuanian Commonwealth, partitioned by its rivals, literally disappeared from the political map, while remaining a cultural player in what the Poles called the Kresy, their eastern borderlands overlapping the Baltic littoral and Pontic steppe. The Habsburgs maintained their standing, but the Ottomans were forced to retreat on the Danubian frontier and in the western Balkans; and Safavid rule collapsed to be replaced by a new dynasty, the Qajars, who gave up territory in the south Caucasus. The Qing reached the apogee of its power and then began to lose influence in Inner Asia to the Russians. Russia gradually gained ascendancy over its rivals, which it maintained with brief interruptions until the second decade of the twentieth century.

During the first of these two periods, social and religious differences were the main sources of resistance to imperial rule in the borderlands. The impulse for autonomy was not yet infused with nationalist sentiments; that was to come only during the nineteenth century, and was more gradual than many nationalist historians are willing to admit. Entangled with these impulses from below, imperial rulers advanced uncertainly toward nationalizing from above.

The Baltic littoral

The Baltic littoral encompassed a coastline stretching from what is today southern Finland to Denmark, the numerous islands and heavily forested hinterland of the Baltic Sea watered by the Neva, western Dvina, Nieman, and Vistula rivers. The land had long been inhabited by tribes of Ests, Letts, and Finns organized in scattered communities engaged in hunting and practicing primitive forms of agriculture. During the late medieval period, the Swedes and Teutonic Knights had gradually occupied most of the northeast (Finland and Karelia) and the eastern shores and hinterland (Ingria and Livonia), and subjugated the indigenous population to serfdom. The Poles controlled the southern shores. The great natural resources of the Baltic littoral were its great forests of pines that provided naval stores, including the famed Riga masts, for the fleets of the Baltic and North Atlantic powers.

Since the sixteenth century, contemporaries had defined the struggle over the borderlands on the Baltic littoral as *dominium maris baltici*, involving primarily Sweden, the Polish–Lithuanian Commonwealth, and Muscovy.[1] The first Russian attempt to break through to the Baltic

---

[1] The following is based on Oscar Halecki, *Borderlands of Western Civilization. A History of East Central Europe* (New York: Ronald Press, 1952), pp. 173–81.

Map 4.1 Sweden at its height, 1660

under Ivan IV during the long Livonian War (1558–1582) radically transformed political alignments in the region. The Teutonic Knights of Livonia adopted the characteristic policy of elites in a contested borderland. They negotiated with both the Poles and the Russians before finally accepting Polish protection in 1559–1561. The Grand Duchy of Lithuania also sought shelter from the Russians by joining the Poles in the Union of Lublin in 1569 to form the Polish–Lithuanian Commonwealth.

For Poland access to the Baltic was vitally important for its external commerce, especially after the sixteenth century when the Crimean Tatars cut off their access to the Black Sea. The borderland of Livonia became the key to their control over the Baltic littoral. Its major ports, Riga at the mouth of the western Dvina, Revel (Tallin), and Narva, linked the ancient trade routes of the hinterland with the Hanseatic ports of the Baltic and the North Sea. For landlocked Muscovy the province was of equal importance in gaining access to European trade. Sweden and Denmark feared the appearance of a powerful Muscovy on the Baltic and entered the struggle in 1560, inaugurating the first "Northern War." The Russians were repulsed and cut off from the Baltic by a Swedish occupation of the southern coast of the Gulf of Finland. The Polish–Lithuanian Commonwealth retained control over most of Livonia, developing Riga into a great port, and sponsored the activities of Jesuit missionaries in a cultural struggle with the German Lutheran Church for the souls of the Ests and Letts.

By the seventeenth century, the Baltic littoral was the northern lock of a system that Cardinal Richelieu – who perfected it – called the *barrière de l'est*. A loose association of France with Sweden, the Polish Commonwealth, and the Ottoman Empire, its dual purpose was to exercise pressure on the flank of France's traditional enemy, the Austrian Habsburgs, and to block Russia from penetrating Central Europe. The system operated like an interlocking mechanism. Whenever Muscovy attempted to break out by attacking one of the barrier powers, the other two would be drawn in. At least that is the way it worked in practice throughout most of the period from the sixteenth to the mid-eighteenth centuries.

A strong argument has been made that Peter the Great's foreign policy aimed not simply to demolish the *barrière de l'est*, but to reverse the geo-cultural slope from Russia toward the West. He intended to forge a security belt by signing a series of treaties of mutual assistance with former enemies and gain freedom of commerce on the inland Baltic and Black seas. As a corollary, he sought to secure leverage over the internal politics of the barrier states, turning them into quasi-dependencies of Russia.[2] The idea of Peter seeking to connect the inland seas gains credence when it is related to his grand design of constructing canals to link Russia's great river system by opening up two continuous all-water routes to the east: one from the Baltic to the Black Sea, and the other from the Baltic to the Caspian Sea.[3] Peter's relations with Sweden, the Commonwealth, the

---

[2] Boris Mouravieff, *Le testament de Pierre de grand. Légend et réalité* (Neuchatel: Éditions de la Baconnière, 1949), esp. pp. 40–46.

[3] John Perry, *The State of Russia Under the Present Czar* (London, 1716). Perry was a Scottish engineer in Peter's service; and K. A. Oppengeim, *Rossiia v dorozhnom otnoshenii. Opyt kratkogo istoriko-kriticheskogo obozreniia dannykh otnosiashchikhsia do razvitiia putei soobshcheniia v Rossii* (Moscow, 1920), pp. 9–17.

Ottoman Empire, and Iran, encompassing three complex frontiers – the Baltic littoral, the Pontic steppe, the Caucasus – were guided by similar principles, even if his actions were not so much planned in advance as inspired by opportunities.[4]

The Swedes were ancient rivals of the Russians for control over the Finnish tribes that separated the two better organized states. In the late sixteenth century there were frontier clashes. But the main contested area was farther south. Moscow had first become a Baltic power in 1478 when it annexed the great trading republic of Novgorod. But this stretch of coast did not possess harbors deep enough to accommodate the large Dutch merchantmen of the sixteenth century that dominated the Baltic trade. During the Time of Troubles, the Swedes closed Muscovy's half open window to the west. Throughout the first half of the seventeenth century, they expanded their Baltic empire, by occupying Estland and Livland (northern Livonia), as well as Karelia and Ingria on the eastern coast, and strong points like Stettin, Stralsund, and Wismar on the southern coast. The overseas provinces provided Sweden with both a springboard to offensive action and a shield to protect the metropolitan center. But its possessions also exposed Sweden to the danger of war on three fronts: against Denmark, Russia, and the German states. As in other multicultural states, the Swedish administrators in the Baltic borderlands divided into two camps: one favoring institutional and legal assimilation, the other seeking cooperation with the German landed nobility.[5]

Economically, the outer provinces earned Sweden a budgetary surplus in peacetime. The German landowning nobility of Estland and Livland benefited from the export of flax and hemp cultivated on their estates. The merchants of Reval and Riga flourished as intermediaries in the eastern Polish and Russian trade. Because they were Swedish citizens, they were exempt from paying the Sound dues when passing from the Baltic to the North Sea in their transit trade with Western Europe. But Sweden had also inherited a social problem with faint though discernible ethnic overtones. The indigenous peasantry of Ests and Letts did not suffer in silence from the twin evils of serfdom and foreign invasion. During the Great Livonian War, spontaneous peasant uprisings broke out, a traditional form of protest. Resistance faltered as the rural population declined sharply during the Russian Time of Troubles in the early seventeenth

---

[4] S. M. Solov'ev, "Publichnye chteniia o Petre Velikom," in *Sobranie sochinenii Sergeia Mikhailovicha Solov'eva* (St. Petersburg: Obshchestvennaia pol'za, n.d.), pp. 969–1116, remains instructive.

[5] Sven Lundkvist, "The Experience of Empire. Sweden as a Great Power," in Michael Roberts (ed.), *Sweden's Age of Greatness, 1632–1718* (New York: St. Martin's Press, 1973), pp. 21, 39–41.

century and again during "the deluge" in Poland at mid-century. But peasants then resorted to flight across the border into Muscovy when economic recovery and the growth of seigniorial estates under Swedish occupation increased the labor corvée.[6] On the eve of the Great Northern War, the social tinder was dry in the countryside.

Sweden's emergence as a great Baltic power with even greater ambitions was largely the result of its participation, indeed, its leading role in the major processes that marked the transformation to the modern European state system. Economically, the high quality of its iron ore and the great demand for its forest products and naval stores made it a much sought after trading partner with Western Europe. "Sweden's career as a great power was built on war and the possibilities which war created."[7] It had rapidly and successfully adopted both the technological and tactical innovations of the "military revolution."[8] Its war-making capacity was due, after the 1620s, to a drastic expansion of its tax structure and efficient administration. Its great Protestant warrior king, Gustavus Adolphus, convinced that war should "feed itself," campaigned on foreign territory all along the eastern and southern rim of the Baltic littoral. These plundering expeditions enabled him to expand the army from 15,000–25,000 to 150,000 men and to enrich the nobility who supported his wars. They also benefited from his alienation of state lands, which they resettled with peasants, thus expanding the tax base.[9] But Sweden's ambitions overstretched its resources. With a population of less than 3 million at the end of the seventeenth century, the tax base remained relatively small compared with its great rival Russia. It had to rely on French subsidies, an agricultural surplus extracted from its Baltic conquests, and control over the bridgeheads in German territories in order to supply and feed its armies.

By the end of the century all these dependencies had created problems. In the early stages of the Great Northern War (1700–1721), the youthful Charles XII of Sweden proved himself to be a brilliant commander, but two decades of campaigning in the German states and Poland against multiple enemies emptied the Treasury and depleted his small army. French subsidies proved to be irregular. Drawn deep into Ukraine, heavily outnumbered, lacking adequate siege artillery, and deprived of supplies by

---

[6] Toivo V. Raun, *Estonia and the Estonians* (Stanford University Press, 1987), pp. 16, 28–31.

[7] Lundkvist, "The Experience of Empire," p. 42.

[8] Michael Roberts (ed.), "The Military Revolution," in *Essays in Swedish History* (London: Weidenfeld & Nicolson, 1967), pp. 195–223.

[9] Paul Douglas Lockhart, *Sweden in the Seventeenth Century* (Basingstoke: Palgrave Macmillan, 2004), pp. 75–77.

hostile peasants, he was defeated by Peter the Great at Poltava in 1707, virtually ending Sweden's bid for greatness.[10]

In the long run, the Swedish empire collapsed not only because of overextension. More important in the long term, the Swedish monarchs alienated elements in the nobility without breaking their power. The slippage of support was nowhere more damaging than in the Baltic provinces, where the defection of the German nobility to the Russians in the Great Northern War significantly weakened Sweden's strategic position. Sweden had first acquired the territory from Poland during "the deluge," and had won the loyalty of the German-speaking nobles and merchants by recognizing their corporate rights, extending to their estates a large measure of self-government, and granting them access to military and civil service positions. But by the end of the seventeenth century, the crown sought to cover its heavy military expenses from the Thirty Years War through a massive confiscation of landed estates, called "the reduction." The centralizing policies of Charles XI (1660–1697) further alienated the Swedish nobles by abolishing their political and social privileges. They were also offended by his legislation – hailed elsewhere as "a unique document" in European agrarian history – to defend the personal and property rights of state peasants.[11]

Dissident Baltic nobles plotted revenge by helping to organize the great coalition of Denmark, Poland, and Russia that touched off the Great Northern War. Their actions once again ignited widespread peasant unrest; it has been estimated that 14 percent of the seigniorial estates experienced some form of mass action. Although directed against the German landlords, the disturbances disrupted the rear of the Swedish army. However, a full-scale civil war never developed in the Baltic borderlands. The Ests and Letts lacked the experienced military leadership that the Cossacks supplied to the Ruthenian peasants in Ukraine. The subsequent loss by Sweden of its seaboard colonial empire was due, then, in part to its failure to grant or repress regional autonomy in its Baltic provinces, a mistake that Peter the Great and his successors were careful to avoid.[12] Once Sweden had been deprived of the resources and strategic position provided by its Baltic colonies, the country never recovered its

---

[10] Lundkvist, "The Experience of Empire," p. 43; Sven-Erik Astrom, "The Swedish Economy and Sweden's Role as a Great Power, 1632–1697," in Roberts (ed.), *Sweden's Age of Greatness*, p. 67.

[11] Ia. Ia. Zutis, *Politika tsarizma v Pribaltike v pervoi polovine XVIII v.* (Moscow: Gosudarstvenoe sotsial'no-ekonomicheskoe izd., 1937), p. 9; A. F. Upton, *Charles XI and Swedish Absolutism* (Cambridge University Press, 1998), pp. 190–200.

[12] Lundkvist, "The Experience of Empire," pp. 44–48; Alf Åberg, "The Swedish Army from Lützen to Narva," in Roberts (ed.), *Sweden's Age of Greatness*, pp. 264–87, who points out

rank as a great power. The Swedish army was a superb fighting force, its bureaucracy a model of efficiency and fiscal responsibility. But the country could not match Russia's massive superiority in human and natural resources mobilized by Peter's harsh measures.[13] By the Treaty of Nystad in 1721, Russia acquired a defensive glacis for St. Petersburg that included Vyborg and part of Finnish Karelia, which was rewarded with a degree of autonomy to the German and Swedish nobles.

After Peter's death his successors were determined to prevent Swedish *révanche* by constructing a web of alliances and interfering directly in Swedish politics. Through bribery, intrigue, and intimidation, they encouraged party strife in the Swedish parliament, as had been done so successfully in the Polish Sejm, in order to undermine a strong monarchical government. Although Swedish kings sporadically rekindled their imperial ambitions, the Swedish nobles gradually reconciled themselves to the loss of empire. Like the Poles, they hampered the king in increasing military expenditures. In Sweden's two misguided attempts in 1741–1743 and 1788–1790 to wage war against Russia, the ruling elites may have been more concerned with defending Swedish independence than with restoring their Baltic possessions.[14] But the Russians kept chipping away at Sweden's borderlands. By the treaty of Abö in 1743, Russia added another slice of territory to "Old Finland."

In 1809, after Russia's fourth war with Sweden, Alexander I finally acquired all of Finland. Although Sweden renounced all further efforts to recover the province, Alexander I's suspicions were aroused when a year later the Swedes elected as the crown prince one of Napoleon's marshals, Jean Baptiste Jules Bernadotte. The tsar reacted strongly, fearing that Napoleon was resurrecting the *barrière de l'est*: "I see that Napoleon wishes to put me between Stockholm and Warsaw," that is, to thrust Russia back to its pre-Petrine frontiers.[15] But Bernadotte's influence swung Sweden

---

that Charles XI committed a grave strategic error by devoting almost all his attention to the frontier with Denmark, despite his advisors, and allowing the fortresses facing Russia to fall into disrepair. See also Zutis, *Politika tsarizma*, pp. 6–15.

[13] Sven-Erik Astrom, "The Swedish Economy and Sweden's Role as a Great Power, 1632–1697," in Roberts (ed.), *Sweden's Age of Greatness*, pp. 36–53; Lundkvist, "The Experience of Empire," p. 43, who estimates that the Treaty of Nystad deprived Sweden of between 500,000 and 1 million inhabitants, destroyed the budget surplus extracted from the outer provinces, and deprived it of the strategic position that enabled its armies to launch operations on the southern and eastern littoral of the Baltic and live off the enemy's land. See also Lockhart, *Sweden*, pp. 151–52.

[14] Romuald J. Misiunas, "The Baltic Question after Nystad," in Arvids Ziedonis, Jr. *et al.* (eds.), *Baltic History* (Columbus, OH: Association for the Advancement of Baltic Studies, 1974), pp. 71–90.

[15] A. N. Sytin, "Rossiia i padenie imperii Napoleona," in O. V. Orlik *et al.* (eds.), *Istoriia vneshnei politiki Rossii. Pervaia polovina XIX veka* (Moscow: Mezhdunarodnye otnosheniia, 1995), p. 79. Alexander I was convinced only an autonomous Poland unifying as

behind the great coalition that defeated Napoleon. The Swedes then exchanged their last foothold on the Baltic littoral, Pomerania, for Norway. And after ascending the throne, as Charles XIV (1818–1844), Bernadotte was more interested in reestablishing royal power than in recovering the lost territories. Sweden was out of the game.

The western Balkans (Triplex Confinium)

The western Balkans acquired the name of the Triplex Confinium or triple frontier at the Treaty of Karlowitz in 1699, but its geocultural configuration took shape long before that.[16] The main geographic features of the western Balkans were the long eastern coastal plain of the Adriatic Sea from Trieste to the Peloponnesus, the offshore islands from Krk to Corfu, the central range of the Dinaric mountain range, and the Drina and Sava tributaries of the Danube. Neither commerce, nor conquest or conversion, was checked by the Aegean or the Straits, that narrow body of water separating "Asia Minor" from "Europe." In his historical-anthropological analysis of the Balkans, the Serbian scholar Jovan Cvijić identified its three major interrelated structural characteristics as Euro-Asiatic, unity and openness, and isolation and separateness. He overlaid four major zones of cultural influence throughout the peninsula: modified Byzantine, Turko-Eastern, west European, and indigenous-patriarchal. These were shaped in large part by migrations spurred by conquests. From Hellenistic times through the Byzantine and Ottoman periods, it had served as the crossroads of civilizations. Its unity was assured by the great river valleys that permitted communications between the northwest to the southeast and its lengthy seacoast. It was open in the north to the influence of Russia and the Pontic steppes, and to central Europe through the Sava and the Danube. But natural barriers also contributed to its isolation and separateness. It was, Cvijić argued, not so much mountains, which had served from time immemorial as sites of pastures and transhumance, but deep gorges, thick forests, and swamplands. Barriers yes, but not insurmountable; much depended on the strength of human migrations. In the less accessible regions of the peninsula the population has remained more or less isolated. There can be found the survivals of the most ancient and patriarchal structures, and the home of the fiercely

many Poles as possible under Russian imperial rule could guarantee security in the western borderlands. See Dominic Lieven, *Russia Against Napoleon. The True Story of the Campaign of War and Peace* (New York: Viking, 2010), pp. 82, 132, 299–300, 332–33.

[16] Drago Roksandić, *Triplex Confinium. Ili o granicama i regijama Hrvatski povijesti, 1500–1800* (Zagreb: Barbat, 2003).

independent mountaineers, a region where the Turks rarely penetrated. These were not stagnant communities but evolved over time.[17]

In the early sixteenth century, the frontier in the Adriatic, the northern Croatian, Dalmatian, and Bosnia hinterland became a contest zone between the Venetian Republic, the Habsburg Monarchy, and the Ottoman Empire. For each of the three major powers the frontier had a different meaning. For the Habsburg Monarchy, it represented the western anchor of its defense of Christianity against Islam. The Venetian Republic viewed the Triplex from the point of view of a maritime power for whom control over the Adriatic littoral was a matter of supreme commercial importance, if not survival itself. For the Ottomans, it was another front in its holy war (jihad), with particular strategic significance in its campaign for naval supremacy in the Adriatic–Mediterranean and its overland advance into Central Europe. The confrontation and interaction between three major religions, Latin Christianity, Orthodox Christianity, and Islam, were complicating factors, but they did not provide the sole or even the major determinant of Great Power rivalry or conflicts among the indigenous people.[18]

From the earliest period fortresses, castles, and other fortifications rather than a linear boundary marked the frontier. For the Venetians, Zadar was the key to their military power, serving also as the administrative center of the Venetian province of Dalmatia. For the Habsburgs, Senj was the key maritime stronghold, blocking Ottoman access to the upper Adriatic. For the Ottomans, the strong point was the capital of the Sanjak of Bihać at the northern limit of their penetration into the Triplex. Other great border fortresses like Knin, first conquered by the Ottomans in 1522, changed hands several times before the Venetians finally reconquered it in 1688. The physical reality of these strong points was enhanced, as an emblem of possession, in symbolic and rhetorical terms

---

[17] Jovan Cvijić, *La péninsule balkanique* (Paris: A. Colin, 1918), pp. 12, 7–29, quotation on p. 28.

[18] The main sources for this section come from the Triplex Confinium Research Project founded in 1997 by Karl Kaser, University of Graz, and Drago Roksandic, University of Zagreb. It has sponsored the following studies: Drago Roksandic (ed.), *Microhistory of the Triplex Confinium* (Budapest: CEU Press, 1998); Drago Roksandic and Natasa Stefanec (eds.), *Constructing Border Societies on the Triplex Confinium, 1700–1750* (Budapest: CEU Press, 2000); Egidio Ivetic and Drago Roksandic, *Tolerance and Intolerance on the Triplex Confinium. Approaching the Other on the Borderlands, Eastern Adriatic and Beyond, 1500–1800* (Padua: CLEUP, 2007). See also Wendy Bracewell, "The Historiography of the Triplex Confinium. Conflict and Community on a Triple Frontier, 16th–18th Centuries," in Steven G. Ellis and Raingard Esser (eds.), *Frontiers and the Writing of History, 1500–1850* (Hanover-Laatzen: Wehrhahn Verlag, 2006), pp. 211–27.

by extensive mapping by cartographers on all sides.[19] After the Treaty of Karlowitz in 1699, the Military Frontier along the Danube stabilized. But the Ottomans and Habsburgs continued to introduce the most advanced technological changes in weaponry and military architecture. The most formidable fortresses were designed on the model of the Italian trace as a response to the destructive power of artillery on curtain walls. But neither the Habsburgs nor the Ottomans had sufficient financial resources to build many of them. Less expensive to construct, and more widely used by the Ottomans, was the *palanka*, a small earthwork with a timbered palisade fronted by a ditch.

Frontier fighters

The Ottomans garrisoned the frontier fortresses with janissaries, and recruited the local Christian population to serve as paramilitary militia. In order to reduce expenses, the frontier troops were allowed to engage in local trade and crafts. Behind the fortifications the Ottomans constructed bridges, mosques, churches, and other civic buildings, seeking to demonstrate to the local population the cultural and economic benefits of imperial rule and the attractions of serving the state. During the first four decades of the eighteenth century, they deepened the border areas and built new fortresses as the frontier became more stable over longer periods.[20] The new system, which lasted until 1835, was based on military units called *kapetanija*. Muslim peasants were largely freed from their feudal obligations in order to serve in various military capacities: "the entire Muslim population was wholly militarized."[21]

During the long Habsburg–Ottoman war at the end of the seventeenth century, a majority of the combat forces on the Venetian and Habsburg

[19] Palmira Brummett, "The Fortress. Defining and Mapping the Ottoman Frontier in the Sixteenth and Seventeenth Centuries," in A. C. S. Peacock (ed.), *The Frontiers of the Ottoman World* (Oxford University Press, 2009), pp. 31–56; Gábor Ágoston, "Where Environmental and Frontier Studies Meet. Rivers, Forests, Marshes and Forts along the Ottoman–Habsburg Frontier in Hungary," in Peacock (ed.), *Frontiers of the Ottoman World*, pp. 81–94.

[20] E. Radushev, "Ottoman Border Periphery (*Serhad*) in the Nikolpol Vilayet, First Half of the Sixteenth Century," *Études balkaniques* 3/4 (1995): 140–60; Kl. Hegyi, "The Ottoman Military Force in Hungary," in G. David and P. Fodor (eds.), *Hungarian–Ottoman Military and Diplomatic Relations in the Age of Suleyman the Magnificent* (Budapest: Loránd Eötvös University Press, 1994), pp. 131–48; Rossitsa Gradeva, "War and Peace along the Danube. Vidin at the End of the Seventeenth Century," in *Rumeli under the Ottomans, 15th–18th Centuries. Institutions and Communities* (Istanbul: Isis, 2004), pp. 107, 132.

[21] Marko Attila Hoare, *The History of Bosnia. From the Middle Ages to the Present Day* (London: Saqi, 2007), p. 47.

side were mercenaries made up of frontier fighters. As Drago Roksandic has pointed out:

the way war was waged, which the later Middle Ages in South East Europe already knew as *akindzijski* or *martoloski* [mercenary], where the main aim was to expel and murder, or to take captive the population and destroy their material culture and economic resources, existed in the triple-borderland area for two full centuries, and was mainly known as *mali rat* ("small war").[22]

As early as the first half of the sixteenth century, Dinaric herdsmen communities had periodically moved into the *terrea desertae*. Variously known as Vlachs or Morlacchi, they spoke Slavic dialects and adhered mainly to Orthodoxy (the Catholic Vlachs were called Bunjevichi).[23] As the Turks advanced into the region, much of the local Catholic population either fled or was driven out. The Turks repopulated the deserted areas and mountain passes with Vlach herdsmen from the interior of the Balkan peninsula, who introduced the Orthodox faith into the region for the first time with fateful consequences.[24] Although the Turks granted the Vlachs hereditary privileges, many of them later crossed over into Venetian and Habsburg lands, offering their services to the frontier defense forces. Their new hosts perceived them as representatives of "barbarism" in the region. The Venetians, who called them Morlacchi, considered them courageous, but "coarse," "self-willed," and "disobedient," even though they continued to employ them as irregular troops against the Turks. The Vlachs continued to serve as auxiliary military forces on both the Ottoman and Habsburg sides at least into the eighteenth century when the Ottoman state gradually replaced them with regular troops.[25]

On the Habsburg side of the frontier, the Uskoks of Senj constituted a different kind of military frontier community, though coming from the same social background. Composed mainly of Vlach frontiersmen, they began to migrate from Ottoman into Habsburg lands in the 1530s and reached a peak in a massive influx in the 1590s. The Habsburgs granted them privileges including *de facto* land ownership, exemption from taxes,

---

[22] Drago Roksandic, "Stojan Jankovic in the Morean War, or of Uskoks, Slaves and Subjects," in Roksandic and Stefanec (eds.), *Constructing Border Societies*, p. 248.

[23] For a social analysis of the Vlachs, see Nenad Moacanin, "Introductory Essay on an Understanding of the Triple-Frontier Area. Preliminary Turkologic Research," in Roksandic (ed.), *Microhistory*, pp. 126–35.

[24] Ivo Banac, *The National Question in Yugoslavia. Origins, History, Politics* (Ithaca, NY: Cornell University Press, 1984), pp. 42–43, 46.

[25] Sanja Lazanin and Drago Roksandic, "J. W. Valvasor and J. Rabatta on the Croatian Military Borders in 1689 and 1719. Stereotypes and Mentality in the Triple Frontier. Comparative Perspectives," in Roksandic (ed.), *Microhistory*, pp. 102–5; see also Stanford Shaw, *History of the Ottoman Empire*, 2 vols. (Cambridge University Press, 1976), vol. 1, pp. 122–31.

and self-government (but no monetary payment) in return for military service. For their livelihood the Uskoks often turned to raiding and plundering both across the porous frontier with the Ottomans and at sea. They had their own code of conduct, and interpreted their self-definition as "the enemies of the enemies of Christ" according to their own lights. This is how they could justify plundering Christians on the Ottoman side of the frontier.[26]

Map 4.2 Habsburg–Ottoman Military Frontier, c. 1790

[26] Catherine Wendy Bracewell, *The Uskoks of Senj. Piracy, Banditry and Holy War in the Sixteenth Century Adriatic* (Ithaca, NY: Cornell University Press, 1992); and for a case study of the Sichelberger District, see Karl Kaser, *Freier Bauer und Soldat. Die Militairisierung der agrarischen Gesellschaft und der kroatisch-slowanischen Militärgrenze (1535–1881)* (Wien: Böhlau, 1997), ch. 2.

Following each successful advance into the western Balkans, the Habsburg rulers extended and strengthened the Military Frontier. They recruited special frontier troops (*Grenzer*) drawn from German colonist-agriculturalists, Serbs, Vlachs, and Szeklers, and granted special privileges, including religious toleration to the Orthodox during periods of Catholic resurgence. What were once the most undependable and undisciplined levies had evolved by the mid-nineteenth century into the most reliable and loyal forces under imperial command.[27]

Farther south along the Adriatic, the Albanian lands were profoundly, if indirectly, affected by the frontier wars between the Ottomans, the Habsburgs, and the Russians. Geographically, their land was not suitable for extensive agriculture or cattle raising, but it did raise renowned infantrymen (*sekbans*). The Ottomans employed them to guard the coast against the Venetians and to defend other more far-flung frontiers. After the middle years of the eighteenth century, local notables armed Albanian peasants from their estates to fight against the Habsburg and Russian armies, plunging the region into turmoil. Following every war with the Habsburgs and Russians at the end of the century, more demobilized *sekbans* returned home; some were incorporated into private armies, others resorted to banditry for a living. Istanbul lacked the resources to repress what they called "mountain bandits," who remained a constant source of disorder until the early nineteenth century when they were recruited to fight for the empire in new wars against the Russians.[28]

The "small war" not only created highly unstable and violent patterns of life, but it also encouraged opposite tendencies toward survival and accommodation. The entire region was "criss-crossed by numerous legal and illegal trade routes." There was a great deal of smuggling, especially in salt. Herdsmen frequently ignored the military boundaries in moving their livestock from winter to summer quarters.[29] Moreover,

---

[27] Gunther E. Rothenberg, *The Military Border in Croatia, 1740–1881* (University of Chicago Press, 1966), pp. 42–46, 116–17, 136–37, 163–64; Gunther E. Rothenberg, "The Habsburg Military Border System. Some Reconsiderations," in Béla Király and Gunther E. Rothenberg (eds.), *War and Society in East Central Europe, vol. I: Special Topics and Generalizations on the 18th and 19th Centuries* (New York: Brooklyn College Press, 1979), pp. 380–87; Drago Roksandic, "Religious Toleration and Division in the Krajina. The Croatian Serbs of the Habsburg Military Border," in *Christianity and Islam in Southeastern Europe*, Occasional Papers of the Woodrow Wilson Center, No. 47 (Washington, DC: Woodrow Wilson Center, 1990).

[28] Frederick F. Anscombe (ed.), "Albanians and 'Mountain Bandits,'" in *The Ottoman Balkans, 1750–1830* (Princeton University Press, 2006), pp. 87–115.

[29] Roksandic, "Stojan Jankovic," pp. 243–44, based on the important work of Bernard Stulli, "Kroz historiju Sinske krajine," and "Gospodarsko-drustvene i politicke prilike u Cetinskoj krajini sredinom 18. stoljeca," in *Iz povijest Dalmacije* (Split: Knjženi krug, 1992), pp. 25–128, 129–208.

despite their clashes, Christians and Muslims engaged in peaceful cultural exchange, ranging from blood brotherhood and intermarriage to shared beliefs in honor, manliness, and courage. Wendy Bracewell interprets the phenomenon as embodying two referents: religiopolitical differences, on the one hand, and common cultural values, on the other.[30]

The example of Dubrovnik illustrates that the Military Frontier was not impenetrable, but rather an arena of cross-border commercial and cultural contact. The Ottoman sultans perceived the great financial advantages of granting the city-state a special status as a "dependent principality"; they collected a substantial tribute in return for permitting the city to govern itself free from an occupation by Ottoman troops. As a vassal of the Ottoman Empire, Dubrovnik was allowed to trade in the Balkans, purchasing raw wool, skins, and hides, and selling Venetian or Florentine woolens. Under Ottoman protection its merchants were insulated against the incursions of their primary competitors, the Venetians. Dubrovnik also served as a neutral point of culture contact with the outer Christian world. Its international trade extended to the Indies.[31] Its existence illustrates how complex frontiers could promote peaceful exchange as well as engender fierce conflicts.

Warfare repeatedly transformed the ethnoreligious profile of the western Balkans. After the Ottoman defeat in the Long War with the Habsburgs and Venetians, thousands of janissaries, Muslim officials, and timar holders fled Hungary into Bosnia, where they crossed paths with Orthodox Serbs and Bosnian Catholics moving north into the Habsburg lands. Following three more wars in 1711, 1718, and 1739, epidemics and famine piled on top of defeat cut deeply into the predominant Muslim population of eastern Bosnia, where they were replaced by Serbian migrants. Another migratory wave in the 1770s and 1780s swelled the number of Serbs in the Austrian frontier forces. But this was not one-way traffic. Serbs, perhaps equal in numbers to those fleeing north, returned to Ottoman Bosnia in order to escape the heavy Habsburg taxes.[32]

The influx of Muslims transformed the landed elite.[33] The newcomers took advantage of the weakness of the Ottoman center to gain control of

[30] Wendy Bracewell, "Frontier Blood-Brotherhood and the Triplex Confinium," in Roksandic and Stefanec (eds.), *Constructing Border Societies*, pp. 29–46.
[31] Suraiya Faroqui, *The Ottoman Empire and the World Around It* (London: Tauris, 2004), pp. 89–91.
[32] Bruce McGowan, "The Age of the Ayans," in Halil Inalcik and Donald Quataert (eds.), *An Economic and Social History of the Ottoman Empire, vol. 1: 1600–1914* (Cambridge University Press, 1994), pp. 647–48.
[33] Colin Heywood, "Bosnia under Ottoman Rule, 1463–1480," in Inalcik and Quataert (eds.), *An Economic and Social History*, pp. 33–39.

the local administration and local militia. Under their command, a Bosnian Provincial Army defeated the Austrians in 1727 and regained Belgrade. Increasingly obliged to rely on their own resources for defense against the Austrians, and after 1804 the Serbs, they found themselves increasingly at odds with the Ottoman power center. Conversion did not automatically ensure loyalty to the Ottoman center of power. Between 1830 and 1832 the province was rocked by rebellion. The Bosnian elite was outraged by a decision of Sultan Mahmud II to cede six municipalities to Serbia; they feared that his plans to create a centralized army would absorb their local militia. Although Mahmud suppressed the rising, their resistance to the Tanzimat reforms lingered into the early 1850s. Like other risings on the frontiers of the borderlands, it was enshrined in popular memory to become part of a national myth.[34]

The widely accepted argument that the occupation of Belgrade ended Habsburg interest in expanding further into the Balkans is not entirely convincing. In 1739, Austria joined Russia in another war against the Ottoman Empire. They may have entered the war as "a reluctant" ally of Russia in order to keep their alliance intact, as Karl Roider, the principal historian of the war, insists. But, as he admits, once they had stormed the fortress of Niš, their appetite grew and they planned to annex the whole of Bosnia, Albania to the mouth of the Drina, and western Wallachia. In their negotiations with their Russian ally, they pressed for a dominant role in the principalities, but were rebuffed. In the event, the Austrians conducted an ill-conceived and badly mismanaged campaign, and were forced to surrender Belgrade. They succeeded in recovering it again, though only briefly, at the end of the century.[35]

The impact of the French Revolution

The rivalry among the powers for hegemony in the Triplex Confinium entered a new phase under the impact of the French Revolution and the Napoleonic Wars. Napoleon's ambitions to extend French power into the eastern Mediterranean had a profound effect on the subsequent political and cultural development of two widely separated borderlands of the Ottoman Empire, Egypt, and Dalmatia. In both cases, but in different ways, local adaptation of French administrative and ideological models

[34] For the subsequent development of a Bosnian nationalism that fused Serb, Croat, and Muslim traditions, see Heywood, "Bosnia under Ottoman Rule," pp. 51–61.
[35] Cf. Roider, *The Reluctant Ally*, pp. 17–24, 35–36, 60–67; G. A. Nekrasov, *Rol' Rossii v evropeiskoi mezhdunarodnoi politike, 1725–1739 gg.* (Moscow: Akademiia nauk SSSR, 1972), pp. 255–59.

led to movements for reform and autonomy that challenged Ottoman imperial rule. The projection of French influence into Egypt, in particular, increased British interest and intervention in the affairs of the Ottoman Empire. The extension of the old Franco-British rivalry into the borderlands forced the Habsburgs and Russians to adjust their policies as well.[36]

During the brief French expedition in Egypt (1798–1801) and the subsequent English occupation, the local ruling class, the Mamelukes, was fatally weakened. The new Ottoman governor, Muhammed Ali, was himself a man from the western Balkan frontier, an Albanian chieftain who brought with him Albanian and Bosnian troops to establish his authority. He became the founder of a ruling dynasty and one of the major reformers within the Ottoman Empire. He forged an independent power base by creating a modern army and a centralized, autocratic administration on the Napoleonic model with the assistance of French advisors. His subsequent attempts to reestablish order throughout the Ottoman Empire and then to take power himself led to a large-scale European intervention and the loss of Greece.

French intervention at the other end of the empire had an altogether different outcome. In 1797, following a victorious campaign against Austria, Napoleon annexed the Venetian Republic along with Habsburg Croatia, Carniola, and part of the Military Frontier, in fact most of the Triplex Confinium. The French also occupied the Ionian Islands, which gave them an important naval base in the central Mediterranean. They consolidated all these conquests into the Illyrian provinces of the Empire. Napoleon's intervention in the western Balkans should be seen as part of his grand scheme to reorganize the borderlands from the Baltic littoral, where he created the Duchy of Warsaw, to the Danubian frontier. It was a latter-day attempt to reconstruct Richelieu's *barrière de l'est*. It was, however, short-lived.

The attempt of the French to forge a south Slavic identity out of Slovenes, Croats, and Serbs on the basis of a common language and the Code Napoléon provided the first model for subsequent versions of the Yugoslav idea.[37] After the defeat of Napoleon, the Congress of Vienna awarded the territories of the old Venetian Republic to the Habsburgs, creating a new strategic situation in the western Balkans. The provinces of

---

[36] The best guide to these complex entanglements is A. M. Stanislavskaia, *Russko-angliskie otnosheniia* (Moscow: Akademiia nauk SSSR, 1962), which delivers far more than the title suggests.

[37] Elinor Murray Despalatovic, *Ljudevit Gaj and the Illyrian Movement* (Boulder, CO: East European Monographs, 1975).

Venetia and Dalmatia flourished economically under Habsburg rule, but the flame of Venetian patriotism continued to burn brightly. In the revolutions of 1848 the Venetian rebels under Daniel Manin declared a short-lived republic. When Venetia was finally incorporated into the Kingdom of Italy in 1870, the local intelligentsia continued to celebrate the pivotal role of the medieval republic as the shield of Christendom against the Ottoman Empire and the defense of Western civilization.[38]

The first response of the Ottomans to the French incursion was to sign a treaty of alliance with Russia in 1799, and to launch a joint naval expedition to expel the French from the Ionian Islands. The two powers created the Republic of the Seven United Islands and placed it under their joint protection from 1800 to 1807. They had different perceptions of what this meant. The Ottomans considered the Seven Islands as a tributary state in the same category as the Danubian principalities and the Republic of Ragusa. Russian policy was muddled, reflecting confusion between the imperial center and local commanders.[39] The islands rapidly became a pawn in a complex diplomatic game. At first, Alexander I toyed with the possibility of establishing a Russian naval base in preparation for the campaign of the Third Coalition against Napoleon. The Ottomans refused to join the coalition and were persuaded by Napoleon that their greatest enemy was Russia. Facing a Serbian revolt in 1804 and maneuvered into a war against Russia (1806–1812), the Ottomans were forced to surrender their protectorate over the Ionian Islands, which the French reoccupied in 1807 under the terms of the peace treaty of Tilsit with Russia. The French were finally driven out by the British, whose occupation of the islands in 1815 was only recognized by the Ottoman sultan in 1820. Entangled in these multiple rivalries among the Ottomans, French, and Russians, the local inhabitants, mainly Orthodox Christians, sympathized with their fellow Orthodox Russians against the hated Catholic French and the Muslim Ottomans. But the Russian government failed to pursue its first and last breakout to the Mediterranean. It yielded control over the Ionian Islands to the British.

Throughout these diplomatic and military shifts the Ottoman center was forced to rely upon the talents of its ambitious pro-consul in the region, Ali Pasha, Governor General of Ioannina from 1787 to 1820, who was often called "the Muslim Bonaparte." He gained prominence

---

[38] David Laven and Elsa Damien, "Empire, City, Nation. Venice's Imperial Past and the 'Making of Italians' from Unification to Fascism," in Stefan Burger and Alexei Miller (eds.), *Nationalizing Empires* (Budapest, CEU Press, forthcoming).

[39] This section follows Kahraman Şakul, "Ottoman Attempts to Control the Adriatic Frontier in the Napoleonic Wars," in Peacock, *Frontiers of the Ottoman World*, pp. 253–70.

in the struggle over the Triplex Confinium as a defender of the Ottoman coastal islands and enclaves against the Venetians and the Western powers.[40] Having earned a reputation there, like Muhammed Ali, he went on to become a key figure in the Ottoman attempt to repress the Greek revolt.

The Serbian revolt

The configuration of power in the western Balkans was dramatically altered by the Serbian revolt of 1804. Serbian resistance to Ottoman rule had a lengthy pre-history. The Serb frontier society resembled that of the Cossacks with its independent, semi-nomadic way of life based on cattle raising rather than on agriculture. They took pride in their military prowess and the fierce defense of their religion, in their case against both Catholic and Muslim pressures to convert. Russia was a distant source of inspiration and potential support, without threatening the Serbs with conquest and assimilation. By the end of the eighteenth century, the Habsburg Serbs had emerged as the most highly conscious of all the Slavic people in the Monarchy. They were primed to respond to any signal of armed resistance by their brethren across the Ottoman frontier, where migrations had greatly increased their numbers in the key Ottoman border *paşalik* of Belgrade from about 60,000 in 1739 to 200,000–230,000 in 1800.[41]

Resistance to Ottoman rule was rooted in the collective life of the peasant village, encouraged spiritually by the Orthodox Church, and armed by their experience on the Military Frontier. Its territorial center was the *paşalik* of Belgrade, where the shift from the timar to the çiftlik system had not yet taken place. As a result, the peasant, although a sharecropper, was personally free and retained his traditional rights over use of his plot. The villages were all Serbian; the Muslim landowners usually lived in the towns. The tight social organization of the peasants gave them a strong sense of collective identity based on the *zadruga* and a council of elders or notables who elected a district chief (*knez*). To discuss common problems the notables periodically met at a central location. Initially, they were content to collaborate with the Ottoman government, and often used their position to acquire land or a tax farm. But they were

---

[40] For this aspect of his career, see Frederick Anscombe, "Continuities in Ottoman Centre–Periphery Relations, 1787–1915," in Peacock, *Frontiers of the Ottoman World*, pp. 236–45.

[41] Wayne S. Vucinich, "The Serbs in Austria-Hungary," *Austrian History Yearbook* 3(2) (1967): 1–17; Roger V. Paxton, "Identity and Consciousness. Culture and Politics among the Habsburg Serbs," in Ivo Banac *et al.* (eds.), *Nation and Ideology. Essays in Honor of Wayne S. Vucinich* (Boulder, CO: East European Monographs, 1981).

also natural leaders of the Christian community. In the villages a lively oral tradition glorified the pre-Ottoman past, sustaining the myth of the heroic defeat of a Christian coalition by the Turks at Kosovo in 1389, although the long written version of the epic was a nineteenth-century creation.[42] Serbian peasants were better equipped by virtue of their social organization and cultural outlook than were Russian serfs to take independent, armed action in defense of their interests.

When the Ottoman power center showed signs of weakness, the local Serbian notables organized self-defense units; or else they helped to lead protests against high taxes and armed uprisings, such as those under the founders of the two rival ruling houses of Serbia: Karadjordjević Petrović in 1804 and Miloš Obrenović in 1815. Yet even at the height of the rebellions in 1804 and 1815 the prospects for the political unity of all Serbs appeared to be dim. They were divided between two empires, rent by splits in the leadership, and exposed to disruptive population movements, migrations, and flight back and forth across the Military Frontier, and encroachments on their ancestral lands by Albanians from the south. The only institution that represented a unifying force was the Orthodox Church.

The Serbian Orthodox Church enjoyed special standing in the Habsburg, Ottoman, and Russian empires. By the early nineteenth century the cultural and educational center of Serbian Orthodoxy was the seat of the Metropolitan at Sremski Karlovci (Karlowitz) in Habsburg territory. Tolerance for the Orthodox Church was an important part of the Habsburg frontier policy. The Serbian clergy took full advantage and turned the church councils, which represented the entire Serbian community, into a substitute for a secular government. The metropolitanate enjoyed a sound financial base. The strongest theological influences did not come from the patriarch in Constantinople, but from the monastery of the Caves in Kiev, which supplied trained clerics and sacred literature. Like the oral literature, the Church kept alive the medieval tradition of Serbian statehood. It regarded Latin Christianity as more of a greater danger to its spiritual mission than Islam. Within the Ottoman Empire the Orthodox Church under the Patriarch of Constantinople was dominated by the Greek clergy and cooperated closely with the government. Only in the *paşalik* of Belgrade and in Montenegro were there Serbian ecclesiastics who led the resistance to Ottoman rule, and looked north to Sremski Karlovci for guidance and inspiration.

---

[42] Albert Bates Lord, *Epic Singers and Oral Tradition* (Ithaca, NY: Cornell University Press, 1991), pp. 108–9.

The renewal of frontier wars between the Habsburgs and the Ottomans in the late eighteenth century was a further fillip to Serbian national aspirations. During the war of 1788, in alliance with St. Petersburg, Vienna formed the Serbian *Freikorps* to harass the Ottoman lines of communication. When the Austrian army withdrew from Belgrade they left behind the well-armed, but embittered Serbian volunteers who were disillusioned with a century of futile cooperation with the Monarchy. The Porte, shaken by the Russian successes on the Danube, offered a series of concessions in order to reestablish control over their fractious Serbian subjects. The key provisions were an amnesty for the Freikorps and the right of Serbians to collect their own taxes and to maintain an armed militia. The janissary garrison of Belgrade was forbidden to return. This touched off a revolt by the janissaries supported by the local Muslim notables. The sultan found himself in the awkward position of relying heavily on the Serbian militia of 15,000 veteran fighters to supplement loyal regiments in repressing his own elite military formation.

The unlikely alliance unraveled after the sultan was forced to withdraw his troops to meet the threat of the French invasion of Egypt. The janissaries returned in triumph and launched a rule of terror. The Serbs found a new leader in Karadjordjević Petrović, a veteran of the Freikorps, to lead their self-defense. The sultan firmly held to his promises until the Serbs took steps to internationalize what had been a purely internal problem. They appealed for aid from Serbs throughout the borderlands, including the thousands who had fled into Austrian territory. The complex frontier was thrown open in both directions. The Serbs also turned to Russia, beginning six years of a torturous relationship.

Characteristically, the Russians regarded the Serbs as pawns in their struggle over the borderlands, to be supported by weightier pieces. They provided arms and a military mission. Yet they were prepared to sacrifice everything they had invested, depending on the fortunes of war and the changes in the international situation. During the Russo-Turkish War of 1806–1812, the Russians shifted their position several times. They ended up abandoning the Serbs. The Treaty of Bucharest in 1812 provided for the full reoccupation of the *paşalik* of Belgrade by the Ottoman forces. Russian advisors left Serbia, and Karadjordjević fled to Austria. A return to the status quo was hardly possible in the atmosphere of bitterness between the Christian and Muslim population. Despite a return by the Ottomans to a policy of conciliation, local uprisings broke out, mushrooming into a large-scale rebellion in 1814, this time under the new leadership of Miloš Obrenović, a prominent local notable. Preoccupied with reform and nudged by the Russians, Mahmud II granted Obrenović all that had been promised the Serbs under Karadjordjević and more.

Serbia emerged from eleven years of strife a semi-autonomous state with Obrenović as prince. But it was a small, impoverished country still embedded in the Ottoman administrative system. The majority of Serbs lived outside its boundaries, their feelings of cultural solidarity more and more assuming a national consciousness colored by the years of resistance and disappointment with foreign assistance. The western Balkans was a time bomb waiting to explode.

The Danubian frontier

To the east the Triplex Confinium merged with the Danubian frontier, which extended from the big bend in the river at Belgrade (which the Ottomans referred to as "the lock") to the Black Sea.[43] The great river was the major trading artery from Central Europe to the Black Sea and the ancient route for Eurasian migrations into Central Europe. Its three major northern tributaries, flowing south from the Carpathians – the Tisza, the Sereth, and the Pruth – linked the Danube to the plains of Hungary on the western flank of the mountains (the Carpathian Basin), and to the plains of Moldavia and Wallachia on the eastern side. The main tributary to the south, the Morava River, opened two routes to the Aegean Sea, the first to Niš and then across the Dragoman Pass to the headwaters of the Maritsa, which flows past Edirne (Adrianople) into the sea, and the second down the Vardar to Saloniki. The Ottoman advance from the south along these river valleys crossed the Danube in the sixteenth century when in 1526 their defeat of the Hungarians at Mohács opened a complex frontier. Over the next century and a half, a free Hungary in northern Transylvania balanced precariously between the Habsburg and Ottoman empires, both competing for its control. By the eighteenth century, the looming presence of the Russian Empire over their duel on the Danube shifted the center of the struggle to the principalities of Wallachia and Moldavia.

The Romanians

The Romanian ruling elites of the principalities, like the Hungarians in Transylvania, maneuvered to maintain their autonomy by shifting their support from one multicultural power to the other. The Russians entered the game late when Peter the Great launched an abortive campaign to free the principalities from Ottoman suzerainty. Throughout the eighteenth century and the first half of the nineteenth century, the principalities were

---

[43] Kurt Wesseley, "Reply to Rothenberg's Comments," *Austrian History Yearbook* 9/10 (1973): 119.

repeatedly occupied for longer or shorter periods by the Austrians and the Russians. Only the rivalry between them saved the principalities from being incorporated into one of the two empires.

The Ottoman advance into the Danubian frontier at the end of the fifteenth and beginning of the sixteenth centuries had broken up two state-building projects by the elites of the Kingdom of Hungary and the Principality of Moldavia. Their struggles to restore their independence embroiled them in one of the most prolonged political rivalries in Eurasian history, matched only by that between the Poles and Russians over the Kresy. Their dispute centered on Transylvania, which had emerged as an autonomous principality in the mid-sixteenth century. A shatter zone, its ruling elites were made up of Catholic Hungarians, the closely related Széklers in the southeast rural areas, and Protestant German, mainly Saxon, colonists in the cities. Orthodox Wallachian peasants constituted a majority of the population, but they did not enjoy any political rights.

The two principalities had succumbed separately to the Ottoman onslaught. Wallachia, more geographically exposed to both Hungarian and Ottoman pressure, was the first to be conquered. Moldavia under its prince, Stephan the Great (1457–1503) held out longer. Both had sought aid from the Polish–Lithuanian Commonwealth by paying homage to the Jagiellonian dynasty. Unable to maintain their independence without external support, the provinces became a contested frontier between the Ottomans, the Hungarians, and the Poles as early as the late fifteenth century. Once the Ottoman conquest had been completed in the early sixteenth century, Constantinople sought to control the principalities through its appointment of their princes. But the princes maintained contact with Polish magnates and frequently conspired to free themselves from Ottoman suzerainty. Their big chance came at the end of the sixteenth century when the Habsburg Monarchy entered the struggle all along the Danubian frontier.

In 1593, Emperor Rudolph II launched the first major war of many against the Ottomans. Ostensibly it was a holy war to expel the Muslims from Europe. Rudolph's main aims, however, were more practical: to secure the military frontier, possibly gain control of Transylvania, and to extend Habsburg influence into the principalities. Vienna had been work-ing for several decades to support the Wallachian boiars against Turkish efforts to transform the principality into an Ottoman province. In Moldavia by contrast they lent their support to peasant insurgents against the boiars, who preferred an association with the Poles in the hope of emulating the privileged position of the szlachta. Rudolph found a val-uable, but unreliable, ally in the Wallachian boiar, Michael "the Brave."

Appointed hereditary *voevode* of the province by the Ottoman sultan in an effort to confound Habsburg intrigues, he turned the tables on everyone, including the prince of Transylvania, the redoubtable Stepan Báthory, later elected King of Poland, who nursed his own ambitions for expansion into the principalities. Michael aspired to unify all three Romanian territories, Wallachia, Moldavia, and Transylvania. As an ally in the holy war he revolted against the Ottoman Empire and defeated the Turkish armies sent against him. Initially, he summoned the peasantry to a war of liberation, but then betrayed them in order to placate the boiars by dissolving the peasant militia and instituting legal serfdom.

Failing to turn the war into a popular uprising against the Ottoman power, Michael weakened his army and sacrificed any support he might have won among the Bulgarian peasantry when he crossed the Danube in a large-scale raid. By this time, most of his army was composed of boiars, mercenaries, and haiduks. Armed by the leaders of the allied armies, the haiduks were an undisciplined force, hardly distinguishable from bandits. They were effective as guerrillas in disrupting Ottoman lines of communication and supplies, occasionally raiding towns like Sofia in 1595. But their plundering alienated the peasantry.[44] It was only later that they were celebrated in popular culture as heroes in the wars of liberation against the Turks.

The holy war ended inconclusively in 1606, but not before it had devastated the principalities, reducing them to a chaotic condition for a quarter of a century. To administer them the Ottoman rulers began to rely on the Greek colony in Constantinople (the Phanariotes) to recommend candidates for the voevodes of Moldavia and Wallachia. Once installed, however, the appointees tended to court potential support in neighboring Christian countries throughout the seventeenth century in the hope of resisting incorporation into the Ottoman governing structure. Meanwhile, the Ottomans were just as content to maintain a loose control over distant territories with vulnerable frontiers and no substantial Muslim population just as long as their suzerainty was acknowledged and tax revenues were guaranteed. The peasantry paid the price.

Peasant resistance took the form of flight or rebellion, the most significant being the so-called Şeiment Revolt in 1655. It was triggered, as were other revolts in the Ottoman Empire at the time, by the demobilization of mercenary forces following a war. The Wallachian peasants joined in, although their grievances were different. Lacking adequate military forces on the spot, the local elites with Ottoman permission called in George

---

[44] Dimitrije Djordjevich and Stephen Fischer-Galati, *The Balkan Revolutionary Tradition* (New York: Columbia University Press, 1981), pp. 6–17.

Rákóczi of Transylvania to put down the rebellion. It proved to be a dangerous precedent. The subsequent rulers of Wallachia frequently betrayed their Ottoman masters and earned a Europe-wide reputation for deceit. But given their position as a beleaguered frontier their actions appear to be at least rational if not honorable.

The Habsburg war against the Ottomans from 1683 to 1699 provided the elites of Moldavia and Wallachia with another opportunity to play their game of shifting alliances. While the Habsburg forces advanced in the western Balkans after they had raised the siege of Vienna, their Polish allies invaded the Danubian principalities, raising suspicions in Vienna that the Polish king, Jan Sobieski, had designs on Transylvania as well. There was no need to worry. The population of Moldavia did not welcome the Poles. The boiars were not disposed to trade a loose Ottoman imperial rule, tolerant of their Orthodox religion, for the Catholic Poles, who were still enmeshed in the Counter Reformation and led by a king with dynastic ambitions. But there was another tempting alternative.

Peter the Great, fresh from his victory over the Swedes at Poltava, allowed himself to be drawn into a war with the Ottoman Empire for which he was not prepared. Russia's debut in their many wars on the Danubian frontier was not auspicious. Once committed to fight, Peter faced a strategic dilemma. Having dispatched major elements of his regular army north to drive the Swedes from their Baltic strongholds, he hesitated to launch a major offensive in the south. Yet to fight a defensive war with an unsettled Cossack population to his rear was also risky. To permit a second Ottoman invasion of Ukraine, possibly to retreat all the way to Kiev might lead to a mass defection of the entire Ukraine under the banner of the rebellious hetman of the Zaporozhian Cossacks, Mazepa, who had fought on the side of the Swedes and was riding in the baggage train of the Turkish army. Peter's alternative strategy was to turn the tables and arouse the Christian population of the Balkans against the sultan.

Peter's Danubian gambit in 1711 was the first of many to come. The adventure, which is what it turned out to be, illustrated once again the growing complexity and interconnectedness of the frontier wars. A war along one of the complex frontiers would almost inevitably trigger a chain reaction along adjacent frontiers. And an armed conflict between two multicultural powers frequently involved the subjugated people of the borderlands, who saw the opportunity to free themselves from imperial rule. Peter's campaign on the Danube aroused fears in the Habsburg court that the Orthodox population of the Balkan borderlands would rise in rebellion against their Ottoman overlords in response to the tsar's appeal for their support. Vienna still regarded itself as the *antemurale christianitatis* in the southeast, a view shared by the papacy, and was not prepared to cede this role to Russia.[45] The immediate danger was twofold. The Serbs manning the Habsburg Military Frontier might desert en masse to Russia, despite the attempt to retain their loyalty by having granted them a measure of religious freedom. This in turn would weaken the Habsburg forces in the Kuruc War against the Hungarian rebels. Their leader, Ferenc Rákóczi, had already in 1707 been in contact with Peter in the hope of getting him to influence the Serbs to cross over to the Hungarian side. After Poltava, he proposed to Peter an alliance of Hungarians, Poles, and Russians against the Austrians. The Austrians were even more concerned about the prospect of Wallachia and Moldavia falling under Russian control. The hospodars were involved in a typically borderland game of playing the Poles, Russians, and Austrians against one another in order to enlist the support of a powerful external ally in order to advance their own interests. Prince Eugène of Savoy warned Joseph I that a victory for the tsar might encourage Peter to go all the way to Constantinople.[46]

It was even more difficult to coordinate a Russian invasion with a mass uprising of the Orthodox population in the Triplex Confinium. To be sure, the Serbs and Montenegrins looked to Russia as their only possible savior in their struggle to break free of Venetian, Austrian, and Ottoman control. Wedged between the Muslim Turks and the equally dangerous "Latins" (Venetians), they were ready to revolt in support of the Russians without guarantees. But they were too weak and distant from the front to affect the outcome of the fighting.

From a military point of view the most important rising would have to occur in the theater of operations on the Danube frontier. But could the local Orthodox Christian elites be trusted? Dmitrie Cantemir, Hospodar of Moldavia, promised to join the Russians once they crossed the Danube. But he insisted that his agreement with Peter should remain secret. It contained two sets of provisions: one in case of Russia's victory and another in case of defeat. Accordingly, Cantemir would either become the hereditary ruler of a Greater Moldavian state stretching from the Danube to the Dnieper "eternally under the protection of his Imperial Majesty," the Russian tsar; or else he would retire to a comfortable house in Moscow with a generous pension. Having assured himself against any eventuality, Cantemir withdrew to a safe refuge to await the Russian advance. The equally cautious Hospodar of Wallachia, Constantin

---

[45] Edouard Winter, *Russland und das Papsttum* (Berlin: Akademie Verlag, 1961), p. 33.
[46] A. V. Florovsky, "Russo-Austrian Conflicts in the Early 18th Century," *Slavonic and East European Review* 47(108) (January 1969): 101–9.

Bráncoveanu, informed Peter that he would give the signal to rise when Russian troops entered his principality.

When Peter's armies failed to reach the Danube, his erstwhile Moldavian allies copped out. Once the rising failed to materialize, the Russian force and Tsar Peter were caught in an encirclement on the Pruth by a huge Ottoman army. Forced to surrender, Peter was faced with the prospect of losing everything he had gained in his war against the Swedes. The Austrians were greatly relieved. Cantemir fled to Russia. The victorious Ottomans let slip a unique opportunity to reestablish their hegemony over the Danubian and Pontic frontiers and to restore Sweden's place in the Baltic littoral. They let Peter off cheaply. He was obliged to surrender only Azov and to raze newly built towns like Tagenrog on the Sea of Azov. He also had to promise not to interfere in Poland and leave the Cossacks alone. But these terms were easy to circumvent in subsequent negotiations. During the campaign, the Ottomans had also resorted to the tactic of stirring up their co-religionists among the Crimean Tatars and nomads of the Pontic steppe. Peter responded by seeking his own allies among the nomads.[47] Thus, for a short period the first linkage was made, however tenuous, between three complex frontiers: the Triplex, the Danubian, and the Pontic. The main outcome in the Danubian frontier was the Ottoman decision to end the rule over the principalities by native princes and to appoint Greek candidates from among the Phanariotes. Moldavia and Wallachia were fated to remain under Ottoman suzerainty for another century. The princes and boiars waged bitter feuds among themselves and conspired with foreign powers against their Ottoman sovereign. But underneath the surface of petty politics the principalities enjoyed a cultural and economic renascence.

Although the principalities had not gained their independence, the princes enjoyed sufficient autonomy to cultivate the transfer of ideas across the borders in all directions. The courtly academies in Iaşi and Bucharest attracted writers and teachers from throughout the region. In the two capitals, Greek, Albanian, Hungarian, and Bulgarian scholars published books in their own languages. Under the umbrella of a great empire, the Romanian merchants benefited from access to a large market, engaging in profitable trade in wheat and timber with Istanbul.[48] Contrary

---

[47] S. M. Solov'ev, *Istoriia Rossii s drevneishikh vremen*, 2nd edn (St. Petersburg: Obshchestvennaia pol'za, n.d.), vol. XVIII, p. 650.

[48] Martin Graff, *Le réveil du Danube. Géopolitique vagabonde de l'Europe* (Strasbourg: La Nuée bleu, 1998); Roxana M. Verona, "The Intercultural Corridor of the 'Other' Danube," in Marcel Cournis-Pope and John Neubauer (eds.), *History of the Literary Cultures of East Central Europe. Junctures and Disjunctures in the 19th and 20th Centuries* (Amsterdam: John Benjamins, 2004–2010), vol. III, pp. 232–43.

to subsequent nationalist narratives, all was not gloom under Ottoman rule.

The Hungarians

Farther west the Habsburgs were steadily improving their position on the Danubian frontier at the expense of the Ottomans and their Hungarian allies. Since the early sixteenth century, the once mighty Hungarian state had been reduced to a pawn caught in the middle of the great duel between the Habsburg and Ottoman empires. From the end of the fourteenth century, Hungary had been at the forefront of defending Christian Europe against the Ottoman advance. The famous Hunyadi family of Transylvania, Janos and his son Mathias (Hunyadi) Corvinus, were successful in defending the Danube line throughout most of the fifteenth century. Corvinus laid the basis for the first of three major Hungarian military frontier systems. In its original form the military frontier extended along two lines from the Dalmatian coast with Bihać as one anchor to Transylvania and Wallachia.

In the 1520s the Ottoman armies under Suleiman the Magnificent broke the center of the system by capturing the key fortress of Nándorfehérvár in 1521, and inflicting a crushing defeat on the Hungarian–Wallachian army at Mohács in 1526. The Austrian archduke, Ferdinand I, had already begun to send German infantrymen to defend the western section of the line, gradually taking over the garrisons in Croatia and laying the foundation for the Austrian Military Frontier in the western Balkans.[49] The Hungarian state collapsed and Mohács became a symbol of national humiliation and mourning. The Magyar nobility split into two camps: the partisans of the Habsburgs and the so-called, but misnamed, national party, which sought to avoid a decisive clash with the Ottomans. Hungary fell into three parts. The large central plain remained under Ottoman control for 150 years; a small strip of independent Hungary elected a Habsburg king, beginning an uneasy association that lasted to 1918; and in Transylvania a local Hungarian dynasty maintained the independence of the principality to 1699.

From the end of the sixteenth century to the end of the seventeenth century, the Protestant princes of Transylvania achieved a precarious balance between the Habsburg and Ottoman empires. During the Fifteen Years War, 1592–1606, the Protestant magnate, István Bocskai,

---

[49] Géza Pálffy, "The Hungarian–Habsburg Border Defense Systems," in Pál Fodor and Géza Dávid (eds.), *Ottomans, Hungarians, and Habsburgs in Central Europe. The Military Confines in the Era of Ottoman Conquest* (Leiden: Brill, 2000), pp. 12–16.

led a revolt against the Habsburgs which rendered considerable assistance to the Ottoman forces. Elected prince by the local diet, his title was confirmed by the peace treaty of 1606. He was succeeded by a series of able princes, among them Gábor Bethlen, an outstanding example of a borderland statesman. Known as the "Hungarian Machiavelli," he reined in the unruly haiduks who had supported the revolt against the Habsburgs, improved the country's devastated economy, and established a court of renaissance splendor. His participation in the Thirty Years War against the Habsburgs demonstrated his mastery of international politics in a dangerous region of Europe. His successor, György I Rákóczi, cautiously continued his policies, repressing the more extreme Protestant sects without being drawn into leading a crusade against Catholic Europe. He chose his moment to intervene on the anti-Habsburg side at the end of the Thirty Years War, and obtained international recognition for Transylvania as signatory of the Peace of Westphalia in 1648. The successes of the Transylvanian princes divided opinion among the nobility of royal Hungary. The majority regarded Transylvania as an outpost of the Ottoman Empire; a minority saw it as the nucleus of a united and independent Hungary. In the long run, Transylvania lacked the resources to complete a major state-building project. In attempting to do so by pursuing the will-o'-the-wisp of a Polish crown, György II Rákóczi fell victim to the temptations of "imperial overstretch." The Ottomans, enjoying one of their periodic revivals under Grand Vizier Mehmed Köprülü, attacked from the rear and devastated the country, ending Transylvania's independence and turning it into a puppet state, while the Habsburg emperor, Leopold I, passively looked on with satisfaction.[50]

After this last victorious Ottoman incursion into Hungary, ending in 1664 with the Treaty of Vasvár, the Hungarian nobles under Habsburg rule rebelled against centralizing control and heavy taxation. They appealed for Ottoman protection that would recognize their autonomy. In the 1670s, they launched uprisings along the Ottoman–Habsburg frontier in the name of defending the rights and privileges of the noble estate, although they couched their appeals in rhetoric that appealed to the whole of society. In the end, the so-called kuruc uprisings failed to address the social and economic grievances of the serfs and fell far short of a national liberation.[51]

---

[50] Dominic Kosáry, "Gabriel Bethlen. Transylvania in the 17th Century," *Slavonic and East European Review* 17 (1938): 162–74; László Kontler, *Millennium in Central Europe. A History of Hungary* (Budapest: Atlantisz, 1999), pp. 165–75.

[51] Cf. László Benczédi, "Hungarian National Consciousness," *Harvard Ukrainian Studies* 10(3/4) (December 1986): 424–37, who pleads the case for the rise of Hungarian national consciousness in this period despite the compelling evidence he presents that these movements were inspired and carried out by the nobility in their own interests.

Nevertheless, ably led by the charismatic Count Imre Thököly, the kuruc forces scored a number of successes in the field, convincing Sultan Mehmed IV that with their support he could finally break Habsburg power. However, Thököly, like the Romanian hospodars, preferred to keep his options open while the situation remained fluid. He did not join the Ottomans in their last campaign in the Danubian frontier. Their siege of Vienna failed, leading to the precipitous withdrawal of the Ottoman forces from Hungary and the incorporation of the entire country, including Transylvania, into the Habsburg Empire. The Habsburg armies then crushed Thököly's forces. But the spirit of kuruc lasted into the eighteenth century.

The wars of the seventeenth century were very destructive. By uprooting local populations, they set off a train of forced migrations. A pattern of demographic disruption on the Danubian frontier had already been established in the late fifteenth century when Serbian sheep herders fled the Ottoman advance into Hungary where Matthias Corvinus had granted them religious toleration. Since that time a typical frontier pattern of raiding and trading across the open plains became a way of life. A frontier society emerged on both sides based on the *komor-spahi* tenure system and a fluid but clear social hierarchy.[52] But the depopulation of the central Danubian lands and Transylvania continued during the Fifteen Years War (1592–1606), again during the Hungarian phase of the Thirty Years War, and yet again during the last great Ottoman campaign in Hungary in 1657–1664. Finally, in the midst of the Great Habsburg–Ottoman War of 1683–1699, the Orthodox patriarch, Arsenije Camojevic, led as many as 30,000 Serbian families out of Kosovo into southern Hungary, an epic enshrined in Serbian history as "the Great Migration."[53] As a result of these forced population movements, a dramatic change took place in the ethnic composition of Hungary. From three directions Slovaks, Romanians, and Serbs moved into the abandoned villages and empty farmlands in the wake of the Habsburg advance. Encouraged by the Magyar nobility, which needed labor, and the Habsburg government, which needed tax revenue, the immigration and colonization of the southern counties was mainly responsible for the increase in population from 3.5 million in 1720 to 9 million in 1787. In the process Hungary was transformed into a multicultural state in which Hungarians counted for less than half the population.[54]

---

[52] Thomas Cohen, "The Anatomy of a Colonization Frontier in the Banat of Temesvar," *Austrian History Yearbook* 19/20(2) (1983/4): 3–6.

[53] Vucinich, "The Serbs in Austria-Hungary," p. 11.

[54] Horst Haselsteiner, "Cooperation and Confrontation between Rulers and the Noble Estates, 1711–1790," in Peter F. Sugar *et al.* (eds.), *A History of Hungary* (Bloomington, IN: Indiana University Press, 1990), pp. 142–43.

The Habsburg liberation of Hungary in 1699 did not reestablish a Hungarian state. Rather, the Austrian emperor Leopold I was determined to impose imperial rule by incorporating the country into his empire as a borderland. Because most of the Magyar magnates had lined up with the Ottoman forces during the recently concluded war, he regarded them as "the enemy of Christendom" and himself as "a bulwark of Christendom."[55] Hungarians of all classes resented the increased taxation, the stationing of German-speaking troops, and the resettlement of the devastated but fertile Alföld by German or Serbian colonists who were used to collect the unpopular war tax. The resistance to Habsburg sovereignty, led by Ferenc Rákóczi, a hero in the Hungarian national pantheon, touched off another eight-year Kuruc War beginning in 1703. Rákóczi's leadership turned an initial peasant rising into something larger, approaching a national insurrection, although the term is a more an invention of latter-day Hungarian historians. One problem for the Hungarians, which reoccurred again in the revolution of 1848, was that the non-Magyars who had settled into the depopulated regions, Saxons, Romanians, and Germans from the Rhenish provinces, and Serb colonists, as well as some local Magyar Protestants, remained loyal to the monarchy.

A second problem was the lack of a professional Magyar army to match the Habsburg forces. The traditional form of the armed forces in the Kingdom of Hungary had been the noble levy or *insurrectio*, which was ill-suited to conduct conventional warfare.[56] A third recurrent problem was the unwillingness of the nobility to commute feudal dues or free their serfs. Finally, the reluctance of the Catholics to abandon the religious intolerance of the Counter Reformation soured the Magyar Protestants who initially supported the rebellion. The resort to a form of guerrilla warfare, as Charles Ingrao calls it, could only prolong the struggle. Without outside assistance the rebellion failed to achieve Hungarian independence.[57] But defeat embellished the heroic myths and sanctified

---

[55] Kontler, *Millennium*, p. 182.

[56] Only Matthias Corvinus had broken with the tradition by creating an army, the feared Black Host of German and Czech mercenaries. But it was disbanded at his death. After the defeat of the Rákóczi rebellion, the imperial authorities insisted on the need to convert the insurrection into a professional standing army for the defense of Hungary. But the nobility resisted, and the Austrians remained suspicious of appointing Hungarians to the *Hofskriegsrat* or positions of command. A century later the tradition of insurrection proved to be an inadequate instrument in the battles with Napoleon's armies. Moral courage was no substitute for modern arms and training. Zoltan Kramar, "The Military Ethos of the Hungarian Nobility, 1700–1848," in Sugar *et al.* (eds.), *History of Hungary*, pp. 67–76.

[57] Charles W. Ingrao, "Guerrilla Warfare in Early Modern Europe. The Kuruc War (1703–1711)," in Király and Rothenberg (eds.), *War and Society*, pp. 47–66.

the insurrectionary spirit that the Magyar nobles shared with the Polish szlachta.

Both nobilities perceived themselves as the sole embodiment of the nation and the representatives of European civilization, battling the barbarians to the east and southeast. Sharing a long military tradition, which was, however, often tarnished by defeat, they also dominated the social and economic life of their countries. The decline of the urban economy throughout eastern Europe in the sixteenth century and the imposition of a second serfdom on the peasantry enabled them to monopolize political power at the local level, claiming defense of their ancient "liberties." Like the szlachta, the Hungarian nobles also enjoyed many of the cultural benefits and the intellectual stimulation of the Renaissance, the Reformation, and the age of the Baroque. But the veneer of high culture could not compensate them for their loss of independence; it could barely mask the archaic pattern of their economic and social lifestyles. Nor were they ever able to resolve the question of ethnic diversity in their own borderlands. They clung precariously to their status as part of Europe. But in the eyes of foreign observers and latter-day historians they appear to have retained much of the pre-modern outlook characteristic of elites in the Eurasian borderlands.

For all their similarities, the Polish and Hungarian nobles exhibited striking differences of political temperament. In dealing with the Habsburgs the Hungarians successfully combined strategies of resistance and accommodation, transforming themselves from conquered peoples exposed to threats along an unstable military frontier into co-sovereigns of a multicultural empire. Among the Poles, who might have played a similar role in the evolution of the Russian Empire, adherents of the insurrectionary tradition overcame the collaborators and steadily lost whatever opportunity they may have had to gain a share of power with the imperial center.

In their struggles with the Habsburgs and the non-assimilated ethnic groups, the Hungarians like the Poles faced three critical problems: how to resist sporadic efforts from the imperial center of power to whittle away their privileges and draw them further under the control of the central bureaucracy; how to reconstitute their vanished statehood; and how to integrate their own borderlands, that is, Transylvania, the Danubian Military Border, Slovakia, and later the Banat of Temesvár, when after 1718 the Habsburgs won it back from the Ottomans.[58] They struggled to resolve these problems for a century without much success.

---

[58] Ferenc Szakaly, "The Early Ottoman Period, including Royal Hungary, 1526–1606," in Sugar *et al.* (eds.), *A History of Hungary*, pp. 83–99; David P. Daniel, "The Fifteen Years War and the Protestant Response to Habsburg Absolutism in Hungary," *East Central Europe/L'Europe de Centre-Est* 1/2 (1981): 38–51.

Contest over the principalities: the Austro-Russian advance

Having checked the Ottoman advance at the gates of Vienna, Vienna faced a new rival along the Danubian frontier. By the Treaty of Karlowitz the Habsburgs had obtained Transylvania, driving a deep wedge between Moldavia and Wallachia and bringing a substantial Romanian population under their imperial rule. But the shadow of Russia first cast by Peter's abortive campaign on the Pruth in 1711, now hovered over the Danube. At a meeting of the Privy Council in Vienna, in 1710, Austrian statesmen for the first time expressed their concern over the Russian penetration of the Balkans. Real worries surfaced only in mid-century when they began to consider the alternatives of partition, conquest, or maintaining the status quo. Nonetheless, during most of the eighteenth century, the Austrians accepted the Russians as allies in the struggle with the common Ottoman enemy, joining them in four wars during which either Austrian or Russian troops occupied the principalities. The most ambitious attempt of the Habsburgs to realize their civilizing mission on their Balkan frontiers before the annexation of Bosnia in 1907 followed the signing of the Treaty of Passarowitz in 1718, by which they acquired not only Belgrade but also the province of Oltenia in southwest Wallachia. For almost twenty years the Austrian administration imposed a series of fiscal, judicial, and financial reforms in the spirit of the early *Aufklärung*. They were forced to restore the province to Wallachia after their poor performance against a revived Ottoman army in the war of 1736–1739. But their main object, shared by the Russians, remained unchanged: to replace the Ottoman Empire as the patron of the principalities.[59]

Taking advantage of the Russian victory in the war of 1768–1774, the Habsburg diplomat, Count Kaunitz, in a masterly diplomatic stroke engineered a bloodless Habsburg annexation of the province of Bukovina. He negotiated with the Russians to replace their troops and bluffed the Ottomans into accepting a *fait accompli*. Initially, it appeared that Vienna intended to insert the province into its interlocking system containing Hungary by placing it under military rule. It encouraged Romanian immigration from Transylvania, Bessarabia, and Moldavia, and was largely successful in co-opting the local Romanian elites. Yet Vienna refused to allow the Romanians to have it all their own way. The

---

[59] Cf. Karl Roider, *Austria's Eastern Mission, 1700–1790* (Princeton University Press, 1982), who argues that the Habsburg Monarchy failed to solve the Eastern Question when it could have because of its lack of enthusiasm for acquiring "poor land" and more Orthodox believers. But he provides evidence that undermines his case.

Habsburg military government set up German-language schools, encouraged the settlement of German craftsmen in the towns of Moldavia and Wallachia, and, in the early nineteenth century, promoted agricultural modernization by German specialists.[60]

The decision in 1786 to incorporate Bukovina into Austrian Galicia further complicated social relations within the province by imposing a German bureaucracy and opening the way for Polish cultural influences. To add to the growing ethnic mix and social conflict, many Romanian and Ruthenian peasants from Galicia crossed into Bukovina in the early nineteenth century. Their resentment toward the seigniorial oppression of Polish landlords flared into repeated uprisings throughout the first half of the nineteenth century, culminating in the great rising in 1842/3 under the leadership of Luk'ian Kobilitsia. Austrian efforts to control this borderland by alternating policies of centralization, assimilation, and colonization led to an impasse that was never resolved throughout the life of the Monarchy.[61]

As part of his expansionist design, Kaunitz also favored occupying Moldavia and Wallachia when the Russians annexed the Crimea in 1783, or, alternatively, occupying Bosnia as compensation. Catherine offered something more. In a dramatic display of personal diplomacy, she proposed to Joseph II nothing less than a dismemberment of the Ottoman Empire and a parceling out of its territory between the two empires. Her so-called Greek Project reserved for Russia the Crimea, the Black Sea coast to the Dniester with the fort of Ochakov, and territory in the north Caucasus. More imaginatively, she proposed establishing two virtual Russian protectorates in the Danubian frontier. The first, to be called Dacia, would be composed of Moldavia and Wallachia, formally independent but ruled by a Russian prince; the second would be a small, reconstituted version of the Byzantine Empire in Europe, including Rumeli (Bulgaria), Macedonia, and Greece, with Constantinople as its capital and Catherine's well-named grandson, Constantine, as emperor. The Habsburgs were to receive part of the *paşalik* of Serbia, Bosnia, Hercegovina, Istria, the Dalmatian coast, and Little Wallachia (Oltenia). Venice would be compensated for its Adriatic losses to the Habsburgs with Crete, Cyprus, and part of Greece (the Peloponnesus). Like subsequent ambitious schemes of partition in the nineteenth and twentieth centuries, the Greek Project ignored the desires of the inhabitants who

[60] Erich Prokopowitsch, *Die rumanische Nationalbewegung in der Bukowina und der Dako-Romanismus* (Cologne: Böhlau, 1965).
[61] D. Kvitkovs'kyi, A. Žukovskaia, and T. Brindzan (eds.), *Bukovina. Ii minule i sušasne* (Paris: Zelena Bukovina, 1956), pp. 211, 214, 217–18, 225–27.

nourished their own aspirations to be free of imperial rule. But the peoples of the borderlands were not yet strong enough to achieve their cherished goals by themselves. Throughout the nineteenth century, the liberators and the liberated were seldom in agreement about the desired outcome. It would be no different in 1918 or 1945.

The fourth Ottoman war of the eighteenth century (1788–1792) was touched off by the Russian annexation of the Crimea. Anticipating the fulfillment of the Greek Project, Joseph sent in his armies. There was nothing "defensive" about the Austrian war plan of 1787. Five Habsburg armies were to invade the Ottoman Empire. By the end of the first year, the plan was to overrun all the Danubian provinces, Serbia, and most of Bosnia. The following year, Albania would be invaded. During the fighting, the Habsburg forces occupied Bucharest and Belgrade.[62] Once again the Russian armies, this time led by the brilliant Suvorov, defeated the Turks. Upon the death of Joseph II, the new Habsburg monarch, Leopold II, quit the fray. He was concerned by the extent of Russia's victories, as well as the threat to Austrian possessions in the Netherlands by the armies of the French Revolution. By the Treaty of Iaşi, in 1792, Russia obtained a common border with the principalities (Bessarabia) for the first time. But the Habsburgs returned what they had won by force of arms. The Greek Project was dead.

The Ottoman response

The Ottomans were unwilling to stand by idly while their empire was carved up. But their response to external threats varied in different borderlands. They managed to cling to their precarious hold over the principalities by granting them a degree of autonomy. This indirect rule was managed by reliable clients, named Phanariots from a district in Istanbul, originally appointed as hospodars (princes) to replace the untrustworthy local families who had lined up with Peter the Great in 1711. The Phanariot regime, lasting from 1711 to 1821, earned a largely undeserved reputation for corruption by ostentatious Greek outsiders. The hospodars were not all Greeks, however, but more frequently came from local Romanian or Albanian families who shared a cosmopolitan culture.[63] The long-lasting misconception of their role may be attributed to their

---

[62] Roider, *Austria's Eastern Mission*, pp. 148–49, 166, 180–81, who nevertheless calls this an unwanted war.
[63] Vlad Georgescu, *The Romanians. A History* (Columbus, OH: Ohio University Press, 1991), pp. 73–74.

flexible and pragmatic policies, oscillating between a return to the Byzantine imperial model and a restoration of princely power.

The Phanariotes were responsible for strengthening the economic power of the boiars in the countryside, with their reforms in the 1740s leading to the abolition of serfdom. After the Treaty of Kuchuk Kainardji broke the Ottoman monopoly on trade with the principalities, the Phanariotes encouraged the rise of a local commercial middle class. Among the reforming princes, Constantine Mavrocordato, who ruled for ten separate terms in Moldavia and Wallachia, adopted the Austrian administration of Oltenia as a model for his centralizing policies in both principalities.[64] But his reforms ran into the opposition of boiars who denounced the princes as representatives of foreign rule and who looked to the Habsburgs or Russia for help in restoring their political power. Freed but heavily taxed, the peasantry increasingly resorted to flight into Transylvania or the lands beyond the Dniester. They often met peasants from Ukraine fleeing in the opposite direction. The Russian government was concerned about the movement of this floating population, which was similar to that taking place farther north into Poland. The last gap in the porous frontier of the Pontic steppe provided St. Petersburg with a further excuse to intervene in the principalities.[65]

The judicial and administrative reforms introduced by the hospodars in the second half of the eighteenth century followed the flow of cultural transfers from the surrounding empires. In addition, Byzantine law, directly borrowed from an earlier tradition of imperial rule, shaped the substance of the legislation. But these centralizing and rationalizing policies did not create "a new elite political culture predicated on the ethos of state service." Instead, a deep tension arose between the hospodars and the boiar opposition, and between foreign and autochthonous elements. These tensions were exploited by the Ottomans to keep the borderland submissive, and by the external powers, Austria and Russia, to subvert Ottoman control and replace it with their own. The princely–boiar conflict and the intervention of the three external powers long delayed the emergence of a Romanian national movement.[66]

---

[64] C. Papacostea-Danielopolu, "État actuel des recherches sur l'époque phanariote," *Revue des études sud-est européen* 24(3) (July–September 1986): 227–34; Paul Cernovodeanu, "Mobility and Traditionalism. The Evaluation of the Boyar Class in the Romanian Principalities in the 18th Century," *Revue des études sud-est européen* 24(3) (July–September 1986): 249–57.

[65] Charles Jelavich and Barbara Jelavich, *The Establishment of the Balkan National States, 1804–1920* (Seattle, WA: University of Washington Press, 1977), p. 110.

[66] Victor Taki, "Russia on the Danube. Imperial Expansion and Political Reform in Moldavia and Wallachia, 1812–1834," Ph.D. dissertation, Central European University, 2007, pp. 50–54.

On the Ottoman side of the Danube frontier, after Karlowitz a specific frontier ecology took shape in response to the protracted struggle for dominance over Wallachia. As in the western Balkans, the Ottomans relied on a network of fortresses to anchor their defense. The key was Vidin, next to Belgrade the most important fortress on the Danube. It had changed hands twice during the long Habsburg–Ottoman War between 1683 and 1699. After the Habsburg conquest of the Banat and Belgrade in 1718, Vidin became the last great Ottoman stronghold on the frontier. Following the Treaty of Belgrade in 1739, which restored that fortress-city to Ottoman rule, large numbers of demobilized irregular, local militias and janissaries, who had, typically, constituted the frontier troops, sought to replace or supplement their lost or meager incomes by engaging in commerce and agriculture on both sides of the Danube. Some succumbed to the temptations of raiding and banditry. Their presence in Wallachia violated the provisions of the treaty, and there were local clashes between the Muslim and Christian populations, as well as rebellious outbursts by discontented janissaries. As was so often the case in the Ottoman Empire, the center of power could not control the floating population on the porous frontier.[67]

By the end of the eighteenth century the endemic violence and instability of the frontier around Vidin, and the loss of territory at the end of a second war within a generation to the Russians, cut deeply into the power and prestige of the sultan. The situation was ready made for a daring and enterprising figure of local importance to organize the malcontents in a rebellion aimed at establishing an autonomous power center on the frontier. In the early 1790s, Osman Pazvantoğlu, a local Ottoman notable, led a rebellion that spread throughout the Danubian paşaliks. Sultan Selim III (1789–1807) committed enormous resources and manpower in a vain attempt to repress it. Pazvantoğlu enjoyed widespread popularity among the Muslims and initially among Christians as well, though this relationship later deteriorated when the Serbian rebellion of 1804 began to acquire a more pronounced anti-Muslim character. Like a true man of the borderlands, he also attempted to engage the support of the major Eurasian powers competing for influence in his frontier provinces – the Habsburgs and the Russians – in order to enhance his bargaining power with the sultan for recognition of autonomy or perhaps even something more. In a bold initiative he appealed for French aid, tempting their

[67] Rossitsa Gradeva, "War and Peace Along the Danube. Vidin at the End of the Seventeenth Century," in Kate Fleet (ed.), *The Ottomans and the Sea* (Rome: Istituto per Oriente, 2001), pp. 149–75; Virginia Aksan, "Whose Territory and Whose Peasants?" in Anscombe (ed.), *The Ottoman Balkans*, pp. 61–86.

ambitious pro-consuls with the vision of winning over the entire Ottoman Empire to the ideals of the French Revolution. His influence faded when one after another the Great Powers opposed his ambitions and the Christians abandoned him.[68] A more serious threat to Ottoman rule erupted with the Greek Revolution when the Great Powers finally decided on a fully-fledged intervention in a borderland of the Ottoman Empire.

The Greek revolt

The Greek Revolution wove together many strands of opposition to Ottoman rule.[69] Following a familiar pattern in the struggle over the borderlands, imperial rivals stoked the fires of domestic resistance. The external sources of the conflict emerged from the Austro-Russian rivalry over the Danubian principalities and the activities of the Greek diaspora. The Treaty of Kuchuk Kainardji in 1774 provided for the appointment of Russian consuls in Bucharest and several other towns, laying the groundwork for future contacts with disaffected elements among the Orthodox populations. But during the war the Russians had disappointed the Greeks, as was so often the case in their relations with their Orthodox brethren. Catherine II's favorites, the Orlov brothers, had stirred up a Greek revolt, but then failed to extend sufficient Russian support. The Ottomans put down the rising with characteristic brutality. Understandably, the Greeks did not stir when a decade later at the outbreak of the Russo-Turkish War of 1788–1792 Russia showered manifestos on them.

The strategic situation on the Danubian frontier changed when Russia secured a common frontier with Moldavia by the Treaty of Iaşi in 1792. Under Russian pressure, the Porte was obliged to make further concessions to Moldavian autonomy. The Russian government also promoted Greek commercial interests in the Black Sea and the Mediterranean, appointed Greeks as their consuls, and used them as their political agents throughout the Ottoman Empire. Greek mercantile interests took advantage of the naval warfare in the Mediterranean, which inflicted heavy

[68] Rossitsa Gradeva, "Osman Pazvantoğlu of Vidin. Between Old and New," in Anscombe (ed.), *The Ottoman Balkans*, pp. 115–62. Statesmen of Republican France saw in Pazvantoğlu, as they were later to see in Muhammed Ali of Egypt, a force capable of unifying the peoples of the Ottoman Empire into a federal reformist regime under the protection of France. See Rachida Tlili Sellaouti, "La France revolutionnaire et les populations musulmanes de la Turquie d'Europe," in Antonis Anastasopoulos and Elias Kolovos (eds.), *Ottoman Rule and the Balkans, 1760–1850. Conflict, Transformation, Adaptation* (Rethymnon: University of Crete, 2007), pp. 105–20.

[69] Leften S. Stavrianos, *The Balkans Since 1453* (New York: Holt, Rhinehart & Winston, 1961), pp. 269–86.

damage on British and French merchant shipping, to expand their ship-building program. Greek commercial connections with Western Europe and the activities of agents of revolutionary France spread subversive ideas among a small group of intellectuals and elements of the new middle class. Wherever they met there was talk of throwing off the Ottoman imperial rule and restoring their ancient liberties, although the merchants were by no means united in advocating revolution. Russian diplomatic and con-sular agents cultivated the impression among merchants in Russia's Black Sea ports as well as in the Peloponnesus that the Russian government was committed to freeing Greece from Ottoman rule. A secret organization, the Philike Hetairia (the Society of Friends), founded in Odessa in 1814 by Greek merchants, was dedicated to freeing Greece from Ottoman rule. It gradually expanded its network throughout the diaspora, often with the assistance of Greeks in Russian service.

In the principalities, the Phanariotes were split over supporting a revo-lutionary movement. The boiars, always a restless group, hesitated between winning concessions from the sultan in local affairs and appeal-ing for protection to a foreign power, either Russia or Austria; in the event of violence breaking out they could always rely on their armed retainers. The mass of the peasantry was unarmed, but a militia of free peasants in Wallachia, known as pandours, had been created to combat banditry and had gained military experience in the Napoleonic Wars and in the war of 1806–1812, fighting on the Russian side. The early leaders of the revolu-tion had close connections with the Russians. One of their commanders, Tudor Vladimirescu, a free peasant cum entrepreneur, had proudly worn a Russian military decoration. Alexander Ypsilantis, son of a Wallachian prince, had served as an officer in the Russian army and as a former aide-de-camp to Alexander I. From his base in the recently conquered Russian province of Bessarabia, he prepared the rising by establishing contacts with some of the boiars and Vladimirescu, but apparently without the knowledge of the Russian tsar.

In confronting a Greek revolutionary movement, the reforming sultan, Mahmud II, faced several concurrent threats to his authority among powerful local Muslim notables along several frontiers who sought to win autonomy for their own putative states.[70] One was Ali Pasha and the other was Muhammed Ali. Both were Albanian tribal leaders who had been appointed to important administrative positions in the empire: Ali Pasha serving as governor of Rumeli (1799–1820), and Muhammed Ali as

---

[70] Fikret Adanir, "Semi-Autonomous Forces in the Balkans and Anatolia," in *Cambridge History of Turkey, vol. 3: The Later Ottoman Empire, 1603–1839* (Cambridge University Press, 2006), pp. 170–85.

governor of Egypt (1805–1848). Successive Ottoman defeats in 1774 and 1792 encouraged them to carve out their own autonomous regions. Migrations bolstered their strength. In the Peloponnesus, demobilized Albanian soldiers (*sekbans*) flocked to and settled in Morea, forcing large numbers of Greeks to migrate into the mountains or emigrate. Ali Pasha nourished territorial ambitions to absorb Greek Epirus where he had ensconced himself in the fortress city of Janina. He was perfectly willing to enter into relations with the Greek rebels and Albanian Christians in order to win support to construct his own multicultural state in the western Balkans. In 1820, Sultan Mahmud II ceased to bargain with him and unleashed a full-scale attack. Within two years, Ali Pasha had been defeated and was executed. The power struggle within the Ottoman Muslim elites, in which the Albanians occupied a key position, encouraged the Greek rebels to plan their uprising.

In January 1821, the Greek revolution broke out in the principalities when Ypsilantis and Vladimirescu separately raised the standard of revolt. Their combined forces were a motley and ill-disciplined crew, and their leaders quarreled over tactics and aims. They carried out several fearful massacres of Muslim civilians in Iaşi and Galati. After having occupied Bucharest, Vladimirescu was murdered by his own subordinates, and Ypsilantis was forced to flee to Habsburg territory. The Ottoman army moved quickly to suppress the rebels and remained in occupation of the principalities for eighteen months.

Tsar Alexander I had been following these events with dismay. He was opposed to revolution in principle, but reacted strongly to reports of Muslim reprisals against the Christian population. At the height of the rebellion in 1821 he broke off relations with the Ottoman Empire. He was determined to maintain the treaty rights protecting the Orthodox Christians without encouraging them to overthrow the legitimate Ottoman government. When the social dimensions of Vladimirescu's peasant rebellion became clear, the tsar openly disowned Ypsilantis. Without Russian assistance the revolt had collapsed. But Alexander was not satisfied with the Ottoman attempts to restore order in the principalities and demanded administrative reforms.

The sultan was in a difficult position. The Russians had encouraged Iran to attack the Ottoman Empire from the rear, and Mahmud was struggling in his own capital to consolidate his reforms. He had no choice but to meet all the Russian demands. He abolished the rule of the Phanariots, and reestablished rule by native princes and the boiars who had opposed the rebellion. He reconfirmed Russia's right to be consulted on internal matters regarding the administration of the principalities. But the Russians insisted on the additional right to review candidates to the princely thrones. Tension remained high. Meanwhile, a more serious conflict had broken out in the Peloponnesus.

Taking advantage of the Ottoman difficulties with Ali Pasha and the rebellion in the principalities, local Greek leaders called *kapitanios* led a series of risings. They were the elected or hereditary heads of the Christian militia (*armatoles*) authorized by the Porte to protect the villagers against bandits (*klephts*) and to collect taxes. But, as in the Triplex Confinium, the dividing line between militia and bandits was blurred; they often passed from one social role to the other depending on their circumstances.[71] They belonged to the floating population that had become such a common phenomenon in the social landscape of the late Ottoman Empire. Both, but especially the klephts, enjoyed a reputation as fierce fighters and were celebrated in the folk culture like the *hayduks* elsewhere in the Balkans. Many of them had seen service in the French or Russian forces on the Ionian Islands during the Napoleonic Wars, and found themselves without any steady employment in peacetime. For reasons that are not clear, in 1821 the *kapitanios* turned against the unarmed Muslim population, killing an estimated 15,000 out of a total Muslim population of 40,000 in the Peloponnesus.[72] The Turks retaliated. The massacre of several thousand Christians on the island of Chios was immortalized in Delacroix's painting. The Muslims had nothing to match it, or Byron's poetry, in what throughout the nineteenth century was to become a one-sided propaganda war focused on the "terrible Turk."

The rebel bands could not defeat the Ottoman regular troops and the latter could end the guerrilla war conducted by the bands in the mountains. In desperation, Sultan Mahmud II called for aid from his powerful subordinate, Muhammed Ali, whose Egyptian army had already been revamped by French officers. Under the leadership of his son, Ibrahim Pasha, a talented commander, the Egyptian forces cleared the rebels out of Crete and most of the Peloponnesus. The main weakness of the rebels was their internal divisions along geographic, ethnic, and social lines. The *kapitanios* represented the interests of the tight-knit village communities; the merchant diaspora projected broader commercial aims; Phanariots from Constantinople sought greater administrative autonomy; klephts were interested solely in loot; the *armatoles* aspired to replace Muslims

---

[71] See especially D. Skiotes, "Mountain Warriors and the Greek Revolution," in Vernon J. Parry and Malcolm E. Yapp (eds.), *War, Technology and Society in the Middle East* (London: Oxford University Press, 1976), pp. 308–29; Nicholas C. Pappas, *Greeks in Russian Military Service in the late Eighteenth and Early Nineteenth Century* (Thessaloniki: Institute for Balkan Studies, 1991), pp. 288–324.

[72] Douglas Dakin, *The Greek Struggle for Independence, 1821–1833* (Berkeley, CA: University of California Press, 1973).

as loyal servants of the sultan; and Albanians joined both sides for material gain. The Greek Church was, unlike its Serbian counterpart, more cautious, having been integrated into the ruling elite under the patriarch in Istanbul. Village priests, who shared the depressed economic conditions of the peasantry, were more likely to join the revolutionaries.[73] What they had in common, however, was the recognition that their aims could be achieved only with the help of a foreign power. But even here they were divided into factions that looked alternatively to Russia, Britain, or France as their savior. The Serbs and Romanians had also been in search of a Christian patron. But the Greek case was different in two ways. First, the competition was no longer just among the regional powers and, second, factional differences erupted into civil war.

Each of the Great Powers had a vital interest in the outcome of the uprising. But none of them desired the dissolution of the Ottoman Empire. The Habsburg Monarchy under the baton of Metternich pursued what had by then become its familiar role: striving to maintain the status quo by restraining Russia and promoting its own interests. France and Britain differed from one another as well as with Russia over the best course of action. From the time of the Napoleonic Wars, Britain was firmly wedded to its policy of preserving its naval predominance in the Mediterranean. Its leaders preferred to maintain the territorial status quo for fear that an autonomous Greece would become a Russian or French outpost. But public opinion was caught up in the powerful currents of philhellenism and idealized the rebels as descendants of the Attic heroes. France sought a balance of power with the British by protecting its position in Egypt and Syria, and gaining a foothold in Greece and Algeria. Its intellectuals were also influenced by the romantic vision of an embattled Greece confronting Asia. Philhellenism was an intrinsic element of the all-European Romantic movements. Sympathy for the heroic Greek revolutionaries in Europe masked the brutal reality of the struggle.

The spread of the Greek Revolution created immense difficulties for Russia. Alexander's policy was a highly modified, moderate version of Catherine's Greek project. Instead of anticipating the dissolution of the Ottoman Empire, he favored the creation of a number of autonomous states in the Balkans under Ottoman sovereignty, but enjoying Russian

---

[73] Christine Philliou, "Breaking the Tetrarchia and Saving the Kaymakam. To be an Ambitious Ottoman Christian in 1821," in Anastasopoulos and Kolovos (eds.), *Ottoman Rule*, pp. 181–94, challenges the use of the terms "Greek" and "Turk" as problematic in describing the cultural and social identities of the participants in what was a many-sided conflict, rather than a revolution in the conventional sense.

protection through a guarantee of the religious rights of the Orthodox Christians. With the Austrians looking over his shoulder, he could not afford to act alone in pursuing his goals in the principalities or even in Serbia. His advisors on foreign policy were split over supporting the uprisings in the principalities and the Peloponnesus. The Russian foreign minister, the mercurial Greek, Ioan Capo d'Istria, sympathized with the rebels. With his acquiescence, Russian consuls quietly encouraged the idea that Alexander I was secretly in favor of their cause. The Greek rebels hoped that Capo d'Istria would lead them, and when he refused they thought he might play a role similar to that of Czartoryski in Poland, namely, that of a high-ranking Russian official who could use his influence with the tsar in order to advance their national aims. But Alexander's more sober foreign minister, Count Karl Nesselrode, regarded a new war with the Ottoman Empire as abhorrent and revolution as unthinkable.[74] Alexander oscillated between a desire to protect fellow Orthodox and enhance Russia's influence. In 1824, he circulated a plan to the European chanceries for three autonomous Greek states under Great Power protection. But the British rejected it, preferring to support Greek independence, which London believed was a better guarantee of freedom from Russian influence.[75]

The climax and collapse of Russian ascendancy

The new tsar, Nicholas I (1825–1855), inherited the legacy of Russia's dilemma in the Balkans. Temperamentally he was disposed to take a more forthright stand than his brother. Disillusioned with the idea of joint action or non-action by the Concert under Metternich's direction, he was prepared to act alone if necessary. Within a year of his accession, he had unilaterally brought pressure on the Ottomans to sign the Convention of Akkerman (October 1826), which established a virtual Russian protectorate over Serbia, Moldavia, and Wallachia, and regulated the Caucasian

[74] Capo d'Istria wrote to Alexander as early as 1807 or 1808, stating that: "It will only be by force that Russia will be able to forge a road to Greece to renew her ties there and to consolidate that beneficent system of influence through which she has long regulated the destinies of the Ottoman Empire." Patricia Kennedy Grimsted, *The Foreign Ministers of Alexander I. Political Attitudes and the Conduct of Diplomacy, 1801–1825* (Berkeley, CA: University of California Press, 1969), p. 231; for an extended analysis of Capo d'Istria, see pp. 228–68, and for Nesselrode, see pp. 270–71; G. L. Arsh, *I. Kapodistriia i grecheskoe natsionl'no-osvobozhditel'noe dvizhenie, 1809–1822 gg.* (Moscow: Nauka, 1976), pp. 230–34, provides additional documentation from the archives illuminating in particular the activities of the network of Grecophiles in the group of officials around Capo d'Istria in St. Petersburg and throughout the Russian diplomatic service in the Near East.
[75] Jelavich, *History of the Balkans*, p. 226.

frontiers. Shortly before (in April 1826), he had concluded the Convention of St. Petersburg with Britain, subsequently adhered to by France, clearing the way for joint mediation by the Great Powers in the Peloponnesus.[76] When the Porte refused their offer, the three powers blockaded the Ottoman coasts, threatening to isolate the Egyptian forces under Ibrahim Pasha. More by accident than by design, the allied and Ottoman fleets clashed at Navarino Bay, and the Ottoman fleet, largely manned in tragic irony by Greek sailors, was destroyed. A wave of popular revulsion swept over Muslims within the Ottoman Empire, directed at all foreigners, but mainly at the Russians.

The Porte denounced the Convention of Akkerman and the Russians declared war. Launching a two-front offensive on the Pontic and Caucasian frontiers, Russian armies invaded the principalities and eastern Anatolia. The Ottoman army, fighting without its janissaries, was no match for the Russians, who swept to the gates of Constantinople. But there they stopped. The Russian Empire under Nicholas I had abandoned his grandmother Catherine's grand design. He sought, not altogether successfully, to eliminate the ambiguity inherent in Alexander's policy. During the war, the Russian army under General (later Field Marshal) I. I. Dibich welcomed assistance from Bulgarian volunteers, but discouraged a general rising of the Christian population.[77] In the principalities General Vitgenshtein took the same position.[78] By the Treaty of Adrianople (Edirne) in 1829, Russia obtained control of the Danube delta, and gained parts of Nakhchevan and Erevan in the south Caucasus inhabited mainly by Armenians who had assisted the Russian troops.[79] A Russian army of occupation was stationed in the principalities for five years as security for the payment of a large war indemnity.

In the aftermath of the Greek Revolution, another conflict within the Muslim ranks opened the path to Russia's greatest, though temporary,

---

[76] M. S. Anderson, The Eastern Question, 1774–1923. A Study in International Relations (London: Macmillan, 1966), pp. 64–65.

[77] Dibich feared that "arming the Bulgarian population would touch off an insurrection of Christians at the gates of the capital [Constantinople] and jeopardize peace negotiations." Dibich to Greig, June 9/21, 1829, Ministerstvo innostranykh del Rossiiskoi Federatsii, Vneshniaia politika Rossii, series 2, vol. VIII, Doc. 85, pp. 226–27. Dibich also felt constrained to reassure the Porte that Russia was not encouraging Bulgarian emigration, that is, resistance of a different sort. But he admitted to Nicholas that it was not possible to deny refuge to those Christians who feared repression for having assisted the Russian army. Ibid., supplementary note No. 303, p. 651. In this way, the dilemma that had faced Alexander persisted.

[78] V. Ia. Grosul, Reformy v Dunaiskikh kniazhestvakh i Rossii (20–30 gody XIX veka) (Moscow: Nauka, 1966), pp. 153–54.

[79] According to Shaw, "Thus, did the so-called Armenian question have its beginning," History of the Ottoman Empire, vol. II, 31.

success in establishing its ascendancy over the entire Ottoman Empire. Muhammed Ali and his son Ibrahim Pasha had gained nothing but humiliation from their efforts to shore up the sultan's power in the Peloponnesus. When their demand for Syria as compensation was rejected, Ibrahim Pasha led his army north, occupying the country and decisively defeating the regular Ottoman forces. Faced by British indifference and French sympathy for the rebels, Mahmud II appealed to Nicholas I for aid. He granted permission for Russian naval and army units to enter the Straits in defense of Istanbul. The Muslim population of the capital was outraged and alarmed, but Ibrahim Pasha agreed to negotiate. Mahmud appointed him governor of Syria, and confirmed his father as governor of Egypt and Crete. Nicholas pressed home his advantage. He extracted the Treaty of Unkiar Skelessi (Hunkar Iskelesi), signed in 1833, from the Porte, a defensive alliance including a much-debated clause containing the sultan's promise to close the Straits to all foreign warships in wartime. In Britain the treaty was misinterpreted as granting Russia a virtual protectorate over the Ottoman Empire. News of the storming of Warsaw to crush the Polish insurrection and the Treaty of Unkiar Skelessi arrived in London simultaneously, touching off a storm of Russophobia in Britain that had long been brewing.[80] Thereafter, any sign of Russian influence or expansion in the borderlands of the Balkans, the Caucasus, or Inner Asia was perceived as a threat to British imperial interests in the Mediterranean and the approaches to India.

The Crimean War (1853–1856) was a major setback to the ascendancy of the Russian Empire in the borderlands of the Danubian, Pontic, and Caucasian frontiers. The causes of the war have become one of the most disputed questions in European diplomatic history, rivaling the controversy over the origins of the First World War. The immediate diplomatic prelude, complex and often murky, cannot be disentangled from the web of relations among the Great Powers, who perceived the weakening of the Ottoman Empire not only as a threat to the peace of Europe, but also as an opportunity to expand their influence, or to check that of others, throughout its restless borderlands. There is ample room to parcel out responsibility for the war. Ostensibly, the crisis erupted over Russia's efforts to reinterpret its rights to represent the Christian population, first narrowly

---

[80] John Howes Gleason, *The Origins of Russophobia in Britain. A Study of the Interaction between Policy and Opinion* (Cambridge University Press, 1950). William Pitt had been the first to sound the alarm when Russia seized the port of Ochakov in 1791. Although this caused only a brief crisis between the two countries, "It marked a stage in the slow growth in Britain of a widespread distrust of Russia and her ambition . . . [which] had by the 1830s become the most single important element in Britain's attitude toward Near Eastern affairs." Anderson, *The Eastern Question*, p. 21.

defined by the Treaty of Kuchuk Kainardji, by claiming to protect all the Ottoman Christians. Behind these claims loomed larger issues. Russia's statesmen had witnessed with growing concern the erosion of its once dominant position within the borderlands along the Danubian frontier. The gradual effects of the French and Industrial revolutions were undermining Russian influence. Russia's autocratic power structure and agrarian-serf economy offered little attraction for Balkan intellectuals enthralled with Western liberal ideas, or among merchants enjoying mutually profitable commercial relations between their agrarian economies and the industrializing powers of the West. All that was left to project Russian power were the ties of Orthodoxy and the hovering presence of the Russian army. Not surprisingly then, in negotiating with the Porte, Nicholas I relied on the religious issue to maintain Russia's influence and the army to enforce it. When the sultan balked over the issue of protecting the Christians, Nicholas sent his armies back to occupy the principalities, still under Ottoman suzerainty, as a bond of security.[81]

The Ottomans pursued their traditional dual policy of calling upon the Western powers to assist them in resisting external Russian pressure, and promising internal reforms that habitually never quite matched their promises. British statesmen vacillated between accepting the assurances of Nicholas that he did not intend to dismember the Ottoman Empire or even to dominate the Straits, and their fears that this was precisely what he had in mind. The alarmists, personified by Lord Palmerston, won out. Napoleon III seized upon the dispute over protection of the holy places as a way of breaking up the Concert of Europe to the advantage of France, winning points with the Vatican and the Catholic Party at home, and insinuating himself back into the eastern Mediterranean. In the complex diplomacy preceding the outbreak of the Crimean War, misunderstanding and miscalculation built upon a half a century of imperial rivalries over the borderlands stretching from the Baltic to Trans Caspia.

At the heart of the disagreement that triggered the conflict was the refusal of the Porte to accept the so-called Vienna Note, a compromise drafted by the Great Powers that would have committed the sultan to confirming previous agreements (the treaties of 1774 and 1829) regarding the privileges of the Orthodox Church, and to undertake to make no

---

[81] For a stimulating exchange on Russian policies and motivations see the chapters in Hugh Ragsdale (ed.), *Imperial Russian Foreign Policy* (Washington, DC and Cambridge: Woodrow Wilson Center and Cambridge University Press, 1993), by David M. Goldfrank, "Policy Traditions and the Menshikov Mission of 1853," pp. 119–58, and by V. N. Vinogradov, "The Personal Responsibility of Emperor Nicholas I for the Coming of the Crimean War. An Episode in the Diplomatic Struggle in the Eastern Question," pp. 159–72.

changes in the status of his Christian subjects without prior approval of the French and Russian governments. He only agreed to make such a concession in the form of a voluntary gift to his subjects. Clearly, the object was to avoid giving the appearance of caving in to Russian pressure, which could only encourage further demands by the Balkan Christians backed up by more threats of Russian intervention. What turned another Ottoman–Russian war into an international conflict was the refusal of the Russians to evacuate the principalities as a prelude to a peace conference. As a consequence, France and Britain declared war.

Nicholas I had counted on Austrian benevolent neutrality to protect his flank and secure his control of the principalities. But Franz Joseph, after some hesitation, broke with the long-standing policy of cooperation with Russia along the Danubian frontier. Over the years the Austrian statesmen had become increasingly worried over the destabilizing effect on the south Slavic populations of Russian interventionist politics in the Ottoman Empire. These fears even outweighed the promises made in January 1854 by Nicholas' favorite and personal envoy to Franz Joseph, Prince A. F. Orlov, to guarantee Austrian possessions in Italy and to share equally protectorates over Serbia, Bulgaria, and the principalities if the Russians won the war.[82] Perhaps the Austrians, following a tradition going back to Metternich, felt safer in an alignment with the more distant Western powers, than in the embrace of the Russian bear.[83] In any case, an Austrian ultimatum demanding Russian evacuation of the principalities was followed by an Austrian–Ottoman treaty transferring Ottoman sovereign rights over the principalities to Austria. Around 1850, the view that the "Balkans are our India" was gaining ground among Austrian ruling circles.[84] This was clearly the first step in an Austrian drive to the Black Sea, which would have cut Russia off from an overland access to the Balkans. As the Russian army withdrew, it was replaced by Austrian

---

[82] V. N. Ponomarov, "Krymskaia voina," in Orlik *et al.* (eds.), *Istoriia vneshnei politiki Rossii*, p. 392. This was the occasion when Nicholas I, whose intervention in the Hungarian Revolution of 1849 had saved the Habsburg Monarchy from dissolution, reversed the portrait of Franz Joseph in his study and scrawled on the back of the canvas, "Die Undenkbar."

[83] Paul W. Schroeder, *Austria, Great Britain, and the Crimean War. The Destruction of the European Concert* (Ithaca, NY: Cornell University Press, 1972), argues that Austria was attached to the idea of the Concert as the best means to deal with the threat of Russian expansion, summed up cogently by Count Fiquelmont as, "always to resist Russia without breaking with her," p. 417.

[84] Zoltan Szasz, "The Balkan Policies of the Habsburg Empire in the 1870s," in Béla K. Király and Gail Stokes (eds.), *Insurrections, Wars and the Eastern Crisis in the 1870s* (New York: Columbia University Press, 1985), p. 86; Tofik Islamov, "The Balkan Policies of the Habsburg Monarchy and Austro-Russian Relations," in Király and Stokes (eds.), *Insurrections, Wars*, pp. 32–34.

troops. The full extent of Austria's ambitions in the borderlands was revealed in its negotiations with France in the summer of 1854.

The war fever on both sides did not abate with the withdrawal of the Russian army from the Danube, rather, it intensified. The British cabinet wavered on the issue of war aims. Lord Palmerston, a fierce Russophobe, represented the most extreme position. He demanded that Russia be stripped of its borderlands: Georgia, the Crimea, and possibly Circassia would be given to the Ottoman Empire; "some of the German provinces of Russia on the Baltic" to Prussia; and "a substantive Kingdom of Poland" established as a buffer state. Palmerston assigned the principalities and Bessarabia to Austria. If Sweden could be persuaded to join the war, then it should have Finland.[85] Extravagant as these projects may appear, the fear of dismemberment played an important role in the decision of Alexander II to conclude peace in 1856.

It was left to the Austrians and the French to draft the Four Points that outlined the realistic war aims of the anti-Russian coalition. The Austrians, having declared armed neutrality, served as the messenger. As was often the case in the struggle over the borderlands, once the fighting began the belligerents abandoned the goals of diplomacy for a much larger design. The Four Points required Russia to surrender its exclusive protectorate over the principalities in particular, and the Christian population of the Ottoman Empire in general, to a collective body of the five European powers. Similarly, the five powers would guarantee freedom of navigation on the Danube and control over its mouth. Finally, the Straits Convention of 1841 would be revised "in the interests of the European balance."[86]

The Russian war aims were equally expansive. According to Nicholas I, all the Christian regions of the Ottoman Empire should become independent and "as such enter into the European family of nations." Their internal organization, guarantees of the freedom of religion, and mutual relations were to be discussed at a special congress in Berlin. But implicit in his statements was the idea that Russia should be the protector of the young Balkan governments.[87] The death of Nicholas and the failure of Russian arms in the Crimea forced Russia to the bargaining table. Russian diplomats conceded points one and two of the Four Points in order to stave off the prospect of Austrian intervention in the war; Russia dug in its heels on points three and four. The fall of Sevastopol ended any possibility

---

[85] Schroeder, *Austria*, pp. 150, 171, 194, 283, 325.
[86] Ponomarov, "Krymskaia voina," p. 395.
[87] V. N. Vinogradov, "Nikolai I v 'Krymskoi lovushke,'" *Novaia i noveishaia istoriia* 4 (1992): 39–40.

of further resistance, although the new tsar, Alexander II, did not at first realize the seriousness of Russia's position. At two conferences in the winter of 1855/6, his advisors warned him that continued resistance would precipitate certain defeat, bring Austria, and possibly Prussia and Sweden, into the war, and mean the loss of Poland and Finland.[88] To defend against a possible Swedish war of *révanche* a Russian army of 270,000 men was immobilized on the Baltic littoral, though men were desperately needed in the Crimea.[89]

For the first time since the Napoleonic Wars, Russia faced the prospect of being stripped of its western borderlands and deprived of its influence beyond the Danubian frontier. The Treaty of Paris in 1856 was less punitive than feared, but still deeply humiliating for Russia. The Black Sea was neutralized. Both Russia and the Ottoman Empire were forbidden from maintaining warships or naval installations on its shores. Russia was obliged to decommission its coastal fortresses, including the great base at Sevastopol that had heroically withstood an allied siege. Russia was deprived of its protectorate over the principalities; Moldavia and Wallachia were to enjoy an "independent and national" administration under Ottoman sovereignty and a joint guarantee by the Great Powers. Russia also ceded southern Bessarabia to the principalities, thereby losing its control over the mouth of the Danube. The Ottoman Empire was admitted to the Concert of Europe, with the Great Powers jointly guaranteeing its independence and territorial integrity. The Straits were closed to warships of all nations.[90]

Although the Ottomans were, for once, on the winning side in a war against Russia, they paid a high price for victory. The demographic effects of the war rippled out for another decade. At the end of hostilities, a fresh torrent of refugees poured into the Ottoman Empire from the north. Among them, 176,000 Tatars from the Nogai Horde and the Kuban settled in central Anatolia. They joined the earlier flow of refugees from the north Caucasus after the suppression of the Murid uprising. In the following decade a million more came in, a third of them settling in Rumeli. They included Slavs, like the Cossacks fleeing Russian army

[88] S. S. Tatishchev, *Imperator Aleksandr II. Ego zhizn' i tsarstvovanie* (St. Petersburg: A. S. Suvorin, 1903), vol. I, pp. 182–87; E. V. Tarle, *Krymskaia voina*, 2 vols. (Moscow: Akademiia nauk, 1950), vol. II, pp. 546–49.

[89] Ponomarov, "Krymskaia voina," p. 407.

[90] The British proposal to add to the term of the ultimatum defining the war aims "the independence of Cherkesssia," the secession of Georgia and other territories south of the Kuban River was opposed by the French and Austrians as unrealistic. The British also failed to have the Polish Question raised at the peace conference. Ponomarov, "Krymskaia voina," pp. 410, 414.

service, and Bulgarians, who had been settled in the Crimea by the Russian government, but elected to return to their homes in the Ottoman Empire. In an attempt to regularize the flow of refugees, the Ottoman and Russian governments reached an agreement in 1860. The Russians estimated that the total number of Muslim immigrants would not exceed 50,000. On the basis of these estimates, the Porte created a General Migration Administrative Commission to handle the administrative problems, but it was soon swamped. By 1864 almost 400,000 Circassians and Abkhazians had left their homelands. The Russians insisted that the migrants should not be settled in frontier regions. Equally insistent, the British, supporting the Greek government, opposed the settlement of Circassians in Thessaly in order to preserve the area for its Greek inhabitants and to avoid "disorder and demoralization." Consequently, the migrants were scattered over Dobrudja, along the Danube, in Macedonia and Thrace in Rumelia, and throughout Anatolia and Syria in Asia, where they suffered very high mortality rates.[91]

The war left deep marks on the internal governance of the Ottoman Empire. The conflict over the holy places placed the accommodationists among the Ottoman Christians, especially the Phanariotes, in an impossible position. By affirming their Orthodox faith while protesting their loyalty to a Muslim ruler, they sought to maintain the flexible, multicultural ethos of the empire. But they failed to satisfy their co-religionists, the central authorities, the British, or the Russians.[92] Their cosmopolitanism was rapidly becoming outmoded, an ominous sign that the Osmanlılık foundations of imperial rule were crumbling. Twenty years later the confessional divide opened into a chasm.

The great Ottoman retreat

In 1875 the struggle over the borderlands entered a new phase. The rebellion of the Orthodox peasantry in Hercegovina and Bosnia spread into the Ottoman Danubian vilayets where, ironically, the Tanzimat appeared to promise great results. Under the reforming governor, Midhat Pasha, the Danube province of Niš had undergone an economic revival. But his attempt to blunt the edge of Bulgarian nationalist

---

[91] Marc Pinson, "Ottoman Colonization of the Circassians in Rumeli after the Crimean War," *Études balkaniques* 3 (1972): 71–85; Kemal H. Karpat, *Ottoman Population 1830–1914. Demographic and Social Characteristics* (Madison, WI: University of Wisconsin University Press, 1985), pp. 65–70.

[92] As seen in the career of Stephanos Volgorodis, in Christine M. Philliou, *Biography of an Empire. Governing Ottomans in an Age of Revolution* (Berkeley, CA: University of California Press, 2011), pp. 158–69.

sentiment by creating mixed administrative councils and courts encountered strong opposition from both the Bulgarians and the Muslims.[93] The
reforms had come too late – an old refrain in Ottoman politics – to
overcome the social and political pressures for change that had been
building for decades. Agrarian disorders in Bulgaria had a long pre-
history. Uprisings had broken out in 1835, 1841, 1841/2, and 1850,
with the participation of *haiduks* who became entrenched in Bulgarian
rural society. Ever since 1845, the Bulgarian Church had been agitating
for religious autonomy (autocephalous status) to match that of Serbia and
the principalities. The Porte finally recognized a Bulgarian exarchate in
1864 with jurisdiction over those areas of Macedonia where at least two-
thirds of the population voted to join it. Under the administration of
Midhat Pasha, the Bulgarian exarch demanded political autonomy as
well, despite the fact that a third of the population was Muslim, including
the Pomaks who were converted Slavs. Thus began the contest in
Macedonia for influence and subsequently for territory that was to poison
Greek, Serbian, and Bulgarian relations for another half a century, culminating in one of the most violent episodes of the Greek Civil War in the
1940s.

When the Bulgarian rebels turned against their Muslim neighbors in
1877, slaughtering great numbers, the Ottoman government was unable
to prevent reprisals led by Tatar and Circassian refugees who had fled
from the Russian occupation of their ancestral homes in the north
Caucasus, and who blamed the Bulgarian peasants for their plight. The
European press seized upon the reports of the killings of Christians by
Muslims (having ignored the earlier and more numerous deaths of
Muslim villagers at the hands of Christians), and launched a massive
propaganda campaign against the "Bulgarian horrors." The public out-
rage, embodied by William Gladstone, leader of the Liberal Party, undercut pro-Turkish opinion that had helped to sustain Britain's opposition to
Russian expansion in the Balkans since the Treaty of Unkiar Skelessi in
1833. Its practical effect was to neutralize Britain in the looming conflict
between Russia and the Ottoman Empire. There would be no repeat of
the Crimean War.

Acting under pressure at home, the Russian government reached an
agreement with Vienna that it would remain neutral in the event of a war.
Russia would recover the territory it had lost after the Crimean War;
Austria-Hungary would be compensated in Bosnia and Hercegovina;

---

[93] Maria Todorova, "Midhat Pasha's Governorship of the Danube Province," in C. E. Farah
  (ed.), *Decision Making and Change in the Ottoman Empire* (Kirksville, MO: Thomas
  Jefferson University Press, 1993), pp. 115–28.

Serbia, Montenegro, and Greece would receive additional territory; and three autonomous states, Albania, Bulgaria, and Rumelia, would be created out of the remaining Ottoman territories in Europe. No large Slavic state would be formed. Another in the many attempts of the two empires to divide the Balkans into spheres of influence, the arrangement was fatally flawed in two ways: future territorial boundaries were left undefined; and the interests and aspirations of the local population were ignored.

Still, Russia hesitated. The long-time reforming ministers of finance and war, Mikhail Reitern and Dmitri Miliutin, warned that Russia could not afford a war without jeopardizing its financial stability and its prospects for future economic development; and the army had not yet had time to implement the military reforms of 1874. Their advice was ignored. The Russian and Ottoman empires both entered the war before their military and financial reforms had had a chance to take hold. After initial difficulties, the Russians broke through in the Balkans, with the help of the Romanians, and in eastern Anatolia. The preliminary peace of San Stefano was negotiated by the Russian pan-Slav ambassador, Nikolai Ignat'ev, who ignored the agreement with Austria and the predictable reaction of the Great Powers. He designed a Greater Bulgaria, truly a large Slavic state that included territory on both sides of the Balkan Mountains, all of Macedonia, and part of Thrace with an outlet to the Aegean Sea. Montenegro was to be tripled in size and given an outlet on the Adriatic. Serbia would receive very little territory and was advised to look to Austria for protection. The Romanians were obliged to return Bessarabia, which they had obtained after the Crimean War, in return for the much poorer land of Dobrudja. Flushed with victory, the Russians clearly aimed at carving out another large client state, but this time Slavic in culture and indebted solely to them for its existence. Dominating the approaches to Constantinople, it would guarantee them permanent strategic hegemony in the southwest borderlands. The Great Powers registered their disapproval. Britain, back under Disraeli's baton, sent the fleet to the Dardanelles. The Austro-Hungarian leaders were outraged by Russia's betrayal – Andrassy called it "an Orthodox Slavic sermon" – and demanded their pound of flesh in Bosnia. Bismarck offered to be the "honest broker" in presiding over an international congress at Berlin. A new treaty was drafted, still without the participation of the Balkan states.

The Great Powers obliged the Russians to mitigate their victory. Russia retained southern Bessarabia and on the Anatolian frontier, Kars, Ardahan, and the port of Batumi. The sultan promised reforms to the Armenians. Bulgaria was cut back and the remainder split into two parts between an autonomous tributary principality north of the Balkan

Mountains, and a semi-autonomous territory to be called Eastern Rumelia south of the mountains with a Christian governor appointed by the Ottomans but under the protection of the Great Powers. The assumption was that Russia would become the dominant power in Bulgaria. It was an artificial and impermanent solution. To balance things, Austria-Hungary was allowed to occupy and administer Bosnia and Hercegovina, and to occupy the Sanjak of Novi Pazar, a strip of land separating Serbia and Montenegro. It was another makeshift improvisation that in the end satisfied no one. Serbia, Montenegro, and Romania received full independence. But the treaty left all the smaller powers dissatisfied and determined to claim what they regarded as their irredenta. The Albanians, never an easy mark, immediately mounted an armed protest, and the Great Powers were obliged to restore some of the territory inhabited by them that had been handed out to Montenegro and Serbia.

Although the Romanians initially felt cheated by the exchange of Bessarabia for northern Dobrudja, the political elites performed the neat trick of turning the new territory from an unwanted burden into the symbol of their European mission. In the words of one of its prominent leaders, Dobrudja was "a land given [us] by Europe and [one] which sets us in contact with Western Europe." Control over the Danube delta would make Romania a Western military bastion against Russia and a guarantor of political stability in Eastern Europe.[94] The governing elites energetically embarked on a campaign to integrate the new province. Their methods were strikingly similar to those employed by the state-builders of their imperial Habsburg, Russian, and Ottoman neighbors in seeking to incorporate multicultural borderlands under a centralizing monarchical rule. The success of their efforts relied heavily on a triad of colonization, cultural assimilation, and economic integration. Over a period of thirty-five years the ethnic composition of the province changed dramatically. The government encouraged massive immigration of Romanians from the Regat (Moldavia and Wallachia) and all over the Balkans, including Transylvanian shepherds (*Mocani*) from the Habsburg Empire who adapted well as farmers, landowners, and merchants. The cultural offensive focused on placing local Orthodox Greek and Bulgarian churches under the jurisdiction of the Romanian Orthodox Church and, less consistently, on schooling. Economically, the major effort was directed toward creating a rail system and developing the port of Constanza to open Romanian trade to the wider world.

---

[94] Constantin Iordachi, *Citizenship, Nation and State-Building. The Integration of Northern Dobrogea into Romania, 1878–1913*, Carl Beck Papers, No. 1607 (Pittsburgh, PA: University of Pittsburgh Press, 2002), p. 15.

The war and peace settlement had widespread repercussions on all the major and minor powers that had struggled for control over the borderlands. In the Ottoman Empire the gap widened between religious groups by making religious identification "the psychological basis for nationality." The traditional practice of mutual toleration withered. An estimated 200,000–300,000 Muslims in Bulgaria, Serbia, and elsewhere had been killed and more than a million forced to flee their homes. The war and migration upset the demographic balance and turned the empire into a preponderantly Muslim state. The fighting inspired the remaining large Christian groups, the Greeks and Armenians, to realize their national ideals. The British consul in Van reported that the Armenians "look to the autonomy of Bulgaria and are beginning to dream of a similar autonomy for themselves, and if reform is delayed, may call upon Russia to obtain it for them." Exclusionist ideologies found a recipient audience among embittered Muslims in the form of pan-Islam, pan-Turkism, and Turkish nationalism. The new sultan, Abdülhamid II, revived the long dormant title of caliph, promoted pan-Islamic ideals, and suspended the constitution virtually bringing the Tanzimat to an end.[95]

The ostensible victor failed to capitalize on its gains. Accompanying the Russian army of occupation, Russian officials drafted a constitution for the new state. Like previous constitutionalist experiments in the borderlands, including the Kingdom of Poland, the Grand Duchy of Finland, and the Danubian principalities, they introduced progressive institutions combining elective assemblies with centralized bureaucratic administrations under the rule of law. By turning their "enlightened face" toward the west, the imperial reformers sought to create model states that would legitimize their sphere of influence in the eyes of Europe and gain acceptance of Russian hegemony from the local population. Their avowed aim in the words of Cyril Black was "to see a Bulgaria which would be independent in an administrative sense but which would associate itself with Russian policy in the Balkans and would also provide a trained militia able and willing to cooperate with Russian troops."[96] For six years after the Treaty of Berlin Bulgaria was virtually a Russian protectorate. The Bulgarian army was officered and trained by the Russians, and the first two ministers of war were Russian officers. The Russians lost ground

---

[95] Kemal Karpat, "The Social and Political Foundations of Nationalism in South East Europe after 1878. A Reinterpretation," in *Studies on Ottoman Social and Political History. Selected Articles and Essays* (Leiden: Brill, 2002), pp. 352–84, quotation on p. 379.

[96] C. E. Black, *The Establishment of Constitutional Government in Bulgaria* (Princeton University Press, 1943), p. 57. As an American representative in Sofia after the Second World War, Black discerned a similar policy pursued by Soviet officials.

when in 1885 Alexander III opposed Bulgaria's unilateral declaration of a union with Eastern Rumelia, and then refused to recognize the prince as the ruler of the unified country for the next ten years. Bulgarian politicians continued to be divided between those who collaborated with Russia and those who resisted its interference in Bulgarian domestic affairs.[97]

Domestically, the Russian Empire also paid a heavy price for its victory. The reforms ground to a halt. Once again, as in 1815, the empire had extended more liberal institutions to non-Russians inhabiting the borderlands facing Europe than it was willing to grant to its own people. The moderate elements in educated society were alienated and the revolutionaries unleashed a campaign of terror that culminated in the assassination of Tsar Alexander II. His son, Alexander III, like Abdülhamid, turned toward a more exclusionist ideology, in his case, a Russian nationalist spirit. For the rest of the century these trends in both empires increased the tensions between their centers of power and the borderlands.

The Pontic steppe

The Pontic steppe extended from the Danube delta to the Caspian Sea, along a wide belt of fertile grasslands broken by arid stretches all along the northern shores of the Black Sea. For centuries after the devastating impact of the Mongol invasions upon the Kievan principality in the thirteenth century, the frontier remained sparsely populated, providing vast grazing zones for the herds of the mounted steppe warriors and open to continuous and ruinous raids by nomads.[98] From the east came the Nogai, Bashkirs, and Kalmyks; from the south, beginning in the fifteenth century, the Crimean Tatars. Spatial and environmental obstacles confronted sedentary powers seeking to establish firm control over the lower reaches of the Pontic frontier. Although four main waterways connected the Black Sea to the hinterland – the Dniester, the Dnieper, the Don, and the Volga – their head waters and deltas had long been under the control of different state structures with different socioeconomic systems. The rivers were separated by open steppe, where conventional armies were forced to endure extremes of weather, the absence of potable water, frequent drought, and disease. Major Ottoman and Russian expeditions

---

[97] Richard J. Crampton, *Bulgaria 1878–1918. A History* (Boulder, CO: East European Monographs, 1983), pp. 115–73, 241–86.

[98] A. I. Baranovich, "Naselenie predstepnoi Ukrainy v XVI v.," in *Istoricheskie zapiski*, 32 (1950), who revises upward earlier population estimates, but does not essentially change the picture.

from the sixteenth to the eighteenth centuries suffered terrible losses from the hostile environment.[99] The wars and endemic raiding long delayed the spread of agriculture and preserved the natural environment, enabling nomadic and semi-nomadic populations, like the Nogai and Kalmyks, to survive and occasionally threaten the security of the frontier settlements.

The entanglement of Polish, Russian, and Ottoman interests in the Pontic steppe was linked to the struggle in the Baltic littoral and to the Ottoman–Habsburg imbroglio on the Danubian frontier. By the early sixteenth century, three major powers were poised to compete with the nomadic tribes for control of the region.[100] For each of them there were clear strategic as well as economic and cultural advantages to be won. For the nobility of the Commonwealth, the region offered the prospects of exploiting highly productive agricultural land, establishing a direct over-land trade connection between the Baltic and Black Sea under their control, and erecting a territorial buffer against raids by the steppe nomads.[101] For the Muscovite rulers, expansion to the south meant the unification under their control of the great river system from the Baltic to the Black Sea, and the opening of the fertile Black Earth region to colonization. Domination of the steppe would fulfill the needs of both external security and internal stability by defending against nomadic raids on settled areas and containing the flight of peasant-serfs from the center who were legally bound to their landlords by the Law Code of 1649.

For the Ottomans, the Black Sea littoral was an important link in its economic and strategic system. Their incorporation of the Crimean kha-nate as a vassal state into their imperial rule in the fifteenth century provided the keystone that cemented the outer perimeter of the Ottoman defenses against the advance of the Russians and Poles to the shores of the Black Sea. Control of the khanate assured safe passage of Muslim pilgrims from Trans Caspia to the holy places of Islam. The

---

[99] Michael Khodarkovsky, *Russia's Steppe Frontier. The Making of a Colonial Empire, 1500–1800* (Bloomington, IN: Indiana University Press, 2002), p. 116.

[100] The complex interaction of the three powers in advancing their aims included at times temporary alliances directed against one another. See A. B. Kuznetsov, "Rossiia i politika Kryma v vostochnoi Evrope v pervoi treti XVI," in B. A. Rybakov (ed.), *Rossiia, Pol'sha i prichernomor'e v XVI–XIII vv* (Moscow: Nauka, 1979), pp. 62–70; and B. N. Flora, "Proekt antiturestkoi koalitsii serediny XVI v.," in *ibid.*, pp. 71–87, which, however, interpret the struggle exclusively as Russian resistance to Tatar and Polish expansionism.

[101] In the 1640s, the Polish king, Władysław IV, nourished the most ambitious plan to organize a great anti-Turkish campaign in order to evict the Tatars from the Crimea and liberate the Balkans with the help of the Cossacks. J. Tazbir, "The Commonwealth of the Gentry," in Aleksander Gieysztor *et al.* (eds.), *History of Poland* (Warsaw: Polish Scientific Publishers, 1979), p. 208.

khanate was also a major source of food, raw materials, and slaves.[102] The annual plundering expeditions of 30,000–40,000 Tatar horsemen into the Commonwealth, Muscovy, and the north Caucasus yielded tens of thousands of prisoners who were then sold in Kaffa, the largest slave market in Europe in the seventeenth century.[103] As vassals Tatar khans, like the Romanian hospodars, were not always reliable subjects. Moreover, their semi-nomadic way of life provoked conflicts with their northern neighbors that often involved the Ottomans in unwanted wars. But the Poles, Russians, and Tatars not only had to deal with one another, but also manage the turbulent Cossack population.

The Cossacks

In the late fifteenth century, the Russian chronicles begin to speak of a new social phenomenon in the "wild fields," known by the Turkish word *kazak*, meaning free warrior or wanderer.[104] Originally, the term may have been first used by the Crimean khans in their diplomatic protests against the employment of renegades from their armies who were hired as mercenaries by Muscovy and the Commonwealth.[105] Subsequently, Russian, Polish, and Tatar governments applied the term to military organizations of the floating population in the "wild fields." As the princes of Moscow consolidated their power, the frontier had become a place of refuge for adventurers, freebooters, anchorites and their followers, gangs (*vatagi*) of fishermen and hunters, discontented servicemen, runaway peasants – by far the largest group – and, later in the seventeenth century, religious dissidents.

When they first took notice of them, Muscovite officials described these people in a variety of unflattering terms, calling them "fugitives fleeing from government obligations," or more simply "marauders" (*sharpolniki*), or sometimes "thieves" (*vory*), but most frequently "rovers" (*guliashchie*

---

[102] Halil Inalcik, *The Ottoman Empire. The Classical Age, 1300–1600* (New York: Praeger, 1973), pp. 129–33, 144–45; Halil Inalcik, "The Closing of the Black Sea under the Ottomans," *Arkheiov Povtov* 35 (Athens, 1979): 74–110.

[103] For the pattern of economic life, see A. L. Iakobson, *Srednevekovyi Krym. Ocherk istorii i istorii material'noi kultury* (Moscow: Nauka, 1964), esp. ch. 6. According to one estimate the Tatars carried off 150,000–200,000 inhabitants of Muscovy during the first half of the seventeenth century. A. A. Novosel'skii, *Bor'ba moskovskogo gosudarstva s tatarami v pervoi polovine XVII veka* (Moscow: Akademiia nauk, 1948), p. 426.

[104] On the origins of the Cossacks, see Gunter Stokl, *Die Entstehung des Kosakentums* (Munich: Isar Verlag, 1953); Philip Longworth, *The Cossacks* (London: Constable, 1969); Robert H. McNeal, *Tsar and Cossack* (Basingstoke: Palgrave Macmillan, 1987).

[105] Linda Gordon, *Cossack Rebellions. Social Turmoil in the Sixteenth Century Ukraine* (Albany, NY: State University of New York Press, 1983), p. 61.

liudi). As early as 1502, Ivan III instructed the prince of Riazan to punish those who "disobeyed and went to live on their own as free-booters (*molodechestvo*) on the Don River."[106] To no avail. Irresistibly they moved along the great rivers, fanned out in the fertile if dangerous "wild fields," or else trudged across the "Rock" into Siberia. For the individual the risks against survival were enormous. It was better to seek refuge with one of the larger groups that had provided itself with arms and formed military brotherhoods. By the mid-fifteenth century, the Moscow chronicles had already begun to identify them as Riazan Cossacks. But it was not until the mid- to late sixteenth century that the records located the main centers of their activities farther south at the big Dnieper bend "beyond the rapids" (*Zaporozhe*), and along the Don, Terek, and Ural (Iaik) rivers.

The Cossacks were an archetypical frontier people of the Eurasian borderlands. For more than a century they occupied the intermediate space between the three rival multicultural empires, which they uneasily shared with other frontier peoples like the nomadic Nogai, Kalmyks, and Bashkirs. Their internal organization was rooted in notions of rough egalitarianism and self-government, but they were not anti-monarchical. Rather, they cherished the ideal or illusion of a popular tsar who would destroy the power of "the boiars" and grant freedom to all his subjects. The most successful Cossack leaders of large rebellions against the central power – Bolotnikov, Razin, and Pugachev – claimed to be the true tsar (*samozvanets*) or his self-appointed representative.[107]

The Zaporozhian and Don Cossacks were overwhelmingly Russian and Ruthenian (Ukrainian), but they accepted Tatars and others into their ranks. At first, they disdained private ownership of land and lived by hunting and fishing, or from the proceeds of raiding and pillaging. Up to 1690, the cultivation of grain on the Don was forbidden on pain of death. When in the seventeenth century Moscow asked the Don Cossacks to send in an embassy "the best people," the haughty answer came back: "we have no 'best people,' the best people are elected by the Host and they will be sent."[108] They took under their protection peasant cultivators who

---

[106] Quoted in S. G. Sviatnikov, *Rossiia i Don, 1549–1917. Issledovanie po istorii gosudarstvennogo i administrativnogo prava i politicheskikh dvizhenii na Donu* (Belgrad: Izd. Donskoi istoricheskoi komissii, 1924), p. 9.

[107] Paul Avrich, *Russian Rebels, 1600–1800* (New York: W. W. Norton, 1976), pp. 156–57, 176–77, points out that one of the weaknesses of Kondraty Bulavin's rebellion in 1707/8 was his failure to pose as the pious or true tsar, or to bring forward a claimant to the throne. For the persistence of popular monarchism, see Daniel Field, *Rebels in the Name of the Tsar* (Boston, MA: Houghton Mifflin, 1989).

[108] Sviatnikov, *Rossia i Don*, pp. 24–26, quotation on p. 26.

did not join the Host and monasteries, but they elected their own priests and decided on the construction of churches. The Cossacks themselves were not a unified social stratum. There were divisions between those who were privileged by virtue of being registered by the Poles or were receiving monetary payment from Muscovy, and those who were unprivileged, between the old timers and the newcomers, between those who gradually acquired property and those who were propertyless. These differences persisted in various forms throughout their history, and at critical moments such as the Russian Civil War in 1918–1920 and the German invasion in 1941–1942 tore their social fabric asunder.

The external relations of the Cossacks reflected their desire for independence and the value attached by others to their military prowess. They made and broke alliances with equal facility, fighting on one side and shifting to another, depending on circumstances and payments for their services. The competing empires sought to enroll them in their armies, but had to acknowledge that they were unable to control the plundering of "their own Cossacks." For example, as early as the mid-sixteenth century the Nogai complained bitterly about Cossack raids on their herds. In response, Ivan IV could only plead his helplessness to control the frontiersmen on his side:

And which place does not have bandits, you know. There are many Cossacks in the steppe – Kazan, Azov, Crimean Cossacks and other independent Cossacks. And the Cossacks from our frontier also leave for the steppe and they are criminals to you just as they are criminals to us; no one instructs them to commit banditry. And having committed banditry, they leave for home.[109]

Russia was more successful than its competitors in stabilizing the frontier and incorporating the Cossack lands into its empire. But it was a long and often violent process marked by rebellions and civil wars. The relationship between the Great Russian center of power and the steppe frontier complicated the process of state-building immensely. The great crisis of state power at the beginning of the seventeenth century, the Russian Time of Troubles, testified to the challenge posed by the tradition of freedom (*volia*) on the frontier to principle of power (*vlast'*) at the center. From 1603 to 1613, the country was plunged into a many-sided civil war with the Cossacks involved at every stage, supporting first one claimant to the throne and then another, split between the so-called "free Cossacks" made up of former slaves, service men, and runaway peasants, who were fighting a class war against the nobility, and the

---

[109] Cited in Khodarkovsky, *Russia's Steppe Frontier*, p. 50. See also p. 122 for Nogai complaints against the Volga and Iaik Cossacks.

Don, Dnieper, and Terek Cossack Hosts, who were mainly interested in securing their traditional privileges.[110] The Time of Troubles contained many of the ingredients of subsequent internal–external conflicts merging civil wars and interventions that reached its climax in the twentieth century.

The Crimean Tatars, their Ottoman overlords, and the Polish–Lithuanian Commonwealth contributed to prolonging the Cossack phenomenon. The large-scale frontier warfare and lesser raids into the Commonwealth by the Crimean Tatars spurred the Poles in 1524 to propose the registration and enrollment of the Zaporozhian Cossacks as a permanent frontier force in the service of the crown. It was only later at the end of the century that the terms of the Cossack service and their religious differences with the Catholic Poles during the Counter Reformation would create endless difficulties and lead to conflicts that seriously undermined the power of the Commonwealth in Ukraine.

For over a century the Cossacks proved to be formidable fighters, repeatedly inflicting heavy losses on the Tatars. They turned the tables on their enemies by launching their own raiding and pillaging expeditions deep into Crimean territory. By the early seventeenth century, they were disrupting Ottoman–Tatar trade on the Black Sea by effectively employing their small maneuverable ships (*saykas*) along the shallow coastal waters. They even seized and held the key naval base of Azov for five years (1637–1642), a fortress that fifty years later would long resist the Russian armies of Peter the Great.[111]

By the mid-seventeenth century, the Cossacks had become the focal point for widespread social and confessional discontent throughout the Pontic frontier. But they were not the natural leaders of a great rebellion, rather, they had leadership forced upon them. The Commonwealth consistently antagonized the Cossacks by hiring them as mercenaries against the Tatars and then failing to meet their promises of payment and privileges. In particular, they mismanaged the registration of Cossacks. In 1591, local quarrels sparked the first Cossack rising. Once aroused, the Cossacks became the champions of larger confessional and social

---

[110] A. L. Stanislavskii, *Grazhdanskaia voina v Rossii XVII v. Kazachestvo na perelome istorii* (Moscow: Mysl, 1990), pp. 21–33, 44–45, who rejects the view prevailing in the Soviet period that this was a peasant war. See also B. V. Anan'ich *et al.*, *Vlast' i reformy ot samoderzhavnoi k sovetskoi Rossii* (St. Petersburg: Dmitrii Bulanin, 1996), p. 99.

[111] For a general picture of Cossack raids, see Alan Fisher, "The Ottoman Crimea in the Mid-Seventeenth Century. Some Problems and Preliminary Considerations," *Harvard Ukrainian Studies* 3/4 (1979/80): 215–26. For vivid accounts of Cossack naval warfare, see Victor Ostapchuk, "Five Documents from the Topkapi Palace Archive on the Ottoman Defense of the Black Sea against the Cossacks (1639)," in Raiyyet Rusumu (ed.), *Essays Presented to Halil Inalcik on his Seventieth Birthday by his Colleagues and Students, Journal of Turkish Studies* 2 (1987): 49–104.

protests. The proselytizing activities of the Jesuits during the Counter Reformation fueled the smoldering resentment of the Orthodox population of Ukraine. Even before, but especially after, the Union of Brest in 1596, a fierce propaganda war had broken out between Catholics and Orthodox. The Polish government denounced the Orthodox spokesmen as fanatical heretics and opposition to the establishment of the Uniat Church as criminal.[112] That same year the Cossacks responded to the appeal of the Orthodox lay brotherhoods in the towns. Their first big revolt was suppressed with heavy losses. Their commitment to their co-religionists as well as to the peasantry was sporadic and unpredictable. But a pattern of greater involvement began to emerge. From 1591 to 1638, the Cossacks launched no less than seven major uprisings. The Pontic frontier was fast becoming an arena for a protracted civil war.

The Cossack insurgencies gradually assumed more sharply etched religious and social characteristics, although they still lacked consistency of purpose and a clear-cut political program. The Cossacks remained attached to their free-booting frontier culture. When defeated in the field by the Poles or offered renewal of their privileges, they abandoned their peasant allies and forgot their promises to the Church. In their demands for autonomy they rose above the level of primitive bandits, but they fell short of being leaders of a national independence movement.[113] In the 1620s and 1630s they were aroused to action once again by the government's attempts to reduce the numbers of registered Cossacks and to convert the "self-governing" Cossacks into peasants who were legally bound to the szlachta. Each successive rebellion against the Poles increased the level of Cossack demands for "satisfaction of the needs" of the Orthodox Church. When in 1648 the government again violated promises to restore "former privileges and Cossack liberties," the long civil war reached its climax and engulfed the entire region.

During the major insurrection led by Bogdan Khmel'nits'ky, the disparate elements of a peasant war, a religious conflict, and a struggle for Cossack autonomy fell into line. The civil war exposed the Pontic frontier of the Polish–Lithuanian Commonwealth to foreign invasion, first, by the

[112] Polish and Russian historians have long differed over a wide range of issues connected with the creation of the Uniat Church. For representative views, see Solov'ev, *Istoriia Rossii*, vol. II, pp. 1404–412, 1419–446; and Halecki, *Borderlands*, pp. 181–85.

[113] Gordon, *Cossack Rebellions*, is excellent on the internal dynamics of the movement, but clings to the model of the Cossacks as primitive rebels. Hans-Joachim Torke, "The Unloved Alliance. Political Relations between Muscovy and Ukraine in the Seventeenth Century," in Peter Potichnyj *et al.* (eds.), *Ukraine and Russia in their Historical Encounter* (Edmonton: Canadian Institute of Ukrainian Studies, 1992), p. 42, detects the first signs of an awakening political consciousness of the Cossacks in 1632.

Tatars who sought to weaken the Commonwealth without creating an independent Cossack state, then by Muscovy. The Russians donned the mantle of the defender of Orthodoxy only hesitantly and reluctantly, aiming initially at regaining control over the left bank Ukraine. Few events in the history of Ukraine have given rise to such a passionate historiography as the Khmel'nits'ky rising.[114] None had a more profound and lasting effect on the struggle over the frontiers until revolution and civil war from 1918 to 1920.

The leaders of the Commonwealth and the more moderate landowning elements in Ukraine were deeply divided over a solution to the Cossack problem. The majority of the Polish magnates were determined to crush the rebellion and restore the old order. A smaller group favored concessions. A few others, like the tragic figure of the Orthodox Ruthenian magnate, Adam Kysil, sought a compromise solution that would preserve the Cossack rights, guarantee the magnates their property and their serfs, and satisfy the needs of the Orthodox Church. He also proposed to turn Cossack energy outward in a great coalition with Muscovy against the Tatars. His "patchwork solutions," as his biographer Frank Sysyn writes, reveal the dilemma of a man of the borderlands who sought to preserve a frontier culture in the midst of powerful opposing forces that tore such regions apart.[115]

In 1654, Muscovy appeared to have gained the edge in the competition for control over the Pontic steppe by signing the Treaty of Pereiaslavl with the Cossacks. The agreement recognized the rights and privileges of the Cossacks, as well as those of the peasants and townsmen who had supported their uprising against the Poles in return for acknowledging the sovereignty of the tsar. Almost immediately, however, problems arose in interpreting its clauses. Scholars have counted at least eleven definitions of what kind of constitutional order it created. The controversy led to innumerable political disputes.[116] Moreover, the treaty did not end the fighting, but only signaled a new phase. For the next fifty years Ukraine was plunged into a series of wars, rebellions, occupations, and fresh treaties that overrode the earlier ones. The outcome was not at all predictable.

---

[114] Frank Sysyn, "The Changing Image of the Hetman. On the 350th Anniversary of the Khmel'nyts'kyi Uprising," *Jahrbücher für Geschichte Osteuropas* 46(4) (1998): 331–45.

[115] Frank E. Sysyn, *Between Poland and Ukraine. The Dilemma of Adam Kysil, 1600–1653* (Cambridge, MA: Harvard University Press, 1985).

[116] V. Prokopovych, "The Problem of the Juridical Nature of the Ukraine's Union with Muscovy," *Annals of the Ukrainian Academy of Arts and Sciences in the US* 4 (1955): 926–46; O. E. Gunther, "Der Vertrag von Perejaslav im Wiederstreit der Meinungen," *Jahrbücher für Geschichte Osteuropas*, New Series, 2 (1954): 243–50.

The Treaty of Pereiaslavl touched off another great frontier war (1654–1667) that involved the Commonwealth, Moscow, Sweden, the Crimean Tatars, and the Cossacks. The effects on Poland were comparable to those on Muscovy in the Time of Troubles. During "the deluge" or "the ruin," as it is alternatively called in Polish historiography, the entire country was devastated by invading armies from Sweden, Muscovy, and the Crimea. In the 1650s, the first plans for partitioning the country were advanced by Sweden, Brandenburg-Prussia, and Transylvania. They were premature, but were a sign of things to come.[117] Belatedly, the Poles offered the Cossacks an alternative compromise to Pereiaslavl. The Treaty of Haidach in 1658 was an extraordinary document that would have created a triune state of Poland–Lithuania–Ruthenia, with the full recognition of the Orthodox Church and co-optation of the Cossack elite into the Commonwealth nobility. But it came too late.[118]

Even before the Khmel'nits'ky rebellion the Cossack starshina began to consider the advantages of accepting the protection of the Ottoman sultan. On numerous occasions the Crimean Tatars had offered to conclude a temporary military alliance with the Cossacks against their common Polish and Russian enemies. By becoming a protectorate of the Ottoman Empire, the Cossacks thought they could obtain an autonomous status similar to that which the Ottomans had granted to Transylvania, the principalities, and the Crimea. This would mean greater security without a loss of freedom. But they failed to overcome popular antipathy toward the Tatars among the Orthodox peasant population of Ukraine.[119] They made one last try.

In the midst of the conflict in 1665 the right bank Cossacks elected as their hetman, Peter Doroshenko, who turned to the Ottoman Empire for assistance and signed a treaty with them.[120] The Crimean khan extended assurances of "protection and defense," and promised to assist Doroshenko in a war against Poland that would make him hetman of "both sides of the Dnieper."[121] A year later the Ottomans took advantage of internal weakness within the Commonwealth and their treaty with the

---

[117] Tazbir, "The Commonwealth," p. 211.
[118] Ivan L. Rudnytsky, "Polish–Ukrainian Relations. The Burden of History," in *Essays in Modern Ukrainian History* (Edmonton: Canadian Institute of Ukrainian Studies, 1987), pp. 56–57.
[119] Orest Subtelny, "Cossack Ukraine and the Turco-Islamic World," in Ivan L. Rudnitsky (ed.), *Rethinking Ukrainian History* (Edmonton: Canadian Institute of Ukrainian Studies, 1981), pp. 127–30.
[120] For Doroshenko's treaty with the Ottomans, see Józéf Wereszczyński (ed.), *Sbornik statei i materialov po istorii Iugo-zapadnoi Rossii* (Kiev: N. T. Korchak-Novitskago, 1916), p. 75.
[121] I. V. Galaktionov, "Rossiia i Pol'sha pered litsom turetsko-tatarskoi agressii," in Rybakov, *Rossiia, Pol'sha*, p. 383, citing TsGADA, f. 89, Dela turetskie 1666, d. 1, l. 89.

Cossacks to launch their last great invasion of Ukraine under the vigorous leadership of Grand Vizier Fazıl Ahmed Köprülü, the son of the founder of a great dynasty of Ottoman statesmen in the seventeenth century. The Ottoman conquest of the Polish province of Polodia in 1672 and its great fortress, Kamieniec, appeared to consolidate Ottoman hegemony along the Pontic frontier. The territory secured Ottoman rule over Moldavia and strengthened its control of the Crimea.[122] The Cossack cause was lost when the Poles and Russians came to an agreement.

The terrible thirteen-year war had drained the military resources of both Muscovy and the Commonwealth. All sides won some great battles, yet the effects of victory in the field were ephemeral. Coalitions disintegrated, usually when the Cossacks or Tatars switched sides or simply went home, and then reassembled with different partners. Reduced to a state of mutual exhaustion, the Poles and the Russians signed the Treaty of Andrussovo in 1667, which brought the left bank of the Dnieper and Kiev (initially for twenty years and then permanently) under Russian rule. A period of relative security from Tatar and Polish raids followed, and the population grew rapidly, swelled by tens of thousands of immigrants from the right bank. In 1681, the Ottomans and Russians signed a twenty-year treaty of peace that recognized Ottoman possession of the devastated right bank of the Dnieper, which had been virtually depopulated by war and famine. It had become in the words of Hetman Doroshenko, "a dreadful wilderness."[123] The long-term significance of Khmel'nits'ky's rebellion was mainly symbolic, but no less powerful. It left a legacy of collective memories and legends of Cossack freedoms and heroism, and provided Ukrainian intellectuals of the nineteenth century (and post-communist Ukraine as well) with the stuff of which national myths are built.[124]

Muscovy's problems in the struggle over the Pontic frontier were not only multiple and external, but also linked to internal developments. As the war with the Commonwealth was winding down in the 1660s, a crisis sparked by three powerful, interconnected, social movements erupted in the Don: the flight of schismatic Old Believers following their official condemnation by the Church hierarchy in 1666/7; the rising tide of

[122] Dariusz Kolodziejczyk, *Ottoman–Polish Diplomatic Relations (15th–18th Century)* (Leiden: Brill, 2000), pp. 141–45, also points out that, except for the turbulent seventeenth century, the Ottoman Empire and the Commonwealth enjoyed long periods of peace as both shared a common interest in checking Russian expansion and suppressing "emancipation movements" in Moldavia and Ukraine.

[123] W. E. D. Allen, *The Ukraine. A History* (New York: Russell & Russell, 1963), p. 178.

[124] Zenon Kohut, *Russian Centralism and Ukrainian Autonomy. Imperial Absorption of the Hetmanate, 1760–1830s* (Cambridge, MA: Harvard University Press, 1988).

runaway peasants reacting to the juridical institutionalization of serfdom by the Law Code of 1649 (*Ulozhenie*); and the migration of Russian peasants from the right bank of the Dnieper River after the partition of Ukraine in 1667 between the Polish Commonwealth and Muscovy. The newcomers to the Don overwhelmed the delicately balanced ecology of the region, which lacked the means to feed them. Outright banditry became endemic even within the Cossack territory and all along the Volga. The "thief Cossacks" founded their own town, which became the center of the revolt. A dissident Cossack, Stepan Razin, ignited this smoldering mass with his slogans of social leveling. The lower and middle Volga was in danger of breaking loose from the Muscovite center of power. Recognized by the ruling elite as a typical man of the borderlands, Razin did not respect state frontiers. He led raids deep into Iranian territory, and did not hesitate to enroll Tatars in his forces.[125] The older Don Cossacks remained neutral in the struggle until Moscow denounced them as traitors. Then they turned against the rebels and captured Razin. By surrendering him to Moscow, they compromised the right of refuge that had been the mainstay of their autonomy.[126]

Before the Razin rebellion, the Don Cossacks had been willing to serve the tsar on a regular basis, but they had refused to take the oath of allegiance or enroll in the Moscow service books. In return Moscow had agreed to make no claims on fugitives once they entered the Don territory. It had requested only that "recent runaways" should not be sent on official missions. All this ended with the suppression of the Razin rebellion. Moreover, the central government made clear its understanding of the organic relationship between the frontier and its foreign policy. It cut off all payments to the Cossacks and suspended trade until they finally took an oath of allegiance to the tsar and renounced the right to conduct foreign relations with the Poles. But repression did not solve the basic problems of frontier control.

The next major advance of Russian power into the Pontic steppe was an unexpected outcome of the Great Northern War (1700–1721) against Sweden, illustrating once again the entangled relations between foreign and domestic conflicts throughout the west Eurasian borderlands. The campaigns of Charles XII not only contributed to the precipitous decline of the Commonwealth, but also stimulated a revival of rebellion all along Russia's southern frontiers, in Ukraine, the Don territory, and among the Bashkirs. Having inflicted a severe defeat on the incompletely reorganized

---

[125] Paul Avrich, *Russian Rebels, 1600–1800* (New York: Schocken Books, 1972), pp. 71–73.
[126] Sviatnikov, *Rossiia i Don*, pp. 101–2.

Russian army at Narva in 1703, Charles plunged into central Poland where, for the following six years, he got "stuck," as Peter put it. The Poles were once again descending into chaos. They had recovered briefly from "the deluge" under the leadership of their last great king, Jan Sobieski, but even he was unable to tame the szlachta. The election of his successors from the ruling house of Saxony, who took little interest in Polish affairs, proved to be disastrous for the Commonwealth. For two centuries the frontier policy of the szlachta had contributed to weakening the authority of the crown. Three times in the eighteenth century, in 1716, 1733/4, and 1767/8, Cossacks, peasants, and *haidamaks* (armed gangs, from the Arab–Turkish word meaning troublemaker) took advantage of Poland's domestic weakness to plunge the right bank Ukraine into civil war. The struggle over the borderlands of the Pontic frontier was not the only factor in Poland's final disappearance from the map of Europe, but it turned social and institutional instability into a security nightmare. The Commonwealth, once a major contestant for hegemony in the region, had itself become a contest zone.

With Poland once again a battleground in the Great Northern War, the Swedes and the Russians supported alternative claimants to the throne and the szlachta divided their loyalties. Charles promoted as his candidate the enlightened Polish noble, Stanisław Leszczynski, while Peter propped up the Saxon king, Augustus II. Russian policy was complicated by the outbreak of rebellion against the Poles in the right bank Ukraine.

At the end of the seventeenth century, the Commonwealth had regained the right bank Ukraine from the Ottoman Empire, and Polish landlords poured back into the territory. The Sejm then sought to curb the Cossacks once and for all by abolishing all their privileges. Predictably, the Cossacks revolted and declared themselves to be subjects of the tsar. But Peter was more concerned with keeping the Poles in the field against Sweden than in acquiring the right bank. He ordered the Cossacks to support their king and sent in a trusted ally, the Cossack hetman Ivan Mazepa to pacify the Zaporozhians. But when Charles invaded Ukraine in 1708, Mazepa defected in the hope of leading a great uprising that would reestablish Cossack autonomy with himself at its head. Only a handful of Cossacks followed, and they were defeated with Charles's Swedish army at Poltava in 1709. Peter ordered the destruction of the Cossack fortress, the Sich, "that damned place which is the root of evil," in his words. He curtailed the powers of the new hetman, Skoropads'kyi, and soon after he abolished the hetmanate as an elective office – although it was restored after his death – writing to the Cossack officers: "As is well known, from the time of the first hetman, Bogdan Khmel'nits'ky, right up to Skoropads'kyi, all hetmen have been traitors." As if to confirm Peter's verdict, Mazepa's successor, Filip Orlyk, continued in exile to collaborate with the Ottomans in the hope of restoring Cossack autonomy.[127]

Peter's state-building policies had a paradoxical effect on the country's social stability. The greater the centralization imposed by Peter, the greater the flight to the frontiers, and the fiercer the resistance of the frontier peoples to the expansion of the imperial center. The region of the Don had replaced the Dnieper bend as the main refuge of discontented elements in Russian society.[128] Prominent among these were the traditional military corps of musketeers (streltsy) who resented Peter's military reforms that deprived them of their privileges and, indeed, threatened their whole way of life. When their southern regiments were disbanded they were ripe for rebellion. Old Believers, already alienated from the official church and banished to the frontiers of the state, were further shocked by Peter's cavalier attitude toward religion and his importation of foreign cultural models. The stream of runaway peasants escaping the heavy burdens of taxation and recruitment continued despite government efforts. The Don Cossacks were increasingly resentful of state intervention in their economic life, and they resisted the repeated attempts of state officials to recover runaways who had sought refuge with them. Peter's challenge to the traditional right of sanctuary touched off a Cossack rising led by one of their hetmen, Kondrat Bulavin, which engulfed much of the lower Don for two years.[129] In many ways it duplicated the revolt of Razin, drawing upon the same discontented frontier population. But it failed to draw in the native tribesmen or to coordinate with Mazepa and the Zaporozhian Cossacks who were intriguing with Charles XII. Nevertheless, at the height of the Great Northern War, with Charles moving east toward Ukraine, Peter was forced to send a large regular army to crush the rebels on the Don. The fighting devastated hundreds of thousands of acres of fields that were cultivated by state peasants, and leveled towns and churches. The repression was savage: 7,000–10,000 Cossacks were executed and thousands fled across the Ottoman borders to serve the sultan. In effect this spelled the end to Don Cossack

[127] Quotation in Solov'ev, *Istoriia Rossii*, vol. XIV, p. 154; vol. XXVIII, p. 826; Orest Subtelny, "Political Cooperation and Religious Antagonism. Aspects of Pylyp Orlyk's Relations with Turks and Tatars," in *Zbirnyk na poshanu prof. doktora Oleksandra Ohloblyna* (New York: Ukrains'ka vil'na academiia nauka u SShA, 1977), pp. 454–65.
[128] Historians of the Don Cossacks have identified six subsequent stages in the process: from independence to vassalage (at the end of the Time of Troubles); autonomy within the Moscow state (1671–1721); provincial autonomy (1721–1775); military–civil government (1775–1797); transitional (1797–1835); and special administration (1835–1917). Sviatnikov, *Rossiia i Don*, pp. 2–3.
[129] Avrich, *Russian Rebels*, Pt. 3, remains the most vivid and balanced treatment of Bulavin's revolt.

autonomy, but not to rebellion or the popular tradition of the Don as a place of refuge. Throughout the eighteenth century, the incorporation of the Don Cossack borderland into the Russian state, like that of Ukraine, was marked by violent resistance and state intervention. After a century of peace, the Don Cossack struggle for autonomy revived during the Russian Revolution and civil war between 1918 and 1920. Fainter echoes could even be detected during the Second World War. The frontier tradition died hard.

The third of the major frontier rebellions during the Great Northern War enveloped the Ural–Kama territories of the Bashkirs. It was touched off by Peter's policy of requisitioning horses for the war in the west and searching for deserters. Bad relations between the tribes and Russian officials had already prepared the ground. Supported by the Muslim clergy, the rebellion spread from the Kama River to the north Caucasus. The Russians lost control of most of the central and southern Urals. The Bashkirs inflicted heavy damage on the mines and metallurgical factories that produced vitally needed iron products for the Russian army.

When the Ufa Bashkirs appealed to their co-religionists for aid, the rebellion threatened to bring in the Crimean Tatars and the Ottoman Empire. Peter resorted to the steppe policies of his predecessors by inciting the nomadic Kalmyks to attack the rear of his enemies. By employing the Kalmyks against the Bashkirs, Peter caught the rebels in a reversal of roles. Following the pattern of social change on the frontier, the Bashkirs had begun to shift from a nomadic to a more settled agricultural life. Now it was their villages that were exposed to savage raids by Kalmyk horsemen. After six years of confused fighting (1705–1711), Peter had to settle for the restoration of the status quo and abandon his tax and recruitment policies. After his death a new treaty was signed with the Bashkirs granting them a large measure of autonomy in return for an annual payment of fur tribute. But relations remained inherently unstable between the Bashkirs, the advancing Russian colonists, and ambitious pro-consuls attempting to open up trade with Trans Caspia. The clash of cultures sparked three subsequent Bashkir uprisings in the eighteenth century before the region was finally subjugated.[130]

The Kalmyks represented the wild card in the tripartite struggle over the Pontic steppe. A Mongol people who adopted Lama Buddhism, they had arrived in western Eurasia in the mid-seventeenth century under pressure from the Oirat Mongols of Dzhungaria. They raided Russian frontier posts in Kazan Province, drove the Nogai from their pastures, and

---

[130] Boris Nolde, *La formation de l'empire russe. Études, notes et documents*, 2 vols. (Paris: Institut des études slaves, 1952), vol. I, pp. 208–30.

raided deep into the Crimean khanate. Muscovy appreciated their usefulness as a counterweight to its enemies and signed a treaty with them in
1655. Its terms committed both sides to promote peace, trade, and
military cooperation. However, like most treaties with the steppe people,
this one was interpreted differently by the two sides. For the Russians, it
was a permanent acceptance of recognition of the tsar as sovereign. For
the Kalmyks, it was a temporary agreement among equals.

Over the following decades the Russians repeatedly tried to bind the
Kalmyks more closely, and the Kalmyks continued to raid, trade, and
bargain with the least threatening neighbor, including the Crimean
Tatars, Ottomans, and Iranians. Peter employed them to quell rebellions
along his southeast frontier. But their raids on the lower Don devastated
the region and weakened the Cossack hosts for a generation. They refused
to help Peter against the Swedes or the Bashkirs on the grounds of
"Chingizide solidarity." Over the following half a century the Russian
government gradually wore down Kalmyk resistance, depriving them of
pasture lands and co-opting members of their elites. When Catherine the
Great attempted to complete their absorption into the Russian armed
forces, the majority decamped for the east. A greatly reduced number,
perhaps only a third, reached Dzhungaria where they were incorporated
into the Qing Empire. It took another generation of Russian administrative practices to deprive the remaining Kalmyks of their autonomy.[131]

In dealing with Sweden, the Commonwealth, and the Ottoman
Empire, Peter's aim was to weaken his competitors permanently not
only by force of arms, but also by interference in their domestic policies.
He took advantage of the Swedish depredations during the Great
Northern War in order to turn the Commonwealth into a vassal of
Russia. The Poles were unable to defend themselves or maintain order
over their own population. After Poltava, Peter restored Augustus II to the
throne, but the Saxon king had lost the support of the szlachta. His Saxon
troops and the Polish forces were at daggers drawn. A Confederation at
Tarnogord in 1715, organized by the Polish supporters of Leszczynski, led
to virtual civil war. The confederates threatened to call in the Crimean
khan if the Russians intervened. But the Russians were able to exploit the
religious and political differences among the szlachta in order to impose
their will. Under the watchful eye of the Russian army, the warring parties

---

[131] Michael Khodarkovsky, *Where Two Worlds Met. The Russian State and the Kalmyk
Nomads, 1600–1771* (Ithaca, NY: Cornell University Press, 1992), pp. 133–46;
Alexandre Bennigsen (ed.), "Les Kalmicks de la Volga entre l'empire russe et l'empire
ottoman sous le règne de Pierre le grand d'après les documents des archives ottomanes,"
Cahiers du monde russe et soviétique 7(1) (January–March, 1966).

reached a compromise at the so-called "Silent Sejm" in 1717, when no delegate was permitted to speak. The one thing the szlachta could all agree upon was to limit the powers of the king. They imposed a limit of 24,000 men on the crown army at a time when the armies of Poland's neighbors, Prussia, Russia, and the Habsburg Monarchy, numbered in the hundreds of thousands.[132] It was another step on the Polish road to self-destruction.

At the same time that the szlachta virtually incapacitated the crown, they failed to maintain control over the peasantry, especially in the ever volatile right bank Ukraine. As the Swedish and Russian armies grappled in central Poland, a new disruptive social force made its appearance in the Kiev voevode. A Polish legislative document of 1717 was the first to record the activities of the haidamaks. The real "primitive rebels" of Ukraine, they shared the same hostility to serfdom and polonization as the Cossacks, but were never incorporated into anyone's armed forces or government service. Resorting more to banditry than insurrection, they drew upon peasants, artisans, Russian army deserters, religious dissenters, Don Cossacks, Kalmyks, and dissident Polish noblemen – the flotsam and jetsam of the frontier. They were frequently supported by Orthodox monks. Their main targets were Polish landlords and Jewish estate managers. They met little resistance because the Polish army in Ukraine numbered no more than 1,000 men and several units of Court Cossacks in Polish service. At every successive outbreak of civil strife within the Commonwealth the haidamaks mounted a large-scale uprising.

In the struggle over the borderlands, the Crimean Tatars steadily lost ground throughout the eighteenth century. For centuries they had constituted the "Northern Shield" of the Ottoman Empire. In the Holy War of 1683–1699, the sultan appealed to the Crimean khan, Halji Selim Giray, to "extend his protecting wings over both borders of the Empire" (Hungary and Azov). The khan spent fifteen years on horseback leading his cavalry from Kaments-Poldolsk to Belgrade and back to Azov.[133] By the eighteenth century, the Crimean cavalry, while still a formidable force especially in combination with the Ottoman army, was more adept at raiding than at occupying and incorporating territories into their state. It

---

[132] Norman Davies, "The Military Tradition of the Polish Szlachta, 1700–1864," in Király and Rothenberg (eds.), *War and Society*, p. 40. Prince V. V. Dolgorukii, the victor over Bulavin who intimidated the Sejm, wrote to Peter in a characteristic Russian response that he would rather have been in a meeting with the Don Cossacks than with "these Poles who from seven to four scream at each other and do nothing." Solov'ev, *Istoriia Rossii*, vol. XVI, p. 260.

[133] Alexandre Bennigsen, "Peter the Great, the Ottoman Empire and the Caucasus," *Canadian–American Slavic Studies* 8(2) (Summer 1974): 312.

became notorious for bolting under artillery fire. Its leaders often left the battle to plunder the enemy camp when victory on the field was not yet secured. The tribal and religious leaders maintained their authority and blocked the efforts of reforming khans to lay the foundations of a modern state system. But for the Ottoman Empire, the loss of its "Northern Shield" would have meant the end of its monopoly over the Black Sea trade, and the opening of a strategic gap between its Danubian and Caucasian frontiers.

In its competition with Russia for domination of the Pontic steppe, the Crimean khanate suffered from several disadvantages. Its semi-nomadic traditions made it almost impossible to reach an agreement with the Russians on a common boundary line. Its dependence upon the Ottoman Empire meant that the Russians would always consider them to be a permanent security problem, and an obstacle to the exploitation of rich agricultural lands and to the development of commercial outlets on the Black Sea.

The power relationships between the Commonwealth, Russia, and the Crimean Tatars were affected as much by colonization of the fertile steppe as by military campaigning. Russia's military victories were due only in part to its superior leadership and technical mastery of European warfare. What tipped the balance in Russia's favor, particularly between the second and third war, was the steady, if often uncoordinated and spasmodic, advance of agricultural settlements into the open steppe. These settlements diminished the space across which it was necessary to transport a regular army. They furnished the Russian army with recruits and reliable Cossacks, and also provided the supplies and provisions that were indispensable to overcoming the logistical problems of conducting overland campaigns against the Crimean Tatars.

Ukrainian borderlands

By the early eighteenth century, as the result of a long historical process, the outlines of several distinctive Ukrainian borderlands began to emerge in the Pontic steppe: Slobodskaia Ukraine, Zaporozhe, the hetmanate (Little Russia), and the right bank. Although their separate development long delayed the emergence of a unified independent Ukrainian state, each part contributed in one way or another to the evolution of a national awareness in the nineteenth and twentieth centuries. In the mid-seventeenth century, Cossack regiments began the settlement of Slobodskaia Ukraine in order to defend the towns and agricultural population against Tatar raids. Together with the local population, they erected wooden fortifications mainly on their own initiative without much state support. Unlike the

Zaporozhians or Don Cossacks, they rapidly adapted to the prosaic routines of agriculture and manufacturing. These occupations were their sole means of livelihood, for again, unlike the warrior societies of their brethren on the Don and Dnieper, they did not receive any state subsidies. The influx of migrants into the right bank by Cossacks after the suppression of Khmel'nits'ky's rebellion considerably swelled their numbers. The new-comers were rapidly absorbed into the local way of life.[134] Consequently, the Slobodskaia regiments did not take part in any of the major frontier uprisings. Subsequent immigration from the Great Russian provinces strengthened their traditional ties to the center. Throughout the internecine struggles of the twentieth century, the former Slobodskaia Ukraine remained most closely attached to the Great Russian core.

The most volatile of the Ukrainian borderlands was Zaporozhe. Throughout the first three-quarters of the eighteenth century, the Zaporozhians fought a persistent if losing battle to maintain their free-doms. Having passed over to the Swedish side on the eve of Poltava, they suffered Peter's vengeance. In 1709, he declared the abolition of the Sich and forbade the Cossacks from crossing into Russian territory except as unarmed individuals. Most of them preferred to flee to the Habsburg and Crimean Tatar lands. They reestablished the Sich in Crimean territory, and served in the armies of the Crimean khan while retaining their own internal organization. During the Polish succession crisis in 1733 they shifted allegiance once again. Invading the right bank with the blessing of the Crimean khan, they then obtained a pardon from Empress Anna, reentered Russian service, and reestablished their Sich in a new location. They reoccupied some of their old lands as frontier guards and received the traditional payment from the Russian government. They elected their own ataman and officers. They took up their former occupations of cattle raising, fishing, and trading. Agriculture never interested them. As befit-ted a frontier people in peacetime, they became commercial intermedia-ries between Russia, the hetmanate, the Commonwealth, the Crimea, and the Ottoman Empire. In resettling them, the Russian government not only restored their privileges, but it assigned them a well-defined territory for the first time in their history. This gave the Cossacks a juridical basis for making claims on their neighbors. It also allowed them to collect their own taxes and establish internal tariffs. As Boris Nolde has suggested, they began "to acquire aspects of a state that they had never before possessed,"

---

[134] D. I. Bagaleia, "Ocherki iz istorii kolonizatsii stepnoi okrainy moskovskogo gosu-darsvstva," in *Chteniia v imperatorskom obshchestve istorii i drevnostei rossisskikh pri mos-kovskom universitete* (Moscow: Universitetskaia typografiia, 1887), vol. I, pp. 334, 379–81, 474–75.

although, as he acknowledged, they lacked any juridical rights over the vast territories that they claimed.[135]

During Russia's wars with the Ottoman Empire in 1736–1739 and 1769–1774 the Zaporozhian Cossacks served faithfully in the imperial armies, yet, true to form, they remained fractious and unpredictable. The Russian authorities did not trust them and stationed a Russian garrison in the Sich; for good reason as it turned out. The Cossacks were involved in constant border disputes with their Polish, Tatar, and Don Cossack neighbors. They opposed new settlements in the steppe by state-sponsored immigrants from Serbia. When large-scale disturbances broke out in the right bank – the haidamak movement – they joined the rebels against their old foes the Poles. The Russian government tolerated their existence as long as the Crimean khanate remained dangerous. Once its power was broken at the end of the Russo-Turkish War of 1769–1774, their fate was sealed.

To the north of Zaporozhe the borderland known as the hetmanate was a truncated part of Khmel'nits'ky's great realm that stretched along the left bank of the middle Dnieper from below Poltava to above Starodub. After the Treaty of Pereiaslavl, Muscovite officials began to call it Malorussiia, or Little Russia, and the name entered into local usage. Over the following century up to the 1780s the hetmanate, or Little Russia, gradually lost its autonomous status. The central state bureaucracy gradually chipped away at its special "rights and liberties" until by the early nineteenth century it was completely incorporated into the administrative structure of the empire. The social and cultural life of the old frontier zone gradually underwent a profound transformation. A new elite began to emerge in the early eighteenth century composed of former Polish szlachta and the Cossack officers. Their response to the erosion of their political rights was to campaign for admission into the Russian nobility. The borderland also witnessed a shift in language use from Slavono-Ukrainian to Russian. The rank-and-file Cossacks lost their former social status and economic independence. By the end of the period of autonomy, most were reduced to the level of state peasants. During the reign of Catherine II, the overwhelming mass of the peasant population was bound to their landlords as private serfs.[136] Although it lost most of its characteristics as a borderland, the social and cultural integration of the former hetmanate was neither complete nor permanent.

[135] Nolde, *La formation*, vol. II, pp. 43, 50.
[136] Kohut, *Russian Centralism*; Zenon Kohut, "The Development of a Little Russian Identity and Ukrainian Nation Building," *Harvard Ukrainian Studies* 10(3/4) (December 1986): 565–67.

The two most distinctive features of Little Russia were the particular social structure of the peasantry and the survival of a historic memory of past glories. While over 90 percent of the population of the Great Russian provinces was made up of peasants, the number in Little Russia was closer to 50 percent. Serfdom had been imposed much later than in the central regions of Russia, and the village organization and land-holding practices were distinctly different. The Ukrainian peasants cultivated hereditary individual plots in contrast to the repartitional strip holdings in the north. This gave rise to their relatively more individualist mentality with respect to tenure and cultivation than existed among Russian peasants. They also retained their Ukrainian speech and local customs that served in the mid-nineteenth century as a cultural reservoir upon which the earliest champions of a national identity among the intelligentsia would draw for inspiration.

The right bank Ukraine was the most polonized of the four borderlands. After "the ruin" and the depopulation of the region, the Polish szlachta slowly reoccupied their lands, granting substantial tax privileges to peasants whom they enticed to settle on their estates. Once the labor shortage had been overcome, they reverted to their traditional tactics of reducing the peasants to a servile status. This triggered the new haidamak uprisings that assumed major proportions following the Polish succession crisis in 1733/4 when the Russian candidate, August III, took the throne. When the crisis was over, the haidamaks refused to disband, reoccupying the Sich instead. They organized themselves politically and raided into Poland every spring. In 1750, they launched a big uprising, forcing the Polish authorities to create a local militia. But it preferred to plunder the inhabitants rather than fight the haidamaks. In 1768, when the szlachta formed a big confederation at Bar against a Russian occupation, the haidamaks raised the standard of revolt for the last time. Joining with dissident Cossacks allegedly to defend the Orthodox faith from the Polish "fanatics," they claimed to be acting under a "Golden Charter" from the Empress Elizabeth. But the daughter of Peter disavowed them; she had other interests in Poland. The Russian army ruthlessly suppressed them and turned their leaders over to the Poles for terrible retribution. With the Russian annexation of the right bank during the First Partition of Poland, the haidamaks disappeared, though their exploits like those of the Cossacks enriched the heroic tradition in Ukrainian folklore.[137]

A major breakthrough in Russia's ascendancy on the Pontic frontier came in the first decade of Catherine's reign, when the Gordian knot that

---

[137] Jaroslav Pelenski, "The Haidamak Insurrections and the Old Regimes in Eastern Europe," in *The American and European Revolutions, 1776–1848. Sociopolitical and*

had for so long tied together Poland, Ukraine, and the Ottoman Empire was cut. In rapid succession the First Partition of Poland in 1772, the Treaty of Kuchuk Kainardji in 1774, and the abolition of the Zaporozhian hetmanate in 1775 led to the formal closing of the Pontic frontier. In 1783, Catherine's pro-consul, Prince Grigory Potemkin, engineered the annexation of the Crimean khanate, removing, as he put it, the "pimple from the face of Russia." The Treaty of Iaşi in 1791 deprived the Turks of their last strategic fortress in the region. Within a few years most of the Tatar population, perhaps as many as two-thirds, had emigrated to the Ottoman Empire despite Russian efforts to retain them by offering religious toleration and other concessions to the Tatar elite.[138] The Second and Third Partitions (1776 and 1791) completely eliminated Poland from the contest over Ukraine, leaving Russia with the lion's share of the spoils.

Catherine's strategy in Poland, initially devised and implemented by Nikita Panin, was to continue the policy of Peter the Great: "We will lose a third of our strength and advantage if Poland is not dependent upon us," Panin wrote to the Russian ambassador in Vienna.[139] Three persistent problems linking the Baltic and Pontic frontiers remained to disturb relations between the two states: the large-scale flight of Russian serfs into Poland; social conflict in the right bank Ukraine; and competition over the control of the Duchy of Kurland.

With the extinction of the Saxon dynasty, Catherine's three-pronged plan was to elect a pro-Russian king, Stanisław Poniatowski; win over some of the magnates like the Czartoryski family to Russia's side; and unilaterally guarantee the Polish constitution. Together with Panin, she manipulated the issue of religious dissidents – more of an excuse than a matter of genuine concern to Russian leaders – in order to create "a firm and trustworthy party with the legal right to take part in all Polish affairs." Their policy foreshadowed a series of attempts over the following 200 years to manage Polish affairs by combining the threat of external intervention with the creation of a domestic, collaborationist regime.

The Polish response also echoed down the corridors of time. Poniatowski and the Czartoryskis were willing to cooperate with the Russians in order to promote their own interests. They hoped that once

Ideological Aspects (University of Iowa Press, 1980), pp. 228–47; Zenon Kohut, "Myths Old and New. The Haidamak Movement and the Koliiushchyna (1768)," *Harvard Ukrainian Studies* 1(3) (1977): 359–78.

[138] Isabel de Madariaga, *Russia in the Age of Catherine* (New Haven, CT: Yale University Press, 1981), pp. 364–65.

[139] Solov'ev, *Istoriia Rossii*, vol. V, p. 1517. At this early stage in 1763, Panin's only territorial claim on Poland was the region called Polish Lifland, an irregular quadrilateral centered on the fortress of Dunaburg that would give Russia full access to navigation on the western Dvina from the central provinces to Riga on the Baltic.

in power they could strengthen royal power at the expense of the szlachta privileges and the rights of the dissidents who were under Russian guarantee. This did not accord with Catherine's plans and she allowed herself to be drawn into the morass of Polish internal politics. In 1767, she sent troops into the Commonwealth, sponsored a confederation at Radom, and arrested members of the Polish senate in order to intimidate Poniatowski. Russian intervention triggered a chain reaction, as was so often the case with Poland, turning an internal crisis into a major international conflict.

In the first of a series of explosive events, a group of szlachta that was both anti-Russian and anti-royal declared themselves a confederation in the frontier town of Bar on the volatile Dniester–Dnieper steppe. They appealed for support to the Ottoman sultan, who took no immediate action. But a band of Crimean Tatars used the appeal as an excuse to pillage across the border. At the same time, a number of small confederations sprang up all over Poland, and a haidamak rising against Polish landlords broke out in the right bank Ukraine. The Russian army moved in and with its Polish allies repressed the risings, but not before they had spilled over the Ottoman frontier, leading to a massacre of the Jewish population of the town of Balta. Panin sought to reassure Istanbul that the criminals would be punished. But the sultan was worried about Russian military activity violating his border. France, now seeing an opportunity to restore its defunct *barrière de l'est*, distributed an enormous bribe to the leaders of the war party in Istanbul. This tipped the balance, and the Ottoman Empire declared war.

Russia's massive intervention in Poland and initial victories in the war with the Ottomans aroused concern in Berlin and Vienna that the balance of power in the borderlands was shifting ominously in Russia's favor. Their response was to advance their own territorial claims at the expense of Poland. Troops of both countries set up "cordons" on Polish territory to contain the contagion of the rebellious confederations. Russia scored spectacular victories in the early stages of the war. Catherine's ambitious war aims, which Frederick the Great wrote "made his hair stand on end," initiated a complex set of diplomatic negotiations that reached a climax in 1772 in the First Partition of Poland.[140] Though the Austrians had not

---

[140] There is still no clear answer to the question of who was responsible for the First Partition of Poland. Chechulin insists that Panin had this in mind since 1763 and his diplomacy was aimed mainly at controlling the timing and size of the partitions. N. D. Chechulin, *Vneshniaia politika Rossiia v nachale tsarstvovanniia Ekateriny* (St. Petersburg: Glavnago upravleniia Udelov, 1896), vol. II, pp. 1762–774. Herbert Kaplan places the responsibility for the war on Catherine, but blames Austria for initiating "the scramble." *The First Partition of Poland* (New York: Columbia University Press, 1962). Isabel de Madariaga

spilt a drop of blood, they were able to obtain territory from both Poland and the Ottoman Empire through the skillful diplomacy of Count Kaunitz. In fact, of the three partitioning powers Austria gained the most populous and productive share of Polish territories as well as Ottoman Bukovina. For his pains, Frederick obtained West Prussia, which cut off Poland from the Baltic and united the separate parts of his possessions in East Prussia and Brandenburg.

The Russo-Turkish War may have been "unwanted," as Nolde argues, but once the Russians were in it they kept raising the ante. They had no plan at the outset. Gradually, the fighting shifted more to the south toward the Black Sea littoral and away from the west, that is, Poland. Beginning with the War Council of November 1768, the Russian leaders were focused on securing navigation rights on the Black Sea and the independence of Crimea. Their plan to detach the khanate illustrates the complexity of frontier diplomacy. Initially, Catherine had no desire to annex the Crimea. The Tatars, she thought, would not be ideal subjects in light of their flighty reputation. What Russia needed, in her eyes, was a naval base "like Gibraltar," and the right to send a few warships through the Straits and into the Mediterranean. Russian diplomats launched several initiatives, but the Crimean khan ridiculed their offer to restore the "old liberties." Panin had the bright idea of winning over the Nogai, who were willing to swear allegiance to Russia if they could resettle along the Dnieper. But the Zaporozhian Cossacks were not about to share the spoils from their participation in the Turkish campaign. They attacked the Nogai, forcing some to flee to the Crimea. The Russian government intervened, indemnified the Nogai, and resettled the rest in the uninhabited but fertile lands along the Kuban. More successful was the Russian effort to depose the khan and replace him with a Russian candidate – à la polonaise. This enabled them, at least, to obtain a naval base. But the Tatars still resisted Russian pressure to declare their independence, a move they regarded as contrary to Islamic law that bound them to the sultan.[141]

The most ambitious Russian war aim surfaced late and caused the greatest difficulty. In the wake of Field Marshal Rumiantsev's brilliant campaign across the Danube, the Russian army occupied parts of Moldavia and Wallachia for the first, but not the last, time. Catherine's desire to establish the independence of these two principalities triggered Austria's strong opposition. It had no desire to see a Russian protectorate

points out the gaps in documentation, but comes round to the position that Frederick II used the threat of Austrian intervention to force Catherine's agreement on partition. *Russia in the Age of Catherine*, pp. 235–36.
[141] Nolde, *La formation*, vol. I, pp. 80–82, 113.

in control of the Danube outlet to the Black Sea. Under pressure, Catherine decided to renounce the independence of Danubian principalities in exchange for annexing Polish Livonia, a fateful move that initiated the First Partition of the Commonwealth.

Working in tandem, the Russian commanders and diplomats engineered a breakthrough to the Black Sea, exceeding Catherine's expectations. The Treaty of Kuchuk Kainardji in 1774 was a decisive, if not final, marker in Russia's triumph in the long struggle along the Pontic frontier. The Ottoman Empire ceded to Russia a strip of the Black Sea coastline from the Bug to the Dnieper, including the river port of Kherson. The Ottomans still held on to Ochakov, which dominated the estuary of the Dnieper. But Russia obtained the right to free navigation on the Black Sea. On the eastern flank of the Crimea, Russia gained the forts of Kerch and Enikale that dominated the entrance to the Sea of Azov.

Catherine had cut an aperture to the south, matching Peter's window to the west. Poland was forever sealed off from the Black Sea. The Crimea lost its overland connection with the Ottoman Empire to the west, although it retained its sovereignty over the Nogai to the east. The treaty forced independence on Crimea, which then hung like a ripe plum to be picked by Russia. The Zaporozhian Cossacks had fought loyally on the Russian side only to find that victory deprived them of their best guarantee of autonomy. Hemmed in by Russian territory on three sides, their room for maneuver was virtually closed down. As part of her policy of crushing autonomous regions on the imperial frontier, Catherine ordered an attack on the Sich by her troops returning from the Turkish campaign. The ataman and most of the leaders were arrested and exiled. The host numbering 14,619 men was scattered. Some fled to the Crimea. A strong contingent made one last bid for freedom, relocating on Ottoman territory at the mouth of the Danube. Others were settled in the newly acquired "empty lands" between the Bug and Dnieper. The rest were reorganized ten years later as state Cossacks into the Black Sea Host and settled on the Kuban to guard the restless north Caucasus frontier.[142] The Sich was no more, but the exploits of the Zaporozhian Cossacks acquired enormous symbolic significance in the later formation of a Ukrainian identity.[143]

---

[142] Kaiuk Svitlana Mikolavna, "Zadunais'ka Sich (1775–1828)," Kandidat dissertation, Dnieprpetrovsk University, 1999. I am grateful to Andryi Posonko for providing me with a copy.

[143] John Armstrong, "Myth and History in Ukrainian Consciousness," in Peter J. Potichnyi et al. (eds.), Ukraine and Russia in their Historical Encounter (Edmonton: Canadian Institute of Ukrainian Studies, 1992), p. 132, writes of "an enduring myth of a savior from the frontier" dating from the time of Khmel'nits'ky.

As we have seen with the security provided by the key fortresses on the Black Sea, colonization entered a new phase. Administratively, Ukraine was divided between two governor-generalships, Little Russia and New Russia. The Cossack leadership (*starshina*) was assimilated into the Russian nobility, while the rank-and-file were allowed personal freedom. The Crimea was annexed in 1783 following time-honored methods of armed intervention in support of a Russian candidate as khan. The occupation was prepared by Potemkin's innovative policy of persuading the Greek and Armenian population, by promising extensive privileges, to abandon the khanate for resettlement in Russian territory. Once the territory was integrated into New Russia, the Tatar landowning class was offered Russian noble rank; religious toleration was extended to the Muslim population. These concessions fell on barren ground. In the largest single forced migration of the eighteenth century, over 200,000 Crimean Tatars left their homeland for the Ottoman Empire, many settling in the Dobrudja, contributing to its character as a frontier shatter zone. Undaunted, Potemkin opened the doors wide to immigration. State peasants, ex-soldiers, and Old Believers joined Christian refugees arriving from the Ottoman Empire.[144] Potemkin was indifferent to the social and ethnic origins of the new arrivals. Greeks, Jews, Armenians, Ukrainians, as well as Russians, and "settlers under Muslim law" (*poseliane magometan-skogo zakona*) like the Nogai, rubbed shoulders with the remaining Tatar population, which numbered only one-third of the original population. The nomadic Buddhist Kalmyks were organized as a separate group.[145] The lands of the departing Tatars were redistributed among the new settlers. Peter's dreams of uniting the great river system linking the Baltic and the Black Sea and of securing the southern frontier had been realized.

The Caucasian isthmus

The geographic frontier between the northern subzone of the Caucasian isthmus and the Pontic steppe was formed by the Terek River, which divided the pasture land from the piedmont of the slopes of the Caucasus

---

[144] Roger Bartlett, *Human Capital. The Settlement of Foreigners in Russia, 1762–1804* (Cambridge University Press, 1979), pp. 81 ff, 126 ff; de Madariaga, *Russia in the Age of Catherine*, pp. 361–66; Marc Raeff, "The Style of Russia's Imperial Policy and Prince G. A. Potemkin," in Gerald N. Grob (ed.), *Statesmen and Statecraft of the Modern West. Essays in Honor of Dwight E. Lee and H. Donaldson Jordan* (Barre, MA: Barre Publishing, 1967), pp. 1–51.

[145] E. I. Druzhinina, *Iuzhnaia Ukraina v 1800–1825 gg.* (Moscow: Nauka, 1970), pp. 72–76.

range where nomadic migrations over the millennium had created a shatter zone of great social and ethnic complexity. The main range of the Caucasus Mountains divided the northern and southern subzones, but did not serve as a barrier. The mountains provided natural defenses for the defeated but unvanquished and proved difficult to subjugate, but they could be flanked along the coastal plains of the Black and Caspian seas. The traditional invasion path to the south Caucasus was along the western shores of the Caspian, where south of Baku the Araxes and Kura river valleys offered a highly favorable environment for herding and raising silk. Generations of conquerors from the north had wintered in the fertile plains flanked by high mountains with abundant summer pasturages. Once densely populated, as the remains of irrigation systems testify, the fertile steppe had by the eighteenth century reverted to grazing lands for nomads who migrated every winter from Iran. A typical frontier agglomeration, the Shahsevan tribal group was composed of Turkmen with a strong admixture of Kurds and other indigenous peoples, subjected by various rulers to "systematic policies of breakdown, dispersal, re-groupment and resettlement."[146] In the late nineteenth century, they were forbidden to cross the Russian–Iranian frontier because of their clashes with Cossacks.[147] But by this time another kind of transborder migration was taking place: migrant industrial workers who were to play a key role in the revolutionary movements in Russian and Iranian Azerbaijan.

The main prize in the frontier wars in the south Caucasus was the borderland of Azerbaijan. In contrast to the rest of Iran, Azerbaijan was relatively densely populated and possessed a high percentage of fertile agricultural land and a flourishing silk industry. The dominant language was Turkic, with Persian being spoken only in the cities by the upper classes, though Christian Armenians and Nestorians made up a substantial part of the population. The main center of urban life was Tabriz, which dated back to Turkic-Mongol times. No longer the Safavid capital by the end of the sixteenth century, it remained the most populous city in Iran into the twentieth century and an alternative center of power.[148]

---

[146] Richard Tapper, *Frontier Nomads of Iran. A Political and Social History of the Shahsevan* (Cambridge University Press, 2006), pp. 72–73.

[147] "Baku," *Entsiklopedicheskii Slovar'*, vol. IV, p. 772.

[148] James D. Clark, *Provincial Concerns. A Political History of the Iranian Province of Azerbbiajan, 1848–1906* (Costa Mesa, CA: Mazda, 2006), pp. 11–12, 58–61, 79–82. See also Touraj Atabaki, *Azerbaijan. Ethnicity and the Struggle for Power in Iran* (London: Tauris, 2000).

The Ottoman–Iranian–Russian duel

There were roughly three phases in the Ottoman–Iranian–Russian struggle over the borderlands of the Caucasian isthmus: from the middle
decades to the end of the sixteenth century, when Russia was forced
temporarily to withdraw from the competition; from the early sixteenth
to the early seventeenth centuries, when the Ottomans and Iranians
partitioned Azerbaijan after several long and costly wars; and from the
early eighteenth to the early nineteenth centuries, when Russia returned
to the region in force, virtually eliminating Iran from the competition,
driving back the Ottomans, and leaving the Muslim (Azeri) and Christian
(Armenian) peoples divided between Orthodox Russia and the two
Islamic powers. This rather overly neat chronology does not always
apply to the history of the indigenous peoples. Periodic devastation and
depopulation of the small Christian principalities and kingdoms and the
Muslim khanates followed a different rhythm, contributing to the long
delay in the emergence of national independence movements and the final
achievement of statehood in the late twentieth century.

In their campaigns to conquer the Caucasian isthmus, the Ottoman
rulers were motivated by commercial and religious interests. They aimed
to control the overland silk trade from Iran and the annual pilgrimage
routes from Trans Caspia, and to establish contact with their Sunni
Muslim brethren among the Uzbeks on the northeastern flank of their
Shi'ite rivals in Iran. The Russian conquest of Astrakhan in 1557 and the
Iranian bid for power in the rich province of Azerbaijan threatened to cut
them off. Finally, the Ottoman rulers sought to stabilize the turbulent
frontier with Iran. They were fully aware of the potential power of movements originating in frontier provinces. After all, the empire traced its
roots to the old Byzantine–Persian frontier where as holy warriors (*gazi*)
the Ottoman Turks had launched their drive to the west.

Under the Safavids, the qizilbashi were never completely absorbed into
the older social and political structures, and retained much of their semi-
nomadic frontier character. Along the old frontier zone between the
Ottomans and the Iranians, which could be traced back beyond the
Byzantine–Seljuk to the Roman–Sasanian period, the religious fervor of
the qizilbashi provoked revolts among the Anatolian peasants, enraged the
orthodox Sunni administration in Constantinople, and led to repeated
clashes with regular Ottoman forces.[149] In the battle of Chaldiran (1514)

---

[149] Jean-Louis Bacque-Grammont, "L'apogée de l'empire ottoman. Les événements
(1512–1606)," in Robert Mantran (ed.), *Histoire de l'empire ottoman* (Paris: Fayard,
1989), pp. 142–43.

between the Ottoman and Safavid forces the firepower of the Janissary Corps musketeers and artillery destroyed the qizilbashi cavalry, and the Ottomans briefly occupied Tabriz. The defeat revealed the weakness of a military force inspired by religious disdain for firearms and weakened the shah's quasi-divine authority. In the wake of defeat, as we have seen, the Safavids took their first steps toward the building of a more stable secular monarchy based on institutions rather than on the ephemeral enthusiasm of the qizilbashi chiliasts.[150]

In the great duel along their ill-defined frontier, the Ottomans and Iranians vied with one another for the allegiance of the Kurdish tribes. The Kurdish tribes had been rapidly Islamicized and integrated into the Arab culture world before two major Mongol invasions in the thirteenth and fourteenth centuries devastated their homeland. They remained in a highly fragmented and weakened condition, and were easily absorbed into the Safavid Empire. When Shah Ismail's centralizing policies antagonized them, they initially welcomed Ottoman proposals to employ them as a counterweight to the qizilbashi along the frontier. Then, in the character-istic style of a frontier people, the Kurds exploited their intermediary position by shifting their allegiance in order to extract maximum conces-sions from both the Ottomans and Iranians. Throughout the sixteenth and seventeenth centuries, the Ottomans proved to be much more flexible than their rivals in granting the Kurds privileges and a high degree of autonomy. They also preserved and consolidated the power of the Kurdish nobility. They skillfully varied their administrative practices depending on the availability of land for distribution, and the strategic significance and internal strength of each tribe or confederacy; those closest to the Iranian frontier generally enjoyed the greatest autonomy. As the Ottomans improved their frontier security they cut back on Kurdish autonomy.[151] The opportunistic tactics of the Kurds enabled them to preserve tribal autonomy in both the Ottoman and Iranian empires, but at the cost of achieving unity in an independent state.

In the first phase of their duel with the Ottomans lasting to the end of the sixteenth century, the Iranians managed to hold on to the rich silk-producing eastern provinces of the southern Caucasus. After almost fifty years of warfare, they also joined with the Ottomans to overwhelm the three indigenous Georgian kingdoms, and in 1555 divided the south

---

[150] Roger Savory, *Iran under the Safavids* (Cambridge University Press, 1980), pp. 37–49.

[151] Hakan Özoğlu, "State–Tribe Relations. Kurdish Tribalism in the 16th and 17th Century Ottoman Empire," *British Journal of Middle Eastern Studies* 23(1) (May 1996): 5–27, includes a valuable analysis of the complex tribal structure of the Kurds; Hakan Özoğlu, *Kurdish Notables and the Ottoman State. Evolving Identities, Competing Loyalties and Shifting Boundaries* (Albany, NY: State University of New York Press, 2004), pp. 43–67.

Caucasus into spheres of influence. The Ottomans then turned their attention to the burgeoning Russian threat.

The first Russian incursion into the complex frontier of the south Caucasus proved to be premature. After the conquest of the khanate of Astrakhan in 1556, Ivan IV took the first steps in penetrating the region. He supported the English Muscovy Company in their exploration of an alternative all-water route along the extensive Russian river system from the Baltic to the Caspian in order to reap a share of the rich Iranian silk trade. He married a Kabardian princess and established a Cossack settlement and fort on the Terek River in support of his father-in-law in the eastern Caucasus. By the sixteenth century, the lands along the Terek and Kuban rivers had already been settled by free Cossacks. They were Slavic settlers from the north engaged in small-scale agriculture, cattle raising, and fishing. Occasionally they entered the service of the Muscovite princes. Mainly, they engaged in launching raids by land and sea against the local tribes, Ottoman and Iranian commercial travelers, and diplomatic missions. In many ways they resembled the Uskoks of the Triplex Confinium in their way of life and the ecological niche they occupied on the frontiers. They intermarried with women from the tribes and welcomed recruits into their ranks from the indigenous populations, so that the line between Cossack and native was blurred and in some cases effaced. Thomas Barrett has best defined them as "the stateless people who came into being in the interstices between states . . . Muscovy/Russia, Iran and the Ottoman Empire. They were defined by what they were not – servitors or subjects."[152]

Although the Cossacks raided and plundered one another, they appeared to have more in common than with the imperial forces that sought to subdue them. Their nomadic life followed the seasonal movement of herds, ignoring sovereign boundaries and state institutions.[153] Through the customary institution of *kunak/kunichestvo*, the mountain people and the Cossacks performed similar services for one another, such as mediators, bounty-hunters, traders, and escorts. Like other free agents in complex frontier zones, they took casual oaths of loyalty and submission only to renounce them when a better opportunity arose. State systems found it difficult to co-opt the elites of the mountain peoples because

---

[152] Thomas M. Barrett, *At the Edge of Empire. The Terek Cossacks and the North Caucasus Frontier, 1700–1860* (Boulder, CO: East European Monographs, 1999), p. 19.

[153] George A. Bournetunian, "The Ethnic Composition and the Socio-economic Condition of Eastern Armenia in the First Half of the Nineteenth Century," in Ronald Grigor Suny (ed.), *Transcaucasia, Nationalism and Social Change. Essays in the History of Armenia, Azerbaizhan and Georgia*, rev. edn (Ann Arbor, MI: University of Michigan Press, 1996), p. 76.

of the fragmented character of political authority among the clans.[154] The Cossacks not only raided and plundered Russian caravans and merchants, but participated in the major social rebellions of the seventeenth century. Up to 1720, they resisted formal subordination to Russian authority (the governor of Astrakhan). Long after that date their lands were a refuge for fugitives, the most famous of whom appeared under the rule of Catherine the Great. The Cossack rebel, Emelian Pugachev, was the last of the pretenders to the throne, claiming to be her murdered husband Peter III.

It was partly in order to break the connection between Ivan IV and Kabardia and to forestall a Russian–Iranian alliance against them that the Ottomans launched a campaign to reconquer Astrakhan in 1569 with the aim of building a Don–Volga canal across the steppe. Success would have meant breaking the Iranian monopoly over contacts with the English Muscovy Company and keeping open the commercial and pilgrimage routes to their Sunni co-religionists in Trans Caspia. Ottoman forces successfully expelled the Russians from Kabardia with the assistance of their nomadic allies, the Nogai, but failed to achieve their larger strategic aims. Ironically, they were hampered by their unpredictable Crimean Tatar ally, Devlet Giray, who was worried about a strong Ottoman presence on his flank. He preferred to send his cavalry off to raid and burn the suburbs of Moscow, which contributed little to the Ottoman cause. At this point, events demonstrated dramatically the overlapping and tangled connections between the Pontic, Caucasian, and Baltic frontiers. The Russians were able to preserve their position at Astrakhan – the southern hinge of the all-water route Ivan sought to secure between the Caspian and the Baltic – only because of the rivalry between the Crimean Tatars and the Nogai, the attacks on the Tatar rear by the Zaporozhian Cossacks, and the Ottoman preoccupation with the war against Safavid Iran.[155]

Ottoman expansion in the Caucasus reached its apogee in 1590 when, after a thirteen-year war, they drove the Iranians out of the region and reached the Caspian Sea. It was a Pyrrhic victory. Their communication lines were stretched over the wild terrain of the Caucasus Mountains, and were exposed to guerrilla warfare and raiding by local chieftains. Moreover, the Iranians, at the very nadir of their power, were about to undergo one of their periodic revivals under their greatest Safavid ruler, Shah Abbas (1588–1629).

---

[154] Chantal Lemercier-Quelquejay, "Cooptation of Elites of Kabarda and Daghestan in the Sixteenth Century," in Marie Bennigson Broxup (ed.), *The North Caucasus Barrier. The Russian Advance towards the Muslim World* (London: Hurst, 1992), pp. 18–44.

[155] Carl Max Kortepeter, *Ottoman Imperialism during the Reformation. Europe and the Caucasus* (New York University Press, 1973), pp. 28–29, 32, 45.

The Iranian revival, which inaugurated the second phase of the struggle over the south Caucasus complex frontier, imposed a crushing burden on the indigenous population. The wars of the sixteenth century had plunged Georgia into a long economic decline; the wars of the seventeenth century almost led to its extinction. Already divided into three kingdoms and several principalities, Georgia underwent further political fragmentation, while the nobility lost its rights to the local princes. In order to survive at all between the grinding millstones of the Ottoman and Iranian empires, the Georgian princes sought to ally themselves first with one then with another of the competing powers. It was natural for the Christian Georgians to turn first to Russia. But by the end of the sixteenth century, Moscow was beginning to enter its own "time of troubles" and could offer only vague promises of support. The king of the Georgian kingdom of Kakhetia lamented in 1596: "Sixteen years have passed since I grasped the tail of the Muscovite Sovereign's coat, but I have seen no help."[156] The Georgian princes then enlisted the aid of Shah Abbas, hoping to free themselves from Ottoman domination. This proved to be a very bad bargain. Abbas played the rival Georgians against one another. He placed his own candidates on the thrones of the local Muslim khanates. When faced with a rebellion of the Khakhetians in eastern Georgia, he ordered a massive deportation of the population, replacing them with Turkmen nomads.

A second partition of the south Caucasus between the Ottoman and Iranian empires in the 1620s failed to snuff out internal resistance to either. Punitive reprisals increased in ferocity and the entire economic structure of western Georgia collapsed. The subjugated Georgian population divided their allegiances. In the west, much of the reduced population was Islamicized; in the east, many of the local leaders and their auxiliaries were forced to enter Safavid military service as slave soldiers. They were effectively deployed in Iranian wars against the Afghans along the Trans Caspian frontier where they acquired a formidable reputation. A few Georgian leaders placed their hopes on distant Moscow and, in extremis, voluntarily emigrated to the north. At the same time, the Armenian population was also severely reduced. During the early seventeenth century, a large-scale emigration inaugurated the Armenian diaspora. Statistics for this period are hard to come by. But what may have been an Armenian majority in eastern Armenia in the mid-fourteenth

---

[156] Ronald Grigor Suny, *The Making of the Georgian Nation*, 2nd edn (Bloomington, IN: Indiana University Press, 1994), pp. 46–53, quotation on p. 49.

century had shrunk by the early nineteenth century to about 20 percent of the population in the region where Muslims numbered 80 percent.[157]

The third period of the struggle over the complex frontier in the southern Caucasus began in the early eighteenth century. By this time the long-term effects of internal resistance and external wars on the frontiers had led to a shift in the balance of power in the region. In comparison with Russian power, the Ottomans underwent a relative decline and the Iranians a precipitous decline. Although Peter the Great had suffered defeat on the Danubian frontier by the Ottomans in 1711, he treated it as a temporary setback to his ambitions in the Caucasus. Two related concerns informed his policy. First, in the north Caucasus he sought an ally among the mountaineers to flank the nomads of the Nogai horde who had raided deeply into the Volga provinces during Peter's ill-fated campaign on the Danube. Second, he explored the possibility of extending Russian influence in the south Caucasus. He launched an expedition to occupy the northern provinces of Iran as part of his general policy to make Russia the intermediary in the west–east trade by realizing the old dream of Ivan IV: to control the all-water route from the Baltic to the Caspian. One of Peter's most active promoters of expansion to the east, Artem Volynskii, reported from Isfahan that Iran was in a parlous condition, was fearful of a Russian attack, and incapable of repressing domestic rebellion. He pressured the Iranians to granting Russian merchants the right to trade and to buy raw silk for export anywhere in the country. Peter appointed him governor of Astrakhan with instructions to prepare an invasion of Iran. He sent intelligence officers to reconnoiter Gilan Province and urged Peter to incite the Caucasian tribes to throw off Iranian rule. When the Kabardians responded by swearing one of those ephemeral oaths to the tsar, Volynskii enthusiastically called them "the most poverty stricken and best warriors" he had ever seen in the region.[158]

The Russian invasion was triggered by the news in 1722 that the Afghans had driven the shah from Isfahan, and the Ottomans were on the march against a weakened Iran. It was clear to Peter that the Turks would use the occasion to reoccupy the southern Caucasus, cut off the Russian penetration of Iran, and jeopardize Russia's commercial and strategic position all along the Caucasian and Pontic frontiers. Personally leading the Iranian expedition, Peter offered to assist the beleaguered shah or whoever was in power in return for a cession of the Caspian provinces. He instructed his agents to pressure local merchants to reorient their trade to Russia. He encouraged the settlement of

---

[157] Bournetunian, "The Ethnic Composition," pp. 77–78.
[158] Solov'ev, *Istoriia Rossii*, vol. XVIII, p. 655.

Armenian and other Christians in the provinces of Gilan and Mazanderan. The Armenian patriarchs urged Peter to liberate them from Iranian rule and to take their flock under his protection. Peter hesitated. He was fearful that this would set a precedent for a religious war, inciting the Ottomans to respond to appeals from the Lezghians and other Muslims to take them under the sultan's protection. The invading Ottomans might also respond by occupying Iranian ports on the southern shores of the Caspian.[159]

Iranian resistance rapidly crumbled. The Kabardians welcomed the Russian forces. One of the local Georgian kings, Vakhtang, who had reluctantly converted to Islam, renounced the faith and sought to raise the Georgian and Armenian Christians against their Iranian overlord. He vainly appealed to Peter as "the indistinguishable lamp at the grave of Christ and the crown of the four patriarchs and himself – the descendant of David and Solomon."[160] The Russian army successfully occupied the coastal plain, but was unable to penetrate the mountains and rescue Vakhtang and his rebels from the advancing Ottomans. Vakhtang and a thousand of the Georgian elite fled to Russia and entered Russian service.

The victorious rivals agreed to partition the Caucasus, this time at the expense of Iran. The Treaty of Constantinople in 1724 gave the Ottomans all the Georgian kingdoms and western Azerbaijan, while leaving the Russians in control of the west and south coast of the Caspian. Once again, however, neither of the victorious sides could maintain its position. The Russians were plagued by the persistent problems of lengthy supply routes exposed to attacks by mountaineers and disease in the malaria-infested lowlands, which carried off 100,000 Russians between 1722 and 1735.[161] The main victims were, as usual, the indigenous peoples, who were forced to throw in their lot with one or another of the rival empires and then be exploited or abandoned by them. A periodic revival of Iran, this time under Shah Tahmasp but really managed by Nadir Shah, confronted the Russians with the alternative of a large-scale campaign to maintain their position or withdraw. Peter's successors decided to withdraw. By the treaty of 1732 the Russians renounced all their authority south of the Kura River. Three years later, Nadir Shah had driven their forces back to the Terek line. Throughout the 1730s, 1740s, and 1750s the

---

[159] G. G. Paichadze, *Russko-Gruzinskie politicheskie otnosheniia v pervoi polovine XVIII veka* (Tblisi: Sabchuta Sakartvelo, 1970), pp. 35–49. Peter's conscience bothered him to the extent that his last message to the sultan before his death included the words, "it is impossible for us by virtue of being Christian to refuse [our] protection of Christians." Solov'ev, *Istoriia Rossii*, vol. XVIII, p. 656.

[160] Solov'ev, *Istoriia Rossii*, vol. XVIII, p. 657.

[161] Muriel Atkin, "Russian Expansion in the Caucasus to 1813," in Michael Rywkin (ed.), *Russian Colonial Expansion to 1917* (London: Mansell, 1988), p. 151.

hapless Georgian principalities of Imeretia and Karteli vainly appealed for aid. The Russians continued to rebuff them for fear the sultan would unleash the Crimean Tatars against their exposed Pontic frontier. Another half a century would pass before the Russians were able to reenter the south Caucasus in force.

In the meantime, the see-saw struggle between the Ottomans and Iranians raged until the death of Nadir Shah in 1747. His vigorous campaigning had expelled the Ottomans from the south Caucasus, enabling his east Georgian royal clients to undertake a rebuilding of a Georgian state. But the depredations of the Iranians continued to disrupt Georgian economic life. It became increasingly clear to the rulers of Georgia that their best hope for stability and a permanent revival lay in the north. Unfortunately for them, the return of the Russians to the region throughout most of the eighteenth century was marked by repeated disappointments and betrayals.

The most lasting religious consequence of the three-way struggle for the Caucasus was the spread of militant Islam. In 1717, Sultan Murad IV apparently permitted or encouraged the infiltration of the Sufi order of the Naqshbandi into the east Caucasus under Ottoman control. They gradually won over elements of the Chechen, Daghestani, and Cherkess people. These conversions had momentous consequences when the Russians attempted to conquer the north Caucasus in the first half of the nineteenth century.[162]

Russian advance

The Russian advance into the Caucasian isthmus gained momentum under the reign of Catherine II. Her policies, inspired and shaped by Prince Potemkin, proceeded on two levels. North of the mountains his aim was to pacify and incorporate the tribes; south of the mountains it was to resolve the problems of the complex frontier by driving out the Ottomans and Iranians, and consolidating Georgian and Armenian states under Russian tutelage. Religious solidarity was never an end in itself.

---

[162] There is some disagreement over the introduction of the Sufi among the mountain tribes. Cf. Bennigsen, "Peter the Great," p. 318, who, based on Ottoman archives, is cautious about the sultan's role; F. A. Shcherbin, *Istoriia kubanskogo kazach'iago voiska*, 2 vols. (Krasnodar: Sovetskaia Kuban, 1912), vol. I, pp. 26–27, on the basis of Russian archives states that Murad IV ordered the Crimean khans to spread Islam among the Caucasian tribes without mentioning the Naqshbandi and that the Cherkess retained some pagan practices; Anna Zelkina, *In Quest for God and Freedom. Sufi Responses to the Russian Advance in the North Caucasus* (New York University Press, 2000), pp. 100–1, also using Russian archives, is the most comprehensive study of the Naqshbandi and the penetration of Islam into the Caucasus, but dates the introduction of the Naqshbandi teachings in Daghestan from Azerbaijan to the early nineteenth century.

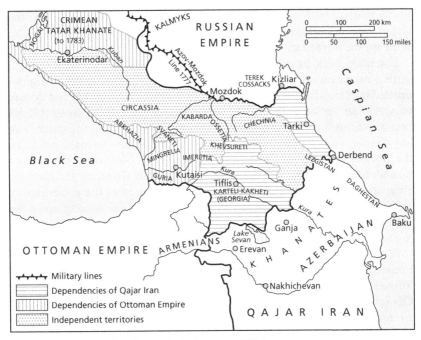

Map 4.3 The Caucasian isthmus, *c.* 1790

Russian protection of the Christian population was highly opportunistic and was never allowed to interfere with official policy.[163]

Potemkin proceeded against the Kabardians in the northeast more systematically than any of his predecessors. He sought to build up the Caucasian Line defenses to protect the Russian settlements against both Ottoman and mountaineer attacks. He convinced Catherine to employ former "loyal" Zaporozhian Cossacks to form a Black Sea host to help fight the Ottomans on the Danubian frontier. In 1792, they were resettled on the right bank of the Kuban as part of Potemkin's strategy to create a Black Sea Cordon Line against the constant raids of the Cherkess. Their numbers were swelled by a large influx of legal and illegal migrants from the borderlands stretching from Lithuania and Poland to Ukraine. As in the past, landowners attempted to recover runaway serfs, while local officials rejected some of their claims as exaggerated. The immigrants represented many non-Russians, including Jews, Romanians, Greeks,

---

[163] Muriel Atkin, *Russia and Iran, 1780–1828* (Minneapolis, MN: University of Minnesota Press, 1980), pp. 24, 29–31.

Turks, and Tatars. In 1808, in one of those typical shifts of allegiance by frontiersmen, 500 former Zaporozhian Cossacks returned from the Ottoman Empire, where they had fled after the abolition of the Sich, to settle on the Kuban as colonists.[164]

Potemkin built new forts, garrisoned them with retired soldiers, and settled state peasants around them. He distributed land grants to impoverished nobles. Many Kabardians reacted by pulling up stakes and fleeing to Ottoman territory or to the more remote mountain areas. Under pressure from the large numbers of Russian troops and in the absence of any alternative external source of support, others chose to make peace. In the frontier style of subjugation, the Kabardian chiefs were required to take an oath of loyalty, pay tribute, and to provide livestock and food for Russian troops. They pledged to refrain from opposing the settlement of their countrymen on the Caucasian Military Line. The Russians used the opportunity to encourage migration to the Russian side in order to weaken the unity and break down the hostility of the Kabardian elite.[165]

It was only in the early 1780s that Catherine finally extended a protectorate over Georgia. The strategic key to the Russian advance was the fortress of Vladikavkaz. Founded in 1784 as the northern terminus of the Georgian Military Highway, it became the model for the construction of strong points around which Kabardians and then Ossetians could resettle under the protection of the Russian Empire.[166] The Georgian Military Highway was built through the mountains to provide a strategic and commercial link between Russian territory and embattled Georgia. But even Catherine discovered that the Russians could not maintain their commitments to Georgia under pressure from the Ottomans occupying the western shores of the Black Sea. The evacuation of their troops in 1787 and again in 1797 resulted in harsh punitive incursions by the Iranians.

Once the new Qajar dynasty took power in Iran, they sought to restore the frontiers of the Safavid dynasty at its height, including the south Caucasus. Their chroniclers interpreted the campaigns of the first of the Qajar shahs, Aga Muhammed Khan, as a restoration of the "natural frontiers of Iranshahr" – which meant not only the Caucasian khanates, but also the principalities of Afghanistan, Central Asia, the province of Ottoman Iraq, all the Kurdish regions, and the islands of the Persian Gulf.[167]

---

[164] Shcherbin, *Istoriia kubanskogo*, vol. II, pp. 40–41, 60–65.
[165] Atkin, "Russian Expansion," pp. 157–58.
[166] Barrett, *At the Edge of Empire*, pp. 19, 150.
[167] Firoozeh Kashani-Sabet, *Frontier Fictions. Shaping the Iranian Nation, 1804–1946* (Princeton University Press, 1999), pp. 209–10; Abbas Amanat, *Pivot of the Universe. Nasir Al-Din Shah and the Iranian Monarchy, 1831–1896* (Berkeley, CA: University of California Press, 1997), p. 4.

In his first contact with the Russians in 1781, Aga Muhammed Khan forced them out of a commercial base they had set up on the southeast coast of the Caspian. Within five years he twice invaded Gilan province, whose ruler supported trading relations with Russia. By occupying Tehran and making it his capital, he shifted the locus of power in Iran closer to his tribal homeland along the northwest frontier and signaled his intention to center his military operations on the south Caucasus. Aga Muhammed laid claim to Georgia as heir to the Safavid legacy: "as most of the provinces of Persia have come into our possession now, you must, according to ancient law, consider Georgia part of the empire ..."[168] His campaign in the south Caucasus in 1795 spread terror among the Christian population of Georgia and Armenia. He occupied, sacked, and burned Tiflis. The Georgian king, Irakli II, appealed to Catherine II for help. Preoccupied with affairs in Poland and the prospect of war with the Ottoman Empire, Catherine approved only a limited intervention with instructions to its commander, V. A. Zubov, "to give the Ottoman Porte no reason for concern or alarm."[169] The Russians lacked the means and possibly the desire to carry out an annexationist policy. Zubov followed Peter the Great's campaign trail along the Caspian coast as a way of demonstrating Russia's interest in protecting its commercial interests and keeping the south Caucasus free from domination by either the Qajars or the Ottomans.

Paul I fashioned a more coherent plan for Russian influence in the south Caucasus aimed at creating a federation of states under Russian protection which would spare Russia from intervening militarily in the region. It proved to be unrealistic. The rivalries among the Muslim khanates and between them and the Christian population could not be settled without *force majeure* applied from the outside, and the Russians were still unwilling to provide it. The Qajars showed no such reluctance. Exploiting the fragmentation of local authority, Aga Muhammed Khan renewed his incursions. After his assassination, his successor, Fath Ali Shah, kept up the pressure on Georgia to submit to Iranian rule. His hand forced, Paul I finally authorized the incorporation of Georgia into the Russian Empire, but agreed to retain the king. The arrangement was upset when Georgii XII, who proved to be the

---

[168] Gavin Hambly, "Aga Muhhamed Khan," in *Cambridge History of Iran*, vol. 7, pp. 119–28, quotation on p. 128.

[169] N. S. Kiniapina, *Kavkaz i Sredniaia Aziia vo vneshnei politike Rossii. Vtoraia polovina XVIII–80e gody XIX v.* (Moscow: Izd. Moskovskogo universiteta, 1984), p. 92, citing N. F. Dubrovin, *Istoriia voiny i vladychestva russkikh na Kavkaze*, 3 vols. (St. Petersburg: Departmenta udelov, 1871), vol. III, p. 80.

last Georgian king, died and Paul was assassinated. In the fall of 1801 the new tsar, Alexander I, abolished the reigning dynasty, following the advice of the chief administrator of the Caucasus, General K. F. Knorring, who believed that the Georgians were incapable of defending or governing themselves.

The difficulties of integrating Georgia into the empire bear some resemblance to the Polish case, although resistance in Georgia was not so strong or well organized. The Georgian nobility, like the Polish, had traditionally enjoyed far more privileges than their Russian counterparts. And like the Poles, too, they could boast of a long history of independence against fearsome odds that at times came close to overwhelming them. Christianity came to Georgia earlier than to Russia and the Church was autocephalous when Georgia entered the empire. A long literary tradition stretched back to the medieval period, and the Georgian elite in the late eighteenth century kept in touch with trends in Paris. The Russian attempts to integrate the nobility were, as in the Kingdom of Poland, erratic and depended even more heavily on the personal preferences of Russian military administrators on the spot.[170] In order to consolidate their rule, the Russians recognized the feudal rights of the Georgian nobles and co-opted them into the Russian nobility. Although there were some signs of discontent arising from losses in their economic and political privileges, most of the noble elite took advantage of opportunities to enter Russian universities and government service. A modest literary renaissance centered on several Georgian periodicals in the 1820s and 1830s. Only a small number were attracted by liberal sentiments and established personal contacts with Decembrist exiles in the Caucasus.

In contrast to the Kingdom of Poland, the local military commanders in the Caucasus often took advantage of the distance from the center and difficulties of communication to take independent action. Firouzeh Mostashari has characterized two tendencies among these tsarist administrators: "the integrationists," who sought to undertake a rapid and forceful assimilation of the Caucasian borderlands; and the "localists," who recognized the importance of local customs and traditions, acted

[170] The following is based on Stephen F. Jones, "Russian Imperial Administration and the Georgian Nobility. The Georgian Conspiracy of 1832," *Slavonic and East European Review* 65(1) (January 1987): 53–76. For the early history of Georgia, see David Marshall Lang, *The Georgians* (New York: Praeger, 1966), esp. ch. 5 on the "Georgian Feudal Monarchy," and ch. 7 on "Literature and Learning." For a clear account of the background to the conspiracy, see David Marsall Lang, *The Last Years of the Georgian Monarchy (1668–1832)* (New York: Columbia University Press, 1967).

more cautiously and judiciously while moving toward the same goal.[171] General Prince Paul Tsitsianov (Tsitishvili), a Russified Georgian noble who held the titles Inspector of the Caucasian Line, Chief Administrator of the Caucasus, and Military Governor of Astrakhan (1802–1806), was a terrifying example of an integrationist, denigrating the Muslim population as "treacherous Asiatic scum." By contrast, Baron Grigorii Rosen, Chief Administrator from 1831 to 1837, favored working with the Muslim local elite.[172]

When in 1830 Paskevich shifted from a localist to an integrationist position, he inaugurated a Russifying policy. The replacement of Georgian by Russian administrators in the civil bureaucracy ignited a conspiracy in the early 1830s among a small but distinguished number of nobles. Unlike the contemporary Polish rising, it was an amateurish plot, isolated from the rest of the population, and quickly broken up. The punishments were milder than for the Poles, mainly taking the form of exile to distant parts of the empire. Several of the conspirators went on to become important poets of the Georgian Romantic movement. Among them were Alexander Chavchavadze, who lamented the loss of Georgian independence in his celebration of the country's heroic past; Grigol Orbeliani, who rose to be an adjutant general and, for a brief period, Viceroy of the Caucasus; Vakhtang Orbeliani, another mourner over the loss of independence; and the dramatist, G. Eristavi, who celebrated the rise of an urban trading class.[173] They provided the inspiration for a national school that nourished the Georgian Populist and Marxist revolutionaries at the end of the nineteenth century.

Once the decision had been taken to annex Georgia, Alexander I was determined to anchor its eastern flank in Daghestan and northern Azerbaijan. He proposed a modified version of Paul's federation scheme to attract the local Muslim khanates along the Caspian coast. His initiative failed to neutralize what was rapidly becoming a complex and violent resistance to Russian penetration of the region. Within two years of the annexation, uprisings had broken out among Ossetians along the Georgian Military Highway; a noble *fronde* had developed in Georgia supported by a member of the royal family and dozens of Georgian princes in exile in Iran. In Iran, Fath Ali Shah, emboldened by a treaty with Britain, declared that Georgia "is a part of the domain of the all-powerful

---

[171] Firouzeh Mostashari, *On the Religious Frontier. Tsarist Russia and Islam in the Caucasus* (London: Tauris, 2006), p. 20.

[172] Mostashari, *On the Religious Frontier*, pp. 14–15, 29–30.

[173] For brief biographies, see I. V. Abashidze (ed.), *Gruzinskia sovetskaia entsiklopediia* (Sak'art'velos SSR: mećnierebat'a academia, 1975–1987), pp. 265–66.

ruler of Iran."[174] Alexander embraced the view of his military commanders that the Iranians were treacherous, cunning, and inferior, and had to be driven out of the south Caucasus. He dismissed General Knorring as too conciliatory and replaced him with Prince Tsitsianov, who took a series of initiatives to consolidate Russia's strategic position. He improved the Georgian Military Highway and put pressure on local khans in northern Azerbaijan to recognize Russian suzerainty. Resistance to his arbitrary and often cruel measures, strategically justified as they may have been, spread among the local Muslim khanates. Caught in between two powerful neighbors, they tried in vain to play Iran against Russia in time-honored frontier tactics.[175]

Alarmed by the Russian policies and the spread of the Ossetian uprising, the shah declared war in 1804, proclaiming that Kabarda, Ossetia, Ingushetia, and Chechnia should belong to Iran. Once the fighting had begun he appealed for support from the peoples of the region.[176] The Muslim khans on the Caspian coast went over to the Iranian side, but failed to convince the mountaineers of Daghestan to follow them. The Ottomans, seeing a chance to divert the Russians from the Danubian front and recover their influence in the Caucasian borderlands, sent agents to stir up the tribes in Kabarda.[177] Shortly after the Russians were engaged with the Iranians, in 1806 the Ottoman sultan declared war. Russia simultaneously faced two rivals in the struggle over the Caucasian borderlands, both supported alternately by France and Britain, reflecting the changing constellation of European alliances during the Napoleonic Wars.

Russia emerged from a potentially dangerous situation with substantial gains due mainly to its military superiority over Ottoman and Iranian forces that had not yet completed their reforms of the army along European lines. The belated and grudging mediation of the British also played a part. London needed the Russians to devote their full energies to resisting Napoleon's final bid for European supremacy. The treaties of Bucharest in 1812 and Gulistan in 1813 secured Russia's position on both flanks of the Caucasian isthmus. At Bucharest, the Ottomans accepted the loss of Bessarabia and a number of fortresses on the Pontic frontier. But,

---

[174] *Akty sobrannye Kavkazskoiu arkheograficheskoiu kommisseiu. Arkhiv Glavnogo upravleniia namestnika kavkazskago*, 12 vols. (Tiflis: Kavkazskaia arkheograficheskaia kommissia, 1866–1904), vol. I, pp. 527, 693.

[175] Atkin, *Russia and Iran*, pp. 43, 61, 75, 94–95. During the war Alexander I rejected negotiations claiming that the Iranian claims were "mad." He insisted on the Aras River border because "this barrier is necessary to prevent the incursions of barbarian peoples who inhabit the land." *Ibid.*, p. 101.

[176] *Akty sobrannye*, vol. II, pp. 804–5, 807, 822.   [177] *Akty sobrannye*, vol. III, p. 651.

encouraged by French and British diplomats, they at first resisted any concessions to Russia in the Caucasus. In the end they agreed to recognize Russian's sovereignty over Georgia, Imeretia, Mingrelia, and Abkhazia, while the Russians agreed to return Anapa, Poti and Akhalkalaki which they had taken in the war. Although the Ottoman rulers did not reconcile themselves to these losses, they never again threatened the Russian position in the south Caucasus.

The Treaty of Gulistan officially transferred the northern khanates of Azerbaijan to Russia, including Baku, which was to become the center of the Russian oil industry in the nineteenth century, and the coastal plain with its important silk- and tea-producing plantations. Iran also recognized Russian sovereignty over Daghestan. The treaty also gave the Russians the exclusive right to maintain warships on the Caspian and it opened Iranian harbors to Russian merchant ships. Thus, Peter the Great's dream of a great commercial artery stretching from the Baltic to the Caspian was finally realized a century later. But the new land frontier with Iran remained ill-defined and porous, storing up problems for the future.

Annexation brought more Muslims into the Empire along with a substantial Armenian Christian population in Karabakh, creating the potential for ethnic conflict within Russia's new south Caucasian borderland. In the 1840s, the imperial administration confirmed the traditional privileges of the local Muslim elites and partially restored their confiscated property. Co-optation was carried out at the expense of the peasant population, both Christian and Muslim, who were kept in economic dependence on their former Iranian and Turkish landlords.[178] Ironically, Russian administrators generated some of the same ethnic and social conflicts between Muslim landlords and Christian peasants as had arisen under Ottoman administrators in Rumelia. Colonization was the second arm of imperial rule in the south Caucasus. Plans for settling Cossacks on the Iranian frontier were mooted as early as the 1830s. Sectarians constituted the first wave of settlers. By 1866 there were over 31,000 Russians in the region. In the 1880s, the government began to confiscate the pasture lands of the nomadic tribes and settle Russians on their land. The peak of colonization occurred during the viceroyalty of Prince G. S. Golitsyn (1896–1904) when Armenian and Muslim landlords were dispossessed in favor of Russians.[179]

[178] Vartan Gregorian, "The Impact of Russia on the Armenians and Armenia," in Wayne Vucinich (ed.), *Russia and Asia. Essays on the Influence of Russia on the Asian Peoples* (Stanford University Press, 1972), pp. 175–80.
[179] Gregorian, "The Impact of Russia," p. 184; Nicholas Breyfogle, *Heretics and Colonizers. Forging Russia's Empire in the South Caucasus* (Ithaca, NY: Cornell University Press,

The Treaty of Gulistan did little to discourage the shah and ruling elite of Iran from continuing to regard Georgia as an integral part of Iranshahr. They interpreted Russia's annexation of the last remaining independent Muslim khanates of the eastern Caucasus as a threat to Iranian dignity and security. Their views emerged most clearly in one of the great works of Iranian epic poetry, which defined the struggle over the Caucasian border-lands as one between two civilizations. The author was Mirza Abdul-quasim Qa'im-maqam Farahani, a high-ranking government official, descended from an old Safavid bureaucratic family that had helped to introduce Persian administrative and literary traditions into the Qajar state and court, particularly in Azerbaijan. His oft-repeated phrase "Russian intrusion into the 'Guarded Domains'" – the official title of the country in the Qajar period – became, in the words of the historian Abbas Amanat, "almost a slogan for defense of the homeland," and in particular its Azerbaijan frontiers. The poet-statesman associated the Russians with two legendary barbarian tribes, Gog and Magog, seeking to despoil the land. In opposing them, Qa'im-maqam proposed an inno-vative approach to jihad. Depending upon circumstances, the duty of the state, and specifically the Azerbaijan frontier government, was to "act like the wall of Iskandar" (Alexander the Great) or "attack like a lion."[180]

In 1826 Fath Ali-Shah opted for the latter course, egged on by the ambitious heir, Abbās Mīrzā. The ruling elite counted on the improved army trained in part by French and British officers. The Iranians were aware, too, that Russia's international position was vulnerable. Its nego-tiations with the Porte had reached a delicate stage on a host of questions arising from disputes over the interpretation of the Treaty of Bucharest with regard to the Danubian provinces, Serbia, and the Black Sea coast. Moreover, the British were subsidizing the Iranians, actively encouraging them to resist Russian diplomatic pressure to settle disputed frontier issues. The new tsar Nicholas I (1825–1855) had been shaken by the Decembrist revolt. The Caucasian army was engaged in repressing an uprising in Chechnia.[181] Russian rule over the khanates was also far from secure. It was based on a hybrid system of military supervision of the

---

2005); Nicholas Breyfogle, "The Politics of Colonization. Sectarians and Russian Orthodox Peasants in 19th Century Azerbaizhan," *Journal of Central Asian History* 1 (1996): 16–29.

[180] Abbas Amanat, "'Russian Intrusion into the Guarded Domain.' Reflections of a Qajar Statesman on European Expansion," *Journal of the American Oriental Society* 113(1) (January–March 1995): 39–41; Firoozeh Kashani-Sabet, "Fragile Frontiers. The Diminishing Domains of Qajar Iran," *International Journal of Middle East Studies* 29(2) (May 1997): 210–12.

[181] The best guide to these entanglements is O. B. Orlik, "Rossiia v vostochnyi krizis 20x godov," in Orlik *et al.* (eds.), *Istoriia vneshnei politiki*, pp. 189–228.

traditional administration of justice and tax-collecting by the khans. The Iranians were convinced that the time had come to recover their position in the south Caucasus. Once Abbās Mīrzā's army crossed the frontier, anti-Russian revolts broke out in three of the khanates.[182]

Despite a few initial successes, the Iranian offensive stalled. Tribal rivalries and a breakdown in military discipline contributed to a disastrous defeat. In Russia, once again differences surfaced over the conduct of the war between the more cautious Nesselrode and the army commander General Paskevich, a favorite of Nicholas I. Paskevich wanted to occupy the frontier provinces of Iranian Azerbaijan, not to annex them, but to extract a heavy indemnity from Iran. He also advocated the annexation of the khanates of Erevan and Nakhichevan. Once victorious, the Russians ended up compromising. The Treaty of Turkmanchai in 1828 was in its way as decisive a victory for Russia in its struggle over the borderlands with Iran as the Treaty of Kuchuk Kainardji had been in their struggle with the Ottomans.

The treaty provided for the cession of the khanates of Erevan and Nakhichevan to Russia. Iran was required to pay an indemnity within six months or else forfeit all the khanates of Azerbaijan to Russia. The subsidy was paid, thanks to a loan by the British who were increasingly alarmed by the Russian advance on the flank of India. The boundary line that split Azerbaijan was, nonetheless, strategic. The treaty had long-range economic and political effects. Deprived of some of its most productive provinces, the Iranian government was forced to take a number of financial measures that further impoverished the peasantry and ruined a large part of the urban population. The center of Iranian Azerbaijan, Tabriz, was particularly hard hit, and became a center of religious factionalism in the 1840s.[183]

Although the Treaty of Turkmanchai effectively expelled Iran from its last foothold in the south Caucasus, the Iranians appeared to have salvaged something. The Russians had recognized the right of the Crown Prince, Abbās Mīrzā, to the throne. Yet even here, there was a catch. By guaranteeing the hereditary line, Russia gained an excuse, if not a right, to intervene in Iranian politics at the highest level. Faint echoes of Poland in the eighteenth century might have been heard by those Iranians who had the wit to worry.

The demographic and economic consequences of the war were even more important for the future of Russia's Caucasian borderlands. After

[182] *Akty sobrannye*, vol. VI, p. 368.
[183] Tadeusz Swietochowski, *Russia and Azerbaizhan. A Borderland in Transition* (New York: Columbia University Press, 1995), pp. 6–8.

the Iranian defeat, over 40,000 Christian Armenians left Iran for Russian territory even though this meant significant financial losses for them. The emigration was part of the Russian plan, endorsed by Paskevich and developed by the famous diplomat-poet, A. S. Griboedov, to secure the region permanently for Russia. Paskevich ordered most of them to be settled in the annexed khanates of Erevan and Nakhichevan, "because of the particular desire to ensure the growth of the Christian population here." He assigned others to the district of Karabakh in northern Azerbaijan. In the absence of sufficient state lands in Nakhichevan, most of the Armenians ended up there as well. Yet the imperial government left Karabakh outside the Armenian province. This was a calculated move reinforced by administrative reorganizations of internal boundaries in 1840, 1844, 1849, 1862, 1868, 1875, and 1880, all designed to check regional and ethnic separatism and to prevent any nationality from becoming the "preponderant majority in any major province."[184]

When in the wake of the 1828 war an unknown number of Sunni Muslims left for the Ottoman Empire, the Azeri inhabitants of the khanates found themselves suddenly in the minority.[185] Discussions on how to reconcile the Armenian newcomers with the Muslims were recorded by Griboedov, who was later assassinated in Tehran. He did well to wonder. The Armenian enclave in Azerbaijan proved to be another ethnic time bomb on the borderlands, waiting to explode as it did in 1905, 1918–1920, and again in 1992. Later in the century, the Russians also became disillusioned with the Armenians as a Christian bulwark against Islam, accusing them of economic exploitation of the Georgians and alarmed by their growing nationalist agitation. The Treaty of Turkmanchai was also a landmark in the struggle over the Caucasian borderlands, marking an end to the threat of a common Iranian–Ottoman front against the Russians. No sooner had the treaty been signed in 1829 than Nicholas I ordered the occupation of the Danubian principalities, so beginning the Russo-Turkish War. The exhausted Iranians remained neutral. Another unintended result of the treaty was to turn the Qajars toward their Trans Caspian frontier, where they sought compensation for their losses in Azerbaijan by recovering the lost province of Herat. That would embroil them, as we shall see, in a prolonged conflict with the British.

---

[184] Gregorian, "The Impact of Russia," pp. 183–85.

[185] Mostashari, On the Religious Frontier, pp. 41–43; Sulejman Alijarly, "The Republic of Azerbaizhan. Notes on the State Borders in the Past and the Present," in John F. R. Wright et al., Transcaucasian Boundaries (New York: St. Martin's Press, 1995), pp. 126, 128.

The Russian conquest of the south Caucasus could not be consolidated without closing the frontier with the north Caucasus. North of the mountain chain the Russian advance against the Ottomans, with the Iranians only indirectly involved, had been forced to deal with the highly militarized frontier society that had evolved between the Terek Cossacks and the mountain peoples (Kabardians, Chechens, and others). It was only in 1824 that the Russian government officially enrolled the Terek Cossacks, obliging them to pay taxes and assume service obligations. When it forced them to participate in regular campaigning against the mountaineers, desertion became a serious problem. In the 1840s, the mountain leaders, particularly the legendary Shamil, rewarded Cossack deserters with important posts in military units, especially if they converted to Islam. The Russian authorities learned the hard way to distrust both their Cossacks and the auxiliary units recruited from mountaineers under their nominal suzerainty. Their policies of strengthening and consolidating the Caucasian Military Line were inconsistent on two levels. First, they oscillated between promoting and discouraging settlement of peasants and dissident religious groups in the region.[186] Then, they alternated between toleration and repression with respect to the customs and religious beliefs of the mountain people.[187]

In the north Caucasus, Russia pursued the same policy of colonization that had enabled it to consolidate its position in the adjacent frontiers of the Pontic steppe and Trans Caspia. By settling and protecting the agricultural population engaged in a mixed economy, the government achieved its aim of making the north Caucasus self-sufficient in grain. Before that the Cossacks had been obliged to rely on trade with the mountain people, who supplied them with agricultural products. For several centuries, their economic interdependence had kept the political situation in balance. In the 1840s and 1850s, when a sufficient number of state peasants had been settled in the north Caucasus, the region was able to provision the forts and Cossack stations as well as the resident armed forces. The exchange economy was no longer viable; the mountaineers had become superfluous. Within the next two decades, the Russian army with the Cossacks in tow crushed their resistance, closing the Caucasian Military Frontier.[188]

The ideological sources of the resistance to the Russian conquest and consolidation of the north Caucasus has become a matter of scholarly

---

[186] Breyfogle, *Heretics and Colonizers.*
[187] Ia. A. Gordin (ed.), *Rossiia v Kavkazskoi voine; istoricheskie chteniia* (Moscow: Zvezda, 1997), Pts. 5 and 6.
[188] Barrett, *At the Edge of Empire*, ch. 6.

dispute. The traditional view, initiated by nineteenth-century Russian historians and reproduced for different political reasons in the twentieth and twenty-first centuries, emphasized the role of a political-religious movement, the Naqshbandi, an allegedly militant brotherhood in the Sufi tradition (called Muridism by the Russians). The critics claim that this characterization is a product of tsarist and Soviet imperialism and the Western Orientalist gaze mediated, paradoxically, by Cold War hopes for its renewal against Soviet power. In any case, the mountaineers were imbued with an egalitarian spirit, loyalty to their military leaders, and messianic expectations. They fought tenaciously against the Russians. From its ranks came the leaders of the Great Chechnia Revolt of 1825/6, and the thirty-year *ghazavat* (holy war) that culminated with the defeat of Shamil in 1860.[189]

The conquest of the north Caucasus borderland was the work of a long line of Russian military pro-consuls who perceived their mission as both strategic and civilizational. The most representative figure in this enterprise was Field Marshal Prince A. I. Bariatinskii, Viceroy of the Caucasus (1857–1862), the man whose policies broke the back of the Murid revolt and led to the capture of Shamil. A protégé of Prince Mikhail Vorontsov and a decorated hero of the Caucasian campaigns, Bariatinskii had ambitious plans for assimilating the Caucasian peoples. His proposed instruments were a reformed local bureaucracy, a crusading religious order in alliance with the Armenian Church, a Trans Caspian trading corporation to challenge the British in Iran, and a railroad linking Tiflis with the central provinces. The latter would, in his words, "free Russia's hands and make [it] master in Asia." The army could then "descend like an avalanche on Turkey, Persia and the road to India."[190] Bariatinskii was running ahead of opinion in St. Petersburg. But, as we shall see, his

---

[189] Moshe Gammer, *Muslim Resistance to the Tsar. Shamil and the Conquest of Chechenia and Daghestan* (London: Frank Cass, 1994). A leading critic, Alexander Knysh, "Sufism as an Explanatory Paradigm. The Issue of the Motivations of Sufi Resistance Movements in Western and Russian Scholarship," *Die Welt des Islam* 42(2) (2002): 139–73, reviews the literature.

[190] Alfred J. Rieber (ed.), *The Politics of Autocracy. Letters of Alexander II to Prince A. I. Bariatinskii, 1857–1864* (Paris: Mouton, 1966), pp. 65–71; I. L. Babich, V. O. Bobrovnikov, and L. I. Solov'eva, "Reformy i kontrreformy v Kavkazskom namestnichestve. Voenno-narodnoe upravlenia," in V. O. Bobrovnikov and I. L. Babich (eds.), *Severnyi Kavkaz v sostave rossiiskoi imperii* (Moscow: Novoe literaturnoe obozrenie, 2007), pp. 187–201; on the cultural reforms, Austin Jersild, *Orientalism and Empire. North Caucasus Mountain Peoples and the Georgian Frontier, 1845–1917* (Montreal: McGill-Queens University Press, 2002), pp. 38–58. Quotation from A. L. Zisserman, *Fe'ldmarshal' Kniaz' Aleksandr Ivanovich Bariatinskii, 1815–1879* (Moscow: Universitetskaia tipografiia, 1890), vol. III, pp. 151–55.

administration promoted the men and ideas that helped to fashion imperial rule in Trans Caspia as well.

Bariatinskii's population policy combined resettling Cossacks and
expelling Muslims in order to secure and stabilize the frontiers. As part
of his reorganization of the Caucasian Military Line in 1861, he recruited
settlers from the Black Sea Cossacks. He hoped thereby to stimulate
agriculture and manufacturing along the Black Sea coast. Initially, the
Cossacks resisted the transfer, fearing that being placed under regular
army orders would lead to the loss of privileges granted by Catherine II.
They were pacified by concessions of land grants in hereditary tenure.
Bariatinskii also ordered the expulsion of the Muslim population from the
area beyond the Kuban. He was concerned that in time of war they would
constitute a potential threat to the rear of the Russian army, a precaution
that proved its value in the Russo-Turkish War of 1877/8. He entertained
the fantastic plan of using Shamil to help in the resettlement by persuading
the Ottoman sultan to grant him empty lands in Anatolia for that purpose.
A great admirer of his opponent, Bariatinskii assured the tsar that Shamil
would organize and discipline the emigrants who otherwise would be
"abandoned to an arbitrary fate." The cleared lowlands of the Caucasus
could then be entirely colonized by the Cossacks.[191] Ethnic cleansing with
a heart! The plan was never implemented.

After the suppression of the Murid revolt, local uprisings in Chechnia,
Ingushetia, and Daghestan broke out. They lacked an organizational
center, but this did not make them any easier to suppress. Between
1859 and 1877 there were eighteen risings against Russian authority in
Daghestan alone. The last one was preceded by the activity of Ottoman
agents, promising aid for a jihad. Among them was the son of Shamil who
had become a general in the Ottoman army. With the outbreak of the
Russo-Turkish War, rumors of an advancing Ottoman army touched off
guerrilla warfare. Fortunately for the Russian authorities, most of the
former military elite of the mountaineers remained loyal to the empire
and even participated in repressing the uprisings. The incident demonstrated both the strength and weakness of imperial rule. The policy of
accommodation had won over important elements of the local elites. The
regular army was too strong for the rebels, who lacked a charismatic leader
like Shamil. They also lacked cohesion and a common program, and they
failed to coordinate their attacks. But the risings increased the fears of the
Russian government, leading it to reverse its policy of permitting local
self-government. In contrast to the generous treatment afforded to

[191] Zisserman, *Bariatinskii*, vol. II, pp. 370–87.

Shamil, the Russians inflicted harsh punishments on the rebel leaders and their villages. After the rising several thousand rebels were exiled to internal Russian provinces. Bitter resentment was kept alive in the laments and chronicles of popular culture; Alexander II was remembered not as the tsar who had emancipated the serfs but as a merciless despot.[192] Russians tend to remember the conquest differently, nurturing romantic and literary legends comparable to those celebrated by the British in India.

The Russian conquest of the north Caucasus was punctuated by flight abroad or the expulsion of large numbers of Muslims. In the first eighty years of the nineteenth century an estimated 180,000 Abkhasians and other smaller tribal peoples migrated or were expelled into the Ottoman Empire, the big waves coming in two bursts in 1864 and following the Russo-Turkish War of 1877/8. Their places were taken by Mingrelians, who were regarded by the Russians and Georgians "just as Russian as the Muscovites."[193]

By the 1860s, the Caucasian frontiers both north and south of the mountains had been closed. Russia's supremacy in the region appeared assured. But concern over internal security ran like a red thread through Russian policy in the second half of the nineteenth century, particularly in light of the strong influence of Iranian Shi'ia ulama on the local population. Russian policy toward the Muslim population of the north Caucasus borderlands was inconsistent, reflecting regional differences, the personal preferences of the viceroys, the views of the central bureaucracy including the Holy Synod, and levels of resistance by Muslim mullahs. Up to the end of the nineteenth century, the Russian authorities implemented a policy of toleration, conversion, and bureaucratic co-optation of the Sunni ulama in order to stabilize the area.[194] But none of these strategies proved to be entirely effective in ensuring the submission of the Muslim population. In the twentieth century, the north Caucasian borderland was convulsed by four major crises involving both the tsarist and Soviet governments: the two revolutions of 1905 and 1917–1921, the Second World War, and the collapse of the Soviet Union. That legacy continues to weigh heavily on the life of the region in the twenty-first century as well.

[192] V. O. Bobrovnikov, "Poslednie volneniia i politicheskaia ssylka," in *Severnyi Kavkaz*, pp. 143–51.
[193] B. G. Hewitt, "Abkhazia. A Problem of Identity and Ownership," in John F. R. Wright *et al.* (eds.), *Transcaucasian Boundaries* (New York: St. Martin's Press), p. 200.
[194] Firouzeh Mostashari, "Colonial Dilemmas. Russian Policies in the Muslim Caucasus," in Robert P. Geraci and Michael Khodarkovsky (eds.), *Of Religion and Empire. Missions, Conversions, and Tolerance in Tsarist Russia* (Ithaca, NY: Cornell University Press, 2001), pp. 229–49.

Trans Caspia

Trans Caspia (often referred to as Central Asia) merges on the west with the Caucasian isthmus, on the northern and southern shores of the Caspian, and on the east with Inner Asia at the Altai and Tianshan mountains. The physical geography of the region is dominated in the north by the Kazakh steppe, and in the south by the Kara Kum and Kyzl Kum deserts, and the great oases of Samarkand, Khiva, and Bukhara watered by the two major river systems, the Syr Darya and the Amu Darya (Oxus), flowing into the Aral Sea. No clear-cut physical barrier separated the nomads and the settled population. After the Arab conquest of the eighth century, both the desert nomads and the oases peoples of Transoxenia had been incorporated into successive Mongol and Turkic empires.

Beginning with the Mongol invasion, which had been devastating, Trans Caspia suffered from a long period of natural and man-made disasters that reduced its population and depleted its resources. The outbreak and rapid spread of plague in the fourteenth century appears to have been a demographic calamity from which the region was slow to recover.[195] By the early sixteenth century, the region had broken up into rival khanates. The great cities of the oases like Samarkand, Khiva, and Bukhara, which had flourished as intermediaries in the international caravan trade, began to lose their prosperity. They suffered from competition with the shift from the overland routes to the sea-borne trade that announced the first stage of west European commercial expansion into the Red Sea and Indian Ocean. The merchants in the Aral basin (Transoxania) were marginalized. Trade became increasingly local. The highly refined skills of the urban craftsmen were half forgotten, and the urban population of the oases cities suffered a long decline. According to the Russian Orientalist V. V. Bartol'd, the result was the return of society to an earlier, more simple structure organized around landlords, peasants, and officials.[196] A feudal reaction set in with local notables contending for control over land and herds.[197]

Yet one should not underestimate the vitality of the steppe people. In the sixteenth and seventeenth centuries there were two sustained efforts

[195] William Hardy McNeill, *Plagues and Peoples* (New York: Anchor Press, 1976), esp. pp. 149–65, 190–96.

[196] V. V. Barthold, *Four Studies on the History of Trans Caspia* (Leiden: Brill, 1958), vol. I, p. 65; V. V. Barthold, *La découverte de l'Asie. Histoire de l'orientalism en Europe et en Russie* (Paris: Payot, 1947), pp. 50, 129.

[197] N. G. Apollova, *Khozistvennoe osvoenie Priirtysh'ia v kontse XVI pervoi polovine XIX v.* (Moscow: Nauka, 1976), for a review of the literature.

by tribal confederations to create nomadic empires: first, by the Shaibanids in Transoxania and, second, by the Dzhungarian khanate in eastern Turkestan. They were finally defeated and destroyed by the Safavids and Qing, but only after a prolonged and stubborn resistance.

Shaibanids, Safavids, and Mughals

In the mid-fifteenth century the last great attempt to bring the Trans Caspian frontier under the sway of a single power triggered a great three-way struggle in which none of the participants was able to prevail. The Shaibani tribe unified twenty-four other Turkic tribes originally inhabiting northwest Siberia into a federation under the charismatic leadership of Abu'l Khayr, "a Jenghiz Khan who did not succeed," in the words of René Grousset.[198] They became known as the Uzbek, but the name, like so many of those subsequently applied to complex formations of tribal loyalties, concealed a highly heterogeneous ethnic mix. As Abu'l Khayr led his great expedition into the oases of the Aral frontier, his fractious confederation broke up. The breakaway tribes, calling themselves *kazaki*, meaning "people free as a bird," turned against him, crushed his forces, and roamed the steppe to harass the Uzbeks from the rear. (The Russians called these *kazaki* Kirghiz or Kirghiz-kaisak, a corruption of kazak, but even though they finally fell under Russian control in the eighteenth century they managed to keep their original name and are today known as Kazakhs.) Abu'l Khayr's grandson, Muhammed Shaibani, restored the Uzbek fortunes. A pious Sunni Muslim, well educated and endowed with linguistic and artistic skills, he modeled himself on the legends of Alexander the Great. As a religious leader, he sought to convert the pagan Kazakhs and break the power of the Shi'ite Iranians. As a state-builder, his aim was to arrest the economic decline, revive the arts, and overcome political fragmentation of Transoxania. By 1503 he had conquered all of the great oases before he was killed at Merv on the edge of the newly consolidated Safavid Empire. But this did not end the struggle.

In their tussle over the Trans Caspian borderlands the Shaibanid Uzbeks and the Safavid Iranians shared a number of similar characteristics in their state-building efforts.[199] However, the Shaibanids were even less successful than their Safavid rivals in integrating the nomadic and

---

[198] René Grousset, *The Empires of the Steppes. A History of Trans Caspia* (New Brunswick, NJ: Rutgers University Press, 1970), p. 480.

[199] Anatoly Khazanov, *Nomads and the Outside World*, 2nd edn (Cambridge University Press, 1994), pp. 261–62.

sedentary cultures of their realm. Part of the tribal federation remained strongly attached to the nomadic way of life. The dynasts and their followers made Bukhara their capital and began to acquire landed properties, although they failed to restore the great literary and artistic traditions of the oases.[200] In order to create a viable state they needed to retain the loyalty of the tribes who furnished them with their best warriors; but the tribesmen were also a source of instability. The urban groups remained culturally and ethnically distinct from the nomadic Uzbek population and even acquired a different name in local parlance. They were called Sarts, a term that was subsequently applied to the entire sedentary population. Increasingly, the Shaibanid rulers used the term Uzbek as a pejorative in order to suggest anarchy and disorder, meaning the nomads whom they could not control.[201] The deep cultural and social divisions within the Shaibanid state ultimately undermined its stability to the point where a major military defeat would destroy its foundations.

For the following 200 years, the Safavids, Shaibani, and Mughals engaged in a three-way struggle over the Trans Caspian borderlands. None of them was able to establish firm control. The problem was a familiar one for state-builders in shatter zones. Two conflicts illustrate the complexity of the regional, religious, and ethnic mix on the Trans Caspian frontier; the first occurred between the Uzbeks and the Iranians in the Safavid province of Astarabad; the second, farther east where the Uzbek khanates bordered on the Afghan tribal confederacies.

The population of Astarabad was predominantly Sunni, unlike the rest of Iran, with strong ties to their Uzbek co-religionists across the border. The local merchant elites and tribal groups drifting in from the Trans Caspian steppes resisted the administrative centralization of the Safavid provincial ruling elite drawn from Shi'ite qizilbashi families. From across the border the Uzbeks frequently intervened in support of their Sunni co-religionists. Caught in the middle, the peasantry was disaffected, suffering from over-taxation and the depredations of border warfare. Fueled by these diverse social discontents, five major rebellions ravaged the province from the early sixteenth century to the mid-eighteenth century. As public order broke down the rebellious elements split and fell upon one another.[202] Although none of these uprisings achieved their aims, they

---

[200] Maria Eva Subtelny, "Art and Politics in Early Sixteenth Century Trans Caspia," *Trans Caspiatic Journal* 27 (1983): 121–48.

[201] Edward Allworth, *The Modern Uzbeks from the Fourteenth Century to the Present* (Stanford, CA: Hoover Institute Press, 1990), pp. 42–43.

[202] James J. Reid, "Rebellion and Social Change in Astarabad, 1537–1744," *International Journal of Middle East Studies* 13 (1981): 35–53.

contributed to the breakdown of central authority all along the Trans Caspian frontier from the south Caucasus to the borders of Mughal India.

The second arena for a three-way struggle among Uzbek Shaibanids, Iranian Safavids, and Indian Mughals spread over a forbidding terrain of semi-desert, barren hills, and high mountains inhabited by one of the two most ethnically heterogeneous populations in the Eurasian borderlands (the other being the Caucasus). Contemporary Afghanistan occupies most of this area.[203] Its strategic position astride the transverse and north–south trade and invasion routes exposed it to a thousand years of intermittent violence. At the end of the sixteenth century, the Safavids and Mughals partitioned the region after Shah Abbas had put an end to Shaibani ambitions in his great victory over them at Herat.[204] Although the Uzbeks were never again able to threaten Iran, they continued to harass the Mughal garrisons.

In the cauldron of this three-way struggle the Afghan tribes resorted to their traditional form of resistance against more powerful external enemies. They allied themselves with first one and then the other of the two major contestants. Although the Safavids and Mughals employed their superior firepower and military tactics to occupy the country, they were unable to stabilize the frontier or pacify the tribes. Superior technology, as many were to learn, does not guarantee domination over the fierce Afghan tribes. Without subjecting themselves to the yoke of unity, the tribes rose in a series of revolts against the occupiers. By the 1670s, the Mughals after repeated attempts to secure the northern part of the country finally abandoned it. By the turn of the century they were out of the rest of Afghanistan for good. The Safavids fared even worse. Their exploitative financial and intolerant religious policies sparked a revolt of the Ghilzai tribe, who were Sunni Muslims. In a series of bloody campaigns during the first quarter of the eighteenth century, they repeatedly defeated the royal forces, occupied Isfahan in 1722, and plunged Iran into fourteen years of anarchy.[205]

As we have seen, none of the charismatic warrior chieftains of the eighteenth century, Nadir Shah, or Ahmad Shah Durrani, were able to incorporate these Trans Caspian borderlands into a stable dynastic empire. It was not until the 1880s that some of its constituent parts, the khanates of Kabul, Qandahar, and Herat were joined together in the state

---

[203] By one estimate there were 345 separate tribal units in the region during the sixteenth and seventeenth centuries. Louis Dupree, *Afghanistan* (Princeton University Press, 1973), pp. 57–65, 321.

[204] Grousset, *The Empire of the Steppes*, pp. 480–84; V. V. Bartol'd, *Istoriia izucheniia vostoka v Evrope i v Rossii* (St. Petersburg: n.p., 1911), pp. 190–91.

[205] Lawrence Lockhart, *The Fall of the Safavid Dynasty and the Afghan Occupation of Persia* (Cambridge University Press, 1958), p. 42.

of Afghanistan, though subsequent events testify to the fragility of its unity.[206] The history of this small region represents the most extreme example of resistance to external control by a culturally diverse, ethnically mixed population, organized along tribal lines and inhabiting a difficult terrain. The same conditions militated against the creation of a centralized and stable state. But the situation was not much less chaotic in Transoxania.

The series of frontier wars following the end of Shaibani rule led to a break up of the core of their empire. A number of independent khanates formed around oases like Bukhara, Khiva, and Samarkand, with Uzbek tribal chiefs setting up their own hereditary dynasties. In the absence of central authority, political fragmentation increased. The petty rulers failed to maintain irrigation canals and alienated state properties, which increasingly fell into the hands of private landowners and Muslim religious foundations (*vaqf*). The peasantry became increasingly dependent on the landlords. International trade shriveled.

As the power of the khans declined, local emirs acquired more administrative and judicial functions. Frequent bloody conflicts broke out between the khan and local elites, who also feuded with one another.[207] Lacking a strong military force, their lands were constantly exposed to nomadic raids, especially by Kazakhs from the steppe to the north. By the end of the seventeenth century, the Kazakhs, who had earlier split off from the Uzbeks and maintained their nomadic life, reached the height of their power when their influence spread over the sedentary population as far south as Tashkent.[208] The legacy of the Shaibani collapse did not pass to Iran, but to Russia. The fragmentation of the khanates and disunity among the nomadic tribes, as well as the linguistic and religious differences separating Shi'ite Iran and Sunni Trans Caspia, allowed the Russians easier access in penetrating the area in the eighteenth century.

By the end of the seventeenth century, a perceptible shift in power relations took place among the Islamic military patronage states in Trans Caspia. By the third quarter of the eighteenth century the decline had become pronounced, and in the early nineteenth century it had

[206] Dupree, *Afghanistan*, chart 21, "Political Fusion and Fission in Afghanistan," following p. 343.
[207] P. P. Ivanov, *Ocherki po istorii Srednei Asii (XVI–seredina XIX v.)* (Moscow: Izd. Vostochnoi literatury, 1958), pp. 68–69; V. V. Bartol'd, "K istorii orosheniia Turkestana," in *Sochineniia* (Moscow: Izd. Vostochnoi literatury, [1914] 1965), vol. III, pp. 110–11.
[208] C. E. Tolybekov, *Kochevoe obshchestvo kazakov v XVII–nachale XX veka. Politiko-ekonomicheskii analiz* (Alma Ata: Nauka, 1971), pp. 259–60; V. V. Bartol'd, *Istoriia turetsko-mongol'skikh narodov* (Tashkent: Izd. Kazakskogo vysshego pedagogicheskogo instituta, 1928), p. 98.

become precipitous. The central question, to which there is still no satisfactory answer, is why they did not complete the transition between tribal-based societies led by ruling elites imbued with a warrior mentality to a modern state system with permanent bureaucracies and strong financial institutions. It no longer appears possible to attribute the failure, if such it was, simply to endemic warfare or inferior military technology. The shift in trade routes and decline of urban centers had something to do with it. So did the persistence of the nomadic way of life that dominated the eco-system.

Qajars, Russians, and British

By the early nineteenth century, two powerful imperial rivals were beginning to move toward one another in Trans Caspia: the Russians across the steppe and the British up to the Indus River. On the way, they would overthrow the local khanates of Transoxania and the Mughal guardians of northwest India, only to face once again the seemingly intractable problem of how to deal with the Afghan tribes.

When Russia expelled the Qajars from the south Caucasian borderlands in 1829, they sought compensation on their Trans Caspian frontiers. In 1831, Abbās Mīrzā, determined to restore dynastic greatness, campaigned to recover the provinces of Herat. He was patronized and supported by the Russians, who were happy to see the Iranians diverted to another front and embroiled with the British. For a quarter of a century the Iranians fought frontier wars to gain control over Herat in 1838, 1852, and 1856. Each time they were opposed by the British who feared that Iran was acting as an advanced guard of the Russians.

These last attempts of the Qajars to reestablish an Iranian empire became entangled in the encounter between British and Russian empire-builders. British historians have tended to focus on the defense of India, dubbing it "the Great Game," a term invented by an English political agent in India and immortalized by Rudyard Kipling.[209] But accepting the original meaning of this term narrows the playing field. The Anglo-Russian rivalry was broader and deeper; broader in the sense of its extension from the Danube to the Pacific, and deeper in the sense of its being embedded in layers of cultural and commercial conflict. To

---

[209] The literature on the Great Game is large and contentious even on the British side. See, for example, Edward Ingram, "Approaches to the Great Game in Asia," *Middle Eastern Studies* 18(4) (October 1982): 449–57, in a duel with Malcolm Yapp, "British Perceptions of the Russian Threat to India," *Modern Asian Studies* 21(4) (1987): 647–65. On the Soviet Russian side, for a broader, well-documented, albeit strongly Marxist-nationalist, interpretation, see Kiniapina, *Kavkaz.*

understand the origins of their competition, it is necessary to return to an isolated but pregnant incident at the end of the eighteenth century.

Britain's concerns over Russian expansion first surfaced when William Pitt the Younger sounded the alarm in 1788 over the Russian storming of Ochakov, an Ottoman fortress on the Black Sea coast. The rumbling quieted down as British statesmen concluded that they needed an alliance with Russia against revolutionary and Bonapartist France in order to counter the greater danger to their imperial position. Britain's main concern was to extricate Russia from its wars along the Caucasian and Danubian frontiers with Iran (1804–1807) and the Ottoman Empire (1806–1812) so that it could concentrate its full military might in Europe against Napoleon. But the Russians were not always cooperative.

During this period Russia's two brief alignments with France were ominous signs of things to come. From the perspective of London, they posed a threat to the British in India, however remote this appears in retrospect. In 1800, Paul I authorized an overland expedition from Orenburg in the direction of India which proved abortive. A similar idea was floated at Tilsit in 1807, when Napoleon and Alexander I agreed to coordinate measures for an invasion of India through Iran where French influence had temporarily replaced the British. British concerns mounted, as we have seen, when they suspected Abbās Mīrzā of being Russia's stalking horse in his campaign to seize Herat in 1831.

In pursing the theme of Anglo-Russian rivalry, a rough parallel may be drawn between the British conquest of the Indian subcontinent and the Russian conquest of the Caucasian and the Trans Caspian borderlands.[210] Both exhibited a similar mix of imperialist motives. They perceived themselves as the bearers of European civilization in the face of disorderly and backward peoples unable to maintain peace and order. It may be argued that the Russians had the better excuse insofar as the disorder which was real existed on the frontiers of their homeland, whereas for the British it lay on the edges of colonial possessions thousands of miles from the metropolis. In any case, they both employed the same learned and literary discourse adapted from the writers of the Enlightenment, modified by Romantic ideas depicting indigenous populations of the East as "Oriental" in that curious blend of tropes that admitted nobility together with barbarism, topped off by the sciences of statistics.[211] In its most intensive phase, from 1864 to 1885, the Russian

[210] See, for example, A. S. Morrison, *Russian Rule in Samarkand, 1868–1910. A Comparison with British India* (Oxford University Press, 2008).
[211] Cf. Daniel Brower, *Turkestan and the Fate of the Russian Empire* (London: Routledge-Curzon, 2003), pp. 9–14.

advance into Trans Caspia proceeded along two fronts, encountering two ecologies but one Islamic culture, posing different problems of assimilation. From the north along the fringes of the steppe, the frontier lines pushed forward into the pasture lands of the Kazakh nomads (known as Kirghiz to contemporaries). From the west, military expeditions moved toward the oases cities of Bukhara, Kokand, and Khiva. The peoples of the oases had embraced Islam in the early years of the Arab conquest, while the nomads had been converted to Islam much later.

The conquest was not centrally planned, but rather the result of initiatives by local military commanders made possible by conflicting bureaucratic interests in St. Petersburg. Initially, the Russian forces had to deal only with the opposition of the nomads and the khanates. But the advance in the direction of India and the Chinese frontier transformed the regional character of the struggle over the Trans Caspian and Inner Asian borderlands. It became the centerpiece of the rivalry with Britain, touching off a long period of tension over delimiting imperial frontiers, and signaling the opening gambit of the Russian penetration into Chinese territory.

From 1840 to 1907, statesmen on both the British and Russian sides periodically explored the possibility of reaching agreements on their mutual interests and establishing spheres of influence. But suspicions, misinterpretations, and bad timing disrupted these efforts.[212] (The parallel with similar Habsburg–Russian negotiations in the Balkans is suggestive.) At the centers of power British and Russian ruling elites frequently found themselves disagreeing over the extent and pace of their respective imperial advances. Advocates of a forward policy clashed with more cautious policy makers. On the frontiers, adventurers and local officials on both sides evaded or ignored instructions from London and St. Petersburg. They preferred to promote their own careers, claiming to act in the best interests of empire-building, which in their minds was often the same thing. Mixed motives and contradictory impulses shared by statesmen, political agents, and military officers bolstered the natural tendency to perceive the opposite side as duplicitous or untrustworthy. At times, most notably on the eve of the Crimean War, this led to disastrous consequences.

Once Britain and Russia lost their common enemy in Napoleon, they found themselves at odds all along the western and southern frontiers of Eurasia. At the Congress of Vienna, as we have seen, Alexander I precipitated a major crisis with Great Britain by insisting on reconstituting most of pre-partition Poland under Russian control. Even before the

[212] Yapp, "British Perceptions," pp. 659–61.

Congress, the Anglo-Russian wartime alliance had already begun to show signs of wear on the Trans Caspian frontier. Following the Treaty of Gulistan in 1813, the Iranians turned to the British for protection and signed a treaty that pledged Britain to come to the aid of Iran if it were attacked by a European power. Although the British managed never to honor the treaty, it served notice to the Russians that Iran had now become vital in British eyes to the defense of India. The British were even more alarmed over the signing of the Treaty of Turkmanchai in 1828, which appeared to make Iran a Russian protectorate. In rapid sequence the Polish revolt in 1830 and the Treaty of Unkiar Skelessi in 1833 aroused British opinion on two additional counts: ideological in reaction to the suppression of Polish liberties and strategic in reaction to the apparent acceptance by the Ottoman Empire of the same status of protectorate that had been imposed on Iran.

From Russia's perspective the rivalry took off in the 1830s when the British contested its sovereignty over the Black Sea coast by trading freely with the Circassians who were in a state of rebellion. Private initiatives by the British adventurer David Urquhart enjoyed support from manufacturers and commercial agents in England for his schemes to open the west coast of the Black Sea to British trade and to supply arms to the rebellious Circassian mountaineers. He established contact with Prince Czartoryski in Paris, who by the time of the second Polish Revolt in 1863 had joined him in the extraordinary belief that the Circassian rebels were the key to securing Polish independence and guaranteeing security for the Ottoman Empire. Failure to support them, he believed, would mean sacrificing Iran to Russia and threatening India.[213]

More serious for the future of Anglo-Russian relations was a renewal in 1838 of the Iranian attempt to gain control of Herat. This time the confusion in Russian policy making, the complication of regional politics, and the overreaction of the British brought the two rivals close to war. The Russian minister in Tehran, the flamboyant Colonel I. O. Simonich, an advocate of a forward policy in the region, enjoyed the protection of like-minded, high-ranking figures such as Governor General V. A. Perovskii at Orenburg, among the military elite, and in the Asiatic Department of the Foreign Ministry. Furnished with funds from the Iranian indemnity, Simonich supported the plans of Mohammed Shah to attack Herat. At

---

[213] G. H. Bolsover, "David Urquhart and the Eastern Question. A Study in Publicity and Diplomacy," *Journal of Modern History* 8(4) (1936): 446–47; Peter Brock, "The Fall of Circassia. A Study in Private Diplomacy," *English Historical Review* 71(2) (July 1956): 401–27, for the Polish connection. The British involvement is magnified in importance by Kiniapina, *Kavkaz*, pp. 131–38.

the same time, one of his agents, the colorful Polish ex-revolutionary convert to pan-Slavism, J. V. Witkiewicz, worked zealously to conclude an alliance joining the Iranians with the Afghan rulers in the khanates of Qandahar (Kohundil Khan) and in Kabul (Dost Mohammed). The Afghans attempted to play the British against the Russians in order to secure their own position. The British agents in Tehran and Kabul sounded the alarm. Britain dispatched a naval force to occupy the island fortress of Kharg in the Persian Gulf, threatening war with Iran and Kabul. Russian Foreign Minister Nesselrode repeatedly reassured the British as to Russian intentions. But he seemed unable to control his subordinates, who were also taking instructions from the General Staff and Perovskii at Orenburg. It was another case of the lack of coordination in the loose organization of the Russian bureaucracy.

When Nicholas I recognized the dangerous waters into which his enterprising agents had sailed, he recalled Simonich; Witkiewicz was discredited; and Nesselrode was authorized to reassure the British that "Great Britain and Russia must have one and the same interests at heart: that is to maintain peace in the center of Asia and to see that a general conflagration does not begin in this vast part of Asia." He proposed that a system be recognized "above all else to respect the independence of the intermediate countries which separate us."[214] On the British side, Lord Palmerston acknowledged that conflict over Iran was not worth the candle as Russia held the geographical advantage. The idea of Iran as a buffer state would be too expensive. The British retreated to the position that control of the Gulf was a sufficient guarantee of the security of India.[215] Yet it would require another seventy years for the two rivals fully to realize this idea.

Pious affirmations did not prevent both Russia and Britain from pursuing the struggle over the borderlands, but rather redirected their efforts to avoid a direct confrontation. Once the crisis was over, Lord Auckland, the Governor General of India, launched an invasion of Afghanistan and deposed Dost Mohammed. But the British were unable to sustain a presence in Kabul and their retreating army was annihilated. Taking advantage of their difficulties, Governor General Perovskii dispatched an expedition to Khiva in the hope of finally establishing a secure and profitable commercial link to the oases of Central Asia and ending the

---

[214] Nesselrode to Pozzo di Borgo, October 20/November 1, 1838, cited in Harold N. Ingle, *Nesselrode and the Russian Rapprochement with Britain, 1836–1844* (Berkeley, CA: University of California Press, 1976), pp. 84–85; see also Philip E. Mosely, "Russia's Asiatic Policy in 1838," *Essays in the History of Modern Europe* (Freepoint, NY: Books for Libraries Press, [1936] 1968), pp. 48–62.

[215] Yapp, "British Perceptions," pp. 654–56.

slave trade in the region. But it too almost perished in the ice storms of the Ust Urt desert. Both powers salvaged something from the debacles. The Khan of Khiva released Russian prisoners and promised not to take any more. The British completed their task of subjugating the remaining Indian principalities. In 1841, Sir Charles Napier occupied Sind, dispatching his witty telegram "I have Sind," and in 1849 the British annexed the Punjab. They restored Dost Mohammed in Kabul, who reciprocated by remaining loyal to them during the Indian Mutiny.

In the post-Crimean period British and Russian statesmen and soldiers found themselves once again deeply divided over the proper course of action on the Trans Caspian frontier. The Russian advocates of a forward policy acquired powerful new voices, including the Minister of War, Dmitri Miliutin. The Crimean War had brought home the realization that the confrontation with Britain was Eurasian in scope. The Viceroy of the Caucasus, Bariatinskii, had stressed the links between the Caucasus and Trans Caspia. He advocated a policy to counter the British defeat of Iran in 1857, which he considered nothing less than a continuation of the Crimean War, by urging St. Petersburg to authorize a Russian occupation of the area beyond the Atrek River. From that position Russia could dominate the northern frontiers of Iran and Afghanistan, and balance the British position in the Gulf. "Otherwise, war, inevitable in the future, would place us in a more difficult situation," he wrote; "for the English, disposed along the Persian Gulf, in Kandahar and Kabul and Herat will make contact with the Central Asian khans and distribute gold among them."[216] At the height of the Polish insurrection in 1863, Miliutin, his former subordinate, another old Caucasus hand recently promoted to Minister of War, echoed and expanded these sentiments. Noting how strained relations were with the Western powers, he wrote: "In case of war we cannot engage the English in Europe – there remains only Asia." If necessary an expedition there would be important "if not for the invasion of India, then at least to draw off English forces from Europe and inflict possibly greater damage to their trade relations."[217]

Similar motivations inspired other ardent advocates of a forward policy, an impressive list including Count Ignat'ev, the ardent pan-Slavist who led expeditions into Trans Caspia in the 1860s, and later emerged as Britain's arch rival at Istanbul; General Chernaev, the conqueror of Tashkent and commander of volunteers in Serbia in 1875; the Governor General of West Siberia, G. Kh. Gasford; the Governor of Orenburg,

---

[216] Zisserman, *Bariatinskii*, vol. II, p. 121.
[217] "Zapiski N. G. Zalesova," *Russkaia starina* 115 (1903): 322–23; 114 (1903): 24–25.

G. G. Bezak; and Governor General Korsakov of East Siberia.[218] Ignat'ev's career exemplifies the most ambitious aspirations for an imperial stretch from Peking to Constantinople. As the chief negotiator of the Treaty of Peking in 1860, he won back the Priamur and Ussuri regions that had been ceded to the Chinese in the late seventeenth century, and opened trade for Russian merchants in the towns of western Turkestan, including Kashgar and Ili. Seventeen years later he was the chief negotiator of the Treaty of San Stefano (1878) that established Russia, briefly, as the preponderant power in the Danubian frontier. Ignat'ev was no wild-eyed fanatic, but a shrewd practitioner of geocultural politics. He perceived the vital importance of the Straits for "the security and prosperity to [Russia's] south and from the political-economic point of view." Russia's control could be direct or indirect, its methods peaceful or not depending on the reaction of the European powers. If Russia were to occupy Constantinople, it would have to use the Bulgarians, Greeks, and Armenians as "an obedient weapon of Russian policy and as constant allies eliminating any possibility of their moving into the enemy camp." The old alliance with Austria was doomed by the *Ausgleich* of 1867, which enslaved the south Slavs, placated the Magyars and Poles, Russia's traditional enemies "with whom sooner or later there must be a war to the death for supremacy in the East, for the unity and integrity of Russia, for the opportunity to maintain and develop the historical position achieved by centuries of toil which the Most High predestined for Russia – the protector of the Orthodox and the most numerous and powerful of the Slavic tribes."[219]

The chief opponent of a forward policy, the Foreign Minister, Prince Gorchakov, was supported by N. O. Sukhozanet, Miliutin's predecessor as War Minister, and Lt. General Diugamel, Gasford's successor as Governor General of West Siberia and Commander-in-Chief of the Siberian army.[220] Gorchakov consistently sought to avoid a conflict with Great Britain in the Eurasian borderlands.[221] He favored peaceful penetration of Trans Caspia through diplomacy and trade. His famous

---

[218] N. A. Khalfin, *Politika Rossii v Srednei Azii, 1857–1868* (Moscow: Izd. Vostochnoi literatury, 1962), pp. 94, 104–5, 107–8, 119, 125, 130–32. Ignat'ev wrote in 1857: "In case of a break with England only in Asia can we fight them with any chance of success and [also] threaten the existence of Turkey." *Ibid.*, pp. 84–85.

[219] "Zapiski Grafa N. P. Ignat'eva," ed. A. A. Bashmanov, *Istoricheskie zapiski*, 135 (1914): 53–54.

[220] Sukhozanet summed up his reaction in a report to officers of the General Staff on the advantage of occupying Central Asia as a threat to Britain in case of war with the pithy phrase: "This is a chimera." "Zapiski Ignat'eva," p. 133.

[221] In 1857, Gorchakov declared dangerous "any step in the East touching on English interests or even capable of giving the English an excuse to protest." "Zapiski

memorandum to the European powers in 1864 outlined his vision of Russian policy in the region. Security and the advance of civilization, he claimed, were Russia's mission, one not unlike those of the major European colonial powers and the United States.[222] Ignat'ev's differences with Gorchakov extended all along the periphery of the Russian Empire. "The basic difference between our views," he wrote in his memoirs, "was that he believed in Europe, in 'the European concert,' thirsted for conferences and congresses, preferred resounding phrases and brilliant diplomacy, belle-lettrist productions to practical action."[223]

Characteristically, Alexander II appeared to encourage both policy options, often at the same time. He kept Gorchakov and Miliutin as ministers and close advisors throughout the 1860s and 1870s when the internal debate was at its height. He did not encourage the most risky and adventurous moves, such as Chernaev's seizure of Tashkent in 1865, but neither did he disown them when they succeeded.[224] As a result, the British dismissed as deceitful the protestations of Gorchakov and others that Russia's policy was peaceful.[225] What they did not perceive was the disagreements within the Russian government over the best means to secure the volatile frontier. The conqueror of Tashkent, Chernaev, backed by numerous military and civil officials, urged annexation. Gorchakov, ever concerned about British reaction, preferred to create a separate khanate under Russian protection. In the end, Chernaev's view prevailed.[226]

Threatened by Russia's advance, the khanates attempted to introduce reforms. From the mid-eighteenth century the middle-sized khanates of

Ignat'eva," p. 67. Cf. Firuz Kazemzadeh, *Russia and Britain in Persia, 1864–1914. A Study in Imperialism* (New Haven, CT: Yale University Press, 1968), for a well-documented survey of the Anglo-Russian contest, which views the Russian advance as steady and calculated with Gorchakov serving as a willing dupe of the forward party led by Miliutin.

[222] For a full English translation of the memo, see W. K. Fraser-Tytler, *Afghanistan. A Study of Political Developments in Central Asia* (London: Oxford University Press, 1950), app. II, pp. 305–7.

[223] "Zapiski Ignat'eva," p. 51. Although written within the context of the Eastern Question, his view applied equally to the Caucasus and Central Asia.

[224] David MacKenzie, "Expansion in Central Asia. St. Petersburg and the Turkestan Generals (1863–1866)," *Canadian Slavic Studies* 3(2) (Summer 1969): 287. Success could also influence Gorchakov's opinion about military action if it did not involve British interests. A. L. Popov, "Iz istorii zavoevaniia srednei Azii," *Istoricheskie zapiski* 9 (1940): 211.

[225] Martin Aust, "Rossiia i Velikobritaniia. Vneshniaia politika i obrazy imperii ot krymskoi voiny do Pervoi mirvoi voiny," in *Imperiium inter pares. Rol' transferov v istorii Rossiiskoi Imperii (1700–1917)* (Moscow: Novoe literaturnoe obozrenie, 2010), pp. 244–65, notes that the real surge in British Russophobia came after the Crimean War and centered mainly on the perceived threat to India which was not well founded.

[226] Kiniapina, *Kavkaz*, pp. 273–78.

Trans Caspia – Bukhara and Kokand – were able to mobilize considerable resources and maintain the irrigation networks. The khans of Bukhara progressively centralized their administration and formed a professional army equipped with artillery and trained by deserters from the Indian army.[227] But the khanates engaged in almost continuous warfare with one another that sapped their resources, while their cross-border raiding and slave trade provoked the Russian colonial administrators. Bukhara's seizure of the smaller khanate of Kokand, in which Tashkent was located, sparked a Russian campaign, forcing the khan of Bukhara to seek a compromise, preserving his control over internal affairs but promising to "not to send troops and raiding parties across the Russian frontier." The Russians agreed to prevent Kirghiz and other nomads from raiding Bukhara. Russian traders and colonists were to be granted extraterritorial rights. But the khan then refused to sign the agreement and, urged by his retainers and the ulama, declared a jihad, despite the fact that his appeals for aid from the Ottoman sultan were discouraged.[228] The Russian forces were victorious under the command of General K. P. von Kaufman, who was appointed to head the newly created governor generalship of Turkestan. The peace treaty recognized the khanate's autonomy, but also its *de facto* dependence on the Russian Empire.

The conquest of Bukhara touched off another wave of Russophobia in New Delhi and London. Negotiations between the two empires focused on the problem of defining their relations with Afghanistan. In 1872, they reached an informal agreement on enlarging its territory to the north and recognizing its independence. But no clearly defined boundary between Bukhara and Afghanistan was worked out until 1885. Meanwhile, the Russian advance continued. A campaign against the khanate of Khiva picked up strong backing from the Viceroy of the Caucasus, the tsar's brother, Grand Duke Mikhail, and von Kaufman in Turkestan, who recognized the need to provide Russia with connecting commercial and strategic links between the Caucasian and Trans Caspian frontiers. The Russian descent on the east bank of the Caspian aroused Iranian fears over the absence of a well-defined border. The shah obtained Russian recognition of Iranian sovereignty up to the Atrek River, where the border remains to the present day. These agreements avoided international complications and facilitated the Russian conquest of Khiva in 1873, despite

---

[227] A. S. Morrison, *Russian Rule in Samarkand 1868–1910. A Comparison with British India* (Oxford University Press, 2008), pp. 13–15.

[228] Kiniapina, *Kavkaz*, p. 280. In the capital of Bukhara, Samarkand, a virtual civil war broke out between the ulama, who urged resistance, and the merchants, who favored surrender and accommodation. *Ibid.*, p. 281.

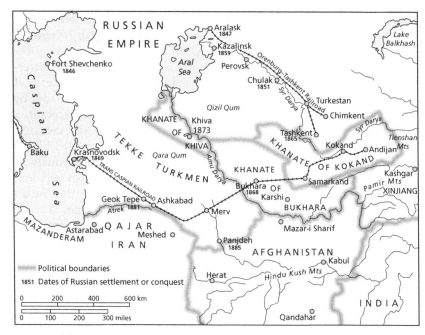

Map 4.4 Trans Caspia to 1886

the khan's attempt to gain support from the British and Ottoman governments.

Unexpectedly, in 1875, the Russian attempt to achieve stability in Trans Caspia by establishing protectorates broke down in Kokand. Open revolt flared under the leadership of Russia's perennial foes in the Sufi brotherhoods. Once the revolt was suppressed, Kokand was incorporated into Turkestan as the province of Ferghana. Only the Turkmen tribes on the eastern shores of the Caspian retained their freedom. But the British and Russians already had them in their sights.

The Russo-Turkish War of 1877/8 illuminated dramatically the dynamic and interactive relationship of the struggle over the borderlands all along the complex frontiers of the Danubian frontier, the Pontic steppe, the Caucasian isthmus, and Trans Caspia. As we have seen, simultaneously with the outbreak of fighting in the Balkans a Muslim revolt broke out in Chechnia and Daghestan. It was prepared and encouraged by the Ottoman Governor General of Erzerum and Caucasian exiles operating out of Ottoman territory. Among the leaders were radical elements of the Sufi brotherhoods calling for jihad. It took a year for a

Russian army of 25,000 men to crush the uprising, but its memory was long-lasting, fueling fears of pan-Islam among Russian officials.[229] Meanwhile, the confrontation on the shores of the Bosporus, where the British fleet and the Russian army faced off almost within shooting distance of one another, resonated in Trans Caspia. If Disraeli was determined to oppose Russia's domination of the Balkans, the new Viceroy of India, Lord Lytton, was equally determined to check Russia's advance by reviving a forward policy in Afghanistan. In a familiar counterpoint, a Russian mission in Kabul responded by seeking an alliance with the emir, Sher Ali. In Europe, war between the two powers was avoided by the compromise at the Congress of Berlin. In Trans Caspia, negotiations broke down when the Afghans refused to accept a British mission. Acting against instructions from London, Lytton ordered the Indian army to invade Afghanistan, touching off the Second Afghan War.[230] The Russian government was not alone in failing to control adventurous spirits among its imperial pro-consuls.

Once in occupation of Afghanistan, the British exerted pressure on Iran to exercise its influence with the Turkmen tribes in order to block the Russians from seizing the oasis of Merv. Hot heads in New Delhi argued that a Russian occupation of Merv "would be regarded as the first step to Herat which is the key to India."[231] Tension drained away when the election in 1880 brought Gladstone, the Little Englander, to power. Once again the British reversed their policy, evacuated Afghanistan, and reached a settlement with the new emir, Abdur Rahman, granting Britain control over foreign relations and establishing the foundations for a buffer state that lasted forty years. They failed, however, to persuade the shah of Iran to claim the Merv oasis on the Afghan frontier. Despite the activities of British intelligence agents working among the Turkmen tribes, the Russians advanced toward the edge of Afghan territory. The Minister of War, Miliutin, finally restrained the ambitious Russian general, M. K. Skobolev, a veteran of the Russo-Turkish War, who wished to press south into Iranian territory. Instead, St. Petersburg secretly negotiated

---

[229] Bobrovnikov, "Poslednie volneniia," p. 151.

[230] Andrew Roberts, *Salisbury. Victorian Titan* (London: Weidenfeld & Nicolson, 1999), pp. 212–24. The Foreign Secretary, Lord Salisbury, repeatedly warned Lytton not to engage in provocative behavior. He contemptuously dismissed alarming rumors of Russian designs on India fueled, among other sources, by the publication of Frederick Burnaby's bestseller, *Ride to Khiva* (London, 1876), which portrayed Russia's advance on India as "slow, silent and certain." It is hard to resist drawing parallels with many Western observers of Soviet conduct during the origins of the Cold War.

[231] *Arkhiv vneshnei politiki Rossiia, f. glavnyi arkhiv*, I-9, op. 8 (1879–1882 gg.), d. 4, l. 58–59, as cited in Kiniapina, *Kavkaz*, p. 307. For the British forward policy and the occupation of Afghanistan, see Fraser-Tytler, *Afghanistan*, pp. 137–52.

an agreement with Iran that drew an arbitrary boundary line dividing the Turkmen tribes and committed the signatories to a policy of non-intervention in tribal affairs on both sides of the frontier. Unfazed, Skobolev occupied Merv, the last oasis on the Afghan border, provoking another crisis of "Mervisness" between London and St. Petersburg. A prolonged and tense period of negotiations ended in 1885–1887 with a final delimitation of the Russian–Afghan border.

The Russian advance was greatly facilitated by the construction of strategic railroads in Trans Caspia. In 1880, a line from the Caspian port of Uzun-Ada deep into Turkmen territory was crucial to the success of Skobolev's campaign against the Teke tribesmen and his occupation of Merv. Five years later, the second stage of the Trans Caspian railroad, passing close to the Iranian border at Ashkabad, strengthened Russia's strategic position in negotiations with the British over the Afghan borders. In 1888, the third leg to Samarkand was completed, realizing the dream of General von Kaufman, the first governor-general of Turkestan (1867–1881).[232]

Turkestan

Turkestan was in the words of Daniel Brower, "a work-in-progress from the time of the conquest of Tashkent in 1865 until the empire collapsed in 1917."[233] From the earliest planning on the governance of Turkestan, Russian policy makers differed over whether to impose a tough military administration or to introduce structural reforms that would incorporate both the nomads of the steppe and the inhabitants of the khanates into a Russian civil order (*grazhdanstvennost'*). The first group was fearful that "fanatical" pan-Islamicists whom they linked to Muslim uprisings in the Caucasus and in Chinese western Turkestan (Xinjiang) could spread to the Turkic population. The second group sought to continue the policies

---

[232] A. M. Solov'eva, *Zheleznodorozhnyi transport Rossii vo vtoroi polovine XIX v.* (Moscow: Nauka, 1975), pp. 196–97. This was the first railroad in the world crossing a waterless desert, the Kara Kum. The British were also building strategic lines toward Afghanistan, but they rebuffed Russian proposals to link the two networks. As Lord Curzon wrote in 1905: "Any attempt to make a railway in Afghanistan in connection with the Russian strategic railways would be regarded as an act of direct aggression against us." Vartan Gregorian, *The Emergence of Modern Afghanistan* (Stanford University Press, 1969), p. 202.

[233] Brower, *Turkestan*, p. 26. Brower uses Russian archives to build on the previous work of Hélène Carrère d'Encausse, "Organizing and Colonizing the Conquered Territories," in Edward Allworth (ed.), *Central Asia. A Century of Russian Rule* (New York: Columbia University Press, 1967), who stresses the administrative side; and the magisterial work of V. V. Bartol'd, *Istoriia kul'turnoi zhizni Turkestana* (Leningrad: Akademiia nauk SSSR, 1927), to whom all these scholars owe a debt.

first enunciated under Catherine II, followed by the old Caucasus hands from Vorontsov and Bariatinskii to Miliutin and his protégé, von Kaufman.

From the outset, the Russians faced three major problems. First, their knowledge of the Trans Caspian frontier was incomplete and faulty. In dealing with the nomads they exaggerated the powers of the Kirghiz khans as their agents and pursued a policy of dissolving clan ties. This led to a decline in the nomadic way of life, but increased the fusion of the Kirghiz and Turkmen with the Sarts. The urbanized nomads were exposed to an artificial literary language with Arabic and Persian words, and a general Muslim scholastic education that increased the difficulty of introducing the Russian language and European culture.[234] Second, the bureaucracy was not united and was often corrupt. Its policies were hesitant or contradictory, reflecting the conflicting views within the ministries, between the center and periphery, and among the successive governors general. The Russian administration ended up being an unwieldy compromise between the two competing policies. Third, the Russians had to deal with different types of authority relations, representing distinctive local ecologies. In the post-Mongol period, the tribal populations of the oases adhered either to the ideal of political equality or to patriarchal authority, while the non-tribal population settled in and around the towns formed the core of patriarchal states. Among the tribes, local leaders were more often elected; in the towns, the officials were appointed by the khans or the beg. While the urban centers observed Islamic law, the nomadic tribesmen had little understanding of the Shari'a.[235] These differences were never overcome by the Russian administrators or, for a time, even by their Soviet successors.

Turkestan could be absorbed into the Russian imperial system only by the conscious and consistent action of the state. At its most idealistic, von Kaufman's administration envisaged a transformation of Turkestan along utopian lines, although it was riddled with contradictions.[236] He set up a hierarchical military administration, and also recognized a degree of autonomy for local judicial administrative and fiscal institutions. But he sought to eliminate the political power of Kirghiz tribal leaders through tax and land reform. His policies of urban development, especially the construction of a European-style quarter of Tashkent, and colonization of rural areas by Cossack and Russian settlers created a residential

[234] Bartol'd, *Istoriia*, p. 122.
[235] Paul Georg Geiss, *Pre-Tsarist and Tsarist Central Asia. Communal Commitment and Political Order in Change* (London: Routledge Curzon, 2003), pp. 159–61.
[236] Brower, *Turkestan*.

separation between the two cultures. Yet he created integrated schools to educate both Russian and indigenous children in the same classrooms. He established a bilingual newspaper to inform the local population of important decisions of the tsarist administration and to spread useful knowledge about the region. But there was no major effort to co-opt local elites into the administration.[237]

Kaufman's attitude toward Islam was summed up in his formulation to "ignore" it rather than to persecute it. He pinned his hopes on his misperception that, left alone, Islam would decay when confronted with a superior Russian civilization. His main concern was to blunt the "fanatical" edge of Islam and to win over the "best people" to collaborate with his administration. He attempted to liberate Muslim women from their most onerous social bonds. He promoted a number of environmental schemes, encouraged the more rational use of land, and supported ethnographic research into the customs and laws of the indigenous population.[238] Kaufman was sensitive to the international dimensions of his policies. Because the khanate of Bukhara shared a common frontier with Afghanistan, he treated the khan with care in order to avoid offending the British, particularly after the Afghan claimant to the throne and future amir, Abdurrahman, sought refuge there in 1870. Similarly, the Russians recognized the importance of Kokand in their competition with the British and Chinese over the khanate of Kashgar, a borderland under the rule of the ambitious adventurer, Ya'qub Beg.[239]

Kaufman's views on colonization reflected his ambivalent attitude toward Islam. He favored it in the fully settled areas of Turkestan, but he opposed it in the steppe region where the government had been settling Cossacks since the 1840s. The Orenburg and Ural Cossacks arrived in two waves, followed by the Siberian Cossacks. They were settled on Kirghiz grazing lands, which led to clashes with the nomads. Kaufman believed Cossack communities would provide security and a bulwark against the Islamic influence of Muslims moving out of the oases into

---

[237] Geiss, *Pre-Tsarist and Tsarist Central Asia*, pp. 197–211, who argues against Carrère d'Encausse that Russia "did not seek to integrate the conquered people." *Ibid.*, p. 204. One of the rare successful examples of co-optation was Ch. Ch. Valikhanov, a Kirghiz graduate of the Siberian Cadet Corps and a strong advocate of adapting Russian culture to combat the fanatical and backward influence of the mullahs. Ch. Ch. Valikhanov, *Sobranie sochineniia*, 5 vols. (Alma Ata: Izd. Akademiia nauk Kazakhskoi SSR, 1984), vol. I, pp. 22–29, 73–76; vol. II, pp. 71–75.

[238] Brower, *Turkestan*, pp. 31–43; Carrère d'Encausse, "Organizing and Colonizing," pp. 151–53; David Mackenzie, "Kaufman of Turkestan. An Assessment of his Administration, 1867–1881," *Slavic Review* 26(2) (June 1967): 265–85, offers a most positive evaluation.

[239] For Ya'qub Beg, see the following section on Inner Asia.

the steppe. But he was disappointed by the results and suspended colonization. He left behind an important legacy, but like other pro-consuls of borderlands his paternalistic methods failed to overcome the enormous obstacles of incorporating a borderland with a radically different culture under imperial rule.

At the end of the nineteenth century, Russian policy makers increasingly took a broader perspective on the commercial and strategic links between the Caucasian, Trans Caspian, and Inner Asian borderlands. General A. N. Kuropatkin personified this trend. Succeeding von Kaufman as Governor General of Turkestan, he went on to become Minister of War. He consistently supported Finance Minister Sergei Witte's policy of peaceful penetration of Iran and Manchuria. As early as 1895 he had been sent on an extraordinary mission to Tehran. In his subsequent report to Nicholas II, he argued that the empire needed to secure control over commerce on the northern frontier with Iran, and possibly beyond to the central and southern regions as well. Witte had already been preparing the ground by purchasing shares in the private Loan Bank of Persia, which he converted into a branch of the Russian State Bank. Taking advantage of Iran's large external debt to Britain, Witte designed a strategy of loans in exchange for commercial and financial concessions. Engaged in a fierce rivalry with Britain for control over Iran's finances, the Russians were successful in negotiating two big loans in 1900 and 1902. In exchange, they obtained concessions to build and exploit a paved road from the Caucasian frontier to Tehran, to construct a parallel telegraph line, and to permit tariff-free importation of Russian goods. Sandwiched between these agreements, a commercial treaty in 1901 gave Russia an advantageous position in Iran's trade.[240]

Ever since the 1870s the Russian government had debated the merits of constructing a railroad linking the Caucasus provinces to northern Iran. In 1881, the commander-in-chief and principal administrative officer of the Caucasus, Prince Dondukov-Korsakov, urged that Russia should strengthen its position in Trans Caspia "as an advanced post from which Russia can act successfully against the hostile designs of England." He proposed a revision in the 1881 frontier, arguing that the Trans Caspian railroad ran too close to the boundary line and that the headwaters of the streams that irrigated the fertile valleys on the Russian side were located on the Iranian side. He foresaw a succession crisis in Iran that would touch off disorders that could easily spread across the porous frontier. He advocated working with the tribal leaders in Khorāsān to bring that

---

[240] Boris V. An'anich, *Rossiiskoe samoderzhavie i vyvoz kapitalov. 1895–1914 gg (Po materialam uchetno-ssudnogo banka)* (Leningrad: Nauka, 1975).

restless province under Russian control. He envisaged using it to bargain with a claimant to the throne, offering Russian support in exchange for a frontier rectification. Although the crisis did not materialize, Russian agents sought to prepare for it by spreading anti-Shi'ite propaganda among the Sunni tribes of Khorāsān and Seistān.

Lacking adequate resources, the Russians were forced to postpone their railroad plans. When the British sought to obtain their own concession, the Russians wrung a promise from the shah not to build any lines for five years. They continued to press successfully for a moratorium on rail construction in Iran until the end of imperial rule.[241] The Russian government was brought round to British proposals to resolve their rivalry over Iran by partitioning the country only after defeat in the Russo-Japanese War forced them to reconsider their entire policy in the borderlands.

Inner Asia

The Inner Asian complex frontier extending from the Altai Mountains to the shores of the Sea of Japan falls into two geocultural subdivisions. The first is centered on the river valleys at the margins of the cultivated land and the steppe where the Chinese, Mongol, and Manchu cultures intersected and interacted. The second coincides with the province of Xinjiang, but is also subdivided between Dzhungaria and western Turkestan, respectively, and the lands north and south of the Tienshan Mountains. The key military strong points on the Inner Asian complex frontier were located in the lower reaches of the Liao River valley, called "the Chinese Pale" by Lattimore, in southern Manchuria, the Ordos bend in the Yellow River, and the oases of the Tarim basin in western Turkestan.[242] The Ordos is one of the handful of places on the margin of the steppe where lakes and rivers produce enough moisture to sustain agriculture and, with irrigation, to expand the cultivation. The Chinese, including the early Ming emperors, made repeated attempts to control it. When they abandoned it to the Mongols, the Ming renounced *de facto* their forward policy of aggressive military action in exchange for a purely defensive strategy based on building walls.[243]

---

[241] Firuz Kazemzadeh, "Russian Imperialism and Persian Railways," in Hugh McClean et al. (eds.), *Russian Thought and Politics* (Cambridge, MA: Harvard University Press, 1953), pp. 180–82, 356–73.

[242] Larry Moses, "A Theoretical Approach to the Process of Inner Asian Confederation," *Études mongoles* 5 (1974): 115–17.

[243] The importance of the Ordos is central to the argument of Arthur Waldron, *The Great Wall. From History to Myth* (Cambridge University Press, 1990), pp. 68–69, 84, 110, 120–39.

416   Imperial frontier encounters

The Qing–Russian encounter

For the Qing, security on the Inner Asian frontiers was the overriding concern in delimitating an international boundary line with the Russian Empire. During the initial period of their conquest, Manchu border troops had clashed with Cossack hunters and colonizers who had sought to bring tribal vassals of the Qing in the Amur valley under their control. The Russian government had built a series of forts on the Amur and its tributaries to establish their sovereignty over the region. As we have seen, the Oirats of Dzhugaria were in touch with the Russians during their war with the Qing. An alliance between the Oirats and the Russians would threaten stability along the entire Inner Asian frontier of the Manchus. The Russians had to be neutralized.

The Manchus enjoyed two advantages in the negotiations with the Russians leading to the Treaty of Nerchinsk in 1689. On the frontier they commanded a numerically superior military force armed with muskets and artillery on the same technological level as the Russians. They brought with them Jesuit priests, who served as translators and intermediaries using Latin as the "neutral" language of diplomacy acceptable to both sides. The Russians should have learned from their experience with the Jesuits in their western borderlands not to expect even-handedness. What they could not have known was that the Jesuit Order had already won points from the Kangxi emperor by supplying him with weapons and information about the European world. The Jesuits anticipated that these services and their diplomatic assistance at Nerchinsk would further advance their plans to convert the Qing Empire to Latin Christianity. In this they failed. But their role in negotiating the treaty gave the edge to the Manchus. The treaty granted the Russians the right to trade across the frontier, in return for renouncing some of their territorial claims. More important, they committed themselves to adopting a neutral position in the struggle shaping up between the Qing and the Dzhungars.[244]

Peter the Great may have been tempted to intervene. The Dzhungar leaders repeatedly renewed their requests for aid, and the Russians were simultaneously receiving appeals from the Kazakh nomads who complained about the infringement of the Oirats on their pasture lands. The tsar's imposition of a state monopoly on trade with China was not working well, and there were rumors of gold to be found in Dzhungaria. He sent missions to both the Qing and the Dzhungars, but distracted elsewhere he

---

[244] For Nerchinsk, see Peter Perdue, *China Moves West. The Qing Conquest of Central Eurasia* (Cambridge, MA: Belknap Press, 2005), pp. 164–73.

hesitated to become actively engaged in the struggle over the Inner Asian borderlands.

Following Peter's death the negotiations leading up to the Treaty of Kiakhta in 1727 were prolonged and painful for the Russians.[245] At times during the six-month visit to Beijing, their mission was confined and half-starved. Twenty drafts of the treaty were discussed and rejected. Initially, the Chinese demanded huge territorial concessions in eastern and western Siberia. They were also, in the words of the chief Russian negotiator, "intent on stripping away by treaty or by arms all the Mongolian lands from the Russian Empire."[246] In the treaty the Russians for the second time ceded substantial territories to the Chinese, including some of their own settlements. In exchange for *de facto* neutrality in the Chinese conflict with Dzungaria, the Russians obtained the right to trade on a regular basis at two frontier markets, Nerchinsk and Kiakhta, to send three caravans directly to Beijing, and to establish a resident Russian church there. Elaborate machinery was put in place on the frontier to regulate all manner of possible disputes. When in mid-century the Qing prepared to unleash their full force against Dzhungaria, their leader, Galdan, again turned to Russia for assistance. Kangxi then played his diplomatic trump card, warning the Russians that any support for the Oirats would be considered a violation of their "peaceful agreement."[247]

In the early nineteenth century, the threats to Qing power in the Inner Asian borderlands came from the coastal frontier, although in the long run the Russians benefited. As we have seen, Chinese foreign relations had traditionally been focused on regulating relations with the barbarians of the north, a policy that the Manchus inherited. Their frontier policies continued to be shaped by the Confucian world view of China as the Middle Kingdom with the emperor exercising the Mandate of Heaven. In relations with the barbarians this meant cultivating reciprocal relations in the form of trade, gift giving, and tribute. But the tributary system also meant the formal subordination of the barbarians to the emperor expressed in the form of the ritual of submission (kowtow). An exception had been made with regard to the Russians during the negotiation of the treaties of Nerchinsk (1689) and Kiakhta (1727), which were conducted on the basis of equality; subsequently, the Qing ambassador to St. Petersburg even performed obeisance before the tsar.

---

[245] For the negotiations, see Marc Mancall, *Russia and China. Their Diplomatic Relations to 1728* (Cambridge, MA: Harvard University Press, 1971), pp. 223 ff.

[246] B. P. Gurevich, *Mezhdunarodnye otnosheniia v tsentral'noi Azii v XVII–pervoi polovine XIX v.* (Moscow: Nauka, 1979), citing AVP f. snosheniia Rossii c Kitaem, 1726.

[247] Gurevich, *Mezhdunarodnye*, pp. 51–56; see also Perdue, *China Marches West*, pp. 175–80.

Preoccupied by the Inner Asian frontiers, the Qing ruling elites did not grasp that traders from overseas represented a different kind of security problem. The Westerners were treated initially in what might be called a strict interpretation of the tribute system. When the British attempted to press the limits of the system by demanding an expansion of the opium trade, Qing resisted on the grounds that opium, unlike horses on the northern frontier, was not a necessary or desirable item of commerce; besides, the Chinese could grow their own. An influential faction of scholar-officials strongly opposed any concession in enforcing the tribute system.[248] Conditioned by fighting on land frontiers in the north, and lacking experience in naval matters, they seriously underestimated British naval power. They were stunned by the defeats on the coast and rivers that lost them the Opium War in 1840–1842.

In the long term the consequences of the war were almost catastrophic. The dislocation caused by the spread of opium increased social instability in the southeast frontier province of Guangxi. Under the inspired leadership of a failed student of the examinations and a Christian convert, Hong Xiuquan, a powerful anti-Manchu revolutionary movement threatened to overthrow the dynasty. Although it was repressed, the Taiping Rebellion (1849–1864) severely weakened the government for the next round of its confrontation with the Western powers and Russia. Beginning in the late years of the Qianglong emperor, imperial rule had begun to show signs of breaking down. One persistent symptom of the crisis was the growth of resistance to central power in the borderlands on the periphery of the empire and the border regions within the interior provinces which shared similar sociocultural characteristics.

The Russian incorporation of Turkestan posed serious problems for the security of the Qing even as it opened up a vast domain for economic exploitation. In Dzhungaria, the caravan route along the so-called northern road of the Tarim basin, passing through the oases of Turfan and Aksu to Kashgar, was the main line of communications that ran the entire length of the region superseding the ancient silk route. It had been "for centuries the strategic key to Chinese imperial policy among the Turkestan oases as a whole . . ." Its strategic importance was further enhanced by the fact that to the west the trade routes passed through the Chinese Muslim provinces of Ningsia and Gansu, where in the nineteenth century endemic rebellion threatened to cut off the whole of western Turkestan from the center of

---

[248] These conclusions represent an attempt to supplement the traditional view of John K. Fairbank (ed.), *The Chinese World Order. Traditional China's Foreign Relations* (Cambridge, MA: Harvard University Press, 1968), with James M. Polachek, *The Inner Opium War* (Cambridge, MA: Harvard University Press, 1992).

power. Exposed to the steppe, western Turkestan suffered from periodic invasion, devastation, and forced migrations. The land, though rich, was undeveloped and contained an amalgam of ethnic groups. The key to its wealth and strategic center was the Ili valley populated by Mongols, Kazakhs, Kirghiz, Manchus, and Chinese. The valley opened up toward the Kazakh steppe, where by the mid-eighteenth century the Russians were advancing to challenge Chinese hegemony all along the frontier. Geography favored their cross-border trade even after the Chinese had incorporated the region as the new province of Xinjiang.[249] By the mid-nineteenth century the Russian penetration of Trans Caspia had carried them to the edge of Chinese territory, poised to intervene in the domestic rebellions across the frontier.

Rebellions in the borderlands

The Muslim uprisings in Gansu and western Turkestan had their origins in the tangled relations among the frontier region's great variety of ethnic and religious groups, and the Qing center of power. The conquests of the eighteenth century had brought into the empire a substantial number of Turkic adherents to the Naqshbandi, the Sufi order that, as we have seen, fiercely resisted the tsarist conquest and consolidation of the north Caucasus. Their doctrines permitted them to employ the two apparently opposite responses of accommodation and resistance in their encounters with imperial rule. They reserved the internal world for the mystical life, but observed the law (Shari'a) in their external behavior where that was the norm. They could respond to a harsh exercise of non-Muslim authority by unleashing jihad, but could also withdraw into a world of pure spirituality, allowing them to collaborate with the infidel.[250] In Trans Caspia they carried out widespread conversions among the Uzbeks, including prominent members of the powerful Khoja clan. The rule of the Khojas from 1679 to 1759 in southern Turkestan was one of the many revivalist Islamic movements that sought to encompass both the nomadic and sedentary populations of the steppe and oases. By managing shrines and religious endowments (*waqf*), and engaging in trade, they acquired considerable wealth. They transformed the economic foundations of local society in their efforts to centralize fragmented tribal authority and to build a stable state. But like other tribal confederations in Trans Caspia,

---

[249] Owen Lattimore, *Inner Asian Frontiers of China*, 2nd edn (New York: Capitol Publications, 1951), pp. 173–81; Owen Lattimore, *Pivot of Asia. Sinkiang and the Inner Asian Frontiers of China and Russia* (Boston, MA: Little, Brown, 1950), pp. 171–73.

[250] Malise Ruthven, *Islam in the World* (London: Penguin Books, 1984), pp. 273–86.

they were unable to build strong central institutions or create a professional army, without which they could not compete with the powerful Chinese and Russian empires. The expansion of the Qing into the region ended Khoja rule in 1759, but did not end resistance.[251]

After the conquest and true to their multicultural policies, the Qing extended a good deal of autonomy to the local mixed Turkic Muslim population of the new province of Xinjiang. But Beijing also extended special protection to the Chinese traders. Small irritations grew under subsequent lax and corrupt Qing colonial administrators. Discontent flamed into rebellion under the leadership of the Khojas who, although deposed by the Qing, continued to control the oases of the khanates across the frontier. The combination of Khoja raids and local Muslim (Naqshbandi) revolts repeatedly shook the region in 1760, 1765, 1815, 1830/1, several times in 1847, again in 1857, culminating in the great rebellion of 1864/5 that enveloped both the north and south of Xinjiang.[252]

The rebellion of 1864 illustrated the central dilemma facing both the Russian and Chinese empires in dealing with the most fervent defenders of the Shari'a among the Sufi orders. Whatever tolerance was extended to local Muslim elites, the fact remained that the imperial rulers were perceived as "infidels" and hence they possessed no legitimacy, no charisma. What sparked the rebellion of 1864 was the widespread discontent over heavy financial exactions to pay for the local Qing administration expressed in the language of jihad. Encouraged by the Taiping rebels, it spread rapidly in an uncoordinated fashion to Kashgar, Urumchi, Yarkand, Ili, and Khotan, involving both Chinese-speaking Muslims (Tungans) and Turkic Muslims.

From 1862 to 1877 a series of Muslim rebellions engulfed the entire northwest of China, including the provinces of Shaanxi, Gansu, and Ningxiam. The rebels espoused "a militant, revivalist and millenarian

---

[251] Joseph Fletcher, "The Naqshbandiyya in Northwest China," in Beatrice Forbes Manz (ed.), *Studies on Chinese and Islamic Inner Asia* (Aldershot: Variorum, 1995); James A. Millward, "The Qing Formation, the Mongol Legacy and the 'End of History' in Early Modern Central Eurasia," in Lynn Struve (ed.), *The Qing Formation in World Historical Time* (Cambridge, MA: Harvard University Press, 2004), pp. 103–4; Isenbike Togan, "The Khojas of Eastern Turkestan," in Jo-Ann Gross (ed.), *Muslims in Central Asia. Expressions of Identity and Change* (Durham, NC: Duke University Press, 1992), pp. 134–48.

[252] For the Qing conquest, administrative, and commercial policies, Joseph Fletcher, "Ch'ing Inner Asia *c.* 1800," in *The Cambridge History of China* (Cambridge University Press, 1980), vol. 10, pp. 60–83; L. J. Newby, "The Begs of Xinjiang. Between Two Worlds," *Bulletin of the School of Oriental and African Studies* 61(2) (1998): 278–97. For the history of rebellions, Immanuel C. Y. Hsu, *The Ili Crisis. A Study of Sino-Russian Diplomacy, 1871–1881* (Oxford University Press, 1965), pp. 18–29.

form of Islam" called the New Sect. The Muslims who called themselves Hui had been settled in these provinces by the Mongols under the Yuan dynasty, who trusted them more than the Han. They served as soldiers, scouts, land reclaimers, merchants, and craftsmen. Fully integrated into Chinese society, they had never abandoned their Islamic faith. In order to repress the rebellion the Qing forces were stretched to breaking point and had little to spare for the major uprising in western Turkestan.

The rebellions revealed all the problems of establishing firm control over an Inner Asian borderland. The weakness of the imperial administration at the center had sparked internal rebellions that spread to the periphery, where ethnic and religious differences between the frontier peoples and the ruling elites and among themselves exacerbated the conflict. Rival empires, Russian, British, and Ottoman, were drawn in when the Chinese lost control of the province to the insurgents.

After the initial victories, the rebel forces were unified under the leadership of Ya'qub Beg. A reassessment of Ya'qub Beg has portrayed him as a latter-day Nadir Shah. He sought to marshal a professional army and maneuver diplomatically in a complex international environment. He proved to be a quintessential man of the borderlands. Initially, his relations with Russia were strained. The Russian government was haunted by persistent fears that the creation of a large Muslim state on the Inner Asian frontiers could only benefit the British.[253] They were also concerned that Ya'qub Beg would not honor the commercial treaties they had signed with the Qing. After they occupied Kokand, Russia put pressure on him to adjust his boundaries in their favor. Tension mounted until in 1872 the two sides finally reached a compromise agreement. The Russians recognized Ya'qub Beg as *de facto* ruler of Kashgar and Urumchi, and he acceded to a commercial treaty.

At the same time, he was negotiating with the British, who had dispatched a mission to evaluate the potential threat to India of Russian domination in the region. In 1874, he signed a commercial treaty with Britain on essentially the same lines as that with Russia. For him the main advantage was not trade, but an opening to purchase arms from the government of India. Even earlier, he had recognized that he needed a stronger source of legitimacy than the kind of local dynastic rule the Khojas had established. Seeking the protection of the sultan-caliph as head of the greater Muslim world, he dispatched a trusted advisor to Istanbul. The Ottomans might provide him with a more dependable, alternative source of weapons. In return, he was willing to accept the

[253] Aleksei Voskresenskii, "Genezis 'Iliiskogo Krizisa' i russko-kitaiskii Livadskii dogovor 1879," *Cahiers du monde russe* 35(4) (October–December 1994): 766–68.

sultan's sovereignty. But he also continued to improve his diplomatic contacts with Russia, working first through Ignat'ev in Istanbul and then von Kaufman in Tashkent.[254]

The Chinese could not deal with Ya'qub Beg until they had suppressed the Muslim rebellions in their northwest provinces. A simultaneous crisis with Japan over Formosa touched off a great debate in Beijing over the relative importance to the security of the country of the land frontier with Inner Asia and the coastal frontier with the West. Those who dismissed Xinjiang as a barren, remote, and costly colony lost out to those who feared that a Russian advance there would lead to a loss of Mongolia which would endanger the capital.[255] The suppression of the western Turkestan rebellions confirmed the long-standing rule of Chinese foreign policy that defending the northern frontiers took precedence over defending the sea coast.

During the initial stages of the rebellions, the Inner Asian frontier with Russia was overrun by refugees, nomadic raiding increased, and trade collapsed. In 1871, the Russians proposed a joint expedition with the Chinese to subjugate the rebels. Receiving no response, Miliutin at the War Ministry decided to intervene unilaterally by occupying the Ili River valley as a precautionary measure to prevent the spread of the rebellion into territories under Russian control. Russian troops remained there for ten years.

Ya'qub Beg relied heavily on his large army and the revival of the Islamic spirit to consolidate his power. Although he had defeated his rivals, he failed to create a strong central administration. His officials proved to be no more honest and efficient than those they had driven out. Moreover, allegiance to Islam could not overcome the ethnic and regional rivalries that undermined his authority. Ya'qub Beg himself lacked legitimacy. In 1877, having resolved the policy debate over the primacy of the northern frontiers, the Qing emperor dispatched his armies to defeat Ya'qub Beg and restore order. The Chinese had brushed aside British offers to mediate and now demanded that the Russians evacuate Ili. The Russians stalled until 1881, coming dangerously close to war with China over a delimitation of the frontier. In the meantime, Russia had occupied the oases of Khiva and Kokand, destroying the last centers of power of the Khojas. The Qing responded by abolishing local rule in

[254] Hodong Kim, *Holy War in China. The Muslim Rebellion and State in Chinese Central Asia, 1864–1877* (Stanford University Press, 2004), pp. 141–57.
[255] C. Y. Hsü, "The Great Policy Debate in China, 1874. Maritime Defense versus Frontier Defense," *Harvard Journal of Asiatic Studies* 25 (1964/5): 22–28.

western Turkestan, and in 1884 incorporated the region as the "new dominion," Xinjiang, as a province in the imperial administrative structure.[256] The partition of Turkestan divided its peoples, like other complex frontiers, leaving Kazakh and Kirghiz on both sides and creating the potential for further conflict in the twentieth century and beyond.

---

[256] The standard treatment is Hsu, *The Ili Crisis*. See also Joseph Fletcher, "China and Central Asia, 1368–1884," in Fairbank (ed.), *The Chinese World Order*, pp. 217–24; James A. Millward, *Beyond the Pass. Economy, Ethnicity and Empire in Qing Central Asia, 1759–1864* (Stanford University Press, 1998).

5   Imperial crises

From 1905 to 1911 all five multinational empires were shaken by constitutional crises that prefigured the greater upheavals and collapse of
imperial rule in the period from 1917 to 1923. While each crisis had its
particular domestic sources, all shared certain common characteristics.
They signaled a major destabilization of imperial rule and a profound loss
of legitimacy. They were precipitated both by the growing strength and
militancy of socialist or nationalist movements in the borderlands, and by
the pressure for economic and political change from powers outside the
boundaries of Eurasia, primarily Britain, France, and Japan. The reactive
impulses of the rulers, whether Franz Joseph, Nicholas II, Abdülhamid,
Nasir al-Din, or the dowager empress – all of whom followed contradictory policies that promoted de-stabilizing institutional reforms while at
the same time seeking to revive traditional ideologies – tended to intensify
rather than disarm the forces of internal resistance and further to splinter
the ruling elites. Disorders within one of the old rival powers often had
consequences in the borderlands of neighboring states. A major reciprocal
shock reverberated from the 1905 revolution in Russia. The centrality of
Russia in the multiple crises of the first decade of the twentieth century
was due to a number of factors: its contiguous and porous boundaries with
all the other Eurasian states; the vigorous, not to say aggressive, conduct of
its foreign policy in the west Balkans, Danubian frontier, Trans Caspia,
and Inner Asia; and, finally, the widespread, if more diffuse, influence of
the Russian revolutionary movements that spread across its frontiers
either by imitation or direct transfer. The crises often, if not always,
originated in conflicts over the borderlands where the ruling elites had
failed to solve the most fundamental security problem of imperial rule;
their first line of defense rested on unstable and vulnerable frontiers.

Although the dynastic rulers managed to weather the initial shock of the
constitutional crises, they were all swept away in the second great period
of revolution. The collapse of central authority in China after 1911, and
the simultaneous defeat of the Habsburg, Ottoman, and Russian empires
in 1917–1918, led to the dissolution of the empires, the breakaway or

attempted breakaway of the borderlands, and a complex process of reconstituting new state systems on their ruined foundations.

Crisis in the Habsburg borderlands

In the last two decades of the nineteenth century Habsburg imperial rule became increasingly tenuous in Hungary, Bohemia, Galicia, and Bosnia. Two sources of the conflicts were similarly entangled in all four borderlands. Resistance of the local elites to the cultural policies of a predominantly German central administration intensified local ethnic clashes between the same elites. As the political stakes increased, it became increasingly difficult to resolve either set of grievances to the satisfaction of all the parties concerned. The ruling elite in Vienna did not lack imagination in devising different policies to deal with the growing restiveness in its borderlands, recognizing the peculiarities of the cultural dynamics in each. But in the end the complexities of the problems overwhelmed them.

Before proceeding to the growing ethnic and religious struggles in each separate borderland, mention should be made of one of the last major efforts by the bureaucracy to resolve all the nationality conflicts by employing the newest technologies of communication. In the Habsburg Empire recognition of the importance of the telegraph and the railroad in shrinking time and space came early. In 1841, Carl Friederich von Kübeck, an energetic would-be reformer of Habsburg administration under Metternich, planned both a state rail (1841) and telegraph (1846) network that gave primacy to political, especially strategic, considerations. Security and the struggle with Prussia for hegemony in Germany dominated construction up to 1866. Like Russia, however, high construction costs forced the government as early as 1854 to turn increasingly to private capital, which meant building economically viable lines tied to centers of industry. After 1880, also running parallel to developments in Russia, the Vienna government pursued its most ambitious railroad policy designed to create an interregional network without paying special attention to industrial development. The lack of coordination between an industrial policy and a politically integrative function failed to overcome the Monarchy's relative backwardness in relation to Western Europe without solving the nationality problem. The vision and fate of the Koerber Plan illustrates the dilemma.[1]

---

[1] Karl Bachinger, "Das Verkehrswesen," in Adam Wandruszka and Peter Urbanitsch (eds.), *Die Habsburgermonarchie, 1848–1918* (Vienna: Österreichische Akademie der Wissenschaften, 1973), pp. 319–22.

In 1901, following a series of bruising political conflicts with the Czechs, Prime Minister Ernst von Koerber drafted a comprehensive transportation project for the Austrian half of the Monarchy. A network was designed to link Prague, Galicia, Bosnia, and Hercegovina, to Trieste through Linz and Salzburg. The law also provided for the regulation of river traffic in Galicia, Bohemia, and Austria. Koerber made it clear that the aim of his project was to promote an economic development program that would resolve regional–national conflicts by offering something to everyone. A successful example of Habsburg bargaining strategies, it easily passed a normally fractious parliament.[2] Unfortunately, the vision failed to materialize. The problem was not so much the conditions of relative economic backwardness with respect to Western Europe, or the uneven development of regional economies within the Monarchy.[3] Rather, it was the resistance of the nationalities to integration on other than economic grounds.

Galicia

The Austrian compromise of 1867 in Galicia had handed over the political and cultural life of the province to the Polish aristocracy, stabilizing the administration but breeding discontent among the Ruthenian majority of the population with fateful consequences in the twentieth century. According to Ivan Rudnytsky, the conflict was not "racial" or even fundamentally religious. Rather, the division "was an extension of the age-old boundary between the worlds of the Roman and Byzantine civilization." Both sides continued to imagine the religious divide between Latin and Greek Christianity as they had during the seventeenth-century wars between the szlachta and the Cossacks, vividly depicted in the popular novels of Henryk Sienkewicz. On the Ukrainian side, the publicist Ivan Franko put it this way: "we wish the Poles complete national and political liberty, but they have to give up lording over us and forming a 'historic' Poland ... they must accept as we do the idea of a purely ethnic Poland."[4]

---

[2] Alexander Gerschenkron, *An Economic Spurt that Failed. Four Lectures in Austrian History* (Princeton University Press, 1977), but cf. David Good, *The Economic Rise of the Habsburg Empire, 1750–1914* (Berkeley, CA: University of California Press, 1984), pp. 180–83; David Turnock, *The Economy of East Central Europe, 1815–1989. Stages of Transformation in a Peripheral Region* (London: Routledge, 2006), pp. 127–31.

[3] John Lampe, "Redefining Balkan Backwardness," in Daniel Chirot (ed.), *The Origins of Economic Backwardness in Eastern Europe. Economics and Politics from the Middle Ages until the Early Twentieth Century* (Berkeley, CA: University of California Press, 1989), p. 194.

[4] Ivan Rudnytsky (ed.), "The Ukrainians in Galicia," in *Rethinking Ukrainian History* (Edmonton: Canadian Institute of Ukrainian Studies, 1981), pp. 40–42.

Embracing a policy of "new Galician conservatism," the Polish aristocracy had rejected the insurrectionary tradition. They gained intellectual respectability from the Krakow school of historians who blamed the eighteenth-century partitions on the reckless domestic actions of the szlachta. The accommodationist Poles borrowed from the Josephine tradition the idea that they were the bearers of enlightenment in the east. Their cultural campaign to polonize the province through the use of Polish in the administration, control of Jagiellonian University and the Galician Academy of Science antagonized the Ruthenian (Ukrainian) intellectuals. For them the cultural option was to adopt either a Russophil or Ukrainophil perspective. To be a Russophil did not necessarily mean to identify with the Russian Empire. Rather, the Russophil or Old Ruthenian camp sought inspiration in the linguistic and ecclesiastical traditions of Byzantine culture. Their motto was: "If we are to drown we prefer the Russian sea to the Polish swamp." Their strength was centered in the northern districts bordering on Russia. In the early twentieth century, the Austrian authorities suspected their cultural activities of being an espionage network.[5] This attitude was characteristic of the spy mania that permeated the intelligence agencies on all sides of the old Polish frontiers. In the rest of Galicia, the Russophils steadily lost ground to the secular, dynamic intellectuals of the Ukrainophils led by M. P. Drahomanov. After the Ems Decree in 1876 forbade the printing of Ukrainian books in Russia, they made eastern Galicia the center of publication for Ukrainian literature. They were the first to conceive of the "Piedmont complex," the idea that Galicia would become the base for the unification of all Ukrainians.[6] Although the notion proved to be unrealistic, it haunted Polish, Russian, and Soviet leaders – Stalin in particular, during the Russian Civil War, the interwar period, and the Second World War.

In the half century after the reforms of 1848, the Monarchy had not pursued its earlier agrarian policy of making concessions to win over the Ruthenian peasantry. By 1902, the farms of two-thirds of those who still held land were on average just over twelve acres. Nineteen percent of the peasants were landless, living in dire poverty. Influenced by agrarian disturbances across the Russian frontier, the east Galician farm laborers went on strike against their Polish landlords in 1902 and again in 1906, winning the right to keep a larger share of the harvest. Nevertheless, the

---

[5] Andriy Zayarnyuk, "Mapping Identities. The Popular Base of Galician Russophilism in the 1890s," *Austrian History Yearbook* 41 (2010): 140–41.

[6] Rudnytsky, "The Ukrainians in Galicia," pp. 46–51; Alexei Miller, *The Ukrainian Question. The Russian Empire and Nationalism in the Nineteenth Century* (Budapest: CEU Press, 2003), pp. 156–89.

Monarchy discouraged attempts to organize the peasantry into a political party that might have offset the hegemony of Poles in the regional administration.

In 1908, the smoldering resentment of the Ruthenians toward Polish cultural, economic, and political domination erupted in violence. A Ruthenian student assassinated the Polish viceroy, Andrzej Potocki, who had tried and failed to reconcile the social and national conflicts that were tearing his province apart. As Larry Wolff has pointed out, the incident anticipated the assassination of Archduke Ferdinand in 1914 by symbolizing the failure of Habsburg imperial rule to reconcile the national antagonisms.[7] On the eve of the First World War, the Habsburg bureaucrats finally worked out a complex compromise that broke the Polish monopoly over Galician political life, but did not lead to an administrative partition of the province along ethnic lines as the Ukrainians desired. The outbreak of war revealed the deep splits in Ukrainian society. One group favored a Supreme Ukrainian Council and an Austrian victory; another group, composed of émigrés from the old Left Bank, desired a democratic, federated Russia which Ukraine would freely join.[8]

Bohemia

Resistance to imperial rule in Bohemia was less complex but more widespread, virtually paralyzing the Austrian parliament on the eve of the war. The dualist settlement of 1867 disappointed and angered the leaders of the Czech national movement. Ever since 1848 the national feelings of a few intellectuals had been spreading among the growing Czech-speaking urban classes and the peasantry who, unlike the Ruthenians, were increasingly prosperous and involved in local politics through elections to communal councils. In 1860, they took over the Prague municipal council. The Old Czech Party led by the men of 1848, František Palacký and František Rieger, were willing to ally with the Bohemian aristocrats, mainly German, in the hope of creating a federal state. Their policy of accommodation crumbled in the face of opposition by the Young Czechs, who had supported the Polish rising in 1863 and rejected the historic rights of Bohemia in favor of universal suffrage and natural rights as the basis for a reconstruction of the Monarchy. Czech–German cultural rivalry centered on the language question and its institutional expression, the establishment of competing secondary schools. But there were signs of

[7] Larry Wolff, *The Idea of Galicia. History and Fantasy in Habsburg Political Culture* (Stanford University Press, 2010), pp. 331–34.
[8] Rudnytsky, "The Ukrainians in Galicia," pp. 60–61; Wolff, *The Idea of Galicia*, pp. 331–32.

Czech resistance in all aspects of life. As Robin Okey has put it: "The tendency was to chip away at German hegemony."[9]

The Czech–German clash over the language question was one of several in the Monarchy that erupted into a constitutional crisis at the turn of the century. The Old Czechs steadily lost ground and parliamentary seats to the Young Czechs, creating a *crise de gouvernement*. The new premier, Count Kasimir Badeni, seized the opportunity to win over Palacký's successors by offering the Czechs linguistic equality with the Germans in Bohemia. This triggered a *crise de régime*. Like many *Kaisertreu* bureaucrats, Badeni concealed his bargaining from public scrutiny. Once it became known, the indignant Bohemian Germans engaged in obstructive parliamentary tactics, paralyzing the government. Badeni resigned after his police clashed with demonstrators and the decrees were withdrawn. The cost of failure was high. Obstruction became the tactic of both Czechs and Germans, with the government frequently resorting to rule by imperial decree. Confidence in the parliamentary system withered along with Czech–German cooperation.[10] The only political refuge left for advocates of multiculturalism in Bohemia was the Austrian Social Democratic Party.

The Austrian Social Democrats had inherited from Marx and the German liberals in Austria the idea that the Habsburg Monarchy was the main bulwark of Central Europe against Russian expansion under the banner of pan-Slavism. In their Brünn Program of 1899 they offered concessions to the non-German nationalities with the object of preserving the Monarchy. Their nationalities program envisaged a transformation of the Monarchy into a democratic federation by creating autonomous ethnoterritorial units to replace the crown lands, and guaranteeing the rights of national minorities. The debates preceding its endorsement exposed the underlying ethnic antipathies between the Czech and German socialists that were only papered over by their internationalist ideals. (At this time the Hungarian Social Democrats already constituted a separate party.) The Czech delegates successfully opposed the idea of designating German as a common language of convenience. They went on to press for the replacement of the crown lands by nationally delimited, self-governing areas governed by "national chambers elected on the basis

---

[9] Robin Okey, *The Habsburg Monarchy c. 1765–1918. From Enlightenment to Eclipse* (New York: St. Martin's Press, 2002), p. 304. See also pp. 217–20, 225, 231, 257, 273, 287, for the evolution of the Czech national movement in all spheres.

[10] Okey, *The Habsburg Monarchy*, pp. 306–9; Robert Kann, *The Multinational Empire. Nationalism and National Reform in the Habsburg Monarchy 1848–1918*, 2 vols. (New York: Columbia University Press, 1950), vol. I, pp. 203–6; Joseph Redlich, *Emperor Francis Joseph of Austria* (New York: Macmillan, 1929), p. 44.

of universal, direct and equal suffrage." Nevertheless, both the German and Czech factions recognized the critical need to preserve the Habsburg Monarchy. Subsequently, the Brünn Program became the touch point in the debate between Lenin, Stalin, and the Austrian Social Democrats on the nationalities question, with the Bolsheviks insisting on national self-determination, which implied the break up of multinational states. Meanwhile, two younger members of the Austrian party, Karl Renner and Otto Bauer, were already challenging the conservative design of the Brünn Program and offering more original proposals.

Although Bauer and Renner are often coupled as the twin pillars of Austro-Marxist thinking on the nationalities question, they differed on important aspects. Renner's early experience as a soldier in the Habsburg army first made him aware of the variety of national groups in the Monarchy and stimulated his interest in their problems, a subject of life-long concern. He always took a more legalistic and moderate view of social change than Bauer. He proposed the reconstruction of the Habsburg Monarchy as a federation based on a complicated two-tiered organization, one administrative and the other ethnic. Socioeconomic interests would define newly delimited administrative provinces, replacing the outdated crown lands that were based on historic factors. Recognizing that any territorial administrative unit would not correspond to the ethnic mix of a multicultural society, Renner introduced his most original contribution. Ethnic groups would be organized on the basis of the identity of individuals no matter where they lived. By detaching ethnicity from a territorial base, he sought to free a federated multicultural state from several potentially fatal dangers to its existence. First, each ethnic group in the shatter zones would no longer be justified in claiming the sole right to define the boundaries and cultural character of its territorial autonomy. Second, separatist movements would be discouraged by demonstrating the greater advantages of membership in a large federal state that guaranteed equal cultural rights to all its citizens. The ideas of Renner and Bauer stirred Lenin and Stalin to even more passionate criticism. The two Bolsheviks were struggling against the idea of national–cultural autonomy embraced by the Jewish Bund and the Georgian Social Democrats, who cited approvingly the example of Austro-Marxism.[11]

---

[11] Arthur G. Kogan, "The Social Democrats and the Conflict of Nationalities in the Habsburg Monarchy," *Journal of Modern History* 21(3) (September 1949): 204–17; Kann, *The Multinational Empire*, vol. I, pp. 147–57. Cf. *Austro-Marxism*, texts translated and edited by Tom Bottomore and Patrick Good with an introduction by Tom Bottomore (Oxford University Press, 1978), which does not include the key texts on Renner's idea of personal autonomy.

A variation of their program may have had a slim chance of acceptance in the Austrian half of the Monarchy, but only if the Social Democrats gained a majority in parliament. The difficulty of applying this formula to Hungary proved to be intractable. Renner did not even attempt it, but he thought the Austrian example would exercise a moral pressure on Hungary. Renner's ideas met with Oscar Jászi's sympathetic response, though he thought them too utopian. For a brief moment in 1918 the two men were important figures in the republican governments of Austria and Hungary, but events moved too fast for them to engage in what might have been a fruitful alliance.[12]

Hungary

In Hungary a second constitutional crisis in 1905 shook the Dual Monarchy to its very foundations. The crisis had been building throughout the 1890s. Two major sources of conflict were the nationalities and the social question. They remained at the heart of Hungarian politics right down to the outbreak of war and revived in the truncated Hungary after the Treaty of Trianon. A third perennial problem was the constitutional relationship with Austria, which erupted again in 1897 during negotiations over the periodic ten-year renewal of the *Ausgleich*. Having acquired autonomy, the Magyar ruling elite proceeded to apply the very same distasteful policies of assimilation to the national minorities on the periphery of their country as Vienna had imposed on them during the campaigns to centralize the empire under a German bureaucracy. Publicists preached the doctrine of 30 million Hungarians (properly Magyarized in language and political ideals) in order to dominate the south Slav population of the Hungarian borderlands. The celebration of the millennium of the Magyar arrival on the Danubian plain emphasized the triumph of the "lordly Scythians," the heroic tradition of the steppe warriors. Public demonstrations by the national groups, mainly Romanians and Slovaks, to gain the kind of autonomy the Hungarians had won from the Austrians were severely repressed. In 1907, Hungarian police killed twelve Slovak protesters who were protesting the consecration of a new church by a priest other than of their own choosing.[13] Pressure mounted to learn the Magyar tongue.

---

[12] Oscar Jászi, *The Dissolution of the Habsburg Monarchy* (University of Chicago Press, 1929); György Litván, *A Twentieth-Century Prophet. Oscar Jászi, 1875–1957* (Budapest: CEU Press, 2006), p. 131.

[13] László Kontler, *Millennium in Central Europe. A History of Hungary* (Budapest: Atlantisz, 1999), pp. 294–98; Géza Jeszenszky, "Hungary through World War I and the End of the Dual Monarchy," in Peter F. Sugar *et al.* (eds.), *A History of Hungary* (Bloomington, IN: Indiana University Press, 1994), pp. 268–70.

The development of social democracy in Hungary took a peculiar turn soon after the foundation of a Marxist party in 1890. The dominant moderate wing of the Social Democratic Party struck a bargain with the government which ensured its legality, but only at the cost of virtually abandoning any efforts to organize the poor peasants and agricultural workers. Yet rural exploitation and poverty constituted the most pressing social problem in the country. Wage disputes and land hunger drove the peasants into radical action, which culminated in 1897/8 in widespread agrarian disorders. The Social Democrats returned to the more comfortable legal path after the collapse of the Monarchy and the revolution of 1919 by signing a pact with the authoritarian government of Admiral Horthy, assuring them of a fragile legal status in exchange for giving up agitation in the countryside. This policy exposed them in the period after the Second World War to the opportunistic tactics and taunts of the communists.

On top of all this, a new generation of Hungarian politicians insisted on extensive changes to the constitutional compromise of 1867 on the expiration in 1897 of the recurrent ten-year period of renewal. By this time, differences over the national and social questions were pulling the two halves of the Monarchy in different directions. Franz Joseph flatly refused to accept the Hungarian demands for revision. The stand-off inaugurated a period of growing tension between Budapest and Vienna known as "the years of obstruction" from 1897 to 1903, culminating in a full-scale constitutional crisis in 1905. During these years, the complex maneuvering in Hungarian parliamentary politics took on the aspects of a political circus. In the words of Peter Sugar: "the image of the Lower House created after 1897 was that of an ineffective, selfish, often ridiculous debating society whose behavior had nothing to do either with the problems of the country or effective government."[14] Its shenanigans seriously undermined the country's much vaunted constitutional tradition. The crisis itself broke out over the two most inflammatory questions facing the Monarchy in general and the Hungarian half in particular: the language question and army reform.

In 1902, both the Austrian and Hungarian governments introduced an army bill to raise the number of annual recruits in each half of the Monarchy by about a quarter for a total of 125,000. The Independence Party, also known as "the Forty-eighters" for never having accepted the Settlement of 1867, saw the opportunity to bargain by demanding the

---

[14] Peter F. Sugar, "An Underrated Event. The Hungarian Constitutional Crisis of 1905–6," *East European Quarterly* 15(3) (September 1981): 292. In general I follow Sugar's analysis and interpretation.

introduction of Hungarian as the language of command, thus asserting the full sovereignty of parliament. They picked up surprising support from a few members of the so-called national aristocracy, a group drawn from distinguished families including members of the ruling Liberal Party. In the ensuing political maneuvering, the Liberals were forced to resign. They were then defeated in an unprecedented electoral upset ending their thirty-year rule. The new majority led by the Forty-eighters blocked the formation of a new government, demanding concessions on the army. It was an issue on which Franz Joseph refused to compromise. He appointed a caretaker government. For the first time since 1867 the structural weakness of the system was exposed. The dual responsibility of the king-emperor and parliament could work only if a majority could be formed in the lower house that agreed with the king-emperor on Hungary's constitutional rights. The crisis was exacerbated by a wave of strikes clearly inspired by the outbreak of the Russian revolution of 1905. A year later, Habsburg army units occupied the houses of parliament in Budapest, bringing the paralysis of government to an end at the expense of constitutional norms. Meanwhile, the traditionally loyal Croats, who had surprisingly linked up with the Serbs to form their own coalition in the Hungarian parliament, were outraged by another language bill in 1907 that made Magyar the obligatory language for all employees on state railroads. The outbreak of disorder in Croatia forced Vienna to suspend the Croatian parliament and to reintroduce absolutist rule.

The impasse was resolved only when the monarch threatened to introduce universal suffrage. This would have spelled an end to the dominance of the Magyar nobility, and they backed down. The army bills were only forced through parliament, illegally, in 1912 by István Tisza, representing the national aristocracy. He sought to resolve the crisis by piecemeal concessions, slightly enlarging the electorate from 6 percent to 10 percent of the population, patching up relations with the Croats–Serbs – but not the Romanians or Slovaks – and reestablishing constitutional rule in Croatia. He also tightened up internal security. He could not, however, undo the damage. The country was deeply split along class and ethnic lines. The accelerated Magyarization of their co-nationals in Hungary further antagonized the governments of Serbia and Romania, eroding the Monarchy's strategic position along its vulnerable west Balkan and Danubian frontiers. Most damaging of all was the aftershock of the Hungarian constitutional crisis on the Austrian half of the Monarchy. When in 1906 the threat of electoral reform hung over the Hungarians, the Austrian parliament, in order to keep pace, passed a law introducing near universal suffrage in Cisleithenia. The electoral results were disastrous. The multiplicity of mutually hostile ethnic parties made it impossible to form a government. Austria could only be ruled by imperial decree. Hungary suffered a similar fate. The real beneficiary of the declining influence of the ruling Magyar elite was not a coalition of urban social groups, but as László Péter has written, "the state machinery ... not the ascendancy of the bourgeoisie but that of the *hivatalálla*, the East European authoritarian state."[15]

In Hungary, as in the Austrian half of the Monarchy, a few enlightened intellectuals put forth proposals to resolve both the social and ethnic questions. The lead was taken by bourgeois radicals not by the Hungarian Social Democratic Party. The principal theorist of the nationality question in the context of social reform in Hungary was Oscar Jászi. He was the guiding spirit of a group of bourgeois radicals, many like him of Jewish origin, who were associated with the magazine *Huszadik Század* (*The Twentieth Century*), founded in 1900. Advocates of broad social and economic reforms, including emancipation of the peasantry, democratic local government, and universal suffrage, their main theoretical contribution focused on the nationalities. Jászi proudly claimed that he was the first person in Hungary to reconcile socialism and nationalism. His position raised obstacles to cooperation with the Hungarian Social Democrats whom he found to be dogmatic on the subject of nationalities, even though they endorsed the Brünn Program in 1899 and agrarian reform.

Inspired by a form of scientific evolutionism more indebted to Herbert Spencer than to Marx, Jászi argued for acceptance of the awakening of national consciousness in the Hungarian borderlands as an inevitable stage in human evolution, laying the foundation for a genuine federation of free peoples within the Carpathian basin to include Greater Hungary within the Austro-Hungarian Monarchy. Kossuth had been moving in the same direction after 1859. By then he had had ample time to reflect soberly on the failure of 1848. In his view, consistently held to his death in 1894, Hungary's historic mission was to provide a bulwark against German and Russian imperialism by forming a Danubian federation composed of Greater Hungary, Romania, and the south Slavs.[16] But for Kossuth, this was a revolutionary means of breaking up the hated Habsburg Empire; for Jászi, a broader Danubian confederation was the

---

[15] László Péter, "The Aristocracy, the Gentry and their Parliamentary Tradition in Nineteenth Century Hungary," *Slavonic and East European Review* 70(1) (January 1992): 109. See also Géza Jeszenszky, "Hungary through World War I and the End of the Dual Monarchy," in Sugar *et al.* (eds.), *A History of Hungary*, pp. 267–91; Okey, *The Habsburg Monarchy*, pp. 330–35, 356–60.

[16] Kann, *The Multinational Empire*, vol. I, p. 111; Oscar Jászi, *Der Zusammenbruch des Dualismus und die Zukunft der Donaustaaten* (Vienna: Manz, 1918), pp. 40–41.

way of preserving it under the banner of equal rights and the preservation of national languages. His scheme combined the ideas of Karl Renner for a union of autonomous states with the Hungarian liberal József Eötvös's principle of retaining the historic boundaries of established states. It would include five federal states: Austria, Hungary (without Croatia-Slavonia), Bohemia, a unified Poland, and a southern Slav Illyria headed by Croatia, with the possibility of Romania joining later as a sixth state. If forced to choose, as he was in 1916, Jászi, like most Hungarian intellectuals and statesmen, expressed greater fear of the Russians than of the Germans. However reluctantly, he supported Germany in the war.[17] His small Radical Party of intellectuals never gained mass support. But as Minister of Nationality Affairs under the republican government of Károly in 1918/19, he led the campaign to persuade the leaders of national groups in the borderlands, mainly Romanians, Slovaks, and Ruthenians, to remain within Hungary's borders by offering them full autonomy.[18] It was, however, too late. As most historians agree, on the eve of the First World War the possibilities for non-violent solutions in Austria-Hungary had all but vanished. Even a radical transformation of the imperial structure along federalist lines, being considered by the heir to the throne, Archduke Franz Ferdinand, would in all probability have ignited large-scale resistance by one or another ethnic group that perceived itself victimized by the new arrangements.

Bosnia

The third and fatal crisis over the Habsburg borderlands erupted in Bosnia and Hercegovina. A great rebellion of the Bosnian peasantry triggered a major international crisis that toppled dominos all along the Eurasian frontiers from the west Balkans through the Danubian basin, the Caucasian isthmus, and Trans Caspia to the edge of Inner Asia. This linkage has hardly been noticed by historians. Bosnia and Hercegovina exhibited all the features of a shatter zone. Muslims numbered 40 percent of its population, mainly converted Slavs; 42 percent were Orthodox, and 18 percent were Catholic. The Muslim population was concentrated in the towns. The Orthodox peasants toiled on the properties of Muslim landlords. They were legally free, but *de facto* they lived in a state of virtual serfdom. Under Ottoman rule the Orthodox Church, however, had flourished. From the 1850s to the 1870s wealthy Orthodox merchants helped to construct new churches and church schools in Mostar and Sarajevo.

---

[17] Litván, *A Twentieth-Century Prophet*, pp. 104–5, 131.
[18] Litván, *A Twentieth-Century Prophet*, pp. 137–41.

They won concessions by bribing the local Ottoman officials who were lax and corrupt. Russian and European consular officials vied with one another in applying pressure to support the claims of the Orthodox and the Catholic population, respectively, in the hope of strengthening their influence.[19]

Habsburg interest in an expansionist policy in the Balkans gained ground after Austria's expulsion from the German federation and the unification of Germany. The economic crisis of 1873 increased the pressure from certain industries to safeguard the Balkan market against the competition of cheap goods from Britain and Belgium; others were attracted by the prospect of exploiting the rich forest and mineral deposits of Bosnia and Hercegovina.[20] Austrian military officials, supported by local Habsburg bureaucrats of Croatian and Serb background, argued that a conquest of Bosnia and Hercegovina was essential for the defense of the long Dalmatian littoral. They persuaded Emperor Franz Joseph to undertake a month-long voyage along the Dalmatian coast with the object of stirring unrest across the border. In the meantime, Ottoman attempts at agrarian reform ran into opposition from the local Muslim notables, slowing its implementation. In 1875, the long-suffering Orthodox peasantry in Hercegovina rose in rebellion. The disorder spread rapidly into Bosnia. The neighboring Serbs and Montenegrins supported what was originally a social movement in the hope of furthering their national aims by expanding their territorial boundaries.[21] Austrian and Russian officials lent assistance to the rebels, with the Austrians offering asylum to refugees fleeing Ottoman reprisals. The Russians intervened diplomatically to prevent the Serbians from being crushed by superior Ottoman forces much improved by the military reforms. Beyond that the Russian government faced a dilemma.

The Russian Foreign Ministry opposed unilateral action and sought to work with Germany and Austria-Hungary to resolve the crisis. But members of the Oriental Department of the Foreign Ministry, including the

---

[19] Al. Kharuzin, *Bosniia-Gertsegovana. Ocherki okkupatsionnoi provintsi Avstro-Vengriia* (St. Petersburg: Gosudarstvennaia tipografiia, 1901), pp. 274, 280–81.

[20] Zoltan Szasz, "The Balkan Policies of the Habsburg Empire in the 1870s," in Béla K. Király and Gale Stokes (eds.), *Insurrections, Wars and the Eastern Crisis in the 1870s* (New York: Columbia University Press, 1985).

[21] As early as 1873 the Habsburg diplomatic representative in Belgrade had warned his government that "the mistaken notion that Serbia is called upon to play the role of Piedmont among the Slavs of Turkey is so strongly rooted that the Serbs can no longer understand that the Slavs of the different Turkish frontiers should seek aid and protection from any state except Serbia." R. W. Seton-Watson, "Les relations de l'Autriche-Hongrie et de la Serbie entre 1868 et 1874. La mission de Benjamin Kállay à Belgrade," *Le monde slave* 3 (August 1926): 283.

Russian Minister in Istanbul, Count Ignat'ev and other agents in the Balkans, who were ardent pan-Slavs, favored a policy of liberation for the Balkan Slavs with Russia's assistance. They could count on the support of a network of Slavic committees in Russia to provide volunteers to fight shoulder to shoulder with their Serbian brothers and the backing of powerful voices in the Russian press. The existence of public organizations and a popular press free of preliminary censorship were products of the Russian reforms. In a certain sense, then, this episode in the struggle over the borderlands was a test between two reforming empires.[22] In 1877, carried away by pan-Slav agitation, Russia declared war. The Russian army crossed the Danube, opening up a new front in the struggle over the borderlands.

The Russian military victory and diplomatic defeat at the Congress of Berlin enabled the Austrians to annex the provinces as a form of compensation for the creation of a small Bulgarian principality. After the Habsburg occupation in 1878, Vienna treated Bosnia more like a colony than an integral part of the empire. Under the authority of the imperial Finance Ministry, it was run on the principle of "administrative absolutism." In the words of Benjamin von Kállay, the Minister of Finance who embodied that principle, imperial rule over Bosnia fulfilled an old and honored Habsburg tradition. "Austria is a great Occidental Empire," he told an English journalist, "charged with the mission of carrying civilization to Oriental peoples."[23] Kállay was one of a small number of likeminded Hungarian Balkanists who included his successor István Burián and their bureaucratic subordinate, the scholar, Lajos Thallóczy. They shared a variation on the Hungarian national mission of serving as an alternative source of civilization and modernity to Austria within the context of the Dual Monarchy.[24] A Hungarian noble who had served as consul general in Belgrade from 1868 to 1875, Kállay's "idea was to make Bosnia-Hercegovina the model land of the Balkans, of whose cultural development and organization the Monarchy should be proud."[25] Kállay, like earlier Habsburg pro-consuls in Bukovina and Banat, worked to promote economic development through state-sponsored

[22] For this section I have relied on B. H. Sumner, *Russia and the Balkans 1870–1880* (Oxford University Press, 1937); David MacKenzie, *The Serbs and Russian Pan-Slavs, 1875–1878* (Ithaca, NY: Cornell University Press, 1967).

[23] Robert J. Donia, *Islam under the Double Eagle. The Muslims of Bosnia and Hercegovina, 1878–1914* (Boulder, CO: East European Monographs, 1981), p. 14.

[24] Robin Okey, "A Trio of Hungarian Balkanists. Béni Kállay, István Burián and Lajos Thallóczy in the Age of High Nationalism," *Slavic and East European Review* 80(2) (April 2002): 234–66.

[25] Quoted in Robin Okey, *Taming Balkan Nationalism* (Oxford University Press, 2007), p. 57.

manufactures, mining, and railroad building. He planned the physical transformation of cities like Sarajevo. Importing architects from Vienna, his aim was to adapt the architecture of the Ringstrasse to fit the local cultural styles of all the Christian and Muslim communities.[26]

Fearful of pan-Serbism and of Russian influence, Kállay sought to create a Bosnian identity by undertaking a complex, perhaps overly subtle, program of nation-building. He recognized the authority of the religious hierarchies of the Catholic, Orthodox, and Muslim communities, and promoted their cultural identities while at the same time seeking to isolate the Orthodox and Muslim populations from their natural association with their wider religious communities in Serbia and the Ottoman Empire. His educational reforms promoted a vague Bosnian historical tradition, while providing functional training for the three different communities. He considered the Muslims to be the key to the success of his enterprise. They were the dominant landowning group and the largest urban group as well. Yet he remained skeptical about the adaptability of Islam to the modern world.[27] Kállay's well-intentioned policy of maintaining religious toleration and confessional balance in the Austrian tradition ran afoul of the Catholic, more specifically the Franciscan, missionaries, who aimed to convert the Muslims. At every step of the way, Kállay's cultural policies encountered the same obstacles as those faced by pro-consuls in the other Eurasian borderlands. His efforts to introduce reforms from above, like theirs, stimulated simultaneous resistance from below by established elites and separatist nationalist movements.[28]

When the Austrian troops occupied the two provinces in 1878, they immediately encountered strong resistance. The armed bands were drawn from lower-class Muslims, encouraged by their conservative religious leaders, and defectors of Bosnian origin from the Ottoman army joined by Orthodox Serbian volunteers. Austria was forced to mobilize 268,000 troops and suffered 5,000 casualties in fighting their way to Sarajevo. The Muslim irregulars retreated to the mountains and continued to resist for several months. Three years later another armed rising ripped through eastern Hercegovina in opposition to the introduction of military conscription. Kállay was entrusted with its repression. After a brief period of calm, disorder erupted again in the late 1880s and spread widely in the mid-1890s sparked by conflict over conversion, conscription, and language policy.

---

[26] Robert J. Donia, "Fin-de-siècle Sarajevo. The Habsburg Transformation of an Ottoman Town," *Austrian Historical Yearbook* 33 (2002): 47–48.
[27] Okey, *Taming*, p. 98.
[28] Cf. Okey, *Taming*, pp. 252–58, for an incisive summary of Kállay's policies.

When compromise seemed unacceptable and rebellion impractical, the Muslims once again resorted to the age-old alternative of flight. Within three years of the Treaty of Berlin (1878), the Muslim population of Austrian Bosnia had declined by a third, losing almost a quarter of a million people to emigration or death.[29] A second big wave of emigration took place in 1900 when 7,000 left for the Ottoman Empire. Although widespread, Muslim resistance was not universal. A small but influential elite of merchants and large landowners were willing to work with Kállay. Unanticipated by him, the accommodationists took advantage of their privileged position to begin to organize politically. Living for the first time under the rule of a non-Islamic state, the Muslim elite devised their own forms of compliance and evasion when it suited them, gradually adapting to the pattern of bargaining characteristic of Habsburg imperial rule in its borderlands.[30]

The Orthodox Serbs in Bosnia and Hercegovina were at the very least equally hostile to the Austrian occupation. The Austrian occupation dramatically changed the privileged position of the Orthodox Church. Tanzimat legislation had extended equal juridical rights to the entire population, depriving external powers of the excuse to aid or protect their co-religionists. Officials were better paid and were no longer venal. The role of the Greek patriarch in Istanbul was reduced to little more than a fiction. The local social organizations – the *sobory* of the Orthodox Church – were still rudimentary. While Russian influence declined, Habsburg policies strengthened the position of the Catholic Church. By signing a concordat with the patriarch in Istanbul, the Austrians obtained the right to appoint the top posts in the Orthodox hierarchy. When Vienna named a Hungarian Serb as metropolitan, he appointed so-called subventionary priests who received special salaries from the government. The new metropolitan refused to confirm priests elected by the *sobory*. This tactic split the Orthodox community between those who accepted and those who rejected the new priests. The Orthodox Church was also losing the struggle over education.[31] Finally, a slow out-migration of the Orthodox reduced their numbers by 7 percent, while the Catholic population held its own. As a result the Orthodox population became increasingly estranged from the government.

---

[29] Justin McCarthy, "Ottoman Bosnia, 1800–1878," in Mark Pinson (ed.), *The Muslims of Bosnia-Herzegovina. Their Historic Development from the Middle Ages to the Dissolution of Yugoslavia* (Cambridge, MA: Harvard University Press, 1996), pp. 80–81.

[30] Donia, "Fin-de-siècle Sarajevo," pp. 44–45.

[31] Kharuzin, *Bosniia-Gertsegovina*, pp. 282–88, 296–303; Donia, *Islam under the Double Eagle*, pp. 18–19.

By the end of his life Kállay's system was in disarray in the face of growing Muslim and Serb opposition to his politics. At his death in 1903, he was succeeded by another Hungarian noble, István Burián, the architect of a new constitutional order in Bosnia. A Hungarian patriot and Habsburg loyalist, he had drawn an important lesson from the Hungarian constitutional crisis of 1905/6. The imperial center had failed to acknowledge the Hungarian demands for a full constitutional order; but the Hungarian nationalist opposition had failed to recognize the need to meet the dynasty half-way. He was determined to avoid those mistakes in his administration of Bosnia by working with the Serbs and Muslims within a new set of autonomous institutions. No less than Kállay, he perceived the main external threat came from the east. He was an ardent foe of pan-Slavism and fearful of local revolutionary movements reacting to an ineffective bureaucracy and inspired by Russian "nihilists." His solution to the Bosnian tangle was to guide the rising discontent of the three ethnoreligious groups into constitutional channels through the granting of cultural autonomy and the establishment of a Bosnian Diet. This could only be achieved following the Austrian annexation of the province in 1908 that he helped to engineer. During his nine-year rule, 1903–1912, his apparent success in strengthening the Serbian school system was subverted by the activities of a growing body of radicalized students who organized under the banner of Young Bosnia.[32]

Under Burián's benevolent gaze the more accommodating Muslims moved toward politically acceptable activities. In rapid succession they founded benevolent societies and, in 1906, a Muslim political party. Two years later they endorsed the annexation and declared their formal allegiance to the empire. In the Bosnian Diet the Muslim politicians learned to work with their Serbian and Croatian counterparts. By applying the lesson of coalition politics and political compromise – the fruits of the "civilizing process" – the Muslim landlords were able to preserve their feudal hold over the peasantry. By 1914, they had become the most loyal subjects of the emperor in Bosnia. These partial successes for Habsburg imperial rule were marred by the contemporary rise of Bosnian, Serbian, and Croat parties, a sign of greater political awareness and activism, but also prone to splintering.

As elsewhere in the Monarchy, bureaucratic, reforming policies stimulated the very national movements they sought to curb. Religion may have been an early focus, but national movements grew increasingly secular. In the early twentieth century a number of loosely associated secret societies

[32] Okey, *Taming*, ch. 8.

collectively called Young Bosnians, mainly by their enemies, sprang up among the south Slavs with important links outside the country from Russia to the United States. The majority were Serbs. Their aim was simply to destroy the Habsburg Monarchy. In Bosnia and Serbia they were predominantly students from the first generation of peasants to be educated in the towns. The students continued to maintain family ties with the villages and their spiritual ties to the Orthodox Church, which may have kindled their yearning for martyrdom.[33] The intellectual cradle of the student movement was the gymnasium in Mostar. In the early years of the century the Young Bosnians fell under the sway of the rationalist and anti-clerical ideas of the Czech philosopher and politician, Tomáš Masaryk. But the annexation of Bosnia and Hercegovina spelled the end of gradualism. Many of the students turned away from Masaryk to embrace the Russian populists. The works of Chernyshevsky, Kropotkin, and Bakunin are frequently cited in their biographies along with Mazzini. They infused the older local tradition of political violence, celebrated in the heroic exploits of primitive rebels like the Uskoks and haiduks, with the newer tactics of political assassination advocated by the revolutionaries of the People's Will. But the Bosnian students were not carbon copies of the Russian revolutionaries; for them national liberation bulked larger than socialism. In this they were more like the Armenians of the same generation.[34]

The assassination of Archduke Ferdinand on June 28, 1914 was the culmination of only one of many terrorist conspiracies by the Young Bosnians. Although armed and penetrated by the Serbian secret society Unification or Death, known as the Black Hand and led by the legendary Serbian Colonel Apis, the Young Bosnians departed from their apparent mentor to pursue their own program of Yugoslavism and plotted their own course. The chief assassin, Gavrilo Princip, came from a Serbian family in the turbulent Ottoman–Habsburg frontier zone. Members of his family had served the Ottoman and then the Austrian administrations. Other conspirators came from mixed social backgrounds; several were sons of Orthodox priests. A few who survived the war became notorious as četnik leaders during the Second World War.[35] All were caught up in the great social and political transformation of the provinces taking place under Austrian administration.

[33] Marko Attila Hoare, *The History of Bosnia. From the Middle Ages to the Present Day* (London: Saqi, 2007), pp. 87–88.
[34] For the classical formulation of these influences, see Vladimir Dedijer, *The Road to Sarajevo* (London: Cassell, 1967), esp. pp. 175–82, 250–60. Cf. Okey, *Taming*, ch. 10.
[35] Hoare, *The History of Bosnia*, p. 88.

The Austrians confronted an almost insoluble set of problems in their newly acquired Bosnian borderland. But they also failed to settle on a consistent policy. They patronized the Muslims, then sought to win over the Serbs, and in the final years, under the incompetent administration of General Oscar Potiorek, aided and abetted by Franz Ferdinand, they shifted to support of Catholicism, which meant the Croats. To be sure, after 1910 they had to deal with unstable coalitions in the Diet – Muslims together with Serbs, Serbs together with Croats – depending on the issues. In the end none of the major groups were satisfied and the student radicals were determined to bring down the entire structure.

The Austrian administration and annexation of Bosnia and Hercegovina assumed truly dangerous international proportions when Vienna aggressively pursued its civilizing mission by promoting a colonization project that antagonized all the political groups. In 1886, there were only 16,275 Austro-Hungarian subjects in the two provinces. By 1910 there were 108,000. Plans were afoot to increase this number by settling retired non-commissioned officers there, a strategy that had been used by the Russians in the Pontic steppe, repeated after the First World War by the Poles in the Kresy. A special bank to promote colonization was opened in southern Hungary to settle Magyar peasants and smallholders. In the economic sphere penetration of the Balkans assumed an even more openly imperialistic aspect.

The Austrian government pursued two lines of economic expansion: railroad construction and commercial agreements both aimed at reducing Serbia to a virtual colony. In 1880, Austria signed a railway convention with Serbia and then rapidly pushed construction of a line from Austrian territory to Belgrade and Niš, where it would link up with branch lines through Macedonia to Saloniki and through eastern Rumelia (soon to unite with Bulgaria) to Istanbul. Completed in 1888, the Orient rail program crowned Austrian efforts to counter British penetration of the Balkans from the sea ports. In 1881, Austria concluded a tariff and commercial treaty with Serbia that made Serbia's foreign trade dependent on the Habsburg Monarchy and severely constrained Serbian industrial development. A political treaty followed hard on its heels. By restricting Serbia's right to conclude agreements with other powers, the treaty reduced it to a political protectorate as well as an economic colony of Austria. At the time Baron Haymerlé, the Austrian Foreign Minister, told Prince Milan Obrenović (who assumed the title king the following year with Austrian support) that:

The Dual Monarchy has no objection to the existence of a truly independent Serbia ... but if Serbia should turn out to be a "Russian satrapy" and were herself

Map 5.1 Between the Treaty of San Stefano and the annexation of Bosnia

to abandon her independence and act on orders from Petersburg, then we could not tolerate such a Serbia on our frontier, and we would as a lesser evil, occupy it with our armies.[36]

The Serbs soon chafed under Austria's protective custody. Domestically, the political opposition to Milan's pro-Austrian policy mounted under the goad of Jovan Ristič, the leader of the pan-Slav leaning Radical Party in the Serbian parliament (*Skupshtina*). But the decisive blow came from abroad. When in 1885 the Bulgarians declared their union with East Rumelia, Austria gave conditional support to King Milan's request for compensation. The Serbs unwisely interpreted this as an endorsement of military action. They borrowed money from

---

[36] William L. Langer, *European Alliances and Alignments, 1871–1890* (New York: Knopf, 1962), p. 328, quoting Count Chedomille Mijatovich, *The Memoirs of a Balkan Diplomatist* (London: Cassell, 1917). Accepting his role as ruler of a contested borderland, Milan assured the Austrians that "Serbia must decide between Austria and Russia … Since [San Stefano] Russia treats us as minors or subordinates. But I do not want to be a prefect of Russia." *Ibid.*, p. 329.

Vienna, marched against the Bulgarians, and were soundly defeated. Austria intervened to demand an end to the fighting and threatened to intervene in order to check the Bulgarian advance. Bismarck warned off the Austrians, helping to cool things down. The Great Powers accepted the union because the alternative appeared to be worse. Reversing their earlier positions, Britain and Austria reluctantly accepted the union, because they thought that a unified Bulgaria would serve more effectively as a bulwark against Russian expansion. Tsar Alexander III was unhappy about the union because the Bulgarians were no longer willing to accept his tutelage. But he too was unwilling to prevent it while he was embroiled with the British in the Trans Caspian frontier and reluctant to challenge the Austrians in the Danubian frontier. The Bulgarians placated the sultan with assurances that the union would not affect his sovereignty. In this instance, the competing interests of the Great Powers over a borderland cancelled out one another.[37] It would not always be so. The Serbs, humiliated on the battlefield and left without compensation, grew increasingly disillusioned with the Austrian orientation. Over the following years, they turned more toward Russia as a protector. The Bulgarians, disillusioned with Russia's meddling in their internal affairs, drifted toward Austria. In both cases politics contradicted geography, leading to a fateful outcome in this struggle over the borderlands of the Danubian frontier.

At the turn of the century, Serbian domestic politics tilted the balance against Austria. In 1903, the pro-Austrian King Milan was assassinated by a group of army officers led by a young Dragutin Dimitrijević, later to be known as Colonel Apis. The new king, Peter Karadjordjević, gained the support of the pro-Russian Radical Party, under the new leadership of Nikola Pašić. Together with the military, they envisaged a Greater Serbia with Russian support. They first seized the opportunity to improve relations with Bulgaria by signing a commercial treaty in the hope of shaking free of Austrian economic domination. The Austrians, goaded by the Hungarians, reacted badly. They set new prohibitive tariffs on the importation of Serbian pork products, touching off the so-called "Pig War." Germany, which had its own reasons for bolstering its economic interests in the Balkans, took up the slack, and the Monarchy suffered another loss of prestige in the region. Although the Balkan states continued to maneuver between the two Great Powers, by 1914 Serbia was firmly in the Russian camp and Bulgaria in the Austrian camp. They ended up paying

---

[37] Richard J. Crampton, *Bulgaria 1878–1918. A History* (Boulder, CO: East European Monographs, 1983), pp. 85–103; see also Leften Stavrianos, *The Balkans since 1453* (New York: Holt Rinehart & Winston, 1961), pp. 426–33.

a high price for what was, in classic geopolitical terms, an anomalous choice.

The big question in the struggle over the borderlands in southeastern Europe continued to be the disposition of the territories that remained under the faltering rule of the Ottoman Empire. The Habsburg Monarchy and the Russian Empire made one last attempt to follow Bismarck's oft-repeated recommendation to divide the region into spheres of influence. It was, unfortunately, a vague and limited arrangement. In 1897, they reached an informal understanding to maintain the status quo in the Balkans as long as circumstances permitted. The two powers agreed to oppose the predominance of one small Balkan state over the others. One point remained unresolved. The Russians took exception to Austria's demand to reserve for itself the right to annex Bosnia and Hercegovina. After a decade of relative peace in the Balkans, the two powers began to negotiate an expanded and expansionist version of the delimitation of spheres. In 1908, the underlying differences between them broke through to the surface, when Austria unilaterally exercised its claim to annex Bosnia, touching off a major international crisis.

The three most active Habsburg bureaucrats in promoting the annexation of Bosnia and Hercegovina, Burián, Foreign Minister Alois Aehrenthal, and Franz Conrad von Hötzendorf, Chief of the General Staff, acted on different motives. Burián saw the integration of the provinces into the Monarchy as a crucial step in his policy of modernizing them by granting them a constitution modeled on that of Hungary. Aehrenthal saw an opportunity to block Belgrade's greater Serbian aspirations, but he was also more calculating. By asserting Austria's independence from Berlin, he hoped to convert the Dual Alliance into a tool for furthering Austria's imperialist designs. Conrad, more bellicose and impulsive, was eager to challenge Serbia when the chances for military success appeared most favorable. He insistently demanded greater expenditures to enable the army to take the offensive in a war against Serbia that he regarded in any case as being inevitable.[38] Aehrenthal prepared diplomatically for the annexation by seeking an agreement with Russia that would confirm their entente over the Balkans, but radically change its terms to their mutual advantage by upsetting rather than maintaining the status quo. According to his proposals, Austria would annex Bosnia and Hercegovina and

---

[38] For Burián, see Okey, *Taming*, p. 177; for Aehrenthal as an aggressive statesman, Jürgen Angelow, *Kalkul und Prestige. Der Zweibund an Vorabend der Ersten Weltkreiges* (Cologne: Bühlau, 2000); for Conrad and a more moderate view of Aehrenthal, Samuel R. Williamson, Jr., *Austria-Hungary and the Origins of the First World War* (New York: St. Martin's Press, 1991), pp. 35–38, 48–51, 66–70.

evacuate the Sanjak; in return he assured Russia of Austria's strong support in revising the Straits Convention of the Treaty of Berlin in 1878 so as to allow the passage of Russian warships in time of peace. The agreement broke down when Russian Foreign Minister A. P. Izvol'skii was unable to gain the approval of the European powers, especially Britain, for changing the regime at the Straits. Without consulting the Russians, Austria then jumped the gun by proclaiming the annexation. Once again, as in 1881 during the Bulgarian crisis, Austria offered no compensation to Serbia. The Serbs were outraged and ordered military preparations. Russia faced a virtual German ultimatum to take no countermeasures and, still recovering from the effects of its defeat in the Russo-Japanese War, it was forced to give up any idea of coming to the assistance of the Serbs.

Both sides drew different lessons from the crisis. Austro-Hungarian statesmen were convinced that in any showdown with Serbia Germany would back them up, and Russia, whose strength they consistently underestimated, would back down. At the same time, they recognized that Serbia had now become an implacable enemy; the logic of politics would dictate its dependence on Russia. This meant in turn that the Monarchy would henceforth confront a strategic threat from Russia on two widely separated fronts: on the Galician frontier to the far northeast and on the Serbian frontier to the south. In the event of a crisis the situation on its other frontiers was also ominous. Although associated with the Austro-German alliance, Italy and Romania could not be counted as loyal allies. They both nurtured irredentist claims on Habsburg territory, Italy in Istria and Romania in Transylvania. Realistically, then, the Monarchy faced a nightmare of encirclement every bit as frightening as that imagined in Berlin. Moreover, the Monarchy had just accepted a Trojan horse with its borders. The secret societies now lodged within the newly acquired borderland of Bosnia and Hercegovina were conspiring actively to destroy imperial rule. The outcome of the Balkan Wars of 1913/14 brought the danger closer by intensifying national feelings in Serbia and enlarging its national territory. Was it any wonder then that the Monarchy's ruling elite saw the assassination of Franz Ferdinand as an opportunity to crush Serbia? Russia drew a different set of conclusions.

Crisis in the Russian borderlands

The causes of a constitutional crisis in the Russian Empire were similar to those that rocked the Habsburg Monarchy. Internally, the social conflicts arising from a late and forced industrialization combined with a failure to solve the problems of governing its borderlands. Externally, an attempt to bring under control yet another neighboring borderland in Inner Asia sparked an international crisis. In the case of Russia, this led to a disastrous war with Japan, revolution, and the concession by the autocracy of the country's first empire-wide elected parliament.

Beginning in the 1880s, imperial rule over the borderlands underwent a qualitative change. A renewed process of centralization and economic integration accompanied an intensification of imperial nationalizing policy. New internal boundaries were drawn, traditional administrative rights and legal systems were eliminated, and the Russian language was promoted as the only language of the bureaucracy.[39] Alexander III presided over the surge in nationalizing the empire through cultural Russification. He surrounded himself with a group of Russian chauvinists, K. P. Pobedonostsev, the Procurator of the Holy Synod; Dmitri Tolstoi, the new Minister of the Interior; and Count I. V. Delianov, Minister of Education from 1882 to 1897, known to his subordinates as "the Armenian zero;" all supported by M. N. Katkov, the extremely influential editor of the mass daily newspaper, *Moskovskie vedomosti*. Their priorities were to uproot the shoots of nationalist movements by administrative centralization and linguistic Russification of the local schools. These measures were inspired by Pobedonostsev's strong antipathy toward Poles, Jews, Armenians, and other peoples of the borderlands. He sought to discredit the reformist Armenian-born Minister of the Interior, Loris-Melikov, with racial slurs, calling him a "frenzied Asiatic" and "a trickster (*fokusnik*) capable of playing a double game … He is not a Russian patriot" was his verdict. After a visit to the Caucasus in 1886, Pobedonostsev wrote to the tsar that "the Armenians and Georgians are seeking to free themselves from Russian culture and nourish the mad dream of reestablishing their national independence."[40]

The Baltic provinces

Under Alexander III the campaign to launch cultural Russifications began in the Baltic provinces. As far back as the 1840s deviant voices on the Russian nationalist right had warned of the German cultural penetration of the Baltic littoral. While the ruling elites celebrated the loyalty of the

---

[39] V. S. Diakin, "Natsional'nyi vopros po vnutrennei politike tsarizma," *Voprosy istorii* 11/12 (5) (1995): 39–53.

[40] For the bureaucratic struggle, see P. A. Zaionchkovskii, *Krizis samoderzhaviia na rubezhe 1870–1880 godov* (Moscow: Izd. Moskovskogo universiteta, 1964); for quotations, see *K.P. Pobedonostsev i ego korrespondenty. Pis'ma, i zapiski.*, 2 vols. (Petrograd: Gosudarstvennoe izdatel'stvo, 1923–1926), vol. I, pp. 315–16; vol. II, pp. 113–17.

Baltic barons who populated the government up to the highest levels of the bureaucracy and army, the early representatives of pan-Slavism, building on Slavophil ideas, drew a cultural frontier between Romano-Germanic and Greco-Slavic Europe. Antipathy toward *Deutschtom* focused first on the Austrian domination of the western and southern Slavs. But the Polish revolt, and even more the unification of Germany under Prussian leadership, further aroused their fears of separatism of the Baltic provinces.[41] These fears were much exaggerated.

The Baltic Germans were steadily losing their dominant position in the economic life of the province. Demographically, they were declining if not in absolute numbers then relative to the rapidly growing Latvian and Estonian population. After 1880, as anti-German feelings grew stronger, the Baltic barons tended to avoid government service where they had long occupied a proportionately large percentage of the higher civil and military posts. Their lack of unity prevented them from proposing reforms of local government under Alexander II and increased their vulnerability to radical administrative and linguistic Russification under his successors.[42] The central bureaucracy had in the 1860s and 1870s undertaken modest Russifying initiatives touching on the agrarian, judicial, and religious affairs of the Baltic provinces; the pace accelerated in the 1880s. In the wake of serious peasant disorders, Alexander III appointed a senatorial commission under N. A. Manasein, soon to become Minister of Justice, to undertake a full investigation of conditions in the Baltic provinces. His report became the basis for widespread cultural and administrative Russification. He recommended the obligatory use of Russian by local officials; the imposition of Russian as the language of instruction in Dorpat University, along with numerous restrictive rules on student corporations; the introduction of Russian legal norms to replace the

---

[41] Among the most influential anti-German voices were those of Mikhail Pogodin, Ivan Aksakov, Iuri Samarin, Fydor Tiuchev, and Mikhail Katkov. See Nicholas Riasanovsky, *Nicholas I and Official Nationality in Russia, 1825–1855* (Berkeley, CA: University of California Press, 1959), pp. 144–46, 156–58, 165; Michael Boro Petrovich, *The Emergence of Russian Panslavism, 1856–1870* (New York: Columbia University Press, 1956), pp. 67–77, 94–96, 118; Stephen Lukashevich, *Ivan Aksakov, 1823–1886. A Study in Russian Thought and Politics* (Cambridge, MA: Harvard University Press, 1965), pp. 117, 131, 158–61; Ivan Aksakov, "Pribaltiskii vopros," in *Sochineniia*, 7 vols. (Moscow: M. G. Volchanninov, 1886/7), vol. VI, pp. 3–157; Boris Nolde, *Iuri Samarin i ego vremiia* (Paris: Navarre, 1926); Michael H. Haltzel, "Russo-German Polemics of the Sixties," in Edward Thaden (ed.), *Russification in the Baltic Provinces and Finland, 1855–1914* (Princeton University Press, 1981), pp. 124–33.

[42] Michael H. Haltzel, "Triumphs and Frustrations of Administrative Russification, 1881–1914," in Thaden (ed.), *Russification*, pp. 150–52.

antiquated and "medieval" German rules; and legislation to promote the interests of the Orthodox Church. He offered only token improvements in the lot of the Latvian and Estonian peasantry. Several of Manasein's more radical reform proposals that would have further reduced the authority of the Baltic German nobility were never implemented.[43]

The selective endorsement and rejection of Manasein's recommendations underscores the dilemma of imperial rule in the borderlands of the Baltic littoral. The zeal of the pan-Slavs, although shared by many at court and by Alexander III in particular, was blunted in practice by the complexity of the ethnic, religious, and social conflicts between the German nobles and Latvian and Estonian peasantry. The small Latvian and Estonia intelligentsia opposed both Germanizing and Russifying cultural policies, but they perceived administrative Russification as offering some advantages in the fight against the German nobility who in their eyes represented the main threat to their burgeoning national identity. The St. Petersburg bureaucrats were wary of encouraging Latvian and Estonian aspirations for fear of providing peasant social unrest that was susceptible to the blandishments of nationalist agitators. There was a danger in weakening the German nobility, which was after all the bulwark of local order.[44] The small Russian population in the Baltic provinces, some of them Old Believers, was a weak reed on which to lean. By the 1890s cultural Russification was opening up new opportunities for young Latvians seeking their fortune outside their native provinces, but it also stimulated dissatisfaction among those who were exposed to the larger world, in particular to the ideas of social democracy.[45] The contradictory effects of Russification in the Baltic provinces were beginning to threaten the entire assimilationist enterprise. The imperial government was obliged to perform a balancing act that, given its own lack of a unified policy on ethnic and religious conflicts in the borderlands, conveyed the impression of weakness and indecision. On the eve of the revolution of 1905 it had retreated from the activist phase of Russification, but the damage was done. Passive resistance had passed over to revolutionary agitation, rural disorder, and strikes.

[43] Edward Thaden (ed.), "The Abortive Experiment. Cultural Russification in the Baltic Provinces, 1881–1914," in *Russification*, pp. 56–74.

[44] Toivo U. Raun, "Estonian Attitudes Toward Russification before the mid-1880s," in Thaden (ed.), *Russification*, pp. 296–305; Andrejs Plakans, "Russification Policy in the 1880s," in Thaden (ed.), *Russification*, pp. 234–42.

[45] Andrejs Plakans, "The Eighteen-Nineties," in Thaden (ed.), *Russification*, pp. 248–64.

The Grand Duchy of Finland

In the Grand Duchy of Finland, Russification and resistance to imperial rule developed more slowly. Up to the 1880s relations between the Swedish–Finnish elites in the Finnish Diet and the imperial center were relatively cordial. Gradually, however, a series of perceived external threats to Russian security by Sweden and a unified German Empire combined with an internal struggle over Finnish constitutional rights to undermine and then to rupture those relations. Although no longer ruling a great power, Sweden's kings in the nineteenth century periodically entertained hopes of regaining Finland. They adopted friendly neutrality toward the Allies during the Crimean War and might well have intervened had Russia not sued for peace. The Swedish press adopted an increasingly anti-Russian tone in the 1870s and 1880s. In the period from 1880 to 1905, Swedish military expenditures increased from 35 percent to 55 percent of the state budget. Swedish commercial and cultural contacts with a unified Germany grew rapidly, accelerating at the end of the century. More and more Swedish officers in the Imperial Finnish army elected to train in Germany. By the outbreak of the First World War, the moderate Finnish socialist leader, Hjalmar Branting, could say, "With the Swedish officer corps one cannot wage war against Germany."[46]

Russian nationalist opinion reacted slowly to these developments. Even Katkov sounded a moderate note. But at the end of the 1880s, a series of disputes over the imperial government's attempts to impose Russian rules on postal and legal transactions soured relations. In the Finnish Diet and press, fears were expressed that St. Petersburg would emulate its Russifying Baltic policies in the grand duchy. The imperial representatives in Helsingfors, while nominally Finnish or German in background, were increasingly caught in the same dilemma facing pro-consuls in the borderlands. Torn between their recognition of local concerns and pressure from the center, when it came to the crunch they were obliged to act as imperial emissaries. They proved unable to bridge the growing gap of distrust. Shortly after the death of Alexander III the first stage of Russification ended, bringing to a close "the period of good will, relative restraint, and the observance of old forms."[47]

The Finns were split between the Swedish-speaking cultural elite and the Finnish-speaking middle classes, intellectuals, and well-to-do

---

[46] This section relies heavily on C. Leonard Lundin, "The International and Military Background of the Russification Dispute in Finland," in Thaden (ed.), *Russification*, pp. 373–81, quotation on p. 377.

[47] Lundin, "Finland," p. 397.

peasants; between the rural landowners and landless peasants (crofters); and between the industrial workers and their employers. The more extreme figures among the Swedish speakers regarded Finland as a cultural frontier. They identified their culture and language with the West as opposed to the East, and regarded the Finnish people, whom they contemptuously called Chud, as lacking in the necessary intelligence and will to achieve freedom and civilization. Not all Swedish speakers agreed. A few even became strong supporters of the Finnish language, further complicating an already confused situation. Although a minority in the grand duchy, the Swedish elite dominated both houses of the Diet. Like Poles, Czechs, and Hungarians, the Finnish speakers were divided between those willing to accommodate (the Old Finns) and those determined to resist imperial rule (the Young Finns). Finns made up a majority of the burgeoning workers movement, but several of the prominent educated leaders were Swedish. Although they were anti-Russian, they were not disposed toward violence during the revolutionary days of 1905. Their turn would come in 1918.

The phase of massive Russification began with proposals to integrate the Finnish army, but rapidly spread to other administrative reforms. The conclusion of a Franco-Russian alliance and military convention in the early 1890s inaugurated an extensive review of imperial military policies. Proposals favoring the extension of the Russian military system to Finland were vigorously advanced in 1898 by the new Minister of War, Alexei Kuropatkin, and the new Governor General of Finland, Nikolai Bobrikov, the former chief-of-staff of the St. Petersburg Military District. On the occasion of his appointment, Bobrikov drafted a plan, subsequently called the February Manifesto, that proclaimed the right of the Russian emperor to determine the form of all legislation for Finland in matters of "general imperial concern."[48] Rejecting Finnish protests, Nicholas II approved what amounted to a violation of Finland's long-standing constitutional rights. The following year, Bobrikov outlined a comprehensive cultural and administrative centralization of Finland, including the introduction of the Russian language into the Finnish Diet, administrative offices, and educational institutions. As tensions mounted, the Russian nationalist press, which had taken a dim view of Finnish separatism since Katkov's days, adopted a shriller tone in backing official policy.[49]

---

[48] Edward Thaden (ed.), "Administrative Russification in Finland, 1881–1914," in *Russification*, p. 82.

[49] Tuomo Polvinen, *Imperial Borderland. Bobrikov and the Attempted Russification of Finland, 1898–1914* (London: Hurst, 1984), pp. 20, 25, 28–33.

The Finnish Senate was split over how to react to the February Manifesto. A majority timidly petitioned the tsar to confirm Finland's constitutional rights and submitted a revised document to the Diet in the prescribed constitutional manner. What shocked the Russian administration, however, was a mass protest movement that gathered 500,000 signatures endorsing a "Great Address" to the throne. It was a stunning refutation of the policy of accommodation. The tsar refused to receive the 500-man delegation that arrived in St. Petersburg to submit it. Bobrikov relentlessly pursued his policy of Russification until his assassination in 1904. His two main accomplishments were the Language Manifesto in 1900, which introduced Russian as the language of all official business in Finland, and the more explosive Army Manifesto of 1901, which virtually disbanded the separate Finnish corps and introduced universal military service. Although approved by the Senate, cowed by purges and pressure, the army reform touched off a campaign of passive resistance. For two years a majority of recruits refused to appear for induction. Disillusioned at home, Finns increasingly resorted to emigration abroad. The number of emigrants per 10,000 of the population rose from 13.2 percent in 1898 to 83.7 percent in 1903.[50]

Bobrikov's policies deepened the social divisions within Finland. The socialist movement became increasingly radical, turning against both the Russian administration and the Finnish bourgeoisie that was leading the resistance. In the countryside Russian officials made a clumsy attempt to court the peasantry, as they had done in Poland after the revolution of 1863, in order to disrupt the political opposition of the landlords. They succeeded only in sowing confusion and raising social tensions. By 1905, the Finns had been largely and unnecessarily alienated from imperial rule. By 1918, as Finland began the violent break with Bolshevik Russia, class conflicts erupted with fearful consequences in the Finnish Civil War along the road to independence.

Crisis in the Pale of Settlement

The pogroms of 1881 marked a new stage in both the government's policies aimed at curbing Jewish economic and cultural influence in the western borderlands and the level of Jewish resistance. The pogroms were the goad that drove greater Jewish political activity.[51] They had been,

---

[50] Lundin, "Finland," pp. 439–41; for the internal debate within the Russian bureaucracy over the army reform which pitted Witte against Kuropatkin, see Polvinen, *Imperial Borderland*, pp. 113–30.

[51] The classic statement remains that of Jonathan Frankel, *Prophecy and Politics. Socialism, Nationalism and the Russian Jews, 1862–1917* (Cambridge University Press, 1981), who dates "the emergence of the new politics" from these events.

according to most accounts, spontaneous, and the government attributed them to popular rage against Jewish exploitation. Although the government did not act rapidly to repress them, neither did it encourage them, fearing the breakdown of public order. As Alexander III famously put it: "in the depth of my soul I am awfully glad when the Jews are beaten, but all the same we cannot tolerate it."[52] In the aftermath, he refused to abolish the Pale of Settlement. Instead, new restrictions, the so-called May laws of 1882, were imposed by the Minister of the Interior, the ubiquitous pan-Slav, Count Ignat'ev, which limited the rights of Jews to settle in frontier areas and reestablished quotas on the admission of Jewish youth to universities.

The Jewish community was deeply divided over a suitable response. Among those who preached accommodation to the new circumstances, the St. Petersburg Jewish elite favored a continuation of "selective integration" into Russian society in the hope of preserving the distinctive Jewish culture. The educational reforms of the 1860s had had the most radical effect in transforming the relations between the Jews and the rest of society. By lifting restrictions on entering universities, the reforms facilitated a closer integration of Jews into both the liberal and radical wings of the Russian intelligentsia. Anti-Semites in the bureaucracy and society viewed the influx of Jews as a new challenge in the culture wars over the borderland of the Pale.[53] The majority of Jewish graduates entered the professions, particularly law. Their hopes of operating within the system were successively shaken by the pogroms of 1881 and the quotas imposed in 1889 on the admission of the Jews to universities and to the bar. By the early 1890s, lawyers were reaching out to the large Jewish community. Their unique formula for assimilation joined together the concept of a juridical Russian citizenship and a Jewish ethnic identity.[54]

Somewhere between accommodation and resistance, the Zionist movement emerged in the 1880s. Reacting to the pogroms, several of its most influential spokesmen, such as Leon Pinsker and Asher Zvi Ginzberg (aka Ahad Ha-Am), advocated the idea of self-help and the colonization of Palestine. Yet in their writings a contradiction surfaced between space and spirit, territory and culture. They acknowledged that Palestine was not adequate for all Jews as a safe asylum. It could serve only as a "spiritual

---

[52] Zaionchkovskii, *Krizis samoderzhaviia*, quoting an archival source, p. 419.

[53] Benjamin Nathans, *Beyond the Pale. The Jewish Encounter with Late Imperial Russia* (Berkeley, CA: University of California Press, 2002), pp. 259–60.

[54] Distinguished jurists like Maksim Vinaver and Genrikh Sliozberg could think of themselves as a "*russkii evrei*," that is, a good Russian and a good Jew, in contrast to the aspiration of full assimilation by enlightened Habsburg Jews and the concept of Poles of a Mosaic persuasion. Nathans, *Beyond the Pale*, pp. 324–38.

national center." Most Jews would have to remain outside in the diaspora. Nevertheless, the Russian "Palestinians" remained attached to the ideal of settling colonists there, opposing the alternative proposals such as those to settle Jews in Uganda. The movement gained a powerful advocate and charismatic figure in Theodore Herzl, whose journalistic and political activity in the Habsburg Monarchy culminated in the publication of *Der Judenstaat* in 1896. The World Congress of Zionism met the following year in Basel where Russian Jews were heavily represented. Herzl's dramatic attempt to gain approval of its aims by the tsarist government encountered the familiar response. In his famous interview with the Russian Minister of the Interior, Vyacheslav Plehve, in 1903, he was fobbed off with vague assurances of sympathy. The government stubbornly maintained its practice of blocking the mass exodus of Jews. The Russian wing of Zionism struggled to reconcile contradictory commitments to colonizing Palestine and to strengthening Jewish culture in Russia. On the eve of the 1905 Revolution, Zionist groups were moving toward a political engagement with the regime.[55]

After the pogroms of 1881/2, Jewish resistance took two forms: flight and revolutionary activity. Emigration without an exit visa was illegal, even though it had been practiced by Jews since the reign of Nicholas I. For a time Ignat'ev had toyed with the idea of letting the Jewish people go, as he put it in his mocking style, before he came out against mass emigration. So too did the St. Petersburg notables. Nevertheless, in the decade after the pogroms almost 135,000 Jews left Russia; in the next decade twice that number headed mainly to the United States.[56] Their departure was opposed by the tsarist government, accommodationist elites in the two capitals, and by the burgeoning radical movements.

Before the pogroms of 1881, Jewish active resistance to imperial rule, like the accommodation, developed from a small numerical base. Still, Jews played a proportionately larger role than any other group in the leadership of the terrorist wing of the Populist movement, although their participation was not directly related to the question of emancipation.[57]

---

[55] Salo W. Baron, *The Russian Jews under Tsars and Soviets*, 2nd rev. edn (New York: Macmillan, 1976), pp. 146–49; Frankel, *Prophesy and Politics*, pp. 114–17, 158–59.

[56] Baron, *The Russian Jews*, pp. 47–50, 69–73. In a conversation with Samuel Poliakov, the Minister of the Interior, Ignat'ev declared that the promotion of Jewish emigration was tantamount to "incitement to sedition." S. M. Dubnow, *History of the Jews in Russia and Poland from the Earliest Times until the Present Day* [1915], trans. I. Friedlander (originally published in 3 vols., Philadelphia, 1916; republished Bergenfield, NJ: Avotoynu, 2000), p. 355.

[57] Norman M. Naimark, *Terrorists and Social Democrats. The Russian Revolutionary Movement under Alexander III* (Cambridge, MA: Harvard University Press, 1983), pp. 92–95, 202–11.

By the 1890s, the shift from populism to Marxism was well under way. Throughout the Pale and the provinces of the former Kingdom of Poland, two currents of resistance met and intermingled: Jewish nationalism and socialism. Jewish Marxist intellectuals found their audience in the emerging Jewish labor force fed by an influx of migrants from the *shtetl* into the cities, and the absorption of craftsmen and artisans into the new factories. The census of 1896 revealed the overwhelmingly urban character of the Jewish population. In European Russia they constituted 4 percent of the population but almost 15 percent of the urban population. They numbered more than 50 percent of the population in towns and cities of the northwest provinces of Minsk, Grodno, Mogilev, Vitebsk, and Mogilev, and more than 40 percent in the provinces of Vilna and Kovno. In the Kingdom of Poland they constituted more than 50 percent of the population in three of the ten provinces, more than 40 percent in three others, and 30 percent or more in all the rest.[58]

The largest, best organized, and most active political organization to emerge in the Baltic littoral was the General Jewish Workers' Union in Lithuania, Poland, and Russia, known as the Bund, the Yiddish word for union. Founded in 1897 after careful preliminary work, it represented social democratic groups in Warsaw, Vilna, Minsk, and Belostok. It continued to be the major socialist organization for the Jewish proletariat until 1917.[59] Jews participated in the other major socialist parties, providing them with some of their most prominent members. This very fact illuminated the central dilemma facing the Bund. It represented a culture aspiring to be a nationality that had no national territory, but inhabited a caricature of one – the Pale of Settlement. There was no way they could turn this territory or a part of it into a Jewish homeland. But to accept a homeland outside it would be to destroy the revolutionary struggle. In their efforts to define their movement as somehow combining social justice and cultural distinction in a society they wished to transform, the Bund faced formidable competitors within the resistance in addition to the autocracy.

Their most serious rivals were the Zionists, who after 1900 were making inroads in the Jewish working class. Its second major competitor was the leadership of the Russian Social Democratic Labor Party (RSDLP), still in its organizational infancy in 1903, even after they split into Mensheviks

[58] F. A. Brokgaus and I. A. Efron (eds.), *Entsiklopedicheskii slovar'* (St. Petersburg: I. A. Efron, 1907), supp. vol. II, appendix, p. xv. These figures slightly underestimated the total Jewish population due to the fact that the census included Russian-speaking Jews as assimilated.
[59] Henry J. Tobias, *The Jewish Bund in Russia. From its Origins to 1905* (Stanford University Press, 1972), remains the standard work, on which I have relied heavily.

and Bolsheviks. In addition, a small group of Jewish socialist intellectuals, including such powerful Marxist theorists as Rosa Luxemburg and Leo Jogiches, founded an anti-nationalist party which fused in 1900 with Lithuanian Social Democrats to form the Social Democracy of the Kingdom of Poland and Lithuania. The most internationalist of the numerous socialist parties in the borderlands, it turned its formidable rhetorical powers against the Polish Social Democrats, the Bund, and the RSDLP. They condemned them all as nationalists.[60] The autocracy did not at first resort just to repressive measures. S. V. Zubatov, the head of the Moscow branch of the secret police, deployed a strategy known as "police socialism." He sought to wean the Jewish working class from revolution by organizing unions under the protection of the police, which would confine their activities to legal activity aimed at winning economic concessions.[61] The movement backfired and had to be aborted. In sum, the participation of Jews in these revolutionary and reformist movements signaled another failure of Russian imperial rule to secure the loyalty of the peoples of the borderlands. It also illustrated, albeit in its extreme form due to the wide dispersal of the Jewish population, the common difficulty facing all movements of resistance from below: how to achieve political unity based on reconciling the national and social questions.

In the early political debates held by the Jewish socialist organizations abroad, the dominant voices favored internationalism. In the Russian Empire, the problems were much more complex because of its multi-cultural population and the existence of widely dispersed ethnic communities in the shatter zones of the western borderlands. Jewish social democrats oscillated between the two extremes, torn between striving for amalgamation into an all-Russian socialist movement and staking an exclusive claim to represent the Jewish worker.

At the first congress of the Bund in 1898 in Minsk, the founders straddled the question of whether class or nation should be given primacy. They agreed that the party should be "an autonomous organization, independent only in questions which specifically concern the Jewish proletariat ... with the Russian Empire" (*rossiiskaia* with its territorial implications, rather than *russkaia* with its ethnic implications). They

---

[60] J. P. Nettl, *Rosa Luxemburg*, 2 vols. (Oxford University Press, 1966), is the most comprehensive on her writings, but see also Elżbieta Ettinger, *Rosa Luxemburg. A Life* (Boston, MA: Beacon Press, 1986), for additional material based on subsequently published correspondence.

[61] Walter Sablinsky, *The Road to Bloody Sunday. Father Gapon and the St. Petersburg Massacre of 1905* (Princeton University Press, 1976); Abraham Ascher, *The Revolution of 1905*, 2 vols. (Stanford University Press, 1988), ch. 3.

soon changed their position under the influence of the ideas formulated by the south Slavic delegates to the Brünn Congress of Austrian Social Democrats and pressure from Bundist youth studying abroad. At their Fourth Congress in 1901, the Bund adopted a resolution in favor of transforming the Russian Empire into "a federation of nationalities, with full national autonomy for each, regardless of the territory which it inhabits."[62] This brought them into conflict with the internationalists. At the fateful Second Congress of the RSDLP, a majority of delegates, including Plekhanov, Trotsky, and Lenin, rejected their proposal to recognize Jews as a nationality like Poles, as well as their claim to be the sole representative of the Jewish proletariat in the Russian Empire. Their delegates then walked out of the Congress, giving a majority to Lenin and the advocates of a tightly knit, centralized party (Bolsheviks) against the minority (Mensheviks).[63] Thus began a tortured relationship between the Bund and the RSDLP. In the intraparty controversies over a nationalities policy, they became a favorite target of Stalin who, as we shall see, had his own very different views on the reconstruction of the Russian Empire along "federalist" lines.

The movement of the Bund toward national autonomy came under pressure from militant workers infused with the spirit of proletarian internationalism. In the decade and a half before the revolution of 1905, socialist youth had been active in organizing workers in Vilna and throughout the northwest Pale. They soon ran into a serious obstacle to further successes. Only a small number of Jewish workers were employed in large industrial establishments where strikes would have the greatest impact.[64] For this reason alone, the left wing of the Bund recognized the importance of keeping close ties with non-Jewish workers. Although they agitated to give preference to proletarian unity by rejoining the RSDLP, they only succeeded in 1906 when the revolutionary wave had passed its peak.

Kingdom of Poland

The prolonged struggle between Russians and Poles over the western borderlands intensified toward the end of the century. Economically, the szlachta managed surprisingly well in their efforts to retain control

---

[62] Frankel, *Prophecy and Politics*, pp. 217–23, quotation on p. 220. This position was also adopted by the Galician Social Democratic Party. See also Tobias, *The Jewish Bund*, pp. 160–76.

[63] See especially the detailed analysis in Tobias, *The Jewish Bund*, pp. 207–20.

[64] Ezra Mendelsohn, *Class Struggle in the Pale. The Formative Years of the Jewish Workers Movement in Tsarist Russia* (Cambridge University Press, 1970).

over their landed estates. From 1863 to 1872, the confiscation of properties owned by rebels affected only 144 domains. The majority of Polish landowners resisted political pressure to sell. They regarded the possession of their estates as a sacred cause and as a substitute for their lost country. Under economic pressure they resorted to leasing the land to Jewish entrepreneurs, rather than selling to Russians, stimulating anti-Semitic feelings as a nasty by-product. The Russian government countered by passing legislation in 1884 to prevent long-term mortgages, followed by other measures to force the sale of Polish estates. The Poles lost 2 million *desiatinas* from 1866 to 1893, but they still held half the land in the former kingdom. Under Nicholas II, a reduction in the special financial contribution of the Poles and their profits from the alcohol monopoly boosted their income, enabling them to avoid further losses. As Beauvois has pointed out, the Russians were not inspired by the same "mystical mission" in the western borderlands. Comparatively speaking, their attachment to their ancestral lands was greater than that of the Russian nobility, which between 1861 and 1914 sold off more than three-quarters of their estates in the empire as a whole. Socially, however, the picture was very different. The szlachta were slow to accept the Polish peasantry as part of the nation.[65]

In the borderlands of Imperial Russia, illegal political movements in the Vistula Lands (the former Kingdom of Poland) displayed a level of national consciousness equaled only by the Armenians. Even before the outbreak of mass demonstrations and violence in 1905, the supporters of accommodation, known as the Warsaw positivists, were largely discredited as a result of the government's policy of Russification.[66] Clandestine political parties began to take shape. The most aggressive right-wing nationalist movement, the National Democrats, or *Endecja*, was under the leadership of Roman Dmowski, a future leader of independent Poland. A broad-based populist movement, it embraced the Church as a national institution, and stigmatized the Jewish and Ukrainian minorities as alien to the national cause. Incorporating Social Darwinism into the insurrectionist tradition, Dmowski believed that Jews did not constitute an organic nation because they never participated in the struggle for survival. Conquest and colonization by progressive forces such as the Polish nation as historically practiced in the east was fully justified, he asserted. His views continued to evolve toward more virulent

---

[65] Daniel Beauvois, *Le noble, le serf et le revizor, 1832–1863* (Paris: Archives contemporaines, 1984), pp. 48–50, 58, 71, 84.
[66] Robert Blobaum, *Rewolucja. Russian Poland, 1904–1907* (Ithaca, NY: Cornell University Press, 1995).

anti-Semitism, culminating in 1902 with his assertion that the Jews had developed a plan to conquer Poland. He also directed his cultural barbs against "Muscovite–Asian despotism" in the name of saving the Lithuanians and Ruthenians for Western civilization.[67] Yet when it came to choosing between Poland's traditional enemies, he grudgingly acknowledged a preference for working within the Russian Empire for Polish independence against the more repressive Prussian rule.

In the early 1890s the socialist movement in the Vistula Lands, as in other urban centers of the empire, rapidly gained ground. Marxist ideas began to penetrate from Germany after the lifting of the anti-socialist laws there in 1890. Simultaneously, illegal strikes rocked the expanding capitalist enterprises, followed by mass arrests and repression. Forced to organize in clandestine conditions, the Polish socialists like their Russian counterparts debated the burning questions of reform versus revolution, and international versus national goals. Similar to other socialist movements born in the borderlands, its leaders assumed different spatial as well as ideological perspectives.

Founded in 1892, the Polish Socialist Party emerged as the champion of a revolutionary struggle for a Polish state. Its foremost spokesman, Józef Piłsudski, was an early and ardent foe of both the nationalist and internationalist tendencies beginning to surface in the Jewish socialist movement. In his open letter "To the Jewish Socialist Comrades in the Occupied Polish Provinces," he leveled his criticism against the promotion of the Russian language and culture in their propaganda among the Jewish proletariat. He predicted that such a Russian-oriented policy – "the cancer of Jewish self-Russification," as he called it – would infuriate the Polish masses. He urged them to recognize that the Russians were more backward, politically and culturally than the Poles. In his eagerness to win over the Jewish social democrats to the cause of recreating an independent Polish national state, he urged and even helped them to introduce Yiddish as the lesser evil in their cultural work as a means of driving out the Russian language.[68]

If in Piłsudski's eyes the Bund was too Jewish in orientation, then the Social Democratic Party of the Kingdom of Poland and Lithuania was too internationalist. It had come into existence in 1893 when a small group of intellectuals led by Rosa Luxemburg, Leo Jogiches, and Feliks Dzierżyński split off from the Polish Socialist Party. From the outset, it rejected the idea that the socialist revolution and the overthrow of imperial rule could

[67] Brian Porter, *When Nations Began to Hate. Imagining Politics in Nineteenth Century Poland* (Oxford University Press, 2002), pp. 180–84, 230, 237.
[68] Frankel, *Prophecy and Politics*, pp. 198–200.

be anything but a unified movement of the world proletariat. In Luxemburg's eyes, the one exception that proved the rule was the Ottoman Empire; she considered it to be so backward that only its dissolution into national units could enable its people to catch up with the normal process of the historical dialectic.[69] It was never able to compete in membership with the other socialist parties in the Vistula Lands and the Pale. But its formidable intellectual leadership demanded attention and engagement in the great theoretical debates over the question of national self-determination. While Luxemburg provided the theoretical power, Dzierżyński provided the organizational muscle. Together they held the party together until 1917 when he went over to the Bolsheviks, to become the first head of the Cheka.[70] Luxemburg persistently adhered to the view that autonomy for Poland was a tactical concession to the bourgeoisie, but the proletariat could find its full liberation only in the context of a Russian revolution. She firmly rejected the Leninist model of a centralized party in favor of a mass, democratic movement of the working class. Yet she and Dzierżyński showed a willingness to join the Bolsheviks along with other parties during revolutionary movements in 1905 and again in early 1917. For them, the Polish Socialist Party was the main enemy in the socialist camp. The socialist parties of the western borderlands were intoxicated by the outbreak of the revolution of 1905 when they enjoyed a brief moment of unity of action, if not of thought, in their resistance to imperial rule.

From the earliest months of the Russo-Japanese War, non-party groups of the Polish intelligentsia began to agitate in the clandestine press for a "unified and independent Poland." Acting "above the parties," they organized illegal rallies that drew in members of the left-wing parties and members of the professions.[71] They immediately supported the general strike of January 1905, and continued to maintain close contact with the workers. In the spring of 1905 professional unions were formed along the lines of the Union of Unions in Russia, and sought to federate with their Russian counterparts. A large number of cultural organizations sprang up in the revolutionary year, some of which survived until 1914. But efforts to reintroduce the Polish language into the public sphere ran

[69] Nettl, *Rosa Luxemburg*, vol. I, pp. 65–66. An appendix to vol. II summarizes her complex views on "the national question."
[70] Robert Blobaum, *Feliks Dzierżyński and the SDKPiL. A Study of the Origins of Polish Communism* (Boulder, CO: East European Monographs, 1984), demonstrates Dzierżyński's tactical skills and his close adherence to Luxemburg's ideological positions.
[71] The following is based on Halina Kiepurska, "Le rôle de l'intelligentsia du royaume de Pologne dans la révolution de 1905," in François-Xavier Coquin and Céline Gervais-Francelle (eds.), *1905. La première révolution russe* (Paris: Institut des études slaves, 1986), pp. 248–60, quotation on p. 248.

into the intransigent opposition of the autocracy. In many ways the revolution of 1905 in Poland was a continuation and expansion of the nationalist movement born in 1863.

South Caucasus

Among the Armenian population of the Caucasian borderlands incorporated into the Russian Empire after wars with the Ottomans and Iranians in 1828 and 1877/8, a national awareness had been gradually growing. In contrast to the Polish case, this occurred under benevolent imperial rule.[72] As had so often been the case in the Russian Empire, church schools became the cradles of the first generation of a national intelligentsia. The government not only permitted the establishment of these schools, but also created a centralized religious authority in the form of the Catholicos at Etchmiadzin, an ancient monastery of the Armenian–Gregorian Church. The monastery had acquired great symbolic significance having survived centuries of occupation and persecution by the Iranians and Ottomans; in 1827, an heroic defense by its Russian garrison had repulsed the siege led by Abbās Mīrzā. The Armenian Church enjoyed special protection within the Russian Empire because of its ancient lineage and its close liturgical relationship to Orthodoxy. The Armenian commercial community also flourished, particularly in Tiflis where Armenians constituted the majority of the population and dominated the municipal council before 1900. The Russian victories in the Russo-Turkish War of 1877/8 had given an enormous boost to the Armenian nationalist cause. Volunteers had poured in to join the Russian armies in eastern Anatolia. They took pride in being commanded by Russo-Armenian generals like M. T. Loris-Melikov, who became Minister of the Interior and the last of the great imperial reformers under Alexander II. But they were disillusioned by the Congress of Berlin where the Great Powers forced Russia to modify the provisions of the Treaty of San Stefano dealing not only with Bulgaria but also eastern Anatolia. The sultan was freed of the obligation to introduce reforms in the Armenian vilayets while still under Russian occupation. It was a formula that guaranteed, once again, the indefinite postponement of Ottoman promises.

Yet up to the 1880s Armenians still looked to the Orthodox tsar as a guarantor of their cultural life and a defense against the Islamic powers to

---

[72] For the following, see Ronald Grigor Suny, *Looking Toward Ararat. Armenia in Modern History* (Bloomington, IN: Indiana University Press, 1993), esp. pp. 36–51, 65–91.

the south. Russia also represented for them the potential source of their unification with their co-nationals living across the Ottoman frontier. In 1881 this optimistic outlook changed with dramatic suddenness. As elsewhere in the borderlands, the assassination of Alexander II by members of the Revolutionary Party of the People's Will touched off a violent reaction against non-Russian nationalities. Russification was the order of the day. Yet in the south Caucasus it took on a curious twist. The man in charge of Russification from 1882 to 1890 was Prince A. M. Dondukov-Korsakov, the head of the civilian administration of the Caucasus and the commander of the Caucasian military district. However, during the same period he acquired a well-deserved reputation as an enlightened reformer. Were Russifying policies and reform incompatible?

Dondukov-Korsakov was an old Caucasus hand, a military hero of the campaigns against the Turks in 1855 and 1877, who served together with Prince Cherkasskii as one of the commissioners of the Russian occupation force in Bulgaria charged with organizing the civilian administration of the new country. His reputation as a reformer in the Caucasus rests on his program of introducing new regulations for the regional administration and abolishing the military administration. He also was responsible for stimulating the economy by regulating the mining industry and promoting the production and sale of the famous Caucasian mineral waters.[73] Yet in 1885, under his administration all the Armenian parish schools were ordered to be closed and replaced by Russian schools. What followed was what might be called "a Russifying reform."

The new educational policy was planned by one of Russia's most well-known pedagogue administrators, Kirill Petrovich Ianovskii. The son of a poor Ukrainian noble family, he rose rapidly in the ranks of educational administrators despite his opposition to the conservative policies of the Minister of Education, Count Dmitri Tolstoi, the champion of classical education. Appointed in 1878 as trustee (*popechitel'*) of the Caucasian educational region by the viceroy, Grand Duke Mikhail Nikolaevich, he spent twenty-two years reorganizing the Caucasian educational system. He was responsible for vastly increasing the number of elementary and secondary schools and teachers' seminaries. He established a wide network of professional and agricultural schools specifically targeted at improving the local economy. He sponsored the publication of twenty volumes of scholarly research on various regions of the Caucasus ranging from ethnographic to linguistic and archaeological works.[74]

---

[73] "Dondukov-Korsakov, A. M.," *Entsiklopedicheskii slovar'*, vol. XXI, p. 17.
[74] "Ianovskii, K. P.," *Entsiklopedicheskii slovar'*, vol. XXI, pp. 82, 674–75.

Russifying reformers were not always satisfied with the willingness of the population to accommodate. By the end of the nineteenth century, Russian bureaucrats charged that the Armenian population had failed to carry out its assigned role as bearers of Christian, civilized values into areas of the south Caucasus still inhabited by nomadic tribes. In 1899, a law limited the redistribution of state lands to peasants of native Russian origin. This ended the lengthy process of resettling Armenian peasant immigrants from the Ottoman Empire. Provincial administrators requested colonizers who could play not only a civilizing but also a state-building role by establishing closer links with the central Great Russian provinces.[75]

That the "Russifiers" in Armenia could be reformers should not cause surprise. Such had been the case in many borderlands since Catherine the Great. Uniform, centralized administration, secularization of education, state stimulus of the economy, and promotion of a common language, that is, Russian, were deemed to be modernizing techniques. But they also generated resistance from those who saw their cultural heritage threatened or who were uprooted from their village societies and plunged into the harsh conditions of early industrialization. In Armenia, Russification, even in the guise of reform, encountered a unique obstacle. On the frontiers of competing empires for over a millennium, the Armenians cherished an ethnoreligious unity, part historical and part mythical, that could be realized only by abolishing the military boundary line that divided them between the Ottoman and Russian empires. This helps to explain why the Armenian resistance to imperial rule in both empires that sought to assimilate them was deeply committed to embracing nationalist and socialist goals.

Socialist ideas in the form of populism filtered into Armenia as in Georgia through the agency of returning students who had studied in Russian and Western universities. Some of them were impressed by the assassination of Alexander II organized by the terrorist wing of the Russian populists. In the early 1880s, small groups of young Armenian populists blossomed and just as quickly died out. In Switzerland, another nursery of Russian revolutionaries, other Armenian students formed small, separate groups. Nationalist sentiments also found fertile ground among students in the wake of the Russian victories over the Turks in the war of 1877/8 and in the formation of a Bulgarian state. In 1887, reflecting these cross-currents, a group of revolutionary students in Geneva founded

---

[75] Iorg Baberovski, "Tsivilizatorskaia missiia i natsionalizm v Zakavkaze, 1828–1914 gg.," *Imperskaia istoriia postsovetskogo prostranstva* (Kazan: Tsentr issledovanii natsionalizma i imperii, 2004), p. 343.

a newspaper, *Hnchak* (*The Bell*), named after the famous organ of Alexander Herzen. It became the core of a party bearing the same name. This was a transition period in the development of Russian revolutionary organizations abroad; a few bold spirits like Georgii Plekhanov were already "half a Marxist." Similarly, the Hnchak program incorporated elements of Marxist vocabulary and thinking. However, it remained populist at heart, committed to the liberation and unification of Armenians in the Russian, Iranian, and Ottoman borderlands into a single independent state.[76]

A second Armenian nationalist party with socialist overtones, the Armenian Federation of Revolutionaries (Dashnaktsutiun or Dashnaks), was founded in 1890 to unify all the revolutionary groups, including Hnchak, under an umbrella organization. Following the precedent set by Greek and Bulgarian émigrés in Russia, the movement grew out of philanthropic societies in Russia with political goals. In the 1870s, the Dashnaks had suffered arrests for revolutionary activity. After the Russo-Turkish War they shifted the main thrust of their propaganda and activities toward liberation of Armenians in the Ottoman Empire. By the 1890s, they were organizing centers throughout the Caucasian and Trans Caspian borderlands from Tiflis and Tabriz to Samarkand and Khiva. They made contact with the Kurds, Young Turks, and especially the Macedonian Revolutionary Organization (IMRO). The Dashnaks were responsible for the famous Ottoman Bank demonstration in August 1896, when twenty-six of their members occupied the bank in Istanbul in the hope of forcing Great Power intervention. The adventure backfired, touching off a massacre of 6,000 Armenians in Istanbul.[77]

Differences arose between the Dashnaks and Hnchak over the relative importance of national and socialist goals. These provoked a split among the intellectual leadership characteristic of all the underground, conspiratorial movements in the Russian borderlands at the time. Hnchak retained its separate existence from the Dashnaks, and the two became rivals despite similarities in their programs. By the late 1890s, the Hnchak party was coming apart, leaving the Dashnaks as the leading force. Both owed much to Russian socialism in its populist form, including terrorism as a tactic. Like the Poles, the Muslim Tatars (later called Azeris), and later on the Mongols, the Armenian revolutionaries took advantage of the

---

[76] Louise Nalbandian, *The Armenian Revolutionary Movement. The Development of Political Parties Throughout the Nineteenth Century* (Berkeley, CA: University of California Press, 1963), pp. 108–10.

[77] Nalbandian, *The Armenian Revolutionary Movement*, pp. 133–45, 151–54, 172–73, 176–77. They obtained arms from Russian workers in the government armory in Tiflis and smuggled them across the Ottoman frontier.

porous frontier in adjacent imperial borderlands to spread revolutionary
ideas of national unity inspired by Russian populism, and later Russian
Marxism.[78]

Trans Caspia

In Trans Caspia, resistance to the Russian administration and influx of
Russian settlers did not assume major proportions until the 1890s. The
government had been careful to avoid recruiting Muslims into the army,
fearing to place firearms into the hands of men trained to use them. The
Sepoy Mutiny in India had been a warning. After the first outbreak in the
Ferghana Valley in 1885 led by an important Muslim landowner, local
outbreaks over the land issue were easily suppressed. Most of them were
led by religious leaders, often from Sufi orders. The Tashkent cholera
riots in 1892 were the largest urban revolt. The riots were sparked by
Muslim fears of poor Russian settlers as bearers of the disease and the
Russian sanitary measures that offended traditional Muslim customs.
They signaled the wide cultural gap that had opened up between the
Russian settlers and the indigenous population.[79] In 1898, tensions
exploded during the Andijan holy war. The revolt was carefully planned.
Led by a highly respected Sufi, it was financed by the brotherhood and
supported by the Muslim tribal elites of the pre-conquest period.[80] The
authorities blamed pan-Islamic propaganda. The Russian administrators
had always entertained exaggerated fears of Muslim rebellions. By the
early twentieth century their suspicions had taken on a sharper edge. The
spread of Islamic reform movements like the Jadid from Crimean Tatar,
Volga Tatar, Ottoman, and Indian sources summoned up visions of a vast
conspiracy to overthrow Russian rule in the borderlands.[81] The

[78] Suny, *Looking Toward Ararat*, pp. 80–92.
[79] Jeff Sahadeo, *Russian Colonial Society in Tashkent, 1865–1923* (Bloomington, IN: Indiana
University Press, 2007), pp. 99–107.
[80] Different interpretations of its origins can be found in Beatrice Forbes Manz, "Central
Asian Uprisings in the Nineteenth Century. Ferghana under the Russians," *Russian
Review* 46 (1987): 69–89, who attributes it to tribal rivalries, and B. M. Babadzhanov,
"Dukchi Ishan und der Aufstand von Andijan, 1898," in Anke von Kügegen *et al.* (eds.),
*Muslim Culture in Russia and Central Asia from the 18th to the Early 20th Centuries, vol. II:
Inter-regional and Inter-ethnic Relations* (Berlin: Schwarz, 1998), pp. 167–91, who attrib-
utes it to religious motives.
[81] Alexander Morrison, *Russian Rule in Samarkand, 1868–1910. A Comparison with British
India* (Oxford University Press, 2008), pp. 53–55, 75–76, 87, 119. In 1910 the last
Russian reformer in Central Asia, Count K. K. Pahlen, noted that "The political tendency
of Pan-Islamism is toward acknowledging the Turkish Sultan as leader. The danger is that
the devotion of the native population of Turkestan to another power will cause a national
religious crisis." *Ibid.*, p. 75.

Turkestan administration was deeply shaken by the revolt and the specialists were divided over the proper response. One group defended von Kaufman's old policy of non-interference. A second group opposed it, declaring: "People speak of our civilizing role in Central Asia. At this juncture our cultural influence is remarkable for its non-existence."[82] Meanwhile, social tensions in Tashkent had been building among the Russian railroad workers who led the first strike against the local administrators in 1899, raising fears that the workers might make contacts with the indigenous population.

No one has argued that the Russian administration of its Central Asian borderlands was a brilliant success. The best that can be said is that it abolished the slave trade, and reduced violent conflicts among the nomadic tribes and between the khanates. But the Russians were divided over the means for advancing their civilizing mission, which were inadequate, and ends, which were ambivalent. In part, this was due to their Orientalist view of Muslims as an alien, hostile, and fanatical population. In part, it arose from the fear that a policy of forced assimilation would trigger rebellions that would appeal to the Ottomans, British, or even the Chinese for protection. An unexpected consequence of the imperial Russian government's half-hearted colonization projects was, ironically, to provide a popular base for a Bolshevik victory in the regional Civil War.

The revolution of 1905

Russia's revolution of 1905/6 had its roots in its imperialist expansion in the Inner Asian borderlands. In the previous decade and a half, the Russians followed up their conquests in Trans Caspia and the delimitation of the Manchurian frontier by undertaking their most ambitious project to bind the Inner Asia borderlands strategically and commercially to the center of imperial power. In 1891, construction began on the Trans-Siberian Railroad. It was the most costly engineering project in Eurasia before the First World War. Up to the 1880s, Russia's rulers and bureaucratic elites had frowned upon the idea of building such a line, or of even undertaking the development of Siberia. Under Alexander III this attitude changed. Close advisors of the tsar among the military and the tsar himself were persuaded that the closer attachment and integration of eastern Siberia to the imperial center was a matter of urgency given their concern over the growth of regionalism and the possibility of a renewed Chinese drive to take back the Amur and Ussuri provinces that they had

---

[82] Carrère d'Encausse, "Organizing and Colonizing," pp. 168–71, quotation from the local press on p. 171.

lost twenty years earlier.[83] The driving force behind this enterprise was the energetic and ambitious Minister of Finance, Sergius Witte. He envisaged the Trans-Siberian as a multipurpose state enterprise to stimulate Russia's domestic production of iron and steel, to colonize a sparsely populated region, to serve as the vehicle for a civilizing mission, and to strengthen the economic power of the state in the struggle over the Inner Asian borderlands.[84]

After some hesitation, Witte also came round to the idea of building a feeder line, to be called the Chinese Eastern Railroad (CER), across the northern third of Manchuria connecting the Trans-Siberian directly to Vladivostok. Meeting opposition within the Russian bureaucracy, Witte pointed out that the line would enable Russia to penetrate all of Manchuria and ultimately bring the entire railroad network of northern China under its control. The plan met with an enthusiastic response from the Chinese elder statesman, Li Hongzhan. A champion of the self-strengthening concept, Li perceived the CER as a key element in his campaign to transfer Western technology to China. In the wake of China's defeat in the Sino-Japanese War (1894/5), he also came to regard the concession as a means of employing the classic Chinese borderland strategy of pitting one barbarian against another. At the time, he judged Japan to be the greater threat to Chinese sovereignty in the northeast provinces (Manchuria). Witte planned to finance the concession through a Russo-Chinese Bank, secured by loans from France.[85] In 1896, he negotiated a treaty of defensive alliance with China aimed specifically against Japan, which granted Russia the right to build a branch line of the Trans-Siberian across Manchuria and also granted extensive extra-territorial privileges.[86] The construction of the CER greatly facilitated the Russian occupation of Manchuria during the Boxer Rebellion in 1900, and aroused Japanese suspicions that the Russian presence would be permanent. Witte then sought to settle the problems with Japan along the same lines as in his previous negotiations with the Habsburgs in the Balkans and the subsequent Russian negotiations with the British in Trans Caspia; namely, by dividing the borderlands into spheres of influence.

[83] Steven Marks, *Road to Power. The Trans-Siberian Railroad and the Colonization of Asian Russia, 1850–1917* (Ithaca, NY: Cornell University Press, 1991), pp. 48–54.

[84] Marks, *Road to Power*, pp. 141–44, 148–69; David Schimmelpenninck van der Oye, *Toward the Rising Sun. Russian Ideologies of Empire and the Path to War with Japan* (DeKalb, IL: Northern Illinois University Press, 2001), pp. 70–71.

[85] B. V. Romanov, *Rossiia v Man'churii (1892–1906)* (Leningrad: Izd. Leningradskogo vostochnogo instituta, 1928), pp. 13–14, 90–94; Dokkyu Choi, *Rossiia v Koree: 1893–1905 gg. (Politka Ministersvtvo finansov i Morskogo minsterstva)* (St. Petersburg: Zero, 1996).

[86] Van der Oye, *Toward the Rising Sun*, pp. 137–45.

Roughly speaking this meant that Russia and Japan would mutually recognize their respective preeminent interests in Manchuria and Korea. But Witte began to lose his influence with Nicholas II in the critical years of the early twentieth century, foreshadowing disasters for Russian policy in the Balkans and Inner Asian borderlands.

Witte's policy of peaceful penetration of the Inner Asian borderlands was only one aspect of his grandiose foreign policy, which required cooperation among Russia's normally fractious bureaucratic interest groups. His efforts to create a unified system of government fell short of complete success. But he managed to influence the tsar's appointment of his clients to several key ministries, enabling him to coordinate his policy of economic imperialism along the great arc from the Danubian to the Inner Asian frontiers.[87] In a striking demonstration of the geocultural links between complex frontiers at the opposite ends of the Russian Empire, Witte was forced to come to terms with the Habsburgs in the west in order to pursue more aggressively his policy in the east. Faced with an outbreak of violence in the Ottoman borderlands on the Danubian frontier, he endorsed an informal understanding with the Habsburg Monarchy in 1897 to maintain the status quo in the Balkans for ten years. The two powers could not agree on several points that, as we have seen, foreshadowed trouble for the future. But the agreement enabled him to shift Russian policy away from its long obsession with the Danubian basin to Inner Asia where, he was convinced, Russian interests could be developed more profitably. At the same time, he envisaged and supported the idea of a continental coalition of Russia, Germany, and France directed against British commercial competition along the great arc of Eurasian frontiers from the Mediterranean to the Pacific.

Although Witte was the architect of the new policy, he was ably seconded by two of his protégés, the Foreign Minister, N. Z. Lambsdorf, and the Minister of War, General A. N. Kuropatkin, who had served as the Governor General of Turkestan up to 1898. Kuropatkin's recommendations for a Manchurian policy were clearly expounded in a memo to the tsar in 1900. In it he acknowledged the necessity of maintaining the status quo in Russia's western borderlands in order to concentrate on extending Russian influence in Iran and northern China. Hostile to the ideas of the pan-Slavs, he rejected any idea of acquiring Galicia, the sub-Carpatho-Ukraine, or other territories inhabited by Ukrainians or Belorussians. "For us," he wrote, "the Slavs of Austria including

[87] Alfred J. Rieber, "Patronage and Professionalism. The Witte System," in *Problemy vsemirnoi istorii. Sbornik statei v chest' Aleksandra Aleksandrovicha Fursenko* (St. Petersburg: Dmitri Bulanin, 2000), pp. 286–97.

the Rusyns [sic] should serve only as a means not an end." He reiterated even more strongly his earlier proposals to reduce Iran to an economic satellite and to pursue aggressively the economic penetration of Afghanistan, Mongolia, and Manchuria. When the Boxer Rebellion broke out, Kuropatkin advocated the occupation of Manchuria, but along with Witte he opposed annexation.[88] Witte also set limits to a policy of expansion where he regarded Japanese interests as paramount. Together he and Kuropatkin lobbied unsuccessfully to restrain members of a court camarilla from pursing an adventurist course in Korea, which was bound to appear to the Japanese as a threat to their security. By involving Tsar Nicholas II in a hair-brained scheme, called the Yalu Timbering Concession, the court camarilla outflanked Witte and Kuropatkin and convinced the Japanese that war was inevitable. In 1904, the Japanese navy destroyed the Russian Pacific Fleet in a surprise attack at Port Arthur, and plunged Russia into war before the completion of the Trans-Siberian Railroad, thus securing their own sea-borne communication with Korea and Manchuria, and forcing the Russian army to fight without a dependable transportation link to its main supply bases in the central provinces.[89]

Russia's defeat in the war with Japan marked the beginning of the end of its ascendancy in the imperial phase of struggle over the borderlands. The unsuccessful war triggered the revolution that shook Russia's control over its borderlands from the Baltic littoral to the Caucasian isthmus. Having apparently recovered from the defeat by negotiating spheres of influence with Japan in Manchuria and Britain in Iran, it renewed its competition with the Habsburgs in the Balkans after the agreement on the status quo expired in 1907. The ripple effects of these struggles over the borderlands foreshadowed a set of entangled crises which was to end in the destruction of all the multicultural empires.

The revolution of 1905/6 was not a revolution in the conventional sense in that it led to the overthrow of the existing government. Instead, it was a series of uncoordinated uprisings that forced the autocracy to accept a

---

[88] A. V. Ignat'ev, "Politika v Evrope, na blizhnem i srednem vostoke," in *Vneshnaia politika Rossii v 1905–1907 gg.* (Moscow: Nauka, 1986), pp. 53–59.

[89] In his classic work, Romanov, *Rossiia v Manchurii*, subsequently revised as *Ocherki diplomaticheskoi istorii russko-iaponskii voiny, 1895–1907*, 2nd edn (Moscow: Akademiia Nauk SSSR, 1955). See also A. V. Ignat'ev, "The Foreign Policy of Russia in the Far East at the Turn of the Nineteenth and Twentieth Centuries," in Hugh Ragsdale (ed.), *Imperial Russian Foreign Policy* (Washington, DC and Cambridge: Woodrow Wilson Center and Cambridge University Press, 1993), pp. 254–60; van der Oye, *Toward the Rising Sun.*

semi-constitutional rule, but retaining the levers of power.[90] Nor was it a dress rehearsal for 1917 as Lenin argued, but rather a foreshadowing of the Civil War between 1918 and 1920. It is not stretching the imagination to see continuities with the civil wars within the Soviet Union during the Second World War and the events leading to the dissolution of the Soviet Union in 1989 when the first serious disturbances against the center took place in Georgia and the Baltic republics.

The revolution of 1905/6 highlighted and deepened social fragmentation and political polarization, two structural faults in imperial Russian society that had reached a critical conjuncture at the turn of the century. They were the products of several particular processes of imperial state-building: the periodic acquisition by conquest of new borderlands; their incomplete and uneven assimilation; and the accretion of new layers of imperial institutions and ideologies, rather than the replacement of the archaic by the new. The outcome of the revolutionary events of 1905/6 provides further evidence that the Russian Empire was a "sedimentary society" where structural reforms were layered on top of existing institutions without replacing them.[91] First, there were several irreconcilable contradictions in the legal documents granted by the tsar that comprised the constitutional structure of the post-revolutionary regime. Nicholas II not only opposed the idea of a constitutional government, but did not understand it. When confronted in 1904 by demands from his own advisors for some form of representative assembly, he shot back: "We did not have feudalism. There was always unity and loyalty (*edinenie i doverie*) ... I do not understand the principle of representative government."[92]

In August 1905, faced by a mounting wave of revolutionary outbreaks, Nicholas II granted a limited constitution, calling into existence an elected imperial parliament, the so-called Bulygin Duma after the Minister of the Interior who proposed it. The decree starkly revealed its limitations:

Whereas, leaving intact the fundamental law of the Russian Empire as it refers to the Autocratic power [defined in the Collection of Russian Laws that came into

---

[90] J. H. L. Keep, *The Rise of Social Democracy in Russia* (Oxford University Press, 1963), p. 150. Cf. Abraham Ascher, "Interpreting 1905," in Stefani Hoffman and Ezra Mendelsohn (eds.), *The Revolution of 1905 and Russia's Jews* (Philadelphia, PA: University of Pennsylvania Press, 2008).

[91] For preliminary sketches of this idea, see Alfred J. Rieber, "The Sedimentary Society," in Edith Clowes, Samuel Kassow, and James L. West (eds.), *Between Tsar and People. Educated Society and the Quest for Public Identity in Late Imperial Russia* (Princeton University Press, 1991), pp. 342–66; Elise Kimmerling Wirtschafter, *Structures of Society. Imperial Russia's Peoples of Various Ranks* (DeKalb, IL: Northern Illinois University Press, 1994).

[92] B. V. Anan'ich, R. Sh. Ganelin, and V. M. Paneiakh, *Vlast' i reform. Ot samoderzhavnoi k sovetskoi Rossii* (St. Petersburg: Dmitrii Bulanin, 1996), pp. 40–81.

force in 1835], We have deemed it desirable to establish a State Duma and to approve its electoral statute, applying these laws to the whole Empire, *except for those changes that will be necessary in the case of a few border regions with special conditions.*[93]

The "few border regions" included the provinces of the Kingdom of Poland, the regions of the Ural and Tugaisk, the provinces and regions of Siberia, the governor generalships of the Steppes and of Turkestan, and the viceroyalty of the Caucasus, as well as the nomadic tribes. There was no time to implement the Bulygin Duma before a general strike forced Nicholas to grant a more liberal document, the October Manifesto. In it he promised to grant "freedom of conscience, speech, assembly and union"; to extend the franchise to those excluded by the special rules following the Bulygin Duma; and "to establish it as an unbreakable rule that no law can become effective without the approval of the State Duma." The critical question was how to reconcile this concession with the principle of autocracy. Throughout the crisis this dilemma split the tsar's advisors and caused him great personal anguish.[94] After much back and forth, the tsar finally accepted a definition of his powers in the Fundamental Law of April 1906 that dropped the word "unlimited" (*neogranichennyi*) from the old formula, but retained the word "autocratic" (*samoderzhavnyi*), at the same time as it confirmed the exclusive right of the Duma to pass new legislation. As Andrew Verner has stated, Nicholas II "refused to see any contradiction between the rights promised by the October acts and the absence of any limits on the autocrat's personal power and prerogatives."[95]

What troubled the tsar greatly was his responsibility to maintain his inherited rights. Better to pile another layer of legislation on previous laws rather than alter his legacy. As if to confirm this sedimentary theory of government, the granting of civil liberties was seriously undermined by the retention of the old emergency provisions in effect throughout much of the empire since 1881 that gave the authorities power to suspend or close newspapers, arrest and sentence individuals without a trial, prohibit meetings and demonstrations, and generally restrict the exercise of civil rights.[96] Adding still another layer to the accumulation of institutions and

---

[93] The document is printed in full in Marc Raeff (ed.), *Plans for Political Reform in Imperial Russia, 1730–1905* (Englewood Cliffs, NJ: Prentice-Hall, 1966), pp. 142–52, citation on p. 143 (italics added).

[94] The best guide to these debates is Andrew M. Verner, *The Crisis of Russian Autocracy. Nicholas II and the 1905 Revolution* (Princeton University Press, 1990). See also Richard Wortman, "The 'Integrity' (*Tselost*) of the State in Imperial Russian Representation," *Ab Imperio* 2 (2011): 34–36.

[95] Verner, *The Crisis*, p. 300.

[96] Peter Waldron, "State of Emergency. Autocracy and Extraordinary Legislation, 1881–1917," *Revolutionary Russia* 8 (1995): 1–25.

laws, the electoral system for the first and second State Duma mixed voting by citizenship and by the archaic and crumbling legal category of estate (*soslovie*). Commenting on the failure of the bureaucrats involved in drawing up the law to understand the principles of representative government, State Secretary S. E. Kryzhanovskii wrote that Russia "lacks the cultural and moral force to carry out an assimilation of the nationalities, especially since some of the periphery stands at a higher cultural level than Russia."[97]

The interaction between the nationalizing (or Russifying) policies of the government and the proliferation of nationalist groups contending with the government and with one another opened up new fissures in society, which in the first flush of revolutionary enthusiasm were pasted over through unity of action against autocracy. When the ill-assorted coalition of revolutionaries of different national and social allegiances appeared to have gained the concession of a constitution, the bonds began to fray and counter-revolutionary groups began to form. Most authorities agree that the failure of the revolution to complete the overthrow of the tsarist autocracy may be attributed to the absence of a unified revolutionary movement.[98] But the determination of the government to repress the disorder should not be underestimated.

After the announcement of the October Manifesto the most serious problem facing the government was the massive breakdown in discipline and open mutiny in the army. The 500,000 reservists serving in the Manchurian army mutinied for two months, demanding to be sent home. Two waves of mutinies peaked in November, with just under two-thirds occurring in the borderlands, and again in the summer of 1906 when they brought the regime close to collapse. But the mutinous soldiers turned against the revolutionaries when it became clear to them that the government was determined to restore public order by taking the most extreme repressive measures.[99] Unlike February 1917 or 1991, the army held the country together. Once it was clear that the government was not going to collapse, the revolutionary wave subsided.

[97] See S. E. Kryzhanovskii, *Vospominaniia. Iz bumagi S. E. Krizhanovskogo, posledniago gosudarstvennogo sekretaria Rossiiskoi imperii* (Berlin: n.p., [1929?]), pp. 98–99, 130.

[98] Abraham Ascher, *The Revolution of 1905*, 2 vols. (Stanford University Press, 1988), vol. I. See also Andreas Kappeler, *The Russian Empire* (Edinburgh: Pearson Education, 2001), pp. 329–41.

[99] John S. Bushnell, *Mutiny Amid Repression. Russian Soldiers in the Revolution of 1905* (Bloomington, IN: Indiana University Press, 1985). For statistics on mutinies by region, see *ibid.*, pp. 141 and 173. See also Oleg Airapetov, "Revolution in the Manchurian Armies, as Perceived by a Future Leader of the White Movement," in Jonathan D. Smele and Anthony Heywood (eds.), *The Russian Revolution of 1905. Centenary Perspectives* (London: Routledge, 2005), pp. 94–118.

Repression from above was not the only weapon used by the government. It encouraged a backlash from below in the form of pogroms. The Jews were not the only targets – other supporters of the revolution were attacked – but they were the main victims. By the fall of 1905 conservative elements in the population began to form the first mass movement of the Russian ultra-right, the Union of the Russian People. It engaged in mass propaganda preaching anti-Semitism and Russification, and organized armed squads to carry out assassinations of its political opponents in a mirror image of tactics adopted by revolutionaries.[100] Most of the counter-revolutionary activity was also concentrated in the borderlands. By combining a few concessions followed by repressive measures, the government was able to drive deeper wedges between the revolutionary forces and then pick them off once it had granted constitutional rights. As a result, the post-revolutionary period witnessed a widening of the social fissures that persisted after the collapse of imperial rule.

Altogether, the mutinies in the Russian army, the strike movement culminating in the general strike of October 1905, and the large-scale peasant disturbances in the central agricultural provinces have justifiably attracted the greatest attention among scholars. However, the borderlands, occupying a wide arc from Finland to the south Caucasus, also witnessed multiple outbreaks which were more sustained and in some cases more violent than those in the core provinces. As Andreas Kappeler has pointed out, there were important precursors to the disorders of 1905 in the borderlands, where in the period from 1895 to 1900 fifty-six of the fifty-nine street demonstrations took place outside the Russian territories, the majority in the Polish provinces.[101] They exhibited characteristics that both linked and distinguished them from the uprisings in the center. In the borderlands a different pattern of class relations was emerging from the uneven development of capitalism, and the ethnic factor frequently added another layer to the struggle of workers and peasants against landlords, factory owners, and officials of the tsarist autocracy. In the core, where communal and repartitional tenure dominated, the risings were largely elemental and uncoordinated. In the Baltic, Pontic, and Caucasian borderlands, where there were stronger traditions of individual land-holding and more highly developed market conditions, the peasant risings were more organized and politically conscious.[102] It would be an

[100] Hans Rogger, "The Formation of the Russian Right, 1900–1906," *California Slavic Studies* (1975): 66–94; Hans Rogger, "Was There a Russian Fascism? The Union of the Russian People," *Journal of Modern History* 4 (1964): 398–415.
[101] Kappeler, *The Russian Empire*, p. 330.
[102] Maureen Perrie, "The Russian Peasant Movement of 1905–1907. Its Social Composition and Revolutionary Significance," *Past and Present* 57 (1972): 127.

exaggeration to characterize the uprisings in the borderlands as national liberation movements. In most cases ethnic clashes did not translate immediately into aspirations for independence. But the involvement of peasants, workers, and other urban groups in mass actions, coupled with the emergence from the underground of incipient parties actively engaged in agitation and propaganda, heightened political awareness and accelerated the process of national identification among the peoples of the borderlands.

Existing Jewish organizations were well prepared for political action in 1905. In 1900, the activists had formed a Defense Bureau which undertook to defend victims of the Kishinev and Gomel pogroms. During the growing political crisis in 1904, members of the Defense Bureau and social activists from the professions joined to form the Society for the Promotion of Enlightenment among the Jews of Russia as a part of the Russian Liberation Movement. They threw themselves into the legal campaign for a constitutional regime. The persistent problem of reconciling issues of Jewish identity and civic equality prevented its members from forming their own political party. Its members entered the ranks of other parties in the Duma elections, but they had all moved from a position of accommodation to resistance, albeit within a legal context.[103] In the years after the revolution, the Society rallied recruits from a new generation of young Jews. Still a small group, they zealously pursued the ideal of a secular yet authentic Jewish education within a legal framework of civic and collective rights.[104]

In the early months of the revolution of 1905 the Bund was at the center of events. As the only Jewish revolutionary party, it led dozens of strikes in the cities of the Pale, manned barricades in street fighting in Odessa and Łódź, raised large sums of money in the United States, and served as a model for other movements which soon came to rival it. Vaulting to the peak of its influence with the October Manifesto, it suffered an equally spectacular crash immediately afterwards. In the most violent pogroms Russia had witnessed, hundreds were killed, sending shock waves through the Jewish community and triggering a mass emigration to the United States. Rival Jewish organizations sprang up. Poale Zion (Labor Zion) was the most active and was dedicated to both international Zionism and the international class

---

[103] Christoph Gassenschmidt, *Jewish Liberal Politics in Tsarist Russia, 1900–14* (Basingstoke: Macmillan, 1995), pp. 8–10, 22–32.

[104] Brian Horowitz, "Victory from Defeat. 1905 and the Society for the Promotion of Enlightenment among the Jews of Russia," in Hoffman and Mendelsohn (eds.), *The Revolution of 1905*, pp. 79–95.

struggle.[105] The Bund's decision to boycott elections to the first Duma proved to be a tactical error as most Jews willingly exercised their right to vote. It was rapidly losing ground to its rivals when the government's repressive measures struck hard at all the Jewish parties. Membership in the Bund fell from 33,890 in 1906 to 800 in 1908; Poale Zion collapsed from 25,000 members in 1906 to 300 in 1908.[106]

The revolution of 1905 had dramatically demonstrated the need for unity of the left, and the Bund responded by moderating their national-autonomist views in order to reenter the RSDLP in 1906. There they remained in the unenviable role as mediators in questions of party organization until the Revolution of 1917 and the Civil War tore the party asunder. They had little choice. In the struggle for influence over the Jewish masses, they perceived their main enemies to be on the right – the Zionists and Piłsudski's Polish Socialist Party (PPS). Their tactics were sound as long as they were struggling for survival in the limited space of the Pale and the Kingdom of Poland. But after 1917 they found themselves in an allegedly proletarian state run by communists who had never accepted their claim to represent the Jewish working class. Abolished as a party, its members joined the Jewish Section of the Communist Party which, until its dissolution in 1930, became the instrument of anti-Zionist propaganda.

In the Kingdom of Poland the Russo-Japanese War provided the underground PPS with an opportunity to surface as the organizer of a public anti-war movement and the leader of a wave of strikes in industries like textiles suffering from the wartime economic dislocation. Their leader, Piłsudski, had taken an uncompromising anti-war, defeatist position and had even journeyed to Japan to put himself and his party at the disposal of the enemy. Workers were the most militant social force in the revolution. More consistently active throughout 1905 than their Russian counterparts in Moscow and St. Petersburg, they continued their strike actions and violent demonstrations into 1906 and 1907 at a higher level than anywhere else in the empire.[107] Students reacted most strongly against Russifying policies in gymnasiums and higher schools, forming their own nationalist and socialist organizations, though often in conflict with one another. Agrarian disorders by contrast developed more slowly and never reached the same level of violence as that seen in the central

---

[105] Jonathan Frankel, "Jewish Politics and the Russian Revolution of 1905," in *Crisis, Revolution and the Russian Jews* (Cambridge University Press, 2009), p. 5. See also Frankel, "The Socialist Opposition to Zionism in Historical Perspective," in *ibid.*, pp. 157–82.

[106] Gassenschmidt, *Jewish Liberal Politics*, p. 70.

[107] Perrie, "The Russian Peasant Movement," pp. 72–73.

provinces of the empire. Nevertheless, the Russian authorities were deeply disappointed that their policy of pitting the Orthodox peasants against Catholic landlords did not engender loyalty to the throne as they had expected. As elsewhere, the demands were mainly economic, but voices were raised to reinstate Polish as the language of the primary schools and local assemblies (*gmina*). The authorities made language concessions in the Polish-speaking provinces, but not among the Lithuanians who quickly became politically radicalized. In the cities and the countryside the fledgling political parties struggled to keep up with the radical actions of the workers and peasants.

Even after the October Manifesto reduced tensions in the cities, the penetration of socialist agitators into the countryside encouraged the anarchic mood of the peasants. Vigilantism spread; armed bands sprang up; Russian officials found themselves targets of assassination; and "state power virtually collapsed as rural communities defiantly substituted 'Polish' for 'Russian' authority."[108] Dmowski's attempt in November 1905 to gain autonomy for Poland along the lines conceded to the Finns by negotiating with Count Witte was short-circuited by the Warsaw governor, General Georgii Skalon, who won over the hard-liners in St. Petersburg. The imposition of martial law crushed the bid for Polish autonomy, but also intensified the violence in the countryside. State repression undermined the concessions on religious practice and language use. Moreover, the active participation of large numbers of Poles in illegal activities created a mass base for a future independence movement, yet left a legacy of political fragmentation and interparty violence that cast a dark shadow on the free Poland that emerged in 1918 from its borderland status as an independent state.

In the period after the revolution of 1905, the Russian government of P. A. Stolypin shifted the emphasis in its struggle with the Poles to securing cultural hegemony in the Baltic littoral and Pontic steppe. Stolypin's new policy aimed not so much at Russifying the Kingdom of Poland, as had been the policy in the previous century, but rather at erecting a cultural barrier between it and the Kresy. The Polish educational societies in Wilno, Minsk, and Nesvezhe were closed. Legislation required the use of Russian in all official internal correspondence in the eight western provinces, and limited the number of Poles in the zemstvos of the western region.[109] Stolypin's most famous and controversial action was to detach the two most southeastern districts of the Lublin and Sedletsk provinces

[108] Perrie, "The Russian Peasant Movement," pp. 142–56, quotation on p. 151.
[109] A. Iu. Bakhturina, *Okrainy rossiiskoi imperii. Gosudarstvennoe upravlenie i national'naia politika v gody pervoi mirovoi voiny (1914–1917)* (Moscow: Rosspen, 2004), pp. 16–17.

of the Kingdom of Poland and to reconstitute them as a new province of Kholm (Chelm).

In the Pontic steppe, peasant disturbances were concentrated on the right bank Ukraine. The peasantry was Ukrainian, but in this case ethnic identity was of little consequence in motivating them.[110] Their illegal activities – strikes, arson, cutting wood, destroying boundary markers – and their demands for land and higher wages targeted equally Ukrainian, Russian, and Polish landlords, and Jewish estate managers. The political parties played little role in organizing or directing the struggle. There are only scattered references in the sources to Socialist Revolutionaries or Social Democrats having been active in the villages. The most visible group on the right bank was the Ukrainian Social Democratic Union (Spilka), an organization of Ukrainian-speaking workers affiliated with the Russian Social Democratic Labor Party. Claiming 7,000 members, it sent delegates into the countryside to help the peasants formulate demands. The cultural gap between urban and rural Ukraine was reflected in the low level of national awareness among the peasantry. In the elections to the First Duma, complex and confusing as it was, the peasants returned representatives who had no clear party affiliation. Once they arrived in St. Petersburg they appeared to sign up, almost at random, with half-formed parties they had heard were supporters of land redistribution, or else they identified themselves simply as "left" or "progressive." Instructions to deputies from the peasant electors revealed no interest in national autonomy.[111]

In the left bank Ukraine the mixture of ethnic groups provided another vivid example of how migration and colonization, spurred by economic development, could produce a shatter zone with a high potential for violence. In the Donbas, for example, a bare majority of Ukrainian speakers uneasily shared space with Russians (about 28 percent) and smaller numbers of Greeks, Germans, Jews, Tatars, Belorussians, and Poles. The official census based on native language hardly conveyed the variety of spoken dialects in the region. A strong tradition of Cossack autonomy was preserved in the administratively separate Don Military

---

[110] Population statistics are misleading because the census was based on religion without discriminating between Ukrainians and Russians, and the small number of Old Believers was probably greatly underestimated. The figures in Kiev for 1894 show that 75 percent of the population were Orthodox, 11 percent were Roman Catholic (Poles), and 8 percent were Jewish. In Kiev province the number of Jews was higher, at 12 percent, and the number of Poles numbered less than 4 percent. *Entsiklopedicheskii slovar'*, vol. XV, pp. 260, 267.

[111] Robert Edelman, *Proletarian Peasants. The Revolution of 1905 in Russia's Southwest* (Ithaca, NY: Cornell University Press, 1987), pp. 162–65.

District. It nourished two contradictory tendencies. One was conservative and anti-Semitic; the other was rebellious. In the Donbas,
as throughout the Pontic steppe, ethnic tensions existed between
Ukrainians and Russians, and between Slavs and Tatars. The main
thrust of ethnic-based hostility, however, was directed against the Jews
by the Christian Ukrainians and Russians.[112] Following the proclamation of the October Manifesto, pogroms spread throughout the urban
settlements of the Pontic steppe. In industrial Iuzovka the workers
unleashed a savage pogrom. The cosmopolitan port city of Odessa was
also badly hit.[113]

The revolution of 1905 in the Baltic littoral began with the workers in
the cities and then spread to the agricultural laborers in the countryside.
The Latvians were the most highly urbanized nationality in the empire
with 40 percent of the population living in towns and cities. While
Latvians and Estonians constituted an overwhelming majority in Riga
district, the city was a multicultural kaleidoscope; in 1897, the population
divided among Germans 47 percent, Russians 25 percent, Latvians
23 percent, Jews 4 percent, and Estonians 1 percent, with Latvians continuously entering the city from the countryside.[114] The workers were
highly concentrated in big factories in Riga, such as the Provodnik Rubber
plant and the Russo-Baltic shipyards. Among Latvian intellectuals,
Marxism had increased its appeal during the 1890s. By the turn of the
century, they had added demands for autonomy and the sole right to
represent the Latvian workers to their socioeconomic program. Their
program was close to that of the Bund, and the two parties found common
ground for cooperation.[115] In light of the high concentration of workers in
large enterprises linked to international capitalism and the growing agitation of social democrats, it is not surprising then that the Latvian workers in Kurland and southern Lifland amassed the highest rate of strikes per
worker in the entire Russian Empire. In the countryside the militancy of
the Latvian peasantry has also been attributed to a combination of ethnic
and economic grievances against the large presence of German

[112] Hiroaki Kuromiya, *Freedom and Terror in the Donbas. A Ukrainian–Russian Borderland,
1870s–1990s* (Cambridge University Press, 1998), pp. 40–47.

[113] Theodore H. Friedgut, "Labor Violence and Regime Brutality in Tsarist Russia. The
Iuzovka Cholera Riots of 1892," *Slavic Review* 46(2) (Summer 1987): 259–60; Shlomo
Lambroza, "The Pogroms of 1903–06," in John Klier and Shlomo Lambroza (eds.),
Pogroms. Anti-Jewish Violence in Modern Russian History (Cambridge University Press,
1992); Robert Weinberg, *The Revolution of 1905 in Odessa. Blood on the Steps*
(Bloomington, IN: Indiana University Press, 1993), ch. 7.

[114] The local press reflected these percentages with eight Russian, eighteen German, and
five Latvian periodicals. "Riga," *Entsiklopedicheskii slovar'*, vol. XXVI(A), pp. 680, 683.

[115] Tobias, *The Jewish Bund*, p. 284.

landlords.[116] When in December the tsarist government resolved to take decisive measures to quell the disorders, it dispatched a punitive expedition to the Baltic provinces that "was far and away the largest military operation the regime undertook against the revolution."[117]

In 1905, the north and south Caucasus appeared to be parts of separate worlds. In the north, relative calm prevailed among the self-contained communities of the tribesmen and the Cossacks. Both groups enjoyed a degree of autonomy in the customs and regulations governing their everyday lives. The Cossacks also benefited economically from their privileges to exploit "in perpetuity" highly productive salt, mineral, and oil resources. Disturbances in the region came from urban and railroad workers caught up in the general strike movement in the central provinces, army units, and the peasantry, especially in the Kuban, expressing their usual economic grievances. Muslim mountaineers often participated along with Cossacks in punitive expeditions against the Russian peasants and workers.[118]

In the south Caucasus the situation was far more complex. Strikes, assassinations, and armed insurrections struck at imperial rule, while ethnic and class conflicts broke out, illustrating the problems of a shatter zone undergoing rapid economic changes. Revolutionary outbreaks in the south Caucasus preceded those elsewhere in the empire. The deepening of the economic depression of 1901/2 had sparked massive strikes, which culminated in a general strike that paralyzed Baku, Batumi, and Tiflis. The government's ill-advised confiscation of Armenian Church property in 1903 had provoked a spontaneous outbreak of Armenian national resistance that took the revolutionary parties by surprise, but inspired them to create an Armenian Committee of Self-Defense inspired by the Jewish Bund's reaction to the pogroms of 1901.[119] In Georgia, two revolutionary currents flowed along separate streams, commingled, and then separated again. In agricultural Guria, literally a frontier province with the Ottoman Empire until 1878, the uprising in 1905 preceded the proclamation of a peasant republic. As Stephen F. Jones' close study of Guria reveals, a complex of factors produced this unusual, rather unique outcome: small

[116] Toivo U. Raun, "The Revolution of 1905 in the Baltic Provinces and Finland," *Slavic Review* 43(3) (Autumn 1984): 453–67; Andrejs Plakans, "The Latvians," in Thaden (ed.), *Russification*, pp. 259–67; for the Baltic littoral as part of the highly developed northwestern industrial region, see Alfred J. Rieber, *Merchants and Entrepreneurs in Imperial Russia* (Chapel Hill, NC: University of North Carolina Press, 1982), pp. 243–49.
[117] Bushnell, *Mutiny Amid Repression*, p. 116.
[118] V. O. Bobrovnikov and I. L. Babich (eds.), *Severnyi Kavkaz v sostave rossiiskoi imperii* (Moscow: Novoe literaturnoe obozrenie, 2007), pp. 286–94.
[119] Anahide Ter Minassian, "Particularités de la révolution de 1905 en Transcaucasie," in Coquin and Gervais-Francelle (eds.), *1905*, pp. 320–24.

but self-sustaining peasant allotments threatened by financial uncertainty; a history of armed resistance to Ottoman and then Russian rule; a high level of literacy; a homogeneous ethnic profile; and a local intelligentsia at the core of Georgian social democracy.[120] In Tiflis, the Georgians constituted only a minority of a highly diverse population. A city in the throes of early capitalist flux, ethnic and class feelings were mixed and shifting.[121] Its multicultural profile mirrored those of other major cities in the south Caucasus, especially Baku, Batumi, and Erevan.

Internal migration and colonization had given the cities their kaleidoscopic character, while the countryside remained more homogeneous. At the turn of the century the ethnic–linguistic composition of Tiflis, for example, was as follows: Armenians 38.1 percent, Georgians 26.3 percent, Russians 24.8 percent, Poles 3.4 percent; Persians 3.2 percent. For Baku, the future capital of the Azerbaijan republic, the figures were: Turko-Tatars 36.8 percent, Russians 34.8 percent, Armenians 17 percent, Persians 3 percent, and Georgians 1.8 percent. The situation in Erevan revealed a bipolar split between 48 percent Armenians and 49 percent Turko-Tatars, with only 2 percent Russians.[122] Although the ethnic mix in the south Caucasian cities was long standing, the clumsy and erratic Russification policies of the government at the end of the century had sharply increased tensions among peoples who had previously lived peacefully in close proximity for decades. Here the revolutions of 1905 took on a more savage inter-ethnic conflict.

Major ethnic rifts in the south Caucasian cities opened up between Russian and Georgian workers, and between Armenian and Muslim Tatar (Azeri) workers. In Tiflis and Batumi, as well as in smaller towns, during the big strikes of January 1905 Georgian workers intimidated or attacked Russian workers who were regarded as representatives of imperial rule. In Tiflis, Baku, and Erevan clashes between Azeri and Armenian workers split the socialist movement.[123] By February a virtual Tatar–Armenian

[120] Stephen F. Jones, "Marxism and Peasant Revolt in the Russian Empire. The Case of the Gurian Republic," *Slavonic and East European Review* 67(3) (1989): 403–34; Stephen F. Jones, *Socialism in Georgian Colors. The European Road to Social Democracy, 1883–1917* (Cambridge, MA: Harvard University Press, 2005), pp. 129–58.

[121] Ronald Grigor Suny, "Tiflis, Crucible of Ethnic Politics, 1860–1905," in Michael F. Hamm (ed.), *The City in Imperial Russia* (Bloomington, IN: Indiana University Press, 1986).

[122] "Tiflis," *Entsiklopedicheskii slovar'*, vol. XXXIII, p. 267; for Baku, *Pervaia vseobshchaia perepis' naseleniia Rossiiskoi imperii* (PVP), 79 vols. (St. Petersburg, 1903–1905), vol. LXI, pp. 154–55; "Erivan," *ibid.*, vol. XLI, p. 15. The Georgians were actually more numerous in Batumi, which had been part of the Ottoman Empire until 1878, than Tiflis: Georgians 39.4 percent, Russians 25 percent, Armenians 21 percent, Greeks 9 percent, Turko-Tatars 7.5 percent. *Pervaia vseobshchaia perepis'*, vol. LXVI, pp. 146–49.

[123] Jones, *Socialism in Georgian Colors*, pp. 169–70.

war had broken out in the cities and rural areas with mixed Muslim and Armenian populations. The Muslims touched off the fighting by launching an anti-Armenian pogrom; then the better organized and armed Dashnaks fought back, inflicting heavy casualties on their rivals. Groups of Muslims, incited by the burgeoning Azeri intelligentsia, reacted by organizing their own defense squads under the name *Difai* (Defense). They attacked tsarist officials as well as the Armenian fighters. The governor general, Vorontsov-Dashkov, was obliged to distribute 500 rifles to the Georgian Mensheviks in an attempt to prevent the Armenians and Muslims from slaughtering one another.[124] The three major national revolutionary movements in the Caucasus shared a common foe in the tsarist autocracy, in their aspirations for some form of local autonomy, and their demands for guarantees of their civic or religious rights. But ethnic, religious, and class differences exploited by revolutionary agitators and radical intellectuals divided them from one another and split their ranks.

Two powerful currents of Caucasian social democracy ran south across the complex frontier to feed the reservoir of domestic opposition in northern Iran: the Muslim *mojaheds* (militants of a sacred struggle) associated with the organization Ferqeh-ye Ejetma'iyoun Ammiyoun (FEA) and the Armenian Dashnaks. In both cases, the transfer of men and ideas typically flowed in two directions. Iranian seasonal workers moved north across the Iranian border, mainly seeking employment in the Baku oil fields; most then returned home, while about 20 percent stayed. There was also a reciprocal, if smaller, traffic of Iranian intellectuals who studied in Russian universities and returned to their own country. Among them, Armenians formed a small but active group. Both groups brought back radical ideas, often honed in labor actions ranging from militant propaganda to strikes.[125]

From the eve of the Russian Revolution of 1905 to the outbreak of the First World War, the migrants in the south Caucasus were exposed to a

[124] Tadeus Swietochowski, *Russia and Azerbaizhan. A Borderland in Transition* (New York: Columbia University Press, 1995), pp. 38–41; Ter Minassian, "1905 en Transcaucasie," p. 324.
[125] From 1900 to 1913 1,765,334 Iranian migrants entered Russia and 1,411,950 returned home in the same period, leaving 353,383 as residents of the Russian Empire. But these were only the legal migrants and other indicators suggest a much larger influx. M. L. Entner, *Russo-Persian Commercial Relations, 1828–1914* (Gainsville, FL: University of Florida Press, 1965), p. 60; N. K. Belova, "K voprosu o tak nazivaemoi sotsial-demokraticheskoi partii Irana," *Voprosy istorii i literatury stran zarubezhnogo vostoka* (Moscow: Izd. Moskovskogo universiteta, 1960), p. 55; and above all the extensive discussion in Cosroe Chaqueri, *Origins of Social Democracy in Modern Iran* (Seattle, WA: University of Washington Press, 2001), ch. 3.

482   Imperial crises

variety of revolutionary movements, including Georgian and Russian social democrats, both Menshevik and Bolshevik; the radical democratic Muslim Himmet (Hemmet) Party, founded by Azeri intellectuals in touch with the Russian Social Democrats; the Armenian Hnchak; and the Dashnaks. The booming oil town of Baku was the center of this political ferment, and it was here in 1907 that the young Stalin found a receptive audience among both Russian and Muslim workers. Along with other Caucasian Bolsheviks, he forged a working alliance with Himmet against his Menshevik rivals.[126] His experience in Baku and his contact with Muslim workers left a profound impression on Stalin and helped to shape his attitude toward the possibilities of revolutionary activity in Iran and elsewhere in the Middle East.[127] In either Baku or Tiflis, another Caucasian Bolshevik, the Azeri revolutionary, Nariman Narimanov, laid the foundations for the main Iranian social democratic party (FEA). In Baku, it recruited mainly oil workers, but in Iran its membership was broadly representative. These movements furnished the most radical currents in the Iranian constitutional crisis.

In Trans Caspia, striking railroad workers in Tashkent spearheaded the revolution in November 1905, but the October Manifesto soon split the anti-government forces. The liberal intellectuals in the state administration and professions feared the excesses of the radicals as well as the growing hostility of the indigenous population whom they regarded as the "dark" Muslim masses needing Russian enlightenment.[128] The law on toleration sparked Muslim efforts in Turkestan to establish an autonomous Spiritual Administration and to broaden the rights of the Muslim jurisconsults (*mufti*). Continuing the policy of von Kaufman, the government suspected potentially political significance and denied their petitions. The fear was that a unified religious institution in Turkestan or under the aegis of the mufti of Ufa would serve as an organizational link between Muslims in Turkestan, the Volga, and Crimea, promoting pan-Islamic ideas. For similar reasons, the government not only maintained

---

[126] Bala Efendiev, "Istoriia revoliutsionogo dvizheniia tiurkskogo proletariata," in *Iz proshlogo. Stat'i i vospominaniia iz istorii Bakinskoi organizatsii i rabochego dvizheniia v Baku* (Baku: n.p., 1923), pp. 39–40; T. Akhmedov, *Nariman Narimanov*, trans. G. Kulieva (Baku: Iazychy, 1988); Aidin Balaev, "Plennik idei ili politicheskii slepets?" *Azerbaizhan* (June 20, 1991).

[127] I. V. Stalin, *Sochineniia*, 13 vols. (Moscow: Gospolitiizdat, 1946–1952), vol. VIII, pp. 173–75.

[128] Jeff Sahadeo, "Progress or Peril. Migrants and Locals in Russian Tashkent, 1906–14," in Nicholas B. Breyfogle, Abby Schrader, and Willard Sunderland (eds.), *Peopling the Periphery. Borderland Colonization in Eurasian History* (London: Routledge, 2007), pp. 150–51; and, in general, A. V. Piaskovskii, *Revoliutsiia 1905–7 gg. v Turkestane* (Moscow: Izd-vo Akademii nauk SSSR, 1958).

but increased its administrative control over Muslim confessional schools and *madrasa* for legal training, including the introduction of Russian as the language of instruction. In 1911, Stolypin issued a regulation "On Measures to Combat pan-Islamist and pan-Turkic Influences among the Muslim population." At the same time, the government endorsed a new policy that would allow any land "deemed in excess" of the needs of the local population to be thrown open to settlement. During the war, the Turkestan region was placed under martial law. But fears of Ottoman penetration proved illusory. Despite their obsession with the threat of pan-Islamism, government officials failed to understand the nature of religious life in Turkestan, administering the region without taking it into consideration. The policy of encouraging colonization was steadily encroaching on the nomads' pasture land. The fusion of religious and economic discontent led to disastrous consequences during the First World War.

In 1916, at the height of the war the government, pressed by a shortage of manpower, introduced a military draft in Turkestan for the first time. Although the recruits were to be used only in the rear areas in supply units, the measure triggered a large-scale uprising. It began among the Kirghiz nomads. The rumor rapidly circulated among them that the draft was really intended to provide cannon fodder for the front so that Russian colonists could take over their pasture lands. The mullahs, who had not been exempted from the draft, rapidly joined the rising. The stunned Russian officials put down the rising with great loss of the nomadic flocks and Russian property. The veteran administrator, Governor General A. N. Kuropatkin, admitted that for thirty years the Russians had failed to engage with the indigenous population. But even he underestimated the religious component of the rising and recommended an administrative solution. Once again, as he had in 1892, he requested the creation of a unified military and civilian administration for Turkestan. Again remedial legislation came too late. The new regulation was put into effect almost exactly a year before the outbreak of the February Revolution.[129]

The Duma and the constitutional crisis

In 1906/7, the holding of elections under conditions of revolutionary ferment created two serious problems for the government.[130] The great

---

[129] Bakhturina, *Okrainy*, pp. 297–314.

[130] The following relies heavily on "Zapadnyi okriany v nachale XX v. Gosudarstvennaia duma," in M. Dolbilov and A. Miller (eds.), *Zapadnye okrainy Rossiiskoi imperii* (Moscow: Novoe literaturnoe obozrenie, 2006), pp. 358–90.

majority of the delegates to the First Duma were committed to a peasant program of massive redistribution of the land, a continuation of revolutionary aims by legal means. Just as ominous in the eyes of the ruling elite were the results from the non-Russian periphery where delegates were returned on a platform of national–regional autonomy, with those elected from Ukraine linking the questions of land and liberty. The best organized faction was the Polish Kolo. They led the charge in demanding local self-government and religious equality. A mass of Duma petitions to the Ministry of the Interior complained bitterly about local administrators who incited ethnic conflict during the revolution. The government reacted swiftly by dissolving the Duma and ordering new elections. Although government pressure reduced the number of non-Russian delegates, the Second Duma proved to be as fractious as the First. But fissures began to open up among the nationalities over the question of local autonomy, and between the non-Russian and Russian representatives in the western borderlands. The new prime minister, P. A. Stolypin, favored concessions, but the tsar opposed them.

Shocked by the radicalism of the first two Dumas, the government introduced a new electoral law (the so-called coup d'état of July 1907), which reduced representation by peasants and the nationalities in the borderlands. The new electoral law entirely disenfranchised the steppe and Turkestan regions, the Turgai, Ural, and Iakutsk oblasts in Siberia, the nomadic peoples of Astrakhan and Stavropol (Nogai and Kalmyks), and the Siberian Cossacks. The number of Polish, Armenian, and Tatar delegates were substantially reduced (the Poles from forty-six to eleven delegates). The law also required that a specific number of deputies from non-Russian regions should be Russian.[131]

The result was more than a little ironic. In the first two Dumas, the Polish Kolo, led by Roman Dmowski, had consisted mainly of accommodationists committed to organic work. The Poles took their place among the delegates of the center, not the left. The Muslim delegates were not even a cohesive group. They lagged far behind the Poles, Armenians, and other peoples of the borderlands in the development of a national consciousness. The most politically active were still under the influence of Gasprinskii. Their highest aspiration was the spread of enlightenment and modest reforms. They too were counted as delegates of the center. Only the Caucasian delegation, especially the Georgian Social Democrats, exhibited a radical face. Yet the government chose to view ethnic representatives with suspicion.

---

[131] Geoffrey A. Hosking, *The Russian Constitutional Experiment. Government and Duma, 1907–1914* (Cambridge University Press, 1973).

When Stolypin renewed his modest proposals to abolish discriminatory laws, he was blocked by the large rightist nationalist groups in the Third Duma and the continued opposition of the court. There were ominous signs, particularly among the military, that ethnicity rather than religion or language was becoming the preeminent category for judging the quality and reliability of the population.[132] By 1914 the growing hostility would become widespread, leading to heightened suspicions among the military about the loyalty of the Finns and the Poles, and to fearful consequences for ethnic Germans and Jews in Russia along the frontiers of the western borderlands exposed to invasion.

Despite calls for autonomy and recognition of cultural distinctiveness, the peoples of the borderlands in the Russian Empire, like the Habsburg Empire, were not agitating for secession. The government may have lost its last chance to mollify them by making concessions along federalist lines; although given the mix of ethnic groups in the borderlands a peaceful outcome could not be guaranteed. Instead, it found itself under pressure for the first time in Russian history by a politically mobilized, nationalist right and at the same time dependent upon these new political forces to pass a reform program in the Duma. The central political problem was that the revolution of 1905, intense as it had been in the borderlands, aroused fear and antagonism among the ruling elites and the most conservative elements in the population who voted for the extreme right parties that dominated the Third and Fourth Dumas.

Any sign of autonomous aspirations aroused the fury of the ruling elites. Stolypin deeply resented the persistent assertions by the Finnish Sejm that the grand duchy enjoyed a special juridical status within the empire. To add insult to injury, its territory lying outside the jurisdiction of the tsarist police had become a refuge for subversive and revolutionary elements. The government was outraged when, after the tsar had prorogued the Second Duma and instituted a new electoral law, a group of Duma deputies gathered at Vyborg to issue a manifesto calling on the Russian people to engage in passive resistance.[133] In retaliation the government renewed its policy of administrative Russification. In June 1910, it introduced legislation imposing further limitations on Finnish autonomy. The Finnish Sejm refused to recognize the new law, and a stand-off continued until the outbreak of the First World War. Although the Finnish press and

[132] Peter Holquist, "To Count, to Extract, to Exterminate. Population Statistics and Population Politics in Late Imperial and Soviet Russia," in Ronald G. Suny and Terry Martin (eds.), *A State of Nations. Empire and Nation-Making in the Age of Lenin and Stalin* (Oxford University Press, 2001), pp. 111–44.
[133] Abraham Ascher, *P. A. Stolypin. The Search for Stability in Late Imperial Russia* (Stanford University Press, 2001), pp. 315–18.

public institutions initially rallied to the throne when war broke out, the Russian government alienated the population by approving a regressive program signed by Nicholas II in September 1914. It diminished the authority of Finnish officials, forbade them from joining political parties, reduced the number of Finnish speakers in the local bureaucracy, and unified the Finnish with the Russian tariff and banking regulations. Public knowledge of these plans stimulated pro-German sentiment. Anger also flared in Sweden among those who agitated for war against Russia for "the salvation of our co-nationals (*soplemennikov*) on the other side of the border."[134] Nonetheless, the overwhelming majority of the Finnish population showed little interest in breaking away from the Russian Empire. Although the Russian military agitated for stricter controls, the civil administration opposed them led by Governor General Franz-Albert Zein, who had made a 180-degree turn from being a strong opponent of Finnish autonomy to become a defender of Finnish interests.[135] The most ominous sign for the future was the defection of a small number of Finnish youth, who crossed into Germany to be trained as volunteers in light infantry battalions. They would return to Finland after the Bolshevik Revolution to play a key role in the victory of the Whites in the Finnish civil war.

A renewed struggle between the Poles and the Russians for cultural hegemony over the Ukrainian peasantry was touched off by an edict in April 1905 that abolished the prohibition on conversion from Orthodoxy to other Christian faiths. Between 100,000 and 150,000 former Uniats in the Kholm region, who had been "voluntarily united" with the Orthodox Church in 1875, promptly returned to the Catholic fold. Tsarist officials denounced this as the work of Polish agitators. The extension of full religious toleration in the October Manifesto made it impossible for the local Orthodox clergy to challenge what they regarded as apostasy. The mass defection aroused concern in St. Petersburg over ensuring Russian representation in the elections to the First Duma. The dilemma was clear. The government would either have to allow the "Poles," meaning Catholics, to take over the province, or provide special protection for the minority of Russians, meaning Orthodox, in violation of the spirit of the reforms.

The idea of creating a separate province was revived after 1906 by the Orthodox bishop of Lublin, Evlogii, whose crusading fervor won over Stolypin, gained strong backing from the nationalist right in the Third

---

[134] Bakhturina, *Okrainy*, pp. 237–40, 246–55, citation on p. 251. The program was shelved in the interests of placating the Swedes and reassuring the Allies.
[135] Bakhturina, *Okrainy*, p. 280.

Duma, and finally became law in 1912.[136] The Poles were furious. But the extreme Russian right in the State Council were no happier. According to one of its spokesmen, the law "strengthen[s] the false idea that there exists some kind of real Kingdom of Poland ... Instead of putting the arrogant szlachta, Jesuits and priests in their place, this draft law ... is limited to shifting them from one place to another."[137]

The episode again exposed the relatively low level of national, as opposed to religious, sentiment among the Ukrainians. This was due in part to the discriminatory measure of the government against the use of Ukrainian. Even the small Ukrainian-speaking intellectual elite willingly accepted a multiple identity as either Ukrainian-Russians or Ukrainian-Poles. Before 1905 there were only small groups of cultural and political activists committed to the national ideal. They played no significant role in the revolution of 1905, and none at all in politics until 1917.[138]

Renewing the imperialist drive

In the post-revolutionary era, Russia adopted a more aggressive and expansionist policy in the ongoing struggle over the borderlands. In the west Balkans and Danubian frontier, its diplomats worked to undermine both the Habsburg and Ottoman presence. It came close to achieving its aims in the Balkans on the eve of the First World War before defeat and revolution overwhelmed the empire. From the south Caucasus to Inner Asia, Russian economic penetration through such agencies as the Russian-Asiatic Bank and Russian railroad policies, as well as deals with Britain in 1907, and with Japan in 1912 to partition Iran and Manchuria into spheres of influence aimed at recovering lost ground and further expanding imperial rule.

Mounting concern among tsarist officials over internal stability ran parallel to their worries about security along the frontiers. Stolypin made clear his views on foreign policy in correspondence with newly appointed Foreign Minister A. P. Izvol'skii. He insisted on the need for a period of international peace and relaxing of tensions, a breathing space so that he

---

[136] Robert Blobaum, "Toleration and Ethno-Religious Strife. The Struggle between Catholics and Orthodox Christians in the Chelm Region of Russian Poland, 1904–1906," *Polish Review* 35(2) (1990): 111–24; Theodore R. Weeks, *Nation and State in Late Imperial Russia. Nationalism and Russification on the Western Frontier, 1863–1914* (DeKalb, IL: Northern Illinois University Press, 1996), pp. 173–92.

[137] Speech of Markov-Two to the State Council, cited in Bakhturina, *Okrainy*, p. 17.

[138] Andreas Kappeler (ed.), "The Ukrainians of the Russian Empire, 1860–1914," in *The Formation of National Elites* (New York University Press, 1992), pp. 122–24.

could devote his energies and resources to the domestic tasks of pacifying the country and reforming the agrarian sector.[139]

Izvol'skii understood his task in terms of restoring Russia's international prestige, maintaining the French alliance without antagonizing Germany, and eliminating the sources of conflict between the empire and its main imperial rivals in the external borderlands.[140] His negotiations were facilitated by the widely held fears among Russia's imperial rivals over the dangers of revolutionary contagion that, together with the defeat of a European by an Asian power, had stirred anti-colonial sentiments throughout the borderlands.

The 1907 Russo-Japanese convention restoring normal relations of peace and friendship masked the real imperialist objectives. In its secret provisions, Manchuria was divided into a Japanese and a Russian sphere of influence where neither side would seek railroad or telegraph concessions. Two-thirds of the northwest provinces were allocated to the Japanese sphere and one-third to the Russian sphere. The allocation of the southern branch of the Chinese Eastern Railroad to Japan and its conversion to narrow gauge meant a break in the connection between northern Manchuria and the Liaotung peninsula, and higher transshipment costs for Russian goods moving south. To compensate, the Russian government strengthened the links between northern Manchuria and Vladivostok by creating a single administration for the Chinese Eastern and the Ussuri Railroad companies. Vladivostok became the main port for the export of Manchurian raw materials to Europe. In its sphere Russia obtained extensive concessions from the Chinese for coal mining and communications. In 1910, a new Russo-Japanese (Izvol'skii–Monoto) agreement on Manchuria confirmed earlier agreements and approved the status quo. But the Russian Foreign Ministry was pressing for more, "through making northern Manchuria ... a dependable buffer," while the military desired the annexation of the region outright. The Japanese government initially opposed the idea, but after the Chinese revolution of 1911 it worked out secret plans with the Russian military for a joint occupation, which were kept ready in the expectation of China's disintegration into anarchy.[141]

---

[139] I. V. Bestuzhev-Lada, *Bor'ba v Rossii po vneshnei politiki, 1906–1916* (Moscow: Akademiia nauk SSSR, 1961), pp. 74, 132.

[140] This approximates the analysis of Baron M. Taube, *La politique russe d'avant-guerre et la fin de l'empire des tsars (1904–1917). Mémoires de baron de Taube* (Paris: E. Leroux, 1928), pp. 115–16.

[141] *Mezhdunarodnye otnosheniia v epokhu imperializma. Dokumenty iz arkhivov tsarskogo i vremmenogo pravitelstv. 1878–1917 gg.*, series IV, 10 vols. (Moscow: Gosudarstvennoe sotsial'no-ekonomicheskoe izdatel'stvo, 1931–1938), vol. XVIII, pp. 2, 90, 134;

The Russians took advantage of the Chinese revolution to press for additional concessions in the Barga region of western Manchuria, inhabited mainly by Mongols. Rich in gold mines, the region had been heavily colonized by Russians settling along the Chinese Eastern Railroad and in the frontier trading cities of Manchuli and Hailar. The tsarist government supported the uprising of the Barga Mongols, who declared their independence from China. Foreign Minister Sergei Sazonov inserted himself as mediator, insisting on Chinese recognition of Russian economic interests in the region and the preservation of Mongol autonomy. In 1915, the government in Beijing finally conceded almost everything the Russians demanded, making the Barga region a virtual condominium of China and Russia.[142] Subsequently, Japan and Russia cooperated within the international consortium of foreign banks in China to block the competition of American investment capital in Manchuria, further consolidating their economic control over China's most productive borderland.[143]

By the agreement of 1907 Russia also renounced any interference in Japanese–Korean relations based on "relations of political solidarity." Japan recognized Russia's special interests in Outer Mongolia and renounced any attempt to interfere in these interests. In a series of follow-up agreements Japan acquired substantial economic concessions in trade and fishing rights in the Russian Far East.[144] After the Chinese revolution of 1911, Russia and Japan concluded another agreement in 1912 delimiting their spheres of "special interest" in Inner Mongolia, "one to the east and the other to the west of the Peking meridian."[145] In Xinjiang, Russia was free to act unilaterally. As in Manchuria, the military made preparations to reoccupy Ili and its capital, Kulja. Briefly restrained by the government, a Cossack detachment occupied Kulja in 1912 without further protests from St. Petersburg.[146]

vol. XIX, pp. 1, 29, 118, 255; and B. Siebert and G. A. Schreiner, *Entente Diplomacy and the World. Matrix of the History of Europe, 1909–14* (New York: G. Allen Unwin, 1921), pp. 24–27.

[142] Peter S. H. Tang, *Russian and Soviet Policy in Manchuria and Outer Mongolia, 1911–1931* (Durham, NC: Duke University Press, 1959), pp. 81–90.

[143] M. I. Sladkovskii, *Istoriia torgovo-ekonomicheskikh otnoshenii narodov Rossii s Kitaem (do. 1917g.)* (Moscow: Nauka, 1974), pp. 317–23; George Alexander Lensen, "Japan and Tsarist Russia. The Changing Relationships, 1875–1917," *Jahrbücher für Geschichte Osteuropas*, New Series, 10(3) (October 1962): 343.

[144] For an account of the negotiations based on Russian archives, see Ignat'ev, *Vneshnaia politika*, pp. 147–57, 172–80.

[145] Sladkovskii, *Istoriia torgovo-ekonomicheskikh otnoshenii*, p. 327.

[146] *Mezhdunarodnye otnosheniia*, vol. XXX, pp. 2, 423, 765, 887, 890.

In preparing to negotiate with Britain, Izvol'skii acknowledged in his report to the tsar that it was the key to unlocking Russia's problems all along its continental periphery:

Next, there is the pressing need to guarantee Russia's security along the entire extensive line from its Far Eastern borders to its European frontiers by means of hammering out a whole set of agreements. Among these, without doubt the most important are agreements with England [sic] making possible together with others for us to remove for a more or less significant period of time the dangers threatening Russia in view of the difficult position in which it finds itself, and consequently to make it possible fully and peacefully to recover its strength.[147]

Coming to terms with Britain over the Trans Caspian borderlands opened up serious splits in the Russian ruling elite. Sobered by military defeat, the tsarist government came round to accepting the idea of dividing Iran into spheres of influence, a proposal that Lord Curzon had advanced in the 1890s. Debate came over defining the spheres. Minister of Finance V. N. Kokovtsov proposed a line determined by Russia's real economic interests. Izvol'skii supported him, but refused to acknowledge Britain's special interest in the Persian Gulf so as to avoid giving Germany an excuse for extending the Berlin to Baghdad railroad all the way to Basra on the coast. The general staff and war minister were guided by strategic concerns and sought to push the Russian zone up to the Afghan frontier. The discussion over spheres in Iran rapidly became enmeshed in discussions that encompassed the whole range of Anglo-Russian relations in the borderlands, including Tibet, Afghanistan, and the Straits.

At the turn of the century, British diplomatic moves to open the borderland of Tibet and replace long-established Chinese influence prompted pro-Russian Tibetans to find a counterweight in St. Petersburg. When the British learned of talks involving Witte, Lambsdorf, and Kuropatkin on the possibility of opening a consulate on the Tibetan frontier, Lord Curzon whipped up a public storm accusing the Russians of seeking to replace the Chinese with a Russian protectorate. The British were skeptical of Russian professions of interest limited to protecting the rights of Russian Lamaists and the safety of scientific expeditions.[148] In 1903, the Indian army invaded Tibet and occupied it until 1906.

The Russian general staff continued to be concerned over British domination of Afghanistan as a strategic launching pad. The Russian government had declared in 1873 that Afghanistan was completely outside its sphere of influence. But times had changed. At the turn of the century, the British were tied up in the Boer War, giving St. Petersburg an

[147] Ignat'ev, *Politika*, p. 112.   [148] Ignat'ev, *Politika*, p. 130.

opportunity to establish direct relations of a non-political nature with the Afghan government. Ever fearful of the shadow of the bear, the government of India feared the request would be the first step toward breaking the British monopoly over the amir's foreign policy. The Russians met British alarm with an offer to negotiate. Like the talks over Tibet, these were suspended until after the Russo-Japanese War.[149]

In August 1907, a month after the Russian–Japanese convention was signed, the British and Russians concluded their agreement on Iran, Afghanistan, and Tibet. In Iran, the division of spheres of influence allotted the north to the Russians and the south to the British, with the two being separated by a neutral zone where, ironically, most of the oil fields were later discovered. The two governments guaranteed the payment of loans to the Russian Discount and Loan Bank and the British Imperial Bank. Britain gave assurances that it had no intention of changing the political situation in Afghanistan. It promised to use only peaceful means to exercise its influence and not to encourage any anti-Russian activity in the country; the Russians again conceded that Afghanistan lay outside their sphere of influence. They promised to conduct political relations with the amir through British intermediaries. But Russian and Afghan frontier authorities were authorized to settle local issues of a non-political character, thus recognizing the problems of controlling movement across a porous frontier. As for Tibet, both sides recognized Chinese sovereignty, but Britain's special interest was also acknowledged in the form of allowing its commercial representatives to deal directly with Lhasa. Provisions were made for the eventual evacuation of British troops from the district of Chumby which they had occupied in 1904. Tehran and Beijing were informed of the terms of the convention on the day it was concluded.[150] The amir of Afghanistan refused to acknowledge the agreement.

The Anglo-Russian agreement of 1907 confirmed that Iran had suffered the same fate as the Polish–Lithuanian Commonwealth more than a century earlier. From being a competitor in the struggle over the borderlands, it had sunk to the level where it had become a borderland between imperial rivals. There was strong disagreement among Russian and British statesmen over the final settlement. Its supporters were limited to a handful of men on both sides over the opposition of powerful voices such as those of Curzon and Witte, who believed too much had been sacrificed for the sake of an agreement. But the two foreign ministers, Sir

[149] W. K. Fraser-Tytler, *Afghanistan. A Study of Political Developments in Central Asia* (London: Oxford University Press, 1950), pp. 174–75.
[150] Ignat'ev, *Politika*, pp. 181–92.

Edward Grey and A. P. Izvol'skii, were willing to bury decades of animosity in order to check the perceived threat from Germany's growing commercial penetration, which the Iranians were encouraging as a counterpoise to an Anglo-Russian occupation.[151] These negotiations have often been portrayed as the last innings of the Great Game. But the verdict was premature.

Convinced that between the two of them they could manage Iranian domestic politics, Russian and British diplomats attempted to reconcile the shah and his liberal opponents in the parliament (*majlis*). But a revolutionary outbreak in Azerbaijan and a revolt of the tribes doomed their efforts. Russia and Britain strengthened their military forces on Iran's borders. The supporters of the shah blockaded the Caucasian revolutionaries in Tabriz, endangering the lives of the foreign colony. The British invited the Russians to intervene, anticipating a temporary occupation. The Russians hesitated at first; some ministers and the viceroy of the Caucasus were worried about being drawn into a lengthy conflict with the civilian population. When the Russians moved in their troops to occupy Tabriz and Meshed, the British landed on the southern coast. Each suppressed the insurrectionary movement in its own zone. The British then evacuated their troops and the Russians set a schedule for withdrawal. But events in Tehran changed their minds. The shah, encouraged by the intervention, mounted a counter-coup against the majlis and dismissed it by force, using his loyal Cossack Brigade commanded by a Russian officer. Domestic order rapidly deteriorated, as we shall see in the section on Iran. The Ottoman Empire took advantage of the situation to occupy territory on their frontier with Iran. The Russians increased their military presence, finally occupying their entire zone to the alarm of the British.

The Russian occupation stabilized the internal situation and secured the frontier, but it did not yield any other advantages. Both the Viceroy of the Caucasus, Prince A. M. Dondukov-Korsakov, and Finance Minister V. N. Kokovtsov complained about the high cost and the drain on the military, and sought some kind of compensation. But the best they could get was a railroad concession from the frontier to Tabriz. Even this proved to be ephemeral when the Russian Discount and Loan Bank began to falter, yielding some of its financial influence to the British. The new

[151] Rogers P. Churchill, *Anglo-Russian Convention of 1907* (Cedar Rapids, IA: The Torch Press, 1939); Firuz Kazemzadeh, *Russia and Britain in Persia 1864–1914. A Study in Imperialism* (New Haven, CT: Yale University Press, 1968), pp. 497–509. British supporters and Russian opponents appeared to agree with Grey's judgment that "What we gained by it was real – what Russia gained was apparent." *Ibid.*, p. 503.

Foreign Minister, Sergei Sazonov, hoped to renegotiate the 1907 agreement, but the moment was unfortunately timed. Iranian oil had just become an important source for the British fleet, which was converting from coal. The incoming First Lord of the Admiralty, Winston Churchill, pushed vigorously for an oil concession and a more active role for the British in the Persian Gulf. Having purchased the Anglo-Persian Oil Company from a private concessionaire, the British government sought to expand the concession into the neutral zone and part of the Russian zone. It was Russia's turn to become alarmed. From this moment onward, the rivalry between the two powers in Iran focused more on oil concessions than on the security of frontiers. Even in the face of growing German commercial penetration, the two powers could not reach an agreement on a Trans-Iranian railroad that would link the Caucasus to India, as the Russians preferred, or to the Persian Gulf, as the British insisted. On the eve of the war new tensions arose between Russia and Britain over the implementation of the 1907 convention in Iran, Afghanistan, and Tibet.[152] Clearly, the Great Game was not over.

Russian aspirations at the Straits proved to be a more complex question and led to increased tensions with the Habsburg Monarchy over the borderlands in southeast Europe. The centerpiece of Izvol'skii's "great national policy" was to obtain the agreement of the Great Powers to the exclusive rights of Russian warships to pass the Straits. Although a long-standing aim of Russian foreign policy, the question assumed special significance during the Russo-Japanese War when the Black Sea Fleet was locked in and unable to join the Russian forces in the Far East, thus depriving them of any naval presence on the high seas after the loss of the Far Eastern and Baltic fleets to Japanese action. Izvol'skii sounded out the British during discussions over spheres of influence in the Central Asian borderlands. The main objective of the Russian diplomats was to avoid a categorical "no" to their proposals whatever reservations and conditions the British might raise in the negotiations for some kind of "agreement." Given their expectations, or lack thereof, what they got from Sir Edward Grey could be variously interpreted, but could hardly be conceived as encouraging. In the British view, the idea of an exclusive right for Russian warships to pass the Straits did not appear realistic. To prepare British opinion for such an eventuality, the cabinet expected corresponding concessions from the Russians in the on-going negotiations on Central Asia and compensation for any changes in the regime of the Straits in related

---

[152] A. V. Georgiev, "1912–1914 gody. Bor'ba za ukreplenie Antanty," in O. V. Orlik *et al.* (eds.), *Istoriia vneshnei politiki Rossii. Pervaia polovina XIX veka* (Moscow: Mezhdunarodnye otnosheniia, 1995), pp. 359–61.

questions like capitulations in Egypt. Discussion on the Straits regime could be advanced only by bringing in the other powers, including the Ottoman Empire. Russia would have to take the initiative in raising the issue.[153]

In making his diplomatic preparations for his master stroke, Izvol'skii made explicit the connection between the regime of the Straits and the situation in the Balkans. Flushed with success over his agreements with Japan and Britain, he toured the European capitals to drum up support for his proposals. He expected a sympathetic reception from his French allies and, with reservations, from the British. But he recognized that the major difficulties would come from Vienna and Berlin. Giving Russian warships the exclusive right to pass the Straits would completely transform the strategic and economic situation not only in the Balkans, where the Austrians were deeply invested, but also in the Mediterranean and throughout the Ottoman Empire, where German interests had begun to penetrate, especially with the construction of the Berlin to Baghdad Railroad. Izvol'skii seriously underestimated the opposition to his aims. It is difficult to imagine any compensation that could have satisfied all the Great Powers on this issue, or even one set of the budding Anglo-French Entente or the Austro-German alliance. Moreover, his combinations omitted one essential element, the populations of the newly formed states in the region that, unlike the helpless subjects of Iran, Afghanistan, and China, were highly energized by the dramatic rise in their national awareness. In 1908, Russia was about to learn a lesson that was to be often repeated. In the borderlands of southeast Europe too many conflicting interests were inextricably entangled for the Russians to dominate either through diplomacy or force of arms.

After 1908, the struggle over the Balkan borderlands became increasingly complicated. The smaller powers became ever more aggressive in their determination to complete the expulsion of the Ottomans from the region, but increasingly quarrelsome over dividing the spoils. The Ottoman Empire appeared to be undergoing another of its periodic revivals with the emergence of the Young Turks. The Habsburg Monarchy had adopted a more bellicose position. Russia's strategic aims remained fixed, but its diplomacy, confused by many voices in St. Petersburg, was increasingly inconsistent and often confusing to others. In part, this was the result of the absence of united government and, in part, it reflected old divisions within the foreign ministry.

---

[153] *British Documents on the Origins of the War, vol. IV: The Anglo-Russian Rapprochment* (New York: N. Johnson, 1967), pp. 279–81.

The role of pan-Slavs and their ideology in the final act of the imperial struggle over the borderlands is both complex and obscure. Although pan-Slavism was never officially adopted as an imperial ideology, its precepts, as we have seen, formed part of the mindset of a number of Russian diplomats. In 1909, a new Russian minister, Nikolai Gartvig (Hartwig), arrived in Belgrade from his posting in Tehran determined to promote a vigorous anti-Habsburg, pan-Slav agenda. His activities went far beyond the cautious policies endorsed by his chief, Foreign Minister Sazonov. Gartvig was associated, like others who shared his views, with the Asiatic Department of the Foreign Ministry where he served as director for five years (1901–1906) under V. N. Lambsdorf. Before that he was a correspondent for the chauvinistic newspaper *Novoe vremiia*. His hopes of becoming foreign minister were shattered with the appointment of Izvol'skii, who shunted him off to Iran. As minister in Tehran in the crucial years of the Anglo-Russian agreement on delimitating spheres of influence, he was nevertheless a bitter antagonist of his British counterpart. In Belgrade, he rapidly assumed a dominant position at the court. As an advocate of "Russia's great Slav mission," which he associated with the establishment of a Greater Serbia, he pressed hard for a Serbian–Bulgarian alliance against the Ottoman Empire based on a division of Macedonia that would be favorable to Serbia.[154] Sazonov favored an alliance, but only as a guarantee of the status quo; a pious hope given the heated atmosphere in the region.

The Serbian–Bulgarian negotiations, mediated by Russia, revealed all the faults of the tsarist government: the lack of firm, consistent, and united leadership at the center; sharp conflicts among its diplomats; and the widely shared illusion that Russia could balance the territorial claims and control the actions of the smaller states competing for the remnants of the Ottoman Empire. Gartvig persisted in fiercely advocating the Serbian position against the more restrained, but equally firm, defense of Bulgaria's claims by the Russian ambassador in Sofia, A. V. Nekliudov. Sazonov finally accepted the Bulgarian demands in the squabble over a small area that they had been promised by the Russians at San Stefano. The crucial dispute over the meaning of the treaty came subsequently. Sazonov assured his French ally that the Balkan powers had secretly promised not to take any offensive action without first consulting Russia. Yet in private both he and Nekliudov were less certain; they worried that the treaty was the prelude to an attack on the Ottoman

---

[154] On Gartvig, see Edward C. Thaden, *Russia and the Balkan Alliance of 1912* (University Park, PA: Penn State University Press, 1965), pp. 65–69; Philip E. Mosely, "Russian Policy in 1911–12," *Journal of Modern History* 12(1) (March 1940): 74–78.

Empire.[155] Within two months Serbia and Bulgaria had signed a military convention without Russian objections that enhanced the offensive potential of their alliance. Greece was drawn in on terms that met objections from St. Petersburg. The final piece in the coalition was added when Montenegro, the wild card of the Balkans, signed on. The Russians had been supplying King Nikita with arms and subsidies in the illusionary belief that this would enable them to control his actions. This was a risky gamble given his unpredictable behavior. In the event, it was Montenegro that gave a final push to the Balkan alliance into a war with the Ottoman Empire. The Russians had lost control of the situation. Their strong warnings to Bulgaria not to expect any Russian support in case of war went unheeded. Their fear of losing their rapidly evaporating preponderance of influence in the region prevented them from appealing to the concert of Great Powers.

Once the fighting had begun, the Russians found themselves in an awkward not to say dangerous position. They backed Serbia's demand for a sea port on the Adriatic, but this brought them face to face with Austria's determination to prevent that from ever happening. The Russians massed troops on the Galician frontier and made other military preparations to deter Austria from intervening in the war. However, Sazonov and Prime Minister Kokovtsov persuaded Nicholas II to restrain the Russian military from taking more provocative measures. There were also belligerent voices in the Viennese cabinet. But neither side desired a war, and their allies, France and Germany, were even less disposed to force a showdown. Russia and Austria backed away from a confrontation and began to reduce the forces on their Galician frontier. The Russians were surprised and dismayed by the rapid Bulgarian advance that threatened to take Istanbul. Although the Russians began military preparations to seize the Straits ahead of the Bulgarians, Sazonov worried that such an action would provoke an Austrian response. Further Austrian expansion in the Balkans could only undermine Russia's policy of protecting the south Slavs and securing the approaches to the Straits. The Russian dilemma

---

[155] Thaden, *Russia*, pp. 94–95, 114–17. In their post-war memoirs both Sazonov and Nekliudov attempted to defend themselves as sober and cautious statesmen pursuing defensive aims. Sergei Sazonov, *Fateful Years 1909–1916. The Reminiscences of Serge Sazonov* (New York: F. A. Stokes, 1928); A. V. Nekliudov, *Diplomatic Reminiscences before and during the World War, 1911–1917* (London: Jonathan Cape, 1928). The most recent survey of Russian foreign policy by a Russian historian endorses their view and expands it to envelop Russian foreign policy in general in the years approaching the war. Disputes within the Foreign Ministry were muted and Gartvig is mentioned, in passing, only twice. Georgiev, "1912–1914 gody," pp. 321–23, 340, 430.

was resolved when the Bulgarian advance stalled.[156] Montenegro's refusal to give up its claim to the town of Scutari threatened to precipitate a new crisis. This too was defused when representatives of the two alliance systems, meeting for the last time as a concert of Europe in December 1912, acted jointly to resolve the territorial disputes in a responsible way; they were still determined not to allow the small borderland powers to drag them into a European war.

In June and July 1914 these restraints no longer held. Historians have long disagreed as to why this was so. Two conclusions seem to be in order. In the prolonged struggle over the borderlands between their imperial domains, the Habsburg and Russian rulers and key figures in their ruling elites had arrived at similar conclusions about the transcendent importance of Serbia in maintaining their vaunted status as a Great Power. Closely related was their belief that Serbia represented a vital link in their security systems. The Habsburg Monarchy had ample historical reasons to fear that Serbian nationalism, if unchecked, would spread across its porous frontier to infect the other Slavs of the empire with the bacillus of separatism. The Russian government remained obsessively concerned with control over the Balkan flank of the Straits, the strategic gateway to its most vulnerable frontier along the Black Sea coast. If it abandoned the Serbs in their hour of need, would it not then appear to abdicate its role as the protector of the south Slavs? And would this not tip the balance in Bulgaria where the ruling elite was divided between the pro-German King Ferdinand with his Prime Minister Vasil Radoslavov and the pro-Russian faction? Their belief that vital interests were at stake and the pressures of mobilization schedules led them to take inordinately high risks. Both sides hoped for a localized conflict. However, the alliance system virtually guaranteed that a local war in the old Triplex Confinium would rapidly metastasize.

Crisis in the Ottoman Empire

At the moment when reform in the Ottoman Empire (Tanzimat 1839–1877) peaked, it suddenly gave way to a counter-reform almost simultaneously with a similar lurch to reaction in Russia. Moreover, the counter-reforming period lasted almost the same time in both empires, culminating in constitutional crisis. The Tanzimat was largely the creation of an elite drawn from a limited number of families, many of whom were Christian, who had hereditary claims on high office. Influenced by

---

[156] Ronald Bobroff, "Behind the Balkan Wars. Russian Policy Toward Bulgaria and the Turkish Straits, 1912–1913," *Russian Review* 59(1) (January 2000): 83–90.

Western currents of thought, they sought to create a constitutional system
in which all religious and ethnic discrimination would be eliminated and
an honest, efficient government would reconcile the Christians as well as
the Muslims to an Ottoman identity (Osmanlılık). By mid-century the
bureaucracy had succeeded in reducing the power of the guilds, subjugating all but the most remote tribes, and whittling down the autonomy of the
provincial dynasts.[157] Its crowning achievement was the constitution of
1876, which for the first time provided for the elections of Christians to a
quota-based representative assembly. Another attempt to stem the tide of
separatism, it was greeted by Jews, Armenians, and Greeks, but not by the
Slavs, with enthusiasm. As we have seen, the new sultan, Abdülhamid,
almost immediately turned against the constitution as a limitation on his
power, suspended it for thirty years, and purged the chief reformers like
Midhat Pasha.[158]

Opposition to political reform was not confined to the sultan.
Resistance developed among the lesser bureaucrats, who were closed
out of the circulation of elites; the ulama, who resented their loss of
influence; and the army, which was also sidelined by the new bureaucrats.[159] The leaders of the opposition, the Young Ottomans, attempted
to combine Western constitutional principles with the Islamic principle of
the *biat* (*bai'a*), that is, the ruler's obligation to consult with the community. They were critical of the bureaucratic reformers for having abandoned
Islamic principles, while at the same time failing to grant the civil rights of
European governments; of having allowed foreign influence to penetrate
all aspects of Ottoman life; and of having allowed the economy to fall into
the hands of foreigners. For them the constitution of 1876 installed by the
bureaucratic reformers was inadequate, although it seemed to embody
many elements of their thought.[160] The split in the bureaucracy between
the centralizers of the Tanzimat and the Young Ottomans supported by
the army and ulama seriously weakened the reforming impulse, and in
1878 facilitated Abdülhamid's restoration of the despotic power of the
sultan over all the contending elements within the political elite.

---

[157] Donald Quataert, "The Age of Reforms, 1812–1914," in Halil Inalcik with Donald
Quataert (eds.), *An Economic and Social History of the Ottoman Empire*, 2 vols.
(Cambridge University Press, 1994), vol. 2, pp. 761–62, 768–70.
[158] Roderic Davison, *Reform in the Ottoman Empire, 1856–1876* (Princeton University Press,
1963), pp. 43–45, 92–98, 115–20, 362–90, 407.
[159] Şerif Mardin, *The Genesis of Young Ottoman Thought. A Study in the Modernization of
Turkish Political Ideas* (Princeton University Press, 1962), pp. 107–32.
[160] Bernard Lewis, *The Emergence of Modern Turkey* (London: Oxford University Press,
1961), esp. ch. 5.

The failure to institutionalize constitutional reform and to introduce Ottomanism as an overarching, supranational, imperial ideology left few political options for the peoples of the Ottoman borderlands outside open resistance to imperial rule. By the mid-1890s three disparate resistance movements were coming to a head in Armenia, Crete, and Macedonia. Each crisis threatened the stability and territorial integrity of the empire, and they were dangerously interconnected. All of them brought intervention by the Great Powers in their wake.

Armenia

Abdülhamid faced a characteristically complex situation in the eastern Anatolian borderland. Although the Ottomans had finally settled their long-contested frontier with Iran, they had never been able to bring the region under their firm control. It was a typical shatter zone with Arabs, Kurds, Turkmen, and Iranians mixed together with smaller populations of Jews, Assyrians, Armenians, and Chaldeans. The situation of the Armenians had become particularly tenuous. On the one hand, they did not occupy a compact territory, but were scattered geographically throughout the empire. Even in the so-called Armenian vilayets of eastern Anatolia they did not constitute a majority of the population. On the other hand, the Ottoman policy of organizing religious communities into millets had provided them with a cultural unity. In the second quarter of the nineteenth century, a cultural revival was inspired in part by the Greek revolution and nourished by Armenian students studying in Venice and Paris. Returning students worked within the insulated confines of the religious community to secularize and democratize the movement, by introducing universal suffrage for the election of the Assembly of the Armenian Church. The reformers were disappointed by the Treaty of San Stefano. It did not provide the same kind of self-government for the Armenian vilayets that had been granted to the Bulgarians. Instead, it only committed the Porte to undertake local reforms and to protect the population against attacks by Kurds and Circassians who had been responsible for the worst of the Bulgarian atrocities.[161] The Armenian delegation to the Congress of Berlin was equally disillusioned. Armenians began to pin their hopes on Britain.

At the Congress of Berlin, Disraeli continued to pursue Britain's long-standing policy of defending the Ottoman Empire against Russian encroachments while extracting concessions from the Porte for services

---

[161] William Langer, *The Diplomacy of Imperialism*, 2nd rev. edn (New York: Knopf, 1960), pp. 147–49, 151–52.

rendered. By concluding the Convention of Cyprus with the Ottomans, he obtained another British island base in the eastern Mediterranean. At the same time, he encouraged the Ottomans to reform their administration and protect the Christian population as the best means of preventing yet another Russian intervention.[162] The British continued to press the sultan to introduce reforms in the eastern Anatolian vilayets inhabited by a mixed Armenian, Kurdish, and Turkish population. True to form, the sultan promised much and delivered little. Abdülhamid's abrogation of the Ottoman constitution in 1878 had already cast an ominous shadow over his government's relations with the Armenians.

The Kurdish question intensified the complexities of Ottoman policy in the Caucasian vilayets and the government's relations with the Armenians. Power was in the hands of the families of landed magnates and the leaders of two rival Sufi brotherhoods. The earliest signs of Kurdish desire for autonomy can be traced back to the 1820s and 1830s, after Sultan Mahmud II suppressed the semi-independent Kurdish principalities as part of his centralizing reforms. In the aftermath of the Russo-Turkish War serious violence broke out, compelling the sultan to intervene. His strategy was to mediate and issue pardons to the rebels despite repeated breakdowns in his peace-making efforts.

A truly nationalist movement only emerged under the leadership of Sheikh Ubayadallah in the 1870s and 1880s. As the head of a local messianic and millenarian Naqshbandi order, he publicly denounced both Turkish and Persian governments and local Christians (Armenians). He proclaimed the unity of all Kurds, denouncing the terms of the Treaty of Berlin that committed the Ottoman government to guarantee the security of the Armenians against the Circassians and Kurds. He created a Kurdish League which was supported by the Ottoman government as a counterweight to Armenian aspirations. In 1880, Ubayadallah's forces invaded Iran. They were driven back and abandoned, and the Ottoman authorities arrested him. He had become something of an international embarrassment since both the Russians and the British opposed his movement for different reasons.[163] Sultan Abdülhamid had not, however, given up the idea of using the Kurds against the Armenians. In the eyes of the ruling elite, local Armenian support for the Russians in the Crimean and Russo-Turkish War had raised questions about their loyalty. When the small but militant Hnchak

---

[162] Dwight E. Lee, *Great Britain and the Cyprus Convention Policy of 1878* (Cambridge, MA: Harvard University Press, 1934), pp. 39–50, 61–65, 155 ff.

[163] Robert Olsen, *The Emergence of Kurdish Nationalism and the Sheikh Said Rebellion, 1880–1925* (Austin, TX: University of Texas Press, 1988), pp. 2–7.

revolutionary movement began to organize in 1890, these suspicions were confirmed. But the allegiance of the Kurdish population was also in doubt. They too had manifested sympathy for the Russians during the war in the hope of gaining greater autonomy from the center. Finally, as we have seen, during the 1860s a large Circassian population had been resettled into eastern Anatolia from the Caucasian highlands as a result of an agreement with Russia. Retaining many of their nomadic practices, they frequently engaged in raids against the local Muslim and Christian population. The Ottoman government of Abdülhamid, reeling from territorial losses and under foreign pressure, particularly from the British government, sought to assert its authority in the region by pursuing a policy of administrative centralization and playing the local Muslim elites against one another. The key was to restrain the Kurds without alienating them. The policy appeared to be working during the decade from 1884 to 1894, according to reports by European consuls, as the authority of the central Ottoman government increased.

In western Anatolia Abdülhamid devised another tactic by recruiting Kurdish tribesmen into a Hamidian cavalry corps, modeled on Russian Cossack brigades. Designed as a concession, it also was a means of disciplining them. The tactic backfired. The Kurdish regiments felt justified in resisting central authority and attacking Armenians.[164] The simultaneous growth of Armenian revolutionary activity and the escalation of Kurdish violence followed a rising curve of conflict. The government reacted to a rebellion by Armenian revolutionaries in the Sasun district by ordering the Hamidian troops to crush the rising, touching off a massacre of the local Armenian population.[165] Once the Armenian massacres had broken out in 1894/5, the sultan was even more reluctant to

---

[164] Stephen Duguid, "The Politics of Unity. Hamidian Policy in Eastern Anatolia," *Middle Eastern Studies* 9(2) (May 1973): 139–55.

[165] Duguid, "The Politics of Unity," pp. 148–49. The literature on the Armenian massacres is very large and contentious. For the view that Armenian revolutionaries bear some responsibility for provoking the attacks and that the violence of the Muslim reaction should be placed in the context of the large-scale deportations of Muslims from the borderlands over the previous century, see Langer, *The Diplomacy of Imperialism*, pp. 160–61, based on the report of the Anglo-French-Russian consular investigation; Erik-Jan Zürcher, "Young Turks, Ottoman Muslims and Turkish Nationalists. Identity Politics, 1908–1938," in Kemal Karpat (ed.), *Ottoman Past and Today's Turkey* (Leiden: Brill, 2000), p. 160; Justin McCarthy, *The Ottoman Peoples and the End of Empire* (London: Arnold, 2001). For the traditional view on exclusive Turkish responsibility, see Suny, *Looking Toward Ararat*, pp. 98, 105; V. N. Dadrian, *Warrant of Genocide. Key Elements of Turko-Armenian Conflict* (New Brunswick, NJ: Rutgers University Press, 1999); Stephen Kinzer, *Crescent and Star. Turkey between Two Worlds* (New York: Farrar, Straus & Giroux, 2001). Cf. Michael A. Reynolds, *Shattering Empires. The Clash and Collapse of the Ottoman and Russian Empires, 1908–1918* (Cambridge University Press, 2011), pp. 145–55.

punish the Kurdish tribesmen on whom he depended. The frontier was still in turmoil when the Young Turk revolution deposed Abdülhamid.[166]

Crete and Macedonia

The Cretan revolt had been simmering since the Porte had evaded the reforms promised in the Treaty of Berlin in 1878. When it broke to the surface in 1897 the Greek government lent support and agitated for union with Crete. After war broke out between Greece and the Ottoman Empire, the powers sought to mediate and occupied the island. None of them wanted to change the balance of power in the region. The two venerable rivals, the Habsburg Monarchy and Russia, had already reached agreement on maintaining the status quo. The sultan accepted the moderate peace terms proposed by the Great Powers, which once again promised local autonomy under a Christian governor.[167] A few Greek nationalists sought to arouse their compatriots from the mood of defeatism by turning their attention to another unredeemed borderland in the north – Macedonia.

The Greek, Bulgarian, and Serbian competition for cultural and then political hegemony over the Ottoman provinces comprising Macedonia flared into a new, more violent phase following the Cretan and Armenian crises. As we have seen, the Greek, Bulgarian, and Serbian competition for cultural hegemony over Macedonia had its origins in the establishment of an autonomous Bulgarian exarchate in 1870. The Greek-dominated patriarchate of Istanbul then concentrated its propaganda attack on local priests for appealing to the Slavic speakers in a language and rhetoric that it condemned as Bulgarian. The patriarchate teamed up with secular Greek literary and patriotic associations to build churches and schools in the province. The Bulgarians countered with their own cultural campaign to mobilize the population, denouncing the double yoke of Ottoman and Greek overlords. The contest intensified with the creation of an autonomous Bulgarian state in 1878 and the cession of the northwest districts of Macedonia to Serbia. The Greeks enjoyed two advantages: their domination of the commercial life of the region; and the high level of literacy of the Greek clergy, although their language was atticized Greek, distinct from the vernacular of the Greek speakers in the region. In

---

[166] Gökhan Çetinsaya, "The Caliph and the Shaykhs. Abdülhamid II. Policy Toward the Qadiriyya of Mosul," in Itzchak Weismann and Fruma Zachs (eds.), *Ottoman Reform and Muslim Regeneration. Studies in Honor of Butrus Abu-Manneb* (London: Tauris, 2005), pp. 97–105.

[167] Langer, *The Diplomacy of Imperialism*, pp. 316–20, 355–83.

histories and school books the Greeks extolled the continuity of Hellenism from the time of Alexander the Great through Byzantium to modern times. The Bulgarians possessed only one advantage and it proved to be the more powerful. The Slavic language spoken by the majority of the Macedonians was close to the Bulgarian used in the churches of the exarchate.[168] The Serbs lagged behind in this contest, although they did expend some efforts in setting up schools in northern Macedonia.

This hotly contested competition raged in a shatter zone inhabited by a highly mixed population. There are no reliable statistics; in fact, there was no clear-cut ethnographic basis for compiling them. Foreign travelers and diplomats generally designated the Slavs as Bulgarians, but indigenous scholars occasionally considered them a separate ethnic group. Several astute foreign observers noted that the peasants expressed no clear notion of their ethnic identification. As we have seen, this was often the case on the frontiers of contested borderlands. Together with Orthodox Slavic speakers, there was a substantial Muslim population, some Albanians, many more Circassians, and other Turkic people resettled in the region in the nineteenth century after the wars with Russia. Scattered throughout Macedonia, Vlach shepherds, farmers, and craftsmen were highly Hellenized, but spoke a dialect close to Romanian. Jews were concentrated in Saloniki and to a lesser extent in other smaller towns.[169]

The shift from cultural competition to political conflict and insurrection took place in the early 1890s. Two competing underground organizations emerged almost simultaneously. The Internal Macedonian Revolutionary Organization (IMRO) was founded in Saloniki in 1893 by a handful of students and intellectuals educated abroad and dedicated to winning autonomy from the Ottomans by violent means. Two years later, the External Macedonian Revolutionary Organization, called the Supreme Committee, unified several associations of Slavic-speaking émigrés from Macedonia in Bulgaria and challenged the IMRO for leadership over the struggle for autonomy. It organized attacks by small bands (*četa*, from which the word *četniks* derives) against Muslims in eastern Macedonia, an area with a long tradition of bandits (*haiduk* in Serbian, *haiduts* in Bulgarian). They aimed to capitalize on the simultaneous disturbances in Armenia and attract the attention of the Great Powers in order to force the sultan to grant concessions in Macedonia.

---

[168] Anastasia N. Karakasidou, *Fields of Wheat, Hills of Blood. Passages to Nationhood in Greek Macedonia, 1870–1990* (University of Chicago Press, 1997), pp. 78–94.

[169] Duncan M. Perry, *The Politics of Terror. The Macedonian Liberation Movement, 1893–1903* (Durham, NC: Duke University Press, 1988), pp. 20–23.

The prince of Bulgaria, Ferdinand, sought in his characteristically devious way to exploit the situation and increase his own influence in the province by allowing the bands to operate from Bulgarian soil and arming them with weapons from the Bulgarian arsenals. Beset by unrest in Crete and Armenia, the sultan bowed to Ferdinand's demands for new bishoprics.[170] The Bulgarian government was unable to control the activities of the armed bands. Russia, having signed the agreement of 1897 with the Habsburg Monarchy "to put the Balkans on ice," had lost interest in the Christian struggles in the Ottoman borderlands and was turning its attention to the Far East.

By 1902 the situation in Macedonia had reached crisis proportions. As the bands grew more active, Muslims countered by organizing their own local militias. Intercommunal fighting broke out. Abdülhamid reinforced the Ottoman garrison, and ordered his governors to "maintain order in their districts in a legal and proper way and not to allow the Muslim population to take the law into their own hands and to take reprisals on the Bulgarian agitators."[171] The sultan was caught in a recurrent dilemma: how to prevent his Christian and Muslim subjects from slaughtering one another without triggering intervention by the European powers. As usual his efforts were half-hearted and crippled by the lack of resources.

At this point Russia and the Habsburg Monarchy jointly intervened. Their proposals for reforming the police and judiciary were reluctantly accepted by the sultan, but almost wrecked by a major uprising in Macedonia. The two powers were committed to a conservative solution of repressing endemic revolts in order to shore up the Ottoman state and to improve security in a borderland torn by warring factions. The reforms featuring international supervision began to take hold; the Ottoman forces repressed two major uprisings and Prince Ferdinand banned all Macedonian organizations. The IMRO disintegrated into factional fighting. The success of the reforms was jeopardized by persistent Ottoman back-pedaling and Abdülhamid's determination to involve all the Great Powers as a means of lessening Austro-Russian pressure; in particular, he could count on British opposition to an Austro-Russian combination. His policy was doomed by the refusal of the indigenous revolutionary forces, supported by outside powers, to accept anything short of autonomy.[172]

---

[170] Perry, *The Politics of Terror*, pp. 38–51.   [171] Perry, *The Politics of Terror*, p. 112.
[172] Stephen Sowards, *Austria's Policy of Macedonian Reform* (Boulder, CO: East European Monographs, 1989).

With the decline of the two major revolutionary movements oriented towards Bulgaria, Serbian and Greek bands began to appear in Macedonia. Between 1904 and 1908 Hellenized Slavs loyal to the patriarch and covertly supported by the Greek government launched attacks against the Slavic speakers loyal to the exarch.[173] During 1905 and 1906 the Greek bands drove the remaining IMRO forces out of the Saloniki region and most of Monastir province. Serbian bands also enjoyed the covert support of Belgrade after the coup of 1903, which had brought back the aggressively nationalistic Karadjordjević dynasty. By 1907 they had gained control over Kosovo.[174] The three-way struggle foreshadowed the partition of Macedonia among Bulgaria, Greece, and Serbia during the Balkan Wars of 1912/13.

Crisis management

Abdülhamid was a representative, if an extreme one, of a late imperial ruler who sought to combine traditional political theologies, resettlement policies, and new technologies in seeking to maintain control over the borderlands. Faced by multiple crises in the Balkans and eastern Anatolia, Abdülhamid rallied the Sufi brotherhoods and sought to wrap himself in the protective envelop of pan-Islam. He undertook a new policy of resettling Muslims who had fled the Balkans and Circassia after 1877/8 in strategic areas on the approaches to the capital in Thrace and the Gallipoli peninsula. He even encouraged immigration from Bosnia.[175] In administrative matters, Abdülhamid instituted an authoritarian centralized regime based on a modern bureaucracy subordinated to his personal rule. At his most innovative, he established new specialized schools to provide the necessary civil and military technicians to run the empire. Following up the tentative initiatives of his predecessors, he pressed for

---

[173] H. N. Brailsford, *Macedonia. Its Races and their Future* (New York: Arno Press, [1906] 1971), pp. 214–17, gives a vivid eye-witness report. Students at the Greek Gymnasium in Saloniki were taught to regard the "Bulgarians as 'murderers, criminals, infidels who should be cleared from the face of the earth.'" Mark Mazower, *Salonica, City of Ghosts. Christians, Muslims and Jews, 1430–1950* (New York: Alfred A. Knopf, 2005), p. 253.

[174] Douglas Dakin, *The Greek Struggle in Macedonia, 1897–1913* (Thessaloniki: Institute for Balkan Studies, 1966); Wayne S. Vucinich, *Serbia between East and West. The Events of 1903–1908* (Stanford University Press, 1954).

[175] Paradoxically, he encountered opposition from the Austrian government who sought to prevent the loss of population and, acting through its agents in Anatolia, to persuade Muslim immigrants to return. Fikret Adanir and Hilmar Kaiser, "Migration, Deportation, and Nation Building. The Case of the Ottoman Empire," in René Leboutte (ed.), *Migrations et migrants dans une perspective historique. Permanences et innovations* (Brussels: Peter Lang, 2000), p. 279.

the development of new technologies of communication – the telegraph and railroads – in order to bind the borderlands more closely to the center.

The first sultan to show an interest in railroads was Abdülaziz. He became an ardent promoter after his visit to Western Europe in 1867, the first by a ruling sultan, during which he traveled almost exclusively by railroad. Before this only a few local lines had been built. The Ottoman state lacked the capital to fund construction and had to rely on foreign entrepreneurs. After the Crimean War half a dozen nations, including Russia, competed for concessions. Their interests, not those of the Ottoman state, guided the direction of the lines. While the British sought to link commercial sea ports with productive hinterlands, such as the two Izmir lines, the Russians aimed at preventing others from building lines close to the northeast provinces. The Russians successfully opposed the proposed section of the planned Berlin to Baghdad Railroad that would pass too close to its Caucasian border, then guarded by the fortress of Kars.[176] A comprehensive plan submitted by a German engineer in 1872 was accepted by the government, but Abdülhamid "preferred to build the sections offering greater military and political benefits than those with high economic potential."[177]

Under his rule 30,000 kilometers of telegraph line were laid. His main interest in the telegraph was to communicate with his intelligence network throughout the empire and to avoid wherever possible reliance on foreign lines.[178] The main rail lines shaped by military considerations included the Oriental Railway, connecting Istanbul to Edirne and Sofia with a branch to Saloniki; the Anatolian Line from Izmir to Ankara; and the notorious and unfinished Baghdad Railroad from Konya deep into the Iraqi provinces. For all his efforts, the strategic lines proved to be inadequate to the demands of modern war in the Balkans in 1912/13 and in the First World War. The absence of a network and the lack of good roads not only slowed mobilization to a snail's pace, but left the troops without

---

[176] Yakup Bektas, "The Imperial Ottoman Izmir-to-Aydin Railway. The British Experimental Line in Asia Minor," in Ekmeleddin Ihsanoğlu *et al.* (eds.), *Science, Technology and Industry in the Ottoman World* (Turnhout: Brepols, 2000), pp. 139–52; Jonathan S. McMurray, *Distant Ties. Germany, the Ottoman Empire and the Construction of the Baghdad Railway* (Westport, CT: Praeger, 2001).

[177] Quataert, "The Age of Reform," pp. 804–15, quotation on p. 807. See also Isa Blumi, "Thwarting the Ottoman Empire. Smuggling through the Empire's New Frontier in Yemen and Albania, 1878–1910," in Kemal Karpat with Robert W. Zens (eds.), *Ottoman Borderlands. Issues, Personalities and Political Changes* (Madison, WI: University of Wisconsin Press, 2003), pp. 253–55.

[178] Marsha Siefert, "'Chingis-Khan with the Telegraph.' Communications in the Russian and Ottoman Empires," in Jörn Leonhard and Ulrike von Hirschhausen (eds.), *Comparing Empires. Encounters and Transfers in the Long Nineteenth Century* (Göttingen: Vandenhoeck & Ruprecht, 2011), pp. 101–2.

sufficient supplies.[179] Moreover, the few strategic lines were built at the
cost of neglecting the economic development of fertile regions in Anatolia,
the commerce of Beirut and the Hejaz. The sultan himself planned the
Hejaz line, the only one to be built with Ottoman capital. By linking
Damascus to Mecca, it fulfilled a multiplicity of integrative aims. By
replacing the caravan route, it facilitated travel by pilgrims on the *hadj*,
thus propagating his pan-Islamic claims as caliph of the world's Muslims;
it symbolized the reconciliation of Islam with science and technology, and
it strengthened ties between the center and the rebellious province of
Yemen. Yet influential elements of the ulama expressed strong disapproval of modern projects such as the telegraph and the railroad. In 1916,
large sections of the Hejaz line were destroyed by Bedouin tribesmen "out
of ignorance or greed or because divisive nationalism proved to be stronger than unifying Islam."[180]

Abdülhamid's secular reforms in secondary and higher education also
worked against his revival of Islamic principles and the caliphate. Thus, as
in China, Iran, and Russia, attempts to reconcile a revitalized imperial
ideology based upon traditional moral or religious codes and secular
education destined to create a new class of efficient bureaucratic servitors
and army officers produced a radical generation bent on constructing its
own program of reform.

The challenge of the Young Turks

The Young Turk movement was initially a loose association of opponents
of the sultan. Its first important organizational center was the Union of
Ottomans formed in 1889 by a group of medical students. A few years
later its leaders adopted the more familiar title of the Committee of Union
and Progress (CUP). Erik-Jan Zürcher has called them "children of the
borderlands." Distinguished by their youth, multicultural backgrounds
(Turks, Arabs, Albanians, Kurds, and Circassians), their varied social
origins, they were almost all educated in the modern schools founded
on the European model under Abdülhamid. Before 1906, civilians dominated; from 1906 to the revolution of 1908, officers were in control. The
majority came from the provinces, mainly the Balkans (48 percent after
1908), where they had been exposed to the small-scale warfare against
Serbs, Bulgarians, and Greek guerrillas and the widening gap between

[179] Erik-Jan Zürcher, "The Ottoman Conscription System, 1844–1914," *International Review of Social History* 43 (1998): 448.
[180] Kemal Karpat, *The Politicization of Islam. Reconstructing Identity, State, Faith, and Community in the Late Ottoman State* (Oxford University Press, 2001), pp. 253–55.

Muslims and Christians in schools and economic activity.[181] But the army
was not united behind the Young Turks. Shortly after they came to power
a counter-revolution broke out, spearheaded by elements of the First
Army in Istanbul allied to an Islamic Party, demanding the restoration
of Islamic law (Shari'a). They were repressed by troops from Saloniki.[182]
It would appear that Turkish nationalism remained a minority ideology
until the collapse of the Ottoman Empire in 1923.

Despite its diversity the committee was united in its determination to
save the empire from misgovernment and the threat of dissolution. It has
been called "a peculiar branch of Ottoman Muslim nationalism, which
was to a very large degree reactive" against the rising nationalisms among
the Balkan, Greek, and Armenian populations.[183] The Russian
Revolution of 1905 in the Caucasian isthmus provided another source
of inspiration for the Young Turk movement. Hundreds of articles in the
Turkish press, including papers of the Young Turks, praised the Russian
revolutionaries. The possibilities appeared to open up for a mutual
exchange of political ideas and joint action across the porous frontiers.
The CUP made contact with Muslim organizations in the Caucasus
through Azeris and Tatars who had taken part in their movement, appealing for a common Turkic front against the Russians and for assistance in
printing and disseminating propaganda. Among the intellectuals they
sought were İsmail Gaspıralı (Ismail Gasprinskii), the Crimean Tatar
champion of a new Muslim educational system, and Hüseyinzâde Ali
and Ahmet Ağaoğlu (Agaev), both journalists who had been educated in
St. Petersburg and Paris and who had participated in the Russian
Revolution of 1905 and the Young Turk Revolution in 1908. Ağaoğlu
returned to the Caucasus in 1918 as advisor to the Ottoman army and
would become a leading figure in the short-lived Azerbaijan Republic.[184]

[181] Erik-Jan Zürcher, "The Young Turks. Children of the Borderlands," in Karpat (ed.),
Ottoman Borderlands, pp. 275–85. In addition to a mixture of Turkism, Ottomanism, and
Islam within the CUP, strong anti-European, mainly anti-Austrian and anti-Russian,
feelings were omnipresent. When expedient, the Young Turks flirted with the possibility
of cooperation with the Armenian Dashnaks and the Macedonian revolutionaries
(IMRO) before the revolution of 1908. Hanioğlu, *Preparation for a Revolution*,
pp. 175–81, 191–97, 243–49, 296–99.

[182] Feroz Ahmad, *The Young Turks. The Committee of Union and Progress in Turkish Politics,
1908–1914* (Oxford University Press, 1969), pp. 40–45.

[183] Ahmad, *The Young Turks*, p. 173, and more generally Erik-Jan Zürcher, *The Unionist
Factor. The Role of the Committee of Union and Progress in the Turkish National Movement*
(Leiden: Brill, 1984).

[184] M. Şükrü Hanioğlu, *Preparation for a Revolution. The Young Turks, 1902–1908* (Oxford
University Press, 2001), pp. 121–23, 157–61; Holly Shissler, *Between Two Empires.
Ahmet Ağaoğlu and the New Turkey* (London: Tauris, 2003).

From the outset the Young Turk movement was fiercely anti-imperialist, condemning in particular the interventions of the Habsburg and Russian empires in Ottoman affairs. Through a successful campaign of propaganda throughout the empire, it steadily gained adherents. In 1907, they merged with a secret organization called the Ottoman Freedom Society. This opened its ranks to disgruntled bureaucrats and junior army officers, who became the backbone of the expanded organization and "gave it control over the most active force in Ottoman society."[185] Throughout its history the CUP shifted its intellectual orientation depending on the occasion and the audience. Like the sultan, they tapped into three diverse traditions in their efforts to strengthen the state: Turkism, Islam, and Ottomanism. Turkism took on a new lease of life where it attracted some elements among the officers of the Young Turk movement. But there, too, it did not meet with universal approbation, being forced to compete with the more numerous advocates of pan-Islam. Particularly during the period from 1902 to 1908, the Young Turks couched their appeals to non-Muslims in terms of Ottomanism. This enabled them to establish contact and cooperation with the Dashnaks in launching abortive uprisings in eastern Anatolia between 1905 and 1907. More importantly, it won them support among Albanian bands, Vlachs, and the right wing of IMRO, while neutralizing the Serbian and Greek bands in Macedonia. In 1908, with their flanks secure, the CUP launched its operations from Macedonia and forced the sultan to capitulate to their demands to restore the constitution of 1876 or risk civil war.[186] Following an abortive counter-coup in 1909, Abdülhamid was forced to abdicate. He was succeeded by two weak sultans who were stripped of any real power by the Young Turk revolution.

Ottomanism had proved to be a double-edged sword. Its Turkish proponents had encouraged Armenian, Albanian, Kurdish, and Macedonian supporters of autonomy without winning their unwavering loyalty. After 1908, the CUP tried its hand at nationalizing the empire by stressing Turkism while simultaneously reaching out to accommodate the local elites. But this tactic no longer had much appeal after the loss of Libya to the Italians in 1911, and Macedonia to the Balkan League in 1913, further reduced the ethnic diversity of the empire. During the Balkan Wars almost 250,000 Rumelian Muslims fled the advancing Bulgarian army and poured into Istanbul.

Defeat in the Balkan Wars marked a decisive turn toward pro-Turkic policies without a complete abandonment of Ottomanism. The lingering contradictions led to disastrous results. The signs were unmistakable in

---

[185] Hanioğlu, *Preparation for a Revolution*, p. 314.
[186] Hanioğlu, *Preparation for a Revolution*, pp. 114–24, 248–78.

two areas: ethnic conflict and economic nationalism. The Greeks were the first to suffer. On the eve of the First World War, about 100,000 Greeks were expelled from the Aegean coast of Anatolia, ostensibly in retaliation for the harassment of the Muslim population in the territories annexed by Greece. Greek Prime Minister Elefthieros Venizelos agreed to a voluntary exchange of populations, but the exchange was never officially implemented. Instead, during the four years of war another almost half a million Greeks were deported into the interior of Anatolia as a security measure. Up to 1916 Muslim paramilitary bands terrorized the Greek minority.[187] The precedent had been set for the more extensive and violent expulsions and exchange of populations in 1923.[188] The Armenians were next.

In eastern Anatolia the unionist initiatives to grant equal rights to Christians and Muslims ran afoul of the hostility between the Kurdish and Armenian populations. The Ottoman crackdown on Kurdish banditry, the appointment of pro-Armenian administrators in the region, the induction of Armenians into the army, and the fears that Armenian lands confiscated and redistributed among the Kurds under Abdülhamid would be returned to their former owners aroused the Kurds to armed resistance. At the same time, the Russian government was playing its own double game by inciting the Kurds against the Ottoman center while also claiming to represent the interests of the Armenians. The unionists retaliated by stirring up the Kurds in Iran against the Russians. On the eve of the First World War the Russians were pressing for an administrative reform that would combine the five provinces inhabited by Armenians under a single Christian, preferably European, governor with broad powers. This was precisely the kind of intervention that the unionists had sought to prevent by their policy of Ottomanism. They succeeded in watering down the reform project before agreeing to it.

The compromise, however, enraged the Kurds. In early 1914 they rose in rebellion. Several of the Kurdish leaders were already in Russia and others fled after the repression of the rising by the Ottoman army. The Ottoman government then shifted back to a policy of courting the Kurds.[189] The

---

[187] D. Ergil, "A Reassessment. The Young Turks, their Politics and Anti-Colonial Struggle," *Balkan Studies* 16 (1975): 62–63; F. Ahmad, "Vanguard of a Nascent Bourgeoisie. The Social and Economic Policy of the Young Turks, 1908–1918," in O. Okyar and H. Inalcik (eds.), *Social and Economic History of Turkey, 1071–1920* (Ankara: Meteksan, 1980), pp. 342–43.

[188] Ayhan Aktar, "Homogenising the Nation. Turkifying the Economy," in Renée Hirschon (ed.), *Crossing the Aegean. An Appraisal of the 1923 Compulsory Population Exchange between Greece and Turkey* (Oxford University Press, 2003), pp. 82–83; Michael Llewellyn Smith, *Ionian Vision. Greece in Asia Minor, 1919–1920* (Ann Arbor, MI: University of Michigan Press, [1973] 1998), pp. 30–31.

[189] Reynolds, *Shattering Empires*, pp. 56–81.

Russian and Ottoman governments not only failed to reconcile the cross-currents of conflict in eastern Anatolia, but their contradictory and manipulative policies intensified the hostility between the Christian and Muslim populations. After the Ottomans declared war on Russia in November 1914, violence between them spiraled to new heights. The government colluded with the Kurds in a massive deportation of Armenians, leading to widespread massacres of genocidal proportions.

The Young Turks were an elitist organization; they were not committed to parliamentary pluralism, and soon revealed their centralizing and authoritarian side. Basking in the aura of their revolution and much better organized than the weak opposition, they swept to victory in the election of 1908. They moved quickly to consolidate their position. Military men played an increasingly prominent role in the movement, especially after the Ottoman defeats in the Balkan Wars of 1912–1913. Two of the so-called ruling triumvirate, Enver Pasha and Cemal Paşa, were graduates of the War College.[190] Attacked for pursuing a policy of Turkification that disregarded Islamic principles, they resorted to a policy of intimidation and fraud to win another overwhelming electoral victory in 1912. The political struggle then assumed an extraparliamentary character. In the wake of defeat in the Balkan Wars, the CUP organized another coup in order to stay in power. Despite their centralizing policies, the CUP was forced, as their bureaucratic predecessors under imperial rule had been, to bargain with local notables from both Muslim and non-Muslim communities. As a result, the elections of 1914, once again manipulated by the CUP, returned a chamber corresponding closely to the new ethnic composition of the empire. But during the war parliament was virtually ignored by the government.[191]

The war also intensified a growing belief within Young Turk circles that for too long the commerce and industry of the empire had been in the hands of Christians and Jews. As early as 1908, the CUP supported a boycott of Greek commerce. Once the war began, the government embraced the belief, already advanced by a few economists in the spirit of Friederich List, that the state should undertake the construction of a national economy. Administrative measures were introduced requiring the compulsory use of Turkish in all business dealings and the introduction of a state-sponsored cooperative movement that discriminated against non-Muslims.[192]

---

[190] Lewis, *The Emergence of Modern Turkey*, p. 221.

[191] Hasan Kayalı, "Elections and the Electoral Process in the Ottoman Empire, 1876–1919," *International Journal of Middle East Studies* 27 (1995): 271–82.

[192] Çağlar Keyder, *State and Class in Turkey. A Study in Capitalist Development* (London: Verso, 1987), pp. 71–90; Fatma Müge Göçek, *Rise of the Bourgeoisie, Demise of Empire. Ottoman Westernization and Social Change* (New York: Oxford University Press, 1996), pp. 108–16.

The outbreak of the war intensified the Turkification of the army. As Minister of War in the cabinet of 1914, Enver Pasha instituted a purge of Arab officers, retiring 300 of them. As military governor of Syria, the third member of the triumvirate, Cemal Paşa, instituted a reign of terror against the Arabs in the belief that they constituted a nationalist movement that threatened the security of the empire. Their policies aroused the Arab leaders to launch a rebellion. Cemal's reprisals radicalized elements among the Arab army officers, who emerged as the main adherents of national independence.[193] The common ties of Ottomanism and Islam broke asunder as the long-gestating national rivalries rose to the surface.

The growing tendency within the Ottoman ruling circles to Turkify the empire had been more of a response to the frontier wars and the crises in the borderlands than a conscious ideological choice. Whatever their intentions, its leaders ended up accelerating the mounting hostility between Turks and Arabs, Christians and Muslims at opposite ends of the empire – eastern Thrace and the Aegean littoral, the Armenian highlands in Anatolia, Syria, and Iraq – preparing the ground for the great Turkish national revival.

Even after the Ottoman defeat in the war and the loss of the Arab provinces, a full-blown Turkish nationalist movement was slow to develop. It came mainly as a response to European plans to partition the empire.[194] When it did come, not surprisingly, it was led by Mustapha Kemal Pasha (Atatürk), another Young Turk member of the War College and a man of the borderlands (Saloniki). Although his relations with Enver and Cemal were not cordial, he came out of the same professional, nationalizing milieu. A century of reforms had produced an army that represented the most secular and modern institution in the Ottoman Empire. For so long the sword and then the shield of empire, the army had produced the Young Turk officers who launched the constitutional revolution of 1908, and then in the person of Mustapha Kemal Pasha overthrew the dynasty. The formative moment of the new state-building project was the campaign of Kemal's new *nationalist* army in 1921 to defeat and expel the Greeks, inaugurating a secular Turkish republic that set the tone for politics over the next eighty years.[195]

[193] Hasan Kayali, *Arabs and Young Turks. Ottomanism, Arabism and Islamism in the Ottoman Empire, 1908–1918* (Los Angeles, CA: University of California Press, 1997), pp. 178, 195, 197.

[194] Reynolds, *Shattering Empires*, p. 256.

[195] Andrew Mango, *Atatürk* (London: John Murray, 1999), pp. 49–54, 71–75, 301, 316, 319–23.

Crisis in Qajar Iran

The constitutional crisis of 1905–1911 in Iran, like those in the Russian and Ottoman empires, ended up heightening rather than reducing the growing tensions between the borderlands and the center of imperial power. But the causes and outcome more nearly resembled what occurred in the Russian Empire. The constitutional movement brought together a wide range of disparate interests, unified only in their opposition to the authoritarian and ineffectual policies of the shah. Initially successful in limiting his power, the movement then splintered and was forced to surrender many of its gains to a counter-revolution. In contrast to Russia, however, the success of the counter-revolution depended on external intervention. The Qajar dynasts had relied too long for survival on manipulating and bargaining with competing groups and interests. They had failed to develop a strong institutional base either in the civil bureaucracy or the army that could sustain them in the event of a major challenge to their authority.[196] During the constitutional crisis it became clear that Iran had become an empire with too many potential power centers – the court and bureaucracy, the ulama, the bazaar, and the tribes – all of which were deeply divided internally and none of which could dominate the others.

The reforms of Amir Kabir in the 1850s were the last serious attempt to complete the modernization of the Iranian army. For the remainder of the reign of Nasir al-Din the army was neglected, disorganized, and demoralized. Commands were bought and sold by men who appropriated the salaries of the rank-and-file. The soldiers were encouraged to make a living on the side and their military training was slipshod and casual. Conservative elements in the court, tribal leaders, and the top hierarchy of the ulama were all opposed to reforms as a threat to their interests.[197] But once the Russians and British had more or less settled on maintaining Iran as a buffer, there were no external threats to galvanize the government into undertaking the reforms that the Ottoman sultans attempted to introduce against the same domestic opponents. Only late in life during a visit to Europe, the first ruler to take such a trip, did Nasir al-Din come face to face with the glamor, if not the efficiency, of the European-trained armies. He invited Grand Duke Mikhail Nikolaevich to send him Cossack instructors. After many frustrating and some hilarious attempts to

---

[196] Mangol Bayat, *Iran's First Revolution. Shi'ism and the Constitutional Revolution of 1905–1909* (New York, Oxford University Press, 1991), p. 11.

[197] Gavin Hambly, "Iran During the Reigns of Fath' Ali Shah and Muhammad Shah," in *Cambridge History of Iran*, vol. 7, pp. 176–77.

introduce discipline, the Russian officers succeeded in forming a Persian Cossack Brigade. It proved itself a loyal bodyguard to the dynasty and protected the claimant to the throne in 1896 on his accession to power, thus guaranteeing the survival of the dynasty for another generation.[198] An exception to the pattern, Iran under the Qajars remained a militarized society without a central professional army.

The most surprising components of the constitutional movement were religious dissidents committed to the destruction of Qajar rule allied with secular reformers influenced by Western ideas. At the end of the nineteenth century, a radical faction among Shi'ia clerics was angered by the government's attempt to limit the jurisdiction of the ulama in courts, schools, and charitable foundations, while at the same time granting extensive economic privileges to foreigners.[199] In 1891/2, the government awarded a tobacco concession to the British which touched off the first significant protest against foreign imperialism in Iran. Anti-foreign sentiment had been growing since the 1860s when religious dissidents, concerned over the spread of Western ideas, denounced the introduction of the telegraph. Merchants blamed the government for the competition from foreigners who enjoyed special privileges. In towns like Shiraz and Isfahan, urban disturbances were on the rise even before the major outbreaks.[200] Open revolt against the concession was led by the intelligentsia, merchants, and ulama of Tabriz and spread rapidly to other cities.[201] The government resorted to its habitual practice of bargaining with the local population and ultimately withdrew the concession. The disorders appeared to close the last door to financial recovery, but it opened the way for constitutional reform. Clearly a fundamental shift was taking place in Iranian urban society. In contrast to the Ottoman Empire where demands from reform came from the ruling elites, in Iran the demands for change emerged from the bazaar, the mosques, and the university under the banner of social justice as defined by the Shari'a.

Like so many political initiatives in Iranian history, the constitutional revolution of 1905–1911 drew powerful support from social groups in the

---

[198] Firuz Kazemzadeh, "The Origin and Development of the Persian Cossack Brigade," *American Slavic and East European Review* 15(3) (October 1956): 351–63.

[199] H. Algar, *Religion and the State in Iran, 1785–1806. The Role of the Ulama in the Qajar Period* (Berkeley, CA: University of California Press, 1969). The ulama subsequently turned against constitutionalism when it did not serve its purposes. Nikki R. Keddie, "The Roots of Ulama's Power in Modern Iran," *Studia Islamica* 29 (1969): 50.

[200] Vanessa Martin, *The Qajar Pact. Bargaining, Protest and the State in Nineteenth Century Persia* (London: Tauris, 2005), pp. 58–61, 77–84.

[201] Ann K. S. Lambton, "The Tobacco Regie. A Prelude to Revolution," *Studia Islamica* 22 (1965), reprinted in *Qajar Persia. Eleven Studies* (Austin, TX: University of Texas Press, 1987).

frontier province of Azerbaijan.[202] Because of their proximity to the Russian and Ottoman frontiers, and their knowledge of the Turkish language, the intellectuals of Tabriz were in a key position to serve as the conduits of Western ideas. In the previous hundred years, about nine-tenths of Iranian representatives abroad came from Tabriz or other parts of Azerbaijan; so did the pioneers of the modern press in the Iranian homeland and diaspora. The printing presses originally came from Russia to Tabriz; the city was linked by telegraph to Tiflis as early as 1868, and by the end of the century it housed American, French, and Russian schools. Large numbers of active participants in the constitutional revolution were born or lived in Tabriz. In Iran, the impact was initially felt more in the economy than in intellectual life, but revolutionary ideas followed hard on the heels of the initial disturbances. Rising discontent over inflation and foreign economic penetration of Azerbaijan gained momentum when the Russo-Japanese War disrupted trade. One of the urban groups organizing the protest demanded that "The government must reverse its present policy of helping Russians at the expense of Iranian merchants, creditors and manufacturers." Hostility fueled three major urban protests, culminating in the revolution of August 1906. At the same time, a small group of Iranian émigré intellectuals operating in the migrant worker communities across the frontier in Baku began to infiltrate its social-democratic program into Iranian Azerbaijan. Russian-inspired revolutionary ideas were diluted by those of French utopian socialists, giving a peculiar caste to Iranian radicalism.[203]

The origins and complex evolution of the constitutional movement were also rooted in Anglo-Russian economic rivalry in Iran and the ascendancy of Russia in the Caucasian borderlands. In the peace treaties that ended the wars in 1813 and 1828, the Russian Empire had permitted the Shahsevan nomads limited access to their historic pasture lands across the new boundary lines. But the nomads, predictably, failed to observe the limitations. The Russian government then exploited the cross-border incidents to bully the Iranian government into abdicating authority over the nomads. Beginning with the appointment of a permanent frontier

---

[202] The following section draws heavily on a remarkable memoir by Seyyed Hassan Taqizadeh, "The Background of the Constitutional Movement in Azerbaijan," *Middle East Journal* 14(4) (Autumn 1960): 456–65, translated from the Persian and annotated by Nikki R. Keddie.

[203] Ervand Abrahamian, *Iran between Two Revolutions* (Princeton University Press, 1982), pp. 76–85; Nikki R. Keddie, "Iran Under the Later Qajars, 1848–1922," in *Cambridge History of Iran*, vol. 7, pp. 198–200; A. U. Martirosov, "Novye materialy o sotsial-demokraticheskom dvizhenii v Irane v 1905–1911 rodakh," *Narody Azii i Afriki* 2 (1973): 116–22.

commission in 1869, the viceroyalty of the Caucasus sought the most effective means to control rather than end the migration, which could lead to economic losses and an increase in raiding: "instead of a unified group of nomads, there would appear on our frontiers numerous mutually aggressive bandits, against whom it would be even more difficult for Russia to protect her frontier population."[204]

Repeated efforts to regulate the migration from both the Russian and Iranian sides could not prevent large nomadic groups from breaking through the border defenses. Repressive measures by the Russians merely led to increased banditry. By the 1890s the entire Iranian province of Azerbaijan had fallen into a state of disorder. The Russians stepped up their pressure and gained control over the appointment of important provincial officials. They increased commercial penetration of the province and established a Russo-Asiatic Bank to extend loans to the Iranian government. The British, who had long been active in seeking to balance Russian influence, promoted their own economic interests through state loans. By 1906, Iran owed a total of three times its annual budget to the two countries.[205]

A second groundswell of revolt began in 1903 when the Secret Committee, one of the first secret "national societies," met in Tabriz, followed by the formation of similar groups in Tehran. For the next two years, these two cities took the lead in demanding a constitution. The opposition to the shah brought together a number of urban groups – merchants, craftsmen, intellectuals, and religious dissenters – in an unstable coalition motivated by different concerns. The urban groups were incensed by the economic concessions to Russia, the establishment of the Russian and British banks, the new customs regulations, and the rising cost of living. They were not so much opposed to economic liberalism as they were eager to control it themselves.

Dissident elements in the ulama joined the movement for reform. They shared the antipathy to foreigners, but were influenced by secular views in their opposition to the Shi'ia elite that supported the state.[206] The defeat of Russia in the war with Japan emboldened the opposition in Iran to

---

[204] Richard Tapper, *Frontier Nomads of Iran. A Political and Social History of the Shahsevan* (Cambridge University Press, 1997), pp. 148, 191–204, 207, quotation on p. 208.

[205] Charles Issawi, *The Economic History of Iran, 1800–1914* (University of Chicago Press, 1971), p. 370.

[206] Historians disagree over the relative importance and cohesion of the ulama in the constitutional movement. Cf., for example, Lambton, *Qajar Persia*, who interprets the ulama as the "natural leaders" of popular movements against despotism and Western influence; Vanessa Martin, *Islam and Modernism. The Iranian Revolution of 1906* (Syracuse, NY: Syracuse University Press, 1989), contradicts the idea of the ulama as champions of social justice and Mangol Bayat, *Mysticism and Dissent. Socioreligious*

challenge its own government's mismanagement, corruption, and dependence on the hated enemy. The movement crested in July 1906 when the government failed to repress the crowds by force and accepted the election of an assembly, the *majles*, with the suffrage based, as in Russia, on class. It lacked a clearly identified political coloring, but it drafted legislation that became the core of the Iranian constitution until 1979.[207]

The reverse flow of radical activists to Iran also centered on Tabriz. Host to important branches of both the FEA and the Dashnak Party, Tabriz led the resistance to the coup d'état of June 1908 when the new Shah Mohammed Ali suspended the constitutional reforms of his predecessor. The provincial council (*anjoman*) of Azerbaijan summoned the other councils to revolt. The local rebels, supported by 200 Caucasian conspirators including Armenians and Georgians, seized control of the province, rallied support in the Caspian province of Gilan, marched on Tehran, and overthrew the shah, reestablishing, if only briefly, the constitutional regime.[208] Despite the international character of the constitutional movement, it proved to be difficult to create a united social democratic party even in the face of a counter-revolutionary threat.[209]

The Russians and British agreed on the desirability of maintaining the dynasty. But the Russians wanted an absolute and the British a limited monarch. As the British ambassador noted, the Russians could not allow the constitutional movement to succeed because "the chief seat of discontent" was Azerbaijan, which was, he added with a slight exaggeration, being "flooded by Russian revolutionaries."[210]

During the tumultuous years of revolution from 1907 to 1908, the sole armed force on which the shah could rely to oppose the constitutionalists continued to be his Cossack Guard. They were the spearhead of his counter coup in 1908. Led by a Russian colonel, they stormed parliament, dismissed the majles, and executed some of the leaders. The British were unhappy. Yet they were unwilling to confront the Russians, preferring to work with them and pressure the shah into making concessions. Their joint efforts could not prevent the revolutionary forces of Azerbaijan and

Thought in Qajar Iran (Syracuse, NY: Syracuse University Press, 1982), and Bayat, *Iran's First Revolution*, who assigns the main oppositionist role among the ulama to religious dissidents influenced by Western ideas.

[207] Nikki R. Keddie, *Qajar Iran and the Rise of Reza Khan, 1796–1925* (Costa Mesa, CA: Mazda, 1999), pp. 55–58, for a concise summary of these events.

[208] Chaqueri, *Origins*, pp. 166–72, 187–97.

[209] Martirosov, "Novye materialy," pp. 116–22; Chaqueri, *Origins*, pp. 114–17, 123–33.

[210] Spring Rice to Sir Edward Grey, January 30, 1907, cited in Ira Klein, "British Intervention in the Persian Revolution, 1905–1909," *Historical Journal* 15(4) (1972): 740.

the Bakhtiari tribes of the south from marching on Tehran, defeating the Cossacks, and deposing the shah. After the shah had twice failed to regain the throne by invading the country, the Russians informed him that they would no longer support him, but granted him asylum in Baku. In the meantime, they blocked the efforts of the constitutional government to reform its fiscal structure. When the majles rejected their ultimatum to dismiss the American financial advisor, W. Morgan Shuster, Russian army units occupied northern Iran and forced compliance. Then they instituted a reign of terror in Tabriz, Mashad, and Resht in reprisals against the revolutionary movement.[211]

Domestic peace was bought at the cost of foreign domination. Lacking a serious army and a vigorous central government, Iran had slipped from the ranks of an imperial power competing with its neighbors for its western and northern borderlands to a condition resembling a borderland between the Russian and British empires. The virtual partition of the country from 1907 to 1914, and especially Russian opposition to the modernization of the army, reform of the bureaucracy, and building rail-roads, severely undermined the legitimacy of the ruling dynasty.[212] Paradoxically, the success of the shah in balancing on the knife's edge by making appropriate concessions to the tribes and ulama further blocked the introduction of fundamental reforms necessary for the dynasty's survival in the twentieth century.[213]

Crisis in Qing China

The constitutional crisis in China that led to the overthrow of the dynasty in 1911 developed out of the last great reforming movement in the Qing period, which was, in turn, a reaction to the encroachment by Russia, Japan, and the Western powers on the Inner Asian borderlands and coastal frontiers. In Inner Asia, the Russian occupation of Ili from 1871

---

[211] Morgan W. Shuster, *The Strangling of Persia* (New York: Century Co., 1912); R. A. McDaniel, *The Shuster Mission and the Persian Constitutional Revolution* (Minneapolis, MI: Biblioteca Islamica, 1974); Chaqueri, *Origins*, pp. 105–9, who reprints photographs of the atrocities and the eye-witness account of the British specialist on Iran, Edward Browne, *The Reign of Terror at Tabriz. England's Responsibility (with photographs and a brief narrative of the events of December 1911 and January 1912)* (Manchester: Taylor, 1912).

[212] Rose Louise Greaves, "Some Aspects of the Anglo-Russian Convention and its Working in Persia, 1907–14 (II)," *Bulletin of the School of Oriental and African Studies* 31 (2) (1968): 290–308.

[213] Saul Bakhash, "The Evolution of the Qajar Bureaucracy, 1779–1879," *Middle East Studies* (May 1971), 139–68; C. Meredith, "Early Qajar Administration. An Analysis of its Development and Functions," *Iranian Studies* 4 (1971): 59–84; Hambly, "Fath' Ali Shah and Muhammed Shah," pp. 157–58.

to 1881 administered a rude shock to Chinese authority in Xinjiang. As a result of its defeat in the Sino-Japanese War of 1894/5, China also lost its influence in Korea. The Boxer Rebellion shook the dynasty and led to the Russian occupation of Manchuria.

While Chinese control over the Inner Asian borderlands weakened and receded, imperial power on the coastal frontiers crumbled in the face of Western and Japanese intervention. The erosion had been steady since the first Opium War in the 1840s, and reached its climax in the early years of the twentieth century. After the defeat by Japan, the scramble for concessions in the treaty ports by the European powers in 1898, and the suppression of the Boxer Rebellion by foreign troops in 1900 reinforced the conviction of the ruling elite that fundamental reforms were necessary to save the dynasty. Demands for change circulated widely among intellectuals, students, and the educated population in general. Two processes that had been gaining momentum, however irregular and interrupted, over the previous half century began to coalesce. The first, the "self-strengthening movement," promoted reform from above guided by eclectic interpretations of Confucianism and carried out by scholar-officials at the imperial court. The second, was a complex mix of uncoordinated anti-foreign and proto-nationalist feelings expressed in periodic outbursts of urban violence, combined with admiration for the achievements of Japan in resisting foreign domination by adopting foreign models of political and economic change. Although they differed on details, the reformers generally sought to preserve the dynasty, their own status, and interests. Their aim in introducing constitutional forms was to concentrate power by extending the authority of the central government deeper into the regional and district levels, building railroads, and creating a modern army.

The spurt in railroad construction at the end of the nineteenth century illustrates how the "self-strengthening movement" was obliged to rely on external aid in order to advance its centralizing aims.[214] In China, the advocates of building railroads among the ruling elites did not initially perceive them as a challenge to the Confucian world view. As in other multicultural states of Eurasia, the practical advantages of building railroads in the struggle over the borderlands emerged after a critical moment in defense of the frontiers. In 1881, following the Russian withdrawal from Xinjiang, the Chinese statesman, Li Hongzhang, expressed his concern that it would be impossible to defend the borderland against future Russian encroachment without linking it to the center by a railroad. He

---

[214] The following is based mainly on Ralph William Huenemann, *The Dragon and the Iron Horse. The Economics of Railroads in China, 1876–1931* (Cambridge, MA: Harvard University Press, 1984), pp. 43–44, 59–65, 70 ff.

continued to champion the construction of railroads and telegraph lines after the Sino-French War in 1884/5 as a means of improving communications on the coastal frontier. Bureaucratic resistance based on fears that railroads would facilitate invasion from abroad delayed an ambitious construction program. During the scramble for concessions, foreign companies were granted rights that clearly served their own economic interests rather than the development of China. Local attacks on railroads in 1899–1900 were part of the anti-foreign reaction of those years. After the Boxer Rebellion, public sentiment reversed itself and demanded that the government construct national, Chinese lines. Local initiatives led to the formation of the Railroad Rights Movement backed by local gentry and wealthy merchants, who also favored a constitutional monarchy. When the government decided to nationalize railroads in 1911 and borrow money from a British-American banking consortium to build new lines, local protest movements again targeted foreigners and government officials. Officers of the New Army joined the chorus of opposition. The Qing faced the classical dilemma of the Iranian and Ottoman empires. In seeking to emulate Western achievements, they became indebted to foreign interests financially and politically, thus triggering strong responses from nationalist-patriotic elements in the population, many of whom also sought reform by relying on their own resources.

The educational reforms that sought to provide China with new leaders trained outside the Confucian classical tradition generated the main source of opposition from below. The impact of the Russian Revolution of 1905 on Chinese intellectuals illustrates the role of transfer in their entangled histories. In the early twentieth century, information on the Russian revolutionary movement was beginning to filter into China, often through the intermediary of Japan. Young intellectuals were particularly attracted by the exploits of Sofia Perovskaia, a member of the People's Will and part of the assassination squad that killed Emperor Alexander II. They were thrilled by the news of an Asian state, Japan, defeating the Russians who had long encroached on the Inner Asian borderlands. They absorbed these sentiments into a more generalized exaltation of revolution, seeking inspiration from other traditions as well.[215]

Repeated attempts to establish modern military schools during the early phases of the self-strengthening movement had been only partially successful. Following the Boxer Rebellion, provincial military schools proliferated, numbering seventy by 1910. They formed a new elite of narrowly

---

[215] Don C. Price, *Russia and the Roots of the Chinese Revolutions 1896–1911* (Cambridge, MA: Harvard University Press, 1974); Jonathan D. Spence, *The Gate of Heavenly Peace* (New York: Viking Press, 1981), pp. 76–87.

trained specialists who were nevertheless exposed to Western ideas. Reacting to China's military weakness, they directed their nationalist-patriotic anger not only at the foreigners, but also at the "foreign" Manchu dynasty.[216] Radical anti-Manchu opposition was fragmented. It drew support from students enrolled in the new schools in China and those returning from education abroad, disaffected literati influenced by Western revolutionary ideas, and officers in the New Army. Massing behind them was a reservoir of malcontents, ranging from poor peasants to a floating urban population of artisans and itinerants. They had served in the past as the rank-and-file of rebellions against the dynasty. The final crisis of Qing rule can be viewed as an interaction of the new generation of reforming elites and an inchoate mass of discontented social groups.

The key to understanding the collapse of the Qing dynasty and the end of imperial rule in China lies with the unintended consequences of the army reform. Since coming to power in the seventeenth century the Manchus had relied on the army to maintain their control over the much larger Han population. The Qing land forces had been divided into three formations: the Eight Banners, the traditional organization of the Manchus; the Green Standard, which was more like a constabulary than a regular army; and the much smaller Huai (Beiyang) divisions. The latter had been created in the 1870s under the auspices of Li Hongzhang as part of the self-strengthening movement. Equipped with modern weapons and relatively well trained, they had been the most effective fighters against the Japanese. But they numbered only 25,000–30,000 men. Outnumbered in one of the key battles against the Japanese, they had been badly mauled. The main shortcomings of the bulk of the armed forces were lax discipline, poor training, and the lack of a professional officer corps.[217]

In revitalizing the dormant self-strengthening movement, in 1901 the ruling elites introduced a series of fundamental changes in the recruitment and training of what after 1904 came to be called the New Army.[218]

[216] Stephen R. MacKinnon, *Power and Politics in Late Imperial China. Yuan Shikai in Beijing and Tianyin, 1901–1908* (Berkeley, CA: University of California Press, 1980), pp. 132–38.

[217] Allen Fong, "Testing the Self-Strengthening. The Chinese Army in the Sino-Japanese War," *Modern Asian Studies* 30(4) (October 1996): 1007–31. The navy suffered from similar problems, see Bruce A. Elleman, "Naval Warfare and the Refraction of China's Self-Strengthening Reforms into Scientific and Technological Failure," *Modern Asian Studies* 38(2) (2003): 283–326.

[218] MacKinnon, *Power and Politics*, ch. 4. For the civil reforms, see Richard S. Horowitz, "Breaking the Bonds of Precedent. The 1905–6 Government Reform Commission and the Remaking of the Qing Central State," *Modern Asian Studies* 37(4) (October 1993): 775–97.

Based on the Beiyang model, the New Army reform introduced for the first time the concept of universal military service. In theory, then, it was only a matter of time before the Manchu dynasty would rest upon the loyalty of an army representing the Han people. Recognizing the danger, the government created a division of Manchu Imperial Guards. But they also allowed Han Chinese to serve in the division, diluting the ethnic homogeneity of the elite unit. They established a special school for sons of high officials and attempted to control senior military appointments. Their fears were real, but their precautions were inadequate.[219]

The army reforms also sought to elevate the common soldier from his low social status by increasing his pay, creating pensions, and limiting service to three years. Officers were to be selected by examinations designed to judge military skills rather than the ability to master the Chinese classics. The government also undertook a program to create an indigenous armaments industry that would produce uniform weaponry. New military academies were established to introduce modern training by foreign, often Japanese, instructors. Promising officer candidates were to be sent abroad for training. The returning officers turned out to be the most receptive to anti-dynastic, nationalist agitation by radical exiles. They, together with graduates of the military schools, were by virtue of their training the most well informed on the vulnerability of China to foreign domination.[220]

The revolution of 1911 that overthrew the Qing dynasty was touched off by a mutiny of elite Han elements of the New Army that had been heavily infiltrated by radical students who served as junior officers. The revolt spread quickly, fed by the powerful currents of national-patriotic sentiments among the youth, literati, and above all the army officers. The key unit in the uprising that overthrew the dynasty in 1911 was recruited and stationed in Hubei Province. It was distinctive in three ways, according to Joseph Esherick: "the size and level of literacy of its New Army, the concentration of that army in a major treaty port and the inability of the provincial school system to absorb all the partially educated and potentially revolutionary youth of the province." In addition, all of its officer corps had either studied abroad or had graduated from the military schools.[221] They were members of anti-Manchu, that is, Han nationalist study groups and literary societies which regarded the Manchu as being as

---

[219] Jonathan Spence, *The Search for Modern China*, 2nd edn (New York: W. W. Norton, 1999), pp. 253–55, 258–63; Bruce A. Elleman, *Modern Chinese Warfare, 1795–1989* (London: Routledge, 2001), pp. 138–45.

[220] MacKinnon, *Power and Politics*, pp. 134–35.

[221] Joseph W. Esherick, *Reform and Revolution in China* (Berkeley, CA: University of California Press, 1976).

foreign as the Japanese or British. Although the disaffected Hubei unit rallied only a small number of troops, no more than 2,000, it was able to seize a modern arsenal and defeat a larger Manchu force sent to repress them. This represented the first time in over fifty years that a Han Chinese military force had defeated troops loyal to the dynasty. The rebellion, led by officers trained in Japan, spread rapidly throughout the country where it assumed more and more the character of a national uprising against a foreign dynasty. Within a year, the forces loyal to the Qing had been defeated in the field. The senior commanders of the Beiyang army urged the court to form a republic. In its final edict, the Qing dynasty abdicated its authority and turned over the government to Yuan Shikai, a former powerful provincial governor and one of the organizers of the Beiyang army. The provisional vice-president of the newly proclaimed republic in 1912, Li Yuanhong, was one of the leaders of the Hubei rising who had helped to spread the rebellion by urging the Han Chinese to overthrow the dynasty before it could consolidate its power by carrying out its centralizing policies.

As president, Yuan Shikai harbored ambitions of founding a new dynasty. He began to re-institute Confucian rituals as a prelude to declaring it China's state religion. He attempted to build his power base on China's traditional elites, the bureaucracy, and the big landlords in the provinces, as well as units of the New Army which he staffed with generals loyal to him. In a series of administrative reforms, he centralized political power in his own hands. He curtailed the authority of regional military commanders, dismissed the parliament, and abolished the cabinet system. However, he failed to reconcile the conflicting political interests in China, polarized between the ardent republican forces and the monarchist groups hoping for a restoration of the Qing dynasty. More damaging to his cause, he sought foreign support for his dynastic ambitions. In 1915, he accepted Japan's Twenty-One Demands, which extracted far-reaching economic concessions for the Japanese in Manchuria and Inner Mongolia as well as other regions. The Japanese used his capitulation to extract further agreements. In return for a series of large railroad loans, they merged the Korean and South Manchurian lines and constructed five other lines that gave them undisputed control over the strategic lines in Manchuria, Mongolia, and Shantung Province.[222] Regional commanders of the Beiyang seized the opportunity provided by a nationwide protest to oppose him openly. When he died suddenly in 1916, they struggled for

[222] His-ping Shao, "Sino-Japanese Military Agreements, 1915–18," in Alvin D. Coox and Hilary Conroy, *China and Japan. A Search for Balance since World War II* (Santa Barbara, CA: ABC-Clio), pp. 39, 47–49.

supremacy over the old centers of imperial power, plunging the country into forty years of civil war.

One of the younger officers, Chiang Kai-shek, had studied in Japanese military schools from 1908 to 1911. Sun Yat-sen had sent him to Russia in 1923 to study the Soviet military system and then appointed him head of the Whampoa Military Academy "to create a new revolutionary army for the salvation of China."[223] This placed him in a strong position in the struggle for control over the Kuomintang after Sun's death. He used it to seize power in a coup in 1926 and consolidated his authority in the south. The Kuomintang was little more than a facade for his personal power based on the military: "the Republic of China's true foundation was the military, and the unification of China [under Chiang] was merely a temporary alliance of warlords."[224] In China, like the Ottoman and Qajar empires, the reforms leading to the creation of a modern, mass army and advanced military technology aimed at strengthening the dynasty against external enemies ended up accelerating the demise of imperial rule.

The immediate effect of the Chinese revolution on the Inner Asian borderlands was to throw into reverse the Qing drive to reassert central-ized control and to initiate movements for autonomy. When the Russians evacuated the Ili valley in 1881, the Qing took the first step away from their eighteenth-century policies that permitted cultural divergence in the bor-derlands. They incorporated Xinjiang as a Chinese province and began to Sinicize it. This meant staffing its administration with Han personnel, encouraging Chinese immigration, and seeking to assimilate part of the Uighur population through Confucian education. The resettlement pro-gram failed for lack of sufficient resources.[225]

In the northeast (Manchuria), the announcement in 1901 of sweeping reforms in every aspect of government, the so-called New Administration, signaled a new campaign to revise the Qing borderland policies by offi-cially opening the region to colonization. Official policy already lagged behind the spontaneous movement of settlers pouring into Manchuria. By the end of the dynasty, the great rush of Chinese settlers had reached a peak. The population of the northeast provinces soared from 12 million in 1894 to more than 18 million in 1912. The Mongol pastoralists were being crowded to the west of the Willow Palisades by the encroachment of

---

[223] F. F. Liu, *A Military History of Modern China, 1924–1949* (Princeton University Press, 1956), p. 8.
[224] Elleman, *Modern Chinese Warfare*, p. 145.
[225] James A. Millward and Nabigan Tursun, "Political History and Strategies of Control, 1884–1978," in S. Frederick Starr (ed.), *Xinjiang. China's Muslim Borderland* (Armonk, NY: M. E. Sharpe, 2004), pp. 63–67.

Chinese agriculturalists into the grasslands. The government also increased the number of Chinese soldiers in the frontier forces who were first introduced into Manchuria in the 1880s. By this time almost the entire population of the northeast spoke Chinese except for the Mongols to the west and the Tungus-speaking population on the Amur frontier.[226]

In Mongolia, as in Manchuria, up to the mid-nineteenth century Qing policies had been aimed at preserving the old martial traditions and nomadic way of life against the "bad Chinese customs." For the dynasty it was vital that the Mongol banners should continue to serve as a military reserve as they had during the repression of the Taiping Rebellion. In the same spirit, the Qing also protected and encouraged the spread of Lama Buddhism in Tibet and Mongolia at the same time that they cut off contacts between Lhasa and the Oirats living outside their boundaries. Their aims were, first, to prevent a regional cultural center from developing that was not under their direct control; second, to erect a cultural screen between the Han and Mongol peoples; and, third, to assure peace, stability, and loyalty among the Mongols under imperial rule by separating power and landed wealth between the church and the princes.[227]

Despite the constant flow of court ordinances discouraging or prohibiting cultural contact between Mongols and Han Chinese, the process of Sinicization proceeded at an accelerating rate, especially in Inner Mongolia. The Mongol nobility had been progressively co-opted into the Qing aristocracy through intermarriage, service in the capital, and the need to appoint Chinese-speaking Mongol officials in the frontier provinces. Mongol nobles seeking to emulate the luxurious life of their Sinicized Manchu counterparts raised taxes and opened grazing lands to Chinese settlers. They sold land illegally and took out high interest loans from Chinese merchants and bankers. The rise in Chinese immigration into southern Mongolia had already commenced in the mid-nineteenth century during the internal rebellions that rocked the central provinces. By the end of the century the Mongol nobility were paying for the costs of their ostentatious lifestyle by opening the flood gates to Chinese immigration.

The Manchu religious policy added fuel to the smoldering discontent. Beijing promoted the development of two Buddhist religious centers in Inner and Outer Mongolia, and encouraged the growth of monasteries through land grants. An unholy triune alliance among banner princes,

---

[226] Robert H. G. Lee, *The Manchurian Frontier in Ch'ing History* (Cambridge University Press, 1970), p. 79 and ch. 5 *passim*.
[227] Owen Lattimore, "Frontier Feudalism," in *Studies in Frontier History. Collected Papers* (London: Oxford University Press, 1962), p. 527.

monasteries, and Han merchants sapped the vitality of the semi-nomadic society and further impoverished the population.[228] Mongol fears that the influx of Chinese immigrants now threatened their entire way of life mounted. Still, the number of colonists in Outer Mongolia remained small compared with the south, where by 1919 Han immigrants made up over 88 percent of the population in four main districts of Inner Mongolia.[229]

Conflicts over land use, the tax burden, and Chinese settlements spurred resistance. Beginning in the mid-nineteenth century with the rise of "Mongol banditry," anti-Chinese violence intensified. A series of major uprisings erupted in the early twentieth century, concentrated in areas where overlords were the most highly Sinicized. The largest of these began in eastern Inner Mongolia in 1908, and within three years had spread to four banners.[230] The announcement by the Qing government in the wake of the Russo-Japanese War that it intended to apply the reforms of the New Administration to Mongolia clearly foreshadowed a determined policy of Sinicization. These steps fit into the general pattern of Qing policies to reestablish their hold over the borderlands. Qing officials began to reorganize the school system and the military. Plans to extend the railroad network aimed to bind Mongolia closer to China and to check the drift of Mongolia into the Russian sphere. Khalka princes denounced the New Administration for offering nothing which benefited the Mongols. In the summer of 1911 an influential group secretly sought Russian aid in St. Petersburg, although their plans remain a matter of dispute to this day. Surprised at first, the tsarist government was uncertain how to react. Economically, Mongolia had little to offer Russia, but the great strategic significance of its long frontier proved to be decisive. For the next three years the Russians vigorously supported "the desire of the Mongols to maintain their autonomy through diplomatic channels without severing their relations to their lord, the Great Qing Emperor."[231] The Russians then pressed Beijing to restore the status quo. When the Qing dynasty collapsed in 1911, the Khalka Mongols proclaimed their

[228] Joseph Fletcher, "The Heyday of the Ch'ing Order in Mongolia, Sinkiang and Tibet," in *Cambridge History of China*, vol. 10, pp. 352–57.

[229] Mei-hua Lan, "China's 'New Administration,'" in Stephen Kotkin and Bruce A. Elleman (eds.), *Mongolia in the Twentieth Century. Landlocked Cosmopolitan* (Armonk, NY: M. E. Sharpe, 1999), p. 44.

[230] Sechin Jagchid, "The Sinicization of the Mongolian Ruling Class in the Late Manchu-Ch'ing Period," in *Essays in Mongolian Studies* (Provo, UT: David M. Kennedy Center for International Studies, Brigham Young University, 1988), pp. 190–203.

[231] Nakami Tatsuo, "Russian Diplomats and Mongol Independence, 1912–1915," quoting Foreign Ministry archives, in Kotkin and Elleman (eds.), *Mongolia in the Twentieth Century*, p. 74.

independence, hoping to rally the Inner Mongolians and establish a Great
Mongol state composed of Outer and Inner Mongolia plus the Barge
region (Hurunui) of western Manchuria. Paradoxically, then, the spontaneous process of Sinicization, long opposed by the Qing, engendered a
national Mongol resistance that matured into an independence movement on the eve of the Qing collapse.[232]

The end of imperial rule cleared the way for the establishment of an
independent Great Mongol state in the form of a theocratic monarchy
headed by the Bog Khan, or Holy Ruler, with a facade of bureaucratic
institutions resembling those of the defunct Qing. For the next several
years, the Mongols appealed for recognition from the Russian Empire and
the new republican government in Beijing, but the two rival powers had
their own agendas. After the Russians had agreed with the Japanese in
1912 to divide Mongolia into spheres of influence, they promoted the idea
of an autonomous Outer Mongolia under their control. This mirrored
their policies in northern Iran and Xinjiang. They even attempted to
create a Mongol Brigade on the model of the Cossack Brigade in Iran.
By contrast, the Chinese sought to limit Mongol autonomy, but were
hamstrung by Japanese pressure to accede to the Twenty-One Demands.

In the tripartite negotiations at Kwacha in 1915, the Russians won most of
the points. The Chinese always viewed Mongolia as part of the Middle
Kingdom, an integral part of the empire, while the Mongols never accepted
this view, but perceived themselves in a different, frontier relationship, as an
"outer vassal" (*Waifan-bu*). The Russians sought to mediate between the
two by translating these terms into Western concepts, shifting the definition
of China's legal status from "sovereignty" to "suzerainty" during the negotiations. The Russians opposed unification of the Mongols in order to avoid
a clash with Japan whose interests in Inner Mongolia it had recognized in
1912.[233] Outer Mongolia would remain a buffer state under Chinese sovereignty, with its autonomy guaranteed by agreements forbidding the
Chinese from dispatching troops, colonists, or administrators into the province. Russia was then free to obtain special economic fights in separate
negotiations with the Mongols. Only the outbreak of the Russian
Revolution prevented them from cashing in their chips.[234]

[232] Thomas E. Ewing, "Ch'ing Policies in Outer Mongolia, 1900–1911," *Modern Asian Studies* 14(1) (1980): 145–57.
[233] Nakami Tatsuo, "A Protest against the Concept of the 'Middle Kingdom.' The Mongols and the 1911 Revolution," in Eto Sinkichi and Harold Z. Schiffrin (eds.), *The 1911 Revolution in China. Interpretive Essays* (University of Tokyo Press, 1984), pp. 129–49.
[234] Thomas E. Ewing, "Russia, China and the Origins of the Mongolian People's Republic, 1911–1921. A Reappraisal," *Slavonic and East European Review* 58(3) (July 1980): 401–7.

The Chinese were more successful in holding on to Inner Mongolia. The republic had been founded on the principle of equality among the five races: the Han (Chinese) and the four peoples of the borderlands, the Manchus, Mongols, Muslims, and Tibetans. But rival governments, in the north under Yuan Shikai and in the south under Sun Yat-sen, could not agree on how to implement it. Yuan Shikai hoped to win back the allegiance of the Khalka Mongols by confirming the power of the local Mongol princes. To gain approval he appointed as general director of the Mongolian–Tibetan Ministry, Prince Gungsangnorbu, a leader of a reform movement influenced by the Meiji restoration in Japan and fore-warned by the failure of the Hundred Days of Reform in China. However, the prince admired Sun Yat-sen and joined the Kuomintang, instituting reforms with the help of young intellectuals trained in Japan. His modest initiatives antagonized the conservative nobles without winning over his more democratically minded supporters.

When Yuan Shikai died in 1916, civil war broke out in north China, threatening to spill over into Inner Mongolia. The Japanese expressed concern over the breakdown of public order in their sphere of eastern Inner Mongolia, arousing fears among the intellectuals that this was the prelude to intervention. The elites were torn between the advocates of the government in Beijing, who wished to preserve the traditional power of the princes, and the democratic regime of the Kuomintang in the south, which promised autonomy; there were only a few enthusiasts for a pan-Mongol unification with Outer Mongolia.[235] Owen Lattimore attributed the failure of Mongol unity to the opposition of the Inner Mongolian princes with their strong economic ties to China, who feared they would be overshadowed by their counterparts in Outer Mongolia and believed that they could secure their power from a weak republican government in Beijing. An even more powerful deterrent was the opposition of the Russians and Japanese.[236]

A third part of the Mongol peoples had been incorporated into the Russian Empire in 1689 by the Treaty of Nerchinsk with China. The Russian attempts to integrate them began with the simple expedient of affixing the name Buryats, a little-known ethnonym, to the great variety of clans which considered themselves part of the original yurt of Chingghis Khan. Some were indigenous to the Trans-Baikal region; others had

[235] Sechin Jagchid, "The Inner Mongolian Kuomintang of the 1920s," in *Essays*, pp. 262–68.

[236] Owen Lattimore, *The Mongols of Manchuria* (New York: n.p., 1934). See also Robert B. Valliant, "Inner Mongolia, 1912. The Failure of Independence," in *Essays in Mongolian Studies* (Provo, UT: David M. Kennedy Center for International Studies, Brigham Young University, 1988), pp. 56–92.

migrated from Manchu territory. They called their region the "back country," to suggest that it was a reservoir of Mongol strength in difficult times or, as one Russian official put it, a kind of "Zaporozhian Sich." Colonization had a drastic effect on the Mongol way of life. Despite the edicts of Peter to safeguard their ancestral lands, Russian colonists gradually occupied large swaths of rich grazing lands in another episode in the ecological struggle over the borderlands.[237] Yet there were also signs of intercultural contact and economic cooperation between the Russians and Mongols, which had their parallel in Inner Mongolia between the Chinese and Mongols. If Inner Mongolia was heavily Sinicized, Buryat Mongolia was equally Russified. When the Russian and Chinese empires collapsed, the two most integrated parts of the Mongol people remained in their respective successor states rather than joining in the movement for Mongol unity.

Parallel to its policies in Mongolia, the Qing government reorganized the military forces in Manchuria with the aim of Sinicizing the officer corps and reducing the banner troops. After the Russo-Japanese War a more ambitious plan was launched to end the frontier character of the entire northeast, break the power of the bannermen, consolidate the three provinces under a single governor general, introduce local elections, and encourage colonization. The reformers inserted a note of urgency into their proposals, fearing that unless China tightened its hold on the region the Russians and Japanese would be certain to extend their control. The reorganization was barely under way when the revolution of 1911 broke out.[238] After the death of Yuan Shikai, local army officers took over the administration of Manchuria, and for the next twenty-five years this borderland was only tenuously attached to China.

Conclusion and comparisons

In the two prewar decades the struggle over the Eurasian borderlands reached a new peak of intensity culminating in the outbreak of the First World War and the collapse of the Eurasian empires. During this period, three historical processes, long under way, reached crisis proportions. First, the calculus of imperial rivalries changed dramatically. Internal weakness in the Ottoman, Qajar, and Qing empires invited increased foreign intervention in their borderlands not only by old rivals (the Habsburgs in the Ottoman Empire and the Russians in all three), but

---

[237] Irina S. Urbanova, "The Fate of Baikal Asia within Russia," *Anthropology and Archeology of Eurasia* (Summer 1994): 62–78.
[238] Lee, *The Manchurian Frontier*, pp. 174–78.

also by the Western colonial powers, especially France and Britain, in the form of indirect imperialism. Second, under the pressure of foreign intervention and the outbreak of violent domestic opposition to imperial rule in the borderlands, the ruling elites embarked on a new series of reforms that were shot through with contradictions, leading to fateful unintended consequences. Third, internal resistance to imperial rule in the borderlands drew inspiration from two major ideologies, socialism and nationalism, that proved to be irreconcilable in addressing the problem of governing multicultural societies.

The intervention of the Great Powers in the governance of the Ottoman, Qajar, and Qing borderlands ranged from agreements over spheres of influence (Habsburg–Russian in 1897, Anglo-Russian in Iran in 1907, and Russian–Japanese in 1909 and 1912) to domination over external trade, banking, financial practices, and railroad construction. Politically, intervention took the forms of detaching borderlands, whether by annexation (Bosnia) or fostering autonomy (Outer Mongolia), bringing pressure for reform (the Armenian question), or encouraging the formation of client state alliances (Balkan League). Although the Habsburg Monarchy and the Russian Empire were also shaken by crises in their borderlands, they survived them, if only briefly, without surrendering their sovereignty but at the cost of leading the world into war.

Responding to crises, divided councils among the ruling elites of the multinational empires led to inconsistent policies, ranging from constitutional reform and concessions in the borderlands to repression of oppositionist movements. At the same time, ruling elites attempted to reconcile nationalizing ideas with the symbols, ceremonies, and political theologies of a patriarchal dynastic order. Under these conditions reforms were bound to have a dialectical result. The reformist thesis generated a revolutionary antithesis, bearing the seeds of its own destruction into a new synthesis. The greater the efforts to reform selective institutions such as elective bodies and cultural practices such as toleration, the more alienated the traditional religious or socially privileged elites became, and the deeper the resistance to imperial rule penetrated the new elites generated by the reforms.

Those most affected by the changes reacted most strongly against expectations. Among the professional officer corps, groups formed in the Ottoman, Iranian, and Chinese imperial armies around the idea that they could rule more efficiently and effectively than the ruling elites. In the borderlands of all the multicultural states, a growing number of intellectuals, reinforced by students and graduates of newly established secular schools and universities, eagerly sought alternative models of change under the banners of socialism, nationalism, and democracy. The socialists wrestled with two interrelated questions: the critique of imperialism, which explored the causes of international rivalry; and the national question, which dealt with conflicts within a body politic. Their theoretical debates, which have long since lost their passionate character and immediacy, but perhaps not their relevance, took place within a highly diverse socialist community, within rather than between parties constituting the Second International. The second question centered on the relationship between the conflicting ideals of a universalist and a particularistic ideology, socialism, and nationalism both preaching liberation from different forms of exploitation, yet each in its purest form demanding total allegiance. They were obliged not only to engage one another, but also to confront the new tendencies among the ruling elites seeking to nationalize imperial rule, that is, to impose the language and cultural practices of the dominant nation upon the peoples of their multicultural state.

The political right reacted to the same questions that excited the socialists by endorsing a nationalizing trend in imperial rule through Russification, Germanization, Magyarization, Turkification, and Sinicization. The multiple sources of conflict produced by proponents of these alternative ways of reorganizing and sometimes transforming their societies were not imprinted on a *tabula rasa*. Rather, they were layered on the vestiges of earlier political and sociocultural processes, the legacy of restless borderlands, contested frontiers, and imperial rivalries. By the early twentieth century the borderlands had evolved into geocultural sites where proponents of incompatible ideologies and political movements – ethnic nationalism, agrarian populism, and industrial socialism – interacted, producing an explosive combination and threatening imperial rule with paralysis, rebellion, and foreign war.

6   Imperial legacies

The wars and revolutions of the first two decades of the twentieth century that destroyed imperial rule have long been treated by historians as a series of ruptures in modern European history. Borderlands broke away from the imperial centers of power. Some followed the siren calls of national self-determination; elsewhere local warlords took regional control. The dynastic idea was dead or dying. The logic and structures of long-established internal markets and networks of transportation and communication were disrupted. The imperial armies disintegrated and their officer corps dispersed; in many cases former comrades-in-arms faced one another across disputed borders. New men, often from the margins of society or the military, rose to power, promoting new ideologies, or radical versions of the old. In the immediate postwar years, the peoples of the borderlands appeared to have taken their revenge for decades or centuries of imperial rule.

Placing too much emphasis on rupture, however, means running the risk of underestimating the legacies of imperial rule and ignoring the persistent factors that confronted the new ruling elites of the successor states. In this chapter historical legacy is employed to mean those elements of institutional, ideological, and cultural structures and practices that survived the demise of imperial rule. They show up most clearly in the nature of leadership and patterns of policy making, as well as in the policies themselves. Legacy in historical context is different from its legalistic meaning as something bequeathed to a successor without manifesting any alteration in its essential features. Historical change being what it is, legacy cannot be the literal equivalent of sameness. Burdened with legacies of imperial rule, the successors could not inscribe their solutions to the problems posed by persistent factors on a clean slate.

The violent passage through war, civil war, and revolution from imperial to post-imperial rule complicates the task of determining what was preserved from imperial rule and what was destroyed. Although many of the imperial officials were driven from power or resigned, others remained in place under new management. Officers of the imperial armies retained their commands under new flags. All the successor regimes valued and rewarded expertise. Parliamentary forms and electoral practices were adopted to new circumstances, but often continued, as in the past, to mask real authoritarian power structures. Armed with these instruments of imperial rule, the new elites faced problems similar to those that had confounded their predecessors.

First, the Eurasian successor states were all multinational except for Austria and Hungary where, however, Jews and Roma were perceived as culturally distinctive, if not alien. Second, the new states were saddled with borderlands of their own that were also located, as under imperial rule, on the peripheries of the centers of power. Third, the borderlands were often inhabited by mixed populations, reshuffled by a new turn of the demographic kaleidoscope. Fourth, the external and internal administrative borders of the successor states were arbitrarily drawn – like those of the empires, almost everywhere as a result of military action – cutting through communities of the same ethnicity, exciting new irredentist claims based on historicist and national grounds. Fifth, this meant that ethnic politics invaded every aspect of cultural policy, especially education.

When the new elites grappled with the problems posed by these persistent factors, their responses often corresponded closely to those of their imperial predecessors. In designing political and social solutions, they too resorted to assimilation, resettlement, or expulsion. The responses of the minorities also replicated those of the subjugated peoples under imperial rule, running the gamut from resistance to accommodation.

Although the successor states were in many ways miniature versions of their imperial predecessors, they exhibited important differences. While remaining multinational, they were ruled by representatives of single dominant ethnic groups. They demanded from the minorities a more all-encompassing allegiance to *the nation* – as they defined it – than did the nationalizing policies of the imperial elites, which were either more flexible or more inconsistent. Moreover, in the vast power realignment engendered by the dissolution of empires, regions that had once constituted a large multinational state had themselves been transformed into borderlands. The forced population movements that accompanied the dissolution of the Habsburg, Ottoman, and Russian empires gave a violent twist to the kaleidoscope of peoples, producing new contested shatter zones. Like the regional parcels of Qing China controlled by warlords, the new borderlands of west Eurasia were vulnerable, exposed to external threats from centers of greater power on their flanks.

Mass population movements

The population mix in the borderlands under imperial rule was stirred ever more violently in the decade between 1914 and 1923. Wars on the Eurasian frontiers had always generated refugees, but the demographic dislocation in the first three years of the First World War was unprecedented. In the great arc of complex frontiers from the Baltic littoral through the Pontic, Danubian, and south Caucasian frontiers, the outbreak of war was followed by mass flight and forced resettlement of peoples on both sides of the military front. By 1917, in the Russian Empire alone an estimated 6 million people were refugees, and the overwhelming number of these had fled or been forced out of their homes in the borderlands.[1] In the Baltic provinces the fighting spurred the flight of an estimated 200,000 Jews and 500,000 Latvians, including half the population of Riga. The Belorussian provinces were swamped with 250,000 refugees. Farther south, by the end of 1915 over 400,000 refugees, mainly Ukrainians, were on the move to the east. Even before the great German offensive of 1915, an estimated 600,000 Jews had been displaced from the Pale of Settlement and over 200,000 people of German origin had been uprooted and sent east. In 1914, on the other side of the Austro-Russian frontier, Ukrainian activists in Galicia fled to Vienna to escape the advancing Russian armies. Tens of thousands of Ruthenians were arrested and sent to internment camps. On the Russian side, this demographic disaster was sparked by suspicions rooted in the previous decades of the struggle over the borderlands. In the words of Peter Gatrell, the deportation of Germans, who had lived for generations in Ukraine and on the Volga, "was a brutal foretaste of the horrors inflicted upon the next generation under the Stalin regime."[2]

Panic had induced some to flee, but the major cause of what was primarily a forced resettlement was the policy pursued by the Russian High Command and local officials. They perceived the non-Russian peoples of the borderlands, particularly Jews and Germans, as security risks. Over the previous several decades, anti-Semitism had grown exponentially, fueled by organizations like the Black Hundreds and a chauvinistic mass press.[3] Germanophobia had deep roots in pan-Slav antipathy toward the "Baltic barons" and their privileges. In the later years of the

---

[1] Peter Gatrell, *A Whole Empire Walking. Refugees in Russia during World War I* (Bloomington, IN: Indiana University Press, 1999), p. 3.

[2] Gatrell, *A Whole Empire Walking*, pp. 22–25, quotation on p. 24.

[3] On Russian anti-Semitism, see Hans Rogger, *Jewish Policies and Right Wing Politics in Imperial Russia* (Basingstoke: Palgrave Macmillan, 1986); John D. Klier and Shlomo Lambroza (eds.), *Pogroms. Anti-Jewish Violence in Modern Russian History* (Cambridge University Press, 1992).

empire, attacks denounced the influence of German entrepreneurs and technical specialists in Russia's growing industrial sector. In the 1890s, the radical shift in Russian foreign policy, breaking with its long association with Prussia-Germany and embracing France, reinforced these trends. Germany's unflagging support for Austria in the Balkan borderlands fostered the belief that Germany would be the enemy in the next war, despite occasional attempts by Nicholas II to mitigate it.[4] Spy mania infected the Russian High Command.[5]

On the eve of the war, nationalizing agitation in the Habsburg and Ottoman empires also focused on the potential disloyalty of alien peoples inhabiting their strategically important borderlands. As in Russia, the growth of intelligence services before the war and the discovery of real or the invention of imaginary spy networks fed into the fears over breaches in security on the frontiers inhabited by minorities. The Habsburg military leadership was obsessed with the belief that the Ruthenian civilian population in western Galicia cultivated subversive links with the enemy. Austrian spy mania focused on the Ruthenian Russophiles who, ironically, had been supported in the last decades of the Monarchy by Polish viceroys as a counterweight to the Ukrainian national movement. A cross-border political-philanthropic association was uncovered which advocated subversive activities directed against the Habsburg government in the event of a war with Russia. On the eve of the war, two public trials of hundreds of Russophiles had been mounted. When hostilities broke out, the High Command ordered the evacuation of thousands of Ruthenians and their resettlement in the interior provinces.[6] The Austrian High Command was also worried about the loyalty of Italians. When Italy entered the war against the Central Powers, the Austrians evacuated 75,000 civilians of Italian background from the South Tyrol frontier and interned them.[7]

---

[4] Eric Lohr, *Nationalizing the Russian Empire. The Campaign against Enemy Aliens during World War I* (Cambridge, MA: Harvard University Press, 2003), illuminates the genuinely mass character of the nationalist "riots" against German residents and their property in the empire in the early phases of the war. To be sure, Germanophobia ultimately turned against the imperial family as well.

[5] For insights into the spy mania in Russia, see Willliam C. Fuller, Jr., *The Foe Within. Fantasies of Treason and the End of Imperial Russia* (Ithaca, NY: Cornell University Press, 2006), esp. ch. 6.

[6] Mark von Hagen, *War in a European Borderland. Occupations and Occupation Plans in Galicia and Ukraine, 1914–1918* (Seattle, WA: University of Washington Press, 2007), pp. 6–7.

[7] Mark Cornwall, "Morale and Patriotism in the Austro-Hungarian Army," in John Horne (ed.), *State, Society and Mobilization in Europe During the First World War* (Cambridge University Press, 1997), p. 176; David Rechter, "Galicia in Vienna. Jewish Refugees in the First World War," *Austrian History Yearbook* 28 (1997): 113–30.

The Young Turks were convinced that the Armenian community represented a major security risk. Divided like the Poles between enemy empires, Armenians volunteered for both the Ottoman and Russian armies despite the aggressive nationalizing policies of both governments. In 1915, Russia's crushing defeat of the Ottoman armies on the Anatolian front set off a massive flight of Armenians to Russian-occupied territory and a savage Turkish reaction. The Young Turk leaders ordered large-scale deportations which ended in the massacre and related deaths from starvation and exhaustion of hundreds of thousands of Armenians.[8] Estimates of the Armenian death toll vary, but most accounts agree on a million or more, with another 250,000 escaping into the south Caucasus as refugees. The killings spread beyond the frontier vilayets to the Black Sea littoral and western Anatolia.[9] In a classic, if poignant, example of frontier politics, the abandoned farms of many Anatolian Armenians were handed over to the 750,000 Turkish refugees who had fled western Thrace during the Balkan Wars.[10] The massacres went far beyond the demands of military security. They had already been foreshadowed by the nationalizing policies of Abdülhamid. The government of the Young Turks used the occasion of the war to accelerate the process of eliminating the Armenians from a body politic that was undergoing a transformation from a multicultural empire to a nation-state. Michael Reynolds has argued that the destruction of the Armenians was part of a "nascent program of ethnic homogenization that involved the resettlement of a multitude of other population groups, including Muslim Kurds, Albanians, Circassians and others in small, dispersed numbers so as to break up clan and tribal ties and facilitate assimilation."[11]

---

[8] Like the earlier massacres in the 1890s, these events have given rise to a large and controversial literature. For a recent Ottoman apologist, see Salaki Ramsdan Sonyel, *The Ottoman Armenians. Victims of Great Power Diplomacy* (London: K. Rustem, 1987); for Turkish voices endorsing the genocide thesis, see Fikret Adanir and Hilmar Kaiser, "Migration, Deportation, and Nation-Building. The Case of the Ottoman Empire," in René Laboutte (ed.), *Migrations et migrants dans une perspective historique. Permanences et innovations* (Brussels: Peter Lang, 2000), pp. 281–84, and Taner Akçam, *A Shameful Act. The Armenian Genocide and the Question of Turkish Responsibility* (New York: Metropolitan Books, 2006); among the many studies from the Armenian perspective, see especially the articles in Richard G. Hovannisian (ed.), *The Armenian Genocide in Perspective* (New Brunswick, NJ: Rutgers University Press, 1986).

[9] Richard Hovannisian, *Armenia on the Road to Independence 1918* (Berkeley, CA: University of California Press, 1967), pp. 48–55; Robert Melson, *Revolution and Genocide. On the Origins of the Armenian Genocide and the Holocaust* (University of Chicago Press, 1992); Manoug Somakian, *Empires in Conflict. Armenia and the Great Powers, 1895–1920* (London: Tauris, 1995), pp. 93–94; Vahakn N. Dadian, *The History of the Armenian Genocide. Ethnic Conflict from the Balkans to Anatolia and the Caucasus* (Providence, RI: Berghahn, 1995).

[10] Gatrell, *A Whole Empire Walking*, p. 26.

[11] Michael A. Reynolds, *Shattering Empires. The Clash and Collapse of the Ottoman and Russian Empires, 1908–1918* (Cambridge University Press, 2011), p. 149. See also the discussion in Ronald Grigor Suny, *Looking Toward Ararat. Armenia in Modern History*

The traumatic experiences of the refugees were too varied to support a simple generalization summarizing the effect of their repatriation on their national consciousness after the war. There was, however, a noticeable tendency among the returnees, or in certain exceptional cases like the Armenians, in the diaspora, to intensify their identification with their adopted or lost national homeland. This could take several forms. Among the large number of Hungarians who fled the lost territories in Slovakia, Transylvania, and the Banat, nationalist sentiment was directed at recovering the irredenta and supporting right-wing organizations. This was, however, exceptional. In Latvia the returnees from Russia appeared to have taken a more activist role in building a nation-state and endowing it with heroic myths, such as the activities of the Latvian Riflemen who, though fighting on the Bolshevik side, could be reinvented as champions of Latvian self-determination.[12] In Lithuania the nationalizing effect took a different turn. Among the 350,000 returnees, many embraced the nationalist ideals of their new country. But the Lithuanian refugees returning from Soviet Russia to the former provinces of Vilna and Grodno found that their homes were situated in territory occupied by the Polish army and that they had to cross a new boundary illegally to get there. They became caught up in a harsh process of selective repatriation involving the Lithuanian, Polish, and Soviet governments that further embittered relations among the three successor states. Moreover, the repatriation of Jews into Lithuania touched off a strong anti-Semitic reaction not only by the nationalist right, but even among social democrats. Official policies toward the refugees took on an increasingly rigid character, which was reflected in "the increasing nationalizing attempts of the state bureaucracy to rid Lithuania of the heritage of the multi-ethnic Russian Empire."[13]

War aims and the borderlands

In the chancelleries of the belligerent powers, the question of war aims was debated without much attention to the turbulence swirling below them,

(Bloomington, IN: Indiana University Press, 1993), pp. 106–15, for a critique of the apologist literature, but also the argument that while the Hamidian policies were profoundly conservative, those of the Young Turks were revolutionary.

[12] Aija Priedite, "Latvian Refugees and the Latvian Nation State during and after World War One," in Nick Baron and Peter Gatrell (eds.), *Homelands. War, Population, and Statehood in Eastern Europe and Russia, 1918–1924* (London: Anthem, 2004), pp. 35–53.

[13] Tomas Balkelis, "In Search of a Native Realm. The Return of World War One Refugees to Lithuania, 1918–1924," in Baron and Gatrell (eds.), *Homelands*, pp. 87–92, 95–96, quotation on p. 95. What effect this might have had on the participation of Lithuanians in the Holocaust twenty years later is still open to question.

although what was happening on the ground would have a far greater effect on the postwar settlement than the dreams of ambitious statesmen. In retrospect, it may appear astonishing that after two centuries of rivalry over the borderlands, the leaders of the Habsburg, Russian, and Ottoman empires found it difficult to decide how to dispose of them in the event of a great victory. But astonishment is no substitute for analysis, and analysis points to complexity. First, as in all wars involving coalitions, the aims of the coalition partners did not always correspond with one another, but often conflicted. Second, the three empires were obliged to negotiate not only with their allies, but also with potential recruits among the neutrals who promoted their own war aims. Third, the Russian, Habsburg, and Ottoman elites disagreed among themselves and often clashed over war aims. Fourth, as the war lengthened and casualty lists mounted, bitterness and war-weariness forced reassessments and compromises. Finally, and perhaps most decisively, the imminent collapse of the three empires thrust into the foreground the war aims and aspirations of the peoples of the borderlands whose initial loyalty to imperial rule had given way to demands for independence.

The following pages make no effort to trace the twists and turns of negotiations, the clash of opinions, and the shifting positions over war aims.[14] Rather, the focus will be on the maximum or ideal war aims in order to demonstrate how the imperial powers envisaged a solution to the recurrent problem of stabilizing their frontiers and reorganizing the borderlands in an effort to obtain the elusive goal of permanent security and economic self-sufficiency.

The Russian government's war aims for the inner and outer borderlands were cast in different molds. In the inner western borderlands of Finland and the Baltic provinces, policies aimed at strengthening administrative Russification, while in Poland the government's tendency was to grant greater autonomy in the face of conservative opposition. In the outer borderlands, the army pursued a policy of fierce Russification, especially in Habsburg Galicia, while in the south Caucasus the treatment of Armenians in the occupied provinces of the Ottoman Empire made it clear that there was no intention of providing a special regime for a united Armenia at the expense of other local nationalities.[15]

Russia's preliminary war aims were outlined in thirteen points drafted in the Foreign Ministry in September 1914 and attributed to Sazonov.[16]

---

[14] A reliable guide to these issues is David Stevenson, *Cataclysm. The First World War as Political Tragedy* (New York: Basic Books, 2004), esp. pp. 104–17, 289–92.

[15] A. Iu. Bakhturina, *Okrain rossiiskoi imperii. Gosudarstvennoe upravlenie i natsional'naia politika v gody pervoi mirovoi voiny (1914–1917 gg.)* (Moscow: Rosspen, 2004).

[16] William A. Renzi, "Who Composed 'Sazonov's Thirteen Points'? A Re-Examination of Russia's War Aims of 1914," *American Historical Review* 88(2) (April 1983): 347–57,

He expressed his views in a friendly conversation with the French and British ambassadors as a kind of wish list in the event of an Allied victory. On the German side, Chancellor Bethmann-Hollweg was engaged, as we shall see, in similar ruminations which were presented in his September Program. Sazonov cast Russia's war aims in the misleading language of idealism. They were, in a curious forecast of Wilsonian and Leninist rhetoric, "to be determined by the principle of nationalities."[17] In fact, it was a program for stripping Germany of its borderlands and advancing those of Russia. Later modified considerably, it never became official policy due to internal wrangling at the highest levels of government, the competing aims of Russia's allies, France and Britain, and the hard bargaining of neutrals like Romania. Moreover, the subsequent manifestation of relative restraint in the statement of aims concerning Germany may also have been a tacit admission by the Russians that after the war they would still need German trade and technology transfer in order to overcome Russia's economic backwardness.[18] Nevertheless, Sazonov's thirteen points demonstrate just how threatened Russia's ruling elites felt by the rise of a united Germany as the new major challenger in the struggle over the borderlands, and how determined they were to terminate their old rivalry with the Habsburg Monarchy by enhancing Slavic power in its borderlands. According to Sazonov, German power was to be reduced, first, by a Russian annexation of the lower course of the Nieman River in East Prussia; second, by adding Posen, Silesia, and eastern Galicia to the Kingdom of Poland; and, third, by restoring independence to Hanover, returning Schleswig Holstein to Denmark and Alsace Lorraine to France (adding part of Rhenish Prussia and the Palatine if France wished), and assigning undefined but "important" border territories to Belgium.

The Habsburg Monarchy would be reconstructed by ceding the eastern part of Galicia to Russia and the western part of Galicia to the Kingdom of Poland; enlarging Serbia by the annexation of Bosnia-Hercegovina, Dalmatia, and northern Albania; transforming the Dual Monarchy into a tri-monarchy by granting the Czechs and Slovaks (mistakenly located in Moravia) a Kingdom of Bohemia; and reducing the "Austrian Empire

suggests that the thirteen points may have been more an imaginative construction of the French ambassador, Maurice Paléologue, than a precise formulation by Sazonov. But he also cites a dispatch by the British ambassador, Sir George Buchanan, which summarizes a "purely academic conversation" with Sazonov in the presence of Paléologue that makes the same points. *Ibid.*, pp. 349–50.

[17] E. A. Adamov (ed.), *Konstantinopol i prolivy po sekretnym documentam. Ministerstva inostrannykh del* (Moscow: Litizdat NKID, 1925), Doc. 15, p. 222.

[18] Horst Günther Linke, *Das Zarische Russland und der Erst Weltkrieg. Diplomatie und Kriegsziele, 1914–1917* (Munich: Fink Verlag, 1982).

[sic]" to its hereditary provinces, while leaving Hungary the task of reaching an understanding with Romania on the subject of Transylvania. The Bulgarians would be kept by gaining land at Serbia's expense. Greece would annex southern Albania, with the exception of the port of Valona which would go to Italy. Russia would thus reaffirm its role as the protector of the Balkan countries by increasing the territory of all of them. The German colonies would be apportioned to England, France, and Japan.[19]

The entry of the Ottoman Empire into the war on the side of the Central Powers immediately opened up immense new possibilities for Russia. In Sazonov's words: "The entry of Turkey would place on the agenda the entire Near Eastern question and would bring about a final resolution of the Straits question." The "entire Near Eastern question" clearly implied resolving the long struggle over the borderlands on the Caucasian and Trans Caspian frontiers as well. The implication disturbed the British, who emphasized the importance of concentrating all forces against Germany. But behind this real strategic concern lurked the old fears of Russia's breaking out of the Caucasus frontier into Anatolia and Iranian Azerbaijan.[20] Ever since Catherine the Great, Russian rulers and foreign policy makers had devised stratagems for gaining free passage through the Straits, and even gaining control of Constantinople, as the key to achieving hegemony in the Danubian, Pontic and Caucasian frontiers. Depending on the international environment, Russian policy makers oscillated between two extremes in advancing their aims. One model was that of Unkiar-Skelessi through alliance; the other was that of San Stefano by force of arms. On the very eve of the war, Sazonov was prepared once again to pursue Russia's interests through diplomacy, fearing that Germany's active economic policy threatened the Ottoman Empire with dismemberment.[21]

In the past, however close its armies or diplomats had come to achieving their ends, the Russians had been frustrated by the intervention of the

[19] Linke, *Das Zarische Russland.* See C. Jay Smith, *The Russian Struggle for Power, 1914–1917. A Study of Russian Foreign Policy during the First World War* (New York: Philosophical Library, 1956), pp. 46–48, contains a full English translation. In November, after Turkey had entered the war against Russia, a very similar but vaguer document was drawn up by the more conservative Interior Minister V. A. Maklakov and Justice Minister I. Shcheglovitov, with an additional demand for the annexation of the Straits and "Tsargrad" (Istanbul). Gifford D. Malone, "War Aims toward Germany," in *Russian Diplomacy and Eastern Europe, 1914–1917* (New York: Kings Crown Press, 1963), pp. 139–42.

[20] Sir Edward Grey was quick to link Russian offensive action in Anatolia with the situation in Iran where, in his words, "it was necessary to act with great caution and foresight." But there was nothing Britain could do to prevent the fighting from spilling over the frontier into Iran. *Konstantinopol i prolivy*, Doc. 18, pp. 228–29.

[21] H. S. W. Corrigan, "German–Turkish Relations and the Outbreak of War in 1914. A Re-Assessment," *Past and Present* 36 (April 1967): 144–52.

Great Powers, mainly the Habsburgs and the British, but also the French. The outbreak of a general European war had broken these restraints; Britain had finally lined up with Russia against the Habsburgs. A *quondam* opponent, France had also become an ally, and in 1914 a very needy one. A set of fortuitous events presented Russia with a unique opportunity. Even Nicholas II grasped this clearly. In November he expansively expressed his views to the French ambassador. He favored expelling the Turks from Europe, guaranteeing Russian free passage through the Straits, and making Constantinople an international city. Repeating Sazonov's plan for the Balkans and Germany, he went even further, advocating virtual dismemberment of the Habsburg Monarchy into its component parts.[22]

Sazonov appeared to have achieved his aims by the Straits Convention of 1915 which pledged Britain and France to support Russia's acquisition of the western shores of the Bosporus, Sea of Marmora, and Dardanelles as well as islands in the Sea of Marmora in the event of a victorious war. Throughout the negotiations, the British showed themselves to be, surprisingly, more accommodating than the French. During the negotiations, Sazonov added almost as an afterthought that it would be desirable to deprive the sultan of the title of caliph, clearly a move designed to diminish his influence on the Muslim population of Russia's borderlands.[23] On paper it was a triumph of Russian diplomacy. But Russia lacked the military power that it had possessed in 1829 or 1878 to realize its aims.[24]

In the aftermath of the Straits Convention, the Russians and British also reached an agreement in March 1915, revising the Anglo-Russian Treaty of 1907 with respect to Iran. At Britain's request, Sazonov, backed by the tsar, acceded to the incorporation of the neutral zone into the British zone. In return, the Russians demanded territorial adjustments which would enlarge the Russian zone to include Isfahan, Yezd, and a strip between the

---

[22] *Konstantinopol i prolivy*, fn. 4 to Doc. 28, p. 236, notes that the archives of the Russian Foreign Ministry do not contain a copy of the telegram of the French ambassador, Maurice Paléologue, reporting this conversation to Paris, although the text is included in his memoirs. See the discussion in Smith, *The Russian Struggle for Power*, pp. 104–8. Cf. Sean McKeekin, *The Russian Origins of the First World War* (Cambridge, MA: Belknap Press, 2011), who argues unconvincingly that Russia's hidden agenda in entering the First World War was to seize the Straits, and that Sazonov deceived not only all his contemporary interlocutors, but most historians who have written on the subject since then.

[23] *Konstantinopol i prolivy*, Doc. 83, p. 284.

[24] See the discussion of the negotiations in Smith, *The Russian Struggle for Power*, pp. 217–43; and V. S. Vasiukov, "Mirovaia voina politika Rossii v 1914–15 godakh," in A.V. Ignat'ev et al., *Istoriia vneshnei politiki Rossii. Konets XIX–nachala XX veka* (Moscow: Mezhdunarodnye otnosheniia, 1997), pp. 463–79, which agree on all the main points. The key documents are in *Konstantinopol i prolivy*, Doc. 59–82, pp. 263–81.

Russian and Afghan frontiers. Sazonov also wanted Britain to recognize Russia's complete freedom of action within its zone, particularly with respect to economic and financial affairs. Finally, he proposed postponing the issue of railroad construction in the formerly neutral zone for future "friendly talks." He renewed earlier demands that the Afghan emir recognize the Anglo-Russian agreement of 1907 and promise not to grant any foreign concessions in the north of his country or any economic monopoly to British concerns. He further insisted that the Afghan government should not authorize the construction of railroads in northern Afghanistan without Russia's previous agreement. In return, the Russians promised to recognize Britain's special rights in Tibet.[25] As the Russian army continued to occupy most of its zone including Azerbaijan and Manderan, having repelled the Ottoman invasion, its grip on northern Iran seemed secure.

In line with Sazonov's views on the complete reopening of the Near Eastern question, that is, the Caucasus and Trans Caspian frontiers, he was determined to extract from his British and French allies a high price for his approval of their plans to partition the Ottoman borderlands into spheres of influence.[26] In the negotiations the British negotiator, Sir Percy Sykes, attempted to block Russia's claims for all of Armenia by invoking the dangers of including territories "inhabited by revolutionary syndicalists" (presumably the Dashnaks) who maintained "close ties with subversive elements in Persia and the Caucasus." He also supported the idea of adjusting the line dividing the French and Russian zones in the neighborhood of the Iranian frontier so as to populate the annexed territories primarily with Muslims who, "from the viewpoint of state security, represents a more hopeful and satisfactory element" than the Armenians.[27] In what justly may be called the "Sykes–Picot–Sazonov" agreement of May 1916, Russia was promised the Ottoman provinces of Erzerum, Trabzon (Trebizond), Van, and Bitlis, plus Kurdistan with their mixed populations of Armenians, Turks, Laz, Kurds, and Nestorian Christians. This time the Russians could back up their claims with military power as their armies advanced along the coast of the Black Sea. Moreover, they could now afford to ignore Armenian hopes for an autonomous region similar to that being debated on Poland. High-ranking Russian military and civil officials on the Caucasian frontiers proposed a familiar alternative: the settlement

---

[25] *Konstantinopol i prolivy*, Doc. 83, pp. 284–85.
[26] The best summary is Richard Hovannisian, "The Allies and Armenia, 1915–18," *Journal of Contemporary History* 3(1) (January 1968): 145–68.
[27] Hovannisian, "The Allies and Armenia," pp. 161–62, quoting from E. A. Adamov (ed.), *Razdel Aziatskoi Turtsii po sekretnym dokumentam ministerstva inostrannykh del* (Moscow: Ministerstvo inostrannykh del SSSR, 1924), pp. 157, 163–64.

of Russian colonists from the Kuban and Don "to form a Cossack region along the border."[28]

With the military and diplomatic situation well in hand, the Russian leadership could also dismiss the contribution of Armenian volunteer units in the army which had supported the Russian offensive. The new viceroy, Grand Duke Nikolai Nikolaevich, ordered the disbanding of these units and imposed strict censorship on all Armenian publications. He further expressed his uncompromising opposition to Armenian autonomy, notifying Sazonov: "It is my profound conviction that there is at present within the bounds of the Russian Empire absolutely no Armenian question, nor should even mention of such a question even be permitted, for the Russian Armenian subjects within the viceroyalty are like Muslims, Georgians and Russians, equal subjects of Russia."[29]

Russian planning for the future of Poland revived all the old debates and revealed the deep splits among policy makers. During the war, the three original partitioning powers vied with one another in promising the Poles some kind of autonomy in order to win support and raise recruits. Both sides had limited success. The Russians were first to go on record. On August 14, 1914, Grand Duke Nikolai Nikolaevich, then commander-in-chief of the Russian army, issued an eloquent proclamation prepared by the Foreign Ministry, greeting "the resurrection of the Polish nation and fraternal reconciliation with Great Russia." Even though the political substance was limited to a vague promise of "self-government ... under the scepter of the Russian Emperor," Polish supporters of accommodation such as Roman Dmowski and Count Zygmunt Wielopolski reacted favorably. For the following two years, they and the Russian liberals pressed for more concrete proposals. A delaying action was mounted by representatives of the Russian right, including Interior Minister Nikolai Maklakov, Minister of Justice Ivan Shcheglovitov, and Procurator of the Holy Synod V. K. Sabler.[30] Finally, in May 1916, Sazonov submitted to a sympathetic Nicholas II a detailed constitution for an autonomous Poland in the hope of forestalling interference by France and Britain; this had been a perennial concern among Russian statesmen since the partitions

[28] Hovannisian, "The Allies and Armenia," p. 158, quoting General Yudenich, the field commander of the Russian army in the Caucasus and subsequently a leading White commander. This view was shared by the Minister of Agriculture, Krivoshein.
[29] Hovannisian, "The Allies and Armenia," p. 163. Like the Poles, the Armenians had also formed a Légion d'Orient under French auspices, which fought well on the Palestinian front. *Ibid.*, p. 151.
[30] Alexander Dallin, "The Future of Poland," in *Russian Diplomacy and Eastern Europe*, pp. 7–13.

and especially during the Polish insurrection of 1863.[31] Despite the strong opposition of Prime Minister Boris Stürmer, Nicholas appeared inclined to approve the constitution until the Empress Alexandra Fedorovna intervened. Whether or not she was instrumental in the dismissal of Sazonov, whom she hated for his "liberalism," there is no question that her fierce opposition to a Polish constitution forced a postponement of its consideration; in fact, it was shelved for good.[32] Once again the ground had been cut from under the accommodationists.

Whatever the domestic differences over Poland, Russia gained a striking, if ephemeral, diplomatic victory. It came at a low point in the French military situation, but also on the eve of the revolution in Petrograd. In March 1917, the two governments agreed to recognize one another's maximum war aims on their frontiers with Germany. The French confirmed their 1915 pledge to support Russia's "age old aspirations" at the Straits, but also "in order to assure its military and industrial security and the economic development of the empire to recognize Russia's full freedom of action in defining its western frontier." In Paris, Izvol'skii, no doubt savoring this reversal of his humiliation in 1907, managed to exclude the word Poland from the agreements.[33] Out of desperation France was obliged to abandon its century-old barrier policy of blocking Russian penetration of Central Europe.

Fully engaged militarily and diplomatically on its Western frontiers, the tsarist government made certain to protect its position on the Inner Asian frontier. In 1916, it signed a secret convention with Japan, officially then its ally, on extending and confirming their earlier agreements "to protect" (*oberegat'*) China from the interference of any third power and to take joint action, if necessary, to prevent it. But negotiating from a position of weakness, the Russians made a number of economic concessions to Japan which foreshadowed a more aggressive Japanese policy in the Inner Asian borderlands at Russia's expense following the Bolshevik Revolution.[34]

---

[31] The constitution reaffirmed the indivisibility of the kingdom and the Russian state. The central government retained control over foreign and military affairs, most of the economy, and the Orthodox Church, leaving the Poles in control of cultural affairs. Dallin, "The Future of Poland," p. 46.

[32] Dallin, "The Future of Poland," pp. 49–59; Smith, *The Russian Struggle for Power*, pp. 398–405.

[33] *Konstantinopol i prolivy*, Docs. 291, 292, 297, pp. 457, 458, 460, quotation on p. 460.

[34] M. I. Sladkovskii, *Istoriia torgovo-ekonomicheskikh otnoshenii s Kitaem (do 1917)* (Moscow: Nauka, 1974), p. 347; George Alexander Lensen, "Japan and Russia. The Changing Relationships, 1875–1917," *Jahrbücher für Geschichte Osteuropas*, New Series, 10(3) (October 1962): 345–47.

In contrast to Russia, the Habsburg and Ottoman empires were much more restricted in defining and pursuing their war aims within a coalition completely dominated by their vastly more powerful ally, the German Empire. The first attempt to state Germany's provisional war aims came from the office of the German Chancellor, Bethmann-Hollweg, but was drafted by his private secretary, Kurt Riezler. The German September Program was a mirror image of Sazonov's thirteen points in its maximalist demands for the reconstruction of the Eurasian borderlands. These were stated in general terms: "Russia must be thrust back as far as possible from Germany's eastern frontier and her domination over the non-Russian vassal peoples broken." Germany's aims in the west were spelled out more specifically, and also involved radical changes in the status and territory of Belgium, Luxembourg, and France, but these did not involve the competing aims of Germany's imperial allies. The pan-Germans presented more detailed plans, demanding that Russia's "frontiers must be reduced approximately to those of Peter the Great." The government's policies shifted as the situation changed on the battlefields. But even when Germany considered a separate peace with Russia through Japanese mediation in May 1916, its list of territorial changes in the borderlands was staggering. Russia was to cede Poland, Lithuania, and Courland to Germany; it was to agree to Turkey's acquisition of Persian Kurdistan, Luristan, and Khuistan; and Russia should disinterest herself in the Balkans. In return Russia would retain the part of Turkish Armenia conquered by its armies, and acquire the rest of Persia, east Turkestan, Dzungaria, Outer Mongolia, north Manchuria, and Gensu and Shensi provinces in north China. Revisions were later introduced, but all aimed at pushing Russia back into Asia and consolidating the German element in the Baltic littoral by population transfers.[35] Once the duo of generals Ludendorff and Hindenburg became the dominant force in Germany's military affairs and assumed broad political powers, their plans for the reorganization of the Baltic littoral under the rubric of *Oberost* involved large-scale administrative changes, massive deportations, and resettlement by German colonists.[36] Despite the consistency of its aims, Germany was obliged to reconcile them with those of Austria-Hungary and the Ottoman Empire.

---

[35] Fritz Fischer, *Germany's Aims in the First World War* (New York: W. W. Norton, 1967), pp. 103–25, 231–36.

[36] Vejas Liulevicius, *War Land on the Eastern Front. Culture, National Identity and German Occupation in World War I* (New York: Cambridge University Press, 2000); Annemarie H. Sammartino, *The Impossible Border. Germany and the East, 1914–1922* (Ithaca, NY: Cornell University Press, 2010), esp. pp. 18–44.

Having launched the war, the Austro-Hungarian leaders were at something of a loss to define its aims. The problem was that any addition of territory was bound to exacerbate the already tense relations between the center of power and the borderlands. The absence of any grand design and the differences within the government leaves the impression that the ruling elites regarded winning the war as its main aim; victory was the sole means of preserving the Monarchy. Nevertheless, the generals and diplomats continued to wrestle with what seemed to be intractable problems. First among these was what to do with Serbia. Here, deep-seated differences showed up between the Austrian and Hungarian views. Ever since the issue was raised during the Second Balkan War, Count István Tisza, the Hungarian Prime Minister, had firmly opposed incorporating Serbia into the Monarchy. His views on foreign policy were entirely dominated by his concern over the security of Hungary's borderlands inhabited by Romanians (Transylvania) and Serbs (the Voevodina). This explains his enthusiasm for a Bulgarian alliance – to hold both the Romanians and Serbs in check. During the July crisis, he alone of all the Habsburg leaders opposed a preemptive war against Serbia and urged a diplomatic solution; in the event that war became unavoidable, he added, the aim should be to conquer Serbia and then to dismember it, distributing parts among Bulgaria, Greece, and Albania, and reserving only a small strategic frontier strip for the Monarchy. When he finally accepted the idea of an ultimatum to Serbia, he continued to insist on a policy of no annexation.[37] In the most detailed rationale for his war aims, contained in a memorandum to the emperor in December 1915, he argued that Serbia should not be destroyed but weakened by the cession of its territory to Bulgaria and Albania, and the merger of its eastern portion with Montenegro to form a new country without a seaboard and thus "economically dependent on the Monarchy." To incorporate more Serbs into the Monarchy "would bring about such a renewal of energy in the ambition of the Serbs of the Monarchy that the Hungarian state would incur the serious danger of losing the unity it possesses." It would create "precisely the situation which the pan-Serb agitation is seeking to bring about," namely, "the dissolution of the Monarchy." Moreover, the annexation of Serbia would not end Russia's intrigues, but intensify them. Russia would never accept the destruction of Serbia unless it was totally defeated, "which does not seem probable."[38]

[37] Gabor Vermes, *István Tisza. The Liberal Vision and Conservative Statecraft of a Magyar Nationalist* (New York: East European Monographs, 1985), pp. 203, 212–13, 222–23, 229.

[38] Letter to Count Burián with enclosure for the emperor, December 3, 1915, in *Count Stephen Tisza, Prime Minister of Hungary. Letters (1914–1916)*, trans. Carvel de Bussy (New York: Peter Lang, 1991), pp. 168–74. He reiterated his opposition in another letter to Burián in January 1916. *Ibid.*, pp. 174–75.

Austrian statesmen were uniformly obsessed with punishing Serbia, but they differed over the best means. For example, Count Leopold Berchtold, the Austrian Foreign Minister, appeared to favor nothing more than a realization of the terms of the ultimatum of July 1914. After Bulgaria attacked Serbia, the aims of a third party had to be accommodated. Once Serbian resistance was broken and both Serbia and Montenegro occupied, the Austrian military government sought to prevent a further deterioration of living conditions in the war-ravaged country. Following Count Tisza's protests that the regime was too mild, a more centralized and authoritarian military governor was appointed. Yet in some ways the Austrian occupation policy resembled that introduced into Bosnia and Hercegovina after 1907. The Muslims of the southern districts of Serbia and in Montenegro were eager to cooperate and raised several thousand volunteers to serve on the Austrian side. They supplemented the Muslim *Schützkorps* which was used to intimidate the Serbian population in Bosnia.

On the positive side, the occupation authorities organized Russian prisoners of war and drafted laborers into work battalions engaged in repairing wartime damage and increasing food production. They brought epidemics under control and established new schools, despite Hungarian protests. The Austrians also undertook constructive activities in occupied Albania, although the resources there were wholly inadequate for a real transformation of the country.[39] There is something almost pathetic in these efforts to revive the ideals of an Austrian civilizing mission in the waning days of the monarchy.

Inevitably, resistance in the occupied areas also manifested itself alongside accommodation. At the end of 1916, a partisan movement began to appear in Serbia as young men fleeing into the woods and hills formed bands of četniks, as they had under Ottoman rule and would do again during the Second World War. Their activities centered in the Bulgarian zone of occupation, but spilled over into the Austrian zone. The Bulgarians had recruited 100,000 men from western (Serbian) Macedonia into the army, and launched a program to construct Bulgarian schools and other cultural institutions in a vain attempt to revive Bulgarian national consciousness that had withered under forty years of Serbian administration.[40]

---

[39] Manfred Rauchensteiner, *Der Tod des Doppeladlers. Österreich-Ungarn und der Erste Weltkrieg* (Vienna: Verlag Styria, 1993), pp. 465–68.

[40] Richard J. Crampton, *Bulgaria 1878–1918. A History* (Boulder, CO: East European Monographs, 1983), pp. 457–58.

The most contentious war aim dividing the Austrians, Hungarians, and Germans was the disposition of the Kingdom of Poland. Austrian officials were neither clear nor united in what they wanted. Count Berchtold was attracted by the idea of incorporating the Kingdom of Poland into the Monarchy by restructuring the Monarchy on tripartite lines, mainly on the grounds that the only alternative was the establishment of an independent Poland. His critics countered that this would merely serve to whet the appetite of Polish nationalists aspiring to reconstitute an even larger Poland by adding Galicia and Posen; in other words, restoring the Commonwealth of the eighteenth century. Conservative Polish leaders in Galicia rallied behind Berchtold. With a population of some 20 million, the Poles could legitimately claim a constitutional position similar to that of Hungary in the Monarchy. The prime minister, Count Karl Stürgkh, distrusted the Poles but saw no good solution. The Austrian Chief-of-Staff, Conrad von Hötzendorf, also distrusted the Poles and preferred to postpone any settlement until after the war. Count Tisza perceived dangers lurking in any solution. He proposed that Austria should incorporate Poland without granting Poland equal status in order to avoid a trialist solution. His close associate, Burián, thought this was unrealistic. His old political enemy, Count Gyula Andrássy, thought it was proof of rigid thinking.[41]

The German military insisted on acquiring a frontier strip of the Kingdom of Poland and economic control over the rest. After two years of war, negotiations, and much hesitation, the Austrians agreed to join Germany in proclaiming the establishment of an independent Polish state as a constitutional monarchy made up of the former Kingdom of Poland, but excluding Austrian Galicia and Prussian Poznan. A shadow government was created with a regency council without any real power. Poland's borders were left vague.[42] At the Brest-Litovsk negotiations in the winter of 1917/18, the Austrians found themselves pinned on the horns of a dilemma over the question of how to define their relations with the Slavic borderlands. With German approval, the separatist government of the Ukrainian Rada obtained representation in the negotiations. The Poles claimed equal treatment, also in the name of self-determination. This created problems for the Austrians. The head of the Austrian delegation, Count Otto Czernin, lamented in his first meeting with the Germans that: "I simply cannot toss the word 'self-determination' into the debate. Otherwise, the

[41] Vermes, *István Tisza*, pp. 264–67, 318.
[42] Fischer, *Germany's War Aims*, pp. 236–44; Piotr Wandycz, *The Lands of Partitioned Poland, 1795–1918* (Seattle, WA: University of Washington Press, 1974), p. 357.

Czechs, the Ruthenes, the South Slavs will come to me and demand self-determination and more self-determination."[43] At the same time, the Germans were bringing heavy pressure on the Austrians to accept their plans to incorporate Poland into their vast design for a customs union in Central Europe (*Mitteleuropa*), which would also include the Habsburg Monarchy. The Austro-German business elite regarded the whole scheme as inimical to their commercial and industrial freedom and firmly resisted, although there was probably nothing they could do about it if Germany won the war.[44]

Austria was also under great internal pressure to reach an agreement with the Bolshevik government in order to smooth the way to a general peace and to gain access to food supplies in Ukraine that were desperately needed in the Cisleithanian half of the Monarchy; the unwillingness of the Hungarians to share their dwindling food supplies had imposed severe hardships on Vienna. Meanwhile, reports from Galicia revealed that Polish peasants were beginning to abandon their traditional *Kaisertreu* sentiments in protest against the requisitioning of food. Czernin attempted to square the circle by offering a convoluted formula. After an acrimonious exchange of views with the Ottoman and Bulgarian delegations, which had their own territorial demands, he endorsed the idea of self-determination as an internal question to be dealt with by each state as it chose rather than as a universal principle. But he could not escape the necessity of choosing between the Poles and the Ukrainians. The Ukrainian delegation at Brest demanded the transfer of the much-disputed district of Kholm to a new Ruthenian crownland comprising eastern Galicia and northern Bukovina with "the full and free national development" of the Ruthenian population. The Austrians caved in. Battered at home by strikes, mutinies, and demands for peace and bread, Czernin agreed to give up his support for Polish claims on Kholm and all of Galicia by signing a treaty with the Ukrainian Rada that met all their demands. The Polish reaction was "immediate and catastrophic." The regency council in Warsaw denounced the treaty; mass anti-Habsburg demonstrations broke out in Poland and Galicia; the Polish Auxiliary Corps serving with the Austrian army mutinied and clashed with imperial troops, with hundreds crossing over to the Russian lines. The final blow was the defection of the Polish representatives

[43] Clifford F. Wargelin, "A High Price for Bread. The First Treaty of Brest-Litovsk and the Break-up of Austria Hungary, 1917–1918," *International History Review* 19(4) (November 1997): 767, quoting Karl Friederich Nowak, *Der Sturz der Mittelmächte* (Munich: G. D. W. Callwey, 1921), p. 8.
[44] Richard W. Kapp, "Divided Loyalties. The German Reich and Austria-Hungary in Austro-German Discussions of War Aims, 1914–1916," *Central European History* 17(2/3) (June–September 1984): 120–39.

in the Reichsrat who joined the opposition, depriving the government of a majority.[45]

By 1918, the Austrians were paying a terrible price for their failure to integrate the economies of the two halves of the Monarchy, and to resolve the conflict between the aspirations of the Hungarians and the nationalities of the borderlands. But even this late in the war, the government in Vienna was not prepared to give up on its belief in an Austro-Polish solution; it appeared to the government as possibly the only salvation of the Monarchy. In September 1918, on the eve of the imperial collapse, they made their final effort to counter German plans to turn Poland into its satellite. In a detailed proposal they offered to meet most of the demands of the Poles for the creation of a genuine tri-monarchy.[46] By this time an imperial solution had lost its appeal. The Poles were on their way to complete independence.

The Ottoman entry into World War I can only be understood in the perfervid atmosphere of rising nationalist feelings following the humiliating defeat in the Balkan Wars stoked by intense desires to prevent further and to avenge past interventions in its affairs by Russia and Great Britain.[47] As a belligerent on the side of a German-led victorious coalition, the chances of securing an economic recovery appeared to be promising despite the danger of greater economic dependence on Germany. Before the sultan entered the war, he took steps to forestall that outcome. In early September 1914, the government unilaterally and extralegally abrogated the capitulary privileges of all the foreign powers. The gambit did not work. Both the Germans and Austro-Hungarians raised objections. Once the Ottomans entered the war, the Central Powers refused to agree, urging the sultan instead to confiscate French and British holdings.

Ottoman war aims were ambitious, but their territorial demands were modest. Perhaps the lesson had been learned from the Balkan Wars that an attempt to regain their lost empire was doomed to failure. The Turks were even willing to cede to Bulgaria a small strip of territory in eastern Thrace as part of an inducement by the Central Powers to bring Bulgaria into the war on their side.[48] At Brest-Litovsk they gained their main territorial claim when the Central Powers forced the Bolshevik government to return the provinces of Kars, Ardahan, and Batumi which the Russians had annexed after the Russo-Turkish War of 1877/8.

[45] Wargelin, "A High Price for Bread," pp. 779–84.
[46] Werner Conze, *Polnische Nation und deutsche Politik in Ersten Weltkrieg* (Cologne: Böhlau, 1958), p. 377.
[47] Mustafa Aksakal, *The Ottoman Road to War in 1914. The Ottoman Empire and the First World War* (Cambridge University Press, 2008).
[48] James M. Potts, "The Loss of Bulgaria," in *Russian Diplomacy in Eastern Europe*, p. 231.

The ambitious aspect of the Ottoman leaders' war aims was to establish one or more buffer states to shield them from a revival of Russian imperialism. Their policy resembled the venerable Ottoman imperial tradition of creating protectorates, such as the Danubian principalities, Hungary, and the Crimean khanate, as borderlands on the periphery of their power as a practical solution to the problem of imperial overstretch. In this same spirit, they supported the independence of Ukraine as "a necessary blow against the Bolsheviks' efforts to recreate a Great Russia." It now seems clear, however, that they did not adopt pan-Turkism or pan-Turanism as their ideological guide to action in the Caucasus.[49] Tentative Young Turk overtures in that direction during the war fell on the deaf ears of the conservative ulama of Trans Caspia. Ottoman hopes for a Caucasian buffer initially appeared most promising after the Russian Revolution of February 1917 when the Ottoman army once again invaded the south Caucasian borderlands. But their aims were repeatedly frustrated by their more powerful German ally.[50]

During the war, Habsburg and Ottoman empires were forced to acknowledge that in the long struggle over the borderlands Germany, which had belatedly entered the contest, had emerged as a major player. Exercising its superior economic and military power, the *Kaiserreich* competed with and subordinated the war aims of its Habsburg and Ottoman allies to that of its own. In 1916, then, it appeared as though victory for either Germany or Russia would result in the ascendancy of one or the other imperial power in the borderlands of the Baltic littoral, the Triplex Confinium, the Pontic, Caucasian, and Trans Caspian frontiers. Unexpectedly, both suffered defeat. This postponed their final confrontation for a generation until the outbreak of the Second World War. In the meantime, the main arena of the struggle over the borderlands shifted to the subject peoples and the successor states, which inherited the heavy burdens of the long struggle wound up to a heightened pitch by the war and the disintegration of imperial rule.

The First World War did not end the fighting in the Eurasian borderlands. In the chaos of 1918–1919, the defeated imperial armies of the Habsburg, Russian, and Ottoman empires broke up into their component national parts which continued to battle over the imperial legacy. After the 1911 revolution, the Chinese New Army also disintegrated, the pieces

---

[49] Michael Reynolds, "Buffers, not Brethren. Young Turk Military Policy in the First World War and the Myth of Panturanism," *Past and Present* 203 (May 2009): 137–79, quotation on 149 paraphrasing a letter from Talât to Enver Pasha, February 1, 1918.

[50] Ulrich Trumpener, *Germany and the Ottoman Empire, 1914–1918* (Princeton University Press, 1968), pp. 38–39, 113–22, 194–99; Reynolds, *Shattering Empires*, pp. 24–25, 188, 196–203, 214–15.

being picked up by virtually independent commanders or warlords in the Inner Asian borderlands and the rest of the shattered Qing inheritance. The Royal Iranian Army, such as it was, also melted away and had to be put back together by the last warrior usurper to the throne, Reza Shah. The central bureaucracies lost touch and control over the borderlands. Imperial ideologies disappeared in the smoke of battle. The institutional glue that had held the multicultural states together for more than three centuries had come unstuck.

Civil wars and interventions

The creation of new Eurasian states and the delimitation of their boundaries were forged during the great social upheavals that began even before the signing of the Armistice in November 1918. The process continued to unfold into the early 1920s. Historians have tended to exaggerate the role, indeed the ability, of the victorious Allies sitting in Paris to draw the boundaries and define the sovereign limits of the successor states. The Allies, like the Central Powers at the height of their military victories, launched major interventions to reshape the borderlands. But neither alliance was successful in resolving the complex problems arising from the persistent factors that had bedeviled imperial rulers. In both cases the outcome confirms Talleyrand's famous maxim: "You can do anything with bayonets except sit on them." When the interventionists withdrew, the ability of a successor state to survive, delimit, and defend its boundaries depended upon its own resources.

The first successor state to inherit the burdens of imperial rule was the Russian Provisional Government. Its attempts to reorder relations between the center and the borderlands vividly illustrate both the inherent difficulty of the problem and the additional complications imposed by the belligerents who set unrealistic war aims for the distribution of the long-contested borderlands. Before the war, liberals and moderate socialists, who became the main supporters of the Provisional Government, had been sharp critics of repressive tsarist policies toward the nationalities and advocates of various forms of self-determination. Once in power, their commitment to continue the war took precedence over all other considerations. They interpreted the separatist demands of the nationalities as a threat to the united war effort and a comfort to the enemy. They grudgingly offered minimal concessions with promises to submit the entire question of the future of the state to a constitutional assembly that was only to be elected after the war. National movements, especially in Finland and Ukraine, considered these gestures to be inadequate. They resented the Provisional Government's refusal to permit the formation of national units in the army. Disillusionment gave way to disaffection. The new regime was no more successful than its predecessor in reconciling the aspirations of the peoples of the borderlands with the security of a multi-national state. Nor could the nationalities rely at this stage on their traditional supporters from the west, who were caught in the inconsistent, if not hypocritical, position of encouraging national liberation in the Habsburg and Ottoman empires, but not in the borderlands of their Russian ally upon whom they relied to maintain an eastern front.[51] The Central Powers were trapped in a similar dilemma. However, their military success in the borderlands enabled the Habsburg and Ottoman empires to postpone, if only briefly, the day of reckoning.

In the first phase of the intervention, the Central Powers reduced Russia to its pre-Petrine core (except for Petrograd) by stripping its borderlands all along the periphery from the Baltic littoral, through the Pontic frontier to the south Caucasus. This was the real meaning of the treaties of Brest-Litovsk with Soviet Russia and Ukraine. While it lasted only seven months, the intervention was massive. In 1918, the occupation force of the Central Powers in Ukraine alone numbered almost 500,000 men. Along the Baltic littoral, the Germans dispatched troops to Finland, the provinces of Estland and Lifland, and the Vistula provinces. Austro-German and Bulgarian troops occupied Serbia and the entire Danubian frontier, driving the Romanians back to the Pruth River. German and Ottoman troops took control over most of the south Caucasus.

In Inner Asia, Japan took advantage of the European war to become the first of the Allied interventionists, bringing heavy pressure on a weakened post-imperial China to loosen its ties with its northern tier of borderlands. Xinjiang, Mongolia, and Manchuria drifted away from the old center of Qing power. Central China split between north and south, and then broke up into smaller pieces under the control of local warlords. After the defeat of the Central Powers, the Allies took over the primary role of interventionist throughout Eurasia, although they were not always eager to force the withdrawal of the German army in the face of advancing Bolshevik forces. The British were the most widely dispersed all along the periphery of Russia from the Baltic littoral (naval and ground troops) and the Caucasian isthmus to Inner Asia. The French took the lead in reestablishing Poland, enlarging Romania, and supporting anti-Bolshevik forces on the Black Sea coast of the Pontic frontier. The Japanese continued to exert pressure on China and sent the largest Allied interventionist

---

[51] Marc Ferro, "La politique des nationalités du gouvernement provisoire (Février–Octobre 1917)," *Cahiers du monde russe et soviétique* 2(2) (April–June 1961): 131–65.

expedition into Siberia. The Americans sent units to Siberia, in part to offset the Japanese, and to north Russia. The Allies also used smaller auxiliary units to bolster their main forces, including Czechs, Italians, Greeks, Serbs, Romanians, Arabs, colonial troops, and Mongols. Overall the interventions were not well coordinated; they pursued different, often contradictory, aims by supporting competing forces within the local resistance movements. Cancelling one another out, the Great Powers were limited in projecting their power throughout the borderlands.[52]

Mainly for reasons of geographic proximity and superior armed force, the Central Powers were more successful than the more distant Allies, if only briefly, in imposing their rule. But defeat in the west cut short their efforts to reconstruct the borderlands. After the withdrawal of the German army and the disintegration of the Habsburg and Ottoman armies, for the first time in half a millennium there were no great powers in west Eurasia. The small Allied military missions on the spot often lacked sufficient forces under their command or the will to impose decisions made in Paris. The Bolsheviks, better organized than their domestic enemies and operating out of strategically favorable inner lines, reestablished control by the old center of power over most of the imperial borderlands.

The main achievement of the intervention by the Central Powers and Allies was to extend political and diplomatic support to independence movements by granting them recognition and by providing arms, equipment, and military advisors to the local combatants. Initially, these were often no more than ad hoc national councils whose authority extended only as far as their small, scattered armed forces could impose it. The Allied powers frequently found themselves internally divided and in conflict with one another over the question of whether their interests were best served by preserving a Greater Russia or encouraging independence movements. Wherever they turned, however, they frequently found themselves limited to remonstrating and bargaining with new elites who were, for the most part, radical intellectuals or army officers, often obscure figures from modest backgrounds.

Diplomatic recognition often proved to be ephemeral, as in the case of Ukraine or the Caucasian republics. With the exception of a few plebiscites in the Polish frontiers (Teschen and Silesia) and the creation of the

---

[52] The multiple and conflicting motives of the Allied intervention are well treated in George Kennan, *Soviet–American Relations, vol. II: The Decision to Intervene* (Princeton University Press, 1958); Richard Ullman, *Anglo-Soviet Relations, 1917–1921*, 3 vols. (Princeton University Press, 1961–1972); James Morley, *The Japanese Thrust into Siberia* (New York: Columbia University Press, 1957).

free cities of Danzig and Fiume, new boundary lines were determined by the local contestants. Never before, and not again until 1989–1991, were the peoples of the borderlands in a position to play such a decisive role in shaping the spatial contours of the Eurasian borderlands. In part, this was due to the collapse of imperial rule which created a power vacuum and, in part, to the forces of resistance that had been building up during the long nineteenth century.

Below the level of Great Power intervention the Eurasian frontiers had once again become shifting, porous, and contested. In the years after 1914, mobilization for total war, the collapse of established authority, forced population movements, and the spread of communal violence worked to transform multicultural communities into more politically conscious multinational societies. Under these conditions the legacy of imperial rule with regard to mixed populations was a ticking bomb. There was no way to draw the boundaries of the successor states on the basis of national self-determination of either the Wilsonian or Leninist variety. The assimilation of different ethnolinguistic groups into the new states had become even more problematic than the nationalizing tendencies under imperial rule for several reasons. First, national feelings had spread more widely and penetrated more deeply among both the dominant and subordinate nationalities. Second, the recognition by the peace treaties of the rights of national minorities merely heightened the perception of difference between the two. For the dominant nationalists, the minorities represented an alien and potentially hostile element of the population. For the minorities, resistance to assimilation had become a mass phenomenon. Third, more ominously for those in power, the minorities were generally located on the vulnerable peripheries of the new states, raising questions of national security. Finally, certain extremist nationalist groups in the successor states entertained larger territorial ambitions with distinctive imperial overtones. They suffered from the complex of "the greater state." That is, they desired to complete the process of nation-building by advancing both historicist claims on territories they had possessed in the past, and ethnolinguistic claims on populations outside their prewar boundaries. The peculiar spatial construction of the postwar settlement guaranteed a renewal of conflicts over the new borderlands between the dominant nationality (Czechs, Poles, Serbs, Romanians, Persians, and Han Chinese) and their minorities.

The possibility of avoiding the fiction of erecting nation-states out of multinational borderlands inspired a number of federative schemes that were floated at the Versailles Conference in 1919, including one by the United States delegation. The Poles and the Russians were the two main protagonists of the idea, but not surprisingly their designs were completely incompatible.[53] One of the skeptics was Sir Halford MacKinder, the arch theorist of geopolitics, who argued that the peoples of what he called the "Middle Tier" – Poles, Bohemians, Hungarians, Romanians, Serbs, Bulgarians, and Greeks – were "much too unlike to federate for any such purpose except defence; yet they are all so different both from Germany and Russia that they may be trusted to resist any new organization of either great neighbour."[54] The father of geopolitics offered a different solution: the exchange of populations, peacefully and by mutual agreement, to be sure. At the time, this had little appeal for successor states with "greater" aspirations. Only the Turks and Greeks arranged such an exchange, but only after another war in which the Greeks attempted ingloriously to carry out their vision of *Megale*, "the Great Idea." In the long term the man who subsequently came closest to realizing MacKinder's suggestion, albeit in a brutal and unilateral way, was Stalin, although he also had some help from the Czechs and the Poles after the Second World War.

With the disintegration of the imperial armies, new armed groups appeared as the main force in state-building or the restoration of order in a society torn by civil war. It was hardly coincidental that many of the new rulers of the successor states were military men: Mannerheim in Finland; Piłsudski in Poland; Horthy in Hungary; Kemal Atatürk in Turkey; Reza Shah in Iran; and Yuan Shikai in China, who was succeeded by his generals as regional warlords and then the supreme warlord of them all, Chiang Kai-shek. Once again, the major exception was the Soviet Union. Had the Bolsheviks lost the civil war, Russia too would have been ruled by military figures such as General Denikin or Admiral Kolchak, who had been prematurely recognized by the Allies as the supreme ruler. These were the men who replaced the dynasts. Self-proclaimed as saviors of their people, they became the object of a new cult of heroes. Like their predecessors, they sought to buttress their personal charisma, often by relying heavily on the army and creating new bureaucratic institutions by both co-opting old elites and recruiting marginal men like themselves.[55]

---

[53] For a discussion of various proposals and counter proposals, see M. K. Dziewanowski, *Joseph Piłsudski. A European Federalist, 1918–1922* (Stanford University Press, 1969), pp. 79–88.

[54] Sir John Halford MacKinder, *Democratic Ideals and Reality. A Study in the Politics of Reconstruction* (New York: Henry Holt, 1919), pp. 213, 200.

[55] Cf. Joshua Sanborn, "Warlordism. Violence and Governance during the First World War and Civil War," *Contemporary European History* 19(3) (August 2010): 195–213, who points out the parallels in the phenomenon of warlordism between China and Russia as "two crippled imperial spaces."

The collapse of imperial rule in the Russian Empire plunged the country into a *smuta*, for which the term civil war is an anemic description.[56] The break up of the state into warring constituencies was a realization of the fear that had long haunted the imperial elites: that a serious defeat in a foreign war would lead to dismemberment, tearing the borderlands away from the center of power, and possibly leading to social revolution. The disintegration of the army, the inability of the Provisional Government to provide strong leadership throughout most of 1917, and the imposition by the Central Powers of the harsh Treaty of Brest-Litovsk in March 1918 on a weak Bolshevik government accelerated the tempo of three disruptive trends in late imperial Russia: social fragmentation, regional particularism, and violent resistance to superordinate authority. The budding institutions of civil society and the weakly developed rule of law were swept aside. The growing feelings of hostility by peasants toward landlords, intellectuals toward capitalists, and workers toward factory owners were entangled with ethnoreligious antagonisms such as those between Christians and Jews, Ukrainians and Poles, Tatars and Armenians, and many nationalities toward the Great Russians, reacting against late imperial Russifying policies.

The major contestants in the struggle for control over the borderlands of the former Russian Empire can be divided for the purposes of analysis into five major groupings, with the important caveat that none of them was unified or consistent in its policies and practices. The Bolshevik leadership, more specifically Lenin and Stalin, were committed in principle to the idea of self-determination exercised, however, by the most progressive social forces, namely, the proletariat. In the initial years of the revolution their outline of the future state remained vague, accompanied by verbal assurances of autonomy for the borderlands. The counter-revolutionary White leaders, most prominently General Anton Denikin of the Volunteer Army, were determined to establish a unitary Great Russian state, ignoring the geocultural diversity of Eurasian space. The various Cossacks Hosts (*voiska*), strung out all along the southern periphery of the former empire, were mainly determined to protect or restore their social privileges and their status as autonomous borderlands. Local nationalists in all the borderlands were divided in their aspirations for various forms of autonomy or independence. "Bandit armies" of anarchists, or Greens opposed any form of state authority.

None of the elites in the successor states sought to construct an overarching ideology aimed at unifying its diverse population with the notable

---

[56] Part of the following is a recapitulation of Alfred J. Rieber, "Landed Property, State Authority, and Civil War," *Slavic Review* 47(1) (Spring 1988): 31–38.

exception of the Bolsheviks in the fledgling Soviet Union. Bolshevik nationality policy may have helped to prolong its existence as a multi-cultural state, but would ultimately prove to be its undoing. The old Muscovite center controlled by the Bolsheviks was predominantly, indeed overwhelmingly, Great Russian. But the Bolshevik leadership included many representatives of different ethnic and cultural origins. Their first government included the unique position of a Commissar of Nationalities headed by Stalin, a Georgian, with a Polish deputy, and staffed by a variety of nationalities including Tatars. Lenin's interpretation of Marxism held out the prospect of national self-determination while at the same time proposing a transnational association based on the equality of nations.[57]

Baltic littoral

In the Baltic littoral the February Revolution loosened the bonds between the Grand Duchy of Finland and the central government, now "provisional," weak, and struggling to redefine relations between the old center of power and the borderlands.[58] Within two years the country was plunged into civil war and foreign intervention, leading to secession. On the eve of the First World War, there were already signs of a polarization of Finnish society. Former officers of the disbanded Finnish army organized a clandestine Military Committee and successfully petitioned the German High Command to train volunteers in Germany. In 1916, Finnish Jäger battalions numbering 2,000 men went into action against the Russian army around Riga. In July 1917, the Military Committee, supported by the extreme right in Finnish politics, requested a German landing on the coast and began to form a clandestine Civic Guard of Protection Corps. Together with the Jäger battalions it would constitute the Finnish White Army that defeated the domestic Reds and with German help drove the Soviet Red Army out of Finland.

The Finnish Red Guards emerged from the same socioeconomic turmoil and displayed the same war-weariness that pervaded urban Russia. By September 1917, soviets of workers and soldiers armed by the Bolsheviks in Petrograd were poised to take power in Finland. But the

---

[57] For the important role in the revolutionary movements of quasi-assimilated intellectuals from the borderlands, especially the Bolsheviks, whose ideology would "sustain imperial structures," see Lilian Riga, "The Ethnic Roots of Class Universalism. Rethinking the 'Russian' Revolutionary Elite," *American Journal of Sociology* 114(3) (November 2008): 649–705.

[58] The following is based mainly on C. Jay Smith, *Finland and the Russian Revolution* (Athens, GA: University of Georgia Press, 1958); Anthony Upton, *The Finnish Revolution 1917–18* (Minneapolis, MI: University of Minnesota Press, 1980).

Finnish left was divided. Stalin, in his first assignment after having been named Commissar of Nationalities, arrived in Finland, urging the Social Democrats to join the revolution. Appalled by the violence of the Red Guards, the Social Democratic leadership wavered. Stalin never forgave them. The situation rapidly disintegrated into civil war. The right drew its main strength from the rural north and center, the left from the more urbanized south. What tipped the balance was the professional competence of the White armed forces led by former Finnish officers of the tsarist army. Their most outstanding leader was the future president of independent Finland, General Baron Karl Gustav Mannerheim.

The Germans made a major contribution to the victory of the Whites. During the negotiations leading to the Treaty of Brest-Litovsk in March 1918, the German High Command relentlessly pressed the fledgling Soviet government to recognize Finnish independence and then to refrain from massively intervening to support the Red Guards. Intervention by soldiers of the Red Army stationed in Finland, numerically superior to any force the Finns and Germans could put into the field, could easily have turned the tide in favor of the Reds. But they were demoralized and discouraged from taking action by their officers. After Brest-Litovsk, the Germans stepped up their supply of arms and dispatched an expeditionary force that drove the Reds out of Helsinki. In return they obtained far-reaching commercial concessions. A White Finland suited the plans of the High Command to create a vast *Mitteleuropa* customs and economic union under German control.

The problem of drawing Finland's eastern frontier with Soviet Russia was settled only after the Finns failed to seize eastern Karelia. This was a vaguely defined region composed of parts of several Russian *gubernii* to the east of the old boundary line separating the grand duchy and Russia which had first been drawn in 1323 between Sweden and Novgorod. At the turn of the twentieth century, it was inhabited by 200,000 people, 61 percent of whom were Karelian Finns and the ethnically related Vepses, and 39 percent of whom were Russians. Mannerheim was eager to annex it as part of his design for a Greater Finland. In March 1918, units of the Protective Corps crossed into Russian territory. The plan was frustrated by the British–German rivalry in the region and the adroit maneuvering of the Bolshevik leaders, who manipulated both the British and Germans in order to restore the old frontier. Valuable resources were at stake: the railroad from Petrograd to Murmansk, the only ice-free port in north Russia, and the copper mines of Pechenga (Petsamo). In a confusing episode, a mixed interventionist force under British command managed to drive out the White Finns, whom they suspected of collaborating with the Germans, in order to secure the region for the White Russian armies.

They only succeeded, however, in making it possible for the Bolsheviks to regain control over the entire region once the White armies had been defeated. The problem for the White Finns, as Mannerheim recognized, was the political necessity of acting independently of any foreign influence, yet the military necessity was to find an ally who would recognize Finnish independence.

Once the Germans had departed, the Russian White governments, obsessed with restoring Greater Russian hegemony, refused to recognize Finnish independence or its boundaries. After an abortive offensive on their own, the Finns reached an accommodation with the Bolsheviks. The Treaty of Tartu in December 1920 ceded Petsamo to the Finns; in return they restored two provinces of eastern Karelia to Soviet Russia, which promised to create an autonomous government of Karelia. When the Bolsheviks reneged, the Karelian Finns launched a local insurrection, supported by Finnish nationalist bands across the border, which had fought to keep Karelia in 1919 and 1920. The Bolsheviks suppressed the rising, but only after making a series of tactical and logistical mistakes that, curiously enough, Stalin repeated in the Winter War of 1940. Having apparently learned a lesson they later forgot, the Soviet government established a Soviet Socialist Autonomous Republic in 1923 as part of the policy of indigenation (korenizatsiia), allowing Finnish-language schools. But the struggle for Karelia had not ended. Finland and the Soviet Union fought two more wars: in 1940, when Stalin raised the status of the Karelo-Finnish republic to all-union status; and in 1941–1944, when the border was finally fixed. The old antagonists, Mannerheim and Stalin, were present at the final act.

From the February to the October revolutions, the peoples of Russia's Baltic provinces began to move along separate paths toward autonomy and independence. The interplay of class and ethnic conflict, together with a foreign, primarily German, intervention was different in Estland, Lifland, and Kurland – emerging from the struggle to form the countries of Estonia and Latvia – and in Lithuania. Estonia did not exist before April 1917, when groups of Est nationalists won recognition from the Provisional Government of a union between Estland and northern Lifland. Middle-of-the-road politicians, backed by the professional and merchant classes, aspired only to autonomy within a democratic Russia. At first they had no armed force to back them up. The Estonians had been permitted to recruit their own army units only after the February Revolution. They were not strong enough to prevent a Bolshevik seizure of power in the northern towns where a Russian-speaking working class was concentrated. Therefore, when they declared independence in February 1918, they were obliged to rely on German troops who occupied most of the Baltic littoral in order to forestall a Bolshevik occupation. The Baltic Germans, joined by collaborators among the Estonians and Latvian middle class, requested that the Kaiser take them under his personal protection.

The Latvians were more deeply divided than the Estonians. The Germans were more numerous and well organized; the Latvian working class, located mainly in Riga, was more radical. The Provisional Government had permitted the formation of a separate Latvian Riflemen's Corps that fell under Bolshevik influence during 1917 and became a vital contributor to the success of the Bolshevik Revolution in Petrograd. The German occupation of the future Latvian territories of Kurland and southern Lifland was as repressive as in Estland. After Germany left the war, a group of Latvians from different parties formed a national council which declared Latvian independence.[59] Both the Estonian and Latvian states were precarious affairs; their survival depended on the protection of the German Freikorps volunteers or the British navy.

After the German surrender in the west, a British squadron was dispatched to the Baltic to enforce the blockade against Germany and render assistance to the anti-Bolshevik forces. The Allies agreed to retain units of the German army (*Freikorps*) in the Baltic in order to check a Bolshevik advance. General von der Goltz, who had led the German force in Finland, assumed command. He was determined to strengthen the German presence in the newly formed states. He could count on local support from the *Baltische Landeswehr* recruited from the Baltic Germans. These forces, together with 3,000 Finnish volunteers, joined Estonian units to drive the Red Army out of Estonia. Von der Goltz followed up this victory by taking Riga from the Bolsheviks, but then overreached himself. His continued advance exposed his forces to the international complexities of the struggle over the Baltic littoral.

While the British needed the German forces to check the spread of Bolshevism, they opposed the establishment of a German sphere of influence in the region. A number of influential politicians in London doubted the ability of the Estonians and Latvians to form viable states, but they thought they could balance the Germans by assisting the White forces assembling in the region in order to repulse the Red Army. They failed, however, to persuade the Whites to recognize the autonomy of Estonia and Latvia within a Greater Russian state. At a crucial moment in this tangled business, the initiative shifted to the local forces.

---

[59] Andrew Ezergailis, *The 1917 Revolution in Latvia* (Boulder, CO: East European Monographs, 1974).

In spring 1919, a joint Latvian–Estonian force defeated the *Landeswehr*, which served as von der Goltz' advance guard, prompting David Kirby to remark that "the twentieth century battle of Wenden was thus as much a turning point as had been the defeat inflicted on the Muscovite forces by a Swedish–Polish army in 1578."[60] Their joint forces went on to expel the White Russians from their territory before separating to consolidate their national aims. The Estonians, having no interest in promoting a Greater Russian state, refused to participate in the last offensive of the White General Yudenich against Petrograd. The Latvians briefly joined the Poles in driving out the last of the Bolsheviks. The leaders of both new states then reached agreements with Lenin's government in 1920 to recognize their independence and establish a boundary along the front lines. Like the Finns, the Estonians and Latvians were able to take advantage of the defeat of Germany and the weakness of Russia to gain independence with a minimum of Western help, a situation that would not be repeated during the Second World War when both Nazi Germany and the Soviet Union would seek alternatively to turn them back into borderlands under their control, while the Western powers looked on helplessly from afar.

What made the situation in Lithuania different from the otherwise similar experience of the Estonians and Latvians was the Polish factor. This complicated the already complex rivalry between Russia and Germany that pervaded the struggle over the Baltic littoral. In the early stages of the Lithuanian national movement following the February Revolution, a national council (*Taryba*) was formed as in other borderlands of west Eurasia. It met under the German occupation, arousing suspicions among Lithuanians living abroad and alienating the Lithuanian socialists.[61] In March 1918, the Taryba bowed to German pressure to form a firm and permanent alliance in order to obtain recognition for their declaration of independence. The German High Command kept a tight rein on Lithuanian political life until its defeat in the west. After the Armistice in November 1918, Lithuania fell into a state of near anarchy. As to its future, a plethora of solutions sprouted from different quarters. The Taryba proclaimed a provisional constitution and formed a government in Vilnius (Vilna, Wilno). Shortly afterwards, the Lithuanians withdrew from their new capital with the retreating German army. Polish legionnaires occupied the city. In Warsaw, the Poles offered

---

[60] David Kirby, *The Baltic World, 1772–1993. Europe's Northern Periphery in an Age of Change* (London: Longman, 1995), p. 279.

[61] The standard work on these events remains Alfred E. Senn, *The Emergence of Modern Lithuania* (New York: Columbia University Press, 1959).

the Lithuanians a federal union similar to that of the Jagiellonian state. The local socialists hoped for assistance from the Red Army advancing from the east, but then opted for fusion with Belorus in a vain attempt to reestablish the territory of Greater Lithuania dating back to the sixteenth century.

By 1919, Lithuania had become a battleground in the Russian Civil War, with Bolshevik forces fighting elements of the White Russian Western Army. Once again it was the Poles who gained the upper hand by driving out both the Whites and Reds. They renewed their proposal to form a union. But the Lithuanian leaders were set on independence and sought to win recognition from the Allied Council in Paris. The British were inclined to approve, if only to place restraints on the French aspirations to create a Greater Poland. For the Lithuanians, one of the main problems was the lack of a strong national army comparable to those of the Finns, Estonians, and Latvians. Thus, the fate of Lithuania as an independent state and of its natural capital, Vilnius, was determined by the outcome of the Soviet–Polish War of 1920.

The Pontic frontier

In Austrian Galicia, Józef Piłsudski led the fight for an independent Poland on the side of the Central Powers. A long-time opponent of imperial Russia and an active revolutionary in 1905, he had already won Austrian permission to organize a network of paramilitary groups in Galicia in the prewar period. When the war broke out, he unified several of these riflemen associations into a Polish Legion that he hoped would become the nucleus of a future Polish national army. Many of its officers were to play a leading role in Poland's postwar government and the Polish government-in-exile in London during the Second World War. Once across the frontier, he was disappointed by the lack of response from the Polish population to his appeals to take up arms against Russia. The spirit of accommodation to Russian rule had gained ground after the constitutional reforms and was buoyed by the generous Russian promises of autonomy. Disillusioned by the reluctance of the Central Powers to grant Poland its independence, he resigned his commission and then advised his men to refuse an oath of allegiance to the kaiser. Before it was disbanded by the Germans, the Legion numbered about 20,000 men. Briefly arrested and then freed by the end of the war, Piłsudski reclaimed command of his former legionnaires from the Germans, expelled their army, and proclaimed himself chief of state.

The second main component of the future Polish army came from Poles recruited in France and prisoners of war from the German army who served on the Western Front. Initially, the tsarist ambassador, Izvol'skii, opposed the formation of separate Polish units, arguing that any decision affecting Poland was an internal affair of the Russian Empire. The 1917 February Revolution in Russia and the critical situation on the Western Front changed all this. France and the Russian Provisional Government reached an agreement on the formation of an autonomous Polish army. At the same time, Polish émigrés in Western Europe, led by Roman Dmowski, formed a National Committee and gradually brought this force under their control. Their ranks were swelled by an influx of Poles from the United States. General Józef Haller was appointed to lead them. A brigade commander of Piłsudski's Legion, he had deserted with his men to the Russians in early 1918 and then fought his way out of a German encirclement before finding his way to France. By 1919 his Blue Army numbered over 68,000 men, fully equipped by the French who envisaged it as a major force in reconstituting a strong Poland as a bulwark against both the Germans and the Bolsheviks.

The reconstitution of Poland was largely the work of these two armed forces reconstituted into a national Polish army. But the political leaders had inherited a divided legacy and disagreed over the nature of the state and the territorial limits of its sovereignty. Dmowski and Piłsudski conceived Poland in different ways. Dmowski's original vision of a purely ethnic Polish state dependent on Russia changed dramatically after the Bolshevik Revolution. He envisaged an independent, much expanded state in order to survive between Germany and Soviet Russia. This meant absorbing all of eastern Galicia, part of Podolia and Volynia, most of Belarus, including two-thirds of Minsk province, and all of the province of Vilnius. These territories would be colonized by Poles from the Vistula lands, who would gradually assimilate the Belorussian and Ukrainian population. He stopped short of advocating a return to the frontiers of 1772, and instead favored reaching an accommodation with the Soviet Union on the basis of dividing the borderlands between their old centers of power. In effect, Dmowski was advocating a centralized, radically nationalizing, multicultural state.[62]

---

[62] One of Dmowski's close collaborators, Stanisław Grabski, subsequently Polish ambassador in Moscow, wrote in 1922: "As long as there are territories in Poland with a majority of Orthodox or even Greek Catholic people, Russia will not cease dreaming about their recovery, that is certain. But it is also certain that when the Polish–Russian borderland becomes Polish territory with a clear majority of Roman Catholic and Polish-speaking people, Russia will relinquish its aspirations for these territories." During the several decades Russia would require to recover, he continued, "we can and should ensure that our state border will simultaneously be Poland's nation [ethnic] border. At that time the age-old conflict between Poland and Russia over the Ruthenian [i.e., Ukrainian] lands

Piłsudski's vision for Poland is more elusive because his plans underwent several changes and he was imprecise in explaining them.[63] He appeared to have favored two different kinds of association between Poland and the Kresy. First, he envisaged some kind of federal arrangement, joining Poland with a historic Lithuania, the land of his birth, and Belarus; this resembled the structure of the former Polish–Lithuanian Commonwealth. Second, he considered forming a political alliance with Finland, Estonia, and Latvia, and concluding a military alliance with the Ukrainian National Republic aimed at securing the independence of the borderland states from Germany and Soviet Russia. Lithuania proved to be the stumbling block. Suspicious of Polish imperial designs and alienated by the Polish occupation of Vilnius, they opposed both a federation and an alliance. Piłsudski's most promising opportunity to expand Poland's frontiers to the east lay in a military alliance with the Ukrainian National Republic.

The wartime struggle over the borderlands of the Pontic steppe contained many of the features at the ground level of the Polish "deluge" in the seventeenth century. The ideological center had shifted, but not completely from the religious to the national. The cast of external powers had also changed, but only partially: Sweden was out, the Ottoman Turks marginalized, Germany was in; but foreign intervention remained a critical element. The fundamental issue was whether the Ukrainian lands – their boundaries as ill-defined as ever – would be constituted as an independent state, a buffer, or else integrated into a multinational Russian or Polish state. Neither the external powers nor the national constituencies on the ground were agreed among themselves as to the preferred outcome.

In Austrian Galicia the Ukrainians were divided between the more moderate pro-Habsburg wing, who advocated the joining together of eastern Galicia and Bukovina in an autonomous crownland free of Polish dominance, and the more radical Russian wing, who agitated for a democratic and independent Ukraine constituted from the borderlands of the Pontic frontier. Mediating between the two groups was another typical man of the borderlands, the Metropolitan of Galicia, Andrei Sheptits'kyi, head of the Greek Catholic (Uniat) Church. His proposal was to create an autonomous Ukraine under the Habsburg emperor, with its own military force based on the Cossack tradition and

would finally be decided and the object of conflict would cease to exist." Cited in Michael Palij, *The Ukrainian–Polish Defensive Alliance, 1919–1921. An Aspect of the Ukrainian Revolution* (Edmonton: University of Alberta Press, 1995), pp. 60–61.
[63] For Piłsudski's thinking and his clash with Dmowski, the Polish anti-federalists, and the Lithuanians, see Dziewanowski, *Joseph Piłsudski*, pp. 88–100, 104–37 ff. and *passim*.

commanded by a hetman, and with its own church hierarchy independent of the Holy Synod in St. Petersburg.[64] Although Sheptits'kyi was destined to be disappointed, he emerged a national hero from imprisonment by the Russians. During the Second World War, he championed the creation of an independent Ukraine in cooperation with the Germans. In 1918, the Central Powers initially favored the more radical group. But the Austrians expressed concern over the growing sentiment in Galicia for the unification of all Ukrainians. The tsarist government was, as usual, divided over a Ukrainian policy. When the Russian offensive of 1916 swept back into Galicia, the civilian cabinet reaffirmed its commitment to incorporating Carpathian Rus into the empire, but the army leaders resisted these irredentist claims.

The February Revolution failed to reconcile competing Russian interests. The Provisional Government was initially sympathetic to the supporters of Ukrainian autonomy, and as a gesture freed Metropolitan Sheptits'kyi from detention. But a rift soon developed between the provincial revolutionary government in Kiev, the Central Rada, and Petrograd. As the Rada stepped up its pressure for a national-autonomous solution, the Provisional Government stalled. The Russian army command ran roughshod over local officials, requisitioned food and supplies, and ignored the breakdown in discipline that led to atrocities against the local population, including savage pogroms against the Jews.[65] Under the Russian occupation the breakdown in public order threatened to plunge Galicia into chaos.

From the moment the Ukrainian People's Republic was proclaimed in Kiev in November 1917, its territory became the most fought over battleground during the Russian Civil War and Intervention. Reduced to a borderland open on all sides to intervention, it was contested by Red and White armies, the Central Powers, and Polish rivals, while the Ukrainians, although deeply divided, struggled to maintain autonomy or achieve complete independence. At Brest-Litovsk the Germans supported Ukrainian as well as Finnish aspirations, and signed a peace treaty recognizing Ukrainian independence. The Ottomans welcomed the establishment of an independent Ukraine as a buffer that would shield them from the ancient "Muscovite" threat and sought to establish "friendly relations." In February 1918, a separate treaty between the Central Powers

---

[64] Von Hagen, *War*, p. 16; Andrii Krawchuk, *Christian Social Ethics in Ukraine. The Legacy of Andrei Sheptytsky* (Edmonton: University of Alberta Press, 1997); Paul R. Magocsi (ed.), *Morality and Reality. The Life and Times of Andrei Sheptyts'kyi* (Edmonton: University of Alberta Press, 1989).

[65] Von Hagen, *War*, pp. 79–85.

and the Ukrainian Rada included a commercial clause that granted favored nation status to the Ottoman Empire, raising hopes in Istanbul (as in Vienna) that access to the granary of Ukraine would nullify the effect of the Allied naval blockade and relieve domestic food shortages. In addition, as Talât Pasha cabled to Enver Pasha, the new state could clear the way for the creation of Muslim governments in the Crimea and the Caucasus.[66] The Crimean Tatars had already announced the formation of a national parliament (*kurultay*) and a cabinet. But local Bolsheviks, backed by sailors of the Black Sea fleet, rapidly overthrew the Tatar government and set up a Soviet Republic of Taurida. Thus began a multi-sided struggle over the future of Crimea.[67]

The Ottoman Empire proved to be the weakest contender for influence in their old Crimean stamping grounds. After the Germans drove out the Bolsheviks in April 1918, they faced a problem similar to that which frustrated the Central Powers in the Polish borderlands: how to reconcile the aims of two competing national movements; in the case of the Crimea that between the Ukrainian and the Tatar. The Ottomans watched, helpless to affect the outcome, as the Germans came down on the side of union between the Crimea and Ukraine.[68] With the end of the war, the struggle continued among the Red, White, and local nationalist forces. The victorious Bolsheviks attempted to square the circle by establishing an Autonomous Crimean Soviet Socialist Republic within the Ukrainian Soviet Socialist Republic. But it was a hollow victory for the Tatars. During the First World War, they would endeavor again with German help to gain independence, but with catastrophic results.

The German Command in Ukraine ignored the interests of its Austrian and Ottoman allies in promoting its own agenda. Invited in to repel a Bolshevik invasion, the Germans arbitrarily intervened in the economic life of the country, hoping, as did its allies, to obtain necessary food supplies to stave off the devastating effects of the Allied blockade. When they met opposition, they overthrew the mildly socialist republican government of the Central Rada in April 1918 and established a more compliant regime under Hetman Pavlo Skoropads'kyi. He was forced to rely on conservative landowners and officials of the old regime from the non-Ukrainian, mainly Russian, population to staff his government and command his embryonic Ukrainian army.

---

[66] Hakan Kirimlı, "Diplomatic Relations between the Ottoman Empire and the Ukrainian Democratic Republic, 1918–21," *Middle Eastern Studies* 34(4) (October 1998): 202.

[67] Richard Pipes, *The Formation of the Soviet Union*, rev. edn (Cambridge, MA: Harvard University Press, 1970), pp. 184–90.

[68] Kirimlı, "Diplomatic Relations," p. 207.

Map 6.1 Ukraine after the Treaty of Brest-Litovsk

Like other aspiring national leaders in the separatist borderlands, but earlier than most, Ukrainian officers in the Russian army had sought as early as May 1917 to organize military congresses and to form national units with Ukrainian as the language of command. Splits rapidly opened up in their ranks; the gap widened between the various Ukrainian units and the Russian army, as well as between the Petrograd Soviet and the Provisional Government.[69] As commander of the 34th Army Corps on the southwestern front, Skoropads'kyi had been skeptical of the Ukrainianization movement in the army. He was contemptuous of the

[69] Mark von Hagen, "The Russian Imperial Army and the Ukrainian National Movement in 1917," *Ukrainian Quarterly* 54(3–4) (Fall–Winter 1998): 220–56.

socialists in the Provisional Government and the Rada in Kiev. But his hatred of the Bolsheviks finally convinced him in June to endorse Ukrainianization as a way of preserving the combat effectiveness of the former Imperial Army. Throughout the summer and fall of 1917 in the disintegrating political situation, his views evolved toward the establishment of a Ukrainian state as a kind of free Cossack society. He found himself torn between loyalty to the vanishing idea of imperial rule and the demands for national autonomy rendered more complex by social conflicts between the Russian right and the Ukrainian left. At the same time, he was suspicious of the Galician Ukrainians whom he regarded as extreme nationalists, pro-Polish, and different socially and culturally from the "Russian" Ukrainians.[70]

Following the Treaty of Brest-Litovsk, Skoropads'kyi hesitated over his various choices, none of which, he apologetically suggested in his memoirs, were ideal. He cast his lot with the Central Powers in the belief he could obtain more concessions from them than from either the Whites or the Bolsheviks. In this he proved to be correct. He was able to promote Ukrainian cultural institutions and secure promises from the Central Powers to incorporate the Crimea, Bessarabia, and the Kuban into his state. He also created a large army of 65,000 men.[71] But he governed as a dictator lacking a broad popular base. The Austro-German policy of confiscating food supplies and supporting landowners seeking to recover estates expropriated by the peasants undermined his authority and ignited peasant insurrections. After the German surrender, he sought support from the Allies who opposed Ukrainian independence and demanded instead a federation with Russia under a White government.

Disaffected Ukrainian nationalist groups now rallied to organize a popular insurrection under a new government called the Directory, evoking the moderate phase of the French Revolution. As in Finland and the Baltic states, the key to Ukrainian independence was an organized armed force that could win endorsement from the Allies. The principal leader in creating a Ukrainian army was Symon Petliura, a well-known journalist and political activist who began to work toward that end in the summer of 1917. He was the spark plug in a series of All Ukrainian Military congresses that sought to win the approval of the Provisional Government in

[70] Mark von Hagen, "'I Love Russia, and/but I Want Ukraine,' or How a Russian General became Hetman of the Ukrainian State, 1917–18," *Journal of Ukrainian Studies* 29(1–2) (Summer–Winter 2004): 123–35.

[71] Yaroslav Hrytsak, *Narys istoriï Ukraïny. Formuvannia modernoï ukraïns'koï natsiï XIX–XX stolittia* (Kiev: Vyd-vo Heneza, 1996), pp. 127–34, who argues that Skoropads'kyi's innovative concept of a Ukrainian nation was founded on loyalty to the state rather than on knowledge of the Ukrainian language.

Petrograd for the Ukrainianization of troops in the imperial army. Although a rival of Skoropads'kyi, he hesitated to assume control over the national movement and failed to provide strong political leadership at critical moments both before the Bolshevik seizure of power and after the Treaty of Brest-Litovsk. In other words, he was no Mannerheim. Yet the obstacles he and other Ukrainian leaders faced in forging a strong army standing behind a unified government should not be underestimated. The main problems were a political split between West and East Ukraine, and an anarchic social revolution in the countryside.

In Galicia during the waning days of the Habsburg Monarchy, a group of Ukrainian military men took power in L'viv and proclaimed a Western Ukrainian Republic, which included the provinces of Galicia, northern Bukovina, and Trans-Carpathia. Initially, the republic appeared to enjoy advantages in state-building over East Ukraine. As we have seen, under the Habsburgs Ukrainians in the province of Galicia had developed a vibrant community life and gained political experience in their competition with the Poles. When the war broke out, the Ukrainian political leaders in Galicia proclaimed their loyalty to the crown and petitioned for the formation of a Ukrainian military unit. The Monarchy conscripted hundreds of thousands of Galicians into the regular army, but also permitted the formation of an elite force, the Ukrainian Sich Riflemen, similar to Piłsudski's Polish Legion. The Austrians used these troops in their occupation of Ukraine.

When the war ended, the West Ukrainian Republic rapidly established contact with the Ukrainian People's Republic in Kiev, and in January 1919 the two governments joined in a fragile union. There were ideological differences and West Ukraine retained an autonomous status. But the real problems crashed in from the outside. In West Ukraine the main external enemy was the new Polish state, which claimed the territory of eastern Galicia. There were others as well: the Romanians occupied Bukovina, and the Hungarians remained in control of Trans-Carpathia until the Czechs drove them out. The West Ukrainians rapidly rebuilt the army that had dispersed after Skoropads'kyi's departure with the Germans. But they were no match for the 100,000-man Blue Army of General Haller, armed, equipped, and encouraged by the French. Meanwhile, in early 1919, the Directory was being squeezed between a renewed Bolshevik attack from the north and the advance of the White Volunteer Army supported by 60,000 French troops who had landed in Odessa. In the words of Serhy Yekelchyk: "Ukraine was about to become a battlefield in the Russian Civil War between Reds and Whites. But the events may also be characterized as a Ukrainian civil war, for ethnic Ukrainians serving in the Directory's Bolshevik and White armies were killing each other for the victory of their respective vision of 'Ukraine.'"[72]

As the military fronts formed and disintegrated – Kiev changed hands six times from 1917 to 1920 – the countryside was ablaze. Tens of thousands of disbanded soldiers, deserters, and armed peasants plunged the countryside into chaos. They drove out the landlords and broke up the big estates; they unleashed orgies of looting and anti-Jewish violence; they often joined up with regular armies, but were not above switching sides.[73] In an effort to salvage something from the wreckage Petliura turned to the Poles. Piłsudski welcomed the possibility of an alliance once it was clear to him that the Whites had lost the civil war in Ukraine and a struggle with the Bolsheviks was inevitable. In April 1920, the Polish government and the Directory signed a political agreement and a military convention. However, the Poles held all the cards and the Ukrainians were forced to accept a subordinate position in the alliance. Their political relationship to Poland and their frontiers were left vague and imprecise.[74] For Piłsudski, the agreements left open the possibility of incorporating Ukraine into his large federative scheme. For the opposite reasons, Dmowski and his supporters opposed the agreement. They preferred to have Russia rather than Ukraine as a neighbor. As Stanisław Grabski declared: "for we, as Poles, have more rights to the pre-partition lands lying east of the [river] Zbruch than the Russians," while Ukraine would demand its rights in eastern Galicia on the basis of national self-determination.[75]

When Piłsudski finally launched his attack on the Bolsheviks, Ukrainian troops strengthened his right flank. But the Poles did not fulfill their promises to supply a large Ukrainian army. Suspecting that they never would, elements of the Sich Riflemen left the front and crossed into Czechoslovakia where they were interned. The Polish–Russian War turned into a see-saw struggle, with the Poles occupying Kiev before being driven back to Warsaw, and then in a counter-offensive recovering most of Galicia and west Belarus.

Mutually exhausted, the Poles and Bolsheviks signed the Treaty of Riga in 1920 that recognized the military front line as the international

---

[72] Serhy Yekelchyk, *Ukraine. Birth of a Modern Nation* (Oxford University Press, 2007), p. 79.

[73] John Reshetar, Jr., *The Ukrainian Revolution, 1917–1920* (Princeton University Press, 1952), remains the standard work.

[74] The political agreement recognized "the right of Ukraine to independent political existence within its northern, eastern and southern frontiers as they shall be determined by means of separate agreements concluded by the Ukrainian People's Republic with the respective border states." For a full English translation of both documents, see Palij, *The Ukrainian–Polish Alliance*, pp. 70–75.

[75] Palij, *The Ukrainian–Polish Alliance*, pp. 78–79.

boundary. This left the Ukrainian army to face the full force of the Red Army. Badly battered, they retreated into Poland where they were interned. Petliura's attempt to organize a resistance movement in Soviet-occupied Ukraine ended badly. Divided once again between two powers, Galician Ukrainians were embittered by the outcome of years of fighting. Hostile to both Polish and Soviet rule, they were the constant source of opposition and resistance. The German conquest of Poland in 1939 and the invasion of the Soviet Union once again raised hopes of independence. West Ukraine again became the locus of a multivalent struggle, with little to choose between the Wehrmacht, Soviet partisans and the Red Army, the Polish underground Home Army, Ukrainian nationalists, and the armed bands who owed allegiance to no one but their leaders; an old and recurrent feature of the struggle over the borderlands.

The outcome of the Polish–Russian War also determined the shape of independent states in the Baltic littoral. The Bolsheviks, having recognized Latvian independence in order to deprive Poland of an ally in the war, recognized Lithuania for the same reason. In a peace treaty in July 1920 the Soviet government also recognized its right to the much-disputed Vilnius in exchange for transit rights for the Red Army in the war against Poland. But the Poles reoccupied the city in their last counter-offensive. The powers in Paris were unable to mediate. At the heart of a shatter zone inhabited by Jews, Poles, Lithuanians, and Belorussians, Vilnius remained in Polish hands (under the name Wilno) until 1939 when the Lithuanians took advantage of Poland's defeat by Germany to re-annex it. Between the wars its contested status continued to poison relations between the Poles and Lithuanians, easing the way for Germany and the Soviet Union to intervene and manipulate the local rivals.

On the southern margins of the Pontic frontier, the civil war and intervention rekindled the dormant struggle of the Cossacks against the center of Russian power. The Treaty of Brest-Litovsk had provided for an independent Ukraine without demarcating its southeastern boundaries. The unimpeded advance of the German army threatened to take control of the Donbass coalfields and the Black Sea ports of Taganrog, Rostov, and even Novocherkassk.[76] They encountered a highly volatile and fluid political situation in the Don borderland.[77] The Don Territory occupied a special

---

[76] Udo Gehrmann, "Germany and the Cossack Country," *Revolutionary Russia* 5(2) (1992): 147–71.

[77] These complexities are clearly sorted out in Peter Holquist, *Making War, Forging Revolution. Russia's Continuum of Crisis, 1914–1921* (Cambridge, MA: Harvard University Press, 2002), on which the following section relies.

place in the imperial system under the authority of the Ministry of War. The Cossacks enjoyed a measure of self-government from which the non-Cossack population of peasants and the growing number of workers were excluded. But economic development had opened up social divisions among them. The war increased tensions between the younger and older generations, and between the propertied and non-propertied groups, as well as widening the social gulf between the Cossacks and the mass of the peasantry. Following the February Revolution, the process of democratization fostered the growth of cross-cutting allegiances among different political organizations – parties, local soviets, Cossack committees – and contributed to a further fragmentation of the social and political order. Different groups of Cossacks advanced competing claims to represent legitimate authority.

The Bolshevik Revolution further deepened the split among the Cossacks and touched off civil war in the Don. The anti-Bolshevik officers of the Imperial Army perceived the Don as a bulwark of counter-revolution and a resource base for the organization of what was to become the main force of the Whites, the Volunteer Army. The Bolsheviks viewed the situation in much the same way. In both cases the stereotype of the reactionary Cossack prevailed over the extremely complex social reality in the Don. A vivid illustration of the dilemma of the Cossacks seeking to defend the Don against external threats, but avoid being drawn into a general civil war, was the visit of a delegation that the Cossack government sent to Moscow to negotiate with the Soviet government. They met with Stalin in his capacity as Commissar of Nationalities, for as Peter Holquist notes: "The shift from defining Cossacks as an estate to seeing them as an ethnic or national group was already under way."[78] Stalin asserted that the Bolsheviks supported "the laboring Cossacks," but not the reactionary leadership. The Cossack delegates insisted they could put their own affairs in order and did not need Soviet punitive expeditions in the Don. What finally led to a collision between the two parties was the Bolshevik reaction to the continued advance of the German army. Although Lenin had nothing against the autonomy of the Don, he accepted the views of local Bolsheviks in Rostov that the only way to check the Germans and deprive them of the specious slogan of self-determination was to practice proletarian self-determination by establishing a Don Soviet Republic. This in turn triggered a series of spontaneous eruptions against the Soviet authorities that became known as the Cossack insurgency.[79] With German assistance the insurgents easily overthrew the Soviet power in the Don.

[78] Holquist, *Making War*, p. 121.
[79] Holquist interprets these risings as an equivalent of the Great Fear in the French

With the withdrawal of the German army after the Armistice of November 1918, the Don Cossacks became one of the mainstays of the anti-Bolshevik forces. But they did not associate themselves fully with the Volunteer Army and the White cause. Characteristic of a people of a borderland, they regarded with suspicion the concept of the highly centralized united Greater Russian state envisaged by the White leaders. This borderland view also influenced their military campaigning. They were willing to join the Volunteer Army when the Red Army threatened their homeland, but they insisted on maintaining their own army outside the White command structure. They were reluctant, or else they refused, to operate outside their own territories. Ataman P. N. Krasnov of the Don went as far as to revive their seventeenth-century battle cry: "Long live the tsar in the Kremlin, but we Cossacks will stay on the Quiet Don."[80]

The Don Cossacks, like the warlord armies in China, were opposed to the establishment of a centralized government, but at the same time were unwilling to cooperate with other organized armed groups like themselves. On the one hand, they cherished their internal democratic order. On the other hand, they maintained a *soslovie* mentality in their relations with social outsiders, whom they called *inogorodnie* (literally, "those from other towns," but meaning "those who come from outside the territory of the Don"). It was as if they had turned their backs on the twentieth century and looked to the traditions of their early history. The disagreements with other Cossack hosts also reflected their exclusivist views. When the Red Army occupied the Don, the Cossack host fell back to the Kuban where they were not eagerly welcomed. The Kuban Cossacks had become increasingly war-weary and their morale had seriously deteriorated. Their hostility toward General Denikin and the Volunteer Army fueled their differences with the Terek Cossacks, who had also sought refuge in the Kuban from the advancing Red Army. In their last effort to reach an accommodation with one another, each Cossack host sent delegates to a meeting of the Supreme Krug in January 1920. By this time the ranks of the Volunteer Army had been seriously depleted. This left the Cossacks to represent the voice of the anti-Bolshevik forces in the north Caucasus. In desperation, Denikin appealed to the Cossacks not to form an independent state and offered them instead "broad autonomy," which he stated

---

Revolution, rooted in the belief that the Bolsheviks were determined to destroy the Cossack way of life by mobilizing the peasants and workers against them, whereas in fact the lines were more complex and tangled. Holquist, *Making War*, pp. 146–54.

[80] P. N. Krasnov, "Vsevelikoe voisko donskoe," *Arkhiv russkoi revoliutsii* 5 (Berlin, 1922): 215.

"was justified by the historical contributions of the Cossacks to the Russian cause." Further promises of a representative assembly, land reform, and a cabinet with Cossack representatives won over the delegates. But it was too late to save the anti-Bolshevik cause.[81]

Triplex Confinium and the Danubian frontier

While the disintegration and partitioning of the Russian Empire was checked and reversed by the Bolsheviks, the disintegration of the Austro-Hungarian Monarchy was permanent. Its borderlands broke away to constitute new multinational states, leaving Austria and Hungary, ironically, as the only homogeneous nation-states in ethnolinguistic terms to emerge from the wreckage of the multinational empires. The patching together of the successor states had only two remotely similar precedents in European history: the Treaty of Westphalia in 1648 and the Treaty of Vienna in 1815. But these exercises in redrawing frontiers were based on different principles: in the first case, religion; in the second case, containment of France. In these previous reconstructions of Europe, the shuffling of peoples involved in territorial adjustments was carried out without their consent, let alone their participation.

The legacy of the Habsburg Empire, duplicated to a lesser extent in other dissolving multinational states, was a mixture of national aspirations and *Staatsräson*, of local initiatives and external intervention. During and immediately after the First World War, the politicians and journalists of the subject populations in the embattled Habsburg borderlands drafted plans for reconstructing the space between German and Russian imperial power. They operated from two bases, in exile and in the homelands. The former group sought to rally their fellow countrymen in the diaspora where they were most strongly influenced by either Wilsonian or Leninist ideas of self-determination. The latter group tended to cling longer, if with diminishing enthusiasm, to the idea of autonomy within the multinational empires. For both groups the Czech political intellectuals often served as an inspiration and a weather vane. In 1915, Thomas G. Masaryk claimed he was the first to bring out "the political significance of the zone of small peoples in Europe that lies between the Germans and the Russians."[82]

---

[81] Peter Kenez, *Civil War in South Russia, 1919–1920* (Berkeley, CA: University of California Press, 1977), pp. 227–33, 240–44.
[82] T. G. Masaryk, *The Making of a State. Memoirs and Observations, 1914–1918* (New York: Frederick A. Stokes, 1927), pp. 86–87, as quoted in Dziewanowski, *Joseph Piłsudski*, p. 80.

South Slavs

There were three centers of political activity working along different lines toward a common goal of south Slavic unity. The Serbian government in exile on the island of Corfu was led by Prime Minister Nikola Pašić of the National Radical Party, who displayed an ominous inability to distinguish between a Greater Serbia and a Yugoslavia. The Yugoslav Committee (*Jugoslavenski odbor*), located in London, represented exiles in the dia-spora, mainly Croats, led by Ante Trumbić, a lawyer, and Frano Supilo, a journalist, from Dalmatia who favored a south Slavic state in which Croats, Slovenes, and Serbs would enjoy equal rights. Stjepan Radić, the founder of the Croat Peasant People's Party, influenced in the prewar period by Masaryk, was an advocate of a federalized Habsburg Monarchy, including an autonomous Croatian federal unit made up of Croats, Serbs, and Slovenes. For the Serbs outside the Monarchy, he proposed a feder-ation with the Bulgarians. At the end of the war he accepted the dissolu-tion of the empire, but proposed a confederal solution for the new state, fearing unification meant Serb domination.[83]

A fourth, and more fractured, center of south Slav agitation within the Habsburg Monarchy was the so-called "declaration movement."[84] During the early years of the war, the Slovene and Croat population generally expressed loyalty to the dynasty, although strident voices in Istria and Dalmatia called for some kind of reorganization of the south Slavs within the Monarchy. By the summer of 1917, war-weariness, economic distress, and arbitrary administration by Austro-Germans in the old Triplex Confinium rapidly eroded these sentiments. A mass movement at the grassroots for an autonomous Croat–Slovene unit in the Monarchy blossomed after Bishop Anton Jeglić of Ljubljana endorsed the action of the south Slav members of the Austrian parliament, the Yugoslav Club, which had gone into opposition. In the winter of 1917/ 18, new tactics of mass rallies and petitions signed by ordinary citizens gained momentum.[85] Local officials confessed their helplessness. The

---

[83] Ivo Banac, *The National Question in Yugoslavia. Origins, History, Politics* (Ithaca, NY: Cornell University Press, 1988), pp. 117–18, 124, 136; Dejan Djokić, *Pašić and Trumbić. The Kingdom of Serbs, Croats and Slovenes* (London: Haus, 2010), pp. 24, 33.

[84] The following is based on Marc Cornwall, "The Great War and the Yugoslav Grassroots. Popular Mobilization in the Habsburg Monarchy, 1914–18," in Dejan Djokić and James Ker-Lindsay, *New Perspectives on Yugoslavia. Key Issues and Controversies* (London: Routledge, 2011), pp. 27–45.

[85] A personal postscript to one of these petitions read: "We love the Habsburg Monarchy, and for that reason we demand for her peoples their own statehood and for us Yugoslavs our own independent state within her, for only thus can the monarchy continue." Cornwall, "The Great War and the Yugoslav Grassroots," p. 33.

movement gradually shifted away from the idea of preserving the Monarchy, although economic and political motives did not always coincide. Divisions appeared among Croats between partisans of a Croatian state and the Yugoslav idea. Upper-class Muslims feared being swallowed up by the south Slavs. Ambivalent attitudes toward the state and social turmoil in those regions help to explain future tensions in postwar Yugoslavia.[86]

The Serbs possessed two advantages in claiming a leading role in the creation of a south Slav (*iugo-slav*) state: prestige and power. Their prestige derived from a century of struggle to transform a contested borderland of the Triplex Confinium into an independent if still embattled state. Their power came from the barrels of their guns. The Serbian government had fled to Corfu after the crushing defeat and occupation of the country by the forces of Austria, Germany, and Bulgaria. It was accompanied by the remnants of the army, which had made a legendary retreat over the mountains and reassembled in Saloniki under the protection of the Allied Expeditionary Force under French command. Pašić was eager for political reasons to prove Serbia's value to the Allied cause. He sought to recruit volunteers from the Serbian diaspora and the Russian prisoner of war camps in order to replenish the ranks of his depleted army. His first success came in 1916 in Odessa with the formation of the First Serbian Volunteer Division. Initially, the Russian government and the tsar had been reluctant to violate the Hague Convention, sponsored by Nicholas II, which forbade the enrollment of prisoners of war in units fighting against their former country. As in the past they also hesitated to embrace fully a pan-Slav movement if it meant undermining legitimate dynastic authority. But the exigencies of war overcame their scruples. The Serb First Division numbering about 18,000 was thrown into fighting against their traditional enemies, the Bulgarians, on the Dobrudja front where it suffered enormous casualties.

Meanwhile, tensions arose between the Serbian National Assembly in Corfu, the Yugoslav Committee in London, and other Yugoslav émigré organizations over the structure of the future state and control over the volunteers. A year later a Second Division was formed in Russia, with Serbs still in the majority, but including more Croats and Slovenes than previously. Although it bore the name of the Serb, Croat, and Slovene Division, its Serb officers considered it a fully integrated unit of the Serbian army. This led to mass resignations by the Croat and Slovene officers and men, who joined Russian units.[87]

[86] Cornwall, "The Great War and the Yugoslav Grassroots," p. 42.
[87] Banac, *The National Question*, pp. 122–23.

The Second Division suffered from additional problems of morale and desertions, especially after the Russian Revolution in February 1917. It was evacuated through Archangel and across Siberia to Vladivostok. Both divisions were reconstituted and rearmed by the Allied Expeditionary Force in Saloniki under French command, where they joined the remnants of the regular Serbian army. As with the case of the Czech Legion, the military exploits of the First Serbian Division on the Saloniki Front were magnified by postwar nationalist literature and turned into a founding myth of the Yugoslav (read Greater Serbian) state.[88]

In the meantime, another Serbian fighting force was taking shape in the mountains of occupied Serbia and Montenegro. In February 1917, a spontaneous Serbian rising took place in the Bulgarian zone of occupation – Macedonia had been a volatile borderland for generations – before it was crushed by German and Austrian troops. But bands of guerrillas, called *comitadji*, sprang up, fighting a "little war" (*maly rat*), and employing the same terms and symbols employed in the struggle against the Turks in the sixteenth and seventeenth centuries. Četnik leaders of the national resistance in the Second World War like Kosta Pećanac and Draža Mihajlovich won their spurs in the guerrilla fighting of 1917–1918. In 1918, the guerrilla war spread rapidly among fugitives from the Habsburg army who were taking refuge in the forests. The comitadji joined the Saloniki force as it fought its way back to Serbia through Macedonia. They even succeeded in liberating some areas before the arrival of the regular Serbian divisions. The unified national army reoccupied Kosovo and launched reprisals against the Albanian bands and alleged collaborators with the Habsburgs. In Bosnia, reinforcements poured in from local guerrilla bands which had been fighting against the Muslim-Croat Schützkorps formed by the Habsburg commander to repress "banditry."[89]

In fall of 1918 Croatia was falling into a state of near anarchy. The most serious threat to the cohesion of the Habsburg army came from the prisoners of war liberated by the terms of the Treaty of Brest-Litovsk. As many as 200,000 had flooded back into the Monarchy; most of them were hostile to a continuation of the war. Although the Habsburg government interned them, fearing the spread of a "red wave," those who were sent back to their units helped to undermine morale; others refused to re-enlist

---

[88] Ivo Banac, "South Slav Prisoners of War in Revolutionary Russia," in Samuel Williamson and Peter Pastor (eds.), *Essays on World War I. Origins and Prisoners of War* (New York: Social Science Monographs, Brooklyn College Press, 1983), pp. 123–40.

[89] Andrej Mitrović, *Serbia's Great War, 1914–1918* (West Lafayette, IN: Purdue University Press, 2007), pp. 167–69, 248–50, 260–61, 275, 303.

and joined the Green bands of peasant guerrillas in the Croatian countryside.[90]

In Bosnia, communal violence broke out between the Serbs and Muslims. In Slovenia and Croatia, local supporters of the Yugoslav movement called on Serbian troops to forestall the advance of the Italian army and to restore public order. The Yugoslav National Council dissolved the Croatian military units of the Habsburg army. Serbian troops also moved into the Voevodina and Banat to challenge the territorial claims of the Hungarians and Romanians and to establish the basis for the final delimitation of the frontiers.[91]

Unitarist or Greater Serbian Yugoslavia was created in December 1918 by a lopsided compromise between the Serbian government and the Yugoslav Committee in London. The advocates of federalism in London had been under pressure to accept a centralized state. The Serbian army was the only real defense against Italian claims on territories inhabited mainly by Slovenes; it was certainly superior to anything the Croats could put into the field.[92] The boundaries of the old Triplex Confinium, where population statistics were much disputed, had always been defined by force of arms.

The conflict with Italy over the final delimitation of the new state sparked one of the major crises at the Versailles Conference. At the end of the war, the Italian army had finally broken through the crumbling Habsburg front, crossed the frontier, and laid claim to the territories promised to Italy by the secret treaty of Rome in 1915; these included the whole of Istria and three-quarters of the Austro-Hungarian province of Dalmatia, turning the Adriatic into "what it been in the day of the Venetian Republic – an Italian lake."[93] In 1921, after prolonged negotiations, Italy and Yugoslavia signed a separate agreement, the Treaty of Rapallo, which followed the main lines of the Treaty of London. Italy retained possession of the entire Istrian peninsula, except for Fiume, leaving 467,000 Slovenes and Croats on the wrong side of the boundary line. In return, the Italians evacuated Dalmatia.[94]

---

[90] John Paul Newman, "Post-Imperial and Post-War Violence in the South Slav Lands, 1917–1923," *Contemporary European History* 19(3) (August 2010): 251–54.

[91] Newman, "Post-Imperial and Post-War Violence," pp. 315–24; Banac, *The National Question*, pp. 129–31.

[92] See the detailed study of unification in Ivan Banac, *The National Question in Yugoslavia. Origins, History, Politics*, corrected edn (Ithaca, NY: Cornell University Press, 1988), pp. 115–40.

[93] Edward James Woodhouse, *Italy and the Yugoslavs* (Boston, MA: Gorham Press, 1920).

[94] Christopher Seton-Watson, *Italy from Liberty to Fascism, 1870–1925* (London: Methuen, 1967), pp. 430, 581.

While the building of a Yugoslav state resulted from a long process of ideological and political preparation, the settlement of its frontiers was largely the accomplishment of the Serbian army. This in turn bolstered the claim of the Serbian leaders to dominate the borderlands in a replication of the Habsburg model of a multicultural state run by Germans. The creation of a multinational state in which there was considerable opposition to the dominant role of the Serbs, especially among the Croats, was a formula for disaster if and when another war challenged its survival. This is what happened in 1941, plunging the country into a civil war that not only tore the country apart but drew the Allied powers into the vortex.

Czechs and Slovaks

The constitution of a multicultural Czechoslovak state, like Poland and Yugoslavia, was mainly the achievement of the armed forces of the best organized and best armed constituent ethnic group – the Czechs, complementing the work of émigré and domestic nationalist politicians. A number of Czech and Slovak officers and men had joined the Serbian First Division in the absence of units of their own. Most of them shortly afterwards transferred to the larger Czechoslovak armed forces gathering in Russia and composed of prisoners of war. Subsequently known as the Legion, it grew steadily, attaining a peak force of 61,000 men. As within the Yugoslav movement, tension developed between Czech and Slovak groups for control over the volunteer forces and implicitly the nature of the future independent state. The Association of Czechoslovak Societies in Russia, composed of prewar emigrants, fought a losing political struggle with the Paris-based Czechoslovak National Council led by Thomas Masaryk. The main problem remained with the attitude of the Russian government. The military were more interested than the civilian ministers in recruiting Czechs and Slovaks. Sazonov in particular regarded any encouragement of Czech national aspirations as dangerous.[95] Even after the February Revolution the Provisional Government opposed the use of the Czechoslovak volunteers in combat for fear of encouraging non-Russian nationalities, especially the Ukrainians under the leadership of the autonomous-minded Rada, from claiming similar rights. On a trip to Russia in May 1917, Masaryk not only won over the volunteers but also

---

[95] Alon Rachamimov, *POWs and the Great War. Captivity on the Eastern Front* (Oxford University Press, 2002), pp. 12–14, 32–33, 117, 124.

persuaded the Russians to commit them to combat. Still, only a fifth to a quarter of the Czech and Slovak prisoners of war joined the Legion.[96]

The Bolshevik seizure of power placed the Czechs in a difficult position. The Western allies viewed them as a means of reconstituting an Eastern Front. The Bolsheviks perceived them as a potentially counter-revolutionary force. The Czechs wanted to go home. The arrangements to repatriate them broke down along the Siberia railroads and led to fighting with the Bolsheviks. The trek of the Legion through Siberia, where it became the main anti-Bolshevik force during the early stages of the Russian Civil War, constituted one of the founding legends of the new republic, comparing it to the Anabasis of Greek mercenaries retreating through Persia. The parallel with the exploits of the Serbs is striking. They returned to the newly created state of Czechoslovakia in 1920 and formed the core of the national army.[97] Although both Czechoslovakia and Yugoslavia were multinational states, their armies were predominantly made up of the dominant Czech and Serbian ethnicities. In both cases, too, the armies had played a crucial role in the consolidation of state power and the delimitation of the frontiers in the period following the end of hostilities. Repatriated elements of the Czech Legion in France fought against the Hungarians to establish the boundaries of the First Republic in Slovakia. The army held its own in clashes with the Poles over Teschen, and occupied the predominantly Ukrainian (Ruthenian) Sub-Carpatho-Ukraine, rounding out the frontiers of the new republic with its own set of borderland peoples – Sudeten Germans, Hungarians along the Slovak frontier, and Ukrainians in the far eastern tip. There at the western edge of the Pontic frontier, the conflict over the borderland variously known as the sub-Carpathian or Trans-Carpathian–Ukraine poisoned relations among three successor states without satisfying the desires of the majority of the population.

After the collapse of the Monarchy, the former province of Rus'ka kraina (the Ruthenian Border) was granted autonomous status by the new Hungarian government of Mihály Károly, appointed by Charles, the successor to Franz Joseph, who had abdicated as emperor of Austria but retained his title as king of Hungary. The initiative came from Oscar Jászi, the Minister of National Affairs, who was desperately seeking to piece together a federal, multinational Hungarian state. The law sparked a

---

[96] Josef Kalvoda, "Czech and Slovak Prisoners of War in Russia during the War and Revolution," in Williamson and Pastor (eds.), *Essays on World War I*, pp. 223–25.

[97] John F. N. Bradley, *The Czechoslovak Legion in Russia 1914–1920* (Boulder, CO: East European Monographs, 1991); David Bullock, *The Czech Legion 1914–1920* (Oxford University Press, 2008).

strong reaction. The Ruthenians opposed the award of three of the seven counties they insisted were ethnically theirs to Slovakia. The Hungarian nationalist press protested against any form of federalism. As elsewhere in the borderlands, national councils sprouted from the local soil. Composed of Ruthenian intellectuals and students, they demanded union with an independent Ukraine. The embattled Ukrainian National Republic, fighting for its life against the Poles and Bolsheviks, was unable to send any aid. Meanwhile, Bucharest sent cavalry into the region seeking to bolster their territorial claims. Facing Hobson's choice, the Carpathian Ruthenian leaders appealed to the Czechs, who were at least fellow Slavs, to send troops. Their arrival virtually decided the incorporation of the territory into the newly forming Czechoslovak Republic.[98] Unfortunately for the Ruthenians, the Czechs, or more precisely Eduard Beneš, set the boundaries of the autonomous territory on political grounds "as a gift from our government," which violated the ethnic principle in delimiting both the internal frontier with Slovakia and the external frontier with Romania.[99]

Romanians

In the creation of a Greater Romanian successor state, the Moldavian population in Bessarabia took the lead. The effects of the February Revolution in Petrograd rippled through all classes of society. Throughout the summer of 1917, peasants demonstrated in favor of an autonomous Bessarabia and priests joined the chorus. Liberal intellectuals and conservative boiars came out in favor of an autonomous Bessarabia within Romania. But the crucial catalysts were the local and national Romanian armed forces. In May, 10,000 Moldavian officers and men declared for autonomy and announced the formation of separate Moldavian army units. When peasant disorders threatened a breakdown in public order and Ukrainian nationalists agitated for the incorporation of Bessarabia into Ukraine, the army officers convoked a national assembly (*Sfat Naţional Român*), which in December proclaimed the establishment of a Moldavian Democratic Federated Republic extending from the Pruth to the Dniester rivers. Its existence was almost immediately

---

[98] Vincent Sandor, *Carpatho-Ukraine in the Twentieth Century. A Political and Legal History* (Cambridge, MA: Harvard University Press, 1997), pp. 8–10. When the issue was brought up at the peace conference, an expert commission concurred, noting that "it is certainly undesirable that Russia should never [sic] extend across the Carpathians down to the Hungarian plain." David Miller, *My Diary at the Conference of Paris, with Documents* (New York: Appeal Printing, 1925), p. 227.

[99] Sandor, *Carpatho-Ukraine*, p. 17.

threatened by an incursion of Bolshevik units. After some hesitation, the Romanian government responded to appeals for help, and the Romanian army drove out the Bolshevik forces in January 1918. But the process of state-building an enlarged Romania had been abruptly interrupted. The collapse of the Russian army and the sweeping victory of the Central Powers over an isolated Romania forced the government to seek an armistice in December 1917 and then to sign the ignominious Treaty of Bucharest.

The peace terms dictated by the Habsburg foreign minister, Count Czernin, were extremely harsh. Romania had to cede territories along the Austro-Hungarian frontier, including strategic passes in the Carpathians, with a population of 750,000 and demobilize most of its army. Germany took over the economy, including a monopoly of the oil fields for ninety years. The unification of the two principalities sanctioned by the Great Powers in 1859 was reversed. The country was virtually broken up. Dobrudja and Wallachia remained under enemy occupation; Moldavia retained its own administration, but was virtually cut off from the rest of the country. In Bessarabia, the Moldavian majority confirmed its union with "Romania" and announced a "de-Russification" of education.[100] While its connection was tenuous, Bessarabia served as a beacon for other Romanians outside the former kingdom.

The rapid recovery of Romania's greater national aspirations followed the defeat of the Central Powers and the arrival of the Allied army from Saloniki on the banks of the Danube. As the Habsburg Monarchy disintegrated, the Romanians of Bukovina and Transylvania who had remained generally loyal to the Habsburg Monarchy, proclaimed their union with the new motherland. Bessarabia quickly followed, giving up its claims for autonomy. Although the Allies had promised these Habsburg borderlands to Romania, the boundaries had been left vague, and Romania's withdrawal from the war gave them an excuse not to honor the secret wartime treaties. A revitalized Romanian army rapidly emerged as the decisive force in drawing the new state frontiers. Carrying out the policies of the Liberal Party under Ion Brătianu, they expelled the Ukrainian troops who had occupied the predominantly Ukrainian districts of Bukovina and the city of Czernowitz, soon to be renamed Cernăuti. The Romanians disparaged the mixed population as steeped in "bukovinism," that is, an "exotic species" of collaborationists with the Habsburgs who continued to use German as the language of conversation.[101]

---

[100] Keith Hitchens, *Rumania, 1866–1947* (Oxford University Press, 1994), pp. 271–79.
[101] Irina Livezeanu, *Cultural Politics in Greater Romania* (Ithaca, NY: Cornell University Press, 1995), pp. 52–59.

A Romanian occupation of the Banat was forestalled by the Serbian army, which got there first. Fighting broke out between the two armies, which was finally brought to a halt by French intervention.[102] In this case, the French intervention was even-handed, clearly due to the desire to satisfy both its former and potential future allies in maintaining French hegemony in Eastern Europe, even at the cost of creating multinational states with hostile minorities. The final disposition of the Banat gave the Romanians about two-thirds and the Serbs (Yugoslavia) one-third, matching their respective share of the population (600,000 Romanians to 300,000 Serbs), while leaving 400,000 German-speaking Swabians unrepresented in both new governments. The Romanians had been battling the Bulgarians in Dobrudja with Serbian help. When Bulgaria left the war in October 1918, Romanian troops rapidly occupied the provinces that they had been forced to cede to Bulgaria in 1878. Dobrudja was incorporated into Greater Romania by the Treaty of Neuilly with Bulgaria in 1920.[103]

The main object of the Romanian army was to drive the Hungarians out of Transylvania and annex the province. Despite the protests of the Allied Supreme Council in Paris, the Romanians invaded purely Hungarian districts and crossed the Tisza River, which had been set in Paris as the armistice line with Hungary. The confrontation with the Hungarians was greatly complicated by the collapse of the moderate Károly government in Budapest and the coming to power of the pro-Bolshevik government of Béla Kún, who had just returned with several colleagues from revolutionary Russia. The Hungarian Soviet government rallied the country's armed forces, checking the Romanian advance and repulsing the Czechs on the Slovak–Hungarian frontier. The Allies, fearing the spread of Bolshevism in Central Europe and failing in their attempts to mediate the conflict, confined themselves to verbal protests. A Romanian counter-attack occupied Budapest, the Soviet Republic collapsed, and a new Hungarian government signed a harsh armistice which foreshadowed extensive territorial concessions to the Romanians. At this point the Supreme Council put pressure on the Brătianu to accept its delimitation of the frontiers, which assigned several purely Hungarian counties to Romania. This led to the flight of tens of thousands of Hungarians into the much-reduced space of postwar Hungary. When the final borders of Transylvania were drawn, the

[102] Zsuzsa L. Nagy, "Peacemaking after World War I," in Stephen Borsody (ed.), *The Hungarians. A Divided Nation* (New Haven, CT: Yale University Press, 1988), p. 36.
[103] Constantin Iordachi, *Citizenship, Nation and State Building. The Integration of Northern Dobrogea into Romania, 1873–1913*, Carl Beck Papers, No. 1607 (Pittsburgh, PA: University of Pittsburgh Center for Russian and East European Studies, 2002).

Romanians barely constituted a majority in their own state, numbering just under 57 percent of the population, followed by the Hungarians with 25.7 percent, the Swabians with 10.8 percent, and smaller percentages of Ukrainians and Jews making up the rest.[104]

Overnight, the previous culturally and politically dominant ethnic groups in Transylvania and the most urbanized part of the population – Hungarians, Germans, and Jews – were reduced to second-class citizens, creating a field for both ethnic and class conflict between the minority in the towns and the majority in the countryside.[105] The settlement profoundly embittered the Hungarians and contributed to their decision in 1940 to ally themselves with Nazi Germany in the hope of recovering the large Hungarian population of Transylvania.

The energetic, not to say aggressive, actions of the Romanians to fulfill the wartime secret agreements were generally supported by the French, who wanted a strong – which they confused with large – set of states to form a *cordon sanitaire* against Bolshevism and a bulwark against the recovery of Germany, a latter-day evocation of the *barrière de l'est*. The expansion of Romania more than doubled its size and increased its population from less than 8 million to 18 million, of which more than one-third were minorities.

The apparent completion of the Greater Romanian state-building project with the acquisition of adjacent borderlands was seriously compromised. The incorporation of Transylvania, Bessarabia, and Dobrudja earned Romania the lasting enmity of Hungary, the Soviet Union, and Bulgaria. Its nationalizing cultural policies alienated the minorities who inhabited the strategically vulnerable peripheries of the state. That the new population was "more urban, more schooled and more modern" than the Romanians meant that Romanian nationalism fastened on the symbol of the peasantry which, in turn, facilitated the shift to the right and heightened the appeal of authoritarian solutions.[106]

Returning radicals

The collapse of the Russian, Habsburg, and Russian empires left a legacy of political radicalism that had no precedent in the long struggle over the

---

[104] For these and other Romanian and Hungarian population statistics, see Elemér Illyés, *National Minorities in Romania. Change in Transylvania* (Boulder, CO: East European Monographs, 1982), pp. 22–23, 34–35, 56–57, 60–61.

[105] The Allies forced the Romanians to sign minority rights treaties providing protection for the Hungarian, Swabian, and Jewish populations, but the postwar Romanian governments ignored their obligations. Illyés, *National Minorities in Romania*, pp. 71–76.

[106] See the argument in Livezeanu, *Cultural Politics*.

borderlands. The strains of war had brought the Bolsheviks to power in Russia; the conversion of prisoners of war to Bolshevism produced the first missionaries of the new ideology in the west Eurasian borderlands. They were among the founders and subsequent leaders of the communist parties of Hungary, Czechoslovakia, Yugoslavia, and Turkey. The Bolshevik withdrawal from the war raised hopes for peace among prisoners of war, a longing to return to their homelands in adjacent empires, and in some cases an eagerness to transfer the revolutionary impulse to their native land in the spirit of reconstructing the social order along either nationalist or internationalist lines. The Bolshevik leadership sought to promote the internationalist character of their revolution and their cause in the civil war by creating national sections of the Central Committee of the Russian Communist Party, incorporating former prisoners of war and deserters into the Red Guards and Red Army, and sending home representatives from their ranks to promote social revolution.[107] The possibilities of their success, which were seriously exaggerated by the reports of Allied diplomats, aroused fears in the West that influenced the decision to support the Czech Legion in its Siberian epic. The reality was something less than threatening to the Allied cause, at least not at the time. It was largely in response to the Bolshevik clash with the Czech Legion that the Soviet leaders helped in May 1918 to form the first Czechoslovak Communist Party out of prisoners of war in Russia. Their aim was to recruit them for the Red Army and prevent them from joining the Legion. The response was not encouraging. The small number of Czech communists in Russia gradually lost their status, being demoted to the same status as the Hungarian and south Slav communists as a section of the Russian Communist Party Central Committee. Only a handful of the original founders returned to Czechoslovakia, where they were absorbed into the various indigenous constituencies of the left, forming the second Czechoslovak Communist Party.[108]

The most successful recruiting appears to have taken place among the south Slavs, who ended up fighting on both sides of the Russian Civil War. A small number of south Slavs joined the Russian Communist Party and recruited an estimated 30,000 south Slavs to fight alongside the Red Army during the first months of the Civil War. But once the war ended in the

---

[107] E. H. Carr, *The Bolshevik Revolution 1917–1923*, 3 vols. (New York: Macmillan, 1953), vol. III, pp. 72–76. Lenin later said these activities were "the real foundation of what has been done to create a Third International." *Ibid.*, p. 74.

[108] F. B. M. Fowkes, "The Origins of Czechoslovak Communism," in Ivo Banac (ed.), *The Effects of World War I. The Class War after the Great War: The Rise of Communist Parties in East Central Europe, 1918–1921* (Boulder, CO: East European Monographs, 1983), pp. 58–60.

west, most of them were repatriated to the new Yugoslav state. Among them were a handful of converts to the Communist cause who were active in helping to organize the Yugoslav Communist Party. They were particularly successful in Croatia-Slavonia and Voevodina where they took an uncompromising stance for a break with the reformist social democrats.[109] Among them was Josip Broz, an obscure Croat soldier later known as Tito.

A much smaller percentage of the 500,000–600,000 Hungarian prisoners of war supported the Bolsheviks. Although they clashed with the Czech Legion in Siberia, their antipathy had more to do with ethnic conflicts in the Monarchy than class warfare. Most of those who supported the Bolsheviks perceived them mainly as opponents of the war and, consequently, the best guarantor of returning to their homeland. Only about 300 Hungarians joined the Bolsheviks after November 1918. But these included some of the men who became prominent leaders of the Hungarian Communist Party, including Béla Kún, Ferenc Münnich, Tibor Szamuely, and Mátyás Rákosi. Of all the postwar Communist parties, the Hungarian party appears to have owed more to the Russian inspiration. Its brief seizure of power in 1919 also had a strong effect on radicalizing the south Slav left-wing social democrats who formed the communist party in Yugoslavia.[110] The smaller pool of Ottoman prisoners of war also showed little interest in joining the Bolshevik movement. But a Red Brigade was formed, and its members founded the Turkish Communist Party in Baku in 1920.[111]

Pro-Bolshevik groups of Romanians were drawn from three groups: social democrats in Moldavia radicalized by the war and the February Revolution in Russia; deserters from the defeated and demoralized Romanian army; and prisoners of war from the Habsburg army. A number of militant Romanian social democrats fled to Odessa in order to escape persecution by the Romanian government. There they were organized by Christian Rakovski, a Bulgarian-born pro-Bolshevik. They did not endorse a fully-fledged socialist revolution in Romania until the

[109] Ivo Banac (ed.), "The Communist Party of Yugoslavia During the Period of Legality, 1919–1921," in *The Effects of World War I*, p. 194, and Banac, "South Slav Prisoners," in *ibid.*, pp. 138–40.
[110] For the Austrians, see Hannes Leidinger's articles in *Zeitgeschichte* 25 (1998): 333–42, and Verena Moritzin Österreich in *Geschichte und Literatur* 6 (1997): 385–403; for the Hungarians, Peter Pastor, "One Step Forward, Two Steps Back. The Rise and Fall of the First Hungarian Communist Party, 1918–1922," in Banac (ed.), *The Effects of World War I*, pp. 87–92, and Rachamimov, *POWs and the Great War*, pp. 120–21.
[111] Yücel Yanikdağ, "Ottoman Prisoners of War in Russia, 1914–1922," *Journal of Contemporary History* 34 (1999): 81.

Bolsheviks took power in Petrograd.[112] Following the collapse of the southeastern front in late 1917, a number of Romanian deserters sought refuge in Odessa and southern Ukraine, where they formed revolutionary battalions supporting the Bolsheviks in the Civil War, fighting against Ukrainian nationalists, the remnants of the regular Romanian army, and the German interventionists. After Brest-Litovsk many were absorbed into the Red Army. Some of its leaders formed a Romanian Communist Committee in Moscow, together with Romanian workers and Transylvanians who had been evacuated to Russia. Like other East European communists they were organized into a section of the Russian Communist Party. They had modest success in recruiting prisoners of war, but most of the Romanian communist activists in Russia became Soviet functionaries. The returning prisoners of war played a minor role in the formation of communist organizations in the former borderlands of the Habsburg Monarchy, Transylvania, and Bukovina.[113]

The two major ideological currents to emerge from the collapse of empires were nationalism and revolutionary socialism. Each constructed its myths of origin in propaganda and historiography; each exaggerating the role of military formations, armies, legions, or internationalist brigades in the attempt to transform imperial borderlands into new states or incorporate them into established states. But beyond the rhetoric was a stark reality. By controlling the armed forces, the nationalists were mainly successful in repressing their major domestic enemies, the socialists. But when the international balance of forces changed during the Second World War, the local communists were able to win in the civil wars and under the protection of the Soviet Union gain full power in the borderlands.

Caucasian isthmus

In the south Caucasus the complexity of the struggle over the borderlands was magnified by a larger number of players and higher stakes. Ancient rivals for hegemony like the Russians, Ottomans, and Iranians competed for influence and control with the British and the Germans. The three major ethnic groups, the Georgians, Armenians, and Turko-Tatars, aspired to independence, rather than simply autonomy as in the past within a shatter zone, where drawing new state boundaries aroused violent

---

[112] Keith Hitchens, "The Russian Revolution and the Rumanian Socialist Movement, 1917–1918," *Slavic Review* 27(2) (1968): 271–75.
[113] Lucien Karchmar, "Communism in Romania, 1918–1921," in Banac (ed.), *The Effects of World War I*, pp. 129–44.

passions. Local forces failed, as they had in 1905, to consolidate their disparate national forces and to cooperate with one another in achieving their common aim of breaking away from the Russian Empire without falling into dependence on another imperial power. The conflict in the south Caucasus once again spilled over into Iran, leading to revolution and foreign intervention by the Russians, Ottomans, and British.

Among the peoples of the south Caucasus, the rapid tempo of industrialization and the concomitant growth of revolutionary parties after 1905 intensified ethnic and social conflict. In Baku province, the Tatar Muslims (Azeri) were more disunited politically than the Russians, Georgians, or Armenians. In the city of Baku, splits in the working class had opened up between the skilled Russian workers, themselves divided between Mensheviks and Bolsheviks, and the unskilled and semi-skilled indigenous Azeri workers and seasonal immigrants from Iran. The Azeri divided their political allegiance between the social democratic *Himmät* Party, which had pro-Menshevik and pro-Bolshevik wings, and the Muslim Socialist bloc, an Azeri version of the Russian Socialist Revolutionaries. The Bolsheviks led by Stalin had managed to make some inroads in recruiting unskilled Azeri workers in Baku, but they were not successful in absorbing the left wing of Himmät. The largest party, the *Mussavat*, was dedicated to Turkic secularism and national autonomy, which they proposed to extend to other Turkic communities in Turkestan and Kirghizia. To complete the jigsaw puzzle, a smaller pan-Islamic party rejected the national idea altogether, appealing to all Muslims in the empire to join a single organization to defend their traditional interests.[114]

In the prewar years, the growth of pan-Islamic or pan-Turkic sentiments among the political parties and the Muslim intelligentsia aroused serious concern among Russian officials. They feared the establishment of links between the Muslims of the Caucasus and the Young Turk leaders. In 1915 the call for a holy war against Russia by Sheik ul-Islam in Istanbul appeared to justify these fears. The Russian government refused to accept Muslim volunteers into the army, relegating their services to labor battalions, a move that further undermined loyalties to the dynasty.[115]

The February Revolution, with its promise of greater autonomy for the borderlands, inspired a widespread revival of enthusiasm among Armenians in Russia for the establishment of a Greater Armenia uniting

---

[114] Tadeusz Swietochowski, *Russia and Azerbaizhan. A Borderland in Transition* (New York: Columbia University Press, 1995), pp. 62–64.

[115] Firouzeh Mostashari, *On the Religious Frontier. Tsarist Russia and Islam in the Caucasus* (London: Tauris, 2006), pp. 143–44.

the Ottoman and Russian Armenian provinces. They were to be disappointed. The Provisional Government failed in the Caucasus as in other borderlands to develop a consistent, coherent, and effective policy. Along with all other pressing issues – land reform, peace, and a constitution – it opted, as we have seen, to postpone a final decision on national autonomy for the borderlands until the election of a constituent assembly. In the meantime, it appointed a Special Transcaucasian Committee (Ozakom) to maintain public order and introduce civilian government into the occupied Ottoman provinces. Although the committee proved to be a weak reed, the Provisional Government established a civilian Armenian administration in the occupied territories, reassigned Armenian troops serving in the Russian army on the Eastern Front to the south Caucasus, and allowed Armenian refugees to return.[116] However, the rapid disintegration of the Russian army of the Caucasus throughout 1917 removed the sword and weakened the shield defending the Armenians, opening the way for a renewed Ottoman advance. The early Bolshevik decrees denouncing the wartime treaties and withdrawing Russian troops from the occupied territories once again doomed Armenian hopes for unity. Perhaps the most serious obstacle to the transformation of Armenia from a borderland to a nation-state was the demographic disasters of the previous decades. In the words of Richard Hovannisian, the dispersal and slaughter of the Armenians meant that "the very foundation of the emancipatory movement had been deeply, perhaps irreparably sapped."[117]

Georgian Social Democrats comprised the best-organized and most experienced revolutionary party in the south Caucasus. Like other social democratic parties in the Russian and Habsburg borderlands, they sought to combine nationalist and socialist ideas, while at the same time find allies among other revolutionary parties without whom they would be sorely pressed to establish and maintain power whether in autonomous or independent polities. This proved to be an impossible task. Nevertheless, their efforts to unify the revolutionary forces of the south Caucasus borderlands began auspiciously.

Following the February Revolution of 1917, the Georgian Mensheviks succeeded in dominating the Tiflis Soviet, although there were divisions on a number of issues, most notably the national question. In Ronald Suny's analysis, the three major revolutionary forces in Tiflis were composed of three different social classes made up of three different ethnic groups, and influenced by three different political parties, although there

---

[116] M. S. Lazarev, *Kurdskii vopros* (Moscow: Nauka, 1972).
[117] Richard Hovannisian, *The Republic of Armenia, vol 1: The First Year, 1918–1919* (Berkeley, CA: University of California Press, 1971), p. 262.

was some overlapping in this tripartite scheme. The workers were mainly Georgian and Menshevik, who supported national equality and autonomy; the units of the wartime imperial army stationed in the city to defend against the Ottomans were composed mainly of Russian peasants, who supported the Socialist Revolutionaries and the unity of Russia; the "progressive bourgeoisie" was largely Armenian, split between the Dashnaks and liberal parties. In addition, the smaller Azeri community rallied behind the Himmät Party. The Georgian Menshevik leadership split into two sections. Their representatives in St. Petersburg, who as members of the Duma and then the Provisional Government were accused by their enemies of having been infected with parliamentarism, and the veterans of the Gurian Republic in west Georgia and Tiflis, who supported the appeals of the Petrograd Soviet for "a democratic peace without annexations and without indemnities."[118]

In May 1917, the local Georgian Mensheviks took the initiative in forming a Regional Congress of Soviets of the Caucasus, which took more radical positions on the key questions of the war, agrarian reform, and national autonomy than the Provisional Government. On the national question, a large majority supported the idea of guaranteeing every nation (*natsiia*) "in Russia (sic!)" the right to "complete internal self-government." In regions of mixed populations where national-territorial self-government was not possible separate national-cultural units within the territory would be formed.[119] Here, then, was a variation on the Austro-Marxist approach.

Nevertheless, the local Georgian Menshevik leaders, Zhordania, Ramishvili, Uratadze, and others were unable to win over the Russian garrisons who went over to the Bolsheviks on the eve of the October Revolution. In a counter coup, the Georgian Mensheviks then seized the local arsenal, formed a provisional executive authority, the Transcaucasian Commissariat, and then a legislature, the Seim, representing all three major ethnic groups. This was the first and last attempt to create an independent multinational government for the south Caucasian borderlands. The membership of the Commissariat reflected the pluralist or fragmented character of borderland politics: two Georgian Mensheviks, two Socialist Revolutionaries, two Dashnaks, four Mussavatists, and one Georgian Federalist. Its main aim was to insulate and defend the south Caucasus from both the Bolsheviks and the

---

[118] Ronald G. Suny, *The Making of the Georgian Nation* (Bloomington, IN: Indiana University Press, 1988), p. 187; S. E. Sef, *Revoliutsiia 1917 goda v Zakavkazii. Dokumenty, materialy* (Tiflis: Zakkniga, 1927), pp. 66–67.

[119] Sef, *Revoliutsiia*, p. 167.

Ottomans. Given the class and ethnic tensions in the borderlands, the prospect that this organ could govern effectively was dim indeed.

Before the Bolshevik revolution none of the revolutionary parties in the south Caucasus or Trans Caspia sought independence, though they all favored autonomy or, in the case of the Bolsheviks, self-determination under specific class restrictions. Even as autonomous republics, they faced the problem of defining their internal boundaries. With the exception of western Georgia, none of the three main ethnic groups – Georgians, Armenians, and Turko-Tatars – occupied a compact and homogeneous core that might have served as the solid territorial base for an autonomous nation-state. The tsarist government had treated the south Caucasus as a single administrative unit under a viceroy or governor general. But it had repeatedly drawn and redrawn the internal provincial boundaries to suit its own political purposes, mainly in order to avoid the concentration and consolidation of a single ethnic group. As a result each province and district contained a complex mix of peoples reinforcing the kaleidoscopic character of the borderlands.[120]

In a related issue, the absence of a strong political and culturally homogeneous capital city was another obstacle to nation-state-building and a source of inter-ethnic friction. The major cities of Tiflis, Baku, and Batumi were all miniature shatter zones. None of the smaller urban conglomerations were even potentially adequate to the task of serving as an administrative center. For example, at the turn of the century Kutaisi, culturally and historically the most Georgian town, had a population of 26,000, of whom 16,000 were Georgian; in addition there were 3,000 Armenians, about 3,000 Jews, and 2,000 Russians, with a sprinkling of Greeks, Persians, Poles, and Turks. Its history was a snapshot of the borderland. Having reached its apogee in the early eleventh century, it

---

[120] Hovannisian, *Armenia on the Road*, pp. 7–15. Hovannisian, *The Republic of Armenia*, vol. 1, p. 91, gives the following statistics for the population of the districts (*uezdy*) of Erevan guberniia in 1916:

Uezd	Muslim	Armenian
Nakhichevan	81,000	54,000
Surmalu	73,000	33,000
Sharur-Daralagiaz	51,000	29,000
Erevan	88,000	107,000
Novo-Bayazit	51,000	129,000
Etchmiadzin	42,000	115,000
Alexandropol	9,000	202,000

was burned by the Seljuk Turks at the end of the century; restored, it became the capital of independent Imeretia in the thirteenth century, before it was destroyed by the Mongols; it was twice sacked at the end of the fourteenth century by the Svanetians and Timur. Rebuilt to become once again the capital of Imeretia, it was pillaged by the Turks and depopulated in the early sixteenth century. It was finally occupied by the Russians in 1810.[121] It was run by Russian bureaucrats and a town council dominated by Georgian nobles. There was no working class or bourgeoisie to speak of.

Although the largest urban and most politically active Armenian population was located in Tiflis and Baku, both cities were politically controlled by minorities of Georgians and Azeri, respectively. Political circumstances forced the Armenians to move their national council out of Tiflis to Erevan, which in 1918 was an unattractive, provincial backwater. In the summer months, it was barely habitable, engulfed in sweltering heat, which was only slightly alleviated by northeasterly winds that enveloped the city in clouds of dust and filled it with swarms of flies and mosquitoes. Many streets and buildings retained their ancient "Asiatic character"; the main economic activity was artisanal. There were only two Orthodox and six Armenian-Gregorian churches as compared to seven mosques. The Azeri not only slightly outnumbered the Armenians in the city, but even more heavily in the surrounding countryside. For four centuries after 1441 the town had been the object of a struggle between the Ottoman and Iranian empires. In 1604, Shah Abbas surrounded the town with new walls. The Russians attempted but failed twice to take Erevan in the early nineteenth century. Finally in 1827, under General Paskevich, thereafter named Count Erevanskii, they successfully stormed the ancient fortress. The town was ceded to Russia by the Treaty of Turkmanchai.[122]

With the withdrawal or flight of Russian troops from the Caucasus in early 1918, ethnic tensions, barely contained, broke into the open. In January 1918, Muslims stopped a troop train of Russians evacuating the region and massacred the soldiers. In Baku, the Armenian-dominated commune with Bolshevik support unleashed a reign of terror against the Muslim Azeri population.[123] As the front disintegrated, Turkish troops

[121] "Kutaisi," F. A. Brokgaus and I. A. Efron (eds.), *Entsiklopedicheskii slovar'*, vol. XVII (1896), p. 135. In sharp contrast to the town, 95 percent of the population of Kutaisi province were west Georgians (Imeretian, Mingrelian, Abkhazian, Svanetian, etc.). "Kutaisskaia gubernia," *ibid.*, p. 132.
[122] "Erivan," *Entsiklopedicheskii slovar'*, vol. XLI (1904), p. 14.
[123] Jörg Baberowski, *Der Feind ist überall. Stalinismus im Kaukasus* (Munich: Deutsche Verlag-Anstalt, 2003), p. 138.

crossed the old imperial frontier, triggering strong and opposite responses from the Christian Georgians and Armenians, on the one hand, and Muslims, on the other. The small Armenian and Georgian volunteer units which had fought alongside the Russians were insufficient to stem the Turkish advance. The local Muslims welcomed the Ottoman troops, but their political parties were divided over the options opened up by the collapse of the Russian Empire. The pan-Islamists welcomed the prospect of incorporation into the Ottoman Empire; the Mussavatists anticipated the creation of a Greater Azerbaijan. Both were disappointed.

Within months of the Treaty of Brest-Litovsk Germany and the Ottoman Empire launched interventions in the south Caucasus, dooming the already dimming prospects for the viability of the Transcaucasian Federation.[124] The Transcaucasian Seim initially refused to acknowledge the cession of Kars, Ardahan, and Batumi, and resisted Ottoman pressure to declare independence from Russia. The Ottoman army rapidly occupied these provinces and then demanded additional territorial concessions that would give them strategic access to northern Iran. In May 1918, under Ottoman pressure, the Transcaucasian Federation broke up into its three constituent parts. In June, the Ottoman government signed treaties of peace with all three new republics, which impinged on their sovereignty, reinforcing the impression that it intended to recover its long-lost position as the dominant power in the south Caucasus.[125]

The Georgian Social Democrats, having formed a government, placed themselves under the protection of Germany. German culture was widely appreciated among the Georgian intelligentsia, especially among the Social Democrats who looked to the German Social Democrats as a Western antidote to Bolshevism and a barrier to Turkish imperialism. The German government welcomed the opportunity to obtain access to Georgia's rich natural resources, particularly manganese, and to restrain the Turks from violating the Treaty of Brest-Litovsk by directing their energies eastward against the British in Iran. The German occupation of Georgia also gave the Georgians an advantage in dealing with Armenians and Azeri over territorial disputes. The withdrawal of the German troops at the end of the war opened the sluice gates to inter-ethnic conflict.[126]

The Armenian National Council in Tiflis had no external protector. Alone in May 1918, they faced and repulsed the Ottoman advance in a

---

[124] For German plans to create a bridge from the Caucasus to Trans Caspia and Iran see, Fischer, *Germany's Aims*, pp. 552–62.

[125] Fischer, *Germany's Aims*, p. 167.

[126] Firuz Kazemzadeh, *The Struggle for Transcaucasia, 1917–1921* (New York: Philosophical Library, 1951), pp. 147–53, 157–62.

series of hard-fought battles. Facing the prospect of a prolonged struggle
without adequate ammunition or reserves, the Armenians then signed the
Treaty of Batumi. By its provisions, the Armenian Republic was reduced
to a small portion of the territory inhabited by an Armenian majority, but
leaving over a million co-nationals outside its boundaries. In addition, the
Armenians were obliged to extend full religious and cultural liberties to
the minority Muslim population, reduce the size of its army, and grant the
Ottoman army unhindered transit rights across its territory.[127] Of the
three republics, its position was the most imperiled. Within a year it
became even more precarious as refugees poured in and food became
scarce. To many it appeared as though the Armenian people would not
survive the collapse of the tsarist empire.

The Armenians were not, however, innocent of precipitating communal violence elsewhere in the south Caucasus borderlands. In the early
months after the Bolsheviks took power in Petrograd, the Dashnaks joined
them in Baku, forming an unstable and shifting coalition of parties controlling the city soviet. In March, an incident involving the protests of the
Tatar population against the disarming of repatriated Muslim volunteers
in the tsarist army sparked an outbreak of fighting. As part of the ruling
coalition with a strong representation in the soviet, the Dashnaks joined
Russian deserters to disarm the rioting Muslim crowds. They went on to
massacre as many as 3,000 Muslims in the city and surrounding countryside. Their Bolshevik allies minimized their responsibility for the attacks
and mounted a coup, excluding the Dashnaks from the administration.
They then faced the prospect of defending the city against the advancing
Ottoman troops supported by an aroused Azeri population.

Bombarded by urgent and fatal instructions from Stalin, the Bolsheviks
were unable to maintain their precarious hold over the city administration. By nationalizing the oil industry, they had precipitated a fall in wages
and a loss of worker support. Under pressure from the majority of Russian
soviet republics and the Dashnaks, who feared the advance of the
Ottoman army, the soviet invited a joint Russian and British force to
come to their aid. Stalin, backed by Lenin, vigorously opposed the decision, but the Bolsheviks were still too weak to reverse it.

In the summer of 1918 a British Expeditionary Force led by Colonel
Lionel Dunsterville (hence the designation Dunsterforce, later called the
North Persia Force), together with 1,000 Russian troops had already left
Baghdad with orders to block the Turkish advance. They were also
instructed to support the embattled Armenians in Baku and elsewhere

---

[127] Hovannisian, *The Republic of Armenia*, vol. I, pp. 36–37.

in the south Caucasus, who were regarded as the only ally of the Allies in the region. The Dunsterforce, weakened by the departure of the Russian contingent which went off to join the anti-Bolsheviks in Daghestan, was unable to hold the city. The Dashnak allies had also proved to be unreliable. After three months the British were evacuated by sea. They took with them as many of the Armenians who had collaborated with them as possible. The rest were left, as we have seen, to the tender mercies of the Muslim population supported by the in-coming Ottomans.[128]

When the Muslim National Council, dominated by the Mussavat Party, proclaimed the independence of a new state of Azerbaijan, it had defined its territory in dangerously vague terms as encompassing "southern and Eastern Transcaucasia."[129] This included the city of Baku. In September 1918, Ottoman troops, ferried across the Black Sea from Romania and supported by Muslim irregulars, drove the Bolshevik and Armenian forces out of Baku, and massacred between 4,000 and 9,000 Armenian civilians. Ethnically cleansed, the city was proclaimed the capital of Azerbaijan. The Ottoman forces continued to advance into the north Caucasus and across the Iranian frontier, occupying Tabriz in their campaign to unite the two parts of Azerbaijan into a buffer state or protectorate under their control. The initially friendly relations between the Ottoman military and the Azerbaijan (formerly Muslim) National Council deteriorated rapidly. The Ottoman commanders, who were conservative, opposed the socialist program of the Mussavat Party and brought to an end the social and economic reforms that it had initiated in 1917.[130] The occupation of Baku was the high point of Ottoman expansion. The German and Ottoman intervention failed to stabilize the Caucasian borderlands, due mainly to the continuous disagreements among the three republics over drawing their sovereign boundaries. The conflict between the Georgians and Armenians erupted over parts of Tiflis province; between the Armenians and Azeri an even larger territory was at stake in Elizavetpol and Erevan provinces. Historic and ethnic claims were intertwined.[131] Although the German and Ottoman forces withdrew at the end of the war, the government in Istanbul allowed Turkish officers who remained behind to join the Azerbaijan army as volunteers. The fighting continued.

---

[128] Pipes, *The Formation*, pp. 200–1.
[129] Hovannisian, *The Republic of Armenia*, vol. I, p. 31.
[130] Pipes, *The Formation*, pp. 204–5.
[131] Hovannisian, *The Republic of Armenia*, vol. I, chs. 3–8, gives the most detailed account of these conflicts, albeit from a point of view sympathetic to Armenian claims. For the view from Baku, see Aidyn Balaev, *Azerbaizhanskoe national'noe dvizhenie v 1917–1918* (Baku: Elm, 1998).

In the postwar years, the struggle of the three borderlands for survival as independent states revolved around three questions. First, their mutual relations continued to center on territorial disputes marked by frontier warfare. Second, their economic viability continued to deteriorate as they failed to recover from the shock of having been cut off from the integrated imperial market and communications system. Third, their lack of an adequate means with which to defend themselves impelled them to seek the protection of outside forces, dragging them deeper into the Russian Civil War and complicating their relations with republican Turkey, Soviet Russia, and imperial Britain.

The major, if not the only, quarrel between Armenia and Georgia erupted over the Borchalo district in Tiflis province. As was so often the case in the competing claims within the borderlands, the opposite sides appealed to two irreconcilable principles of sovereignty: the ethnic (Armenian) and the historicist (Georgian). Although Armenians constituted the majority of the population, the district had once been ruled by Georgian kings and had been administratively part of Tiflis province, considered by the Georgians to be part of their national homeland within the Russian Empire. In the waning days of the First World War, the Central Powers had been unable to resolve the territorial dispute over the area. When they withdrew Georgian troops occupied most of Tiflis province. The Armenians moved into the southern part of the province and the stage was set for a clash. Resentment toward the Georgian occupation forces flared into revolt in December 1918, and regular Armenian troops joined their compatriots. The fighting escalated rapidly. It seems clear that the Armenians had counted on support from the Allies, and were rudely disappointed by the British mediators who restored the situation to the *status quo ante bellum*. The fighting stopped, but the bitterness remained. The Georgians used the conflict as an excuse to arrest, expel, and confiscate the property of hundreds of Armenians in Tiflis, beginning the vast exodus that would transform the city into a Georgian capital inhabited by Georgians.[132] It proved no longer possible for the two republics to unite against the gathering storm from the north.

The conflict between Armenia and Azerbaijan centered on two districts of the mountainous region of Elizavetpol province, Karabakh and Zangezur. Both republics considered the area vital to the security of their frontiers, and both advanced historicist claims over the region. The population of Karabakh was divided between approximately 165,000

---

[132] The most detailed account of the Armenian–Georgian conflict is Hovannisian, *The Republic of Armenia*, vol. I, pp. 95–125; see also Kazemzadeh, *Struggle for the Transcaucasus*, pp. 177–83.

Armenians, 59,000 Muslims, and 7,000 Russians. The ethnic mix was further complicated by the disposition of the Kurdish–Tatar villages separating the Armenian populations of mountainous Karabakh and the lowlands. The Muslim claims were based on economic as well as strategic factors. Their pastoral economy depended on their control over the highlands. The Armenians depended on Baku for supplies delivered along the major primary roads in the district. Thousands of Armenians were engaged in seasonal or permanent employment in the Baku oil fields. In Zangezur, the Armenians dominated the central highlands, although in the district as a whole the Muslims outnumbered them 120,000 to 101,000. The Armenians and Muslims of the district preserved a precarious coexistence until the Ottoman army appeared on its way to occupy Baku. Its commander supported the claims of Azerbaijan. The Armenian villages resisted, and by the summer of 1918 communal warfare had broken out.

The stalemate in the fighting was broken after the withdrawal of the Ottoman army and the intervention of the British. Concern over alienating the Muslim population of India and interest in exploiting Baku's oil reserves disposed the British to favor the claims of Azerbaijan. The Armenians were obliged to concede control over Karabakh in an agreement lavish with promises of local autonomy, but Zangezur held out. The military resolution of the problem was subsequently ratified by the Soviet government in setting the borders of the south Caucasian socialist republics. But that did not end the struggle, which would erupt once more when Soviet power collapsed in 1989 and Karabakh once again became the object of a bitter fight between the two independent republics of Armenia and Azerbaijan.

Despite the intensity of the ethnic conflict, the major threats to the independence of the Caucasian republics after the withdrawal of the Central Powers came first from the Volunteer Army and then from the Bolsheviks, both representing in different ways the historic aspirations of the center of imperial power over the borderlands. When the Germans withdrew from Georgia, General Denikin, who assumed command of the Volunteer Army, was determined to reimpose Russian rule on the south Caucasus. He regarded the Georgians and the Muslims as the primary enemies. He took an ambivalent attitude toward the pro-Russian Armenians; they were a useful counterweight to his main enemies, but he did not endorse their aspirations for independence. In early 1919, he moved his troops against the Georgians and invaded Daghestan, overthrowing the Mountain Republic that had been proclaimed in the spring of 1918 and recognized by Georgia, Azerbaijan, and the Ottoman Empire. For Denikin, it was a den of pan-Turanian sedition. His offensive was only brought to a halt by the British, who sought to mediate between the Volunteer Army and the Caucasian republics in the hope of turning Denikin to the north in order to meet the Bolshevik threat. The pressure from the Volunteer Army brought Georgia and Azerbaijan into a defensive alliance, one of the few cooperative ventures by the south Caucasian republics. Denikin imposed an economic blockade, announcing: "I cannot let the self-styled formations of Georgia and Azerbaijan, which have sprung up to the detriment of Russian state interests, and which are clearly hostile to the idea of the Russian state, to receive food supplies at the expense of areas of Russia which are being liberated from the Bolsheviks."[133] The defeat of the Volunteer Army in the northern campaign in the summer of 1919 and its precipitous retreat to the south forced Denikin to come to terms with both the Cossacks and the south Caucasian republics. He agreed to recognize the independence of the *de facto* governments and the mediation of the Allied governments in establishing mutual relations and signing treaties between his All-Russian government and the governments of the borderlands. Once again the compromise came too late. His forces were already disintegrating and soon surrendered their last stronghold in the Crimea. The south Caucasus was then exposed to the conquest and occupation by the Red Army.

The two heirs to the Ottoman and Russian imperial rivalry over the south Caucasus borderlands, the Turkish nationalists and the Bolsheviks, shared a common interest in eliminating the weak, quasi-independent republics of Armenia, Georgia, and Azerbaijan, any one of which might potentially become an outpost of British influence in the region. Putting aside their ideological differences, they managed, although not without some tense moments, to reach a mutually satisfactory solution. In April 1920, following swiftly on the heels of the British evacuation, the Bolsheviks rapidly carried out the sovietization of Azerbaijan. Although planned in Moscow and carried out mainly by the local Russian and Azeri communists, the leading nationalists and Turkish officers in Baku played an important role in convincing the Muslim leaders that the Bolsheviks did not intend to abolish their autonomy. They argued that the transfer of military aid to the Turkish nationalists fighting in Anatolia for the liberation of Turkey from foreign rule took precedence over supporting the struggle for the independence of Azerbaijan.

---

[133] As cited in Kazemzadeh, *The Struggle for the Transcaucasus*, p. 245. For Denikin's views on the south Caucasus, see Anton Ivanovich Denikin, *Ocherki russkoi smuty*, 5 vols. (Paris: J. Povolozky, 1921–1924, vols. I, II, III); (Berlin: Slovo, 1924–1926, vols. IV, V), vol. IV, pp. 128–35, 171–77. See also Hovannisian, *The Republic of Armenia*, vol. I, pp. 365–73.

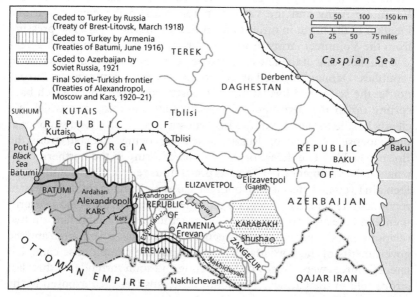

Map 6.2 South Caucasus, 1918–1921

In August, the Treaty of Sèvres imposed by the victorious Allies on a dying Ottoman Empire further stimulated the Turkish nationalists and the Bolsheviks to reach an accommodation. According to its provisions, Turkey was to surrender part of eastern Anatolia to an independent Armenian state and recognize the autonomy of Kurdistan. To prevent the loss of these territories, the Turkish nationalists under Mustafa Kemal concluded an agreement with the Soviet government to establish a common frontier between the two countries. Shortly thereafter a Turkish nationalist force invaded Armenia and seized Kars. Despite protests by the local communists, the Soviet government followed up the Turkish advance by invading Armenia from the northeast. In November, the Dashnak government chose to surrender to the Bolsheviks as the lesser evil; an Armenian Socialist Republic was proclaimed in Erevan.[134] But resistance did not end. An armed rising in the winter had to be put down by the Red Army.

---

[134] Bülent Gökay, *A Clash of Empires. Turkey between Russian Bolshevism and British Imperialism, 1918–1923* (London: Tauris, 1997), pp. 81–88; Pipes, *The Formation*, pp. 225–34.

The proclamation of an Armenian Socialist Republic revived tensions between the Kemalist government and the Soviet leaders. The Turkish nationalists launched a campaign to eliminate the Turkish Communist Party in Anatolia. At the same time, Kemal showed signs of reversing his policy of supporting the Soviet campaign to undermine Georgian independence. Moscow began to fear that the Turks would intervene to protect the Menshevik government. This may have been the decisive reason why Lenin agreed in February 1921 to an intervention by the Red Army. A few weeks after the Red Army entered Tiflis, the Turkish nationalist forces entered Batumi and proclaimed its annexation. The Turks claimed that they were protecting the Muslim population of Batumi and strongly criticized Soviet military operations as inimical to Muslim interests in the south Caucasus.[135] A crisis was avoided between the two governments when the Georgians, like the Armenians, followed historical precedent by opting for submission to Moscow instead of accepting Turkish hegemony. In cooperation with elements of the Red Army, the Georgians drove the Turks out of Batumi. The treaty setting the boundaries of Armenia also restored Batumi to the Georgian Socialist Republic.

The struggle over the south Caucasian borderlands replicated many features of past imperial rivalries, transformed by the effects of war and revolution. In the end, it was the heirs of the two imperial powers in the region – Turkey and the Soviet Union – that decided the fate of the peoples of the south Caucasus. The main reasons for the loss of independence of the three republics may be attributed to a reversal of the factors that enabled them to gain their independence in the first place. First, foreign intervention by the Germans and the British had bolstered the local nationalists; when they withdrew, the protective screen collapsed. Second, the internecine fighting over borders, fed by religious and ethnic rivalries that had long characterized the area, severely weakened the local forces in their efforts to build nation-states and prevented them from uniting in a joint effort to resist external domination. Third, the incorporation of most of the borderlands into the Soviet Union was not just a function of superior force, but of hopes betrayed. The new local elites dominated by the Georgian Mensheviks, the Armenian Dashnaks, and the Azeri Mussavat were all national socialist parties. However much they opposed the centralizing and authoritarian aspects of the Bolsheviks, they still perceived, at this early stage in the building of the Soviet state, an opportunity for both some kind of autonomy and the introduction of

---

[135] Gökay, *A Clash of Empires*, p. 90; Pipes, *The Formation*, pp. 239–40.

social and economic reforms that were long overdue in the region. Finally, there can be no doubt that the deeply rooted hostility of the Georgians and Armenians to a Turkish option played a major role in their decision to give up the hopeless fight and opt for the Soviet solution. As for Iran, its ability to recover its influence among the Muslim population was hampered by its own internal problems, which are the subject of the next section.[136]

Trans Caspia

During the First World War the struggle over the south Caucasus spilled over the porous Trans Caspian frontiers. The Russians, who had occupied Iranian Azerbaijan in 1912, clashed with the Ottoman forces, who invaded northwest Iran in 1915, renewing their duel for domination over the region. Accompanied by pan-Islamic refugees from Iranian Azerbaijan, the Ottomans occupied Tabriz before being driven out the following year by the Russians. Ottoman policy toward Iran was a mixture of official endorsement of Germany's policy of recognizing Iran's independence and an unofficial encouragement of pan-Islamic sentiments and jihad that were shared by Shi'ia ulama in the holy cities of Iran. In the course of this see-saw struggle, anti-Russian sentiment (and anti-British sentiment as well) was building in Tehran.

The Russian and Ottoman occupation forces had antagonized the local population by their harsh policies. Many Iranian constitutionalists, in their hatred of the Russians and British, turned to Germany for assistance. In 1916, they set up an alternative government in Ottoman-occupied Kermanshah, only to be driven out by the British. As all sides scrambled to recruit supporters among the Iranian population, especially the tribes, internecine fighting threatened to tear the country apart. In one little known episode, the large Christian population of Urmia in Kurdistan, battered by the civil war, lost half of its 75,000 inhabitants during a murderous forced exodus to the south.[137] Over the following three years Iran was not only a staging ground for British intervention in the Russian Civil War, but also a country divided by civil war.

---

[136] An initiative of the Azerbaijan government to strengthen its ties with Iran led to a treaty of friendship and commerce in March 1920, and fostered hopes that closer relations with an Iran under British tutelage would enable the Azeri to slip back under the net of British protection. But the rapprochement was stillborn in the face of skepticism in London and open opposition in Iran to the Anglo-Iranian agreement establishing a British protectorate over Iran. See Swietochowski, *Russia and Azerbaizhan*, pp. 83–85.

[137] Nikki R. Keddie, *Qajar Iran and the Rise of Reza Khan, 1796–1925* (Costa Mesa, CA: Mazda, 1999), pp. 68–69.

The Russian Provisional Government condemned tsarist policy in Iran as imperialist, but refused to withdraw Russian troops until the Ottomans did likewise. The stand-off continued until the Bolshevik Revolution. Meanwhile, an anti-Russian guerrilla movement called Jangali ("from the Forest") revived in the dense forests of Gilan province to the east of Azerbaijan on the southern shores of the Caspian. Its leader, Kuchuk Khan, was a charismatic figure, but lacked a talent for organization. He surrounded himself with an assortment of individuals and groups formed into a hodge-podge of committees and consultative bodies. Among them were future leaders of the Iranian Communist Party. He picked up support from defecting Iranian army officers and obtained arms from the Ottomans. The movement was also able to purchase weapons illegally from disaffected Russian occupation troops who were eager to return to their villages. During the war, the imperial Russian army had attempted unsuccessfully to suppress the movement. In the interim the Jangalis gained strength. The Bolshevik Revolution stimulated them to demand greater reforms from Tehran and to shift their focus from the Russians to the British as the main enemy of Iranian liberation from foreign domination. They established an unofficial government (*Ettehêd-i Islam*), like so many other similar national councils in the borderlands, with its own military force and newspapers. Their program was vague, but appealed for national independence from both the Russians and the British. They abolished capitulary rights for foreigners and expelled the European customs officials. But they could not agree on land reform. Kuchuk Khan oscillated between placating powerful landowners and responding on an ad hoc basis to desperate appeals from the poor peasantry. The armed force was better suited to guerrilla fighting than regular warfare. The Ettehêd-i Islam, weakened by internal divisions, began to come apart in early 1918 under pressure from the British, only to revive again when the Bolsheviks gained the upper hand in the south Caucasus in 1920.

The motivations inspiring British intervention were in many ways an extension of their long-term interests in the Caucasian and Trans Caspian frontiers heightened by the exigencies of war. The retreat of the Russians and the advance of the Central Powers in the south Caucasus rekindled traditional fears in London and Delhi over the defense of India. The British had negotiated the settlement of 1907 with the Russians not only to partition Iran into spheres of influence, but also to insulate Afghanistan from foreign, mainly German, influence. That protective wall was now breached. The government of India and the British General Staff were concerned that if the Ottoman forces reached Baku they would then be in a position to cross the Caspian and continue along the Trans Caspian railroad to flank northern Iran and Afghanistan. They conjured up fantasies of the Turks and Germans fanning the flames of pan-Turanism and "Mohammedan fanaticism" in order to descend on India and transform Asia into a German colony. At the same time, there was a realistic need to prevent the Central Powers from gaining control over the Baku oil fields.[138]

On the way to Baku, the Dunsterforce had fought its way through the territory under Jangali control and obtained an agreement with Kuchuk Khan to permit the passage of the British and loyal Russian troops across the border into the newly independent state of Azerbaijan.[139] At the same time, the government of India dispatched intelligence officers to the Iranian border province of Khorasan to blow up sections of the Trans Caspian Railroad if the Turks attempted to launch an attack along the line leading to the borders of Afghanistan. Delhi was also concerned about rumors that the Bolsheviks were organizing Austro-Hungarian prisoners of war to defend against any British incursion. As in the past, London and Delhi did not agree on the extent of the threat from the north or the limits of intervention. The end of the war was the decisive factor in persuading the British to cut their losses and concentrate on securing control over Iran as the first line of defense. In August 1919, they pressured the Iranian government to sign a treaty of alliance that virtually converted the country into a British protectorate. This triggered a radical reaction in Iranian politics and a vigorous counter-offensive by the Bolsheviks.

In January 1918, the Soviet government had denounced the Anglo-Russian Agreement of 1907 as null and void. Several subsequent attempts to make contact with Iran were blocked by the British and rejected by the Iranian government. Reacting to the new Anglo-Iranian Treaty, the Soviet Foreign Commissariat and the Commissariat of Nationalities called for an open struggle against the oppressors. In the south Caucasus, the various social democratic organizations that had sprouted during the revolution of 1904/5 had been moving toward a more radical stance during the war. But many issues and personal rivalries divided them. The Mussavat Party retained its ascendancy over much of the Muslim working class. Its main rival was Himmät, which revived during the war but was split between a pro-Bolshevik and pro-Menshevik wing. A

---

[138] Ullman, *Anglo-Soviet Relations*, vol. I, pp. 304–8; Swietochowski, *Russia and Azerbaizhan*, pp. 72–76.

[139] Cosroe Chaqueri, *The Soviet Socialist Republic of Iran, 1920–21. The Birth of the Trauma* (Pittsburgh, PA: Pittsburgh University Press, 1994), pp. 88–89. The author refutes the view that Kuchuk Khan was collaborating with the Bolsheviks or the Germans. In fact, the Bolsheviks, Stalin among them, viewed the Jangali movement as revolutionary, but without a workers' component, taking place in a "hardly developed" country. Stalin's views did not change over the following decades.

third party, *Ädälät* (Justice) was made up of immigrants from Iran, who represented the most radical elements in the Muslim working class in Baku. They joined the Russian Bolsheviks in the civil war and participated prominently in the campaign to spread revolution in the Caucasus and Trans Caspia. Both the latter two parties had ties with social democracy in Iran (*Ejtima-i Amiyyun*). Future leaders of the Communist Party of Azerbaijan in the Soviet Union and the Iranian Communist Party were drawn from these parties.

Ädälät took the lead in reviving the dormant social democratic branches in the northern provinces of Iran. It dispatched members to Moscow for training, recruited heavily among the impoverished peasantry, and created a "red army." It even won over some officers from the Iranian army. But it too fell victim to the malady of factionalism that plagued the Muslim radicals. In its first congress on Iranian soil in the spring of 1920, it split into two irreconcilable groups, one endorsing a national revolution uniting all classes and the other favoring sovietization of the country, including a federal solution for the borderlands.

Meanwhile, the Jangali movement gained new adherents reacting against the Anglo-Iranian Treaty, and inspired by the success of the Bolsheviks in the Russian Civil War. Kuchuk Khan enthusiastically greeted the landing of a Soviet detachment on the Caspian coast at Anzali in Gilan Province as a sign of support for his movement. After the Soviet forces drove the British out of Gilan, the Jangalis proclaimed a Soviet socialist republic in June 1920. Although Kuchuk Khan flirted with Bolshevik emissaries and adopted a policy of wary cooperation with the local Ädälät leaders, he did not endorse an agrarian revolution. The gap between his revolutionary rhetoric and cautious activities was part of his strategy to put together an autonomous provincial government supported by Moscow. He gradually expelled the Caucasian and local communists from his movement, while appealing to the Iranian landlords, merchants, and peasantry on whom he relied to check the radical demands of his left-wing allies. His program combined radical and traditional elements: the abolition of the monarchy and the proclamation of a soviet republic; the protection of life and property of all inhabitants; annulment of all agreements with foreign powers; and the protection of Islamic principles. Aside from the personalist character of his politics, the Jangali leader adhered to the Islamic concept of the land as belonging to God.[140] His activities fit the familiar pattern of borderland politics. Whatever his ultimate

---

[140] Chaqueri, *The Soviet Socialist Republic*, pp. 167–72, 192–200. Chaqueri concurs with other specialists in Iranian history that the revolutionary movement of the Jangalis replicated the best eschatological tradition of Islam linking armed struggle to piety.

intention – whether to create an autonomous regional regime or to use his base on the periphery to move into the center of power – he was forestalled by a mutually advantageous agreement between Soviet Russia and Iran.

Another revolt in the borderlands broke out in Azerbaijan under the leadership of Sheikh Muhammed Khiabani, a Shi'ite leader who had defended Morgan Shuster in 1911 as a symbol of Iranian independence. In 1915, he opposed the Ottoman occupation, which flaunted its Sunni and pan-Turanian doctrines, as well as the British domination of Iran. After the Anglo-Iranian agreement of 1920, he proclaimed Azerbaijan an autonomous "land of freedom." The Iranian government incited the Shahsevan tribe against him and dispatched the Cossacks to occupy Tabriz, where he was assassinated.[141]

The revolutionary movements had given the Bolsheviks an opportunity to restore Russia's traditional position all along the porous frontiers of the south Caucasus and Trans Caspia.[142] Having repressed the uprisings, the Iranian government sought to free itself from complete dependence upon Britain, and to restore the balance between the two external powers which alone could guarantee it some measure of independence. The Soviet–Iranian Friendship Treaty of February 1921 contained two key provisions that guaranteed Soviet interests in the north. Article 6 stipulated that "Russia shall have the right to advance her troops to the Persian interior for the purpose of carrying out operations necessary for its defense." Article 13 required the Persian government "not to cede to a third power or its subjects the concessions and property" obtained by tsarist Russia "by military preponderance," but restored to Persia by the present treaty. The meaning here is clear. Iran surrendered its sovereign right to rent or lease land or resources in the former tsarist Russian sphere of influence to any foreign power except the Soviet Union. Further provision assured Soviet Russia of exclusive rights to the Caspian fisheries and required the withdrawal of British troops from Iran as a condition of the withdrawal of the Russian detachment in Gilan Province.[143]

The British, who had been negotiating a trade agreement with the Soviet government, acknowledged that once again their forward policy in defense of India had thrown a bridge too far. They scrapped the

---

[141] Michael P. Zirinsky, "Imperial Power and Dictatorship. Britain and the Rise of Reza Shah, 1921–1926," *International Journal of Middle East Studies* 24 (1992): 642–43.

[142] The Soviet communists were reluctant to push for a more radical revolution for fear of antagonizing the British, with whom they were seeking to establish trade and avoid a revival of their intervention in the north, and their skepticism about the social basis for a revolution in Iran. The local communists were split over tactics concerning the agrarian question. Chaqueri, *The Soviet Socialist Republic*, pp. 200, 216–17.

[143] Chaqueri, *The Soviet Socialist Republic*, pp. 284–85.

agreement of 1919, and signed an agreement with the Soviet Union that in effect restored the 1907 sphere of influence agreement. The British abandoned their proposed program of internal reform and threw their support behind a "strong man," Reza Khan, the commander of the Iranian Cossacks. The Soviet leaders also regarded the nationalist elements in Tehran favorably, including Reza Khan. But in their case, he represented the most reliable bulwark against British influence. Their diplomats sought to mediate a settlement between Kuchuk Khan and Tehran. No doubt they perceived reconciliation as a further step in strengthening the nationalist element and also in preserving their influence in the northern provinces. But Reza Khan lost patience, invaded Gilan and dispersed the Jangalis. Kuchuk Khan was assassinated by his former commissar of war who had defected to Reza Khan.[144] His movement fell apart.

The revolutionary movements had been weakened by their failure to address the land problem. In the course of the nineteenth century a new class of landowners – merchants, ulama, and bureaucrats – had joined the tribal leaders in exploiting the peasants. The peasants and ruined artisans emigrated across the frontiers, where they were gradually converted to radical ideas in the mines and oil fields of the south Caucasus. Moving back and forth, they swelled the ranks of the various socialist movements. But their potential leaders among the Tatar population of the south Caucasus and of Iranian Azerbaijan were deeply divided. When the opportunity came in 1918–1920, they failed to unite around a program of agrarian reform. The most formidable obstacles to social change in the countryside came from the tribal leaders, who were also the major landlords in the northern borderlands of Gilan, eastern Azerbaijan, and Mazanderan.[145]

Although Iran had not been a belligerent in the First World War, it had suffered enormous damage from political immobilism and a series of natural disasters. The constitutional revolution proved to be ephemeral because there was no firm institutional or social base on which to build a parliamentary government. Separatist movements threatened the integrity of the state. The Russian (and Bolshevik)–British rivalry had deeply eroded the country's sovereignty. Epidemics, above all the influenza pandemic, had carried off as many as 2 million Iranians, a quarter of the rural population. By 1920, Ervand Abrahamian has written, Iran had become "a classic 'failed state'" ready for salvation by a man on horseback.[146]

---

[144] Chaqueri, *The Soviet Socialist Republic*, pp. 328–42.

[145] J. J. Reid, "Rebellion and Social Change," *International Journal of Middle Eastern Studies* 13 (1981): 35–53.

[146] Ervand Abrahamian, *A History of Modern Iran* (Cambridge University Press, 2008), pp. 60–62.

During the last years of the Qajars, the Cossack Brigade was still the only effective armed force under the control of the dynasty. In 1921, the withdrawal of the British troops created a highly unstable situation throughout the country. In February, Colonel Reza Shah, the head of the Qazvin and Hamadan detachment of the Cossack Brigade, marched on Tehran and in collusion with a few Iranian intellectuals took control of all government establishments while professing loyalty to the shah. In its manifesto the new government referred to the army as the supreme means of the prosperity of the country.

Appointed army commander by the shah, Reza Khan quickly built his own power base. He was a descendant of a military family that had fled the Russian advance into the south Caucasus and settled in the frontier province of Mazanderan. His military training and his skill as a diplomatist in playing off the Russians and British were stepping stones to dictatorship. Like previous usurpers who founded Iranian dynasties, he relied on a body of loyal troops, in his case the Cossacks, even at the cost of splitting the regular army.[147] But Reza Shah was a modern man. He organized his own party that stressed industrialization, expansion of education, separation of church and state, the replacement of foreign investments with native capital, and the formation of a professional army – in short, a nationalizing program. When as minister of war he proposed the introduction of compulsory military service he stirred up a hornet's nest.[148] Powerful elements among the political elites and the bazaar also opposed his preference for a republic. Opportunistically, he shifted his position. In 1925, he deposed the shah, proclaiming himself the founder of a new Pahlevi dynasty based upon the loyalty of the army as the only way to carry out the modernizing reforms.[149] Once again, as had occurred with the founder of the Safavid and Qajar dynasties, a military man from the Turkic borderlands had overthrown the old regime only to reconstitute the state on a new basis. The true independence of Iran, however, still depended upon the benevolent attitudes of its northern neighbor, the Soviet heir to the Russian Empire, and the British still concerned with the defense of India.

---

[147] Stephanie Cronin (ed.), "Reza Shah and the Paradoxes of Military Modernization in Iran, 1921–1941," in *The Making of Modern Iran. State and Society under Riza Shah, 1921–1941* (London: Routledge, 2003), pp. 37–64.

[148] Stephanie Cronin, "Conscription and Popular Resistance in Iran, 1925–1941," *International Review of Social History* 43(3) (December 1998): 451–71.

[149] Vanessa Martin, "Mudarris, Republicanism and the Rise to Power of Reza Khan, Sardar-I Sipah," *British Journal of Middle Eastern Studies* 21(2) (1994): 199–210.

Inner Asia

The end of Qing imperial rule in 1911 and the Russian Revolution weakened two of the three main contenders for hegemony in Inner Asia, enabling local elites in the three borderlands of Xinjiang, Mongolia, and Manchuria to maintain *de facto* autonomy for almost two decades. The failure of Yuan Shikai to establish a new dynasty and his death in 1916 was followed in rapid succession by the disintegration of the empire into its constituent parts and the rise of warlordism. This new phenomenon precipitated an internal debate among Chinese intellectuals over its significance, shedding further light on the questions of continuity in Chinese history and the legacy of imperial rule.

Two leading protagonists in the debate were Chen Duxiu and Hu Shi, both professors at Beijing University and leading figures in the May 4 movement. But they differed in their analysis of what warlordism represented in Chinese society and how to combat it. Chen argued that warlordism represented the periodic fragmentation of China along regional lines. Only a strong centralized authority could break the cycle of violence and end the power of the warlords. This he hoped to accomplish by becoming one of the founding members of the Chinese Communist Party. Hu Shi took the opposite tack, insisting that warlordism emanated precisely from the very tendency extolled by Chen, which was to unify and centralize China by force of arms. He favored a reorganization of China along liberal democratic lines. In the view of Arthur Waldron, their debate reflected an abiding divide in Chinese intellectual thought between the tradition of *junxian*, which placed moral responsibility for order in a centralizing leadership, and *fengjian*, which located it in decentralized civil authority that he viewed as primary and autonomous.[150] Situating the struggle over the Inner Asian borderlands within this context, the tension between centralized and decentralized authority takes on a different cast. The warlords who succeeded to power in Xinjiang, Outer Mongolia, and Manchuria, whatever their ideological outlooks may have been, were similar to one another. They were also distinctive in one important way from warlordism in the rest of China. As men of the borderlands, their fate did not depend solely on domestic factors. The key to their success or failure depended on the intervention of powerful

---

[150] For the relationship between Chen and Hu, see Jonathan Spence, *The Search for Modern China*, 2nd edn (New York: W. W. Norton, 1999), pp. 305–6; for their debate on warlordism, see Arthur Waldron, "The Warlord," *American Historical Review* 96(4) (October 1991): 1095–96; for the two traditions, see Kung-chuan Hsiao, *A History of Chinese Political Thought, vol. 1: From the Beginnings to the Sixth Century A.D.*, trans. F. C. Mote (Princeton University Press, 1979).

external forces, whether the Russians, their Soviet successors. or the Japanese.

As early as the first republican year in 1912, the crumbling of imperial authority opened the way for military officers to take control of large regions with local armies numbering up to tens of thousands of men. Many of them had been trained in the Qing military academies and had served in the Beiyang Army of Yuan Shikai. Others had studied abroad in Japan and Germany. A few had been bandits. They were fiercely anti-foreign. Most were opposed to a centralized government; a few aspired to gain control over Beijing, the old center of power. Typically, they lived off the land, collecting rural taxes, regulating the opium trade, and receiving small subsidies from district governments.[151] According to James Sheridan, the warlords drew their main ideological inspiration from the alternative tradition of the heroic military figure celebrated in popular literature rather than from neo-Confucianism, although they tapped into both legacies of imperial rule.[152]

After the overthrow of the Qing, a small number of radical intellectuals proclaimed Manchuria's independence, but were quickly suppressed by local military figures. Among them General Zhang Zuolin became one of the most famous war lords in China and a key player in the future develop-ment of Manchuria. A typical product of the old frontier, he had been a militia leader fighting against bandits in the Liao River valley during the Sino-Japanese War, and had served as an irregular ally of Japan during the Russo-Japanese War. The Qing court gave him a regular army appoint-ment, and after the fall of the dynasty the republican government made him one of the three provincial governors and commander-in-chief of the provincial army. Through his lieutenants he gained control over the rest of Manchuria.[153]

In Xinjiang, a local official of Han background, Yang Zengsin, took power in a quiet coup during the disturbances accompanying the revolu-tion that deposed the Qing dynasty. Confirmed as governor by Yuan Shikai, he turned the province into a personal fiefdom. Ruling autocrati-cally, he played off ethnic groups (Kazaks, Mongols, Tungans, and Uighurs) and regional interests against one another. Gradually, he extended his favor to the conservative Uighur upper classes in order to

[151] Diana Lary, "Warlord Studies," *Modern China* 6 (October 1980): 439–70; Edward A. McCord, *The Power of the Gun. The Emergence of Modern Chinese Warlordism* (Berkeley, CA: University of California Press, 1993).
[152] James E. Sheridan, *China in Disintegration. The Republican Era in Chinese History* (New York: Free Press, 1975), pp. 98–101.
[153] Robert H. G. Lee, *The Manchurian Frontier in Ch'ing History* (Cambridge University Press, 1970), pp. 130–31.

offset the influence of Bolshevism and Turkic nationalism. Thus, "he followed a policy identical to that pursued by the tsarist empire in its last years in Kazan, Bukhara and elsewhere, namely to attempt to quash liberal influences by bolstering 'the old timer' (*qadimist*) religious conservatives."[154] Fearing that the Mongols would make common cause with their brethren in Outer Mongolia, he forbade them to carry arms, except for a small group of Tungan Mongols along the Russian border, a cavalry force well trained by Russian Cossacks. When the Kazakhs in Russian territory revolted in 1916, Yang allowed thousands of them to cross into Xinjiang and settle there. During the Russian Civil War, he managed to control the flow of White Russians fleeing across the border, and negotiated agreements on trade and refugees with the Soviet government which had no diplomatic relations with China until 1924. Until he was assassinated in 1928, he played the classic role of the regional official in the Inner Asian borderlands who recognized Chinese suzerainty, but in the absence of a strong central authority exercised personal power. His death opened the way for a struggle for power that ended with the victory of a real warlord, Sheng Shicai.[155]

In Outer Mongolia the collapse of the Russian Empire tempted Chinese military men on the frontier to reimpose their control. The senior banner princes turned back to China, fearing the spread of social revolution. Beijing under the rule of the Anfu military clique welcomed their initiative and dispatched an ambitious member, General Xu Shucheng, to abolish the autonomy of Outer Mongolia. Xu may have had ambitions to establish himself as warlord, rivaling Zhang Zuolin in Manchuria. But he was opposed by the younger Mongol officials and intellectuals who had matured after the fall of the Qing. In the course of the struggle, the leaders of the Mongol revolutionary movement who formed the Mongol People's Party emerged to keep power in the hands of the locals. Among them was Sukhe Bator, a Russian-speaking and Russian-trained soldier. Although not among the original prominent figures in the movement, by 1921 he had become its leader.[156] He is rarely described as a warlord. But that is exactly what he was until in 1920 he teamed up with Choibalsang, the future premier of Outer Mongolia, then already half a Marxist. Together they won over the conservatives headed by the Living Buddha in Urga, and appealed to the Bolshevik forces in Siberia to assist them in resisting

---

[154] James Milward and Nabijan Tursun, "Political History and Strategies of Control, 1884–1978," in S. Frederick Starr (ed.), *Xinjiang. China's Muslim Borderland* (Armonk, NY: M. E. Sharpe, 2004), pp. 68–71, quotation on p. 69.

[155] Owen Lattimore, *Pivot of Asia* (Boston, MA: Little, Brown, 1950), pp. 52–69.

[156] Thomas Ewing, "Russia, China, and the Origins of the Mongolian People's Republic, 1911–1921," *Slavonic and East European Review* 58 (July 1980): 409–13.

the renegade White forces operating in the region. This action plunged the Mongols into the Russian Civil War.

In the chaotic conditions on the Russian side of the frontier after the Bolshevik seizure of power, a small number of military adventurers put themselves at the head of a motley assortment of Cossack frontiersmen of the Ussuri and Amur hosts and indigenous Buriat, Kalmyk, and Chinese recruits. Their aim was to oppose the Bolsheviks, overthrow the local soviets in the hands of moderate socialists, and carve out an autonomous territory under their control. They were not, however, successful in tapping the deep reserves of Cossack strength. The Amur and Ussuri Cossacks had been formed only in the 1860s and 1880s. On the eve of war they numbered several thousand and owned extensive properties. But they were indifferent to cultivating the land. They preferred the traditional occupations of hunting, fishing, and raiding across the frontier. In the eyes of some observers, they were prone to idleness.[157]

The most active of the adventurers were Baron Roman Ungern von Sternberg, a Baltic German officer in the imperial army, and Ataman Grigorii Semenov. Because Semenov's band never exceeded several thousand, he needed outside support for his ambitions. In light of his dubious reputation, the White leader in Siberia, Admiral Kolchak, was reluctant to employ his talents. However, the Japanese found him to be the perfect collaborator. They gradually took him under their wing with the aim of creating an independent Cossack government for the entire Trans-Baikal region, a buffer between the new Soviet Russian republic and their interests in Manchuria and Inner Mongolia. When it became evident that Semenov lacked popular support, the Japanese abandoned him and negotiated an agreement with Moscow recognizing an ephemeral buffer state, the Far Eastern Republic, which enabled them to withdraw their interventionist forces without dishonor.[158]

Up to this point the Bolsheviks had been preoccupied by fighting the Whites in western Eurasia. Now they were free to deal with the adventurers. Ungern von Sternberg was shot on a raid into Siberia. Semenov's forces were scattered by elements of the Red Army cooperating with the Mongol partisans led by Sukhe Bator and Choibalsang. In

---

[157] *Aziatskaia Rossiia*, 3 vols. (St. Petersburg: A. F. Marks, 1914), vol. I, pp. 178–99, 383, diagrams following pp. 490 and 492; vol. II, pp. 369, 383–87; O. I. Sergeev, *Kazachestvo v russkom Dal'nem Vostoke v XVII–XIX vv* (Moscow: Nauka, 1983), gives a favorable picture of Cossack economic activity. Steven G. Marks, *Road to Power. The Trans-Siberian Railroad and the Colonization of Asian Russia, 1850–1917* (Ithaca, NY: Cornell University Press, 1991), pp. 16–17, is more skeptical.

[158] M. I. Svetachev, *Imperialisticheskaia interventsiia v Sibirii i na Dal'nem Vostoke (1918–1922)* (Novosibirsk: Nauka, 1983), pp. 116, 179–80, 185–88, 200–4.

February 1921, together they rode into Urga (later named Ulaan Bator), enthroning the Bogd Khan as constitutional monarch. When he died three years later, the revolutionary leaders proclaimed the Mongol People's Republic. The battle of the warlords in Outer Mongolia had been won by the soldiers who wrapped themselves in the mantle of Marxism–Leninism.

Conclusion

On the Western and Italian fronts, the First World War, for all its terrible loss of life and destruction of property, had not resulted in large-scale territorial changes, massive shifts in population, or social revolution. Alsace-Lorraine had been restored to France, Italy had gained the Alto Adige, and Belgium had acquired a small border strip. The only regime change had taken place in defeated Germany, where the kaiser had abdicated, bringing to an end the Hohenzollern dynasty. Scattered revolutionary outbreaks had rapidly collapsed. But no foreign intervention had played a part in these events, and no real change had taken place in the composition of the old ruling elites. The contrast with Eurasia is striking. There the war had been equally destructive. But it rapidly passed over into civil wars and interventions, breaking up empires, ripping open the complex frontiers, fomenting social and political revolutions, inciting mass flight and deportations, and leaving an onerous legacy for the successor states led by new men and movements who were forced to confront many of the same persistent problems that had preoccupied their predecessors.

The successor states were all multinational, having evolved from multicultural societies of different ethnolinguistic and religious groups into more cohesive if still imagined "nation-states." Only Finland, truncated Austria and Hungary in the west, and Outer Mongolia in the east were ethnically homogeneous, or nearly so; but even they were only parts of a larger national community located outside their frontiers in Karelia, Germany, Transylvania–Slovakia, and China, respectively. The boundaries of the successor states, while newly configured, remained arbitrary, disputed, and porous. They were often armistice lines, which mutually exhausted protagonists accepted as permanent. Most of them cut through ethnic national communities, stirring up ideas of unredeemed territories (*irredenta*). The burden of state-building among the successors had been largely shouldered by the military forces – fragments of the imperial armies along with local militias and armed bands – which played an even larger role in the new ruling elites than they had under imperial rule (again with the exception of the Soviet Union).

The new elites forced the nationalizing trends of their predecessors into new channels. By embracing the political theology of integral nationalism, they obliterated virtually all the modest concessions to cultural diversity that had been made under imperial rule. Although they found some willing collaborators among the national minorities, more often they encountered nodes of resistance similar to those opposing imperial rule. More often, too, they resorted to repression rather than seeking to compromise or bargain with minorities over granting autonomous rights. Because the minorities were generally located on the peripheries of the new states with co-nationals living across the boundary lines, the ruling elites doubted their loyalties. Under the threat of a new world war, as happened in the 1930s and 1940s, the doubts became self-fulfilling prophesies. The persistence of problems inherited from imperial rule virtually guaranteed that the struggle over the borderlands in Eurasia had not yet come to an end.

In the decade after the last of the postwar treaties had been signed, the role of the Great Powers in reshaping the borderlands along the complex frontiers was greatly diminished. The successors to the Kaiserreich and the Russian Empire were too weak to recommence their competition. The Japanese leadership remained undecided whether to renew their imperial advance in Inner Asia or to reach an accommodation with Britain and the United States as partners in establishing an international order in the Pacific. China was too deeply divided to recover its borderlands. The British and the French were absorbed in holding down their colonial possessions. None of the smaller successor states could afford to reactivate an open struggle despite unfulfilled territorial aims. But it was just a matter of time before the only potential great power rivals for hegemony in the borderlands, Germany and the Soviet Union, would recover their strength or, in the case of Japan, decide to employ it in what was to become the next and most destructive period in the struggle over the borderlands.

Conclusion: Transition

The long and problematic process of state-building by the multicultural empires of Eurasia had not been completed, in the eyes of the ruling elites, by the end of imperial rule. If they had survived the First World War, the acquisition of new territories and assimilation of wayward borderlands would certainly have continued. Throughout this process, this book has argued, what happened on the peripheries of the centers of power was far more significant than has generally been recognized. Frontier wars of conquest and the incorporation of the borderlands into the body politic had profound effects on the ideologies and institutions of imperial rule.

Frontier wars occurred in a geocultural space long characterized by large-scale population movements within varied landscapes, producing shatter zones of highly diverse ethnolinguistic, religious, and socioeconomic groups, kaleidoscopic in their internal rhythms of change. The military lines of advance and retreat divided rather than united peoples sharing one or more of those defining features, leaving Poles, Ukrainians, Serbs, Armenians, Kurds, Turkmen, Kirghiz, and Mongolians living under different flags.

The imperial elites exhibited considerable pragmatism in their efforts to administer, assimilate, and acculturate the conquered borderlands as a key element of state-building. In their flexible responses to pressures from external rivals or internal opposition, they shifted their policies from imposing centralizing measures to granting autonomy (in the Russian Empire to the Finns and Poles; in the Habsburg Empire to the Hungarians and Poles; in the Ottoman Empire to Crimean Tatars, Romanians, Kurds, and Arabs; in the Qing Empire to Mongols and Uighurs), which helps to explain their dynastic longevity.

In expanding imperial rule they employed a variety of strategies, ranging from outright conquest to colonization, conversion, and co-optation of elites. Colonization and conversion were not, however, solely state-directed, but were often spontaneous and voluntary, while the co-optation of elites required a sympathetic response from below. The conquered peoples responded with their own strategies designed for different ends: to preserve their cultural identity, to acquire autonomy, and, only when imperial rule was on the verge of collapse, to achieve independence. Their tactics ranged along a spectrum from passive acceptance to armed rebellion. Subjugated elites did not constitute a uniform group any more than did ruling elites. Their responses were not consistent or coordinated, often alternating between accommodation and resistance, or incorporating both.

The outcome of wars frequently determined the pace and direction of domestic reform. But the focus remained fixed on the army and the mobilization of resources to shore up sagging defenses or to prevent further loss of territory. Almost all the major structural reforms undertaken by the multicultural empires were generated as a response to defeat, culminating in the nineteenth century with the Tanzimat in the Ottoman Empire, the Great Reforms in the Russian Empire, the Compromise Settlement (*Ausgleich*) in the Habsburg Monarchy, the feeble responses of the last Qajar Shahs, and the New Administration and New Army Reform in Qing China.

By the early twentieth century, constitutional crises had exposed the dialectics of reform in all the multicultural empires. The reforms instituted to bolster imperial rule incorporated the technologies and techniques of the third military revolution: mechanized weaponry; mass armies commanded by officer corps imbued with a rational and nationalizing outlook that proved to be at odds with conservative rulers who were turning back to traditional political ideologies. Under the pressure of war and internal upheavals they abandoned the cause of imperial rule. At the same time, the new schools and universities established to provide professionally trained cadres of civil servants became centers for the diffusion of political and social ideas from the West, stimulating the growth of an intellectual class that was increasingly alienated from imperial rule.

The ascendancy of Russia in the struggle over the borderlands, apparently well established by 1914, may be attributed to four major factors: the establishment by Peter the Great and the consolidation by Catherine II of a centralized state able to mobilize large human and material resources for fighting wars; the generally successful co-optation of elites (except for the Poles after 1863), combined with extensive colonization in the Pontic steppe, Trans Caspia, and Inner Asia; and a reforming tradition that enabled the ruling elite to restore control and rebuild its military and financial institutions after internal revolts as in Poland, or defeats in the Crimean and Russo-Japanese wars. Russia's successes cannot be attributed only to its own actions, but depended in equal measure on the failings of its rivals.

The unprecedented strains of the First World War, the civil wars, and interventions ripped open the fragile fabric covering the seven complex frontiers. The dissolution of empires left unresolved problems arising from persistent factors that had long faced the rulers and ruling elites of the multicultural empires. The successor states were themselves multicultural, with arbitrarily drawn borders dividing ethnic communities along contested and porous frontiers. Their legitimacy was frequently challenged internally by large minorities and externally by more powerful states. Taking advantage of the weaknesses of the successor states, a revived Germany under Hitler and a militarist Japan were prepared by the early 1930s to renew the struggle over the Eurasian borderlands. From Manchuria to the Sudetenland, they began their campaign to destroy the postwar settlement order and erect their own new order based on new ideologies and new levels of violence.

Index

Abbās Mīrzā, Crown Prince (Qajar), 31,
  275, 388–89, 400, 401, 461. *See also*
  reform
Abdülaziz (Ottoman), 134, 259, 261,
  506. *See* Tanzimat
Abdülhamid I (Ottoman), 255
Abdülmecid (Ottoman), 259. *See also*
  Tanzimat
Abdur Rahman, 410
Abu'l Khayr, 396
Ädälät (Justice), 604–5. *See also* Bolshevism;
  social democracy
Adshead, S. A. M., 12, 39
Aehrenthal, Alois, 445–46
Afghanistan, 31, 398–411, 469, 490–93,
  541–42
Aga Muhammed Khan, 205, 273, 382–33
Ağaoğlu (Agaev), Ahmed, 507, 508. *See also*
  nationalism; revolutions; Young
  Turks
Agency of Convert Affairs, 99–100. *See also*
  conversion; religion
Ahmad Shah Durrani, 272, 398
Ahmed Resmi, 256
Aksakov, Ivan, 120. *See also* pan-Slavism
Aksan, Virginia, 27, 255
Albania, 23, 24, 306, 308, 327, 344, 345,
  539–40, 546–47
Aleksei Mikhailovich (Russia), 97
Alexander I (Russia), 31, 111, 204, 228–29
  Anglo-Russian rivalry, 401, 402
  Balkan policy, 57
  Baltic policy, 216–18
  Bessarabia and the principalities,
    218–20
  Caucasian policy, 384, 385–86
  Jews, 237
  Napoleonic Wars, 310
  Ottoman policy, 332–35
  Polish policy, 156, 221–22, 225–26
  reforms, 211

religious policy, 101
succession, 109
Swedish rivalry, 300
Ukrainian policy, 112–13
Alexander II (Russia)
  as reformer, 278
  assassination, 462, 463, 520
  Baltic policy, 114, 448
  Crimean War (1853–1856),
    204, 340–41
  death, 347
  legacy, 394
  Polish policy, 231–33
  reforms, 211–12, 235, 461
  religious policy, 103
  Trans Caspian policy, 407
Alexander III (Russia), 110
  Bulgaria, 444
  Bulgarian policy, 346–47
  death, 450
  nationalism, 123, 347
  pan-Slavism, 121
  pogroms, 453
  Russification, 114, 447–49
  Siberia, 467
Alexandra Fedorovna (Russia), 105–6,
  123, 544
Allied Supreme Council, 584–85
Amanat, Abbas, 388
Amir Kabir, 275–76, 513. *See also* army
Anatolia, 12, 21–22, 60, 127, 135, 242,
  263, 336, 341–42, 344, 393, 461,
  499–500, 501–2, 505, 509–11,
  536, 599–601
Andrássy, Count Gyula, 344, 548
Anglo-Iranian Agreement (1920), 606
Anglo-Iranian Treaty (1918), 604–5
Anglo-Russian Treaty (1907), 491–92, 495,
  541–42, 604
Apis, Colonel, 441, 444. *See also* terrorism;
  Young Bosnians

wars
Anglo-Persian War (1856–1857), 405
Austro-Ottoman War (1683–1697), 27, 254, 322, 329
Austro-Ottoman War (1716–1718), 307
Austro-Ottoman War (1736–1739), 255, 307, 325, 327
Austro-Ottoman War (1788–1792), 191, 313
Austro-Prussian War (1866), 92, 93, 181
Balkan Wars (1912–1913), 1, 446, 496–97, 505, 506, 509, 546, 550
Caucasian War (1817–1864), 393–94
Chinese Civil War (1946–1949), 1
Crimean War (1853–1856), 1, 132, 204, 337–42, 500
Fifteen Years War (1592–1606), 128–29, 307, 316, 320–21, 322
Finnish Civil War (1918), 486, 558–60
Finnish War (1808–1809), 300
First World War (1914–1918), 77, 183–85, 205–6, 537–52, 613
  German war aims, 545
  Habsburg war aims, 546–50
  Ottoman war aims, 550–51
  Russian war aims, 538–44
French Revolutionary Wars (1792–1802), 87, 308–11
Great Northern War (1700–1721), 207, 298–99, 357, 358
Great Ottoman War (1683–1699), 303, 317
Holy War (1683–1699), 362
Hussite Wars (1419–1434), 45
Italian War (1859), 92, 93, 181
Korean War (1950–1953), 149
Kuruc War (1703–1711), 70, 178, 189, 318, 321–22, 323–24
Lignica (Liegnitz), battle of, 18
Livonian War (1558–1582), 294–96, 297
Long War. *See also* Fifteen Years War (1592–1606)
Nándorfehérvár, battle of (1521), 320
Napoleonic Wars (1803–1815), 49, 179–80, 308–11, 401
Opium Wars (1839–1842), 286, 287, 418, 519
Pruth, Campaign (1710–1711), 317–19
Russian Civil War (1917–1921), 58, 77, 351, 354, 470, 557–75
  Inner Asia, 611–13
Russo-Japanese War (1904–1905), 205–6, 224, 415, 446, 460, 469, 475, 491, 493, 515, 526, 610
Russo-Ottoman War (1710–1711), 307
Russo-Ottoman War (1736–1739), 365

Russo-Ottoman War (1769–1774), 255, 365, 368–70
Russo-Ottoman War (1787–1792), 130, 327, 368–70
Russo-Ottoman War (1806–1812), 57, 313, 331, 386, 401
Russo-Ottoman War (1828–1829), 219, 390
Russo-Persian War (1804–1811), 386–87, 401
Russo-Persian War (1826–1828), 388–89
Russo-Swedish War (1741–1743), 300
Russo-Swedish War (1788–1790), 300
Russo-Turkish War (1877–1878), 120, 134, 205, 251, 343–47, 409–10, 412, 437, 500
Second Anglo-Afghan War (1878–1881), 410
Silesian Wars (1740–1763), 186
Sino-French War (1884–1885), 520
Sino-Japanese War (1894–1895), 1, 152, 288, 467, 519
Soviet–Finnish conflict (1921–1922), 559–60
Soviet–Polish War (1919–1920), 563, 570–72
Thirteen Years War (Polish-Russian War) (1654–1667), 355–56, 358
Thirty Years War (1618–1648), 45, 84, 177, 178, 321, 322
War of the Austrian Succession (1740–1748), 80
War of the Spanish Succession (1700–1714), 178
Winter War (1940), 560
Weber, Max, 166
Westphalia, Peace of (1648), 321, 575
Wielopolski, Count Zygmunt, 543
Wielopolski, Marquis Alexander, 232–33. *See also* reforms
Wilson, Woodrow, 539, 555, 575
Windischgrätz, Field Marshal Prince Alfred, 187
Witkiewicz, J. V., 403–4
Witte, Sergius, 414, 467–69, 476, 490, 491
Wittek, Paul, 25–26
Wladyslaw IV (Polish–Lithuanian Commonwealth), 155
Wolff, Larry, 428
Wortman, Richard, 107, 110

Xinjiang, 12, 62, 69, 168, 262, 281, 284–85, 415, 419–20, 489, 518–20, 524, 527, 553, 609–11
  colonization, 39–41

Made in the USA
Middletown, DE
25 January 2024

48472161R00364